COMPUTER ARCHITECTURE

Concepts and Systems

COMPUTER ARCHITECTURE

Concepts and Systems

Edited by

Veljko M. Milutinović

School of Electrical Engineering
Purdue University, West Lafayette, Indiana

North-Holland
New York • Amsterdam • London

Elsevier Science Publishing Co., Inc.
52 Vanderbilt Avenue, New York, New York 10017

Sole distributors outside the United States and Canada:
Elsevier Science Publishers B.V.
P.O. Box 211, 1000 AE Amsterdam, the Netherlands

Library of Congress Cataloging-in-Publication Data

Computer architecture.

  Includes index.
  1. Computer architecture. I. Milutinović, Veljko.
QA76.9.A73C63   1987   004.2'2   86–24335
ISBN 0-444-01019-X

Current printing (last digit):
10 9 8 7 6 5 4 3 2 1

Manufactured in the United States of America

Contents

Foreword

The coming of the computer has created a revolution as profound as the change from the Middle Ages to the Renaissance. Many of the changes that took place around the time of the Renaissance—the invention of printing, the development of systematic experimental science, the invention of oil painting—have analogs today, made possible by the computer. We are moving from printed media communication, with time delays of a year or more for professional publications, to instantaneous communication via computer networks. Computers are revolutionizing the capability of scientific instruments. Supercomputers are enabling man to "see" phenomena not even accessible to experiment—from tomorrow's weather, to the complete billion-year history of a star, to the deep interior of the earth. The ability of computers to sort information is giving mankind unprecedented capability to find needles in our rapidly growing haystack of knowledge.

In the past forty years, the power of computers has advanced by a factor of a million or so. Nevertheless, the computer revolution has only just begun. The technological opportunities for further advances seem almost limitless. Since the bit carries no weight or other mechanical burdens, one can expect the volume assigned to a single bit in processors, communications, and memory, to continue to shrink dramatically, vastly increasing the number of bits that can be handled at a time. The needs for computing power are likely to keep pace with any technological advances that come along, due to the many problems of exponential or close to exponential complexity that computers must deal with—from economic forecasting to probing the secrets of molecules.

Unfortunately, there is one constraint from the discipline of physics which is limiting and shaping computer architectures of today and into the future. There is a maximum speed with which bits can travel, namely the speed of light, and today's computer designs already suffer from this limitation—forcing supercomputers to become smaller and smaller as their speed increases. The speed of light limitation is forcing architects to achieve new levels of processing capabilities mostly through parallelism rather than speed. As silicon chips (or whatever replaces silicon in future) become three-dimensional and the bit continues to shrink, the number of bits that can be processed in parallel could increase in spectacular fashion—is Avagodro's number (the number of atoms in a few grams, or 10^{23}) out of reach? Clearly the challenge to computer architects is to harness the capabilities of bits processed in parallel for the benefits of man- and womankind.

Finally, I remind all readers already deep into the jargon of silicon circuits that the brain puts all silicon to shame. The brain has cycle times of milliseconds, and a size smaller than even a desktop computer, yet it recognizes patterns, analyzes speech, and stores and sorts through databases, all at rates that are untouchable even by supercomputers. Its programming system is natural and user-friendly. Only its fault-tolerance does not meet engineering standards.

Kenneth G. Wilson
1982 Nobel Laureate

Preface

The area of computer architecture is exhibiting an extremely rapid growth, which has been impacted by both technology and application domains. Advances in technology and application result in the introduction of new capabilities, new concepts, and new design approaches. Therefore, a wide variety of different concepts and design approaches currently exists. The state of the art is rapidly changing, and there is a constant need for updated overviews of the field.

This book represents a joint effort of twenty-one authors, recognized experts in various aspects of the computer architecture field. They have been associated with the nation's leading universities and industries. Their knowledge and experience were brought together to create a unique view of twelve different and carefully selected topics, all of which belong to the general area of computer architecture. Special attention has been devoted to a clear and tutorial presentation of concepts and techniques, with simple but effective examples and representative case studies.

This book is intended for computer system architects and designers, as well as for computer managers or users needing deep, broad, and up-to-date knowledge in the area of computer architecture. It can be used as a text for graduate and advanced undergraduate university courses. It also can be used as a research and development reference in the industrial environment.

The book is divided into three parts. The first part of the book concentrates on selected topics in uniprocessing, with special emphasis on VLSI processor architecture. Such an emphasis was chosen to reflect the importance of the subject. Chapter 1 discusses the possible approaches to architectural support for high-level languages. Chapter 2 presents the reduced instruction set architecture approach. Chapter 3 concentrates on various design trade-offs in the area of VLSI processor architecture for GaAs technology. The general approach of the first part can be described as follows: First, a number of different concepts underlying the design of advanced microprocessors and high-level language computer architectures is analyzed. Then one of them, which is currently attracting a lot of interest, the reduced-instruction-set approach, is chosen and analyzed from the various points of view: software, hardware, technology, etc. Finally, attention is devoted to GaAs/Silicon design trade-offs.

The second part concentrates on selected topics in multiprocessing. Essential issues in multiprocessing are overviewed in Chapter 4. Parallel processing is covered in Chapter 5. Chapter 6 is on interconnection networks for parallel processing, multiprocessing, and distributed processing. Chapter 7 is on distributed processing and resource allocation in distributed processing systems. The approach of the second part can be described as follows: First, the general concepts are discussed. Then, the interconnection networks are studied, as an essential element of multiprocessor systems. Finally, one specific problem of vital interest for distributed processing is analyzed.

The third part concentrates on various concepts and systems for numeric and nonnumeric processing. Supercomputers and artificial intelligence machines are discussed in Chapter 8, and the emphasis is on both numeric and symbolic computing. Chapter 9 gives a unique view of dataflow architecture. Chapter 10 is a survey of functional programming architectures. Systolic arrays are treated in Chapter 11, where mapping methodology is stressed. Finally, Chapter 12 concentrates on fault-tolerant computing. The approach of the third part can be described as follows: Five different topics were chosen, to reflect current trends and interests. Each one is treated from both theoretical and practical points of view.

One of this book's goals has been to give maximal exposure to the ''research personality'' of each contributing author; by research personality I refer to each author's background, experience, goals, biases, and subjective opinions. In some cases, similar concepts and systems are discussed in more than one chapter, but from different viewpoints, a few times even with different conclusions. I believe that it is very important to expose the reader to different opinions and to make him/her aware of the fact that many issues are still the subject of research.

I would like to express thanks to all of the institutions and people who have helped during the preparation of this book. Also, I am especially grateful to my colleagues who provided constructive criticism.

All contributing authors did an excellent job, both by writing their own chapters and by reviewing related chapters. The way in which they combined their knowledge and enthusiasm was more than impressive.

Veljko M. Milutinović

Contributors

Paul Chow
>   Center for Integrated Systems
>   Stanford University

Jack B. Dennis
>   Department of Electrical Engineering and Computer Science
>   Massachusetts Institute of Technology

José A. B. Fortes
>   School of Electrical Engineering
>   Purdue University

*King-Sun Fu**
>   School of Electrical Engineering
>   Purdue University

David A. Fura
>   School of Electrical Engineering
>   Purdue University

Daniel D. Gajski
>   Department of Computer Science
>   University of Illinois at Urbana-Champaign

Joydeep Ghosh
>   Department of Electrical Engineering-Systems
>   Computer Research Institute
>   University of Southern California

---

* Deceased

John Hennessy
Department of Electrical Engineering and Computer Science
Computer Systems Laboratory
Stanford University

William Tsun-yuk Hsu
PASM Parallel Processing Laboratory
School of Electrical Engineering
Purdue University

Kai Hwang
Department of Electrical Engineering-Systems
Computer Research Institute
University of Southern California

Jie-Yong Juang
Department of Electrical Engineering and Computer Science
Northwestern University

Roy A. Maxion
Department of Computer Science
Carnegie-Mellon University

David G. Meyer
School of Electrical Engineering
Purdue University

Veljko M. Milutinović
School of Electrical Engineering
Purdue University

Jih-Kwon Peir
Thomas J. Watson Research Center
IBM Research Division
Yorktown Heights, New York

Thomas Schwederski
PASM Parallel Processing Laboratory
School of Electrical Engineering
Purdue University

Howard Jay Siegel
Supercomputing Research Center
Lanham, Maryland

Daniel P. Siewiorek
    Department of Computer Science
    Carnegie-Mellon University

Alexander A. Silbey
    Gould, Inc.
    Computer Systems Division
    San Diego, California

Steven R. Vegdahl
    Computer Research Laboratory
    Tektronix Laboratories
    Beaverton, Oregon

Benjamin W. Wah
    Department of Electrical and Computer Engineering and the Coordinated
        Science Laboratory
    University of Illinois at Urbana-Champaign

COMPUTER ARCHITECTURE

Concepts and Systems

PART   I

Topics in Uniprocessing

1

Advanced Microprocessors and High-Level Language Processor Architectures

Alexander A. Silbey
Veljko M. Milutinović

1.1. Introduction

While most hardware costs have remained steady or have decreased in recent years, software costs have unrelentingly increased. Software design, testing, and maintenance now comprise the largest portion of the cost of a computer (23).

Users seeking maximum performance on conventional machines have usually turned to assembly language code, resulting in low productivity, high design and maintenance costs, and reduced software reliability. To overcome these drawbacks, one of the thrusts in computer architecture has been to tailor computer systems to the support and execution of high-level languages (HLLs), such as FORTRAN, C, Pascal, and Ada. With an HLL computer, there is a low penalty associated with using a high-level language—compiled HLL code runs almost as fast as hand-coded assembly code. Most users have little need to resort to assembly language.

Ditzel and Patterson define a high-level language computer as one in which interaction with the computer occurs strictly at the level of the HLL (9). This means that an HLL computer produces neither ugly machine-code

3

core dumps nor unintelligible error messages that are related to the specific hardware/software implementation of the HLL. HLL computers have one or more HLLs as their "natural" language.

This definition of an HLL computer, however, says nothing about the level of hardware complexity necessary for its implementation. The omission is not accidental. One type of HLL computer, the so-called RISC[1], is characterized by its relatively simple hardware and its relatively efficient (sometimes complex) compiler to bridge the gap between the HLL statements and the simple machine-language instructions. Another type of HLL computer, ˌ̣ ̣̣̣ be quite complex because of CISC-
vident that the HLL computers and
.ˍˍˍˍˍily related.

The architecture of a computer is generally defined from the point of view of the assembly language programmer—i.e., what registers can the programmer access and what instructions can he execute? Conventional definitions of computer architecture deal with the instruction set and the register transfer level.

However, some new research projects under way at leading universities make it less relevant to speak of architecture in terms of registers and instructions only. These projects propose the migration of some functions traditionally performed in hardware into software. In the proposed architectures, the programmer deals not only with registers and instructions, but also with timing dependencies and pipeline conflicts.[2]

For example, let us consider the task of conflict detection and resolution in a pipelined computer. Most mainframe computers rely on sophisticated logic circuits to detect and resolve resource conflicts (e.g., for registers) between different stages of the pipeline. These logic circuits are known by various names, such as internal forwarding, common data buses, or scoreboards. They detect conflicts in hardware and eliminate them through appropriate measures. On the other hand, the Stanford MIPS (17) architecture performs the task of pipeline conflict detection and resolution in software. In this particular case, software conflict detection and resolution were chosen for technology-related reasons. Examples such as MIPS redefine the traditional allocation of functions to hardware and software.

1.2. A Classification of HLL Computer Architectures

Getting a grasp on developments in HLL computer architecture is made more difficult by the wide variety of approaches that can be taken. Some

---

[1] RISC and CISC are acronyms for Reduced and Complex Instruction Set Computer, respectively.
[2] Typically, the only programmers who deal with the machine at this level are the system programmers.

approaches concentrate on hardware, others on software, and still others on implementation technology. In order to unify these diverse ideas, we use a new system of classification for HLL computer architectures (22). This classification is a composition of ideas from Myers, Patterson, and Chu. Its tree-like structure is depicted in Figure 1.1.

We distinguish among various classes of HLL architectures by looking at the sophistication of their machine languages compared to that of an HLL. Different types of computers have different gaps between the HLL and the code that controls the hardware. The first level of our classification tree is the HLL Computer Architecture. We divide all HLL architectures into two groups: Indirect Execution and Direct Execution architectures. Indirect Execution architectures employ one or more levels of translation and/or interpretation in executing HLL programs. Indirect Execution architectures make use of software or hardware to translate the HLL program into a form more suitable for machine execution. Direct Execution Architectures (DEAs), on the other hand, execute HLL source code without intermediate translation. DEAs use hardware to extract the semantics of a HLL program and execute the source code directly.

Continuing down the classification tree, the indirect execution architectures are divided into two types: reduced and complex. One major difference between reduced architectures and complex architectures is the levels of their machine languages in relation to that of the HLL. In reduced architectures, the compiler spans a relatively large gap between the complex HLL statements and the simple machine-language instructions. Most HLL statements translate into several reduced machine-language instructions. In

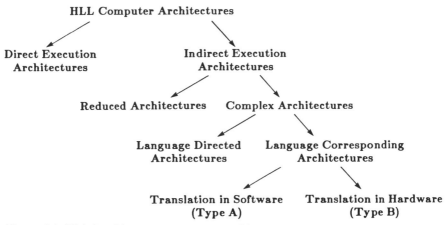

Figure 1.1 High-level language computer architecture classification tree. (From Milutinović VM (ed): Advanced microprocessors and high-level language computer architecture. IEEE Computer Society Press Tutorial, 1986. © 1986 IEEE.)

complex architectures, the level of the machine language is elevated to a higher level, and the gap between the HLL and the machine language is smaller. In a complex architecture, many HLL statements translate into one or two machine instructions.

Complex architectures are broken down into two types: language *directed* and language *corresponding* architectures. The difference between the two is based on the correspondence of HLL statements to machine instructions. If the correspondence is one-to-many, the architecture is classified as a language directed architecture. If the correspondence is one-to-one, the architecture is classified as a language corresponding architecture.

The language corresponding architectures are further subdivided at the lowest level of the HLL architecture tree. The two classes of language corresponding architectures are Type A and Type B. Type A architectures are characterized by their software translators. Type B architectures are characterized by their hardware translators.

The following sections will more carefully define the distinctions between the classes of computer architectures and will also include case studies on each class. More details on the same subject can be found in (22) and (23).

1.3. Reduced Architectures[3]

Machines known as RISCs directly attack one of the crucial problems with high-performance software: they are designed to virtually eliminate the need to write in assembly language or microcode. RISCs execute most programs as efficiently from compiled HLL code than most other architectures do from hand-coded assembly code. They reduce the performance penalty traditionally associated with using HLLs.

A metric called the *penalty ratio* is helpful in determining this penalty. The penalty ratio is the ratio of assembly code execution time to compiled code execution time. The closer the penalty ratio is to 1.0, the lower the penalty for using an HLL. One RISC, the UC Berkeley RISC-II, has a penalty ratio of 0.9. One particularly poor CISC, the M68000, has a penalty ratio of 0.34! Of course, the answer depends on the efficiency of the compiler. However, the efficiency of the compiler depends very much on the characteristics of the machine architecture.

To efficiently execute compiled HLL code, RISC machines are designed to efficiently execute those instructions most often generated by compilers. Before they specify the instruction set for a RISC, computer architects perform extensive studies to determine the most often used HLL

---

[3] See Chapter 2 for another view of this issue.

constructs, the time required to execute these constructs, the frequency of memory references, and many other details.

RISC instruction sets are designed to avoid the unfortunately common situation in which machine instructions are so specialized as to be almost useless (except in specific cases). As indicated by Wulf, some of the specialized CISC instructions are never generated by CISC compilers (35). CISC compilers, presented with a wide variety of choices in addressing modes, instruction formats, etc., must analyze each option to determine the optimal choice. In many instances, the specialized instructions can be replaced by a sequence of simple instructions with the same or even a shorter execution time. On a RISC, only the simple operations are included in the instruction set. Complex operations are performed in software by sequences of simple instructions.

The instructions that are usually implemented in RISC hardware resemble the primitive operations contained in CISC *micro*instructions.[4] Complex instructions are included in a RISC only if they do not slow down the simple instructions, or if they are absolutely necessary for the application. For example, the UCB RISCs and the Stanford MIPS do not include floating point instructions. Floating point calculations for these processors are assumed to be done on coprocessors with specialized hardware. To provide support for floating point in hardware would require a complete revision of the processor (e.g., microcoded implementation), which would be contrary to the RISC philosophy.

So most RISC instructions are very simple. The simple instructions can be relatively easily hardwired, avoiding the extra level of macro-to-microinstruction translation present in CISCs. RISC instructions are in fact so simple that almost all of the examples studied here actually *are* hardwired. Because RISCs do not have an extra level of translation, they have short cycle times and simplified control mechanisms. It should be noted that simple instructions are almost a prerequisite for hardwiring. It would be very difficult indeed to hardwire the instruction set of a typical CISC—say, the Motorola MC68020.

To maximize their execution speed, RISC instructions are set up to simplify their decoding. There is a limited number of instruction formats (sometimes a single one), and most instructions have the same length. For example, the UCB RISC-I instructions' destination register selection field is in the same bit location, regardless of the instruction (29). The decoding process in a RISC is as simple as bit-field selection from the instruction register. Many CISCs, on the other hand, require a complicated instruction parser because the location of the operands varies from instruction to instruction, depending on its format. Once again, the simplicity of a RISC is reflected in the small percentage of the chip area devoted to control.

---

[4] CISC machine instructions are typically microcoded.

Most RISCs use a load/store organization to simplify their design and improve execution speed. In a load/store organization, the only instructions that access memory are the LOAD and STORE instructions. They move data between the register file and memory. A register-based instruction set tends to minimize the number of slow off-chip memory references. All non-memory-reference operations can proceed at the fast speed of the registers, so almost all RISC instructions are single-cycle instructions.

All RISCs rely on improved compiler technology and theory to improve execution speed. Compilers play a big role in the viability of the RISC idea. One advantage of the RISC is that its instructions are easily *generated* by compilers. More importantly, though, they are also easily *optimized*, because RISC instructions have fewer side effects than CISC instructions. This idea will be revisited in the subsection discussing the IBM 801 RISC.

To a varying degree, RISCs require the compiler to handle some of the tasks accomplished in hardware in most CISCs. As discussed before, the Stanford MIPS architecture relies on the compiler to reorganize the code to eliminate all pipeline hazards at compile time. This allows the design of a pipeline without internal forwarding paths and conflict-detection circuitry to resolve pipeline conflicts. The silicon area that would otherwise be used for this purpose can be used for another function.

RISCs use the silicon area freed up by the migration of functions into software to implement architectural innovations which result in higher execution speeds. Examples of these innovations are longer pipelines, larger register files, on-chip caches, and so on. We should note that these innovations are just as applicable to CISCs as they are to RISCs. However, in the world of VLSI, as in any other, nothing is free. RISCs have a reduced complexity in the decoding and execution of their instructions, allowing them the luxury of implementing some or all of these innovations. CISCs, however, often cannot afford the extra silicon area for the innovations because CISCs are inherently more complex. CISCs use much of the available area for large microcode ROMs to hold their inherently large instruction set.

The large register files used by RISCs require compiler intelligence in order to be used effectively. The compiler is required to perform extensive program flow analysis to identify the most often used operands. These operands are assigned to registers, and all others reside in memory. The idea of *data reusability* is the key to the success of the load/store architecture. A simple example illustrating the idea of the load/store architecture is shown in Figure 1.2. The HLL statements in Figure 1.2a are translated into machine instructions for a load/store machine in Figure 1.2b. In Figure 1.2c, the same HLL statements are translated into machine instructions for a machine in which all instructions access memory. Redundant load and store instructions are eliminated by reusing register operands in a load/store architecture. This optimization can also be applied to architectures that do not use the load/store organization. However, the other advantages of the load/store archi-

a)   X = A * B + C
      Y = A/B

b)   LD   R0,A
      LD   R1,B
      MPY   R0,R1,R2
      LD   R3,C
      ADD   R3,R2,R2
      ST   R2,X
      DIV   R0,R1,R1
      ST   R1,Y

c)   LD   R0,A
      MPY   R0,B
      ADD   R0,C
      ST   R0,X
      LD   R0,A
      DIV   R0,B
      ST   R0,Y

Figure 1.2 The load/store architecture allows operands to be reused. (A) A simple sequence of HLL statements. (B) Operands B and A are reused in a load/store machine. (C) Operand A must be reloaded in a register/memory instruction format.

tecture (simplified instruction set, processor design, and interrupt handling), which show up during the design phase, cannot be so applied.

One important byproduct of the simplicity of a RISC is that it requires less time to design, layout, and debug than a comparably performing CISC. Some RISCs originated as university class projects (e.g., UCB RISCs) or thesis projects (e.g., Stanford MIPS). Because of their fast design cycle, RISC chips can take advantage of new technologies years earlier than CISC designs can. Of course, some of the benefits stemming from the simplified hardware of RISCs may be offset by the less simple optimizing compilers that accompany them. Even when one considers the (possibly) more complex compiler that accompanies the RISC processor, the fast design cycle is a strong advantage of the RISC idea.

It cannot necessarily be said that one architecture, CISC or RISC, is better than the other. Although each architectural style has its firm adherents, it is still too early to tell whether RISCs will emerge from the research environment and gain a foothold in the commercial market. Several RISC processors are commercially available—among them the Pyramid 90X and the Ridge 32. A number of RISC-related research projects have been sponsored by the government. The RISC/CISC debate is actively going on, and we have some very good contributions to that debate (8). An in-depth discussion of RISC architectures is offered in Chapter 2. For another discussion, see Chapter 3.

The following subsections consider six RISC examples in some detail: the IBM 801, the UC Berkeley RISCs (I and II), the Stanford MIPS, the Ridge 32, the Inmos Transputer, and the University of Reading RIMMS. Throughout this chapter, the term *RISC* refers to the philosophy of reduced complexity computers. *UCB RISC I* and *UCB RISC II* refer to two specific implementations based on that philosophy.

1.3.1. IBM 801

The IBM 801 is an experimental system developed at IBM's research headquarters in Yorktown Heights, New York. The philosophy guiding the research team was to improve the cost/performance ratio when executing HLL programs. The IBM 801 exhibits a different approach than the other RISCs discussed here because of the different technology used in its implementation and the early date at which the research was begun. The research team swung into action in 1975, and the finished prototype MSI ECL processor was ready in 1979. A highly optimizing PL/8 (similar to PL/I) compiler complemented the RISC processor.

The major RISC-like characteristic of the IBM 801 is that each of its instructions is executed in a single machine cycle. Its instructions are relatively primitive compared with the multi-cycle instructions of a CISC. Three advantages are claimed to result from the single-cycle instruction execution. First, single-cycle instructions can be interrupted efficiently. Second, they are easy for the compiler to optimize. Third, it is easier to precompute (at the time the program is being compiled) certain constants or variables if each instruction is simple. The following subsection discusses these advantages in more detail.

Some background in how processors time their handling of interrupts would be useful in discussing how the IBM 801 interrupt strategy was chosen. There are three common strategies for handling interrupts. They are waiting for an instruction boundary, instruction restart, and instruction continuation. Waiting for an instruction boundary is the simplest method. It queues any interrupts that may occur during the execution of an instruction for later servicing. An interrupt that occurs during the execution of an instruction is not serviced until the instruction is completed. At the end of each instruction, the interrupts are serviced, and execution continues with the next instruction following the one during which the interrupt was recognized. The second strategy, instruction restart, provides a more responsive method of servicing interrupts than waiting for an instruction boundary. Using this strategy, interrupts are serviced immediately as they occur. The processor, upon recognizing an interrupt, saves some state information which will allow it to re-execute the interrupted instruction. Then the processor services the interrupt. After the interrupt service routine is finished, the state information is used to re-execute the entire interrupted instruction. The instruction restart method requires that an instruction not be allowed to permanently change the state of the machine until it has been determined that no interrupts are pending. The third strategy, instruction continuation, is potentially the best-performing strategy. Like the instruction restart method, instruction continuation allows the servicing of an interrupt at any time during the execution of an instruction. The difference is that instruction continuation saves enough information to permit the processor to restore the state that existed when the interrupt occurred. This approach is especially beneficial in processors that have long instructions since it permits the instruction to be resumed, rather than restarted. Unfortunately the amount of information that has to be saved can be huge.

So how does the IBM 801 fit into this framework? Knowing that the IBM 801 is a RISC machine, you might guess that its designers would use the simplest interrupt strategy, waiting for an instruction boundary. That would be a correct guess. The IBM 801 architects decided that the short execution time of the single cycle instructions would make it attractive to simply defer interrupt servicing until the instruction boundary. Since that boundary is at most one cycle (66 ns) away, this is not an unreasonable solution. Particularly advantageous is the fact that very little information has to be saved and restored in order to service interrupts.

The second advantage of single cycle instructions is that they are easier for the compiler to optimize. Because each instruction does a small, self-contained task, it is easy to move some parts of a complex, loop-oriented sequence of instructions outside of the loop. This concept is called invariant code motion, and it is used in many CISC machines also. However, CISC instructions are more difficult to move outside a loop because they are more intricately related to the surrounding instructions.

The third advantage of single cycle instructions is that they make it easier to precompute some parts of a complicated operation at compile time. For example, if one of the operands of a multiply instruction is a constant, it may be possible to replace the multiplication by a more efficient sequence of shifts and adds.

A second major characteristic of the IBM 801 is that its architects used an architectural solution which reduces the penalty associated with branching. This solution is known as the *delayed branch*, and it is also used in various forms by the Stanford MIPS and the UC Berkeley RISCs.

The delayed branch is a branch which does not take effect until after the *n*th instruction following the branch. The *n* instructions following the branch instruction in memory are executed whether or not the branch is taken. This solution makes it unnecessary to flush the pipeline when a branch is executed. However, it does require some intelligence on the part of the compiler to avoid the unnecessary execution of NO-OP instructions.

As shown in Figure 1.3a, the compiler's code generator automatically inserts *n* NO-OP instructions after each branch instruction. It is possible to eliminate some of the NO-OPs by replacing them with instructions from elsewhere. Figure 1.3b shows one possible solution. It is left as an exercise to the reader to determine the effect of delayed conditional branches and unconditional branches.

a) 100   BRANCH   200
           NO-OP   ⎫
           NO-OP   ⎬ $n = 2$
                   ⎭
             ⋮

    200   LOAD   R1,X
           LOAD   R2,Y(R1)

b) 100   BRANCH   201
           NO-OP
           LOAD   R1,X
             ⋮
    201   LOAD   R2,Y(R1)

Figure 1.3 Delayed branches and elimination of NOPs. (A) The code generator inserts two NOPs after the branch. (B) The code optimizer replaces one of the NOPs with an instruction from the branch target.

The IBM 801 provides both delayed branch and conventional branch instructions. The delayed branches are used for the 60 percent of branch instructions where it is possible to replace the NO-OP with a useful instruction (31). The conventional branches are used in the other cases, and they cause the instructions following the branch instruction in the pipeline to be flushed. Providing both forms of branches prevents the insertion of superfluous NO-OP instructions and saves memory space.

Unlike the Stanford MIPS, the IBM 801 performs pipeline interlocking in hardware. Whenever a pipeline resource conflict is detected, the instruction which is deepest into the pipeline is allowed to execute, while the conflicting instruction is forced to wait for one or more cycles. However, pipeline flushes should be infrequent because the compiler arranges code so as to minimize the occurrence of pipeline conflicts.

The third major characteristic of the IBM 801 is that the architecture is geared towards easing the job of the system programmer. The IBM 801 architects assumed that all programs, except for system programs, would be written in a HLL. Accordingly, the architecture provides a regular, orthogonal set of instructions which are easily generated and optimized by a compiler. The compiler does not have to perform extensive analysis to determine the optimal instruction sequence to perform a given task. The *code generation* portion of the compiler can be kept simple. The *code optimization* portion, though, is complex because the compiler is required to perform extensive flow analysis in order to efficiently use the general-purpose registers.

The IBM 801 relies entirely on compiler intelligence to support subroutine calls and parameter passing. It does not use the register windows of the UC Berkeley RISC I and II. George Radin (31) suggests that arguments be passed to/from subroutines through registers for best efficiency.

Another performance improvement is gained by the use of SSI/MSI ECL technology in the implementation of the IBM 801. The technology of the IBM 801 is quite unlike the other RISCs studied here. The use of ECL allowed the 801 to have a very short cycle time of 66ns.

The IBM 801 is proof that RISCs need not be memory hogs. For example, one of the benchmarks used to compare the IBM 801 to the IBM System 370 Model 168 is the inner loop of a heap sort. The 801 requires an average of nine tenths the code size required for this and other HLL benchmarks on the S370/M168, *using the same compiler*. The IBM 801 executes the inner loop in 35 cycles, but the S370/M168 requires 96 cycles to execute the same loop. Part of the performance gain is due to the small object code size of the 801. This small object code size is possible because the instruction set was chosen to allow maximum performance in compiler-generated code.

Accurate performance comparisons between the 801 and the S370/M168 were possible because of the excellent PL/8 compiler that was developed together with the 801 hardware. This compiler can be retargeted to generate object code for a number of processors. When the PL/8 compiler was retargeted to generate System 370 code instead of IBM 801 code, the code executed *fifty* percent faster than with the best System 370 compiler previously available (29). Although a complete discussion of the compiler is outside the scope of this book, a large part of the credit for the high performance of the IBM 801 is due to its outstandingly efficient compiler.

1.3.2. UC Berkeley RISC

A strong research program at the University of California, Berkeley, has resulted in the design, layout and fabrication of RISC I (28), RISC II (20), SOAR, SPUR, and an instruction cache chip for the RISC II processor (27). The philosophy of the UC Berkeley RISC research team is to use simple hardware to provide efficient support for high-level language execution. RISC I was designed and fabricated over the course of 1981–1982 and was completed in the summer of 1982. RISC II was designed and fabricated between 1981 and 1983, and was completed a year after RISC I. We will concentrate on RISC II, which offers higher performance because of a larger register file and a deeper, three-stage pipeline. For another discussion of this and other RISC processors, see Chapter 2.

The RISC II design was undertaken following a series of studies aimed at answering the question, ''What are the most often used HLL constructs, and how much time do they take to be executed?'' The studies used a mix of C and Pascal programs. None of the programs involved heavy number crunching; they were mostly general-purpose programs. The instruction set developed for RISC II reflects the makeup of these benchmarks in that some features, like floating point support, were omitted. Instead, the emphasis was on optimizing the execution of the benchmarks' most frequent and time-consuming HLL constructs. Only those instructions needed to efficiently execute the HLL code were included in the instruction set. For example, the hardware does not support the left arithmetic shift and rotate functions because they are not needed in HLLs.

RISC II has two hardware features that accelerate the execution of HLL programs: register windows and support for local scalars in the form of a large set of registers. The register windows speed up the most time-consuming HLL construct—the subroutine call/return. RISC II provides multiple, overlapping banks of registers, only one bank of which is visible at any time. To execute a subroutine call, RISC II changes a hardware pointer to point to the next register window. Parameters for the called sub-routine are placed in an overlapping area between the calling routine's win-dow and the called routine's window, as shown in Figure 1.4. The lower numbered registers of the calling routine become the higher numbered reg-isters of the called routine. To execute a return from subroutine, the pointer is moved back to its original value, restoring the register window of the calling routine. The register windows eliminate the overhead of placing sub-

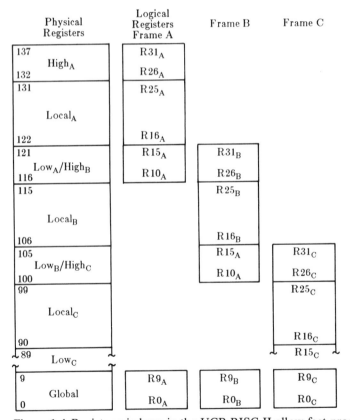

Figure 1.4 Register windows in the UCB RISC-II allow fast procedure calls. (Adapted from Patterson D, Sequin C: A VLSI RISC. IEEE Computer, Vol. 15, No. 9, pp. 8–21. © 1982 IEEE.)

routine parameters on a stack and saving/restoring registers on subroutine calls.

If more parameters are to be passed than can be accommodated in the overlapping area (six), they must be placed in main memory. However, this should occur infrequently because HLL studies indicate that fewer than 2% of HLL subroutine calls involve more than six parameters.

The second hardware feature that accelerates the execution of HLL programs is the large register file. This allows most operands to be kept in registers rather than in main memory. Studies indicate that 75% of operand references are integer constants and local scalars. It is relatively easy to find room for these operands because each register window has 32 visible registers. Global variables (i.e., variables that are shared between windows) are kept in the lowest numbered registers. The lowest numbered registers are accessible from every window.

The RISC II processor has a three-stage pipeline consisting of fetch, read/operate, and write stages. Conflicts between the read/operate stage and the write stage are resolved by a technique called internal forwarding, taking the form of a latch that bypasses the register file when read/write conflicts occur. Typical of pipelined RISC processors, the RISC II uses the delayed branching scheme to reduce hardware complexity and remove most of the penalty associated with branching in a pipelined processor.

RISC II requires the use of a smart compiler to optimally use the hardware. First, the register window scheme may require compile-time prediction of the execution sequence of calls and returns. This may be necessary in order to assign the hardware register windows to the software procedure contexts. Second, keeping the frequently used operands in registers requires that the compiler predict the usage frequencies of scalars and constants. Finally, the delayed branching scheme requires the compiler to reorganize the code in order to eliminate NO-OPs. This migration of complexity from hardware into software is typical of RISC processors. However, we shall see later that the Stanford MIPS requires an even higher level of compiler intelligence than RISC II.

A version of the RISC II chip using 3 micron nMOS has a cycle time of 330 ns, and uses approximately 41,000 transistors. The instruction decode portion of the chip (in the narrow sense) consumes only 0.5% of the total area (20). Much of the chip area is occupied by large, regular data structures (e.g., the register file). There are only 39 opcodes. The RISC II object code is somewhat larger compared with a VAX-11/780 (1.25 times) or MC 68000 (1.1 times).

1.3.3. Stanford MIPS

The Stanford MIPS (Microprocessor without Interlocked Piped Stages) is an ongoing research project at Stanford University. The research is directed toward optimizing the division of functions between software and hardware in a processor for a high-performance, 32-bit workstation. The MIPS project was begun in 1981, and the first chip was fabricated in 1983. Current research concentrates on the MIPS-X and R2000 extensions of the MIPS architecture.

As in most RISC architectures, MIPS instructions are simple so that they may be executed in one machine cycle. The components of the instruction set were chosen as a result of studies similar to the ones used in the UC Berkeley RISC I and II processor design. The frequency of use, time required for execution, and feasibility of implementation in hardware were considered for each HLL construct. The most important functions were chosen for inclusion in the instruction set, but other, nonessential instructions were included only if they did not slow down the execution of more frequent instructions. Exceptions to this rule are some operating system functions that had to be included in the instruction set to achieve minimum functionality—e.g., address translation.

Although similar studies were undertaken prior to the specification of both the RISC I and MIPS processors, the architectures are quite different. For example, the MIPS processor does not support byte addressing of main memory. MIPS studies indicated that byte load/store operations are infrequently used by HLL compilers. Detailed design studies indicated that using a byte aligner in the main data path would require the cycle time to be lengthened by 15 to 20%. If a byte aligner were used, all instructions would be slowed down by a large margin, not just those dealing with byte addressing. Therefore, the decision was made to omit the byte aligner and support word addressing only. Since byte manipulation facility is needed, the architecture provides byte insert and byte extract instructions that operate on word-length data already located in a register. The UC Berkeley RISCs, on the other hand, provide full support for byte operands.

MIPS achieves high performance by way of a deep, five-stage pipeline. Similar to the IBM 801 and UC Berkeley RISCs, MIPS bypasses the penalty associated with branching in a pipelined machine by using a delayed branch. MIPS carries this idea one step further than the others by moving the task of pipeline conflict detection and resolution into the compiler, thereby simplifying the design of the hardware and saving silicon area. The MIPS pipeline has no hardware to prevent resource conflicts between stages. Instead, the instruction sequence output by the compiler undergoes a transformation, or *reordering,* which removes all possible conflicts prior to execution. Reordering is done after compilation by a separate program called the reorganizer.

The reorganizer effectively splits the MIPS architecture into two levels: the assembly-language level and the machine-language level. At the assembly-language level, the code is arranged without regard to pipeline conflicts (including delayed branches). At the machine-language level, the code is reorganized to prevent pipeline conflicts and to take advantage of delayed branches. The transformation between the two levels is highly machine-dependent. A simple example is shown in Figure 1.5 for an HLL assignment

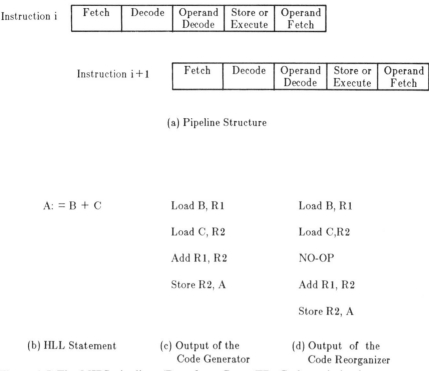

Instruction i

| Fetch | Decode | Operand Decode | Store or Execute | Operand Fetch |

Instruction i+1

| Fetch | Decode | Operand Decode | Store or Execute | Operand Fetch |

(a) Pipeline Structure

A: = B + C	Load B, R1	Load B, R1
	Load C, R2	Load C,R2
	Add R1, R2	NO-OP
	Store R2, A	Add R1, R2
		Store R2, A

| (b) HLL Statement | (c) Output of the Code Generator | (d) Output of the Code Reorganizer |

Figure 1.5 The MIPS pipeline. (Data from Gross TR: Code optimization techniques for pipelined architectures. Proc. COMPCON Spring 1983, IEEE Computer Society, San Francisco, CA, March 1983, pp. 278–285. © 1983 IEEE.)

statement (Figure 1.5b). Straightforward code generation will produce code that cannot execute correctly because of the pipeline conflict (Fig. 1.5c). Specifically, the second LOAD instruction uses the fifth pipeline stage to load register 2 with the contents of memory location C. The ADD instruction requires the same register in its third pipeline stage. This results in a conflict because stage five of the LOAD instruction and stage three of the ADD instruction are executed at the same time. The reorganizer detects this conflict and inserts a NOP between the LOAD and ADD instructions (Figure 1.5d). The reorganizer is usually able to eliminate the NOP instruction, replacing it with another instruction from elsewhere in the program.

Effective use of the MIPS processor requires a sophisticated compiler (and reorganizer). The MIPS system software is even more complex than that of the IBM 801 or UCB RISCs. Not only does it deal with delayed branches, but also with pipeline interlocking.

Performing the interlocking in software has three advantages. First, no instruction is ever delayed in the pipeline because of register conflicts. Second, the basic cycle time of the processor can be decreased because no complicated logic is needed to detect register conflicts. Third, the area that would otherwise be needed for conflict detection logic can be used for some other purpose. It is interesting to note that the code reorganization technique could also be applied to a processor *with* interlocked pipe stages. This would increase performance since instructions would not have to be delayed because of register conflicts. However, advantages two and three would not apply in this case because the conflict detection logic would still be in place.

Several interesting architectural solutions are used in MIPS. The first is that there are no condition codes. The MIPS designers felt that condition code (CC) logic unnecessarily complicates a VLSI design. The CC logic would be irregular because it gathers information from widespread locations on the chip, causing the design to be more complicated and the layout more difficult. Since MIPS is hardwired rather than microcoded, careful decoding would be required to determine which instructions are allowed to affect the condition codes and which are not.

Instead of using the condition codes to control program flow, MIPS uses a "compare and branch" (CAB) instruction. This single-cycle instruction performs a test on an operand, then steers execution either toward the branch target or to the next sequential instruction. Not only is this approach beneficial in terms of simplifying the design of the MIPS chip, but it also saves instructions, compared with performing an explicit compare followed by a branch.

The MIPS designers did not use the register window approach to speed up HLL procedure call/return execution. The large register file (138 registers) in RISC II is only visible in windows of 32 registers. All registers other than the ones in the current window remain unused, resulting in some inefficiency. The large register file increases the length of the buses, and this slows down their operation considerably. The large register file also slows the context switch, since all 138 registers have to be saved in main memory. Instead of using the register windows, the MIPS designers felt confident that a medium-size register file (16 registers) would be sufficient to allow the compiler to efficiently allocate registers *across* subroutine boundaries.

A version of the MIPS architecture was implemented in nMOS VLSI in 1983. The chip has 24k transistors, much fewer than RISC II. The basic cycle time of the chip was 250 ns, with an instruction fetch occurring every two cycles. The performance of the chip was promising. It executed many standard benchmarks, such as the Towers of Hanoi, Quicksort, and matrix multiplication faster than the Motorola 68000 by a factor of about 5.

1.3.4. Ridge 32

The Ridge 32 is the first RISC machine in commercial production. The goal of the Ridge 32 is to provide high performance in integer *and floating-point* calculations, at a moderate price. Unlike some other RISCs, the Ridge 32 is a multiboard processor with virtual memory and built-in floating-point-capability. Like the Stanford MIPS, the Ridge 32 has a streamlined instruction set and a compare and branch (CAB) instruction.

One feature that streamlines the instruction set is the small number of formats. All Ridge 32 instructions conform to one of three formats shown in Figure 1.6 (2). Note that the opcode and register specifiers occupy the same position in all three formats. The uniform format allows decoding to occur concurrently with the prefetching of register operands. This feature alone accounts for much of the performance of the processor.

Having three formats instead of two, as in the UCB-RISC, makes it possible to specify a full, 32-bit memory address when necessary. When a 16-bit address will suffice, the short displacement mode can be used. The extra instruction format for the long displacement mode complicates the decoding of instructions on the Ridge 32. However, the Ridge designers justify the long displacement mode by pointing out that including the long displacement mode would eliminate the need for IBM-like base registers.

The Ridge 32 uses an idea also seen in the Stanford MIPS—it has no condition codes. Condition codes are a liability in a pipelined machine because they complicate the design, make it more difficult to predict branches, and take extra time to set. Condition codes are especially unwieldly because they increase the amount of state information that has to be saved in the event of an interrupt. They make branch prediction more complicated because almost any instruction can modify the condition codes. The design of the execution phase of the pipeline is made more constrained because the condition codes have to be set at the end of the execution cycle.

Instead of condition codes, the Ridge 32 uses a CAB instruction to transfer control. The CAB instruction has a *branch likely bit,* which is tested

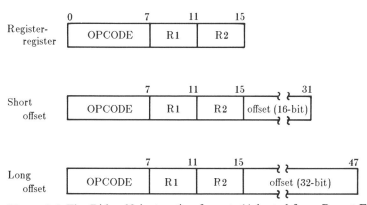

Figure 1.6 The Ridge 32 instruction format. (Adapted from Basart E, Folger D: Ridge 32 architecture—a RISC variation. Proc. IEEE International Conference on Computer Design: VLSI in Computers, Port Chester, NY, Oct. 31–Nov. 3, 1983, pp. 315–318. © 1983 IEEE.)

by the instruction prefetch unit at execution time. If the branch likely bit is set, prefetching occurs at the branch target. Conversely, if it is reset, prefetching occurs at the instruction sequentially following the CAB instruction. The compiler can make intelligent guesses about the likelihood of a branch by examining the semantics of the HLL program. For example, statistics indicate that about 90% of the branches at the end of a loop are taken (27). So the compiler sets the branch likely bit in the branch instruction at the end of a loop. The branch likely bit, together with the absence of condition codes, eliminates many of the pipeline flushes necessary in conventional machines without the complication of multiway prefetching.

The Ridge 32 is implemented in Schottky bipolar logic, rather than as a custom nMOS chip. Using these fast off-the-shelf parts resulted in a 125-ns cycle time, with most register-to-register instructions taking only one cycle. As in most RISCs, the Ridge 32 relies on its compiler to provide some of its speed advantage. In this particular case, the compiler is able to correctly predict branches in 86% of the cases (2).

1.3.5. Inmos Transputer

The Transputer system is a commercial family of compatible, high-performance microprocessors developed by Inmos of the United Kingdom (1). The Transputer design team set forth ambitious goals of providing non-RISC-like features such as multiprocess, multiprocessor, and communications support for industry standard peripheral devices, all on a single VLSI chip.

The Transputer system was designed to be programmed entirely in a high-level language called OCCAM. OCCAM is used to program both system functions and user applications. Because of the flexibility and power of OCCAM, Inmos doesn't even support an assembly language for the Transputer.

The 32-bit T424 Transputer incorporates a mix of CISC and RISC ideas. Unlike other RISCs, the Transputer is microcoded. Like other RISCs, though, the Transputer has a simply encoded, sparse instruction set with only 16 opcodes. Instructions are all of the same length: 8 bits. The upper nibble of the instruction is the opcode; the lower nibble is the function (or the operand). For example, the opcode for the "operation" instruction is 15 decimal, and the function nibble specifies 1 of 16 possible operations (add, shift, etc.).

Transputer instructions are independent of the word length of the processor, so they can be used on other non-32-bit members of the Transputer family. For example, let us consider the handling of immediate operands. Immediate operands are loaded into a register not as a single entity, but by a series of "prefix" instructions followed by a load-constant instruction. The prefix instruction loads a 4-bit data item into the lower nibble of a register and shifts it left 4 bits. The load-constant instruction replaces the lower nibble of the register with the contents of the function field of the instruction.

a) TOS = 17B   ;TOS = Top-Of Stack

b) prefix 1   ; TOS = 1
    prefix 7   ; TOS = 17
    load constant B ; TOS = 17B

Figure 1.7 Transputer efficiently executes typical HLL statements. (A) HLL statement loading the top of stack. (B) Transputer assembly code.

For example, loading the top of the stack with a hexadecimal value of 17B can be synthesized from a sequence of three instructions as shown in Figure 1.7. Together, these instructions allow the construction of arbitrary-size constants up to the word length of the register. The same code could be used to generate a 16-bit operand on either a 16-bit or a 32-bit Transputer.

Similar to the UC Berkeley RISC II, the Transputer has a large register file. It consists of 4 Kbytes of on-chip RAM and is used entirely for storage of data. This gives a total of 1024 registers, any one of which can be accessed at a given time—i.e. the registers are not windowed. Instruction prefetching is done in packets of four 8-bit instructions at a time to match the processor and memory speeds.

The Transputer provides a fast context switching time because of the small number of registers associated with each process. The six registers associated with a process can be stored in memory very quickly. The Transputer provides a microcoded process scheduler and it is used to provide priority-based scheduling among active processes. Microcode also supports communication between processes in the form of messages.

The six registers associated with a process are the A, B, and C registers, the instruction pointer, the workspace pointer, and the operand register, as shown in Figure 1.8. The A, B, and C registers are the primary working registers. The workspace pointer is a type of base address used in accessing operands. The workspace pointer can be quickly changed upon a context switch to point to the new process' workspace. The operand register is used to form operands.

One of the impressive system features built into the Transputer is its support for interprocessor communication. Instead of using a slow global

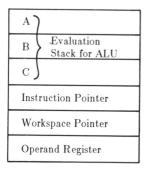

Figure 1.8 Transputer's small register set. (From Barron I, Caville P, May D, Wilson P: Transputer does 5 or more MIPS even when not used in parallel. Reprinted from Electronics, Nov. 17, 1983, p. 109. Copyright © 1983, McGraw Hill, Inc. All rights reserved.)

bus like the one used in RIMMS (discussed in Section 1.3.6), the Transputer uses four serial point-to-point links to communicate with its four nearest neighbors. These links are independent of the memory and I/O buses. The links are controlled by a microcoded protocol to ensure the integrity of interprocessor communication.

Each T424 Transputer has a built-in I/O processor that operates independently of the memory bus. The I/O processor interfaces with industry standard peripherals over an 8-bit bus operating at 4 Mbytes/s.

The T424 Transputer is fabricated in 2-micron nMOS VLSI. The large microcode ROM contributes to the 250k transistor count. It has a cycle time of 50 ns per instruction.

1.3.6. University of Reading RIMMS

RIMMS stands for Reduced Instruction set architecture for Multi-Micro-processor Systems. RIMMS is an ongoing research project at the University of Reading in the United Kingdom (13). The goal of the RIMMS architecture is to provide increased performance by combining many simple processors to form a multi-microprocessor system. This contrasts with the other RISCs studied here in that the emphasis is on making a single processor fit into a global system of processors rather than on building a single, fast processor.

The RIMMS designers reason that low-power MOS VLSI circuits are approaching technological limits that will slow down their tremendous speed gains of the past years. The faster VLSI chips will not be much faster than 10-year-old TTL circuits. Therefore, argue the RIMMS designers, the route to increased performance is through the replication of simple processors. Simple processors are easier to design and are faster because of their smaller size. Complex tasks should be attacked by breaking them into small subtasks.

The current version of RIMMS has a set of seven 16-bit registers. Future plans call for more registers to allow the retention of data on-chip rather than in main memory. RIMMS instructions are doublewords, and have three operand addresses so that the destination register can be explicitly specified. Having an explicit destination register promotes the reusability of operands in registers and can reduce the number of off-chip memory accesses.

The RIMMS architecture can be treated on two levels: the RIMMS level with many processors working together as a system, and the RIMS level with a single processor servicing its resident program and the global bus. On the RIMMS level, the system comprises 255 processors connected by a global token-based bus, as shown in Figure 1.9. Memory addresses consist of 16 bits, the most significant byte being the global address and the least significant, the local address. Normal operand fetches are handled internally to the processor from a local memory. However, when a processor

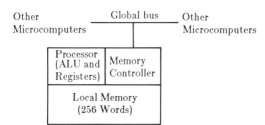

Other   Global bus   Other
Microcomputers   Microcomputers

Figure 1.9 The RIMMS microcomputer: One element of a large system. (Adapted from Foti L, English D, Hopkins R, et al: Reduced instruction set multi-microcomputer system. Proc. 1984 NCC, Las Vegas, NV, Vol. 53, June 1984, pp. 69–75.)

is passed a global address other than zero, during an operand fetch or store, the memory controller sends a remote load/store request over the global bus and waits for a response. In this fashion, each processor has free access to data located both in its local memory and also the memories of all other processors.

Instruction fetches, however, are handled somewhat differently. If a processor attempts to fetch from nonlocal memory, the instruction is actually executed by the remote processor. Execution continues on the local processor with the instruction following the remote fetch instruction.

Communication between the processors is in the form of 34-bit *packets* consisting of a 2-bit operation field, a 16-bit address, and a 16-bit operand. The four possible operations between processors are LOAD, STORE in register, STORE in memory, and EXECUTE. The packets are controlled by the memory controller, which interfaces with the processor, the global bus, and the local memory. When a packet arrives, the memory controller services it independently of the processor. One situation that is handled differently is when an EXECUTE packet is received by a controller whose main processor is busy. In this case, the packet is rejected, and the sending processor tries again when its turn arrives.

On the RIMS level, each microcomputer consists of three major elements: the processor, the memory controller, and the memory. There are two addressable registers: the program counter (C) and the data register (D). When a context switch occurs, only the C and D registers have to be saved/restored. So, for example, when a processor executes a GOTO XXX, where XXX is a nonlocal address, all information needed to transfer execution to the remote processor is contained in the C and D registers. Instructions consist of a 5-bit opcode, three mode bits, and three 8-bit address fields. The mode bits indicate whether the address fields contain memory addresses or literals. Addresses are signed offsets applied to the data pointer register.

The RIMS microcomputer is synchronized with its peers by means of the FORK/JOIN concept. A FORK can be seen as a ''tee'' in the execution of a program: control is transferred to the target of a FORK, but it also continues with the next sequential instruction. Figure 1.10 shows how this works in practice. For purposes of illustration, the code shown in the figure is symbolic; it should not be interpreted to be actual RIMMS assembly lan-

```
        RIMS 1                      RIMS 2                    RIMS 3

100   FORK   200   210        200   ADD                 300   SUB
102   FORK   300   310               ⋮                         ⋮
                                206   GOTO 110          308   GOTO 110
104   pcount    ←2
106   HALT
         ⋮
110   SUB pcount, 1, pcount
112   IF pcount > 0      114
           else 116
114   HALT
116    ⋮
```

Figure 1.10 RIMMS executes the FORK/JOIN operations efficiently. RIMS refers to a single microprocessor in the system; RIMMS refers to the entire microcomputer system.

guage. Processor 1 reaches a point where it wishes to create a parallel program flow at location 100. It executes two FORKs, specifying new C and D values for the new processes, then executes a HALT. As each FORKed process completes, it jumps to a location in Processor 1 that counts the number of FORKed processes that have completed. When all processes have completed, Processor 1 continues execution.

The first, experimental implementation of RIMMS uses 3-micron nMOS VLSI for the processor and memory controller, and uses commercially available chips for the memory. The processor chip required 17k transistors.

1.4. Language-Directed Microprocessor and Minicomputer Architectures

Language-directed architectures fall under the CISC branch of the HLL architecture tree shown in Figure 1.1. Language-directed architectures can be characterized by the migration of complexity from software into microcode. This migration can result in higher execution speed and greater standardization of functions. For example, some processors provide special addressing modes to make it easier to access the complex data structures used in HLL programs. Other processors have an object-oriented architecture for purposes of security, reliability, and modularity.

The machine language of language-directed architectures is elevated to a relatively high level, but not yet to the level of the HLL. The distinguishing characteristic of the language-directed architecture is that an HLL statement generally translates into a small number of machine-language instructions. In language-corresponding architecture, there is a one-to-one correspondence between HLL statements and machine-language instructions.

One can draw an analogy between the microinstructions of a vertically microcoded language-directed processor and the macroinstructions of a RISC processor. Both types of instructions represent simple operations; the difference is that microinstructions are read from a fast ROM and macroinstructions are read from either cache or main memory. The speed advantage of language-directed architectures over classical architectures stems partially from fast ROM technology.

Language-directed architectures represent a logical extension of the trend of past years to incorporate more and more functions in hardware and/ or firmware. The DEC VAX-11 is more complex than the PDP-11; the Intel iAPX 432 is more complex than the 8086; the Motorola MC 68020 is more complex than the 68000—and the list goes on. The danger of this trend, when taken to extreme, is that hardware is more difficult to change than software. Any function done in hardware runs the risk of being inflexible to the needs of its users. If the hardware function does not meet the needs of its users, it will lie unused, inefficient.

Another drawback to the language-directed architecture lies in the very complexity of its instructions. The compiler must analyze many addressing modes and instruction formats to identify the optimal way to accomplish a task. This makes the optimizing compiler more complex and increases compilation time.

In most cases, stack architectures also belong to the language-directed architectures. However, we choose to treat stack architectures as a concept of computer organization rather than as a concept of architectural support for HLLs. Consequently, some elements of the stack architecture can be found in all other classes of HLL computer architecture mentioned in this chapter. Well-known examples of stack architectures include the Burroughs B5500 and the Hewlett-Packard 3000.

In the following subsections, we discuss six 32-bit, language-directed microprocessors: the Intel iAPX 432, the Motorola MC68020, the Hewlett-Packard Focus, the National Semiconductor NS32032, the Zilog Z80000, and the DEC VLSI VAX. Some authors would not classify these complex instruction set microprocessors as language-directed architectures. However, their designers have made every effort to make them efficient for the execution of compiled HLL code. Therefore, we treat them as language-directed architectures. Other members of the class of language-directed architectures include the AT&T WE 32000 (formerly the Bellmac-32) and some Japanese products.

1.4.1. Intel iAPX 432

The Intel iAPX 432 was developed by a design group in Aloha, Oregon, to be a commercial microprocessor for software-intensive applications. The iAPX 432 (432 for short) became commercially available in 1981 (15). A major goal of the 432 is to provide full architectural support for an object-oriented

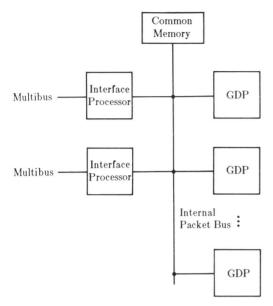

(a) An iAPX 432 Multiprocessor System

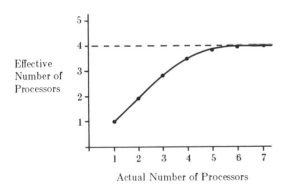

(b) The Efficiency Function

Figure 1.11 Multiprocessing with the iAPX 432. (a) A multiprocessor iAPX 432 system. (b) Additional processors increase throughput. ((a) Adapted from Myers GJ: Advances in Computer Architecture. John Wiley & Sons, New York, 1982; (b) adapted from Gupta A, Toong HD: An architectural comparison of 32-bit microprocessors. IEEE Micro, Feb. 1983, pp. 9–22. © 1983 IEEE.)

operating system and compiler. The 432 was intended for use in low-volume applications in which programming is done only once, or for high-volume applications in which programming may occur often (25). The 432 system incorporates many features to improve the reliability and security of programs and data.

An outstanding feature of the 432 is the ease with which additional performance can be obtained. It is possible to add up to five general data processors (GDPs) to a system *without changing its software*. An example of an iAPX 432 multiprocessor system is shown in Figure 1.11a. Using more than five GDPs, though, is futile. Since all processor-memory traffic uses the global bus, its capacity is used up by as few as five processors. As indicated in Figure 1.11b, memory contention reduces the effective performance of five GDPs to less than four times that of a single GDP.

Reliability of the 432 hardware and software is ensured by the fault handlers. The fault handlers allow programs to fully detect and recover from hardware and software errors. In addition, it is possible to use a redundant processor configuration to compare results from multiple processors for fault detection.

The iAPX 432 can be characterized as an operating system machine. The hardware provides a complete set of primitives for the protection, scheduling, resource management, and interprocess communication functions that are basic to an operating system. The philosophy guiding the architecture was to provide a collection of mechanisms in hardware, leaving the selection of *policies* to the software.

The 432 is an object-oriented processor. This means that all macroinstructions deal with uniform entities known as objects. There are context objects, processor objects, process objects, and others. A processor object, for example, can either be executing instructions or waiting in a queue for dispatching. Access to objects is controlled by means of capabilities. Capabilities allow fine-grained protection of access, modification, and execution of objects.

The hardware implementation of the iAPX 432 is in the form of two chips with a total of about 160k transistors. The 43201 fetches and decodes instructions, while the 43202 performs addressing and arithmetic. Its successor, the Intel iAPX 386, with 270k transistors, is said to make up for their speed shortcomings.

1.4.2. Motorola MC68020

The Motorola MC68020 is an advanced member of the well-known MC680X0 family. It has 32-bit, nonmultiplexed address and data buses, unlike previous members of the family (24). The outstanding features of the 68020 are the on-chip instruction cache, the pipeline, the coprocessor interface, and several complex addressing modes useful for accessing HLL data structures.

The instruction cache is direct-mapped, and it contains 64 blocks of 4 bytes. The data storage capacity of the cache is 256 bytes. Since the cache contains nonmodifiable data, it is less complex than one that has to handle STOREs. The cache is completely transparent to user programs, except for the increase in execution speed. However, the 68020 provides some privileged instructions to allow the operating system to control the cache. For example, the OS has the capability of "freezing" the contents of the cache by setting a bit in the cache control register. When the cache is frozen, cache misses do not cause the cache to be updated. This feature is useful when emulation programs (e.g., virtual machines) wish to avoid reducing the cache hit ratio of the emulated program.

The CPU has a three-stage pipeline to allow the overlapping of operations. The overlapped operations are prefetching, operand extraction, and instruction decoding. The pipeline can operate on either three words of the same instruction or on three separate instructions. The effect of the pipeline is to cause the execution time of some instructions to be entirely hidden.

Further performance improvement comes from the ability of the 68020 to interface with special-purpose coprocessors. For example, floating-point instructions can be executed by the MC68881 chip, and memory management capabilities are incorporated into the MC68451 chip. The protocol for communicating with the coprocessors is implemented in firmware. Coprocessors execute synchronously in a 68020 system. This means that the main processor is idle when the coprocessor is running. Synchronous protocols make future upgrades and extensions of the coprocessor(s) easier.

Like the 68010, the 68020 supports true demand paging. Operand fetches, operand stores, and instruction fetches can cause *page faults* during the processing of an instruction. Page faults occur in a virtual memory system when the targeted page is not contained in main memory. The operating system handles page faults by replacing a memory-resident page with the appropriate page from the backing store.

The 68020 is implemented with 150k transistors, and has a performance of 2.1 to 2.7 MIPS in the ideal case (32).

1.4.3. Hewlett-Packard Focus

The Hewlett-Packard Focus is an advanced 32-bit microprocessor intended primarily for internal use in the Hewlett-Packard company. The goal of the Focus design team was to improve design productivity, testability, and system performance (3). The Focus chip required 450k transistors, and was the most complex CPU chip of its time. The chip has been used internally at HP since 1981.

The most notable feature of the Focus CPU chip is the high level of performance it achieves. The Focus design team determined that the principal potential bottlenecks in the machine's performance were the 32-bit add, qualifier testing, bit extraction, and address computation. Each of these areas was given special attention in the design, and in some cases, additional hardware was devoted to these critical areas. For example, the ALU was given a 32-bit carry lookahead adder of immense complexity. The barrel shifter is capable of shifting an arbitrary amount from 1 to 31 bits in a single cycle.

A large part of the area taken up by the chip is consumed by the 28 general-purpose registers. Having this many registers makes the compiler's task of register allocation easier. An even larger area is used by the 9k word microcode ROM, each word being 38 bits.

As shown in Figure 1.12, the HP Focus chip is pipelined. The stream of macroinstructions is fed through a three-stage pipeline in which fetching, decoding, and execution are overlapped. The microinstructions corresponding to the macroinstructions are also pipelined in order to match the data path time and the fetch time. The micropipeline overlaps microinstruction fetching from the ROM, microinstruction decoding in a PLA (programmable logic array), and microinstruction execution in the ALU or shifter. As a result, microinstructions are executed approximately one per 55-ns cycle.

Since it was impossible to provide a full memory-management unit on the Focus chip, it was decided to provide some limited support for a segmented memory instead. There are four kinds of segments: code, stack, global data, and external data. Each segment is supported by an appropriate number of on-chip, 32-bit registers. For example, the global data segment has a base register and a limit register.

Much of the effort put into the Focus was devoted to making the chip testable and easy to debug. The sheer complexity of the chip required careful organizational and technical management. Heavy emphasis was placed on external visibility paths and special control functions, such as single-stepping and breakpointing. The chip itself has 600 metal probe pads for routing sig-

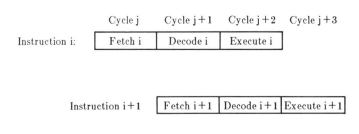

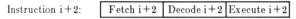

Figure 1.12 The HP Focus pipeline. (Adapted from Beyers JW, Dohse LJ, Fucetola JP, et al: A 32-bit VLSI CPU chip. IEEE Journal of Solid-State Circuits, Vol. SC-16, No. 10, Oct. 1981, pp. 537–541. © 1981 IEEE.)

nals to the outside. This allows precise, efficient testing of the chip during the manufacturing phase. Special hardware allows microcode, macroinstruction, and high-level language single stepping and breakpointing.

The minimum feature size of the Focus chip is 1 micron. The operating speed of 18 MHz is quite high, and the 32-bit integer multiplication takes only 1.8 μsec.

1.4.4. National Semiconductor NS32032

The National Semiconductor NS32032 is a 32-bit CPU targeted toward high-performance applications such as engineering and CAD workstations. The architecture of the NS32032 resembles the DEC VAX in some ways (32). For example, the byte ordering schemes are the same. These similarities make it easier to port the UNIX operating system to the NS32032. One of the goals of the NS32032 is to make the CPU chip more suitable for applications with high bus traffic, by minimizing the number of bus transfers by the CPU (21). Reducing the number of CPU bus transfers allows more transfers by DMA, other CPUs, and graphics devices. The NS32032 data path is given in Figure 1.13.

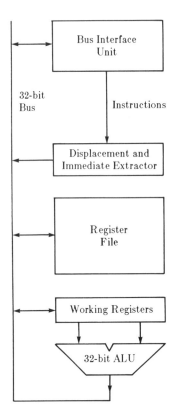

Figure 1.13 The NS32032 data path. (Adapted from Mateosian R: System considerations in the NS32032 design. AFIPS National Computer Conference Proceedings, Vol. 53, 1984, pp. 77–81.)

The NS32032 employs two ways of reducing memory bus traffic: it maximizes the information in each transfer and eliminates transfers altogether by keeping data in the CPU, where it is needed.

The information per bus transfer is maximized by using a wide (for a microprocessor), 32-bit bus and by compactly encoding the instruction set. The memory bandwidth needed to support the instruction set is enhanced by the special addressing modes with variable-size displacements. For example, the register-relative addressing mode allows the displacement to be specified in 1–4 bytes. The commonly used short displacement mode requires only 1 byte. The less frequently used long displacement modes can be accommodated in 2–4 bytes. Using this scheme, only as many bytes are used as are necessary to address the operand.

The reduction in memory traffic is achieved at the expense of increased on-chip complexity. For example, decoding the variable length displacements of the preceding example requires extra circuitry. This can be contrasted with most RISC instructions, where the instruction has a fixed length and the operand fields occupy fixed positions within the instruction. The NS32032 designers view this trade-off as acceptable because they point to the memory bus as the principal bottleneck in a NS32032 system.

As mentioned before, the memory traffic is reduced by keeping data in the CPU, where it is needed. The NS32032 has a total of 16 registers, 8 of which hold floating-point operands. With the help of a smart compiler, data can be kept in these registers rather than in memory. If the most often-used data is kept in the registers, the overall number of memory references is reduced. The number of memory references due to instruction fetches could be reduced by means of an instruction cache, such as is used in the Motorola 68020 and others. The NS32032 does not have an instruction cache, however. Instead, it has an 8-byte instruction prefetch buffer. The prefetch buffer is not as successful in reducing memory traffic due to nonsequential instruction streams as is the cache.

Memory traffic due to operand address translation is reduced by the NS32082 memory management unit. The 32082 has an on-chip translation look-aside buffer (TLB) containing the 32 most recent virtual-to-physical address translations. The size of the TLB is sufficient to avoid all but 2% of the memory references otherwise necessary to support the virtual memory (the hit ratio is typically 98%).

1.4.5. Zilog Z80000

The Zilog Z80000 is a high-performance 32-bit CPU developed for applications such as graphics, array processing, and desktop computing. The Z80000 attempts to provide flexible and simple support for overall systems design (26). The Z80000 incorporates many advanced mainframe-like features such as on-chip virtual memory support, on-chip cache memory, six-stage pipeline, and multiprocessing support.

The register file has 16 32-bit registers, each of which can contain 4-byte operands, two-word operands, or one long-word operand. Registers can be used in ALU operations without affecting the most significant byte(s). Effectively, this quadruples the number of registers for byte-length operands.

The Z80000 has a 4-Gbyte address space that can be modeled in three ways: segmented, linear, or compact. The optimum mode for the application can be chosen by the compiler. The CPU has an adder independent of the ALU for performing virtual-to-physical address translation. This allows address generation to proceed autonomously with respect to other pipeline functions. The 16 most recently used address translations are stored in a translation lookaside buffer. Virtual memory page faults are detected early in the translation process, before the faulting instruction alters the state of the machine. This allows the instruction to be restarted after the appropriate page is transferred to main memory from the backing store.

The Z80000 has a flexible on-chip cache, which can be configured as data-only, instruction-only, instruction and data, and local memory. Any of these configurations can be chosen by an appropriate control register setting. The cache is organized as a 256-byte associative memory. A fully associative placement policy is the most flexible arrangement, and is unusual for a microprocessor cache memory. Most other microprocessors have a direct-mapped cache (e.g., Motorola 68020) (30). The cache is made suitable for a multiprocessor system by its write-through design. The write-through ensures that main memory always contains an updated copy of the data.

The CPU has a very long, six-stage pipeline similar to the Stanford MIPS pipeline. Figure 1.14 shows the breakdown of the pipeline into instruction fetch, instruction decode, address calculation, operand fetch, execution, and operand store. The Z80000 does not have a delayed branching capability, so it suffers a rather severe performance penalty when executing both conditional and unconditional branches. It is probably too much to ask that the Z80000 implement some of the more esoteric schemes (e.g., branch

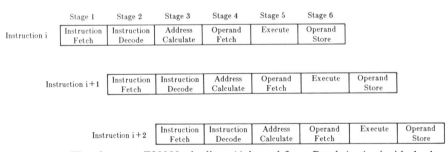

Figure 1.14 The six-stage Z80000 pipeline. (Adapted from Patel A: An inside look at the Z80000 CPU: Zilog's new 32-bit microprocessor. AFIPS National Computer Conference Proceedings, Vol. 53, 1984, pp. 83–91.)

prediction, branch target prefetching) that reduce the penalty associated with branches.

The Z80000 performance was predicted successfully by simulation studies. According to Patel (26) the 25-MHz CPU achieves an average performance of 3.7 mips. This figure takes into account the memory and pipeline delays.

1.4.6. DEC VLSI VAX

Digital Equipment Corporation's VLSI VAX is high-performance, multichip implementation of the VAX architecture. This 8-chip set executes all of the VAX instruction set in hardware (firmware). A parallel project, not discussed here, implements a subset of the VAX instruction set on a single VLSI chip. The goals of the design team were to obtain fast address translation and fast parsing of the variable-length instructions (5). The design was undertaken as an experiment, and should not be treated as an effort toward a commercial product.

The VLSI VAX consists of eight chips: the instruction fetch/execute (IE) chip, the memory-related (M) chip, the floating point (F) chip, and five control store ROM/RAM chips. The IE chip contains the instruction prefetching, decoding, and execution hardware. The M chip contains the cache, translation buffer, and other miscellaneous hardware. The F chip, which is optional, contains a high-performance arithmetic accelerator. A block diagram of a VLSI VAX system is shown in Figure 1.15.

The memory management resources supplied by the VLSI VAX are impressive. The IE chip contains a minitranslation buffer (MTB) containing the five most recently used address translations. Four of the entries are for the data stream, and the remaining one is reserved for the instruction stream. If an MTB miss occurs, the translation request is given to the M chip, which has a 512-entry backup translation buffer (BTB). Main memory is accessed only if both the MTB and the BTB miss. An MTB miss can be serviced quickly by the BTB, so both buffers together give almost the same performance as a 512-entry on-chip translation buffer (19).

MTB translations take one cycle; BTB translations take a total of two cycles, and in the rare cases in which main memory translations are necessary, they take 20 cycles. Address translation uses the same ALU as the instruction stream, unlike the Z80000. In this case, however, a dedicated adder is not necessary because the CPU is not pipelined. There is a small, 8 kbyte direct-mapped cache controlled by the M chip.

The other major goal in implementing the VLSI VAX was to be able to quickly parse the VAX instruction. Instruction parsing is made necessary in the VAX architecture because instructions vary in length from 1 to over 100 bytes (5). The IE chip sequentially decodes the fields of an instruction and places their values in specific microregisters. The speed of

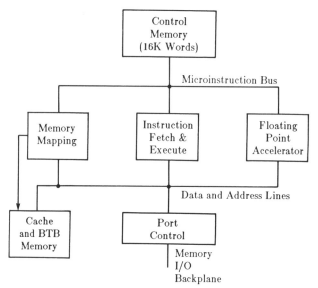

Figure 1.15 VLSI VAX block diagram. (Adapted from Brown JF, Sites RL: A chip set architecture for a high-performance VAX implementation. Proc. of the 17th Annual Microprogramming Workshop, New Orleans, LA, Oct.–Nov. 1984, pp. 48–56.)

the parsing task is accelerated by the use of parallelism in the microcode. During one microcycle, up to three operations can be performed in parallel: a main operation, a length/condition code operation, and a miscellaneous operation. Thus, the IE chip can simultaneously load the microregisters, increment the macroprogram counter, and prefetch instructions.

All eight VLSI VAX chips together have a total of almost 1.4 million transistors. The cycle time of the chip set is 200 ns. The performance of the chip set is comparable to the VAX-11/780. For example, the VLSI VAX integer multiply time is slightly slower, but the integer divide time is twice as fast as in the 780. The VLSI VAX achieves this performance with a 400-fold reduction in the number of integrated circuits.

1.5. Language Corresponding Architectures—Type A

The following subsections describe architectures that one would normally think of as HLL computer architectures. Their natural language is very close to the HLL in concept. The Type A and Type B architectures are Language Corresponding architectures, and their path to the root of the HLL computer architecture tree (Figure 1.1) goes through Complex Architectures and Indirect Execution architectures.

The Type A architecture discussed in this subsection represents an attempt to reduce the conceptual gap between the HLL and the machine language by making the machine language resemble the HLL. Type A and Type B architectures are similar in the sense that both machine languages have a one-to-one correspondence with one or more HLLs. Type A and Type B architectures differ, however, in the method by which the source language is translated into machine language. This task is accomplished by software in the Type A architecture and by hardware in the Type B architecture (25).

The following subsections cover the MIT Scheme-79/81 and the IBM APL machine. Research on these projects began in the 1970s, and ideas from both of these machines are still being used in various ongoing research projects.

1.5.1. MIT Scheme-79/81

The Scheme-79/81 research project at the MIT Artificial Intelligence Laboratory was begun in 1979. The goal of the Scheme research team was to achieve an optimal hardware/software tradeoff in the design and fabrication of a VLSI chip capable of executing a dialect of Lisp called Scheme-79/81. The Scheme-79 architecture is given in Figure 1.16. The term Scheme-81 refers to the follow-up chip (22).

According to the authors, Lisp was chosen as the target language because it is a fundamentally simple language (34). Its complex operations and data structures can be synthesized from simple operators and data types.

Type A architectures, you will remember, have a software translator to convert HLL programs into machine-language programs. The machine language of a Type A closely resembles one or more HLLs. In Scheme-79/81, the machine-language program consists of a sequence of list nodes. Each list node consists of a 24-bit data field, a type field, and a bit used for storage allocation. The data field can be interpreted several different ways, depending on the type field. Examples of data fields are literals, local pointers, global pointers, etc. The normal execution sequence consists of fetching a list node, examining the type field, and interpreting or executing the data field accordingly. Different type field values cause the list node to be processed accordingly, so one might say that the type field is the "opcode" of the Scheme-79/81 chips.

One of the major bottlenecks of the Scheme-79/81 chips is the memory allocation and garbage collection problem. When memory becomes full, a garbage collector microprogram traverses the program list and marks all nodes that cannot be reached by the current program. Then memory is rearranged so that all accessible nodes are located in low memory. Garbage allocation and program execution cannot be done concurrently because there is only one set of registers. Approximately 80% of the machine's time is spent doing storage allocation and garbage collection.

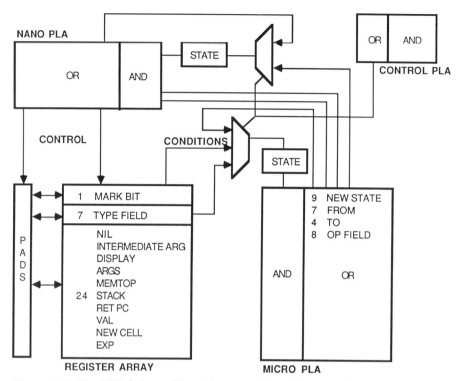

Figure 1.16 The MIT Scheme-79 architecture. (From Sussman GJ, Holloway J, Sterl GL, Bell A: Scheme-79 lisp on a chip. IEEE Computer, Vol. 14, No. 7, July 1981, pp. 10–21. © 1981 IEEE.)

Another limitation is posed by the simplified register file design. The register file has a single bus, and the cells are unbuffered. Having a single bus means that some transfers between registers have to be executed serially, when two buses would allow the operations to be done in parallel. The unbuffered register cells prohibit reading and writing during the same machine cycle. This slows down the increment and decrement operations.

Even with these clear performance limitations, the Scheme-79/81 chips outperform some conventional machines. The computation of the Fibonacci numbers is almost four times as fast on the Scheme-79 as on the DEC PDP-10 when no garbage collection is done.

1.5.2. IBM APL Machine

The IBM APL Machine was developed at the Thomas J. Watson Research Center in Yorktown Heights, N.Y. The hardware/software system was completed in 1973. The goal of the research team was to design and implement a complete system tailored toward the execution of APL programs. The essence of this approach is the implementation of HLL support through extensive microprogramming. We believe that both hardware and firmware approaches may prove efficient in achieving the goals of HLL computer architectures.

The research team chose APL as the target language of the machine because of its usefulness in numeric and data processing, and also because of its power and flexibility (16). However, this choice contributed to some of the difficulties encountered in the implementation of the APL machine. This is because APL is a highly dynamic language, unlike compiler-oriented languages such as FORTRAN, Pascal, and C. The semantics of an APL statement depend very much on the context in which it appears. For example, the statement "A gets B + C" may have a scalar or a vector result, depending on the types of variables B and C. Because of the dynamic, context-dependent environment, APL is not well suited to efficient compilation. Much of the binding must occur at execution time.

The internal representation of the APL program on this Type A machine is very similar to its external representation. A supervisor/translator program is responsible for accepting source programs as input and producing an equivalent reverse Polish representation for internal storage. The reverse Polish representation is used because it is easier to evaluate on a stack.

At execution time, a microcoded statement scanner and syntax analyzer process the code line-by-line. This results in some inefficiency in repeatedly executed statements, such as loops. However, the nature of the APL language eliminates many of the inner loops common to other procedural languages. As the statement is scanned, the analyzer uses the appropriate scalar or vector microcode routine to execute the function. Some of the more complicated APL constructs are actually implemented by APL-coded routines because of microcode storage limitations.

The hardware used to implement the APL machine was the IBM System 360 Model 25. The Model 25 was chosen because of its low cost and its writable control store. The total microcode memory available on the Model 25 is 16 kbytes, and a 4 kbyte auxiliary memory contains the IBM 360 register set. During the power-up sequence, the control memory is first loaded with the IBM 360 emulator, then the APL system routines are loaded. Finally, the system switches to the APL mode.

The performance of the IBM APL machine turned out to be somewhat disappointing. Compared with conventional machines executing APL, the IBM APL machine showed a speed advantage only on long vector operations. Scalar statements and short vector statements actually executed slower on the specialized HLL machine. The loss of speed can be attributed to the need to repeatedly scan and analyze the HLL statements. Whereas a conventional machine performs the lexical and syntactical analysis of an HLL program only once (during compilation), the IBM APL machine must perform this sequence every time the statement is executed. One suggested improvement (16) to the IBM APL machine is specialized scanner/analyzer hardware and vector processor.

1.6. Language Corresponding Architectures—Type B

The Type B architecture, like the Type A architecture, represents an attempt to reduce the conceptual gap by raising the level of the machine language closer to that of the HLL. Unlike the Type A architecture, however, the Type B architecture translates the source language into machine language by means of hardware. The Type B machine does not necessarily have an intermediate software representation.

An interesting question in language corresponding architectures is what to call the translator. Should it be called an assembler or a compiler? Commonly, the word "assembler" is used to denote a program that translates assembly language mnemonics one-to-one into machine language. We use the word "compiler" to describer a translator that accepts HLL source code as its input and produces assembly or machine code as its output. The catch is that the translation process *is* one-to-one in language corresponding architectures. But the translator also inputs HLL source code and outputs machine code (or control information in the case of a Type B). So either designation, compiler or assembler, would be appropriate. Here, we choose to use the word "compiler" to remind ourselves that the machine code of a language corresponding architecture is an HLL.

A potential advantage of the Type B architecture is its compilation speed. Since the compiler of a Type B architecture is implemented in hardware, it is faster than an equivalent software compiler. However, the speed advantage is achieved at the expense of increased design and development cost and at the expense of flexibility. The hardwired or microcoded compiler is difficult and time-consuming to design and modify. Language extensions and enhancements are difficult to add to such a machine.

Further research and experience will tell whether the Type B architecture represents an optimal tradeoff between hardware and software. The answer depends on the application and the importance of fast compilation to the application.

We will consider two examples of Type B architectures in some detail: Symbol and DELtran. However, some other work—see (22) and (23)—also deserves attention. Although the research related to our two examples began in the 1960s and 1970s, the ideas of Symbol and DELtran are still present in a number of current research projects at Intel, IBM, Aerospace Corporation, Stanford, Purdue, and elsewhere (4).

1.6.1. Fairchild/ISU Symbol

The Symbol IIR system was developed by Fairchild beginning in the mid-1960s. The sole operational Symbol IIR system was delivered to Iowa State University in 1971 (10). At ISU the machine was studied, debugged, and finally decommissioned. The goals of the Symbol design team were to increase performance and push the state of the art of technology while providing a cost-effective system. The machine delivered to ISU was intended to be a research tool for HLL operators, memory management, and various other untested ideas. There was to be a follow-up machine called Symbol II, dropping the "Research" suffix.

The Symbol IIR system was designed to provide hardware support for only one HLL: the Symbol Programming Language (SPL). SPL is a block-oriented language with some features of APL, PL/I, and Lisp. There are only two data types in SPL, and all arithmetic is done in arbitrary-precision base 10.

The SPL source code is translated by a dedicated hardware translator, one of eight processors in the system. The translator attained compilation speed of 70,000 statements per minute because SPL was designed for "easy" parsing and no optimization was performed (10). The translator accepted SPL source code and produced a one-for-one reverse Polish representation that was executed by a specialized processor.

An interesting detail of the translator processor is how it handles identifiers (e.g., variables). The translator processor establishes a name table for each block in the source program (25). The name table, similar to an assembler's symbol table, contains two items: the string representing the identifier and the identifier control word. The string is the ASCII name of the identifier, and the identifier control word is a form of descriptor. Symbol stores the complete identifier rather than a compact, encoded representation of the identifier. This approach has an advantage in code debugging because statements can be "disassembled" without reference to the source code.

Another notable feature of the Symbol system is the hardware memory manager processor. The memory manager processor executes many of the same functions as the (software) memory manager of an operating system on a conventional machine. Examples of the functions performed by the memory manager processor are memory allocation, paging, and free memory list management.

The memory itself is divided into 64k pages of 256 bytes each. The central processor uses a FIFO algorithm in conjunction with a priority system to manage the memory-resident pages. The priority system favors the pages belonging to the process currently being executed and disfavors pages belonging to processes that are waiting for execution. An entirely separate processor performs garbage collection functions. The garbage collector reclaims unused memory pages at low priority, using the interprocessor bus only when it would otherwise be idle.

Many computer architects agree that Symbol was a landmark in HLL computer architecture. Symbol IIR was the first system to be built entirely in hardware to support an HLL. All interaction with the system occurred at the level of the HLL, including error messages and debugging features.

The sheer complexity of a complete hardware implementation of an

HLL, though, proved to be the downfall of the Symbol system. Given the technology available when the project was begun (i.e., no semiconductor RAMs, ROMs, MSI, LSI, etc.), it is remarkable that the Symbol system ever worked. Recognizing the limitations faced by Symbol's designers, we must applaud this pioneering effort in HLL architecture. However, we should also question whether the term "architecture" really applies to the Symbol system.

Did Symbol's designers strive to achieve an optimal trade-off between software and hardware functions in this system? The answer is clearly "no." A major limitation of the Symbol system is the lack of flexibility inherent in its hardware implementation of functions. For example, the interface processor of the original Symbol system provided a primitive, pushbutton-operated editor for program entry. The interface processor required special, dedicated terminals that could only be used on the Symbol system. Because the interface processor had no "hooks" for software control, the primitive built-in editor could not be used by the students at ISU. Instead, all text editing was performed by software in the central processor, and the editing hardware was unused. As another example, the Symbol system supported only one language, and that language was not an accepted, popular language. Programmers wishing to use FORTRAN or COBOL were forced to rely on a software translator or a custom hardware translator.

1.6.2. DELtran

DELtran is an experimental system developed at the Stanford Emulation Laboratory beginning in 1977. The DELtran design team strove to reduce the gap between the machine language and the HLL as well as the gap between the machine language and the machine's execution interpreter. DELtran stands for a Directly Executed Language derived from FORTRAN code.

DELs are intermediate languages that represent the optimal balance between a single HLL and the execution interpreter of the machine. As such, DELs are designed to be easily interpreted while also being easy to generate using a one-to-one translation of an HLL. The DEL model for execution architecture is shown in Figure 1.17 (12).

DELtran was designed to support a minimal subset of FORTRAN-II. FORTRAN-II is a simpler language to support than Pascal or PL/I because of the limited scope of its identifiers and its strongly typed nature. Variables in FORTRAN subroutines are either local to the routines or global; subroutines may not access variables that "belong" to their callers. This structure simplifies the dynamic accessing of variables.

It is important to recognize that DELtran's mechanism for referencing identifiers is a major difference between DELtran and traditional architectures. DELtran instructions contain identifiers that are closely related to the

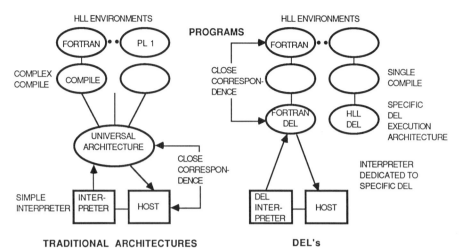

Figure 1.17 The DEL model for execution architecture. (From Flynn MJ, Hoevel LW: Execution architecture: The DELtran experiment. IEEE Trans. on Computers, Vol. C-32, No. 2, Feb. 1983, pp. 156–174. © 1983 IEEE.)

HLL rather than the execution interpreter. This means that the DELtran instruction does not refer to machine registers or memory addresses as does the conventional instruction. Instead, the instruction refers to identifiers in the name space of the HLL.

The particular mechanism used in DELtran minimizes memory usage and interpretation overhead associated with identifier referencing. The DELtran instruction refers to a compact, encoded representation of the identifier. The first variable in a (sub-) program is assigned the number 1 by the compiler, the second one is assigned the number 2, and so on. Thus, N identifiers can be represented in ceiling(log N) bits.

How are these identifier numbers used at execution time to reference variables? This is a situation in which the choice of FORTRAN as the target language of the machine proved to be fortunate. In FORTRAN, the name space is unique for each subprogram because routines at a lower lexical level cannot reference variables at a higher lexical level. This fact simplifies the situation in the DELtran machine. At execution time, an environment pointer points to an access table of descriptors. The descriptor defines the type of the variable and its location in memory. At execution time, the identifier number from the instruction is used as an index into the descriptor table, thus generating the memory address of the identifier with only one level of indirection.

Separate access tables are used for each subprogram, and the access tables are changed upon subprogram call/returns. DELtran speeds up the table access by maintaining the access tables in a high-speed writeable control store.

DELtran's identifier accessing mechanism contrasts with the approach used in the Symbol IIR system in many ways. One major difference is that DELtran uses a compact representation of the identifier, whereas Symbol IIR uses the full literal value of the identifier. The DELtran approach offers efficiency at execution time because of the elimination of comparisons and searches. However, the Symbol approach allows easy HLL-level debugging because machine-language statements can be easily translated into HLL code.

The run-time interpreter in the DELtran machine uses 800 words of control store memory. The small size of the interpreter supports the assertion that DEL computers present less of an interpretive burden than conventional machine languages. In comparison, one model of the PDP-11 uses 1200 words, and a System/360 uses 2100 words (12). DELtran fared well in the Whetstone benchmark against various mainframe computers such as the IBM 370, Honeywell 66, and the Burroughs B1700. In both execution time and program size, DELtran showed a five-to-one advantage over these conventional architectures. It remains to be seen, though, whether the DEL approach will efficiently transfer to such dynamic environments such as Ada, Pascal, and C.

1.7. Direct Execution Architectures

The Direct Execution Architecture (DEA) represents one extreme in hardware/software tradeoffs. All other classes of architectures perform some preprocessing or translation of programs before executing them. The DEA, on the other hand, executes the HLL source code directly, without intermediate translation. The DEA has several potential advantages: no compilation overhead, single-copy program storage, and a high degree of interactiveness (6).

Even more than the Type B indirect execution architecture, however, the DEA suffers from inherent disadvantages stemming from its lack of indirection. The major problem with DEAs is that they are implemented entirely in hardware. Because of their implementational complexity and lack of flexibility, DEAs represent a nonoptimal hardware/software tradeoff, except in specific applications. A DEA developed for the Ada language, for example, is not well suited to executing FORTRAN code. Whereas other architectures allow a compiler to bridge the gap between the HLL and the hardware, the DEA is rigid in its insistence on a strict format.[5]

In addition to the problems related to its hardware implementation, the DEA suffers from increased error-detection delay. When a program is run

---

[5] Actually, one could use a DEA as a language definition tool. The definition of a language can be embodied in the hardware of the DEA.

on a DEA, it is checked for syntax errors at the same time as it is executed. This means that a syntax error on the last line of say, a 1000-line program is not detected until the 1000th line is executed. On a conventional computer, the syntax error would be detected by the compiler *before* execution. Of course, nothing prevents the use of a syntax checker before executing a program on a DEA. However, as long as the lexical and syntax phases of the compiler are being synthesized, why not perform some simple code generation at the same time? The extra effort would be minimal in terms of complexity in software, and the performance gains in executing the intermediate code could be large.

The DEA differs from von Neumann architectures in three ways (6). First, programs and data are kept in separate memories. Von Neumann architectures, by definition, do not distinguish between program and data storage. Second, the central processor black box is separated in practice into at least two separate processors: one for control flow, one for data flow. Von Neumann architectures use a single processor to handle both flows. Third, the control and data flow processors execute concurrently.

The type of DEA we will concentrate on is known as the University of Maryland approach. The program code of a DEA is stored in a program memory, and the data is stored in a data memory, as shown in Figure 1.18. The program code is accepted into the program memory from the input device. At execution time, a *lexical processor* scans the program memory to extract HLL tokens. This phase of execution corresponds to the lexical analyzer of a compiler. Tokens are placed one at a time into a token register, which corresponds to the instruction register of a conventional machine. The lexical processor maintains a pointer to the location from which the

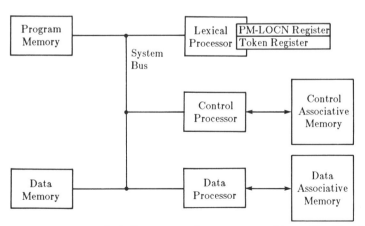

Figure 1.18 A typical direct-execution computer. (From Chu Y, Abrams M: Programming languages and direct-execution computer architecture. IEEE Computer, Vol. 14, No. 7, July 1981, pp. 22–31. © 1981 IEEE.)

token contained in the token register was fetched. This pointer corresponds to the program counter in a conventional processor.

The token register is examined by the control processor and data processor. The data processor executes tokens that perform data manipulation, such as multiplication and shifting. The data processor also manages access to the data memory by means of symbol tables (e.g., a content-addressable memory) and storage management routines. The control processor, on the other hand, executes tokens that change the control flow, such as "repeat," "do," "goto," and "if."

In the following paragraphs, we will briefly examine only one DEA architecture, based on the University of Maryland approach. Some other DEAs should also be mentioned (7, 36).

The PASDEC project (Pascal Interactive Direct Execution Computer) was developed at the University of Tsukuba, Japan (18). The motivation for the PASDEC project was to increase programmer productivity by eliminating the conceptual gap between the HLL and the target architecture. The PASDEC system consists of a complete system involving a terminal, I/O processor, Interactive processor, and a Language processor.

PASDEC executes a small subset of standard Pascal called Tiny-Pascal. Tiny-Pascal has three control constructs, two data types, two data structures, and one data flow operation. Such limited languages are typical of DEAs.

The outstanding feature of PASDEC is that all interaction with the system occurs at the HLL level. PASDEC is a true HLL computer system as defined by Ditzel and Patterson (9). For example, the user enters a program under the interactive direction of an Editor subprocessor, similar in concept to the Symbol IIR editor processor. The Editor subprocessor immediately detects syntax errors and allows the user to correct them, thus avoiding the flood of meaningless error messages often encountered when compiling code on a conventional computer.[6]

Program debugging also occurs at the HLL level. The PASDEC user is able to single-step the program at any desired granularity and immediately observe the program's effect on the data. Debugging is under the control of the Debugger subprocessor, which, together with the Editor subprocessor, forms the Interactive processor.

Actual execution of the code is handled by the Language processor, which consists of a Control subprocessor, a Data subprocessor, a Lexical subprocessor, and a Driver subprocessor. The Control subprocessor handles control tokens (IF, WHILE, etc.), and the Data subprocessor handles data manipulation tokens (declarations, assignments). The Lexical subprocessor obtains the tokens from the program memory. The Driver subprocessor uses

---

[6] Of course, an interpretive language on a conventional computer provides the same capability with greater flexibility, lower risk, and lower cost.

the token fetched by the Lexical subprocessor to decide whether the Control or Data subprocessor is to be activated.

1.8. Summary

The main intention of this chapter is to bring together basic concepts and examples from the areas of advanced microprocessors and high-level language processor architectures. For more detailed information, the reader is referred to earlier versions of this text, which contain classified bibliography listings and suggestions for further readings (22) and (23).

Problems

1. The instruction set of many CISC machines includes memory reference arithmetic instructions, in which one operand is in memory and the other is in a register. This approach is known as the memory reference approach. Other machines, typically RISCs, require that both operands be located in registers, which must be loaded before the operation, and stored away later. This is known as the load/store approach. Describe applications which favor each approach. Which organization is more appropriate for compiler-generated code?

2. Comment on the advantages and drawbacks of multiple, overlapping register sets, as used in the UC Berkeley RISCs. What effect does the frequency of context switches have? How does the implementation technology affect your evaluation of the trade-offs (think of VLSI)?

3. Is it contradictory to claim that RISC machines reduce the semantic gap even though they have a simplified instruction set? If so, what other strategies might shrink the gap? If not, in what other ways do RISC machines shrink the gap?

4. Although Type A and Type B language-directed architectures have similar goals, they offer different solutions to the architecture design problem. What are the essential differences between them? How do these differences affect the suitability of the architectures for different applications? What are the essential similarities which make them belong to closely related classes of HLL architectures? List applications particularly suited to each type.

References

1. Barron I, Cavill P, May D, Wilson P: Transputer does 5 or more MIPS even when not used in parallel. *Electronics*, Nov. 17, 1983, pp. 109–115.
2. Basart E, Folger D: Ridge 32 architecture—a RISC variation. *Proc. of the IEEE*

International Conference on Computer Design: VLSI in Computers, Port Chester, NY, Oct. 31–Nov. 3, 1983, pp. 315–318.

3. Beyers JW, Dohse LJ, Fucetola JP, et al: A 32-bit VLSI CPU chip. *IEEE Journal of Solid-State Circuits*. Vol. SC-16, No. 10, Oct. 1981, pp. 537–541.

4. Bose P, Davidson ES: Design of instruction set architectures for support of high-level languages. IEEE 7111/84/0000/0198, 1984.

5. Brown JF, Sites RL: A Chip set architecture for a high-performance VAX implementation. *Proc. of the 17th Annual Microprogramming Workshop*, New Orleans, LA, Oct.–Nov. 1984, pp. 48–56.

6. Chu Y (ed): Special issue on high-level language computer architecture. *IEEE Computer*, Vol. 14, No. 7, July 1981.

7. Chu Y, Abrams M: Programming languages and direct-execution computer architecture. *IEEE Computer*, Vol. 14, No. 7, July 1981, pp. 22–31.

8. Colwell RP, Hitchcock CY, Jensen ED, et al: Computers, complexity, and controversy. *IEEE Computer*, Vol. 18, No. 9, Sept. 1985, pp. 8–20.

9. Ditzel DR, Patterson DA: Retrospective on high-level language computer architecture. *Proc. of the Seventh Annual Symposium on Computer Architecture*, May 1980, La Baule, France, pp. 97–104.

10. Ditzel DR: Reflections on the high-level language symbol computer system. *IEEE Computer*, Vol. 14, No. 7, July 1981, pp. 55–66.

11. El-Halabi H, Agrawal DP: Some remarks on direct execution computers. *Computer Architecture News*, Vol. 10, No. 1, March 1982, pp. 23–27.

12. Flynn MJ, Hoevel LW: Execution architecture: The DELtran experiment. *IEEE Transactions on Computers*, Vol. C-32, No. 2, Feb. 1983, pp. 156–174.

13. Foti L, English D, Hopkins R, et al: Reduced instruction-set multi-microcomputer system. *Proc. 1984 NCC*, Las Vegas, NV, Vol. 53, June 1984, pp. 69–75.

14. Gross TR: Code optimization techniques for pipelined architectures. *Proc. COMPCON Spring 1983*, IEEE Computer Society, San Francisco, CA, March 1983, pp. 278–285.

15. Gupta A, Toong HD: An architectural comparison of 32-bit microprocessors. *IEEE Micro*, Feb. 1983, pp. 9–22.

16. Hassit A, Lageschulte JW, Lyon LE: Implementation of a high-level language machine. *Communications of the ACM*, Vol. 16, No. 4, April 1973, pp. 199–212.

17. Hennessy J, Jouppi N, Baskett F, et al: MIPS: A VLSI processor architecture. *Proc. of the IEEE Spring COMPCON '82*, Feb. 22–25, 1982, San Francisco, CA, pp. 2–7.

18. Itano K: PASDEC: A PASCAL interactive direct execution machine. *Proc. of the International Workshop on High-Level Language Computer Architecture*, University of Maryland, 1980, pp. 161–169.

19. Johnson WN, Herrick WV, Grundmann WJ: A VLSI VAX chip set. *IEEE Journal of Solid-State Circuits*, Vol. SC-19, No. 5, Oct. 1984, pp. 663–674.

20. Katevenis MG, Sherburne RW Jr, Patterson DA, Sequin CH: The RISC II microarchitecture. *Journal of VLSI and Computer Systems*, Vol. 1, No. 2, Fall 1984, pp. 138–152.

21. Mateosian R: System considerations in the NS32032 design. *AFIPS National Computer Conference Proceedings*, Vol. 53, 1984, pp. 77–81.

22. Milutinović V (ed): Advanced microprocessors and high-level language computer architecture. IEEE Computer Society Press Tutorial, 1986.
23. Milutinović V (ed): High-level language computer architecture. Computer Science Press, 1988.
24. Motorola Inc: MC68020 Technical summary. Motorola Semiconductors Products Inc., 1984.
25. Myers GJ: *Advances in Computer Architecture.* New York, John Wiley & Sons, 1982.
26. Patel A: An inside look at the Z80000 CPU: Zilog's new 32-bit microprocessor. *AFIPS National Computer Conference Proceedings,* Vol. 53, 1984, pp. 83–91.
27. Patterson D, Garrison P, Hill M, et al: Architecture of a VLSI instruction cache for a RISC. *Proc. of the 10th International Symposium on Computer Architecture,* Stockholm, Sweden, June 13–17, 1983, pp. 108–116.
28. Patterson D, Sequin C: A VLSI RISC. *IEEE Computer,* Vol. 15, No. 9, pp. 8–21, 1982.
29. Patterson D: Reduced instruction set computers. *Communications of the ACM,* Vol. 28, No. 1, Jan. 1985, pp. 8–21.
30. Phillips D: Mainframe tricks raise performance of 32-bit micros. *Computer Design,* Vol. 24, No. 7, July 1985, pp. 95–103.
31. Radin G: The 801 minicomputer. *IBM Journal of Research and Development.* Vol. 27, No. 3, pp. 237–246.
32. Serlin O: 32-Bit MPU battle nears climax. *Unix/World,* Aug. 1985, pp. 16–20.
33. Silbey A, Milutinović V, Mendoza-Grado V: A survey of advanced microprocessors and HLL computer architectures. *IEEE Computer,* Vol. 19, No. 8, August 1986, pp. 72–85.
34. Sussman GJ, Holloway J, Sterl GL, Bell A: Scheme-79 lisp on a chip. *IEEE Computer,* Vol. 14, No. 7, July 1981, pp. 10–21.
35. Wulf W: Compilers and computer architecture. *IEEE Computer,* Vol. 14, No. 7, July 1981, pp. 41–47.
36. Vahey M, Mosteller G: High-level language oriented aerospace computer. *Proc. of NAECON 1979,* New York, IEEE, pp. 684–690.

2

Reduced Instruction Set Computer Architectures

Paul Chow
John Hennessy

2.1. Introduction

Reduced Instruction Set Computer (*RISC*) architectures have evolved from
the desire to provide performance for programs written in high-level languages.[1] These designs are simpler and can be implemented without the use
of microcode. This is a trend away from the Complex Instruction Set Computer (*CISC*) architectures that use a large amount of hardware complexity
to provide a high degree of instruction set capability. The RISC approach
is fostered by technology shifts both in software and in hardware. Work on
RISC-style machines began at IBM in 1975, although this was not widely
known. The result was a minicomputer known as the 801 that was built out
of standard ECL parts. Berkeley in 1980 and Stanford in 1981 started projects
to build VLSI processors that demonstrated the RISC design philosophy.
The Berkeley group produced the RISC I and RISC II processors and Stan-

---

[1] See Chapter 1 for more information on this aspect of RISC architectures, and HLL
computer architectures in general.

ford produced the MIPS chip. The result of this work has generated widespread interest in the commercial world.

This chapter describes the ideas and issues behind RISC machines and their implementations. First the goals of a computer architecture are described. Then, the trends in architectural design will be outlined, showing how RISCs are a logical result of these trends. To show two different ways of dealing with some of the issues presented by the RISC approach, the Berkeley RISC processors and the Stanford MIPS processor are used as examples. These will be followed by a section on the implementation issues that must be considered in a RISC design. Finally, some general conclusions and observations about future trends will be given.

2.2. The Goals of an Architecture

The effectiveness of a computer architecture can be measured by how well it can be used to carry out an application and the performance attainable by implementations of that architecture in various technologies. Applications are generally written in a high-level language and compiled to use the instruction set of the machine. This heavy reliance on high-level languages represents a development of the past 10 years. The RISC approach responds to this shift in technology by designing architectures to mesh with compiler technology. Application programs also rely on functions provided by the operating system. Therefore, to carry out an application an architecture must be able to support both the use of high-level languages and the functions required by an operating system.

The cost and the performance of a machine measure how well an architecture can be implemented. Since the ultimate use of a computer is to run programs, the most important of these measures is the performance of the machine or how quickly and efficiently it can be used to execute a program. Thus, an instruction set designer must carefully consider both the usefulness of an instruction set for encoding programs and how the instruction set impacts the performance achievable for the architecture. This last effect is difficult to measure; attempts to investigate the implementation aspects of an architecture would need to consider implementation technology, as well as the relative size of an implementation. In some technologies, such as VLSI, the penalties for a substantial increase in the size of an implementation lead directly to performance disadvantages for such architectures.

Several methods have been used to gauge the performance of a machine. They include instructions per second, total and peak memory bandwidth required, and the static and dynamic count of instructions needed for an application. These measures, however, cannot always be used to make meaningful comparisons of performance, particularly between machines with different architectures. Abstract evaluations completely neglect issues such as clock speed and average instruction execution rate. To a user wishing to run an application, the key performance factor that is perceived is how long it takes to run the application. This time will be a combination of the effectiveness of the machine and the effectiveness of the compiler. Efforts to separate these two issues are becoming increasingly difficult as machines that mate better with optimizing compilers are designed.

Consider the following equation as a way to measure the performance of an implementation running a particular benchmark:

$$Performance = \frac{1}{No.\ Instructions \times Cycle\ Time \times Cycles/Instruction}$$

From this equation it can be seen that to maximize performance it is necessary to

1. minimize the clock cycle time of the system. This means that the overhead per instruction must be reduced and the hardware must be organized to minimize the delays in each clock cycle.
2. reduce the number of cycles required to perform an instruction. Ideally, this suggests that each instruction should execute in one cycle. This may mean that some performance may need to be sacrificed in some parts of the architecture in return for increased performance of the more heavily used parts.
3. keep the number of instructions required as small as possible. This is determined by the effectiveness of the compiler and the functionality of the instructions.

The product of the clock cycle time and the average cycles per instruction is the execution time for an average instruction. Although not strictly true, it is usually the machine organization that defines the cycles per instruction, while the cycle time is largely determined by the implementation technology. An organizational technique that can influence the cycle time is pipelining. The aim is to reduce the number of cycles per instruction, but the hardware required to control the pipeline can have a significant effect on the cycle time.

The balance between compiler support and hardware support of language features is a key challenge for the computer architect. Depending on the programming environment some language features are sufficiently performance critical that they merit special support in the architecture. These features include support for tags, floating point arithmetic, and parallel constructs. A feature that is becoming a standard part of many compilers is optimization, and in this case, the architecture should be designed to allow the optimizer to make the choices between more time-efficient or more space-efficient sequences. Details of the hardware should be exposed to allow the compiler to make the most effective use of the hardware. If this is not done, many computations hidden by an instruction cannot be optimized away. Ideally, the instructions should be simplified to maximize the visibility of all the operations (or machine cycles) needed to execute a program.

An architecture that provides a suitable target for a compiler still needs to be able to support an operating system to make the hardware usable. The operating system requires certain architectural capabilities without which it will either be impossible to implement certain operating system functions, or there will be significant performance penalties in implementing those functions. The most important architectural support includes

- privileged and user modes that protect some special instructions and some system resources while in user mode;
- support for external interrupts and internal traps;
- memory mapping support, including support for demand paging and provision for memory protection; and
- primitives to support synchronization in multiprocessor configurations.

The architecture imposes certain requirements on the hardware at the organizational level, and this affects the performance by restricting what the hardware must be able to do and what flexibility exists in implementation. The detailed machine organization usually has a significant influence on the performance; of course, this organization must be driven both by the architecture and by issues arising from the implementation technology. This compromise is especially important when VLSI is used because the interaction between architecture and implementation is more pronounced. Here are some of the implications on architecture and machine organization that arise from the technology:

- To make up for the limited speed of a technology, parallel implementations are often used. Several slower components are used instead of a smaller number of fast components. This is the trade-off seen between bipolar and MOS implementations. The higher density and lower cost of MOS can lessen the speed advantage of ECL, by exploiting parallelism.[2]
- The complexity of the circuits that can be implemented in hardware limit what can be done. A corollary of this is that no architectural feature is free. Any addition to an architecture impedes the design cycle and often has a direct performance effect as well.
- Communication is more expensive than computation. An architecture that requires a lot of global interaction will suffer in its implementation.
- In VLSI, chip boundaries become a major design influence in two different ways. First, they place a hard limit on the bandwidth onto and off the

---

[2] See Chapter 3 for more information on RISC architecture for GaAs technology.

chip. Second, they create a substantial disparity between on-chip and off-chip communication delays.

2.3. Architectural Trends

Early computers were limited mainly by the speed of the central processing unit (CPU) and by the technology available to build memories. The limited compiler technology and mismatch between machine performance and application requirements encouraged the use of assembly language; there was no other way to write a program that would fit in the limited amount of memory available and achieve the necessary performance. As computer systems developed, the speed of the CPU increased and memory became denser and cheaper. Increasing application complexity made assembly language programming uneconomical. However, there are still many applications being written in assembly language, particularly for microprocessors. The arguments for doing so are generally the need for speed and the limited amount of memory available on a particular processor, exactly as in the early days of computing. Programming in assembly language allows the programmer to take full advantage of the hardware being used. The available compiler technology for many architectures is generally not able to produce code that is as efficient both in time and in space as a carefully coded assembly language program. A better approach than using assembly language would be to develop well-integrated architectures and compilers that together deliver much higher performance.

The evolution from 8-bit to 16-bit to 32-bit microprocessors is evidence of the realization that high-level languages are becoming more important. The 16-bit and 32-bit machines have many more instruction features to support compiled languages. These features have been added in the hardware to try and close the *semantic gap*, or the distance between machine instructions and the statements of a high-level language. This is supposed to make the resulting code more efficient, but the research into RISCs has shown that this is not often true. The machine instructions will always be the target of a compiler, so the compiler should drive the instruction set choices. It has been observed that simple instructions dominate the mix, even on very powerful architectures. This led to the investigations into the RISC architectural approach.

We can use the simple performance equation given in Section 2.2 to illustrate the difference between the RISC and CISC approaches. In a CISC machine, the designer attempts to make powerful instructions. This tends to decrease the numbers of instructions needed, but increases the cycles per instruction, and often increases the cycle time as well. A RISC architecture will attempt to significantly decrease the average execution time per instruction, usually by decreasing cycles per instruction to close to 1, and often by decreasing the cycle time. However, for compiled programs, RISCs can achieve this dramatic decrease in average instruction execution time with only a small increase in dynamic instruction count.

2.3.1. The RISC Approach

The RISC style of architecture shifts complexity from hardware and program runtime to software and program compile time. The designer must consider two major points when evaluating each addition to the architecture:

- The performance advantage gained when the feature is part of the hardware versus that when it is implemented in software.
- The performance loss that may occur because of the increased hardware complexity. Adding a feature to increase performance for some instructions may slow down all the other instructions.

RISCs are machines with simplified instruction sets. Their instruction sets are simpler than most other machines, but they still may have many instructions. The 801 has over 100 instructions and MIPS has over 60. They also may have conceptually complex details such as programmer cache management in the 801 and pipeline dependency hazards that must be considered by the software as in MIPS. The architectures avoid features that need complex hardware control structures, though they may use complex implementation structures if the performance gain merits their use. It may be better to call these machines streamlined instead of reduced. Here are some of the key characteristics of such architectures:

1. Most instructions are executed in a single machine cycle. (This usually means that a new instruction can be fetched every machine cycle even though each instruction requires several cycles to complete.)
2. Functionality has been migrated to software so that only the features that significantly increase performance are implemented in hardware. Compile-time implementation in software is preferred whenever the hardware/software performance trade-off is negligible because extra hardware adds complexity and can increase the cycle time of the machine.
3. The architecture is load/store (also called register–register); only load and store instructions are used to access memory. All actual computations are register–register format.
4. The instruction set is regular and simple, with few addressing modes.
5. Control is hardwired, with little or no microcode.
6. There is a high-performance memory hierarchy including general purpose registers and cache memory.

The advantages of simplified instruction sets are clearly demonstrated when the interaction between the architecture and the implementation is examined. The simple architecture means a simple implementation that leaves room for implementing constructs in the hardware that can significantly enhance the performance of the machine. The advantages of this approach range from implementation performance advantages to a better match with the compiler. Some of the most important advantages are described below.

A Level of Runtime Translation Is Eliminated

Using a simplified instruction set means that the level of translation done in microcoded instruction sets at runtime can be done instead by the compiler. This reduces the hardware requirements, and improves performance by eliminating a level of translation.

Instruction Decoding Is Faster

The simple instruction formats mean that the instructions can be decoded very quickly. This helps to reduce the cycle time of the clock and the pipeline latency.

Execution Is Fast

Most instructions can achieve single-cycle throughput. The register-oriented (or load/store) nature of the architecture provides this capability. Even on complex machines, the simplest instructions are the most frequent, so fast execution of simple instructions is important.

Little Overhead per Instruction

The use of hardwired control simplifies the implementation so that the overhead in logic delay necessary for each instruction is reduced. This also helps to shorten the clock cycle.

Simple Instructions Are a Better Match for a Compiler

The low-level instruction set provides the best target for state-of-the-art optimizing compiler technology. The optimizer can clearly see what the hardware is doing and remove any redundant operations.

Hardware Resources Can Be Devoted to Other Uses

The available hardware budget can be used for features that enhance the performance of the machine in direct and visible ways, instead of implementing complex control structures and instruction set functions that are rarely used. Examples of performance-oriented additions might include caches and translation look-aside buffers. The simpler design also means that the human resources can be concentrated on performance issues instead of just getting the machine to function. These trade-offs are especially relevant in VLSI, where additional silicon resources are expensive.

A Simpler Design Should Require Less Design Time
In the past, design time has not been considered an important issue. However, with the recent rapid pace of technology improvement, designs that take too long can be made obsolete by improved technology. The design cycle for current machines is typically 4 years, while a technology will only remain state of the art for about 2 years.

There are also potential disadvantages to RISC architectures. The first is the effect of decreased instruction density. A simplified instruction set requires more instructions, both statically and dynamically, to perform the same function, putting greater demands on the instruction memory and on secondary storage. The static size increase for RISC machines is typically in the region of 40–50%, while the dynamic size increase (i.e., the number of instruction bytes actually fetched) is 10–30% greater. Thus, a RISC-based computer will need more secondary storage to hold programs and, more importantly, will require higher instruction memory bandwidth than a machine with more densely encoded instructions. The other potential disadvantage is that the software system may be more complex. For example, the software system may have to perform pipeline scheduling.

Two aspects to the memory bandwidth issue must be considered. One is the data accesses; the other is the instruction accesses. For data accesses, it has been shown that register-oriented architectures have significantly lower data memory bandwidth requirements. This is desirable because data access is less predictable, and thus has more impact on performance. The existing streamlined machines use the advantages of having registers in different ways. The Berkeley RISC machines have a large number of registers broken into smaller sets called register windows. The Stanford MIPS processor and IBM 801 have a much smaller number of registers and rely on the compiler doing register allocation. These machines also differ in how memory accesses are handled in the pipelining of the machine. The differences are discussed in Section 2.4 when the Berkeley and Stanford machines are compared.

For instruction accesses, it is important to examine some aspects of the memory system in more detail. First is the peak and average memory bandwidth requirements. The peak bandwidth determines the complexity of a memory hierarchy, whereas the average bandwidth is important in determining the performance of a hierarchy. On any machine, most of the instructions executed are loads and stores, simple ALU instructions, and branches. The execution time of these instructions is largely limited by the instruction and data bandwidth the machine can support. Thus, the peak bandwidth of a CISC machine must come close to that of a RISC machine if the two machines are to achieve the same performance level. This means that the memory system of a RISC machine will not necessarily be more complicated than that of a CISC machine. The second aspect to examine is the details of the implementation of the machine. Issues such as caching, memory hierarchy design, and the implementation technology can affect the instruction bandwidth. For example, in VLSI designs the peak bandwidth at the chip boundaries is a limiting factor.

Designing compilers for RISC machines presents a different set of challenges. The code generation for a simplified instruction set is actually easier than for a more complex machine because the number of possible instruction alternatives is quite limited. Optimization is much more important because it can be more effective and the simple instruction set makes it easier for the optimizer to decide whether a given transformation has a desirable effect. However, there can be more complications because of implementation complexities visible at the instruction set level. An example is the MIPS system, where the software is more complicated because it must take care of instruction scheduling to make sure that all data dependencies in the pipeline are removed. This is not overly difficult, and represents an optimization that can be used on any pipelined machine.

2.3.2. The Effects of Technology

The evolution of hardware technology has had a significant effect in advancing the RISC approach. Rapid progress in integrated circuit technology has resulted in two substantial effects: the production of high-density, high-speed RAM technology, and the creation of a technology suitable for single-chip CPUs. The progress in memory technology represents a shift in the relative performance and cost of memory versus logic. In particular, the availability of fast, dense static RAMs makes the use of large caches attractive, and large dynamic RAMs make large main memories attractive. Thus, this technology encourages the use of higher bandwidth, more memory-consumptive approaches to architecture.

VLSI technology has also made it possible to implement CPUs on a single chip in the form of microprocessors. This requires not only high density MOS, but also high bandwidth packaging that can support a CPU. With increasing densities it is now possible to consider the use of on-chip caches or large register sets in the design of new architectures. An on-chip cache can be a cost-effective alternative to a microstore, with the added benefit that the application dynamically allocates this limited on-chip memory rather than the architect preselecting what is statically stored in microstore.

2.4. Examples of RISC Architectures

The RISC architectures that have been implemented are different in many aspects but all achieve similar goals. A feature that all three research RISC machines (MIPS, Berkeley RISC, and the IBM 801) share is the delayed branch. The idea of the delayed branch demonstrates the basic philosophy of the RISC approach. The best-known simplified instruction set machines are the Berkeley RISC processors and the Stanford MIPS processor. These two machines have taken different approaches to several problems using different trade-offs. The Berkeley RISC machines are particularly known for their use of register windows.

2.4.1. Delayed Branches

When a branch instruction is executed on a pipelined machine, the instruction that should follow the branch is not known till the branch completes execution. This can force the pipeline to stall till the branch is completed, typically causing a performance loss in cycles equal to the number of cycles required to determine the branch destination after the branch instruction has been fetched. Rather than stalling the pipeline, which can cost 30–50% of the machine performance, branch prediction can be used. This can be implemented in hardware or by using delayed branches. Delayed branches is a static software branch prediction technique that is about as effective as hardware branch prediction, but it does not require the addition of hardware resources or hardware complexity.

To see how a delayed branch scheme works, first consider the RISC I pipeline shown in Figure 2.1. This is a simple pipeline that overlaps the execute cycle of one instruction with the fetch cycle of the next instruction. For a branch instruction, the execute cycle is used to compute the branch condition, so it is not possible to affect the instruction fetch of the next instruction. In a delayed branch, the outcome of the branch does not take effect until one following instruction (or more, depending on the pipeline) has already been fetched. This fetched instruction is always executed. Software schedules an appropriate instruction for this *branch delay slot*. The simplest scheme would insert a *no-op* instruction, but a better solution is to find a useful instruction. Figure 2.3 illustrates the scheduling of a delayed branch. In a normal branch scheme, the sequence executed is 1000, 1001, 1005, ... When using a delayed branch scheme with no scheduling, a *no-op* is inserted in the delay slot and the sequence executed is 1000, 1001, 1002, 1006, ... If scheduling is used, a better sequence is 1000, 1001, 1005, ... Here, the *or* instruction has been moved into the slot without changing the program behavior and the branch delay time has been effectively used.

2.4.2. The Berkeley RISC Microprocessor

The first microprocessors to explore the concept of the simplified instruction set were the Berkeley RISC I and II processors. The most notable feature of these processors is their use of register windows. This feature will be explained in more detail shortly. The Berkeley RISC architecture supports 31 instructions and a 32-bit data path. The ALU does only integer operations,

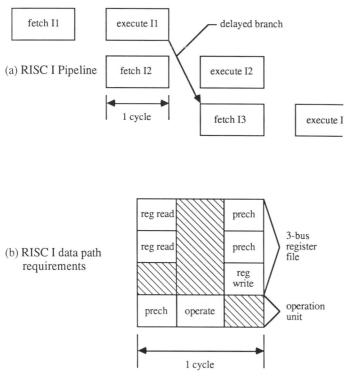

Figure 2.1 The RISC-I pipeline and resource usage.

including add, subtract, logical, and shift instructions, but not multiply and divide. The ALU instructions use a three-operand format with both operands in registers, or with one of the source operands being a 13-bit immediate constant. Condition codes are updated by an instruction if the set condition code control bit is enabled in the instruction. The instruction formats are shown in Figure 2.4. Memory is accessed via load/store instructions, and accesses of bytes, half-words (16 bits), and words (32 bits) are supported. There is only one addressing mode. Addresses are computed by adding an offset to the contents of a register. Absolute addressing is achieved by making the register contents zero, and register indirect addressing can be done by making the offset zero. Also included are a set of delayed conditional branch instructions, call and return instructions, and processor status instructions.

With this very simple set of instructions, the instruction fetch and decode operations are very simple. As a result, the amount of control logic needed on the processor is substantially reduced. The loose encoding of the instructions does mean, however, that the instruction density is lower than other architectures by about 40–70%. The processor is able to achieve single

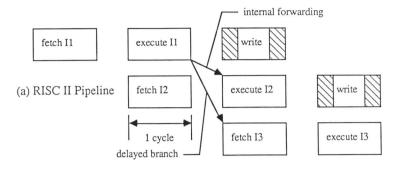

(a) RISC II Pipeline

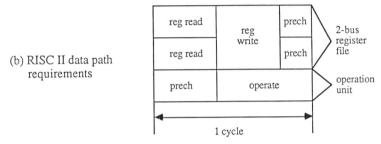

(b) RISC II data path
requirements

Figure 2.2 The RISC-II pipeline and resource usage.

machine cycle execution of register–register instructions and does memory accesses in two machine cycles. The instruction set is summarized in Table 2.1.

There are two implementations of the Berkeley RISC architecture. RISC I was a nearly functionally perfect design, but it did not achieve its projected speed. With a 1.5 MHz clock and three clock phases per machine

Address	Normal Branch		Delayed Branch		With Branch Slot Scheduling	
1000	or	r1,r2	or	r1,r2	branch	1005
1001	branch	1005	branch	1006	or	r1,r2
1002	sub	r3,r5	no-op		sub	r3,r5
1003	sub	r7,r6	sub	r3,r5	sub	r7,r6
1004	add	r5,r6	sub	r7,r6	add	r5,r6
1005	add	r4,r2	add	r5,r6	add	r4,r2
1006			add	r4,r2		

Figure 2.3 The delayed branch.

Table 2.1 Summary of RISC Instruction Set

Instruction	Operands	Comments	
add	Rd,Rs,S2	Rd := Rs + S2	integer add
addc	Rd,Rs,S2	Rd := Rs + S2 + carry	add with carry
sub	Rd,Rs,S2	Rd := Rs − S2	integer subtract
subc	Rd,Rs,S2	Rd := Rs − S2 − borrow	subtract with borrow
subi	Rd,Rs,S2	Rd := S2 − Rs	integer subtract reverse
subci	Rd,Rs,S2	Rd := S2 − Rs − borrow	reverse subtract with borrow
and	Rd,Rs,S2	Rd := Rs & S2	bitwise AND
or	Rd,Rs,S2	Rd := Rs $\mid$ S2	bitwise OR
xor	Rd,Rs,S2	Rd := Rs xor S2	bitwise EXCLUSIVE OR
sll	Rd,Rs,S2	Rd := Rs shifted by S2	shift left
srl	Rd,Rs,S2	Rd := Rs shifted by S2	shift right logical
sra	Rd,Rs,S2	Rd := Rs shifted by S2	shift right arithmetic
ldw	Rd, (Rx) S2	Rd:= M[Rx+S2]	load word
ldhu	Rd, (Rx) S2	Rd:= M[Rx+S2] (align, zero-fill)	load half unsigned
ldhs	Rd, (Rx) S2	Rd:= M[Rx+S2] (align, sign-ext)	load half signed
ldbu	Rd, (Rx) S2	Rd:= M[Rx+S2] (align, zero-fill)	load byte unsigned
ldbs	Rd, (Rx) S2	Rd:= M[Rx+S2] (align, sign-ext)	load byte signed
stw	Rm, (Rx) S2	M[Rx+S2]:= Rm	store word
sth	Rm, (Rx) S2	M[Rx+S2]:= Rm (align)	store half

stb	Rm, (Rx) S2	$M[Rx + S2] := Rm$ (align)	store byte
jmpx	COND, (Rx) S2	if COND then $PC := Rx + S2$	cond. jump, indexed
jmpr	COND, Y	if COND then $PC := PC + Y$	cond. jump, PC-rel.
callx	Rd, (Rx) S2	$Rd := PC$; $PC := Rx + S2$; CWP − −	call indexed
callr	Rd, Y	$Rd := PC$; $PC := PC + Y$; CWP − −	call PC-rel.
ret	(Rx) S2	$PC := Rx + S2$; CWP + +	return
ldhi	Rd, Y	$Rd\langle 31:13\rangle := Y$; $Rd\langle 12:0\rangle := 0$	load immediate high
gtlpc	Rd	$Rd := lastPC$	save value for restarting pipeline
getpsw	Rd	$Rd := PSW$	read status word
putpsw	Rm	$PSW := Rm$	set status word
reti	(Rx) S2	$PC := Rx + S2$; CWP + + ;	return from interrupt
calli			call an interrupt

Rd, Rs, Rx, Rm: a gister (one of 32, where R0 = 0).
S2: either a register or a 13-bit immediate constant.
COND: 4-bit conditioning.
Y: 19-bit immediate constant.
PC: Program-Counter.
CWP: Current-Window-Pointer.
All instructions can optionally set the condition-codes.

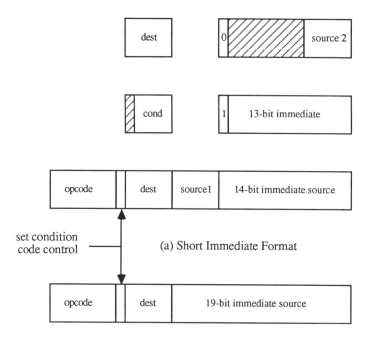

(b) Long Immediate Format

Figure 2.4 The Berkeley RISC instruction formats.

cycle, it can execute a half million register–register instructions per second. A more sophisticated design was used for RISC II. It has a completely new implementation using a 4 μm single-metal nMOS process and an 8 MHz clock with four clock phases per machine cycle. RISC II can achieve a register–register instruction rate of 2 mips. A 3 μm version achieves 3 mips using a 12 MHz clock.

The RISC I pipeline is a simple two-stage pipeline that overlaps the fetch of an instruction with the execution of the previous instruction. The pipeline and associated data path activities are shown in Figure 2.1. The instruction fetch memory cycle occurs in the same amount of time as the register-read, operate, register-write execution cycle. The register file needs three buses so that the read buses can be precharged while the write bus is being used. The register file is idle during the operate part of the cycle.

The RISC II pipeline is shown in Figure 2.2. It is a three-stage pipeline that delays the write-back of the instruction result until the third stage. In this scheme, the write-back does not complete before the start of the execution cycle of the next instruction. This means that instruction *I2* cannot get the results of instruction *I1* by reading the register file. Hardware is used to detect this case and *forward* the result to the next instruction because the result is available in a latch waiting to be written into the registers. This is called *internal forwarding* or *bypassing*.

The use of the three-stage pipeline means the register file can be kept busy all the time, with the write occurring during the time the register file was idle in the RISC I scheme. The write completes in time to precharge the buses, so only two buses are needed in the register file. This means that the register cell can be made smaller and makes it possible to implement a larger and faster register file in RISC II.

Both Berkeley RISC processors suspend activity in the pipeline during a data memory access. This is because there is only one memory port and the memory is not pipelined. It is only possible to do either a data access or an instruction access during a machine cycle. Thus, loads and stores take two machine cycles, while almost all other instructions take one cycle.

2.4.3. Register Windows

The major unique feature of the Berkeley RISC processors is the addition of a large register stack with overlapping register windows to support procedure calls. The register windows provide a significant amount of the performance benefit that the Berkeley RISCs demonstrate. The small control needed for the simple instruction set means that there is space to add the large register file.

The large register file is used to reduce memory bandwidth by allowing the compiler to allocate variables to these registers in an efficient manner. The large register file is more effective than a cache for two reasons. First, it is more space-efficient because tags are not required and the control logic is smaller for the register file. Second, the addressing overhead is eliminated when the register file is accessed. In the Berkeley RISCs, register–register instructions execute twice as fast as memory accesses.

To make a large register set useful, particularly for procedure calls where it is desirable not to have to save a lot of registers, the register file can be organized as a stack of register sets that are allocated dynamically at each procedure call. For each procedure call, a new window of registers is allocated on the stack and the old set is pushed. Each procedure sees a different set of registers. The compiler tries to allocate variables to the register window so as to eliminate memory accesses. On a return, the stack is popped. The push and pop actions are done by manipulating pointers to the current register frame. Another advantage of this scheme is that the software register allocation can be very simple. The automatic saving of registers at procedure call time decreases the need to carefully control the variables in registers because there is little performance penalty associated with over-allocation of the registers.

Although the idea of using register windows seems straightforward, there are numerous complications to consider. Should the windows be of fixed or variable size, and how large if they are fixed? Using variable sized frames means a slower register access time because of the extra hardware needed (an adder to compute the actual position of a register). Using a fixed size for each set yields simplifications in the hardware, but it means that some procedures will waste registers while others may not have enough. Studies have shown that a fixed frame size using about 8 registers is sufficient, and most implementations use a fixed size frame with 8 to 16 registers per frame. RISC II uses 16 in a frame.

Another problem is register stack overflows. Using current technology it is not possible to put a very large number of register sets in a processor, and bounding the number of register sets needed at compile time is impossible. There are also implementation disadvantages in making the register file too large, which will be discussed shortly. In the case of an overflow, the oldest frame can be saved off chip in memory. This can be done in several ways using hardware/microcode assist (possibly using free background memory data cycles to save the oldest frame before an overflow occurs) or—in the case of the Berkeley RISC—by using macrocode. When a procedure returns, the empty frame can be reloaded immediately with a frame that has been previously saved or the frame can be filled when it is needed.

The advantage of register windows depends on the call pattern of procedures. If the call depth varies widely and quickly, there is little advantage because of the high overhead in saving and restoring frames. Studies for the Berkeley RISC register file show that this is not the case and that there is substantial *locality* in the procedure calls. The most frequent pattern is that calls are made to a level k, then a number of calls are made at that level or within a few levels of k before returning from that level. This means that frames may be saved and restored in going to and returning from level k but very little is done once the level is reached. Register windows perform quite well in this situation.

Several software issues must be considered when using register windows. Scalar global variables can be allocated to registers if there is a base-level frame that is accessible to all procedures and does not change during the running of the program, but variables that are visible to multiple, separately compiled routines cannot be allocated to registers unless this function is coordinated by a linker with register allocation capability. Languages that have nested scopes, like Ada, Modula, and Pascal, allow up-level referencing from any nested scope to a surrounding scope. In this event, the processor must allow addressing to all the register frames that are global to the currently active procedure. However, this case is rare, so very little performance is lost if a simple mechanism is available that allows this mode to be slow without slowing the cycle time of the machine. A further complication arises if the desired register set has been swapped out because of a register overflow. The reference must then become a memory reference. A similar problem occurs when a parameter is passed by reference (the address of the parameter is passed) and the variable has been allocated in a register. There is no address to pass.

There are two solutions to the problems of up-level referencing and the passing of reference parameters. One is to use a two-pass compilation scheme to detect up-level references or address references and prevent the associated variable from being allocated in the register stack. This requires a slightly smarter compiler and has some small performance impact. The other solution is to add some hardware that will handle both types of nonlocal references. Assume each register frame (and hence each register) has a main memory address where it resides when it is swapped out. The memory address of an up-level reference can be determined by computing the address of the desired frame using the address in memory of the current frame (based only on the absolute frame number) and the number of frames offset from the current frame based on the difference in lexical levels between the current procedure and the scope of the referenced variable. Similarly, a reference parameter that is in a register can be passed by using the memory address assigned to the register location in the frame. Some of the references will be to frames that have overflowed into memory. These are treated as a conventional memory reference. If the register is currently on-chip, it is only necessary to find the register set and access the on-chip version.

The Berkeley RISC machines also provide support for passing parameters between procedures. Typically, compilers try to speed up procedure linkage by using the registers to communicate parameters and return values. This is not possible in a straightforward register stack because neither procedure can access the registers of the other in a fast efficient manner. The Berkeley RISC processors extended the register stack ideas to solve this problem. The caller and callee window frames overlap by a small number of registers. The caller uses these registers to pass parameters and the callee uses them to return values. RISC II has a total of 138 registers, with 8 frames of 16 registers and 10 global registers accessible to all frames. In each frame, 6 registers overlap with the caller, 6 with the procedure to be called, and 10 are for locals, so that each procedure sees a total of 32 registers. The RISC II window scheme is shown in Figure 2.5.

The disadvantages of the register set idea arise in several areas. First, improved compiler technology, mainly in the form of good models for register allocation, makes it possible for compilers to achieve good usage of the registers and efficiently handle the saving and restoring of registers at procedure call boundaries. Second, as the number of bits in the register stack increase, the cost per bit may become comparable to that of an associative cache of similar size. In this case, a cache can be more efficient in using storage because all of the cache can be actively in use while only one frame in a register stack can be used at any time. Third, when it is necessary to do a process switch, the current state must be saved. A register stack will increase the process switching time because there is much more

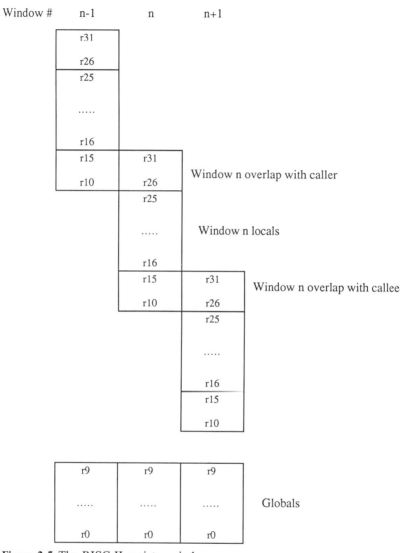

Figure 2.5 The RISC II register windows.

processor state. However, this occurs much less frequently than procedure calls, so the save/restore overhead should be reasonably low. Last, the implementation cost of the register file can be high, particularly in VLSI. There is a trade-off between the desire for a large number of registers and the effect on the speed of the data path. The register file is tightly coupled to the data path, and as the register file increases, the greater the register access time becomes. The best size is difficult to determine because it depends a great deal on both the implementation and the benchmarks chosen to measure the performance.

2.4.4. The Stanford MIPS Microprocessor

The MIPS (Microprocessor without Interlocked Pipe Stages) machine from Stanford is oriented toward the use of optimizing compiler technology. The key idea is to expose in the instruction set all the processor activity that could affect performance. This philosophy, coupled with the concept of a streamlined instruction set, allows a shift of functions from hardware to software. The requirements of the hardware are therefore simplified, making it possible to have a higher clock speed (4 MHz) and a fast pipeline that can fetch a new instruction every two clock cycles, access data memory every two clock cycles, and perform an ALU operation every clock cycle.

MIPS is a load/store architecture but it only supports word-addressing. This choice was made because word addressing dominates in frequency and the implementation is simpler and faster. There are instructions that can be used to manipulate byte pointers and insert and extract specific bytes in a word. There are 16 orthogonal general purpose registers. The ALU is 32-bits wide and supports integer multiplication and division with instructions that will do two bits of a Booth multiply sequence and one bit of a divide sequence; these instructions are put in sequence to obtain a full 32-bit multiply or divide. There is no hardware support for floating point. All ALU instructions use register–register addressing in both two and three operand formats and, as in Berkeley RISC, one of the source registers can be replaced by a small constant. There are no condition codes; instead, branching is done with a compare-and-branch operation, and arithmetic overflow causes a trap. This approach simplifies the compiler and increases performance. The compiler does not have to attempt optimization of the condition code setting, and the hardware is simpler because the implementation of the pipelining and branch handling is easier. Trapping on overflow is preferred to explicit checks on every integer ALU operation. Branches have a branch delay of one instruction except for the indirect branch. It has a delay of two because it requires a memory access to fetch the branch target. MIPS can fetch an instruction and access data in memory without stalling the pipeline by pipelining the instruction and data addresses over a single set of address lines. This scheme requires an instruction cache so that instructions can be accessed in one cycle instead of two.

The MIPS instruction set architecture has been defined at two levels. The first level is visible to the compiler and assembly language programmer and represents the MIPS machine as a simple streamlined processor. The assembly language instructions are summarized in Table 2.2. This is a simple, well-structured instruction set that assumes sequential instruction execution

Table 2.2 MIPS Assembly Instructions

Operation	Operands	Comments	
Arithmetic and logical operations			
Add	src1, src2, dst	dst: = src2 + src1	Integer addition
And	src1, src2, dst	dst: = src2 & src1	Logical and
Ic	src1, src2, dst	dst: = byte src1 of dst is replaced by src2	Insert byte
Or	src1, src2, dst	dst: = src2 | src1	Logical or
Rlc	src1, src2, src3, dst	dst: = src2||src3 rotated by src1 positions	Rotate combined
Rol	src1, src2, dst	dst: = src2 rotated by src1 positions	Rotate
Sll	src1, src2, dst	dst: = src2 shifted left by src1 positions	Shift left logical
Sra	src1, src2, dst	dst: = src2 shifted right by src1 positions	Shift right arithmetic
Srl	src1, src2, dst	dst: = src2 shifted right by src1 positions	Shift right logical
Sub	src1, src2, dst	dst: = src2 − src1	Integer subtraction
Subr	src1, src2, dst	dst: = src1 − src2	Reverse integer subtraction
Xc	src1, src2, dst	dst: = byte src1 of src2	Extract byte
Xor	src1, src2, dst	dst: = src2 ⊕ src1	Logical xor
Transport operations			
Ld	A[src], dst	dst: = M[A + src]	Load based
Ld	[src1 + src2], dst	dst: = M[src1 + src2]	Load based-indexed

Ld	[src1>>src2], dst	dst: = M[src1 shifted by src2]	Load based-shifted
Ld	A, dst	dst: = M[A]	Load direct
Ld	I, dst	dst: = I	Load immediate
Mov	src, dst	dst: = src	Move (byte or register)
St	src1, A[src]	M[A+src]: = src1	Store based
St	src1, [src2+src3]	M[src2+src3]: = src1	Store based-indexed
St	src1, [src2>>src3]	M[src2 shifted by src3]: = src1	Store based-shifted
St	src, A	M[A]: = src	Store direct

Control transfer operations

Bra	dst	PC: = dst + PC	Unconditional relative jump
Bra	Cond, src1, src1, dst	PC: = dst+PC if Cond(src1,src2)	Conditional jump
Jmp	dst	PC: = dst	Unconditional jump direct
Jmp	A[src]	PC: = A+src	Unconditional jump based
Jmp	@A[src]	PC: = M[A+src]	Unconditional jump indirect
Trap	Cond, src1, src2	PC: = 0 if Cond(src1, src2)	Trap instruction

Other operations

| SavePC | A | M[A]: = PC_{-3} | Save multistage PC after trap or interrupt |
| Set | Cond, src, dst | dst: = −1 if Cond(src,dst) dst: = 0 if not Cond(src,dst) | Set conditional |

with no interlocks or branch delays visible, and a single ALU operation per instruction.

The machine-level instruction set of MIPS is closely tied to the pipeline structure, and at this level the implementation details in the pipeline are visible. The complications are handled by a program called the *reorganizer*. In addition to being an assembler, the reorganizer has the added function of reordering the instructions for each basic block to satisfy the constraints imposed by the pipeline. It also packs pairs of assembly language instructions (or *instruction pieces*) into single machine instructions whenever it is possible to use the two ALU cycles available in every machine instruction. This scheduling of instruction execution is done at compile time.

The MIPS pipeline is shown in Figure 2.6. In the figure it is assumed that all instructions are base-offset loads combined with ALU instructions. The pipe is five stages long, with an instruction started on every other stage. The *IF* and *ID* pipestages are for instruction fetch and decode, *OD* and *SX* are for the ALU, and there is one stage, *OF*, that is used for writing data into the registers. Instruction addresses are available at the start of *IF*, and the instruction comes back during the first half of *ID*. For loads and stores, the address is available at the end of *OD* and the load data is back at the end of *OF*.

During the execution of a load instruction, the ALU is only required once to compute the effective address of the data item to be fetched, leaving the ALU free for one cycle. This free cycle is available to do an independent two-operand register–register ALU operation, called an ALU2 piece. Some forms of the load (e.g., long immediate) sacrifice the ALU instruction encoding space for another use. Store instructions and some forms of branch instructions can also be combined with ALU2 pieces into a single instruction word. Another combination is to pack a three-operand ALU operation (ALU3 piece) and an ALU2 piece into one instruction word. The two component pieces of a machine instruction are separate and distinct. Some single instructions that occupy the entire word also break down into two distinct pieces. For example, the compare-and-branch instruction has a condition test and a PC-relative address calculation. Since the resources of the machine are allocated to particular instruction pipe stages, at any particular time the activities of each unit are known, thus simplifying the pipeline control and allowing it to run faster. Some example machine level instruction formats are shown in Figure 2.7.

The reorganizer is an example of how functions can be shifted from the hardware to the software. Because there are no hardware interlocks to handle register access conflicts, the reorganizer is used to generate the machine code that accounts for the pipeline structure and register usage. For example, the reorganizer knows that the load delay is one cycle, so it schedules an instruction piece that is not dependent on the load, during the cycle

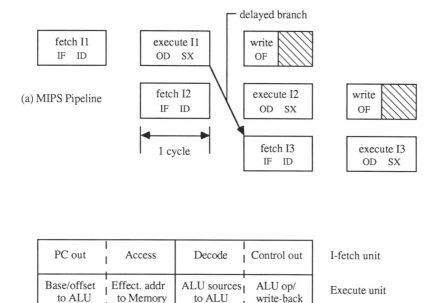

(a) MIPS Pipeline

(b) MIPS data path
requirements

Figure 2.6 The MIPS pipeline and resource usage.

following the load. Only if the memory takes more than two cycles to respond will the entire processor be stalled. This type of scheduling prevents instructions from accessing operands before they are available and is called *operand-hazard* instruction scheduling. Delayed branch scheduling is just a special case that accounts for the absence of interlocks when accessing the program counter.

Software instruction scheduling enhances performance by making the machine do useful work while it would normally be stalled waiting for an interlock to be resolved, and it simplifies the pipeline control hardware so that a shorter clock cycle can be used. The disadvantage of this scheme is that when there is no instruction to execute, a *no-op* instruction must be inserted. This increases code size slightly but does not affect execution speed. It has been found that the combination of a simplified pipeline struc-

(a) Two-operation ALU (ALU3 and ALU2)

00 + Imm. bits	Dest opcode 1	Opcode 1	Dest/source opcode 2	Source 1 opcode 2	Opcode 2	Source 2 opcode 1	Source 1 opcode 1

(b) Load/ Store based & ALU operation

01x + Imm. bit	Load dest Store source	Base register	ALU dest./source	ALU source	ALU opcode	8-bit load offset

(c) Load/ Store direct and load immediate

Load/Store Direct Load Imm.	Load dest Store source	24-bit absolute address for load/store direct 24-bit signed constant for load immediate

(d) Branch conditionally

1111	000 + Immediate bit	Condition	Source 2	Source 1	12-bit PC relative branch offset

(e) Unconditional branch and jump

Unconditional branch/ Jump Direct	24-bit offset for unconditional branch 24-bit absolute address for jump direct

Figure 2.7 MIPS instruction formats (simplified).

ture and the optimization that can be done by the code reorganizer are responsible for about a factor of 2 in performance improvement in MIPS.

2.4.5. Comparing RISC and MIPS

It is worth comparing some of the differences between the architectures of these two processors. Both have a streamlined instruction set but they have some major differences. These include the register file, the pipeline interlock scheme, and the instruction encoding.

The most important difference is how they deal with the high bandwidth data memory access that is required. The Berkeley RISC suspends its pipeline while doing a memory access, making load/store instructions take an extra cycle. This make the external memory system easier to design because it does not need to be pipelined and only one port to memory is needed on the chip. The large register file is used to decrease the number of actual times that memory has to be accessed, reducing the effects of the slower memory instructions. MIPS uses a scheme where the pipeline is not suspended during a memory access. Instead, there is an access slot in the pipeline that is used to allow load/store instructions the time needed to do a memory access. During the delay slot, other parts of the pipeline can still be functioning so other instructions can be scheduled. MIPS reduces the effects of extra time needed for memory instructions by allowing other instructions to be executed during that time. Furthermore, MIPS assumes an external instruction cache with a shorter access time and pipelines the instruction and data addresses on its address pins so that an instruction and data can be accessed in one instruction. The two streams do not interfere with each other as they do on RISC.

RISC uses the large set of register windows to decrease the accesses to memory. The approach taken in MIPS is to have only a small number of registers and rely on register allocation to decrease the times that memory has to be accessed. Since MIPS has separate instruction and data streams and can execute an instruction during memory accesses, a higher percentage of loads and stores can be tolerated without significant performance degradation.

The Berkeley RISC and MIPS both use *delayed branches* to avoid interlocks in the pipeline due to branches but they handle other dependencies differently. RISC II has a data dependency in the pipeline when an instruction requires the result from the previous instruction. *Internal forwarding* requiring some extra hardware is used to avoid stalling the pipeline. MIPS has no hardware interlocks. Instead, the software attempts to schedule the instructions so that there are no conflicts and adds *no-op* instructions if no other instructions can be found. The forwarding scheme could be used in MIPS, but it would not eliminate the delay for *load* instructions.

The instruction formats for the Berkeley RISC are very simple and easy to decode. In contrast, MIPS tries to do more with each 32-bits fetched by encoding a possible second ALU operation in some instructions. This reduces the instruction bandwidth and makes better use of the available resources, but the result is that the instructions are more difficult to decode. Probably some compromise between the two instruction encoding schemes is appropriate.

MIPS has no condition codes to decrease the amount of state in the machine. Instead, the conditions are computed by the branch instruction, simplifying the compiler and the hardware. The Berkeley RISCs use condition codes that can be set by an instruction if the appropriate bit is enabled.

One other difference worth noting between the two machines is the amount of pipelining used. This in many ways is related to how they deal with memory accesses, but not entirely. The RISC I pipeline is a very simple one that overlaps an instruction fetch with the execute cycle of the previous instruction. RISC II adds one stage to use the register file more effectively, with the result that internal forwarding is required. The MIPS pipeline is even more complicated because it has two ALU cycles and inserts a delay for memory instructions. As a consequence, the hardware needed to handle exceptions is more complicated because of the longer, more active pipeline.

2.5. Implementation Issues

The architecture of a machine has a great effect on how it can be implemented. The complexity of the instructions and the functions that must be performed specify the requirements of the hardware and limit the possible organizations. There are still many interactions and trade-offs possible and they will be discussed using the Berkeley RISCs and MIPS processors as examples. These issues are common to most processor designs, as is the goal—to achieve maximum performance within the given cost and hardware constraints.

2.5.1. Pipelining

As seen in the examples of the RISC and MIPS processors, pipelining is a key feature in the organization of the hardware for a simplified instruction set machine. It is a classical technique for enhancing the performance of a processor. The performance can be increased by up to a factor determined by the depth of the pipeline: If the maximum rate at which pipeline operations can be executed is r, then pipelining to a depth of d provides an *idealized* execution rate of $r*d$. Consider the simple pipeline of RISC I shown in Figure 2.1. It is a two-stage pipeline overlapping the instruction fetch of one instruction with the execution step of the previous instruction. Without the overlap, the second instruction does not start until the execution of the first instruction has completed. Since the fetch of an instruction is usually independent of the execution of another instruction, it is possible to overlap these two steps and increase the throughput by up to a factor of 2 (assuming the basic rate is the same) because instructions can now be issued twice as fast.

Even though it is possible to increase performance by pipelining a machine it is not true that performance will continue to get better as the number of stages is increased. There are several other trade-offs. Not all instructions require the same number of pipestages, meaning longer pipelines will waste a number of cycles equal to the difference in the length of the pipeline and the average number of stages needed by an instruction. This suggests that using longer instructions and more pipeline stages is effective, but there are two more important problems: branch frequency and operand hazards.

The length of a pipeline is limited by the frequency of branches because branch frequency determines the average number of instructions executed before the pipeline must be flushed. Pipelining works best when all the pipestages are being used and there are no breaks in the flow of instructions through the pipe. If the number of instructions between branches is small, a long pipeline will be very inefficient because there will always be cycles wasted stalling or flushing the pipe because of a branch. Unfortunately, branch frequencies for most programs are very high—in the range of 15–35%. During a branch, the processor must calculate the effective destination of the branch and fetch the instruction. It may also have to calculate the condition that it is branching on. In general, the pipe must be delayed at least one stage unless both successors of the branch are fetched or the branch outcome is correctly predicted. For most programs and implementations, breaks due to branches cause the most degradation in the performance of a pipeline; branches also add complexity to managing the pipeline and handling the breaks that occur. This function requires additional overhead to the basic pipeline logic, causing a degradation in the clock rate. Using the *delayed branch* scheme described in Section 2.4.1 is one way to reduce the complexity of the controls.

The problem of data or operand hazards occurs when the pipeline is stalled because an instruction requires data that is still in the pipeline. Consider the case of a load instruction in the RISC I pipeline. The data from a load instruction requires an extra cycle before it is available to be used on the chip. To handle this, RISC I stalls the pipeline for one cycle to allow for the necessary access time. MIPS avoids such breaks by requiring that the compiler do pipeline scheduling. This technique can be used even if the interlock hardware that detects such hazards is present, because the scheduling will reduce the actual occurrence of such interlocks. Pipeline scheduling typically improves performance by about 5–10%. In MIPS there is also the benefit of the pipeline hardware being simpler because the hazard detection circuitry is not present, resulting in even more performance gain.

2.5.2. Instruction Fetch and Decode

One goal of pipelining is to approach as closely as possible the target of one instruction execution every clock cycle. This can usually be achieved in the execution unit of the machine except for more complicated operations like floating point instructions, where longer pipeline latencies are encountered. Thus the challenge is to fetch and decode instructions at a rate of one per cycle.

Instruction sets with dense encodings and multiple instruction lengths cannot be decoded in parallel because the instruction fields can be interpreted in many ways and there are many interdependencies among the fields. This is a serious penalty because it is not possible to pipeline the instruction decoding to achieve a fetch and decode rate of one instruction per cycle unless the pipeline is made longer. But densely encoded instructions have very short sequences between branches, so increasing the pipeline length is a bad trade-off. This is a major reason that RISC machines have very simple fixed-length instruction formats.

Another problem with complex fetch and decode is that most of the instructions executed are still simple instructions. The cost of the fetch and decode is often higher than the execution cost. This may cause the speed of the simple instructions to suffer a penalty because of the complexity of the instruction decoding unless there is a very careful design and instruction encoding that simplifies the fetch and decode for the simple instructions.

2.5.3. Control Unit Design

The main function of the control unit is to handle normal processor instruction cycles under usual conditions and to handle exceptional conditions, such as page faults, interrupts, cache misses, and internal faults, when they arise. The most difficult part is to handle the exceptional conditions that require the intervention of the operating system because this usually involves shutting down the execution of the normal instruction stream, saving the state of the execution and transferring to supervisor level code to save user state before handling the exception. Simpler conditions such as a cache miss only require the processor to delay its normal cycle.

Two distinct problems arise because of exceptional conditions and require the interruption of execution. One is saving the state of the processor; the other is stopping the execution of the current instruction. Instructions with internal instruction state that is not visible to the user require extra hardware to assist in saving and restoring the state of a partially executed instruction. Some architectures avoid this problem by forcing the state to be visible. It is generally the multicycle instructions that are dealt with in this way. For instructions that have shorter running times, interrupts are generally prohibited during the execution of the instruction. When an interrupt that cannot be ignored occurs (such as a page fault in the currently executing instruction), the architecture can stop the execution of the instruction, process the interrupt, and restart the instruction. This is straightforward except when the instruction changes the state of the machine before the interrupt occurs. The options are to continue the instruction from the middle or restore the state of the machine to what it was before the instruction started. Both these approaches are very difficult and require hardware assist. Some machines symbolically execute the instruction to determine whether it will page fault first, take any necessary faults, and then really execute the instruction knowing that the faults cannot occur.

Streamlined architectures avoid these problems by prohibiting instructions that can cause these problems. All the state of the machine is visible, and because the instructions are simple, it is easy to arrange that they all change the state of the machine at the same time and change only a very small amount of state. This makes the exception controller much simpler to implement and reduces the delay in one of the possible critical paths of the machine, resulting in shorter cycle times. It also reduces the amount of circuitry required and the space and power needed.

2.5.4. Data Path Design

The data paths of most processors share many common features because most instruction sets require a small number of basic microoperations. The main data path usually has two or more buses serving as a common communication link among the components of the bus. Microarchitectures will vary because of special features designed to improve the performance of some special features of the instruction set. Common components of a data path include the following:

- A register file for the processor's general purpose registers.
- An ALU that provides both addition/subtraction and some collection of logical operations. It may also provide support for multiplication and division. The ALU is discussed in more detail shortly.
- A shifter used to implement shifts and rotates and to implement bit string instructions or assist instruction decoding in some cases.
- The program counter. Having the PC in the data path simplifies the calculation of PC-based displacements. In a pipelined machine, the PC section will usually have its own incrementer so that the next sequential instruction address can be computed more quickly and overlapped with an ALU operation. Often, a pipelined machine also has multiple PC registers to simplify state saving and returning from interrupts.

The data path of the MIPS processor is shown in Figure 2.8. The Berkeley RISC data path is even simpler (except for the register stack); other machines such as the VAX have more complicated data paths to support the data types and more complex instructions that they can accommodate. Other differences in the data path may occur because of pipelining. For example, if MIPS were further pipelined to execute an instruction on every cycle, it would require another ALU. Many pipelined machines use separate ALUs for instruction execution and for address computation. ALU design in streamlined VLSI processors is one area where various designs have made different trade-offs. All designs will support addition and subtraction as well as some collection of Boolean functions. Support for complex instructions such as floating point has not been provided directly on-chip because of the hardware required. Some designs do not even support integer multiplication and division for the same reasons. The Berkeley RISC processor codes these integer operations out of simpler instructions, resulting in multiply or divide performance at the rate of about one bit every three or four instructions. In the MIPS processor there are multiply and divide instructions that can do an add or subtract and a shift in one instruction to reduce the number of

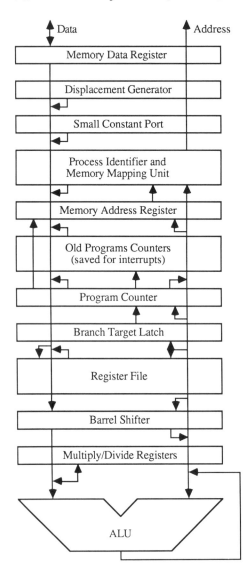

Figure 2.8 MIPS data path block diagram.

instructions needed to do multiplication and division. The resulting speed is the same as an implementation done with microcode. The architect can balance frequency of occurrence with speed of execution to obtain the best trade-off between using hardware or software.

Support for more complicated instructions such as floating point operations can be provided by using a separate coprocessor. The design of the interface is extremely important and must be considered when the instruction set is designed. The dominant factor in the time to execute an instruction on a coprocessor is the time needed for communication and coordination. A RISC-oriented coprocessor design, with its own registers and operations, is an attractive approach to minimizing communication and coordination overhead.

2.5.5. Packaging Constraints

Before concluding this section on implementation, it is important to mention packaging issues. Packaging limitations have a significant influence on the design of an architecture, especially in a VLSI processor chip. However, as integrated circuit (IC) technology improves, these issues must be confronted in every technology. Implementations using CMOS or ECL gate arrays must address similar problems, and all designers face system packaging problems involving design partitioning, communication, and cooling. Of course, as the packaging issues become more global, the interaction with detailed architectural considerations fades.

IC packaging introduces several constraints in the design of a processor. The number of pins limit the bandwidth of information that can go on or off the chip at any time. Another problem is that every time a signal must cross a chip boundary significant delay is incurred. The signal delays on-chip are much smaller than those off-chip because of the distances traveled and the capacitances that must be driven. These constraints force the designer to partition the functional boundaries of the entire system to minimize the amount of interconnection needed. The problem of signal delays increases as technology improves because the delays off-chip do not scale when the on-chip delays decrease. An important example of how these delays affect a processor design is how accessing memory influences the architecture. With the very high-performance machines, fast memory access times become comparable to the cycle time of the machine, and the amount of support logic needed for the memory system becomes very important in determining the delay through the memory system before data is available to the processor. The ways that Berkeley RISC and MIPS handle the access time needed for memory are two examples of how this problem is handled.

In MOS designs, package inductance is also a problem that must be considered. If the processor drives a number of pins simultaneously, such as 32 data lines and 32 address lines, the peak current required can be quite large. The package inductance can lead to a transient in the on-chip supply voltage. Some ways to reduce this effect include using separate power and ground lines or by using more sophisticated die bonding and packaging.

Packaging technology also defines the maximum static power that a chip may consume. Extra power can be used to decrease delays in the critical path so the way that power is budgeted is very important. Figure 2.9 shows how the power used in MIPS is distributed. In nMOS technology, power is usd to overcome delays due to serial combinations of gates, to reduce co-

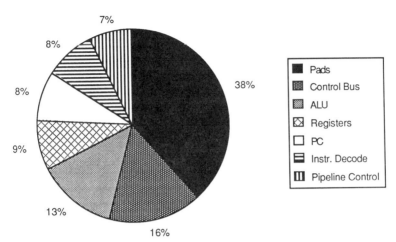

Figure 2.9 MIPS current distribution.

munication delays between functional blocks, and to reduce off-chip communication delays. In the MIPS power distribution plot the major power consumers are the pins with the drive logic, the ALU with its many levels of logic, and the control bus, which provides most of the time-critical intrachip communication. Note that the pads consume the largest fraction of the power. This is because of the need to make off-chip memory access as fast as possible.

2.6. Summary

The RISC approach shows that it is important to consider all aspects in an architectural design, starting from the software right through to the hardware. By making trade-offs across these boundaries, the architect can significantly enhance performance. New instruction set designs must use measurements based on compiled code to determine the effectiveness of any features being considered if the instruction set is to be a suitable target for high-level languages. Features should not be added without first showing that they can significantly benefit the resulting performance of compiled code, or substantially improve operating system performance.

The biggest barriers to using this integrated approach to design exist primarily in the commercial market where there is much commitment to existing assembly language programs and a lack of high-quality compilers. As compiler technology improves and sufficiently fast processors become available, there should be less reason to be driven toward programming in assembly language. This should open the door to proven architectural advances.

Future architectures will probably embrace some combination of streamlined and complex architectures. The important realization is that there are many trade-offs to be examined between the software and the hardware boundary and that there is freedom to move the boundary to obtain better performance in the total system.

Problems

1. In this problem, you will design a simple pipelined data path. Assume a four-port register file that can read two registers and write two registers simultaneously. Also, assume that there are two caches, one for instructions and the other for data. Each cache is pipelined in two stages: the tag and data access takes 50 ns and the tag compare takes another 50 ns (ignore misses). The timing of basic operations is:

Register file read	50 ns
Register file write	50 ns
Instruction decode	50 ns
ALU operation	50 ns
Cache latency	100 ns
Cache throughput	1 access every 50 ns

   a. Design a pipeline for this machine so that it can execute instructions as fast as possible. You may use only one register file, and no more than two caches. Draw a chart indicating what happens in each phase, and a block diagram of the data path. Assume an instruction format that lets your machine start reading the source registers as soon as the intruction has been fetched (no decoding delay for this). The pipeline should execute one instruction every 50 ns. Use delayed branches and delayed loads. Your design should include features that minimize the effects of the two major types of pipeline dependencies.
   b. How long is the branch delay? How long is the load delay?
   c. Some statistics of programs show that 1 out of every 4 instructions is a branch, 1 out of every 10 instructions is a load, and 50% of the delay cycles are wasted. How many instructions per cycle will your machine actually execute?
2. A processor is being considered that has four pipeline stages. They are:

   IF   Instruction fetch.
   RF   Instruction decode and register fetch.
   ALU   ALU or shift operation.
   WB   Write the result into the destination register.

   The proposed branch scheme uses a *compare and branch* scheme where two registers are compared during the ALU cycle and the result is used to determine the outcome of the branch. The pipeline stalls one cycle for a load instruction.

   a. What are the trade-offs between using a *compare and branch* scheme and condition codes? A condition code machine sets condition codes in a status register as a side effect of executing other instructions. The branch instruction will branch according to the value of the condition codes.
   b. What is the branch delay?
   c. A different scheme for evaluating the condition has been proposed. A simple comparator can be placed on the output of the register file that can be used to test whether the outputs of the two registers are equal. The sign bit can also be tested. What types of branches can be implemented with this scheme? How can the other types of branches be implemented? What is the effect on the branch delay?

   Assume that branches are 25% of the instruction mix, that a single branch delay slot can be used 60% of the time, and a second delay slot can only be used 30% of the time. What percentage of the branches must be able to use the new scheme without any additional computation before it is better than the original scheme, neglecting implementation effects?

   If the additional hardware needed to implement this new scheme requires that the cycle time be increased by 10%, how does this affect the number just derived? Assume that 10% of the instructions are loads.

3. The pipeline for the machine given in Question 2 assumes that the processor stalls during a data access. Assume that an extra pipeline stage, called *MEM* is placed between *ALU* and *WB*.
   a. Give the trade-offs between stalling a processor during a memory access and allocating a pipeline stage to make this access time visible.
   b. If the processor is to be implemented on a single chip, give the effects on the bandwidth needed at the pins.
   c. What are the effects on the branch and load delays? What are the effects on the bypassing?
   d. Assume that load delay slots can only be filled 60% of the time. Compare the difference in execution times between stalling the pipeline and using an extra pipeline stage. Redo the calculations for Question 2.

Further Reading

Hennessy JL, Jouppi N, Baskett F, et al: Hardware/software trade-offs for increased performance. *Proceedings of SIGARCH/SIGPLAN Symposium on Architectural Support for Programming Languages and Operating Systems.* ACM, Palo Alto, CA, March 1982, pp. 2–11.

Katevenis MGH: Reduced Instruction Set Computer Architectures for VLSI. ACM Doctoral Dissertation Award 1984, Cambridge, MA, MIT Press, 1985.

Matick RE, Ling DT: Architecture implications in the design of microprocessors. *IBM Systems Journal*, Vol. 23, No. 3, 1984, pp. 264–280.

Patterson DA: Reduced instruction set computers. *Communications of the ACM*, Vol. 28, No. 1, Jan. 1985, pp. 8–21.

Przybylski S, Gross T, Hennessy J, et al: Organization and VLSI implementation of MIPS. *Journal of VLSI and Computer Systems*, Vol. 1, No. 2, Spring 1984.

Radin G: The 801 minicomputer. *Proceedings of SIGARCH/SIGPLAN Symposium on Architectural Support for Programming Languages and Operating Systems*. ACM, Palo Alto, CA, March 1982, pp. 39–47.

3

Computer Design for Gallium Arsenide Technology

David A. Fura
Veljko M. Milutinović

3.1. Introduction

Digital circuit designs employing gallium arsenide (GaAs) technology have been regularly presented since the mid-1970s. The faster switching speed of GaAs and its higher resistance to adverse environmental conditions have created sporadic bursts of enthusiasm throughout the last 10 years. However, not until recent significant advances in GaAs material quality and fabrication technology has GaAs begun to attract serious interest from computer system designers.

A coherent computer system design strategy requires a thorough understanding of the underlying implementation technology. The advances made in silicon technology have drastically improved the capability of silicon-based computer systems. Apart from the performance improvements due strictly to improved technology, technology-driven architectural advances have also played an important role. The effect that the characteristics of silicon very large scale integration (VLSI) has had on computer design strategies is observable in the recent enthusiasm for designs such as dataflow computers (12), systolic arrays (36), and reduced instruction set computers (RISCs) (54).

As GaAs technology is only expected to begin achieving integration levels approaching 10,000 gates by the late 1980s (38), it is not surprising that design strategies appropriate for GaAs should differ from those encountered in VLSI silicon. In fact, GaAs–silicon differences are more pronounced than as indicated by level of integration alone. Two additional key differences are the already mentioned higher speed of GaAs gates, as well as a corresponding relatively higher penalty for interchip communication for GaAs chips. Clearly, it is vital to understand the characteristics of GaAs that influence computer system design before attempting to build GaAs-based computer systems, and it should not be assumed that silicon-based techniques are desirable for GaAs implementations.

The purpose of this chapter is to explore the use of GaAs technology in computer system design. We are interested in *architectural* approaches for fully exploiting the fast transistors of low-density GaAs chips by minimizing the deleterious effects of a slow off-chip environment. System *packaging* approaches for improving this slow interchip communication are also important issues but are not within the scope of this text.

Because the implementation technology plays such a critical role in the design of computer systems, Section 3.2 provides a description of GaAs technology relevant for a clear understanding of the architectural design trade-offs required by GaAs. The characteristics of GaAs we present here are representative of a particular GaAs technology of the mid-1980s. As GaAs technology matures, we can expect to see a greatly increased GaAs capability; however, we emphasize fundamental aspects of GaAs that should remain valid throughout this progress. Section 3.3 discusses the architectural design issues that are affected by the characteristics of GaAs technology, and suggests promising design approaches. Again, the conclusions drawn here are based upon the GaAs characteristics of the mid-1980s.

3.2. GaAs Technology

To provide a sound basis for subsequent GaAs computer system design discussions, this section presents an overview of digital GaAs technology. We discuss the relative merits of candidate device families and their logic gate implementations, and we also present some of the advanced GaAs digital designs that have appeared in the last few years. In order to permit a rational GaAs–silicon comparison, we select the GaAs technology that appears to have the first shot at VLSI levels of integration in production quantities. In comparing this GaAs technology with silicon, we illuminate several differing characteristics. These GaAs–silicon differences will then provide much of the motivation for the discussion of the next section.

3.2.1. GaAs Device Families

Just as silicon technology has undergone major change, GaAs technology has seen rapid advancements in its relatively short history. The first published *digital* GaAs circuits were introduced in the mid-1970s (68). The earliest devices to be utilized in these circuits were depletion-mode metal-semiconductor field-effect transistors (D-MESFETs). Some widely used devices that followed include enhancement-mode MESFETs (E-MESFETs), enhancement-mode junction field-effect transistors (E-JFETs), modulation-doped FETs (MODFETs), also known as high electron mobility transistors (HEMTs), and heterojunction bipolar transistors (HBTs). The first devices to be used in a 32-bit GaAs microprocessor design were MESFETs, HBTs, and JFETs.

D-MESFETs were the first devices to be used in digital circuit designs, and the ease with which they are fabricated is one of their primary advantages over other device technologies. Some additional strengths include high insensitivity to fanout and large noise margins for D-MESFET logic gates (72). Unfortunately, D-MESFET logic designs must utilize complex circuits, resulting in large power and area requirements (14). They require two power supplies and voltage level shifting circuitry to allow logic gates to be cascaded.

E-MESFET and E-JFET circuits require but a single power supply and no voltage level shifting logic, thus requiring less power and area than D-MESFET designs (14, 20, 74). For this reason, they are considered more appropriate for VLSI implementations. E-MESFET logic circuits can also be faster than D-MESFET circuits; however, they are more sensitive to fanout loading and perform poorly in high load environments (14). E-MESFETs also require higher material quality and more complex processing to achieve the high threshold voltage uniformity necessary for working devices (14, 39). E-JFET circuits overcome some of the E-MESFET disadvantages. Because threshold voltage is controlled in the E-JFET by the differential implantation of n and p dopants, the critical channel height can be accurately controlled despite the existing material quality. Also, the placement of the p–n junction within the bulk of the material improves reliability and radiation performance.

MODFETs, also commonly known as high electron mobility transistors (HEMTs), achieve much faster switching speeds than either D-MESFETs, E-MESFETs, or E-JFETs; consequently, they have generated much interest for high-speed computer design. MODFETs utilize a layer of AlGaAs material to supply electrons into an undoped GaAs channel. Because the room temperature mobility of electrons in undoped GaAs is almost twice as high as in n-channel GaAs MESFETs, MODFETs are able to more quickly change their output state with low power consumption (64). At liquid nitrogen temperature (77°K), electron mobilities in MODFETs are improved even further—approximately six times higher than at room temperature (64). Ionized impurity scattering in n-channel GaAs MESFETs denies this higher mobility to MESFET devices (64). The major disadvantages of MODFETs are a more complex processing requirement than MESFETs and the need for a very high-quality AlGaAs layer (64).

HBTs do not suffer from the threshold voltage problems that plague the FETs that we just described, and this is an important advantage for VLSI implementations (13). In addition to their built-in threshold voltage control, HBTs are very fast and have higher output drive capability than FETs, resulting in lower sensitivity to fanout and loading (4). HBTs may also be employed in circuit designs with differential inputs and outputs, which results in decreased switching noise (4). The disadvantages of HBTs are higher processing complexity than FETs, as well as relatively high power and chip area requirements (4).

3.2.2. Some GaAs Logic Families

There are several logic families that utilize these devices. Some widely used families that utilize FETs include buffered FET logic (BFL), Schottky diode FET logic (SDFL), and direct-coupled FET logic (DCFL). Other logic families utilizing bipolar transistors include emitter-coupled logic (ECL) and Schottky transistor logic (STL), and heterojunction integrated injection logic (HI^2L).

Early BFL logic circuits utilizing D-MESFETs exhibited fast switching speeds at high power levels. One reported design had gate delays of 34 ps at 41.0 mW per gate (52). Efforts to reduce the power consumption of BFL gates resulted in low power BFL (LPBFL) designs with a relatively small penalty in switching speed. Advanced LPBFL designs include a 32-bit adder containing 420 gates with gate delays of 230 ps and a power of 2.8 mW per gate (72). To our knowledge, the highest level of integration achieved with a BFL design is an LPBFL 12 × 12-bit multiplier that, including its non-BFL input and output buffers, incorporated 1083 gates (19). The LPBFL gates had switching speeds of 170 ps and a power dissipation of 1.7 mW. Figure 3.1 is an example of a BFL inverter that demonstrates the complexity inherent in D-MESFET-based circuits. However, LPBFL versions require only one or two diodes for voltage level shifting instead of the three shown.

SDFL logic circuits also use D-MESFETs and have a relatively complex logic circuit implementation, as shown in Figure 3.2. However, because of their lower power and area requirements, they have achieved higher integration levels than BFL designs (15). In fact, the first reported GaAs LSI (>1000 transistors) design utilized SDFL gates (37). This 1008-gate 8 × 8-bit multiplier had gate delays of 150 ps and a power dissipation of 0.6–2.0 mW per gate. The highest reported level of integration achieved with SDFL logic gates appears to be a combination gate array/SRAM chip (69). This

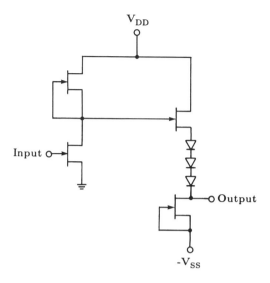

Figure 3.1 BFL D-MESFET inverter. (Eden RC, Welch BM, Zucca R, Long SI: The prospects for ultrahigh-speed VLSI GaAs digital logic. *IEEE Journal of Solid-State Circuits*, Vol. SC-14, No. 2, April 1979, pp. 221–239. © 1979 IEEE.)

design incorporates 432 programmable cells, 32 interface I/O buffer cells, and four 4 × 4-bit SRAMs, for a total of approximately 8000 devices. The average gate propagation delay and power dissipation were 150–300 ps and 1.5 mW, respectively.

DCFL logic circuits utilizing E-MESFET drivers and D-MESFET loads (DCFL E/D-MESFETs) have achieved by far the highest level of integration of any GaAs technology. The use of the simple circuit configuration of Figure 3.3 gives DCFL designs a decided advantage in power dissipation and area requirements, both extremely important for VLSI implementations. Several significant DCFL E/D-MESFET designs have been reported. A 2000-gate gate array exhibiting gate delays of 215 ps and power requirements

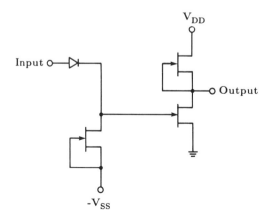

Figure 3.2 SDFL D-MESFET inverter. (Eden RC, Welch BM, Zucca R, Long SI: The prospects for ultrahigh-speed VLSI GaAs digital logic. *IEEE Journal of Solid-State Circuits*, Vol. SC-14, No. 2, April 1979, pp. 221–239. © 1979 IEEE.)

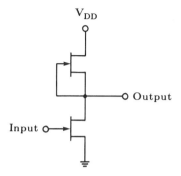

Figure 3.3 DCFL inverter. (Eden RC, Welch BM, Zucca R, Long SI: The prospects for ultrahigh-speed VLSI GaAs digital logic. *IEEE Journal of Solid State Circuits*, Vol. SC-14, No. 2, April 1979, pp. 221–239. © 1979 IEEE.)

of 0.5 mW per gate was reported (67). A 3168-gate 16 × 16-bit multiplier with gate delays of 150 ps and a power dissipation of 0.3 mW per gate has been presented (50). However, the highest reported level of integration achieved to date is a 16K-bit SRAM containing 102,300 devices (32). The access time was 4.1 ns and the total chip power consumption was 2.5 W. Ring oscillator measurements showed gate delays of 115 ps at 0.1 mW per gate. Some recent experiments reported about 50 ps (25).

The DCFL logic circuit design of Figure 3.3 is utilized for MODFET devices. Because of the early state of MODFET development, this promising technology has not achieved the levels of integration experienced by E/D-MESFETs. The highest level of integration achieved thus far is a 4K-bit SRAM (35). This chip had an access time of 4.4 ns and power dissipation of 860 mW at room temperature. At 77°K, access time and power requirements of 2.0 ns and 1.6 W, respectively, were achieved. However, MODFET designs have the distinction of holding the fastest gate propagation times. The current record at room temperature is 11.6 ps, while at 77°K it is only 8.5 ps (56).

HBTs have only recently been used in digital logic circuits and have achieved the lowest level of integration of the devices discussed. Ring oscillator measurements were performed using common mode logic (CML) ECL gates (5). Propagation delays of 60 ps were achieved with a gate power dissipation of 3.0 mW. An example ECL/CML logic gate is shown in Figure 3.4. Thus far, the highest reported level of integration for HBTs is a 1K-gate gate array utilizing an STL-like logic implementation (73). Using a circuit design represented by the inverter of Figure 3.5, a propagation delay and power dissipation of 400 ps and 1.0 mW, respectively, were achieved.

Table 3.1 summarizes the current relative performance levels of the logic circuit families mentioned. The DCFL E/D-MESFET family shows the highest capability in these published designs. Because DCFL E/D-MES-FETs were first to achieve VLSI (>10,000 transistors) densities in laboratory environments, they were among the first to be seriously considered for processor implementation. In fact, the description of an 8-bit GaAs processor using E/D-MESFET technology has already been published (27).

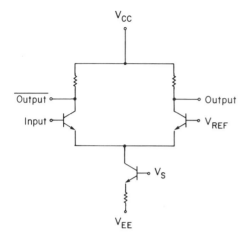

Figure 3.4 ECL/CML HBT logic gate. (Asbeck PM, Miller DL, Anderson RJ, et al: Application of heterojunction bipolar transistors to high-speed, small-scale digital integrated circuits. *Proc. IEEE GaAs IC Symposium*, Boston, MA, Oct. 1984, pp. 133–136. © 1984 IEEE.)

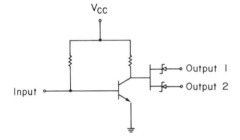

Figure 3.5 STL-like HBT inverter. (Yuan H, McLevige WV, Shih HD, Hearn AS: GaAs heterojunction bipolar 1K gate array. *Proc. 1984 IEEE International Solid-State Circuits Conference*, San Francisco, CA, Feb. 1984, pp. 42–43. © 1984 IEEE.)

Table 3.1 Performance Characteristics of GaAs Designs

Unit	Speed (ns)	Total power (W)	Device count (K)	Reference
Arithmetic				
32-bit adder (BFL D-MESFET)	2.9 total	1.2	2.5	(71)
16 × 16-bit multiplier (DCFL E/D-MESFET)	10.5 total	1.0	10.0	(50)
Control				
Gate array/SRAM (SDFL D-MESFET)	.15/gate	3.0	~8.0	(68)
1K-gate gate array (STL HBT)	.40/gate	1.0	~6.0	(72)
2K-gate gate array (DCFL E/D-MESFET)	.08/gate	0.4	8.2	(66)
Memory				
4K-bit SRAM (DCFL MODFET)	2.0 total at 77°K	1.6	26.9	(35)
16K-bit SRAM (DCFL E/D-MESFET)	4.1 total	2.5	102.3	(32)

3.2.3. GaAs–Silicon Comparison

Because of their early attainment of VLSI densities in laboratory environments, DCFL E/D-MESFETs will be used to represent GaAs technology throughout the rest of this chapter. The performance characteristics of silicon are based primarily on NMOS, which has the same logic gate circuit design as DCFL designs. In addition to its similar circuit design, we select NMOS because most of the RISC silicon processors that are used here for comparison purposes are implemented in NMOS.

Table 3.2 shows performance characteristics of both DCFL E/D-MESFET GaAs and NMOS silicon (8) that are relevant for computer system design. The data in Table 3.2 are for specific silicon and GaAs processes that are typical of those encountered in the early to mid 1980s. In principle, other processes may exhibit different characteristics. From this list, three fundamental differences between GaAs and silicon are evident.

1. GaAs logic gates switch considerably faster than silicon logic gates. This is the most significant advantage that GaAs enjoys over silicon in the context of this chapter. The principal reason for this GaAs advantage is the higher mobility of GaAs electrons. The electron mobility of 4000–5000 cm^2/Vs in n-channel MESFETs is approximately six times higher than the electron mobility of 800 cm^2/Vs for silicon (52). A secondary GaAs speed advantage is the ability of GaAs to be fabricated as a semi-insulating material, which reduces parasitic capacitances (52).

2. The transistor count capability of GaAs is much lower than that of silicon. The limitations of GaAs are due to problems with both power dissipation and yield.

   Power dissipation is a concern of chip designers regardless of the technology. If total chip power consumption significantly exceeds 2 W, the associated heat may cause reliability problems. Special packaging techniques must then be used to remove heat more quickly from the chip. Although GaAs transistors require less power than silicon transistors at similar switching speeds, GaAs transistors operating at maximum speed require more power than slower silicon transistors. GaAs designs requiring 0.2 mW per gate will be limited to approximately 30,000 transistors if a 2-W maximum power dissipation limit is imposed. An example 2-W silicon design, the Motorola MC68020, uses nearly 200,000 transistors (39).

   Because yield is *inversely* proportional to chip area, while transistor count is *directly* proportional to chip area, transistor count may be traded off for higher yields and, hence, lower costs. GaAs material is also currently of lower quality—i.e., it has higher defect densities—than silicon (70). Therefore, GaAs wafers experience poorer yields than silicon wafers with similar areas. This problem is compounded by the fact that the GaAs material is more expensive than silicon because gallium is a rare material, and as a compound material, GaAs requires additional processing to cre-

Table 3.2 Performance Comparison of GaAs and Silicon[a]

	GaAs (DCFL E/D-MESFET)	Silicon (NMOS)
Complexity		
Transistor count/chip	20–30 K	200–300 K
Chip area	Yield and power dependent	Yield and power dependent
Speed		
Gate delay	50–150 ps	1–3 ns
On-chip memory access	0.5–2.0 ns	10–20 ns
Off-chip/on-package memory access	4–10 ns	40–80 ns
Off-chip/off-package memory access	20–80 ns	100–200 ns
IC Design		
Transistors/gate	1 + fanin	1 + fanin
Transistors/memory cell		
static	6	6
dynamic	1	1
Fanin (typical transistor size)	2–3	5
Fanout (typical transistor size) gate delay increase for each additional fanout (relative to gate delay with fanout = 1)	3–4	5
	25–40%	25–40%

[a] This table represents silicon NMOS and GaAs E/D-MESFET used in early RISC processors. Adapted from Heagerty W: GaAs seminar presented at Purdue University, Jan. 1985.

ate it and to verify its composition (49). In order to satisfy cost constraints, some GaAs designs may experience severe area limitations, and hence be limited to lower transistor counts.

3. As indicated by the on-chip and off-chip memory access times, the speed advantage that GaAs enjoys over silicon for the on-chip environment is not matched by an equal off-chip speedup. Interchip signal propagation speed is not significantly different for GaAs and silicon chips because it is primarily dependent on packaging considerations rather than integrated circuit technology. Interchip signals are first limited to the speed of light; however, the media dielectric constant and capacitive loading on the signal lines can reduce signal propagation speeds to one-third the speed of light or lower (47). Because of this, the penalty for interchip communication is higher, in terms of gate delays, for a GaAs design than it is for silicon designs.

3.3. Design Considerations for GaAs Computer Systems

In Section 3.2 we presented an overview of GaAs device and logic families. The characteristics of GaAs were then compared with those of silicon in order to illuminate the relevant differences between the two technologies.

In this section, most of our discussion is based at least indirectly on the results of Section 3.2. We first extend these results by defining more clearly those GaAs characteristics that influence computer design, and describe in general terms the appropriate strategies for dealing with some problems posed by GaAs technology. We then discuss the design approaches that appear to be suitable for computer system hardware and the compiler for a GaAs processor, concentrating on those approaches that are more valuable in GaAs system designs than in silicon designs.

The discussions throughout the rest of this chapter are oriented to GaAs processor systems that execute compiled high-level language (HLL) programs. No specific application area is targeted, as these discussions are intended for GaAs processor system design in general.

3.3.1. The Effect of GaAs Characteristics on Computer Design Strategy

The design of a GaAs computer system is intimately dependent on the GaAs characteristics presented in the previous section; therefore, these characteristics deserve closer scrutiny.

As previously stated, GaAs transistors are significantly faster than silicon transistors. The purpose of this chapter, then, is to determine the best approaches to maximize the exploitation of this GaAs advantage.

Unfortunately, GaAs chips generally have fewer transistors than silicon chips. This obviously has an enormous impact on computer design. Minimizing chip count is desirable for performance, reliability, and cost reasons. Designs that minimize hardware complexity reduce chip count and are therefore very desirable.

A significant problem by itself, low transistor count severely compounds the problem caused by large interchip propagation delays. Together, these two problems may potentially limit the exploitation of the great strength of GaAs technology—its fast transistors.

A GaAs processor is able to execute instructions faster than a silicon processor only if it has a corresponding increase in its supply of instructions and data. A fast GaAs processor should not be forced to spend its time waiting for information from its external environment. There are three methods of resolving this information problem: reduce the processor's need for off-chip information, increase the effective information transfer rate, or overlap the information transfers with processor execution.

Obviously, if the entire system could be built within one GaAs chip, the need to access off-chip information would be minimized. However, because GaAs chips are expected to contain fewer transistors than silicon chips, the need for off-chip information will be even greater. Silicon processors are able to alleviate this problem by incorporating large amounts of on-chip memory in the form of a register file, cache, or microprogram store.

Silicon's abundant transistors may also be used in the design of complex arithmetic units that, while performing complex functions, utilize each data element longer than simple arithmetic units do in performing simple operations. Because of the lower transistor count of GaAs chips, many of these silicon solutions will not be available to a GaAs processor.

Increasing the effective rate of information transfer can be accomplished in two ways: The information content of each transfer can be increased, or the rate of transfer can be increased.

Increasing the information content of transfers can be accomplished either by transmitting more bits per transfer or by eliminating redundancy within the transferred information. Upper limits on the number of bits per transfer are imposed by pin limitations of integrated circuits. However, silicon supercomputers using SSI/MSI components, such as the Cray-1, are able to utilize this technique for data transfers (57), but this technique is limited to operations on very regular data structures such as arrays. This work is not limited to the applications with well-structured data that are necessary for maximum performance on silicon vector supercomputers. Redundancy removal, on the other hand, generally requires an encoding and decoding capability. A compiler can effectively provide the encoding function on instructions; however, the decoding function must be performed by hardware resources within the processor. Many silicon processors incorporate large on-chip microprograms for which a single macroinstruction is mapped into multiple on-chip microinstructions. GaAs processors will likely not have the transistors available to provide such a thorough decoding capability.

A second technique for increasing the information transfer rate is to increase the effective rate of transfer. Silicon computer systems rely increasingly on cache memories, and multiple-level memory hierarchies in general, to provide effective processor–memory transfer rates near the rate required by the processor. These traditional silicon solutions may not be adequate for GaAs processors, because interchip signal propagation delays will take larger percentages of GaAs instruction cycle times.

Overlapping information transfers with processor execution is the final technique that we consider for reducing the GaAs processor information problem. Parallel execution and information transfer imply that information transfers are initiated before the processor has a need for this information. For a completely autonomous information transfer mechanism, separate datapaths and memory are required. This is more easily affordable in silicon implementation than in GaAs.

Clearly, the low transistor count of GaAs chips and the relatively large penalty for communication between them are real obstacles to the successful exploitation of the fast gates of GaAs technology. Silicon computer systems are designed within an implementation environment that has matched increased on-chip switching speeds with enormous levels of integration; therefore, the computer design techniques used in silicon are not entirely compatible with the requirements imposed by GaAs technology. GaAs computer systems require approaches in both hardware and compiler design that differ from those traditionally used in silicon computer design. This is now an important engineering problem (45).

3.3.2. Hardware Design Issues

Given the general GaAs-driven design considerations of the previous section, we are now in a position to discuss design approaches for the hardware of GaAs processor systems.

We begin our hardware discussion by describing design approaches within the processor before moving to the off-chip memory environment. We first discuss our choice of processor configuration, followed by a presentation of suitable design approaches for the instruction pipeline, register file, execution unit, and instruction format. Our memory design discussions include virtual memory, memory hierarchies, both run-time and compile-time memory management, and pipelined memory systems.

Processor Configuration

A number of different processor configurations are available as candidates for a GaAs implementation. Two representative silicon processor designs are the Cray-1 (57) and the Motorola MC68020 (39).

The Cray-1 is a supercomputer implemented in silicon emitter-coupled logic (ECL), and optimized to perform floating point operations on regular data structures such as arrays. Although the use of ECL allowed the Cray-1 to achieve a low 12.5-ns cycle time, a large number of these SSI and MSI parts were required to implement the processor. Because of the severe performance penalty for interchip communication in the GaAs environment, multiple-chip configurations such as these are not especially desirable. In fact, it has been reported that even if gate delays could be reduced to zero, the performance of a well-known supercomputer would only be increased by about 20% because of the dominance of off-chip delays (23). In contrast with the lower transistor count capability of GaAs compared to silicon NMOS, GaAs has a higher transistor count potential than silicon ECL. Therefore, the use of higher-density GaAs parts would improve the performance of vector processors such as the Cray; however, we are not concerned with such special-purpose environments in this chapter.

Processors such as the Motorola MC68020 take the opposite approach of the Cray as they are implemented on a single chip. With this approach, the datapath (execution unit, register file, etc.) is on-chip, and the datapath execution time is not influenced by interchip signal propagation delays. This configuration has obvious advantages in a GaAs implementation environment. In fact, a single-chip processor configuration will achieve a higher relative performance increase through the use of GaAs technology than either silicon mainframes or silicon supercomputers (22). It is because of this large potential increase in performance, in addition to a broader application market, that this chapter is oriented to the study of computer systems utilizing single-chip VLSI GaAs processors.

Single-Chip GaAs Processor Designs
The decoding and control logic (microcode) of the Motorola 68000 requires 68% of that chip's area (33). Although some may argue that this is acceptable for a silicon processor, it is clearly not tolerable for transistor-scarce GaAs processors. In contrast to the 68000, the Berkeley RISC-II processor uses only 10% of its area for decoding and control (33). The characteristics of processors such as the Berkeley RISC-II are worthy of further study for possible incorporation into GaAs processors.

The Berkeley RISC-II (33) is an example of a reduced instruction set computer (RISC). Other well-known RISC processors include the IBM 801 (55) and the Stanford MIPS (28). RISCs are designed utilizing a philosophy that espouses the fast execution of the most frequently used instructions of an application environment, while avoiding the negative aspects of complexity associated with a silicon implementation. One of the Berkeley RISC-II designers presented his view of instruction set design. "First, the most necessary and frequent operations (instructions) in programs were identified. Then, the datapath and timing required for their execution was identified. And last, other *frequent* operations (instructions), which *could also fit* into that datapath and timing, were included into the instruction set (33)." In fact, this same frequency-based justification holds for all hardware resources. The result of this strategy is a processor with low decoding and control requirements and, consequently, low transistor count requirements. The 32-bit Berkeley RISC-II processor required only 41,000 transistors, while the 32-bit Stanford MIPS required but 25,000. These numbers are in contrast to the Motorola 68020, a Complex Instruction Set Computer (CISC), using approximately 190,000 transistors (39). In fact, the low transistor count requirements of the Stanford MIPS led to its being selected by the U.S. government as the architecture for its first 32-bit GaAs processor program (7).

Several processor features result from the RISC design philosophy and will likely be inherited by GaAs processors as well. RISC processors generally implement only a few simple instructions, execute every instruction in one cycle, use a register-to-register execution model, and access off-chip data through explicit data load or data store instructions (54). RISC processors also rely more heavily on the capabilities of optimizing compilers. In fact, functions are implemented in hardware only if they cannot be performed at compile time (55). This constant evaluation of hardware–software trade-offs, implicit in the RISC philosophy, which leads to both reduced

hardware resource requirements, as well as demonstrated superior performance (28, 53), makes the RISC design philosophy very appropriate for GaAs
processor implementations. A more thorough discussion on RISC processors
is given in Chapters 1 and 2.

Instruction Pipeline Design
Instruction pipelining is frequently used in silicon processors to increase
execution speed. An example instruction pipeline for a silicon processor
might resemble Figure 3.6. In this example, the instruction fetch time is
equal to the instruction execution (datapath) time. This pipelined implementation results in approximately twice the execution speed of a nonpip-
lined implementation. The speedup is due to the overlapping of instruction
fetching with execution, which allows the instruction memory system to
completely satisfy the processor's instruction requirements.

A GaAs processor will require instructions at a faster rate than a silicon
processor, and it is very likely that conventional silicon-like instruction pipelines will not satisfy a GaAs processor's instruction requirements for two
reasons. First, the ratio of off-chip memory access delay to both on-chip
memory access delay and arithmetic logic unit (ALU) delay is much higher
for a GaAs processor than for a silicon processor. Second, the lower transistor count of GaAs chips precludes the use of an on-chip cache for memory
access speedup (44). In fact, if a GaAs processor utilizes a typical silicon-
like datapath (i.e., ALU, shifter, register file) design with an on-package
instruction cache, the ratio of instruction fetch delay to datapath delay will
be up to approximately 3 (25). For an off-package cache, the ratio may easily
reach 6. The typical silicon instruction pipeline of Figure 3.6 does not fare
very well under these conditions, as observed in Figure 3.7.

An instruction pipeline should not have a processor datapath under-
utilization built into it. Ideally, the effective instruction fetch time exactly
matches the instruction execution time. The techniques for achieving good
pipeline design in a GaAs processor are part of the discussions of the next
few sections. Pipelines that result from careful GaAs computer system design
approach those shown in Figures 3.8, 3.9, and 3.10. Figure 3.8 is the result
of increasing the effective *rate* of instruction fetches. Figure 3.9 is the result

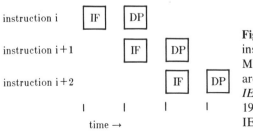

Figure 3.6 Example of silicon
instruction pipeline. (Fura DA,
Milutinović VM: Computer
architecture design in GaAs. *Proc.
IEEE Midcon/85*, Chicago, IL, Sept.
1985, pp. 24/3.1–24/3.7. © 1985
IEEE.)

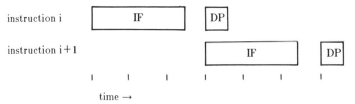

instruction i

instruction i+1

time →

Figure 3.7 Example of silicon pipeline implemented in GaAs. (Fura DA, Milutinović VM: Computer architecture design in GaAs. *Proc. IEEE Midcon/85*, Chicago, IL, Sept. 1985, pp. 24/3.1–24/3.7. © 1985 IEEE.)

of increasing the *content* of instruction fetches. Figure 3.10 is the result of decreasing the *required rate* of instruction fetches.

Register File Design

As already indicated, the RISC design philosophy typically results in processors that use a register-to-register execution model. In addition to its contribution to complexity reduction, the register-to-register execution model has other desirable features for a GaAs implementation.

First, registers are fast on-chip memory. The access time of a register is much shorter than that of off-chip memory, and this difference is more pronounced for a GaAs processor. As stated earlier, maximizing on-chip memory is of great importance for a GaAs processor.

Register files are generally more effective than caches at the small capacities available in a GaAs processor. For example, an instruction cache containing 16 32-bit words can be expected to achieve a hit ratio of only 70%, while an equivalent data cache would hit only 55% of the time (63). Because register file data placement is performed by the compiler instead of a runtime caching mechanism, register file accesses never miss. In addition, register files aren't burdened by the hardware overhead required by caches.

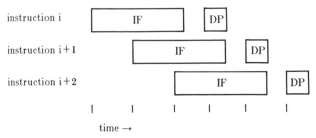

instruction i

instruction i+1

instruction i+2

time →

Figure 3.8 Example of GaAs instruction pipeline with a pipelined memory. (Fura DA, Milutinović VM: Computer architecture design in GaAs. *Proc. IEEE Midcon/85*, Chicago, IL, Sept. 1985, pp. 24/3.1–24/3.7. © 1985 IEEE.)

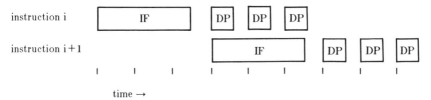

Figure 3.9 Example of GaAs instruction pipeline with instruction packing. (Fura DA, Milutinović VM: Computer architecture design in GaAs. *Proc. IEEE Midcon/85*, Chicago, IL, Sept. 1985, pp. 24/3.1–24/3.7. © 1985 IEEE.)

A register address is directly specified within the instruction. Therefore, an address calculation is not required and no virtual-to-physical translation need be performed. The short length of register addresses leads to compact code that can be expected to increase the hit ratios of program memory accesses at the higher levels of the memory hierarchy.

Given the importance of register files, this section presents the design issues involved with register memory cells and register file partitioning.

Register cell design. In silicon processors, performance depends heavily on the speed of datapath elements such as the register file. For this reason, register cell designs emphasizing fast access speed and multiple read and/or write ports are common. As an example, the microcode pipeline of the HP-Focus processor (9) is shown in Figure 3.11. Because of the fast access time of its on-chip microcode memory, fast register file access was also needed. Figure 3.12 shows the register cell design used in the HP-Focus, which allows two simultaneous data reads or writes and supports the 55-ns cycle time.

In GaAs processors, fewer transistors will be available for register file implementation; therefore, simple register cells are very advantageous. Even if simple register cells reduce the datapath speed, performance may not be negatively impacted. One approach to reducing a high ratio of instruction fetch delay to datapath delay is to increase the datapath delay. This may

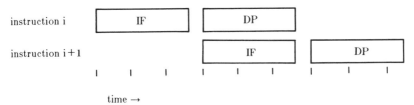

Figure 3.10 Example of GaAs instruction pipeline with long-latency datapath elements. (Fura DA, Milutinović VM: Computer architecture design in GaAs. *Proc. IEEE Midcon/85*, Chicago, IL, Sept. 1985, pp. 24/3.1–24/3.7. © 1985 IEEE.)

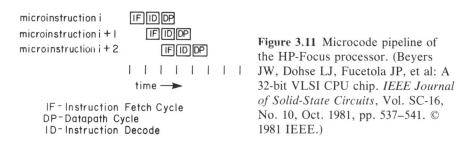

microinstruction i

microinstruction i + l

microinstruction i + 2

time →

IF – Instruction Fetch Cycle
DP – Datapath Cycle
I D – Instruction Decode

Figure 3.11 Microcode pipeline of the HP-Focus processor. (Beyers JW, Dohse LJ, Fucetola JP, et al: A 32-bit VLSI CPU chip. *IEEE Journal of Solid-State Circuits*, Vol. SC-16, No. 10, Oct. 1981, pp. 537–541. © 1981 IEEE.)

seem very undesirable; however, reducing the effective instruction fetch delay, which is intuitively the best approach, introduces new problems. Fast register cells imply that pipelines such as those in Figures 3.8 and 3.9 must be used to match the "effective" instruction fetch delay to a very low datapath delay. However, the degree of instruction packing shown in Figure 3.8 is severely constrained by pin limitations of integrated circuits and information needs of a GaAs processor, while the pipelined instruction memory approach of Figure 3.9 is penalized heavily by program branches.

If a pipelined instruction memory is used with a very fast GaAs datapath, a large number of pipeline stages will be required to match the instruction fetch and datapath delays, while a slower datapath will require fewer pipeline stages. However, the speed advantage of the faster datapath is negated considerably by the execution of program branches and off-chip data accesses. As the level of pipelining becomes large, the ability of the compiler to perform branch fill and data load fill (explained later) decreases, and the fast datapath is used to execute an increasing number of NOOPs associated with branches and off-chip data accesses.

Using slow register cells at least has the advantage of a low resource requirement. Given the decreasing performance benefit of fast datapath designs at high ratios of instruction fetch delay to datapath delay, the use of simple datapath designs is worthy of strong consideration. The selection of an appropriate register cell design must be considered in the context of the

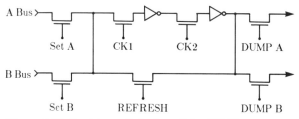

Figure 3.12 Register cell design of the HP-Focus processor. (Beyers JW, Dohse LJ, Fucetola JP, et al: A 32-bit VLSI CPU chip. *IEEE Journal of Solid-State Circuits*, Vol. SC-16, No. 10, Oct. 1981, pp. 537–541.)

entire system. There is certainly a greater disparity in access time between off-chip memory and a slow register cell than between a fast and a slow register cell. It is conceivable that a larger number of slow registers may provide better system performance than a smaller number of fast registers.

Simple register cells that make good candidates for GaAs processors are shown in Figures 3.13 (58) and 3.14 (45). Figure 3.13 shows the register cell design of the Berkeley RISC-II. Its transistor and area requirements are much lower than those of the HP-Focus. Although this register cell allows parallel reads, its read time is slower than the cell of the HP-Focus (58). Figure 3.14 shows a register cell with a single read bus. This cell uses less area than the other cells, but requires sequential reading and writing.

Register file partitioning.   Register files generally succeed in reducing the processor's need to access off-chip data during the execution of HLL procedures. However, at procedure boundaries (calls, returns) the register file values must be stored to memory and new values loaded in. This massive off-chip communication is bad enough in silicon implementations, but is even more damaging to a GaAs processor.

To alleviate this procedure boundary problem, multiple window register file schemes have been introduced by silicon designers, and used in processors such as the Berkeley RISC-II (33). In a multiple window register file, each procedure is allocated one window for its data. Whenever a procedure call or return is encountered, instead of emptying and refilling the register file, a new window is allocated, perhaps by simply changing a pointer

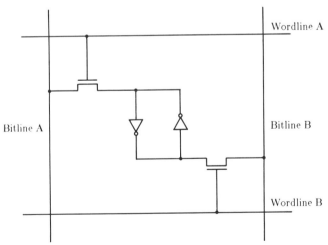

Figure 3.13 Register cell design of the Berkeley RISC-II processor. (Sherburne RW, Jr: Processor design trade-offs in VLSI. Report No. UCB/CSD 84/173, University of California at Berkeley, April 1984.)

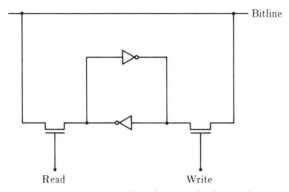

Figure 3.14 Register cell design employing a single read bus. (Milutinović VM, Fura DA, Helbig W: An introduction to GaAs microprocessor architecture for VLSI. *IEEE Computer*, Vol. 19, No. 3, March 1986. © 1986 IEEE.)

value as in the Berkeley RISC-II. The only time that emptying and refilling is required is on an "overflow" or "underflow." An overflow occurs when a procedure call is encountered and no unused windows exist. An underflow occurs when a procedure return is encountered and the values of the returned-to procedure were saved to memory because of a previous overflow. The eight-window scheme of the Berkeley RISC-II was responsible for an approximate 50% reduction in the number of data loads and stores (54). Consequently, this technique shows potential applicability for a GaAs processor implementation. See Chapters 1 and 2 for more discussion of the Berkeley window scheme.

A major problem that prevents the implementation of the Berkeley RISC-II register window scheme in GaAs is the large number of registers required for its implementation—138. In fact, the Berkeley implementation would consume nearly all the transistors available to a 30k transistor GaAs processor. For this reason, two variations of the Berkeley method are potential candidates for a GaAs implementation. They are multiple window schemes with (a) variable-size windows and (b) background loading and storing.

Multiple window register files with variable-size windows have been discussed in the context of silicon implementations (33). The real advantage of this approach is that more windows can be formed from fewer registers compared with a fixed-size approach. The reason for this is that most procedures use very few local variables and formal parameters in well-structured programs (65). A fixed-size window scheme will encounter very poor register file utilization, and this is quite undesirable in a GaAs implementation where off-chip delays are large. When only enough registers are allocated to minimally satisfy each procedure's needs, additional registers are made available to implement more windows and reduce overflows and un-

derflows. The drawbacks to this approach are additional hardware requirements and added delay for register address calculation, and additional overhead for procedure calls/returns and overflow/underflow handling. A compromise approach is to provide multiple windows but limit the number of
sizes that may be used, and choose sizes to reduce complexity (17).

Multiple window register files with fixed-size windows and background
mode loading and storing have also been discussed (33). The advantage of
this approach is that intelligent preloading and prestoring may reduce the
frequency of overflows and underflows. The primary drawbacks to this approach include the additional processor–memory bandwidth required, and
the need for an independent input–output controller capability.

Execution Unit Design

The effect that the low transistor count and large off-chip delays have on
register cell design for a GaAs processor is felt in the execution unit design
as well. Once again, scarce hardware resources should not be used to create
or exacerbate a mismatch between execution unit information needs and off-
chip memory system capabilities. The execution unit design for a GaAs
processor should instead be part of a system-level effort to achieve a match
between these two.

If the effective off-chip memory access time cannot be cheaply reduced
to match the datapath delay, another method of matching the off-chip memory and datapath delays may be appropriate. A useful approach for GaAs
processor execution unit design is to approach the ideal "instruction fetch
delay–datapath delay" equality from the direction indicated in Figure 3.10.
This approach is summarized as "reducing the execution unit's need for off-
chip data in some useful way." There are two methods for accomplishing
this: (1) Remove resources from the execution unit in order to slow down
the execution of primitive operations, and reallocate the resources elsewhere, perhaps to the register file. (2) Maintain or add resources to the
execution unit only to support complex operations that require large amounts
of time. These two approaches will be in evidence throughout this section.

Adder design.   Silicon processors typically require high-speed adders to
maximize their performance. Again, this is because of the relatively fast
access times of silicon memories by comparison with datapath times, especially when the memory is on-chip. For example, the HP-Focus utilized
a full-carry look-ahead adder to satisfy its 55-ns cycle time in a silicon
implementation.

The adder designs available for a GaAs implementation range from the
high-speed, high-resource-requirement full-carry look-ahead adder to the
low-speed, low-resource-requirement ripple-carry adder. Others with speeds
and resource requirements between these two extremes include conditional-
sum and carry-select adders (31).

As in register cell design, simple designs are advantageous for GaAs adders. In addition to transistor count differences, the preceding adder designs exhibit differences in regularity that introduce chip area differences as well.

A VLSI implementation environment introduces complexity into adder performance evaluation (58). In a silicon SSI/MSI TTL (transistor–transistor logic) implementation, adder speed is determined by the number of gate delays required to obtain the final result. In a VLSI implementation, designers have potential opportunities for performance enhancement, such as in varying transistor sizes to improve speed in critical paths. Additional variables are also introduced, such as large signal propagation delays because of long wire lengths, large fanins, and large fanouts.

In a silicon VLSI environment, it has been shown that the regular layouts and low fanin/fanout requirements of adders such as the ripple-carry and carry-select reduce the performance advantage of the traditional carry look-ahead approaches, which are very irregular (54).

From both a performance and implementation cost standpoint, ripple-carry and carry-select adders are more suitable than traditional carry look-ahead adders for implementation into a GaAs processor. This is partially because of their lower sensitivity to fanin and fanout problems, and partially because of reasons discussed in the register cell section.

Multiplier/divider design.   The frequency of use of multiplication and division operations varies from application to application. In a distribution of instructions from a computer aided design (CAD) application environment, multiplies were only 3% of all instructions executed. However, the high frequency of multiplies in signal processing applications prompted the designers of the Texas Instruments TMS320 (41) to include a 200-ns on-chip hardware multiplier. In this section we present multiplication and division techniques that are advantageous for GaAs processor implementations. Designs for both high-frequency and low-frequency usage will be given.

Silicon processors targeted to general purpose applications typically utilize the datapath adder to perform multiplication and division. Silicon CISCs implement multiplication and division with microcode routines, while silicon RISCs use special multiply-step or divide-step instructions that are stored within the program. In special purpose application environments where multiply and/or divide operations are more frequent, silicon processors incorporate additional hardware. Example hardware multipliers include an implementation of the modified Booth algorithm in the TMS320 and an array multiplier in the NEC IPP (51). An example division technique is the "division by repeated multiplication" method used in the IBM 360/91 which requires a fast multiplier.

Multiplication and division operations require relatively large amounts of time; therefore, if justified by frequency of use, additional hardware support is desirable for GaAs processors as well. In addition to faster speed, an advantage in using a hardware implementation of a multiplication/division algorithm is that less off-chip information (fewer instructions) is required than in traditional software approaches. However, candidate approaches must satisfy the limited transistor count typical of GaAs.

The standard add-and-shift multiplication technique and subtract-and-shift division technique require the fewest hardware resources and are quite desirable from this standpoint, especially in general purpose environments. Minor hardware additions, such as those incorporated in the Stanford MIPS (28), improve these two techniques, achieving multiplication in n/2 steps and division in n steps, where n is the word length.

Silicon CISC implementations of these multiplication and division techniques have an advantage over silicon RISC implementations in one respect. A silicon CISC must only fetch one instruction from off-chip memory in order to execute either a multiply or divide, while a RISC must fetch several instructions. A microcoded CISC therefore does a better job of reducing off-chip communication needs; in principle, this is very desirable for GaAs processors. This does not imply that microcoded CISCs are appropriate for GaAs; however, achieving the higher information content of CISC-like instructions is desirable. Modifying RISC principles to allow a single instruction to represent a sequence of add-shift operations (or subtract-shift operations) is worthy of consideration. This idea is presented in greater detail in the next section.

The hardware multipliers used on the TMS320 and NEC IPP require too many hardware resources to be incorporated into a GaAs processor. If the need for fast multiplication is very strong, the following two hardware approaches may be used.

A serial multiplier with moderate hardware resource requirements may be constructed. A serial multiplier presented in (21) requires 64 cycles to perform a 32-bit by 32-bit multiplication. Since each cycle period need only be long enough to allow signal propagation through a flip-flop and minimal logic, a faster clock may be used to achieve a serial multiplication time much lower than that achieved by the datapath adder. This solution makes very good use of the architectural strength of GaAs—its fast gates. This type of iterative approach has also been cited by an early GaAs architecture researcher (23) as being desirable for GaAs. An off-datapath serial multiplier also allows concurrent multiplication and datapath execution.

An alternative approach is to incorporate a hardware multiplier into a coprocessor. The multiplier design in such an implementation is not as constrained as in the processor; therefore, designs with greater hardware requirements are more appropriate here. Of course, this technique may be extended to allow two or more such coprocessors if the application environment demands it. This approach also allows the concurrent operation of the coprocessor and the processor's datapath.

Instruction Format Design

The use of the RISC design philosophy in GaAs processor design might appear to reduce instruction format design to a trivial problem. This is of course not so. A legitimate concern for GaAs processor design is the effect of the instruction format on the timely transfer of instructions to the processor. The instruction bandwidth requirement of a processor is strongly dependent on the instruction format. Although the basing of design decisions on instruction bandwidth alone is not to be encouraged, this architectural metric acquires added significance in the GaAs environment, but should be used within the context of the system design.

Compact programs require a lower memory-processor bandwidth and are more beneficial in GaAs processor systems than in silicon processor systems for at least two reasons.

First, the technology used to implement the memory at the highest levels of the memory hierarchy will likely be GaAs. Because GaAs memory chips will likely remain less dense than silicon memory chips, GaAs caches will be relatively small. It has been shown that cache size is the single most important factor in determining cache hit ratios (59), and that hit ratios increase rapidly at small cache sizes before leveling off at high cache capacities (63). Because a decrease in program size is equivalent to an increase in memory size, compact programs are indeed very desirable in a GaAs processor system.

Second, because of the extremely fast instruction cycle times possible in a GaAs processor, a memory access miss in a GaAs processor system will likely entail a longer delay, in terms of instruction cycles, than a memory access miss in a silicon processor system. It is therefore more important to minimize these misses in a GaAs processor system.

The major disadvantage of the RISC design philosophy in a GaAs implementation is the generally low information content of RISC instructions. Of course, the very simplicity of RISC instructions leads to their low decoding logic requirements. Therefore, any attempt to reduce program size through increased encoding of instructions must be done so as to minimize its impact on decoding complexity.

We discuss two methods for increasing program compactness that can have little impact on the decoding requirements for a GaAs processor. The first approach relies on the high dynamic frequency of short immediate fields and few operand addresses, while the second approach makes use of the repetitive nature of some complex operations such as multiply and divide.

Frequency-based instructions. Techniques based on Huffman codes (30) are frequently considered in instruction set design. Huffman coding is a technique for assigning the most frequent instructions the smallest encodings. A pure Huffman implementation would require sequential decoding and much hardware, and is not a serious candidate for a GaAs processor.

However, the general concept of providing small encodings to frequent occurrences is very applicable for GaAs processor instruction sets.

Compact instruction formats may be designed to incorporate small immediate fields and few address fields. The resulting reduction in program size is not due to an explicit encoding function operating on these fields, but results from the high dynamic frequency of small immediate data values and both one-address and two-address instructions in real programs. In one study of XPL programs (2), it was shown that 61% of the branch distances required 8 bits or less, while 81% could be represented with 12 bits. They also found that 47% of the numeric constants could be represented by only 4 bits, and that 87% required 8 bits or less. It is also estimated that 87% of all assignment statements require only two operand addresses (48).

Compact instruction formats resulting from using short immediate fields and few operand addresses have three beneficial aspects for a GaAs implementation.

First, as just mentioned, the proper design of immediate and operand fields can be expected to reduce total program size and provide the benefits for a GaAs implementation described earlier.

Second, this approach takes advantage of the dynamic characteristics of program behavior. Small immediate values and few operand addresses are not the output of an encoding algorithm, but occur naturally and frequently in real programs; therefore, there is no need for a significant decoding function within the processor to "undo" any additional encoding.

Third, compact operations may be packed into a single instruction. Because pin limitations of a GaAs processor will limit the size of instruction fetch transfers, multiple operation fetching, as shown in Figure 3.9, is only possible for short operations. A well-designed packed instruction format can improve the performance of a processor in a long-latency off-chip environment.

Many silicon instruction sets display varying levels of program compactness, and some even employ operation packing. The longest immediate data values for many silicon processors require 32 bits of information. In order to include immediate fields in single-word instructions to represent 32-bit values, extremely long instructions would be required.

Even relatively sparse instruction formats, such as the Berkeley RISC-II, take advantage of the low frequency of use of such long immediate values by only supporting short immediate values within a single instruction. The use of very large immediate values requires two RISC-II instructions.

The Stanford MIPS limits its maximum immediate field size to 24 bits to allow all immediate values to be used within single instructions. However, the MIPS instruction set takes advantage of small immediate data values by packing a second operation into instructions that require short immediate fields. This operation packing also makes use of the high frequency of one- and two-address operations because the instruction fields for the packed operations are only large enough for two-address operations.

The ability of the Stanford MIPS to execute two operations per instruction fetch is limited by the occurrence of long immediate values and also by the ability of its compiler to find suitable useful (non-NOOP) packing candidates. A more complex instruction format also results from the MIPS style of packing. This results in a 10% increase in the MIPS instruction cycle time (54), in addition to increased decoding hardware requirements.

The Transputer (71) relies very heavily on the high frequency of small immediate values as it only provides four bits of immediate field in every 8-bit instruction. Larger immediate values must be built from multiple instructions 4 bits at a time. The small size of its instruction format allows the Transputer to pack four such instructions—from now on we call these *operations*—into a single packed instruction.

The Transputer is better able to meet its maximum rate of four operation executions per instruction fetch because of a somewhat different definition of "operation." The Transputer uses even more primitive operations than the MIPS or RISC-II. The use of a large immediate data value is implemented by a sequence of "build immediate field" operations. However, these operations have a 50% overhead as only 4 of the 8 bits contain actual data. However, the field boundaries of the Transputer's instruction format can be expected to result in a simpler decoding function than required by the MIPS instruction format.

Compact instruction formats must be designed with a good understanding of the instruction requirements of the intended application environment. However, the exploitation of the high frequency of usage of small immediate values and few operand addresses may provide significant benefits for a GaAs processor implementation.

Context-based instructions. Huffman codes are based on the frequency of usage of data items without considering the environment surrounding the data items. Because instruction executions are not independent of each other, additional compaction opportunities are available.

A compaction technique that uses context information, in addition to the instruction frequency information used by Huffman-based techniques, is conditional coding (26). In this technique, the encoding of the next instruction to be executed is dependent on the probability of its occurrence, in the context of the execution of the current instruction. Therefore, if there are n instructions in the instruction set, each instruction has n different encodings—one associated with each of the n possible preceding instructions. A strict implementation of this scheme is not practical for a GaAs processor; however, the concept of using context information to reduce program size is applicable.

A less rigorous, but simpler technique is to replace frequent instruction sequences with a single instruction (26). In fact, this technique is typically used on microcoded CISCs. A program consisting of CISC macroinstructions is generally more compact than a program containing RISC instructions because each macroinstruction corresponds to a sequence of microinstructions, while each RISC instruction corresponds to a single microinstruction-like instruction. It is possible that this CISC mechanism can be utilized to good advantage in some GaAs processor environments.

If justified by frequency of use, complex instructions such as multiply, divide, and perhaps even multiply-accumulate may be added to the instruction set of a GaAs processor. Even if a transistor-scarce GaAs processor cannot support the hardware to directly execute these operations and must instead use the main datapath, there are advantages to using complex instructions.

For example, the implementation of multiply on a RISC can be performed in a number of ways. A linear sequence of multiply-step instructions can be used for each multiply in the program. For a processor such as the Stanford MIPS, this may require nearly 20 instructions per multiply. If multiplies are 10% of all instructions executed, this technique nearly triples the program size.

Alternatively, a loop containing as few as one multiply-step instruction can be used. However, introducing loops into programs is not generally desirable both because of the time wasted on looping overhead and because of the large number of instructions required to perform branch fill in if the GaAs processor is highly pipelined.

A third technique is to include a linear sequence of multiply-step instructions into a system procedure that is callable from anywhere within the program. This technique therefore requires that a procedure call and return be executed for each multiply instruction. Beyond the normal overhead associated with procedure calls, this method degrades the execution locality, possibly decreasing memory hit ratios.

The implementation of a single multiply instruction entails none of the preceding disadvantages; however, complexity is introduced into the pipeline control mechanism. Single-cycle instruction execution is a feature of "true" RISCs because it leads to simple pipeline control. When a CISC-like multiply instruction is encountered, the processor will likely spend a long time executing it; therefore, the instruction pipeline must be halted. If the instruction memory is also pipelined, a time delay will probably exist before the entire memory pipeline can be halted, and buffering may be needed. Clearly, the benefits of CISC-like instructions must be weighed against this implementation complexity, and the decision to use CISC-like instructions should be considered in the context of the entire system.

Memory System Design

Memory system design is an extremely important issue in a computer system containing a GaAs processor. The capabilities of a fast GaAs processor cannot be fully exploited unless the memory system is able to satisfy the processor's increased information needs. The low transistor count of GaAs memory chips and the long interchip delays, with respect to the cycle time of a GaAs processor, both limit a memory system's ability to provide the capacity and transfer bandwidth required by a GaAs processor.

The role of virtual memory.   The application environment also has a large influence on the design of a memory system for a GaAs processor system, particularly with regard to the issue of virtual memory. A virtual memory system is one that provides a mapping from logical addresses to physical addresses (10). Logical addresses are produced by the compiler, while physical addresses are used for accessing physical memory.

There are several advantages to virtual memory systems. Because virtual memory systems normally contain a large capacity backing store such as a magnetic disk, both the programmer and compiler are able to generate code without regard to the actual size of main memory. The burden of memory allocation is transferred from the programmer to the operating system, and multitasking and protection mechanisms are easier to incorporate. Virtual memory is used extensively in computer systems in universities and industry.

The disadvantage of virtual memory is that the logical-to-physical address translation is necessary. Virtual memory systems therefore have longer memory access latencies than nonvirtual memory systems. In applications that require the speed of a GaAs processor, the performance loss due to a virtual memory implementation is quite expensive. Many silicon supercomputers do not use virtual memory; instead they rely on large main memories. Applications such as these, as well as many embedded applications with special-purpose programs and relatively small memory requirements, will not require virtual memory in GaAs processor systems.

Memory hierarchy.   Large memory systems generally utilize several types of memory components to achieve a favorable cost-performance balance. The fastest memory parts are also generally of the lowest capacity, as well as being the most expensive; slower, higher capacity memory is generally the cheapest. Memory system designers try to provide memory speeds approaching the speed of the fastest technology, while achieving a cost per bit approaching the cost of the cheapest technology. This is achieved through the exploitation of the locality of references that exist within most computer programs.

Two types of program localities exist (11). Temporal locality means that once information is used it will likely be used again within a short time span. Programming constructs that cause this include loops, recursive procedures, and activation record accesses. Spatial locality means that when a unit of information is used, its neighboring information will likely be used within a short time span. Programming constructs that cause this include sequential program execution, activation record accesses, and structured data accesses.

These two localities of reference are responsible for the success of hierarchical memory systems. By keeping the information that is within the current referencing locality in the fastest memory, fast information access will be available to the processor a large percentage of the time. This clearly would not be the case if accesses were uniformly distributed throughout the entire memory system.

The memory technology best able to meet the speed requirements of a GaAs processor is GaAs. Therefore, GaAs memories will likely be used to implement the highest level of the memory hierarchy. The lower levels of a memory hierarchy usually incorporate cheaper, larger, and, hence, slower memories. As the capacities increase at each successive level, fast, less-dense technologies (i.e., GaAs) lose their speed advantage over slow, dense technologies (i.e., silicon). This is because off-chip signal propagation delays are larger for low density chips, which require large amounts of board area. This is especially true when low-density memory chips cause board area capacities to be exceeded, requiring additional interboard communication.

Run-time control of hierarchical memory systems.   Most silicon hierarchical memory systems make extensive use of run-time information control mechanisms. For example, caches, which are often used as the fastest element of the memory hierarchy, use hardware to decide at run-time what information is to be located within the cache. Similar run-time approaches are commonly used for main memory as well.

Two techniques are frequently used in silicon systems to decide what information should be moved into a higher level of the memory hierarchy. The simplest method is to move the information into the higher level when it is needed by the processor and not already at the higher level. The processor is required to wait until the requested information is moved, and this may result in a considerable delay. Another common method, known as prefetching (60), relies on a form of spatial locality known as sequential locality. Sequential locality is caused by the sequential execution of most programs and the sequential access of structured data. In prefetching techniques, information located at addresses slightly higher than the currently accessed addresses is moved into a higher level of the memory hierarchy. This run-time-initiated information movement is potentially very advantageous in a GaAs processor system.

In addition to deciding what information should be moved into a higher level of the memory hierarchy, run-time mechanisms must decide where the information is to be located within the higher level.

Existing silicon memory systems vary in the amount of power they give to the run-time hardware in deciding where in the higher level to locate the moved information. Three placement policies are commonly used in silicon caches: fully associative, set associative, and direct mapped (62). In a fully associative memory level, the run-time hardware is free to locate the information in any location. In a set associative memory level, the run-time hardware is constrained to locate the information within a subset of the memory level called the "set." In a direct mapped memory level, the run-time hardware has only one valid location in which to locate the information.

In silicon caches, the fully associative technique generally achieves the highest hit ratios among these three methods, followed by the set associative and direct mapped techniques (62). However, at small cache sizes, the difference in hit ratios between the three techniques becomes insignificant (59).

In the fully associative and set associative techniques, the run-time hardware decides where in the higher level to locate the moved information. The movement of information into the higher level implies an equal-volume movement of information out of the higher level. Therefore the location in the higher level is chosen so as to hopefully displace information no longer needed by the processor. Of the information candidates for displacement, the information needed by the processor for the longest period of time cannot be predicted by a run-time mechanism.

Three common replacement algorithms are the least recently used (LRU), first in first out (FIFO), and random (RAND) methods (62).

The LRU technique exploits temporal locality by replacing the information that saw the least recent use. A strict implementation of this technique requires excessive overhead if a fully associative policy or set associative policy with large set size is used. A strict implementation is therefore generally restricted to small set sizes; however, LRU approximations may be used for larger sets.

The FIFO method does a poorer job of temporal locality exploitation but requires less overhead for its implementation.

The RAND method makes no attempt to exploit temporal locality but is easily implemented.

If the information being displaced was modified while in the higher hierarchical level, this information must be stored back into memory at the lower levels. Two common techniques are used to achieve this storing.

The copy-back method (62) waits until the information is displaced before storing to the lower levels. In order to avoid storing information that has not been modified, a "dirty bit" is commonly associated with a block of information. If this bit is set, the information has seen recent modification while in the higher level and should therefore be written to the lower level. If the dirty bit is not set, no storage to the lower levels is necessary.

In the write-through technique (62), the information is written to the lower levels as soon as the processor modifies it. If the processor must wait for its data stores to complete before continuing execution, this technique will introduce long delays into program execution. However, if buffering is used, such as in pipelined memory systems discussed later in this chapter, no additional delays are introduced. The write-through method also does not require the overhead associated with the copy-back approach.

As already mentioned, memories consisting of GaAs chips will generally be smaller than silicon versions. Because of the minimal run-time overhead associated with the direct mapped implementation just discussed, as well as its relatively good performance at small memory capacities, this approach is desirable for the memory at the highest level of the memory hierarchy.

At the lower memory levels, the set associative and fully associative techniques become advantageous because of the larger capacity of the lower levels. The LRU, FIFO, and RAND replacement policies are all viable methods at these lower memory levels as well.

If pipelining is employed in the memory system design, the write-through method is preferable to the copy-back approach for the cache and main memory levels of the memory hierarchy. Write-through eliminates both the need for long-latency copy-back operations and reduces coherency problems by ensuring that the lower memory levels are continuously updated.

Compile-time control of hierarchical memory systems. The compiler has three advantages over run-time hardware in the implementation of memory hierarchy information control mechanisms. First, it has a larger base of knowledge from which to make decisions because it has a view of the entire program. Second, it presumably has more time to implement a more optimal strategy. Finally, compiler algorithms do not require additional hardware, which is so important for GaAs implementations.

Although the temporal and spatial localities of reference allow run-time information control mechanisms to work well, there are times when the required locality is missing. LRU-based run-time mechanisms, which exploit the referencing localities, are responsible for bringing information into the higher levels of the memory hierarchy, and for deciding which information at the higher levels should be replaced. Two instances where LRU-based mechanisms fail are the following:

1. Information is accessed for the first time after a long period of nonuse.
2. Information is accessed once but will not be accessed again for a long period of time.

The compiler has the potential to detect this nonlocalized behavior and the power to help the run-time mechanism to perform more effectively. Because the delays caused by nonlocalized accessing patterns are more costly, in terms of instruction cycles, for a GaAs processor, the effort expended on compiler design and the increased time for compilation are offset by greater gains in performance. A more thorough discussion of this issue is presented on page 118.

Pipelined memory systems. Pipelining is a common technique for speeding the execution of long-latency operations. Pipelining is frequently used within the processor to overlap instruction fetching, decoding, and execution, etc. It is also used for implementing complex arithmetic operations as in the IBM 360/91 (3).

Because of the longer relative delays associated with memory accesses in a GaAs processor system, memory pipelining is a very attractive approach. In fact, memory pipelining has already been used in silicon systems, on the Amdahl 470V/6 (60). Memory pipelining is even more feasible in a GaAs processor system because the long access delay of off-chip memory is not necessarily due to slow memories, but to long interchip delays. These delays are easily pipelined. An example of a pipelined memory system is shown in Figure 3.15. This pipeline consists of three stages. In the first stage, the address (and data if write) is propagated from the processor to a latch physically near the memory. In the second stage, the memory is accessed and, for a memory read, the data is stored into another latch physically near the memory. The third stage is used, for a memory read, to propagate the data to the processor.

In a three-stage pipeline such as this, three memory accesses may be concurrently serviced. Assuming a GaAs processor system in which the ratio of instruction fetch delay to datapath delay equals 3, this memory system will produce a pipeline such as in Figure 3.8. Clearly, pipelined memory systems decrease the "effective" memory access delay even though the total memory access latency is unchanged. In general, the number of stages in a pipelined memory system is chosen such that the "effective" memory access delay equals the datapath delay. If the ratio of memory access delay to datapath delay is n, then ideally a pipelined memory system will contain n stages. Pipelined memory systems are extremely valuable in GaAs processor systems because they are so successful at increasing the information transfer bandwidth between processor and memory. However, as discussed later, the increased instruction-pipeline depth resulting from pipelined memory

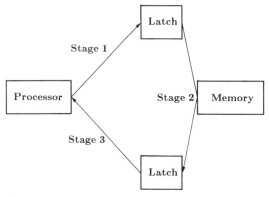

Figure 3.15 Example pipelined memory system.

implementations introduces performance problems associated with program branches. Overall, though, pipelined memory systems should have a positive effect on the performance of GaAs processor systems.

3.3.3. Compiler Design Issues

The high penalty of interchip communication and low levels of integration of GaAs chips combine to increase the importance of the compiler in GaAs processor systems. Without the support of a powerful compiler technology, GaAs processor systems will struggle to fully exploit the speed advantage of GaAs technology, except possibly for selected special-purpose applications.

As discussed earlier, GaAs processor system design utilizes the concepts central to the RISC design philosophy. It is not surprising, then, that the increased reliance on compiler solutions, utilized by silicon RISC designers, is transferred to GaAs processor systems as well. In fact, the characteristics of GaAs dictate that an even increased reliance on compiler solutions be utilized.

Silicon RISC designers have demonstrated the superior performance of RISC computers over silicon CISCs (28, 53). Much of the credit for the improved performance of RISCs is given to simplified instruction sets that allow the rapid execution of the most frequently used instructions. However, the increased role of compiler technology also plays a large part in the success of RISC processors.

In order to minimize the instruction cycle time, RISC designers attempt to eliminate hardware complexity. One technique used to achieve this is the transfer of functionality from hardware to the compiler. There are several examples of this in silicon RISCs. Interlock hardware for sequencing hazards (24) was eliminated on the IBM 801 (55), Berkeley RISC-II (33), and Stanford MIPS (28). This introduced a compiler optimization called "branch delay fillin," a technique commonly used by microcode programmers. Interlock hardware for timing hazards (24) was also eliminated on the Stanford MIPS in order to reduce hardware complexity, with timing hazard detection and avoidance performed instead by the MIPS compiler. Because transistor count limitations will be greater for GaAs processors than for silicon processors, the transfer of even more functionality to the compiler may be desirable for GaAs processors.

RISC instructions are comparable to the microinstructions of a CISC processor. However, a CISC compiler only has access to predefined (by the processor architect) microinstruction sequences in the form of macroinstructions. A RISC compiler, on the other hand, has access to microinstruction-like RISC instructions and therefore has many more instructions to use for both hardware-independent and hardware-dependent optimizations. An increased number of hardware-independent optimizations, such as code motions and common subexpression eliminations, therefore present themselves to a RISC compiler (55). A hardware-dependent optimization called "load delay fillin," which is not available on most CISCs, presents itself to RISC compilers as well (55). In a memory-to-memory or memory-to-register CISC instruction, a data memory read must precede the operation execution. If the read requires a large amount of time, so will the complete execution of the entire instruction. Because RISCs generally use register-to-register and explicit data load instructions, the compiler can schedule the data load instruction in advance, then "fill in" the data load latency with other useful instructions. Because GaAs processors can be expected to have longer data load latencies (in terms of instruction cycles), the burden on the compiler to find candidate instructions for the fillin gap is increased.

A third area where silicon RISCs place increased reliance on compiler technology is the result of their decreased instruction cycle times. Because silicon RISCs have such short cycle times, they are more negatively affected by off-chip delays than silicon CISCs. As a result, the compiler for the IBM 801 incorporated a sophisticated register coloring scheme in order to reduce that processor's need for off-chip information (6). Also, the IBM 801 instruction set included instructions to allow the compiler to override the hardware caching mechanism in some instances when the compiler detected a better strategy for reducing the cache miss ratio (55). The Stanford MIPS incorporated an instruction packing scheme, and required the compiler to perform the packing (28). This approach allows two operations to be executed during the time required for one fetch, and also reduced the program size—both very beneficial characteristics for a processor in an environment with high penalties for off-chip communication. Because GaAs processors will have even shorter instruction cycle times than silicon RISCs, GaAs processors will benefit even more from these types of compiler optimizations. Additional discussions of the importance of compiler technology on silicon RISC performance may be found in Chapters 1 and 2.

Compiler Optimization in Control
The two techniques for reducing hardware complexity, which were just briefly listed, are examples of the migration of control hardware into the compiler. These are both described more fully here.

Sequencing hazard interlocks. Sequencing hazards are caused by branch instructions on a pipelined processor. The problem arises because before the execution of a branch instruction is complete, hence before the decision to jump can be established, successive instructions have already been fetched. In general, the execution of these successive instructions may lead to incorrect results. Silicon CISCs and silicon RISCs usually handle this problem in two different ways.

Silicon CISCs usually employ hardware that halts the execution of the instructions immediately following the branch instruction in the event that the branch is to be taken. This results in a delay in execution until the pipeline can be refilled with the instructions at the destination of the branch. Some CISCs rely on the compiler or run-time algorithms to predict the outcome of the branch condition and fetch the instructions down the appropriate path. However, a wrong guess again requires the emptying of the pipeline. An even more ambitious and hardware-consuming CISC solution involves fetching and decoding instructions down both paths. This can then be expanded to three paths, and so on.

Silicon RISCs use a technique called "delayed branching" to solve the sequencing hazard problem. Most RISCs always execute the instruction following the branch instruction; thus, there is no need for special hardware to halt instruction execution. However, in order to ensure correct program execution, only a subset of all possible instructions are eligible for placement in the "fillin slots" after branch instructions. If eligible instructions cannot be found, the compiler must insert NOOPs into the fillin slots.

Because branches are typically 25% of all instructions in compiled HLL programs (33), their negative effect on performance can be costly. The delayed branching method for sequencing hazard resolution, in addition to promising simpler hardware, offers potentially higher performance as well. Whenever the RISC compiler is able to successfully move a useful instruction into the fillin slot, the delayed branching method exhibits no branching overhead. However, when the RISC compiler is not able to fill the slot, an instruction cycle is lost whether the branch is taken or not. The CISC approach, with sequencing hazard resolution hardware, loses an instruction cycle whenever branches are taken, but loses nothing when sequential operation is maintained.

The performance of the delayed branching scheme, then, depends solely on the RISC compiler. The Stanford MIPS compiler was able to fill approximately 90%[1] of the branch fillin slots (29), so an instruction cycle was lost on only 10% of the branch instruction executions. The CISC approach, with its dependency on dynamic branching probability, does not do so well. Because approximately 75% of all branch instructions change the program flow (61), an instruction cycle is lost on 75% of all branch executions.

However, branch instructions are potentially more costly for the delayed branching scheme in GaAs processor systems than in silicon systems. As discussed earlier, pipelined memory systems are very advantageous in GaAs processor systems because of their ability to decrease effective memory access delays. However, as evident in Figure 3.8, pipelined memory

---

[1] Static count.

systems increase the total pipeline length and, consequently, increase the number of fillin slots following branches. For the pipeline in Figure 3.8, the branch delay contains three slots instead of one. Figures 3.16–3.19 show an example program sequence to demonstrate the branch delay fillin optimization on both a silicon and a GaAs processor. In Figure 3.16, an unoptimized program sequence is shown for a silicon processor with a branch delay of one. In Figure 3.17, the sequence is shown after the successful fillin of the single fillin slot. Figure 3.18 shows the same program sequence in unoptimized form with a branch delay of three. Figure 3.19 shows the sequence after optimization in which two of the slots were successfully filled. The third instruction cannot be moved because its completion is required before the execution of the branch instruction. Therefore, the compiler must search outside this code sequence in order to find a third fillin candidate. This example demonstrates both the instruction interdependencies that limit instruction reorganization and the need for more sophisticated branch fillin algorithms for GaAs processors.

A significant increase in compiler capability is required in order to successfully fill the larger number of slots. Although the Stanford MIPS compiler was able to fill one branch fillin slot 90% of the time, its fill success on the second and third slots was 43% and 39%, respectively (29). Advances

```
add   a,10      'a takes a plus 10'
add   b,a       'b takes b plus a'
add   c,1       'c takes c plus 1'
bgt   c,0       'if c greater than 0 jump'
NOOP
```

Figure 3.16 Example program sequence on a silicon processor before branch fill.

```
add   a,10      'a takes a plus 10'
---
add   c,1       'c takes c plus 1'
bgt   c,0       'if c greater than 0 jump'
add   b,a       'b takes b plus a'
```

Figure 3.17 Example program sequence on a silicon processor after branch fill.

```
add   a,10      'a takes a plus 10'
add   b,a       'b takes b plus a'
add   c,1       'c takes c plus 1'
bgt   c,0       'if c greater than 0 jump'
NOOP
NOOP
NOOP
```

Figure 3.18 Example program sequence on a GaAs processor before branch fill.

```
add   c,1         'c takes c plus 1'
bgt   c,0         'if c greater than 0 jump'
add   a,10        'a takes a plus 10'
add   b,a         'b takes b plus a'
NOOP
```

Figure 3.19 Example program sequence on a GaAs processor after branch fill.

in compiler technology resulting in high fillin probabilities for larger branch delays will result in much higher performance for GaAs processor systems.

Timing hazard interlocks.   Timing hazards generally arise in pipelined processors when multiple pipeline stages have potential access to datapath resources at the same time. Three types of timing hazards have been identified (24). These are called destination–source conflicts, source–destination conflicts, and destination–destination conflicts.

An example of a destination–source conflict is when a pipestage attempts to read from a hardware resource (i.e., register) at the same time that a previous pipestage is writing to the resource. Destination–source conflicts occur naturally in register-to-register architectures whenever an instruction writes to a register that is a source register for the succeeding instruction.

An example of a source–destination conflict is when a pipestage attempts to write to a hardware resource at the same time that a previous pipestage is reading from the resource. Another source–destination conflict occurs when a pipestage writes to a hardware resource before a pipestage of a preceding instruction is to read it. The second type of source–destination conflict occurs when a pipestage reads a resource that is previously written by a pipestage in a succeeding instruction. If an exception of some kind occurs, the succeeding instruction may not be executed before the pipestage of the preceding instruction reads the resource.

An example of a destination–destination conflict is when two pipestages attempt to write to a resource concurrently. This may result when the value of a data load is to be written to a register at the same time that the result of an ALU operation is to be written to the same register.

CISC processors typically utilize hardware to prevent incorrect execution due to timing hazards. An example technique is the "scoreboard" used in the CDC 6600 (66). Some RISC processors such as the Berkeley RISC-II use a hardware technique called "internal forwarding" to resolve destination–source conflicts.

The Stanford MIPS, on the other hand, relies entirely on software to resolve timing hazards. The MIPS compiler is tasked with reorganizing instructions so that all conflicts are removed. If the compiler cannot find a suitable candidate instruction to prevent a conflict, it must insert a NOOP. Figure 3.20 shows an example code sequence with a destination–source conflict, since register a is both the destination of the first instruction and the source of the second instruction. Figure 3.21 shows the default action of a compiler to resolve the conflict, and Figure 3.22 shows a successful reorganization to eliminate the NOOP. It has been reported that the MIPS instruction cycle would have been lengthened by 10% if hardware interlocks were used (54).[2]

Because of its reduction in hardware requirements, software interlocking may be desirable for a GaAs processor. However, this approach again places a great burden on the compiler in order to minimize the number of NOOPs inserted into the program.

Compiler Optimizations in Memory
The low transistor count of GaAs memory chips and the high performance penalty of interchip communication severely hinder the memory system in its attempt to maintain an adequate supply of instructions and data for a GaAs processor. Fortunately, the compiler for such a processor has the potential to greatly increase the efficiency of the hardware resources that implement the memory system.

```
add   a,10        'a takes a plus 10'
add   b,a         'b takes b plus a'    Figure 3.20 Example program sequence
add   c,d         'c takes c plus d'    showing a destination–source conflict.
```

```
add   a,10        'a takes a plus 10'
NOOP                                    Figure 3.21 Example program sequence
add   b,a         'b takes b plus a'    showing default compiler action for
add   c,d         'c takes c plus d'    destination–source conflict. Branch fill.
```

```
add   a,10        'a takes a plus 10'   Figure 3.22 Example program sequence
add   c,d         'c takes c plus d'    showing a successful reorganization of
add   b,a         'b takes b plus a'    destination–source conflict.
```

---

[2] An interesting question, however, is how often the MIPS compiler has to insert NOOPs to implement the software interlocus. Obviously, the answer depends on the application.

A compiler can provide memory system support in two ways. First, it can increase the reusability of information—i.e., it can increase the length of time that useful information is kept in the higher levels of the memory hierarchy. Second, it can overlap the transfer of information into the higher hierarchical levels with the execution of useful instructions through information prefetching. These two techniques are each discussed here for two types of memory.

1. Memory that is normally controlled by the compiler—i.e., the register file.
2. Memory that is normally controlled by run-time mechanisms—i.e., the cache and main memory.

Register file compiler optimizations.   Register file usage is normally directly controlled by the compiler. In fact, registers have absorbed considerable abuse for the very fact that they require this compiler control. Because of the long history of register usage, compiler designers have developed fairly advanced techniques for utilizing registers efficiently. The RISC designers were instrumental in advancing compiler technology in this area in order to exploit their faster execution cycle times. GaAs processors, because of even faster instruction execution, will experience a corresponding benefit from improved register file compiler optimizations.

REUSABILITY.   In a GaAs processor that executes register-to-register instructions, and only accesses off-chip data via explicit data load and data store instructions, data loads and stores are extremely costly. The primary reason for this is the much longer access delay for off-chip memory. A secondary cost is the increase in total program size caused by the presence of data loads and stores. Larger program sizes can be expected to decrease hit ratios at all levels of the instruction memory system.

In typical compiled HLL programs on RISC machines, data loads and stores are approximately 30% of all executed instructions (54). In the silicon environment, larger register files may be incorporated in order to keep more useful data on-chip. As indicated earlier, the designers of the Berkeley RISC-II used 138 registers, divided into eight windows, to reduce their frequency of data loads and stores to approximately 15% (54). Clearly, this solution is not applicable for a transistor-scarce GaAs processor. The multiple window

```
store   a,TEMP        'store a into TEMP'
add     b,c           'b takes b plus c'
load    a,TEMP        'load from TEMP to a'
add     b,d           'b takes b plus d'
add     d,a           'd takes d plus a'
```

Figure 3.23 Example program sequence showing poor register allocation.

```
---
add   b,c                'b takes b plus c'
---
add   b,d                'b takes b plus d'
add   d,a                'd takes d plus a'
```

Figure 3.24 Example program sequence showing good register allocation.

schemes for GaAs discussed earlier, although potentially good approaches, do add hardware complexity to a GaAs processor.

The designers of the IBM 801 relied very heavily on the capabilities of compiler technology. Their PL.8 compiler incorporated a highly sophisticated register allocation scheme to reduce the frequency of loads and stores (6).

Figures 3.23 and 3.24 show the improvement that can be gained from an intelligent compiler. Figure 3.23 shows an example unoptimized code sequence. Figure 3.24 shows the same sequence, but produced by a compiler with a good register allocation scheme. Clearly, a compiler-based approach to reduce the frequency of data loads and stores has an inherent advantage over hardware approaches in the GaAs environment if it can achieve adequate results.

PREFETCHING. As indicated previously, RISC processor designs allow a compiler optimization not allowed on typical CISCs. This optimization, "data load fillin," reduces the negative effect of data load latencies on performance. Because GaAs processors can be expected to have longer off-chip data load latencies than silicon processors, this optimization can have a greater positive impact on performance for a GaAs processor.

In a GaAs processor system, the data memory may execute data loads and stores in parallel with processor execution. In principle, for all data memory accesses, the processor need only initiate the access, and also receive the data value resulting from the load. If the compiler is able to schedule enough useful instructions after the data load initiation, the data load latency is effectively eliminated.

The compiler then is tasked with scheduling each data load instruction so that the data load result is in the processor before or at the time the processor requires it. This optimization is similar to the branch fillin problem described earlier in that only a subset of the possible instructions can be used to perform the load fillin.

This optimization is shown in Figures 3.25–3.28 for a Silicon pipeline represented by Figure 3.6 and a GaAs pipeline represented by Figure 3.8. Figure 3.25 shows an unoptimized program sequence for the silicon pipeline, while Figure 3.26 shows the optimized version. Figure 3.27 shows the same unoptimized program sequence for the GaAs pipeline, and Figure 3.28 shows its optimized form. As in the case of branch filling, data load filling success is limited by data dependencies, and more sophisticated optimization strate-

```
add    a,b            'a takes a plus b'
add    a,1            'a takes a plus 1'
add    c,b            'c takes c plus b'
load   d,A[c]         'load A[c] into d'
NOOP
add    e,d            'e takes e plus d'
```

Figure 3.25 Example program sequence on a silicon processor before load fillin.

gies are required to approach 100% fillin on a GaAs processor. Because data loads are so frequent, the implementation of improved compiler technologies can improve GaAs processor system performance significantly.

Cache/main memory compiler optimizations.   The contents of the LRU-based memory levels of the memory hierarchy (i.e., cache, main memory, etc.) are normally determined by run-time hardware. However, as already indicated, in many instances in which the temporal and spatial localities of reference, upon which LRU mechanisms are based, fail, the compiler is able to provide assistance. Because a similar delay due to memory misses results in greater wasted instruction cycles for GaAs processors than for silicon processors, compiler optimizations to improve hit ratios gain added importance in the GaAs environment.

REUSABILITY.   This section describes two ways in which the compiler is able to increase the useful time of cache blocks, main memory pages, etc. The first technique is to increase the temporal and spatial localities of reference; the second technique involves providing support that is used at run-time to reduce the negative consequences of poor locality.

Increasing referencing locality is more effective for large memory units such as main memory pages or segments, but may also be used with cache blocks as well. What is desired is an increased correlation between high temporal locality and high spatial locality for particular information units. In other words, the information used within nearby time periods should also be stored in nearby memory locations. If the compiler (and linker) knows the page size, etc., then information that exhibits high temporal locality, as determined by the compiler, can be allocated memory locations within the same page, etc. Even without page size information, more spatial locality by itself will decrease miss ratios. A study was performed on a compiler algorithm to increase the spatial locality of data having large temporal lo-

```
add    a,b            'a takes a plus b'
---
add    c,b            'c takes c plus b'
load   d,A[c]         'load A[c] into d'
add    a,1            'a takes a plus 1'
add    e,d            'e takes e plus d'
```

Figure 3.26 Example program sequence on a silicon processor after load fillin.

```
add   a,b          'a takes a plus b'
add   a,1          'a takes a plus 1'
add   c,b          'c takes c plus b'
load  d,A[c]       'load A[c] into d'
NOOP
NOOP
NOOP
add   e,d          'e takes e plus d'
```

Figure 3.27 Example program sequence on a GaAs processor before load fillin.

cality (1). In this study, miss ratios for the unmodified programs were as much as 20 times the miss ratios for the modified programs. Clearly, this type of compiler optimization will have an enormous impact on the performance of a GaAs processor system.

As mentioned earlier, one instance where temporal locality is not present is the use of some particular information followed by a large period of nonuse. Bringing this type of information into a higher level of memory hierarchy will decrease that level's hit ratio because it results in more useful information being replaced. If the compiler detects that an information access will displace information of higher future usefulness, it may override the run-time information control mechanism. One possible method for accomplishing this is the use of special data load and store instructions that inhibit the memory system's run-time mechanism. This technique is used on the IBM 801 (55). A special data store instruction is provided that signals the cache to not perform block replacement. As with many compiler optimizations designed for silicon RISCs, this technique is potentially even more profitable for a GaAs processor.

PREFETCHING. As mentioned earlier, temporal locality is not present in instances where information is accessed for the first time after a long period of nonuse. These instances occur when the present referencing locality is exited and a new locality established. These interlocality gaps are disastrous for LRU-based run-time mechanisms. It is possible for the compiler to detect these interlocality gaps and to assist the run-time mechanism in preparing for them. This technique is more useful for the cache than for the main memory in systems with magnetic disks. Because disk accesses normally

---

```
add   c,b          'c takes c plus b'
load  d,A[c]       'load A[c] into d'
add   a,b          'a takes a plus b'
add   a,1          'a takes a plus 1'
NOOP
add   e,d          'e takes e plus d'
```

Figure 3.28 Example program sequence on a GaAs processor after load fillin.

require milliseconds, page faults are usually handled by switching to another waiting task. Unless the prefetching scheme can detect the prefetch candidate milliseconds before need, nothing is gained by beginning the disk transfer early.

When the compiler detects a prefetching candidate, it requires a method to initiate the prefetch. One technique is to use special memory prefetch instructions, which are executed by the processor as special memory instructions. Thse special instructions may be handled by the memory hardware in much the same way as any memory access. When such an instruction is executed, the processor calculates the memory address and does nothing more. Many of the NOOPs normally executed by the processor, because the compiler was unable to successfully perform branch or load fillin, may be replaced by these special memory instructions. Once again, this compiler support can increase the performance of a GaAs processor significantly.

3.4. Conclusion

The characteristics of GaAs technology certainly demand a reexamination of computer system design methodologies. The lower transistor count of GaAs chips and the high penalty for communication between them reduce our ability to exploit the fast transistors of GaAs technology. The design approaches presented here utilize the strength of GaAs technology while reducing the negative effects of the weaknesses of this new technology.

As GaAs technology matures, its impact on computer design will likely change as well. However, the three major characteristics we based our computer design approaches on will remain valid to varying degrees. Many researchers believe GaAs logic gates will only get faster as MODFET and HBT designs become readily available. GaAs integrated circuits will be limited by heat dissipation to transistor counts much below silicon technologies. For high-speed applications, the much lower mobility of holes in GaAs material restricts the use of low power complementary deigns, such as silicon CMOS, to speed insensitive areas such as register cells. Interchip signal propagation delays will see improvement with advances in packaging technology; however, delays for off-chip communication will remain large in comparison to shrinking processor instruction cycle times.

Although GaAs technology-based computer design is a relatively new discipline, several papers have already been presented. General architectural approaches for GaAs computer design were presented in (23). GaAs processor design, system design, and compiler design were presented in (18, 45, and 47), respectively. Additional GaAs computer issues were covered in (16, 34, 43, and 46). A description of an actual GaAs processor design was provided in (27). An excellent source of information is the IEEE Computer special issue dedicated to GaAs technology-based computer design and computer architecture (October 1986). Another view of the same problem can be found in the former versions of this text (see reference 22 of Chapter 1 and reference 44 of this chapter).

Problems[3]

1. Consider a reduced instruction set GaAs processor-based system in which the ratio of instruction fetch delay to datapath delay equals six. Assume that 40% of all branch fillin slots and data load fillin slots contain NOOPs (i.e., probability of branch fill = probability of load fill = 60%), and that branches and data loads represent 30% and 20% of all instructions executed, respectively. Also assume that the instruction cache hit ratio equals 80%, and a miss results in an additional six-cycle delay. Ignore the effects of data cache misses and data memory references.

   a1. Calculate the expected number of instruction cycles required to execute 1000 instructions using the three pipeline types represented by Figures 3.8–3.10.

   a2. Assume equal values for the probability of branch fill and probability of load fill. For what values (i.e., of probability of branch fill) is the "long-latency" pipeline performance superior to the "pipelined memory" pipeline performance.

   a3. Assume that the average number of non-NOOP operations per instruction fetch for the "instruction packing" pipeline equals three. For what values of probability of instruction cache hit is the "instruction packing" pipeline performance superior to the "pipeline memory" pipeline performance.

   b1. Discuss the appropriateness of the assumed values for the parameters used in part (a). Upon what factors do these parameters depend, including any variations across the instruction pipeline types?

   b2. Discuss the sensitivity of the three instruction pipeline types to these parameters.

2. Consider a GaAs processor-based system with the same parameters as in Problem 1. Compare a "pipelined memory" instruction pipeline implementation, resembling Figure 3.8, with a "long-latency" instruction pipeline, as in Figure 3.10, and with an increased register file size. Assume that for a register file size of 16, 20% of all instructions are data loads, and that each successive doubling of register file size decreases the number of data loads by 50%.

   a1. For what size register file will the "long-latency" pipeline outperform the "pipelined memory" pipeline with 16 registers?

   b1. Now assume that the probability of branch fill (pbf) and probability

---

[3] Feel free to introduce additional assumptions if necessary.

of load fill (plf) vary with the number of slots (nos) to fill according to: pbf = plf = 0.9 − 0.1 × nos. Furthermore, assume that the probability of instruction cache hit (pih) varies with the program size (ps) according to: pih = 0.85 − ps/1000 × 0.05. For a program containing 1000 non-NOOP instructions, compare the performance of the "long-latency" pipeline and 32 registers with the "pipelined memory" pipeline with 16 registers.

3. Discuss the manner in which the NOOPs associated with unfilled branch and data load slots effect the performance of "pipelined memory" instruction pipelines. Present both compile-time and run-time techniques to reduce the negative effect of these unfilled slots.[1]

4. Discuss the suitability of systolic array and dataflow approaches for GaAs implementation. Compare the implementation environments for which these approaches were developed with that presented by GaAs. Consider both fine-grained (i.e., arithmetic operation level) and course-grained (i.e., task level) dataflow approaches.

Acknowledgments

The authors are thankful to Bill Geideman of McDonnell Douglas; Shaun Whalen and Bob Heemeyer of CDC; and William Heagerty, Walt Helbig, and Wayne Moyers of RCA for their helpful comments.

References

1. Abu-Sufah W, Kuck DJ, Lawrie DH: On the performance enhancement of paging systems through program analysis and transformations. *IEEE Trans. on Computers,* Vol. C-30, No. 5, May 1981, pp. 341–356.

2. Alexander WG, Wortman DB: Static and dynamic characteristics of XPL programs. *IEEE Computer,* Vol. 8, No. 11, Nov. 1975, pp. 41–46.

3. Anderson SF, Earle JG, Goldschmidt RE, Powers DM: The IBM system/360 model 91: Floating-point execution unit. *IBM Journal of Research and Development,* Vol. 11, No. 1, January 1967, pp. 34–53.

4. Asbeck PM, Miller DL, Anderson FJ, Eisen FH: Emitter-coupled logic circuits implemented with heterojunction bipolar transistors. *Proc. of the GaAs IC Symposium,* Phoenix, Arizona, October 1983, pp. 170–173.

5. Asbeck PM, Miller DL, Anderson RJ, et al: Application of heterojunction bipolar transistors to high-speed, small-scale digital integrated circuits. *Proc. of the GaAs IC Symposium,* Boston, MA, Oct. 1984, pp. 133–136.

6. Auslander M, Hopkins M: An overview of the PL.8 compiler. *Proc. of the ACM SIGPLAN Symposium on Compiler Construction,* Boston, MA, June 1982, pp. 22–31.

7. Barney C: DARPA eyes 100-mips GaAs chip for Star Wars. *Electronics Week,* Vol. 58, No. 20, May 20, 1985, pp. 22–23.

8. Bass S, Neudeck G: VLSI transistor count and basic delays. *Internal Report,* Purdue University, 1984.
9. Beyers JW, Dohse LJ, Fucetola JP, ct al: A 32-bit VLSI CPU chip. *IEEE Journal of Solid-State Circuits,* Vol. SC-16, No. 10, October 1981, pp. 537–541.
10. Denning PJ: Virtual memory. *ACM Computing Surveys,* Vol. 2, No. 3, Sept. 1970, pp. 62–97.
11. Denning PJ: On modeling program behavior. *Proc. of the Spring Joint Computer Conference,* 1972, pp. 937–944.
12. Dennis JB: Data flow supercomputers. *IEEE Computer,* Vol. 13, No. 11, Nov. 1980, pp. 48–56.
13. Eden RC: Comparison of GaAs device approaches for ultrahigh-speed VLSI. *Proc. of the IEEE,* Vol. 70, No. 1, Jan. 1982, pp. 5–12.
14. Eden RC, Welch BM, Lee FS: Implications and projections of gallium arsenide technology in high speed computing. *Proc. of the IEEE International Conference on Computer Design: VLSI in Computers,* Port Chester, NY, Oct.–Nov. 1983, pp. 30–33.
15. Eden RC, Welch BM, Zucca R, Long SI: The prospects for ultrahigh-speed VLSI GaAs digital logic. *IEEE Journal of Solid-State Circuits,* Vol. SC-14, No. 2, April 1979, pp. 221–239.
16. Fortes JA, Milutinović VM, Dick RJ, et al: A high-level systolic architecture for GaAs. *Proc. of the 1986 International Workshop on High-Level Computer Architecture,* Honolulu, Hawaii, Jan. 1986.
17. Furht B: RISC architectures with multiple overlapping windows. *Proc. of Midcon/85,* Chicago, IL, Sept. 1985, pp. 23/2.1–23/2.10.
18. Fura DA, Milutinović VM: Computer architecture design in GaAs. *Proc. of Midcon/85,* Chicago, IL, Sept. 1985, pp. 24/3.1–24/3.7.
19. Furutsuka T, Takahashi K, Ishikawa S, et al: A GaAs 12 × 12 bit expandable parallel multiplier LSI using sidewall-assisted closely spaced elecrode technology. *Proc. of the International Electron Devices Meeting,* San Francisco, CA, Dec. 1984, pp. 344–347.
20. Geideman B: E-JFET and C-JFET. *Panel of VLSI Processor Design for GaAs,* Honolulu, Hawaii, Jan. 1986.
21. Gnanasekaran R: On a bit-serial input and bit-serial output multiplier. *IEEE Trans. on Computers,* Vol. C-32, No. 9, Sept. 1983, pp. 878–880.
22. Gheewala TR: System level comparison of high-speed technologies. *Proc. of the IEEE 1984 International Conference on Computer Design,* Port Chester, NY, Oct. 1984, pp. 245–250.
23. Gilbert BK: Design and performance trade-offs in the use of SI VLSI and gallium arsenide in high clockrate signal processing. *Proc. of the IEEE 1984 International Conference on Computer Design,* Port Chester, NY, Oct. 1984, pp. 260–266.
24. Gross T: Code optimization of pipeline constraints. *Technical Report No. 83-255,* Stanford University, Dec. 1983.
25. Heagerty W: GaAs seminar presented at Purdue University, Jan. 1985.
26. Hehner ECR: Computer design to minimize memory requirements. *IEEE Computer,* Vol. 9, No. 8, Aug. 1976, pp. 65–70.
27. Helbig WA, Schellack RH, Zieger RM: The design and construction of a GaAs technology demonstration microprocessor. *Proc. of Midcon/85,* Chicago, IL, Sept. 1985, pp. 23/1.1–23/1.6.

28. Hennessy J, Jouppi N, Gill J, et al: The MIPS machine. *Digest of Papers, Spring COMPCON 82,* San Francisco, CA, Feb. 1982, pp. 2–7.
29. Hennessy J, Jouppi, N, Przybylski S, et al: Design of a high-performance VLSI processor. *Technical Report No. 236,* Stanford University, Feb. 1983.
30. Huffman DA: A method for the construction of minimum redundancy codes. *Proc. of the I.R.E.,* Vol. 40, No. 9, Sept. 1952, pp. 1098–1101.
31. Hwang K: *Computer Arithmetic: Principles, Architecture, and Design,* John Wiley & Sons, 1979.
32. Ishii Y, Ino M, Idda M, et al: Processing technologies for GaAs memory LSIs. *Proc. of the GaAs IC Symposium,* Boston, MA, Oct. 1984, pp. 121–124.
33. Katevenis MGH: Reduced instruction set computer architectures for VLSI. *Report No. UCB/CSD 83/141,* University of California at Berkeley, October 1983.
34. Keirn K, Milutinović V: An analysis of the UCB-RISC in the GaAs environment. *Microprocessing and Microprogramming,* Vol. 17, No. 3, March 1986, pp. 119–128.
35. Kuroda S, Mimura T, Suzuki M, et al: New device structure for 4Kb HEMT SRAM. *Proc. of the GaAs IC Symposium,* Boston, MA, Oct. 1984, pp. 125–128.
36. Kung HT: Why systolic architectures? *IEEE Computer,* Vol. 15, No. 1, Jan. 1982, pp. 37–46.
37. Lee FS, Kaelin GR, Welch BM, et al: A high-speed LSI GaAs 8 × 8-bit parallel multiplier. *IEEE Journal of Solid-State Circuits,* Vol. SC-17, No. 4, Aug. 1982, pp. 638–647.
38. Leopold G: New approach promises GaAs interconnections. *Electronics Week,* Vol. 58, No. 22, June 3, 1985, p. 27.
39. MacGregor D, Mothersole D, Moyer B: The Motorola MC68020. *IEEE Micro,* Vol. 17, No. 8, Aug. 1984, pp. 101–118.
40. Matsuoka Y, Ohwada K, Hirayama M: Uniformity evaluation of MESFET's for GaAs LSI fabrication. *IEEE Trans. on Electron Devices,* Vol. ED-31, No. 8, Aug. 1984, pp. 1062–1067.
41. McDonough K, Caudel E, Magar S, Leigh A: Microcomputer with 32-bit arithmetic does high-precision number crunching. *Electronics,* Vol. 55, No. 8, Feb. 24, 1982, pp. 105–110.
42. McDaniel G: An analysis of a mesa instruction set using dynamic instruction frequencies. *Proc. of the Symposium on Architectural Support for Programming Languages and Operating Systems,* Palo Alto, CA, March 1982, pp. 167–176.
43. McNeley K, Milutinović V: Emulation of a CISC with a RISC, *IEEE Micro,* Vol. 7, No. 1, Feb. 1987, pp. 60–72.
44. Milutinović V, Fura D, Helbig W: An introduction to GaAs microprocessor architecture for VLSI. *IEEE Computer,* Vol. 19, No. 3, March 1986.
45. Milutinović V, Fura D, Helbig W, Linn J: Architecture/compiler synergism in gallium arsenide computer systems. *IEEE Computer,* Vol. 20, No. 5, May 1987.
46. Milutinović V: Guest editor's introduction for the special issue on GaAs microprocessors. *IEEE Computer,* Vol. 19, No. 10, Oct. 1986.
47. Milutinović V, Silbey A, Fura D, et al: Issues of importance in designing GaAs microcomputer systems. *IEEE Computer,* Vol. 19, No. 10, Oct. 1986, pp. 45–57.

48. Myers GJ: *Advances in Computer Architecture, 2nd edition,* John Wiley & Sons, 1982.
49. Namordi MR: Advances in GaAs invited lecture. Purdue University, Oct. 1984.
50. Nakayama Y, Suyama K, Shimizu H, et al: A GaAs 16 × 16 bit parallel multiplier. *IEEE Journal of Solid-State Circuits,* Vol. SC-18, No. 5, Oct. 1983, pp. 599–603.
51. Nukiyama T, Kusano T, Matsumoto K, et al: A VLSI image pipeline processor. *Proc. of the 1984 IEEE International Solid-State Circuits Conference,* San Francisco, CA, Feb. 1984, pp. 208–209.
52. Nuzillat G, Perea EH, Bert G, et al: GaAs MESFET ICs for gigabit logic applications. *IEEE Journal of Solid-State Circuits,* Vol. SC-17, No. 3, June 1982, pp. 569–584.
53. Patterson DA, Piepho RS: Assessing RISCs in high-level language support. *IEEE Micro,* Vol. 15, No. 11, Nov. 1982, pp. 9–19.
54. Patterson DA: Reduced instruction set computers. *Communications of the ACM,* Vol. 28, No. 1, Jan. 1985, pp. 8–21.
55. Radin G: The 801 minicomputer. *IBM Journal of Research and Development,* Vol. 27, No. 3, May 1983, pp. 237–245.
56. Rose CD: Speed record claimed for GaAs transistor. *Electronics Week,* Vol. 58, No. 19, May 13, 1985, pp. 19–20.
57. Russell RM: The Cray-1 computer system. *Communications of the ACM,* Vol. 21, No. 1, Jan. 1978, pp. 63–72.
58. Sherburne RW Jr: Processor design trade-offs in VLSI. *Report No. UCB/CSD 84/173,* University of California at Berkeley, April 1984.
59. Smith JE, Goodman JR: A study of instruction cache organizations and replacement policies. *Proc. of the 10th Annual Symposium on Computer Architecture,* Stockholm, Sweden, June 1983, pp. 132–137.
60. Smith AJ: Sequential program prefetching in memory hierarchies. *IEEE Computer,* Vol. 11, No. 12, Dec. 1978, pp. 7–21.
61. Smith JE: A study of branch prediction strategies. *Proc. of the 8th Symposium on Computer Architecture,* May 1981, pp. 135–148.
62. Smith AJ: Cache memories. *ACM Computing Surveys,* Vol. 14, No. 3, Sept. 1982, pp. 473–530.
63. Smith AJ: Cache evaluation and the impact of workload choice. *Proc. of the 12th Annual Symposium on Computer Architecture,* Boston, MA, June 1985, pp. 64–73.
64. Solomon PM, Morkoc H: Modulation-doped GaAs/AlGaAs heterojunction field-effect transistors (MODFET's), ultrahigh-speed devices for supercomputers. *IEEE Trans. on Electron Devices,* Vol. ED-31, No. 8, Aug. 1984, pp. 1015–1027.
65. Tanenbaum AS: Implications of structured programming for machine architecture. *Communications of the ACM,* Vol. 21, No. 3, March 1978, pp. 237–246.
66. Thorton JE: Parallel operation in the Control Data 6600. In Siewiorek, Bell, Newell (eds): *Computer Structures: Principles and Examples,* McGraw-Hill, New York, 1982.
67. Toyoda N, Uchitomi N, Kitaura Y, et al: A 42ps 2K-Gate GaAs gate array. *Proc. of the 1985 IEEE International Solid-State Circuits Conference,* Feb. 1985, pp. 206–207.

68. Van Tuyl RL, Liechti CA: High-speed integrated logic with GaAs MESFET's. *IEEE Journal of Solid-State Circuits,* Vol. SC-9, No. 5, Oct. 1974, pp. 269–276.
69. Vu TT, Roberts PCT, Nelson RD, et al: A gallium arsenide SDFL gate array with on-chip RAM. *IEEE Journal of Solid-State Circuits,* Vol. SC-19, No. 1, Feb. 1984, pp. 10–22.
70. Waller L: GaAs ICs bid for commercial success. *Electronics,* Vol. 57, No. 12, June 14, 1984, pp. 101–102.
71. Whitby-Stevens C: The transputer. *Proc. of the 12th Annual International Symposium on Computer Architecture,* Boston, MA, June 1985, pp. 292–300.
72. Yamamoto R, Higashisaka A, Asai S, et al: Design and fabrication of depletion GaAs LSI high-speed 32-bit adder. *IEEE Journal of Solid-State Circuits,* Vol. SC-18, No. 5, Oct. 1983, pp. 592–599.
73. Yuan H, McLevige WV, Shih HD, Hearn AS: GaAs heterojunction bipolar 1K gate array. *Proc. of the 1984 IEEE International Solid-State Circuits Conference,* San Francisco, CA, Feb. 1984, pp. 42–43.
74. Zuleeg R, Notthoff JK, Troeger GL: Double-implanted GaAs complementary JFETs. *IEEE Electron Device Letters,* Vol. EDL-5, No. 1, Jan. 1984, pp. 21–23.

PART II

Topics in Multiprocessing

4

Multiprocessing

Daniel D. Gajski
Jih-Kwon Peir

4.1. Introduction

In the past several years we have seen many proposed and commercial
multiprocessor architectures, all aimed at increasing machine performance
by an order of magnitude. Although faster hardware is relatively easy to
build these days, there is no agreement on how to achieve this performance
increase for realistic applications.

There are basically four schools of thought as to what is the most
important factor in obtaining higher performance in a particular machine.
The first school of thought believes in faster circuit technology, which will
allow us to retain present architectures, possibly augmented with a mechanism for synchronizing parallel processes. The second school puts priority
on optimizing or vectorizing compilers, possibly interactive, that will detect
parallelism and help users to write better parallel programs. The third school
believes that a dramatic increase in performance will come mainly from new
parallel algorithms, so it supports development of new languages that will
allow easy conversion of algorithms into programs. The fourth school supports new models of computation, such as data flow models, that will allow

dramatic increases in parallelism and can be easily exploited by a multiprocessor architecture to increase performance.

Although each school deals with one part of the solution, none of them shows how to optimally combine application requirements with the capabilities of the new VLSI technology. The first school uses the least risky approach by retaining old programming and architectural models. It takes advantage only of the speed that the new technology offers, not of its density. The second and third schools retain old architectural models, which may no longer be cost effective. Furthermore, the second school retains programming models developed for pre-VLSI architectures. The fourth school, although the most progressive, does not take into account technological limitations. For this reason, machines based on new models of computation do not exhibit impressive performance.

If we assume that at each point in computer evolution an optimal compromise or trade-off between application needs and technological capabilities is achieved, we may say that each of these schools has failed to notice that VLSI technology brought us not an evolutionary step forward but a revolutionary one. In the beginning, a simple combination of processor and memory with a bus between them was most cost effective. In such a machine, data and instructions are stored in the memory, and the processor controls and performs the computation—that is, it generates addresses for data and instructions, fetches the data and instructions, and computes with the data. Thus, the bus is the most frequently used component of the system. To avoid a potential bottleneck, smaller and faster local storage in the form of general registers, local memory, and cache are added to the processor. It is used to save local data and instructions under the assumption that they will be accessed more frequently by the processor.

Vector machines introduced vector instructions for cases in which the same operation is performed on many sets of operands. Only one instruction fetch is needed for many data operations in executing a vector instruction. The bus load drops significantly for large vectors. Vector machines such as the Cyber-205, the Cray X-MP, and the Fujitsu VP-200 depend heavily on pipelining of functional units, interleaved memory modules, and faster vector registers to obtain high performance. However, programs do not consist of vector instructions, and, even worse, if vector data is not evenly distributed in all memory modules according to the referencing order of the data, memory conflicts will occur and degrade performance. Furthermore, the market demand for increased performance cannot be satisfied any more effectively by an increased level of pipelining (more stages in the pipeline) or by faster circuit technology (increased clock speed).

VLSI technology made replication of hardware units affordable. Multiprocessor architectures use several identical processors in parallel to obtain high execution speed. Two types of multiprocessor systems can be identified. In a shared-memory model (Figure 4.1a) data is stored in the shared

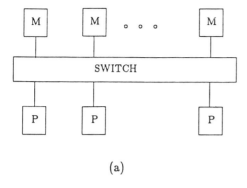

(a)

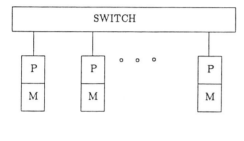

(b)

Figure 4.1 Multiprocessor model. (a) Shared memory. (b) Message-passing.

memory, which can be accessed by all processors through an interconnection network. In a message-passing model (Figure 4.1b), each processor has an associated local memory, and data is passed from the producing processors to the consuming processors through a connection network.

Basically, the difference between vector machines and multiprocessors is how they slice the data flow graph of the program. For vector machines, the graph is sliced to yield long vectors corresponding to the horizontal slicing shown in Figure 4.2. On the other hand, multiprocessors require slicing that minimizes communication between processors, corresponding to the vertical slicing in Figure 4.2, in which the data flow graph is partitioned into four tasks, each executing on one processor. The multiprocessor approach introduces three new requirements that have not been encountered in the uniprocessor environment. First, each problem must be partioned into tasks. Second, each task must be scheduled for execution on one or more processors. Third, synchronization of control and data flow must be performed during execution. In addition, program partitioning introduces several levels of execution control. Parallelism can be exploited on each level, which leads to different hierarchical control structures. Furthermore, the memory latency problem has been aggravated by addition of a network between processors and memories.

$$c_0 = 0$$
FOR i FROM 1 to 8 DO
$$a_i = d_i \,/\, e_i$$
$$b_i = a_i \,*\, f_i$$
$$c_i = b_i + c_{i-1}$$
ENDFOR

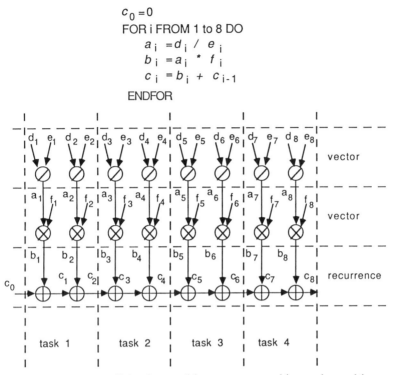

Figure 4.2 Program slicing imposed by a vector machine and a multiprocessor.

We support a fifth school of thought, which believes that only efficient solutions to all the preceding problems will bring an order-of-magnitude improvement in multiprocessor performance. In this chapter, we discuss these essential problems and their solutions. We assume that the problems are axes of a multiprocessor design space and that the solutions are values on the axes. Each point in the space represents a multiprocessor architecture as a set of solutions for the essential problems, which in turn induce a certain computational paradigm that a user must follow to tune his application to the machine and achieve maximal performance.

4.2 Parallel Models of Computation

Backus (5) characterized three models of computation—the simple operational model, the applicative model, and the von Neumann model—based on the criteria of program foundation, history sensitivity, type of semantics, and program clarity. Simple operational models such as Turing machines have very simple and concise mathematical foundations. They use storage to save information that can affect the behavior of later programs, so they are history-sensitive. Their program clarity is very poor, because only simple state transitions are allowed. Applicative models, such as pure Lisp, have concise foundations and use reduction semantics that make their programs very clear. They are not history-sensitive because they have no notion of storage. Von Neumann models are the basis of all conventional languages, such as FORTRAN and Pascal. Their program foundations are complex. They are history-sensitive. Their state transitions are complex and their program clarity can be only moderately clear.

We characterize computational models from a different standpoint. Because we are interested more in understanding how fast and efficiently a program can run in a multiprocessor environment than in looking into its functional semantics and correctness, we define a model of computation by examining program sequencing during the course of execution. A program can be represented by a control graph, in which nodes represent one or more transformations or movements of data, and arcs represent the order in which nodes are executed. Arcs arise from data dependencies, in which data produced by one node are used by its successor, or from control dependencies, in which an order of execution is specified by the user in a language with limited or no capacity to express parallelism.

From the standpoint of sequencing, there are two models. A serial model of computation, corresponding to sequential languages such as FOR-TRAN, has a control graph with serially ordered nodes (Figure 4.3). Nodes are executed one at a time, and each node is executable only when its predecessor has been executed. This model is well suited for a uniprocessor

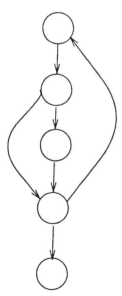

Figure 4.3 Serial model of computation.

machine. A program counter is sufficient for keeping track of the next node to be executed.

A parallel model of computation, characterized by a control graph such as the one shown in Figure 4.4, is better suited for a multiprocessor system. Three basic problems can be identified in the parallel model:

1. The partitioning problem: Partition a program into tasks, each task represented by a node in a control graph.
2. The scheduling problem: Assign each node to one or more processors for execution.
3. The synchronization problem: Assure an order of execution that leads to correct results.

4.2.1. Data-Driven Execution

There are two submodels of parallel sequencing. In data-driven execution, the graph is executed in the direction pointed by arcs—that is, a node is executable when all the data needed for its execution are available. The data-driven computation is implemented by sending tokens down arcs. A token is a logical entity that contains not only a value but the name (address) of the destination node. When all input arcs to a node have a token, the node is executable.

Treleven et al. (54) have identified two types of data-driven computation. In the data flow model, pioneered by Dennis (13) tokens carry data with them, and no preallocated storage is needed for data (Figure 4.4a). In the control flow model, tokens carry pointers to indicate locations where data is stored (Figure 4.4b), or they carry an enable signal to the node in

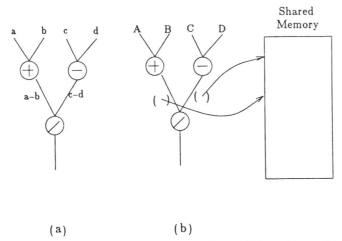

(a)   (b)

Figure 4.4 Parallel model of computation. (a) Data-driven. (b) Control driven.

which the operand addresses can be found. The data flow model is suitable for expression evaluation as well as for problems involving single data items. The control flow model is necessary for structured data, such as matrices, which may be only partially transformed by each node during the course of computation. It is inefficient to carry the entire matrix around if we want to change only one element or perhaps one row of it. Thus, any general-purpose data flow architecture must include tokens with reference to data structures because tokens that carry only values are not efficient. Examples include I-structures in the tagged-token architecture (4) and the proposed structure store in the Manchester data flow machine (27).

4.2.2. Demand-Driven Execution

Demand-driven (also called ''reduction'') execution pioneered by Berkling (6) and Backus (5) processes the control graph in the opposite direction from the data-driven model. In a demand-driven model, the demand for a result triggers its computation, which in turn triggers evaluation of its arguments, and so on. This demand propagation continues until constants are encountered; then a value is returned to the demanding node and execution proceeds in the opposite direction.

Because a demand-driven computer performs only those computations required to obtain the results, it will perform less computation in general than a data-driven computer. In data-driven execution, for example, both *then* and *else* parts of a conditional statement are computed whenever the data are available, with one of them being selected later.

This redundant computation may increase the execution time. If, for instance, computation of the *condition, then,* and *else* parts takes 10, 20, and 100 time units respectively, the entire statement will take 100 time units in the best possible case. On the other hand, if the condition is evaluated first, followed by the *then* or *else* parts, execution time could be either 30 or 110 times units, depending on which part was selected. We gain in performance if the *then* part is chosen in the latter execution method. So in many data flow models, such as Arvind's U-interpreter (4), the condition statement is executed in the demand-driven mode, while the rest of the graph is data-driven. However, this combined model is still less efficient than the demand-driven model because arguments for both *then* and *else* parts are evaluated in parallel, although only one set will be used later.

4.3. Control Model Classification

So far we have been equating a node in the control graph with a task, but we have not defined either task or node. A node may represent almost anything: one arithmetic operation, an arbitrary collection of instructions, or another control graph. We generalize the data flow model introduced by Dennis (13) to include any structure in a node and define four levels of control—job, task, process, and instruction—for programs running on multipressor systems. On the job level, several programs can be executed—in parallel (multiprogramming) or serially (batch) depending upon the operating system.

Each job or program consists of one or more tasks, and each task is a unit of scheduling to be assigned to one or more processors. Each task consists of one or more processes. Each process is a collection of program instructions executed on one processor—that is, a process is an indivisible unit with respect to processor allocation. Processes can be combined into higher level structures. A vector of processes is an ordered set of noninteracting processes, such as a DO loop in which no data is passed between iterations. In a recurrence of processes, each process i supplies some data to process $i + 1$. In a two-sided recurrence, process i produces data for and consumes data from processes $i - 1$ and $i + 1$.

Many other types of process structures can be defined. At scheduling time, a vector of processes can be allocated to n processors, with processor $j(j \leq n)$ working on processes $j, j + n, j + 2n, \ldots$, for example. Obviously, other scheduling algorithms can be applied. On the other hand, even if a task is merely a random collection of interacting processes, it can still be assigned to more than one processor under the assumption that the architecture provides a synchronization mechanism for it. Each process in turn consists of one or more instructions, where each instruction is considered to be a simple unit of execution. A serial or parallel model of control can be used on each of the task, process, and instruction levels. On the basis of this division, we can classify machines into different groups.

A serial, single-level control with a single machine instruction in each node can be found in the majority of uniprocessor architectures—for example, the VAX-11 and the Motorola 68000. In these machines, the entire program is a single process executed serially. Some data flow machines, such as the single-ring Manchester machine (27), have a parallel, single-level control. Each node of the control graph is a single machine instruction. In both cases, each instruction represents a task and a process.

The NYU Ultracomputer (25) has a parallel–serial control. Each node is a sequence of instructions called a task, specified by the programmer. At run time, each active task can spawn another task by calling the distributed operating system kernel. The kernel puts all the active tasks in a queue in the shared memory. The queue can be accessed by all the processors through an enhanced Omega network. Whenever a processor becomes idle, it gets a new task from the front of the queue. Each task is executed serially in a processor. In the NYU machine, tasks and processes are the same and represent a node in the control graph. The RP3 (45) multiprocessor currently under construction at IBM Thomas J. Watson Research Center has essentially the same architecture as the Ultracomputer.

The Cray-1 (49) may be considered to have a serial–parallel control. The control graph is serially ordered, and each node is a single instruction or a vector instruction. Each vector instruction can be considered a vector of processes scheduled on x processors, where x is the number of pipeline stages in the functional unit. When vector instructions are considered, an x-stage pipeline is just a cost-reducing engineering technique to replace x independent processors. The new version, the Cray X-MP-2 (38) can be considered as a serial–parallel–parallel controlled machine. The system consists of two CPUs, each of which is a multifunctional pipelined vector machine like the Cray-1. The CPUs share the central memory and communicate through a number of inter-CPU communication registers (Figure 4.5). The program control graph is serially ordered and each task is a collection of code segments or loops. The parallel portion of code inside a task can be further partitioned into two processes each running on one CPU.

The tagged-token data flow architecture proposed by Arvind (3, 4) has a parallel–parallel, two-level control, in which the whole program graph is

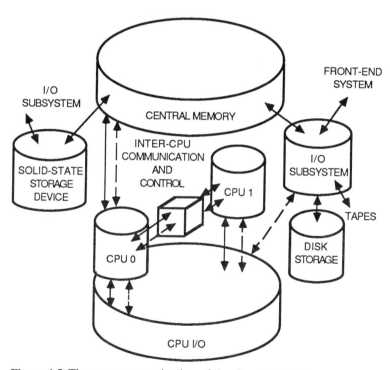

Figure 4.5 The system organization of the Cray X-MP-2.

clustered into tasks called "code blocks," each of which is another data flow graph. Code blocks can be executed in parallel on the same or a different set of processors, called a "physical domain."

There is no process in this architecture, but each instruction in a code block is allocated to a processor at compile time according to its iteration and statement number. Each processor shown in Figure 4.6 contains a matching unit, a fetching unit, a program memory, one ALU, an output section, and a data memory (I-structure). A manager coordinates the execution of a program. When a code block is initiated, all the arguments (tokens) required by that block are passed to the assigned physical domain. Each token contains a destination node address. A node is executable when the last of its input tokens arrives at the matching unit. An executable node fetches its operation code from program memory and is then dispatched to the ALU.

After execution, output tokens are generated and routed to the appropriate processor according to the new destination addresses. If the input token indicates an I-structure operation, it is routed to the I-structure storage. The manager is notified when a code block is finished. All the results

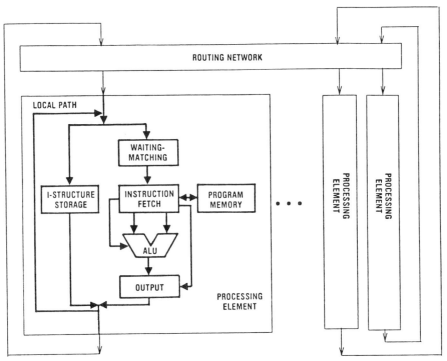

Figure 4.6 The organization of Arvind's data flow machine.

are saved in the I-structure for the subsequent code blocks. The data flow graph in each processor is executed in an instruction pipeline, which allows an increase in performance equivalent to the number of pipeline stages as long as there are sufficient executable nodes. The advantages of the data flow model on a single processor are not obvious, but performance is more complex and more costly than on a von Neumann machine.

The Cosmic Cube designed at Caltech (51) and commercially offered by Intel (under the name Hypercube) has a parallel–serial control mechanism. Each node of the program control graph is a process (also called a task). All processes, once created, execute concurrently, whether by virtue of being in different processors or by being interleaved in execution within a single processor. Each process is executed sequentially by one processor. A significant difference between the Cosmic Cube and most other multiprocessor machines is that it uses message-passing instead of shared-variables for communication of control and data between concurrent processes.

The Cosmic Cube currently in use at Caltech consists of 64 processors connected through bidirectional, asynchronous, point-to-point communication channels to six other processors, to form a network that follows the plan of a six-dimensional hypercube shown in Figure 4.7. The Cosmic Cube

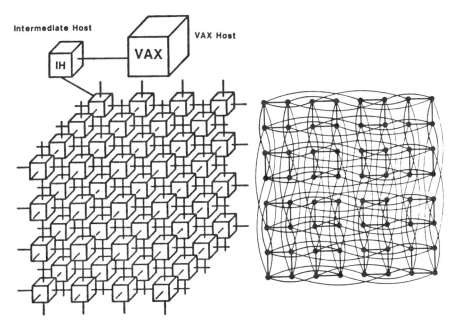

Figure 4.7 The Cosmic Cube six-dimensional hypercube architecture and nodes connection.

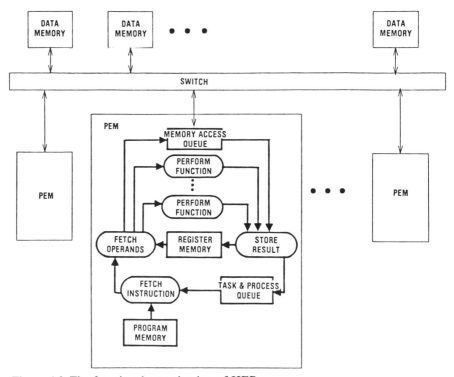

Figure 4.8 The functional organization of HEP.

intermediate host (IH) coordinates the initiation and finishing of a job. When a job is initiated, the IH sends a startup packet to certain processors in the cube to start the computation. The packet provides the job initial state, the ID of the next process in the job control graph, and the total number of processes the job needs to perform. The computation in the cube can run autonomically by spawning and killing processes through an operating system kernel residing in each processor. The IH will be noticed when all processes of the job are finished.

The HEP machine diagrammed in Figure 4.8 has a parallel–parallel–serial control (52). Programmers specify tasks and processes inside a job. Tasks can run in parallel in the same or different processors, called ''process execution modules'' (PEMs), each task allocated to only one PEM. Each PEM contains a task queue, a process queue, a memory access queue, and several pipelined functional units, each with eight stages except for the division pipe. When a task is initiated in the HEP, a PEM is selected and the task status word is stored in the task queue, while the initial process for this task is loaded into the process queue. Each process can create another process in any task. All tasks in a PEM are executed in a round-robin fashion. When a PEM executes a task, it selects a process from the task and sends the current instruction of that process to one of the functional units. For a data memory access, the process enters the memory access queue. Afterward, the PEM switches to the next task in the task queue. If there are fewer than eight tasks in a PEM, several processes from the same task can be executed in parallel. When an instruction execution is completed, the process is reinstantiated in the process queue and waits for the next turn. The instructions inside a process are executed serially.

Cedar (22) also has a parallel–parallel–serial control. As shown in Figure 4.9, it has a shared global memory, a global network, several processor clusters, and a global control unit (GCU). The GCU controls the execution of a program. From the GCU point of view, a program is a directed control graph in which each node represents a task called a compound function (CF). When a job is initiated, the control graph is loaded into the GCU. A task becomes executable when all its predecessor tasks are finished. The task can be further divided into two groups: computational functions (CPFs) and

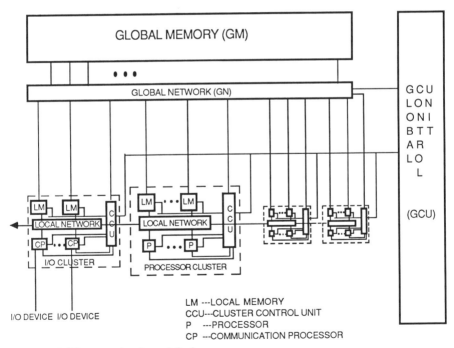

Figure 4.9 The organization of Cedar.

control functions (CFTs). The CTFs specify the execution sequence of the CPFs. For example, they determine which branch in an *if* statement is going to be taken. They are not time-consuming functions and are therefore executed in the GCU. Each CPF is a high-level structure of processes executable in parallel on several processors. Each process is executed serially

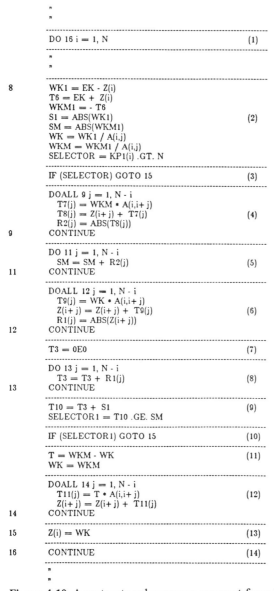

$$
\begin{array}{lll}
 & \text{"} & \\
 & \text{"} & \\
\hline
 & \text{DO 16 i = 1, N} & (1) \\
\hline
 & \text{"} & \\
 & \text{"} & \\
\hline
8 & \text{WK1 = EK - Z(i)} & \\
 & \text{T6 = EK + Z(i)} & \\
 & \text{WKM1 = - T6} & \\
 & \text{S1 = ABS(WK1)} & (2) \\
 & \text{SM = ABS(WKM1)} & \\
 & \text{WK = WK1 / A(i,j)} & \\
 & \text{WKM = WKM1 / A(i,j)} & \\
 & \text{SELECTOR = KP1(i) .GT. N} & \\
\hline
 & \text{IF (SELECTOR) GOTO 15} & (3) \\
\hline
 & \text{DOALL 9 j = 1, N - i} & \\
 & \text{T7(j) = WKM • A(i,i+ j)} & \\
 & \text{T8(j) = Z(i+ j) + T7(j)} & (4) \\
 & \text{R2(j) = ABS(T8(j))} & \\
9 & \text{CONTINUE} & \\
\hline
 & \text{DO 11 j = 1, N - i} & \\
 & \text{SM = SM + R2(j)} & (5) \\
11 & \text{CONTINUE} & \\
\hline
 & \text{DOALL 12 j = 1, N - i} & \\
 & \text{T9(j) = WK • A(i,i+ j)} & \\
 & \text{Z(i+ j) = Z(i+ j) + T9(j)} & (6) \\
 & \text{R1(j) = ABS(Z(i+ j))} & \\
12 & \text{CONTINUE} & \\
\hline
 & \text{T3 = 0E0} & (7) \\
\hline
 & \text{DO 13 j = 1, N - i} & \\
 & \text{T3 = T3 + R1(j)} & (8) \\
13 & \text{CONTINUE} & \\
\hline
 & \text{T10 = T3 + S1} & (9) \\
 & \text{SELECTOR1 = T10 .GE. SM} & \\
\hline
 & \text{IF (SELECTOR1) GOTO 15} & (10) \\
\hline
 & \text{T = WKM - WK} & (11) \\
 & \text{WK = WKM} & \\
\hline
 & \text{DOALL 14 j = 1, N - i} & \\
 & \text{T11(j) = T • A(i,i+ j)} & (12) \\
 & \text{Z(i+ j) = Z(i+ j) + T11(j)} & \\
14 & \text{CONTINUE} & \\
\hline
15 & \text{Z(i) = WK} & (13) \\
\hline
16 & \text{CONTINUE} & (14) \\
\hline
 & \text{"} & \\
 & \text{"} & \\
\end{array}
$$

Figure 4.10 A restructured program segment from LINPACK.

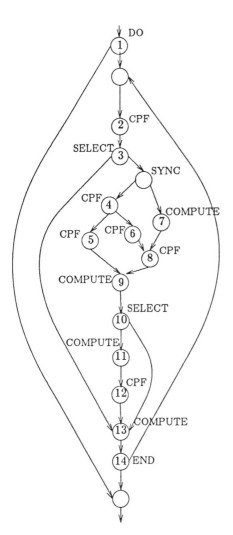

Figure 4.11 The macro-dataflow graph for the program in Figure 4.10.

on one processor controlled by the program counter. Figure 4.10 shows a FORTRAN program segment from linear programming package in its restructured form [using Parafrase (36)]. The corresponding macro-dataflow graph for GCU is shown in Figure 4.11 (43).

4.4. Partitioning

Parallelism and scheduling-and-synchronization overhead are the two most important factors influencing performance. For high performance, we want as much parallelism as possible with the lowest possible overhead. Both of these factors depend on the granularity of nodes in the control graph. Figure 4.12a shows a fine-granularity graph with seven nodes and nine arcs. A time penalty for scheduling each node and for synchronizing each arc must be added to the execution time of the program represented by the graph. However, if we merge nodes 2 and 3, 4 and 5, and 6 and 7, we will obtain the graph shown in Figure 4.12b, which reduces the time penalty. On the other hand, all the parallelism available in the original graph will not be exploited. When we merge nodes 6 and 7 into new node Z, for example, we force sequential execution on nodes 5 and 6 because node Y is executed before node Z.

Thus, as we merge or fuse more and more operations, we pay less in synchronization-and-scheduling overhead but waste more and more parallelism. The parallelism wasted for random structures such as those originated from expression evaluation is much higher than for regular structures such as those originated from linear algebra. For example, addition of two vectors of size 100 can be scheduled on 10 processors so that each processor generates the sum of every 10th element of the resultant vector. The process is synchronized only at the end, after each processor executes all 10 additions. Scheduling-and-synchronization overhead is much lighter if we consider each addition separately. This relationship is shown qualitatively in Figure 4.13.

Every multiprocessor architecture attempts to exploit as much parallelism as possible at the lowest possible overhead. Proponents of data flow architecture (4, 14, 27) believe that each problem can be transformed into

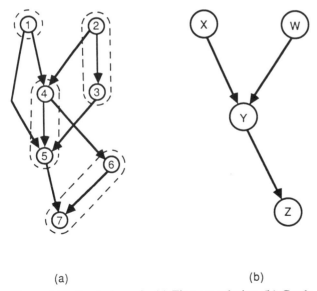

(a)   (b)

Figure 4.12 Control graph. (a) Fine granularity. (b) Crude granularity.

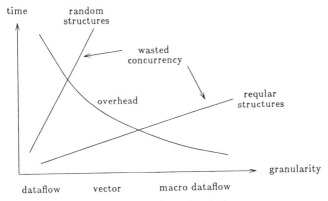

Figure 4.13 Concurrency and overhead plots.

expression evaluation with negligible scheduling-and-synchronization overhead. They have chosen fine granularity as the main principle of their machines. On the other hand, proponents of crude-granularity data flow (22, 23, 25, 30, 51) believe that most of the important problems in science and engineering can be solved with operations on structured data, and they have chosen granularity as an underlying principle of their architectures. In this way they hope to overcome the overhead problem associated with fine granularity.

An obvious solution to the overhead problem is to hide it by instruction pipelining. If a machine has approximately 10 stages including execution in the instruction pipeline, the number of nodes executable in parallel is 10 times the number of usable processors in the machine. For example, if we have five processors, 50 nodes must be executable in parallel at every moment to keep all the processors fully utilized. In other words, a program will run at only 10% of its maximal speed if 100% efficiency of the multiprocessor is required. This relationship is shown in Figure 4.14, which shows a typical program profile with respect to the number of parallel operations. There are areas of high parallelism interleaved with areas in which only a few operations can be executed in parallel.

This kind of profile is the result of partitioning a large problem such as a 2-D or a 3-D simulation into smaller subproblems, then using one processor to solve each subproblem. The areas of low parallelism come from updating the points on the boundary of the subproblem before computing the points inside. A small number of processors can be used efficiently. As the number of processors increases, performance increases and efficiency drops. Therefore, to obtain high performance, we must tolerate some degree of inefficiency but minimize it by avoiding unnecessary scheduling-and-synchronization overhead for computation on regular structures.

The partitioning problem can be divided into two subproblems. Par-

Time

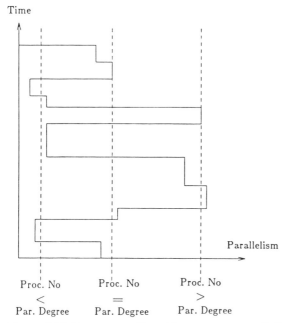

Figure 4.14 Program profile with respect to parallelism.

allelism detection determines all possible parallelism in a program to max-imize the execution speed. Clustering combines several operations into a task and partitions a program into many tasks to increase the throughput or the efficiency of the machine. Although partitioning embodies these two distinct ideas, they are usually performed together by the user, the compiler, or the machine at runtime.

4.4.1. Parallelism Detection

Parallelism can be detected by users during algorithm design. They need a language such as CSP (29) or OCCAM (56), which can define parallel tasks and communication of data between them. It can also be detected by com-pilers such as Parafrase (42) or Bulldog (19), which use program-restructuring techniques to transform a sequential program into a parallel form suitable for multiprocessors. Finally, parallelism can be exploited by machines such as the IBM 360/91 and the CDC 6600.

The traditional way of allowing programmers to specify parallelism is to provide parallel constructors in sequential languages. The Fork and Join suggested by Conway (11) allows the designated routine executing in parallel with the invoking routine. The Parbegin and Parend introduced by Dijkstra (16) declares explicitly the parallel parts of a program. A Process used in

Concurrent Pascal (28) and Modula (57) can be executed in parallel with any other process.

The OCCAM language (41, 56) provides partitioning mechanisms. It has three primitive processes: assignment (: =), input (?), and output (!). Assignment changes the value of a variable, input receives a value from a channel, and output sends a value on a channel. Variables (VAR) and channels (CHAN) are declared by the programmer at the beginning of the program. Three constructors combine processes to form larger processes. The sequential (SEQ) constructor causes its components to be executed one after another, terminating when the last component terminates. The parallel (PAR) constructor causes its components to be executed concurrently, terminating only after all the components have terminated. The alternative (ALT) constructor, operating like an *if* statement, chooses one component process for execution, terminating when the chosen component terminates.

A matrix multiplication of arrays A and B, using a square array of processors, is given in Figure 4.15. Procedure *mult* specifies three sequential steps for each processor. First, the *up* and *left* channels supply data to the processor. The processor then performs the arithmetic operations. Finally, the input data is passed to output channels called *down* and *right*. The main program declares two arrays of channels, which specify the data paths of arrays A and B throughout the array of processors.

Parafrase and Bulldog are two examples of detecting parallelism at compile time. The Parafrase system (36, 42) is a source-to-source restructuring tool that utilizes a sophisticated data dependence test and transforms FORTRAN programs from their original, sequential forms into a form suitable for execution on high-speed multiprocessor systems. The current Par-

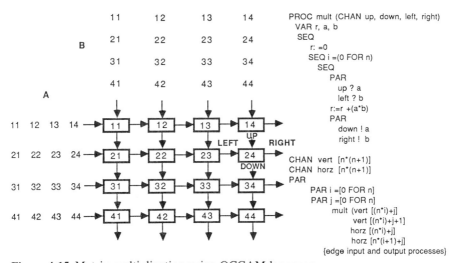

Figure 4.15 Matrix multiplication using OCCAM language.

afrase has two phases. The first phase, called "front-end passes," performs machine-independent transformations and restructures the program into an intermediate form that expresses the maximal parallelism of the programs. In this phase, different program transformation techniques such as scalar renaming, forward substitution, loop normalization, subscript expansion, loop distribution, loop interchanging etc. can be used. The second phase, called "back-end passes," maps the intermediate form into a specific architecture, such as single execution of array instructions, multiple execution of scalar instructions, and multiple execution of array instructions, selected by users.

The Bulldog compiler uses the trace-scheduling algorithm to compact sequential microcode into parallel microcode. Previous work (37) dealt only with compaction of straight-line code blocks (SLCBs). Experiments showed that the parallelism in such blocks is very limited (20). More parallelism can be obtained by code motions between blocks. Trace scheduling, on the other hand, uses a global compaction technique, operating on traces over many SLCBs. A trace (or execution path) is a loop-free execution sequence of instructions selected at compile time by a compiler, which predicts conditional jumps at the end of each SLCB based on how frequent each part of the conditional jump will perform.

The IBM 360/91 (1) has multiple functional units. Instruction execution can be overlapped by decoding an instruction and transmitting it to one of the functional units before its predecessor instruction finishes. However, the operation specified by the instruction is performed only when all the operands are supplied either by memory or another functional unit. Thus, the sophisticated hardware execution mechanism of the 360/91 allows run-time parallelism detection within a window around the current program counter.

4.4.2. Clustering

Several operations are usually clustered into tasks during parallelism detection. The INMOS Transputer uses the OCCAM language, while the Cray, the HEP, the Ultracomputer, and the Cosmic Cube use extended high-level languages such as FORTRAN or C to allow the programmer to partition programs into tasks. Cedar and ELI, on the other hand, cluster tasks at compile time with the Parafrase and Bulldog compilers. Note that parallelism detection and clustering are strongly influenced by the architecture, but are not architectural features. They are trade-offs taken by designers in capturizing the system. Clearly, Cedar can use FORTRAN extensions and allows users to partition programs so that Ultra, HEP, and the Cray can use a restructural compiler.

The criteria for clustering tasks depends upon the organizations of machines. The Cray X-MP has vector registers of length 64. Vector instructions longer than 64 have to be clustered into different tasks. ELI provides 512-bits-long horizontal microcode instructions. Bulldog clusters sequential microcodes into these long instructions. Three criteria are considered in Cedar for clustering tasks: granularity, data movement, and processor requirements. The granularity of tasks is chosen to optimize between parallelism and overhead. Data movement is concerned about how to cluster tasks in order to minimize movement of data between global and local memory. Clustering tasks according to the requirement of processors increases the efficiency of the multiprocessors in a multitasking environment.

So far, we have concentrated on partitioning a program into tasks. Each task is a unit of scheduling to be executed on one or more processors. We now discuss how to map a task onto a fixed number of processors. This mapping problem involves two distinct concepts. First, the task must be further partitioned into processes, each process being a unit of allocation to be executed on only one processor. Usually, each iteration of a loop in a task is treated as a single process. This task partitioning method is very effective when all iterations of a loop can execute independently. When data dependences exist between different iterations, a proper synchronization mechanism must be used to enforce the data dependence during execution. We will discuss the synchronization issue in section 4.6. Second, each process must be scheduled to execute on one processor. This scheduling problem will be discussed in the next section.

4.5. Scheduling

Scheduling is vaguely defined as a function that assigns jobs to processors. In early timesharing, multiple-process operating systems, scheduling played the central role in processor management. Three levels of scheduling are described by Deitel (12). High-level scheduling, sometimes called "job scheduling," selects a subset of all submitted jobs to compete actively for computer resources. Each active job may create one or more processes. Each process performs a subset of functions required by the job. Intermediate-level scheduling responds to short-term fluctuations in system load by temporarily suspending and activating processes to achieve smooth system operation. Low-level scheduling determines the next ready process to be assigned to the processor for a certain time. Different scheduling policies, such as first-in-first-out, round-robin, shortest-job-first, or shortest-remaining-time, can be a applied to each level of scheduling. Many research studies on performance of different scheduling policies were made in the late 1960s and early 1970s (9, 32).

In a multiprocessor system, scheduling assigns to each task one or more processors, with the goal of high performance for a single program or high processor utilization in a multiprogramming environment. Related issues of scheduling are also discussed in Chapter 7.

Scheduling can be static or dynamic. Kruskal and Weiss (34) have compared the performance of the two scheduling methods. Given certain restrictions on the task distribution, they proved that the static scheduling provides reasonable performance relative to an optimal scheme. In static scheduling, tasks are allocated to processors during the algorithm design by the user or at compile time by the compiler. The OCCAM language (41, 56) allows programmers to specify the instruction execution sequence, the channel of communication, and the execution unit. On the other hand, the Bulldog compiler (19), after applying the trace-scheduling technique to determine all the traces (tasks), performs register allocation and binds operations to specific functional units at compile time. Scheduling costs are paid only once, even if the program is run many times with different data. Moreover, there is no run-time overhead. The disadvantage of static scheduling, however, is possible inefficiency in guessing the run-time profile of each task. For this reason, Bulldog runs each program with a set of data in order to determine run-time parameters more accurately.

Dynamic scheduling by the machine at run time offers better utilization of processors, but at the price of additional scheduling time. The dynamic scheduling algorithm can be distributed or centralized. The HEP machine (52) uses a centralized scheduler that assigns each task to run on one of the PEMs. Each PEM can support up to 128 processes. As a result, the maximum number of processes a task will create must be specificd to the system when the task is loaded. Arvind's data flow machine (3) has a centralized scheduler called the "manager," which schedules each code block to a physical domain with several processors. Tasks are serially ordered in the Cray X-MP. So the scheduling problem in the task level does not exist.

Although specialized hardware can accelerate a centralized scheduler, a performance bottleneck may develop when the number of processors becomes large. Assuming that the total number of processors in a multiprocessor system is n, the average number of processors required for a task is p, and the average execution time of a task using p processors is t, then, in order to take advantage of n processors, the scheduling overhead has to be less than $t*p/n$.

The HEP machine uses a distributed self-scheduling technique to balance the execution time of processes in a task. The number of processes in a task is statically defined by the programmer. However, the contents of each process depend on the run time environment. For example, a DOALL task with 100 iterations is partitioned into 10 processes, as shown in Figure 4.16. Self-scheduling allows each process to acquire the next iteration dynamically when it finishes the previous one. In this example, a synchronization variable, represented by a $ in front of the variable, has two states:

```
DIMENSION A(100),B(100),C(100),D(100)
        .
        .
    N = 100
    DO 10 I = 1,N
        A(I) = B(I) +  C(I)
        D(I) = A(I) ** 2
10  CONTINUE
        .
        .
        .
```

(a)

```
    COMMON A(100),B(100),D(100),N              SUBROUTINE DOALL ($NOI, $TOTAL)
        .                                      COMMON A(100),B(100),C(100),D(100),N
        .                            100    I = $NOI
    N = 100                                 $NOI = I + 1
    NP = 10                                 IF (I.GT.N) GOTO 200
    PURGE $NOI, $TOTAL                      A(I) = B(I) + C(I)
    $NOI = 1                                D(I) = A(I) ** 2
    $TOTAL = 0                              $TOTAL = $TOTAL + 1
    DO 10 I = 1,(NP-1)                      GOTO100
        CREATE DOALL ($NOI, $TOTAL)  200    RETURN
10  CONTINUE                                END
    CALLDOALL ($NOI, $TOTAL)
20  IF (VALUE($TOTAL).LT.N)GOTO20
        .
        .
        .
```

(b)

Figure 4.16 Self-scheduling in HEP. (a) Serial source code. (b) Parallel self-scheduling code.

full and empty. The variable can be read only if the state is full and set to empty afterward, and it can be written into only if the state is empty and set to full afterward.

Other types of reads or writes are also allowed, such as VALUE ($NAME), which accesses the variable $NAME regardless of its state. PURGE clears the state of variable. CREATE, similar to CALL syntactically, causes a subroutine to run in parallel with its creator. Two synchronization variables are used in this example: $NOI is used to keep track of the iteration count and assures that exactly 100 iterations are executed; $TOTAL is used to assure that all 100 iterations have been finished before the main program continues. The execution time of each iteration may vary widely because of the unpredictable delay of memory access through the network. When iterations are assigned statically to processes, the total execution time of the task may increase because one process may get all the iterations that require longer execution time. This situation can be avoided with self-scheduling. However, when the number of iterations is not much greater than the number of processes, the advantage of self-scheduling is lost.

The NYU Ultracomputer (25) uses a distributed algorithm to implement self-scheduling in a different way. Tasks are specified by the programmer at algorithm time and put into a central queue in the shared memory at run time. Each processor takes the first task from the queue and executes it whenever the processor becomes idle. A task can be thought of as one iteration in our DOALL example (Figure 4.16). The task queue is not a bottleneck because the Ultracomputer uses its special synchronization instruction called "fetch&add," which allows simultaneous access from all processors to the same memory location without performance degradation. Such a distributed algorithm allows for architectural scalability at the expense of scheduling overhead caused by the global memory access through the network.

Most multiprocessor machines have more than one level of execution control. Either a static or a dynamic scheduling method can be used on each level. For instance, Arvind's data flow machine and Cedar use dynamic scheduling for tasks, while processes and instructions are bound statically at compile time to a virtual processor whose identity number is determined at run time. Furthermore, both centralized and distributed dynamic scheduling schemes may be applied to different control levels of the same machine. For instance, the HEP machine schedules tasks centrally, while each process in a task is self-scheduled distributively.

The Cosmic Cube even uses both static and dynamic scheduling strategy in the same control level. The programmers can control the distribution of process to processors using an extended high-level language. On the other hand, they can also use a library process that assigns a newly created process to a processor considering load and storage utilization in neighboring processors.

Different dynamic scheduling schemes, such as first-come-first-serve, least-service-time-first, and random-choice, can be used in multiprocessor systems (30). When a task is allocated to more than one processor, a more sophisticated processor scheduling strategy is needed. In Cedar, for example, the maximal number of processors needed by a task is determined at compile time. When the number of available processors at run time is not adequate, the scheduler can either wait or fold the task on a smaller number of processors. Simulation experiments have shown that folding the task will provide better performance and processor utilization than waiting (60).

4.6. Synchronization

Synchronization originated from resource management in multiple-process operating systems in which each shared resource is accessed by only one process at a time. Various methods such as mutual exclusion and conditional synchronization can synchronize concurrent processes (2, 47). In this section we are concerned with the synchronization methods for coordinating parallel execution of tasks and processes in multiprocessor systems. We define two mechanisms, each of which can be implemented by shared-variable or message-passing methods.

4.6.1. Control-Level Synchronization

In control-level synchronization, a program counter synchronizes sequential execution; in a parallel control graph, execution is synchronized by allowing a node to execute only when all its predecessors have finished. All the sequential uniprocessors, such as the VAX-11 and the Motorola 68000, use the program counter method; data flow machines, such as Dennis's and Arvind's, use directed control graphs.

In a control graph, tokens traveling on arcs communicate the completion of the computation in each node. If there are two loops in the control graph, with one producing the data and the other consuming it, and if the producer loop is faster than the consumer loop, tokens accumulate on the input arc of the consumer loop. For example, in the control graph for the trapezoidal rule shown in Figure 4.17, tokens will accumulate on the input arc A of function f if the execution time of f is longer than the $+ h$ and the $\leq n - 1$ operations.

Two practical solutions exist (21): (1) the use of data flow graph is limited by restricting tokens on each arc of the graph to only one at any time; (2) the tokens are allowed to carry their index and iteration level as a label. The first approach, which implies sequential but pipelined execution of the control graph, is used in static data flow architecture (14). Pipelining is implemented through the use of acknowledge signals, which are returned to the nodes in the graph that generated those values by the nodes that consumed the values. The second approach, which allows a node to be executed only if all input tokens have the same label, is used in labeled-token data flow machines (4, 27).

The labeling method permits the use of pure static code and enables maximal use of any parallelism that exists in the problem specification. However, because label generation is inherently a serial process, it introduces overhead between the initiation of two consecutive iterations. In order to generate a *label* for one iteration in the trapezoidal rule example, serial execution of five nodes (a merge, a compare, a switch, an increment, and

(INITIAL $s \leftarrow (f(a) + f(b))/2$;

$\qquad x \leftarrow a + h$

FOR i FROM 1 TO $n-1$ DO

$\qquad$ NEW $x \leftarrow x + h$;

$\qquad$ NEW $s \leftarrow s + f(x)$

$\qquad$ RETURN s) * h

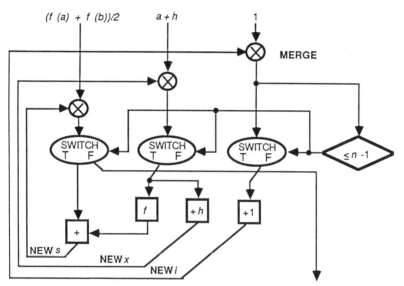

Figure 4.17 Dataflow graph of the trapezoidal rule. (From Arvind, Iannucci RA: A critique of multiprocessing von Neumann style. *Tenth Symposium on Computer Architecture*. Stockholm, 1983, pp. 426–436.)

an update-label node) is required. Even though the updates to the function f can be executed in parallel, they are pipelined by a stage delay of five sequential nodes as described above.

4.6.2. Data-Level Synchronization

Data-level synchronization is used whenever two or more processes inside a task share the same variable. It is very effective when a task represents an operation on large structured data. For example

$$\sum_{i=1}^{n} (a_i + b_i)*c_i$$

can be computed as two processes, a vector addition followed by a vector multiplication. However, the vector multiplication process may start before the vector addition process is finished, if consumer multiplication does not overrun producer addition. In the Cray X-MP, this is called *chaining*, and synchronization is accomplished through proper clocking of two functional units, an adder and a multiplier. A different synchronization mechanism must be used for general processes that are not executed in a lockstep manner.

Shared-variable synchronization can be used to coordinate execution of general concurrent processes. Each shared variable has many states. When a shared variable is in a state inappropriate for executing a particular operation, any process attempting such an operation should be delayed until the state of the data object is changed by other processes. Multiprocessor machines usually include hardware synchronization primitives, which provide an efficient way of implementing data-level synchronization.

The IBM 360/370 (17) uses a test-modify-write instruction called "test&set," which reads a value from memory and writes all 1s back into memory as a single uninterruptible machine instruction. Test&set can be used to guarantee mutual exclusive access of shared data, as shown in Figure 4.18. While the content of the synchronization variable a is 0, the first process that gets the 0 from test&set is allowed to access the shared variable. The other processes will be blocked by getting all 1s. After the successful access, a process will reset a to 0 and allow other processes to compete for the shared variable.

C.mmp (58) uses a "lock" instruction for low-level, mutual-exclusion primitives operating below the process level. Lock is implemented with two counters, which can be indivisibly decremented and tested, and a bit mask to record waiting processes. Instead of continuous polling for the waiting processes, C.mmp uses interprocessor interrupts to avoid the memory contention problem. Both test&set and lock can be used to implement any kind of data-level synchronizations. However, before accessing the data, an extra fetch to the shared memory for testing and modifying the state of the shared variable is necessary, but it decreases machine performance.

Smith introduced a full/empty (F/E) bit in each memory location in the HEP (52). Each register or memory word can be used to synchronize two processes in a producer–consumer fashion. For example, assume that process A produces a result and stores it into variable x and that this data is consumed by process B. Initially, the F/E bit of x is cleared for process A to store the result in. Afterward, process A will set the F/E bit so that process

```
PROCESS Mutual (a);
    WHILE Test&Set (a) ≠ 0 DO
        Nothing;
    Access The Shared Variable;
    a = 0
END
```

Figure 4.18 Mutual exclusion implemented by Test&Set.

B can read it. If B rushes ahead of A, the empty bit will block B from reading until the bit is full. The testing and modifying of the F/E bit, along with the proper memory operation, are performed indivisibly.

This method is very elegant for "single-assignment" languages. However, for languages that allow the reassignment of variables, a single F/E bit can synchronize only alternating reads and writes to the same location without preserving an exact order. Arvind applied this synchronization method to the I-structure of his data flow machine, using a single-assignment language. Presence bits are associated with each I-structure location to solve the read-before-write race problem.

A fetch&add synchronization instruction (F&A (V, e)) using integer addition in each network element and memory module was introduced in the NYU Ultracomputer (25). F&A (V, e) performs an indivisible operation of fetching the integer variable V and replacing it by $V + e$, where e is an integer expression. Moreover, fetch&add must satisfy the serialization principle: If V is a shared variable and many fetch&add operations simultaneously address V, the effect is the same as if they occurred in some (*unspecified*) serial order. For example, if P_i executes $ANS_i \leftarrow$ F&A (V, e_i), if P_j simultaneously executes $ANS_j \leftarrow$ F&A (V, e_j), and if V is not simultaneously updated by yet another processor, then either

$$ANS_i \leftarrow V; ANS_j \leftarrow V + e_i$$

or

$$ANS_i \leftarrow V + e_j; ANS_j \leftarrow V$$

and in either case, the value of V becomes $V + e_i + e_j$. Combining the requests is implemented through each switching element in the network. For example, if F&A (V, e_i) and F&A (V, e_j) meet at a switch, the switch forms the sum $e_i + e_j$, transmits the combined request F&A $(V, e_i + e_j)$, and stores the value e_i in its local memory (see Figure 4.19). When the value of V returns to the switch, the switch transmits V to satisfy the original request F&A (V, e_i) and $V + e_i$ to satisfy F&A (V, e_j).

Fetch&add can be used to perform many important algorithms in a completely parallel manner. Gottlieb et al. (26) used an essentially equivalent instruction, replace&add, to solve the readers–writers problem in parallel. They also presented a highly concurrent queue management technique that can be used to implement a decentralized operating system scheduler. However, fetch&add cannot preserve the order of a sequence of memory reads and writes more efficiently than a simple test&set instruction because parallel access to a memory location is executed in an unspecified serial order.

Zhu and Yew (61) introduced a synchronization scheme for Cedar. They define a key field for each synchronization variable and use it as a counter. Each synchronizing instruction tests the key and performs a memory read or write only if the tested condition is satisfied. After this operation,

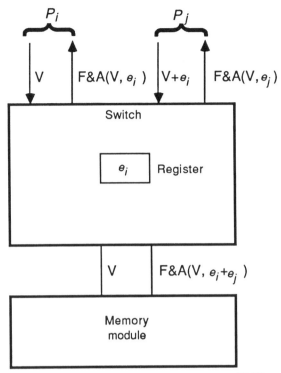

Figure 4.19 A switching element in the NYU Ultracomputer.

the key is incremented or decremented in order to allow the next operation on the same variable. All these operations are performed in an indivisible manner in the accessed memory module. For example, if four processes P_1, P_2, P_3, P_4 access a shared memory location x in the order P_4, P_3, P_2, P_1, then the sequence numbers given to process P_4, P_3, P_2, P_1 are 1, 2, 3, and 4 respectively. Initially, the key field of variable x contains the value 1. When P_4 reaches the accessed memory module, it is allowed to perform the memory operation because the tested sequence number is matched. Afterward, the key of x is incremented so that P_3 is allowed to access x. Processes out of sequence must wait for their corresponding access sequence number.

The counter method makes it very difficult to preserve the reference order when a repeated referencing pattern of each data element occurs and a counter is updated by two or more overlapping sequences of memory operations. For example, if each processor computes one grid point in the two-point finite-difference problem shown in Figure 4.20, each grid value such as A(3, 3) must be read once by the processors computing A(2, 3) and A(3, 2) in either order before a new value can be written into A(3, 3). This sequence of references is repeated on each iteration of the outer loop. If all

```
DO r = 1, TIMES
  DO i = 1,N
    DO j = 1,N
      A(i,j) = ((A(i+1,j) + A(i,j+1))/2.
    ENDO
  ENDO
ENDO
```

(a)

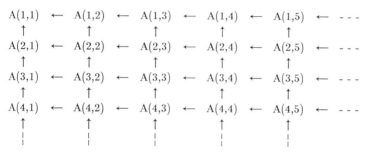

(b)

Figure 4.20 A finite difference problem. (a) Source code. (b) Data processing.

processors are allowed to proceed to the next iteration of the outer loop, and the processor computing A(3, 2) is delayed by one iteration, the processor computing A(2, 3) decrements the counter of A(3, 3) twice, and A(3, 3) is updated out of order. Two errors are made: the processor computing A(2, 3) gets an old value of A(3, 3) twice, while the processor computing A(3, 2) computes with a new value of A(3, 3).

Yet another difficulty of the counter method is resetting the key to its initial value for each grid point after each iteration of the outer loop. Resetting the key allows each processor to proceed to the next iteration independently regardless of the speed of other processors. To avoid these problems, Zhu and Yew (61) introduced a second key to identify each iteration of the outer loop and a separate test&reset instruction to reset the first key. The second key makes their scheme complicated in this application.

A bit-map synchronization method (44) solves this problem by treating the key field as multiple F/E bits. Each synchronizing memory instruction,

$READ/WRITE, Address, Mask

where Mask is used for testing and setting the F/E bits, is implemented as the following indivisible sequence of microoperations. For READ, the sequence is defined as follows:

$$\bigwedge_{i=1}^{n} (Mask_i \text{ OR } Key_i): \text{Register} \leftarrow \text{Memory(Address)};$$

$$Key \leftarrow Mask \text{ AND } Key;$$

For WRITE, the sequence is:

$$\neg \left(\bigvee_{i=1}^{n} (Mask_i \text{ AND } Key_i) \right): \text{Memory(Address)} \leftarrow \text{Register};$$

$$Key \leftarrow Mask \text{ OR } Key;$$

For example, if a sequence of memory operations to the same memory location is W_5, R_4, W_3, R_2, R_1 (from right to left), the correct referencing order can be preserved by using the key and mask values as shown in Table 4.1. This method can be used successfully for the example shown in Figure 4.20.

Data-level synchronization can also be implemented through the message-passing method (2). When message passing is used for communication and synchronization, processes send and receive messages instead of reading and writing shared variables. Communication is accomplished because a process obtains values from some sender process. Synchronization is accomplished because a message can be received only after it has been sent, which constrains the order of these two events. The basic architectural requirement for the message-passing method is a channel of communication between the sender and the receiver processes.

The Cray X-MP-2 has a set of binary semaphore registers for interprocess communication and control. On the other hand, the Cosmic Cube has hypercube connections between processors for message passing channels. Concurrent tasks (or processes) synchronize each other by SEND and

Table 4.1 A Bit-Map Synchronization Example

	SYNC or MASK value					
	W_5	R_4	W_{32}	W_{31}	R_2	R_1
Init SYNC Value	1	0	1	1	1	1
Mask of R_1	1	1	1	0	1	0
SYNC after R_1	1	0	1	0	1	0
Mask of R_2	1	1	0	1	0	1
SYNC after R_2	1	0	0	0	0	0
Mask of W_3	0	1	1	1	0	0
SYNC after W_3	1	1	1	1	0	0
Mask of R_4	0	0	1	1	1	1
SYNC after R_4	0	0	1	1	0	0
Mask of W_5	1	0	0	0	1	1
SYNC after W_5	1	0	1	1	1	1

RECEIVE procedure calls to the operating system kernal to accomplish message-passing functions.

4.7. Memory Access

The interconnection network in a multiprocessor plays a crucial role in system performance. A fully connected network, called a "crossbar switch," is very expensive because its complexity grows proportionally to the square of the switch size. Only small networks are built as crossbars—for example, the 16 × 16 crossbar used in the S1 machine (18) and in C.mmp. (58). Usually, a limited-access network is built—for example, the shuffle-exchange in Cedar (10, 22), the Banyan in TRAC (7), or the Boolean-cube in the Cosmic Cube machine (51). The interconnection network issue is discussed extensively in Chapter 6. These interconnection networks introduce an unavoidable delay in accessing data stored in the shared or distributed memory. Furthermore, because access to memory may be blocked temporarily because of conflicts in the network or the accessed memory module, access delays are unpredictable and the data arrival order may differ from the order of request.

One solution to conflict problems is to buffer network elements. A request will be queued in the buffer when a conflict occurs (15). The Ultra-computer uses this buffered method in its multistage interconnection network (33). Another solution is to delete all but one of the conflicting requests; processors will retry after they receive a blocking signal. Either scheme reduces performance. To minimize performance degradation, Ultra combines requests in the switching element where a conflict occurs and the requests want to access the same memory location. Cedar and the HEP provide multiple paths between each processor and each memory module to reduce accessing conflicts. In Ultra, the method not only resolves the conflicts but allows concurrent reads and writes to the same shared memory location.

In addition to the conflict problem, a memory request may be unsuccessful when the required data is not available. Then, a processor can "busy-wait" or its request can be queued in the accessed memory module. Busy-waiting wastes processor bandwidth, memory bandwidth, and network bandwidth. Queuing unsuccessful requests has been used with P and V semaphores for process synchronization (2). Semaphores are implemented by operating system calls to a kernel to prevent the processor from busywaiting. Each process in the kernel can either be ready to execute or be blocked, waiting for the completion of a P operation.

Arvind applied this queuing idea to memory requests. In the I-structure storage, presence bits are associated with each memory cell. If, for example, a memory module receives a read request to a certain location and its presence bits indicate that the data object has already been written into, the read operation will proceed. If the bits indicate an empty location, the request will be queued and the location marked. When a write request arrives later, the memory module will notice a pending read request, and the new value will be sent to the process that issued the read request.

Queuing requests in an I-structure requires a single-assignment language. If more sophisticated synchronization primitives are provided, such as the counter or the bit-map method described in the previous section, the queued-requests method can be used without restricting the language to the single assignment rule. All unsuccessful requests can be queued in the same memory module in their accessing order. Whenever a data item is read or written successfully to a memory location, the queued requests for that location will be answered.

4.7.1. Cache Memory

The memory access, or latency, problem exists even in a conventional uniprocessor system. It increases with memory size. As soon as a certain capacity is exceeded, the memory becomes the bottleneck in the system. A traditional way of circumventing the latency problem is to provide a processor with a small, high-speed buffer storage (10) in the form of local memory, or cache. Data and instructions are moved to the high-speed buffer as required by the processor. Under the assumption of temporal and spatial locality, these data and instructions will be referenced more frequently in the near future.

A cache is designed to be user transparent. Special hardwares are required to translate the memory address (virtual) to cache address (real). A block of data is moved to the cache automatically by hardware when a required datum is not found in the cache. This is called a "cache miss." When a cache miss occurs, a significant penalty has to be paid for moving the data from the main memory. Thus, the hit (or miss) ratio representing the fraction of program reference found (not found) in the cache is usually used to measure the effectiveness of a caching scheme in capturing localities. The capacity of the cache, the size of each block of data, and the choice of placement and replacement policy affect the hit ratio greatly. The speeds of main memory, cache, and address mapping are also important factors for the cache performance (31, 48, 53).

The local memory scheme, on the other hand, relies on programmers or compilers to specify the data movement instructions explicitly. In this way, users have the control of the local memory. If the address is known, a prefetching scheme can move a block of data to the local memory before the data is required by the processor. Most existing machines, such as the

IBM 3090 and the VAX-11, use a caching scheme. The Cray X-MP, on the other hand, uses the prefetching method to move blocks of 64 elements into its vector registers.

Either of the above schemes will work on a multiprocessor system if data coherence is maintained. A memory scheme is coherent if the value returned on a load instruction is always the value given by the latest store instruction with the same address. In uniprocessor systems, the write-through scheme allows write operation to update the data both in the cache and in the main memory, so that data in the cache is never different from its copy in main memory. This scheme cannot solve the coherence problem in a multiprocessor system where each processor has its own private local memory. Even though in the write-through scheme the main memory lo-cation can always keep the most recent data, the possible copies of a variable in other caches are not automatically updated.

There are three solutions to this multiple-cache coherence problem. The easiest solution, obviously, is to move into cache only the data that is either read-only or locally read-write to the processor. Longer delay occurs in accessing the shared read-write data. The Ultracomputer adopted this solution for its caching scheme.

The second solution is to use the shared-cache organization (59). The write-through scheme solves the coherence problem because there is only one copy of data residing in the shared cache. However, data access to the shared cache requires an interconnection network. The latency problem may still exist, especially in a large, shared-cache system.

The third solution is to use a dynamic coherence check through hard-ware or software interlocks (8). Each data block in cache and shared memory has several flag bits for indicating the state of that block. Whenever a pro-cessor issues a read or a write request to shared read/write data, certain coherence check, data validation, and state modification actions are taken by the cache and the shared memory. This scheme introduces a substantial performance degradation and, in general, works only on a machine with a small number of processors, such as the S1 machine.

The multiprocessor configuration of the IBM 308X and 3090 (55) use the directory method to maintain the cache coherence. The cache directory table records the state of each block of data in any cache. In order to write into a data block, an exclusive state must be obtained from the system control element (SCE), which invalidates the same data block existing in any other cache. Goodman (24) proposed a write-once dynamic coherence check method for a bus-connected multiprocessor system to reduce the bus band-width requirement while maintaining the cache coherence.

Cedar combines the first two methods to solve the coherence problem (40). Data can be declared as private local, cluster-shared, or global shared. Private local memory provides the fastest access time for data accessed only by its own processor. Cluster-shared memory is a shared-cache organization that stores data locally to the cluster. A crossbar switch is used for accessing the cluster-shared data. Obviously, data not in these two groups is global-shared. A direct connection placed between each processor and its corresponding global memory module reduces the global access time for data located in that module. Caching and non-caching options are provided for all three levels of data. Programmers determine an appropriate scheme to use.[1]

4.7.2. Time Multiplexing

Another method for solving the memory latency problem is time multiplexing of processors. Whenever a memory access is required, a processor switches to another instruction or another process. Hiding latency this way, obviously, requires high-level parallelism in a program. High-performance processors, such as the IBM 360/91, using run-time instruction look-ahead to detect parallelism, allow multiple memory accesses in a pipeline fashion. This introduces extra complexity in the control unit to check the data dependence between active instructions. Furthermore, the look-ahead mechanism can be performed only on a small window around the program counter.

Vector machines such as the Cray X-MP exploit parallelism by vector instructions for pipelining memory access. After an initial setup delay, data arrives at the processor at pipeline speed. The latency problem still exists for nonvectorized data. The structured memory access architecture (46) introduced a fetch and an execution processor in each conventional processor. A FIFO queue is used between these two processing elements. Address generation, data fetch, and operation execution can be overlapped to increase the performance. However, a data dependence problem between the fetch and the execution processors is not easily solved.

The HEP has multiple processes in each processor and performs context switching while one process waits for the data from memory. An extra set of register files is needed for each active process to avoid overhead associated with saving registers. This scheme requires a high level of parallelism in the running program; whenever a process requests a memory access, the queue of processes waiting to be executed must not be empty. The number of processes waiting in the queue is proportional to the ratio of memory access time to the time of one stage in the instruction pipeline. Data flow machines, such as Arvind's, use parallel models of computation to obtain parallelism. They may have several executable nodes in each processor and perform context switching on the instruction level. Whenever an

---

[1] The Cedar prototype constructed at Center for Supercomputing Research and Development, University of Illinois, uses Alliant FX/8 as a cluster. FX/8 has a 128 K bytes shared cache for all 8 processors. Therefore, the private local memory does not exist in the prototype system.

I-structure request node in the data flow graph is executed, the processor automatically switches to the next executable node.

4.7.3. Message Passing

Finally, a third method solves the latency problem by message passing. With respect to data communication, we mentioned two types of multiprocessors in the introduction. In the shared-memory model, the data is in a preallocated location in the shared memory, where it can be accessed by each processor without interruptions from other processors. In the message-passing model, there is no global shared memory. Each processor has an associated local memory, and data is passed from the producing processor to the consuming processor through a connection path. Data flow computation is usually associated with the message-passing model, in which an operation is performed upon arrival of all its operands. The message-passing model passes data whenever data becomes available and not when it is needed. Thus, longer delay through the connection path can be tolerated when data is not used immediately after its generation. Arvind indicated that data flow machines using the message-passing model can tolerate the memory latency under low parallelism. However, this model is not applicable to shared storage such as the I-structure in Arvind's machine.

The Cosmic Cube minimizes the impact of memory latency on performance by using the message-passing model—that is, data is sent by the producer processor at the data generation time, not by the request from the consumer processor. Furthermore, the number of stages that a message travels in a hypercube connection increases with the distance between the sending and the receiving processors. Thus, in a cleverly partitioned program, the average distance data travels is shorter than in any other logarithmic switching network, where the distance is always $\log_2 n$, n being the number of input ports.

4.8. A Classification Scheme

In this chapter, we have conjectured that real progress in computer architecture will come from solutions that compromise between application requirements and technology limitations. In particular, we have specified and surveyed the five issues we consider crucial to such solutions: hierarchical control, partitioning, scheduling, synchronization, and memory access. Furthermore, these issues may serve as a crude classification scheme for comparison of multiprocessor machines.

Previous works related to comparison of machines concentrated on their architectural and topological features. Flynn considered control unit taxonomy based on instruction and data streams. He classified three computer organizations: Single Instruction stream–Single Data stream (SISD), Single Instruction stream–Multiple Data stream (SIMD), and Multiple Instruction stream–Multiple Data stream (MIMD). The same classification scheme is used in Chapter 5. Kuck (35) added one more dimension to Flynn's taxonomy: execution stream. This allows for 16 different types of systems, which covers a wide range of machine organizations. Recently, Schwartz (50) made a new taxonomic table of parallel computers based on 55 designs. He defined two groups of parallel architectures with respect to the size of the processors used: coarse and fine grained designs. Within each group, he divided machines according to the type of connection between processors. Although Schwartz gave a detailed classification for multiprocessor systems based on their main architectural features, the consideration of how a program is actually executed in multiprocessors was not included in his taxonomy.

Using our classifying scheme, we summarize in Table 4.2 the machine most cited in this chapter. The Cray X-MP has three levels of control mechanisms. A program is partitioned either by users or by a vectorizing compiler. The Cray uses a set of semaphore registers for interprocess communication, and memory latency is handled by vector caching and vector parallelism. Arvind's data flow machine has two levels of control mechanisms. Program partitioning is defined by the data flow language with help from the compiler. This machine uses a dynamic centralized-scheduling scheme for tasks and a static scheduling scheme for instructions. The F/E bit synchronization method is implemented in the I-structure, and memory latency is handled by message passing and instruction-level parallelism.

The HEP machine has three levels of control mechanisms. A program is partioned by users. The HEP uses dynamic scheduling of both tasks and processes, but task scheduling is centralized and process scheduling is distributed. The F/E bit synchronization method was invented for HEP, and register caching and process-level parallelism handle memory latency. The NYU Ultracomputer has two levels of control mechanisms. A program is partitioned by users. Ultra uses a dynamic distributed-scheduling scheme for tasks. Synchronization is accomplished by the fetch&add instruction, which allows concurrent access to the same memory location. Private caches are provided for handling memory latency.

The Cosmic Cube has two levels of control mechanisms. Users control both the program partitioning and the process scheduling. However, processes can also be scheduled in a distributive manner by the operating system kernel at runtime. The message-passing model is used for synchronization and reduction of memory latency. The Cedar machine has three levels of

Table 4.2 A Comparison Table for Eight Machines

Machines	Model of control	Program partitioning	Scheduling	Synchronization	Memory access
Cray X-MP-2	3-level: Task: serial, PC Process: parallel, Dd, Cf Inst: parallel, Dd, Cf	User, FORTRAN ext. Vectorizing compiler	Task: static Process: static	Semaphore registers	Vector registers Vector parallelism
Tagged token machine	2-level: Task: parallel, Dd, Cf Inst: parallel, Dd, Df&Cf	User, dataflow lang. Compiler	Task: dynamic cen. Inst: static	F/E bit in I-structure	Message-passing (scalars) Inst. parallelism
HEP	3-level: Task: parallel, Dd, Cf Process: parallel, Dd, Cf Inst: serial, PC	User, FORTRAN ext.	Task: dynamic cen. Process: dynamic dis. self-scheduling	F/E bit	Register cache Process parallelism
NYU (IBM RP3)	2-level: Task: parallel, Dd, Cf Inst: serial, PC	User, FORTRAN ext.	Task: dynamic dis.	Fetch&Add	Private: cache
Cosmic cube (Intel hypercube)	2-level: Process: parallel, Dd, Cf Inst: serial, PC	User, C ext.	Process: static, or dynamic dis.	Message-passing	Message-passing Hypercube connection
Cedar	3-level: Task: parallel, Dd, Cf Process: parallel, Dd, Cf Inst: serial, PC	Parafrase compiler	Task: dynamic cen. Process: static	Synchronization key	Private cache Shared cache

Key: PC: program counter; Dd: data-driven; Df: dataflow; Cf: control flow; cen.: centralized; dis.: distributed.

control mechanisms and relies upon the advanced Parafrase compiler to partition programs. Cedar uses a dynamic centralized-scheduling scheme for tasks, but a process is bound statically to a processor. The counter method synchronizes concurrent processes, and both private and shared caches are provided to handle memory latency.

We can see that Arvind's data flow machine and the HEP differ basically on two points: granularity and partitioning. The HEP exploits parallelism on the process level, while the data flow machine uses instruction-level granularity. The HEP requires users to implement partitioning; the data flow machine uses a data flow language and its compiler for partitioning. Both machines exploit parallelism to solve memory latency. However, the data flow machine obtains extra tolerance for memory latency on scalar data by using the message-passing model.

Furthermore, our table shows that Cedar and the Ultracomputer are not as close as their topology would suggest. Cedar has a process-level of control that does not exist in Ultra. Cedar performs partitioning through a compiler, while Ultra requires a user to do it. Scheduling is distributed in Ultra but is centralized in Cedar. Synchronization primitives are also different in the two machines.

The way these and other implementations resolve the issues we have discussed here will determine the performance and efficiency of future multiprocessor systems. These issues are essential because they are concerned with the user's view of the computing process instead of the engineering view of the machine.

Problems

1. What are the most essential issues in solving problems on multiprocessor systems? Why do these issues follow the users' view of how to use the systems instead of the architectural view of the systems?
2. Using the control-model classification scheme, can you classify the following machines: IBM-3090, Cray-2, ETA-10, FPS T-series, Alliant FX-8, and the Connection Machine.
3. What are the differences in concept between program partitioning, clustering, scheduling, and mapping?
4. In the following figure, if two processors execute the fine granularity graph, then 4 units of time are required. (Assume each node takes 1 unit of time to execute, and scheduling-and-synchronization overhead is omitted.) On the other hand, it requires 6 units of time to execute the crude granularity graph. How do you partition this program graph into 4 processes so that 5 or less execution time units can be achieved?

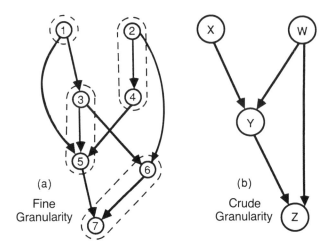

(a)

Fine
Granularity

(b)

Crude
Granularity

5. Parallelize the following program segment using (1) the full/empty, and
(2) the bit-map synchronization methods:

DO i = 1, 20
  DO j = 1, 20
    $A(i, j)$ = .25 × $(A(i - 1, j) + A(i, j - 1) + A(i, j + 1)$
    + $A(i + 1, j))$
  ENDO
ENDO

6. Using the synchronization insructions of the HEP machine illustrated in
Figure 4.16, rewrite the following program segment into 16 parallel dynamic (self-scheduling) execution processes:

DO i = 1, 100
  DO j = 1, 100
    $A(i, j)$ = $B(i, j) + C(i, j)$
    $D(i, j)$ = $E(i, j)$ × 5.
  ENDO
ENDO

References

1. Anderson DW, Sparacio FJ, Tomasulo FM: The IBM system/360 model 91:
Machine philosophy and instruction-handling. *IBM Journal,* Vol. 11, No. 1, Jan.
1967, pp. 8–24.
2. Andrews GR, Schneider FB: Concepts and notations for concurrent programming. *Computing Surveys,* Vol. 15, No. 1, March 1983, pp. 3–43.

3. Arvind: The tagged token dataflow architecture. Unpublished Memo, Laboratory for Computer Science, MIT, Nov. 1982.
4. Arvind, Iannucci RA: A critique of multiprocessing von Neumann style. Tenth Symposium on Computer Architecture, Stockholm, 1983, pp. 426–436.
5. Backus J: Can programming be liberated from the von Neumann style? A functional style and its algebra of programs. *Comm. ACM,* Vol. 21, No. 8, Aug. 1978, pp. 613–641.
6. Berkling KJ: A computing machine based on tree structure. *IEEE Trans. on Computers,* Vol. C-20, No. 4, April 1971, pp. 404–418.
7. Brown JC: TRAC: An environment for parallel computing. COMPCON, Spring, 1984, pp. 294–298.
8. Censier LM, Feautrier P: A new solution to the coherence problems in multiprocessor systems. *IEEE Trans. on Computers,* Vol. C-27, No. 12, Dec. 1981, pp. 18–27.
9. Coffman EG, Kleinrock L: Computer scheduling methods and their counter measures. *Proc. AFIPS, SJCC,* Vol. 32, 1968, pp. 11–21.
10. Conti CJ: Concepts for buffer storage. *Computer Group News,* 2, March 1969, pp. 9–13.
11. Conway M: A multiprocessor system design. *Proc. AFIPS Joint Computer Conference,* Spartan Books, NY, 1963, pp. 139–146.
12. Deitel HM: *An Introduction to Operating System. Revised First Edition,* Addison-Wesley, Reading, MA, 1984.
13. Dennis JB: First Version of a Data Flow Procedure Language. *Lecture Notes in Computer Science,* 19, Springer-Verlag, Berlin, 1974, pp. 362–376.
14. Dennis JB: Dataflow supercomputer. *IEEE Computer,* Vol. 13, No. 11, Nov. 1980, pp. 48–56.
15. Dias D, Jump J: Analysis and simulation of buffered delta networks. *IEEE Trans. on Computers,* Vol. C-30, No. 4, Apr. 1981, pp. 273–282.
16. Dijkstra EW: Cooperating Sequential Processes. In Genuys F (ed): *Programming Languages.* Academic Press, NY, 1968.
17. Falkoff AD, Iverson KE, Sussenguth EH: A formal description of system/360. *IBM Syst. J.,* Vol. 3, No. 3, 1964, pp. 198–261.
18. Farmwald PM: The S-1 Mark IIA Supercomputer. In Kowalik JS (ed): *High Speed Supercomputers.* Springer-Verlag, NY, 1984.
19. Fisher JA: Very long instruction word architectures and the ELI 512. *Tenth Symposium on Computer Architecture,* Stockholm, June 1983, pp. 140–150.
20. Foster CC, Reisman EM: Percolation of code to enhance parallel dispatching and execution. *IEEE Trans. on Computers,* Vol. C-21, No. 12, Dec. 1972, pp. 1411–1415.
21. Gajski D, Padua D, Kuck D, Kuhn R: A second opinion on data flow machines and languages. *IEEE Computer,* Vol. 15, No. 2, Feb. 1982, pp. 58–69.
22. Gajski D, Lawrie D, Kuck D, Sameh A: Cedar. *COMPCON,* Spring, 1984, pp. 306–309.
23. Gannon D, Rosendale JV: Parallel Architectures for Interactive Methods on Adaptive, Block Structured Grids, In Barkoff G (ed): *Elliptic Problem Solvers,* in press.
24. Goodman J: Using cache memory to reduce processor-memory traffic. *Proc.*

Tenth International Symposium on Computer Architecture, June 1983, pp. 124–131.

25. Gottlieb A, Grishman R, Kruskal CP, et al: The NYU ultracomputer—designing an MIMD shared memory parallel computer. *IEEE Trans. on Computers,* Vol. C-32, No. 2, Feb. 1983, pp. 175–189.

26. Gottlieb A, Lubachevsky B, Rudolf L: Basic techniques for the efficient coordination of very large numbers of cooperating sequential processes. *ACM TOPLAS,* Vol. 5, No. 2, April 1983, pp. 164–189.

27. Gurd JR, Kirkham CC, Watson I: The Manchester prototype dataflow computer. *Comm. ACM,* Vol. 28, No. 1, Jan. 1985, pp. 24–52.

28. Brinch Hansen P: The programming language concurrent Pascal. *IEEE Trans. Soft. Eng.* SE-1, 2, June 1975, pp. 199–206.

29. Hoare CAR: Communicating sequential processes. *Comm. ACM,* Vol. 21, No. 8, Aug. 1978, pp. 666–677.

30. Hwang K, Su SP: Priority scheduling in event-driven dataflow computers. TR-EE 83-36, School of Electrical Engineering, Purdue University, Dec. 1983.

31. Hwang K, Briggs FA: *Computer Architecture and Parallel Processing.* McGraw-Hill, New York, 1984.

32. Kleinrock L: A continuum of time-sharing scheduling algorithms. *Proc. AFIPS, SJCC,* Vol. 36, 1970, pp. 453–458.

33. Kruskal CP, Snir M: The performance of multistage interconnection networks for multiprocessors. *IEEE Trans. on Computers,* Vol. C-32, No. 12, Dec. 1983, pp. 1091–1098.

34. Kruskal CP, Weiss A: Allocating independent subtasks on parallel processors. *Proc. International Conference on Parallel Processing,* Aug. 1984, pp. 236–240.

35. Kuck DJ: *The Structure of Computers and Computations,* Volume 1. John Wiley & Sons, New York, 1978.

36. Kuck DJ, et al: The effects of program restructuring, algorithm change, and architecture choice on program. *Proc. International Conference on Parallel Processing,* Aug. 1984, pp. 129–138.

37. Landskov D, Davidson S, Shriver B, Mallet PW: Local microcode compaction techniques. *Computing Surveys,* Vol. 12, No. 9, Sept. 1980, pp. 261–294.

38. Larson J: Multitasking on the Cray X-MP-2 multiprocessor. *IEEE Computer,* Vol. 17, No. 7, July 1984, pp. 62–69.

39. Lawrie DH: Access and alignment of data in an array processor. *IEEE Trans. on Computers,* C-24, No. 12, Dec. 1975, pp. 1145–1155.

40. Lawrie D: Memory access mechanisms in Cedar. Cedar Docu. No. 1, Center for Supercomputing R&D, University of Illinois at Urbana-Champaign, Aug. 1982.

41. May D, Taylor R: OCCAM. Unpublished paper, INMOS Limited, Whitefriars, Lewins Mead, Bristol BS1 2NP, UK, 1983.

42. Padua DA, Kuck DJ, Lawrie DL: High-speed multiprocessor and compilation techniques. *IEEE Trans. on Computers,* Vol. C-29, No. 9, Sept. 1980, pp. 763–776.

43. Peir J-K, Gajski DD: Preliminary global control unit design and its instruction set. Cedar Docu. No. 26, Center for Supercomputing R&D, University of Illinois at Urbana-Champaign, Nov. 1983.

44. Peir J-K, Gajski DD: Dataflow execution of FORTRAN loops. *Proc. First International Conference on Supercomputing Systems,* Dec. 1985.
45. Pfister GF, et al: The IBM research parallel processor prototype (RP3): Introduction and architecture. *Proc. International Conference on Parallel Processing,* Aug. 1985.
46. Pleskun AR, Davidson ES: Structured Memory Access Architecture. *Proc. International Conference on Parallel Processing,* Aug. 1983, pp. 461–471.
47. Presser L: Multiprogramming coordination. *Computing Surveys,* Vol. 7, No. 1, March 1975, pp. 21–44.
48. Rao GS: Performance Analysis of Cache Memories. *J. Assn. Compt. Mach.,* Vol. 25, July 1978, pp. 378–395.
49. Russel RM: The Cray-1 computer system. *Comm. ACM,* Vol. 21, No. 1, Jan. 1978, pp. 63–72.
50. Schwartz J: A taxonomic table of parallel computers, based on 55 designs. Ultracomputer Note #69, Courant Institute, NYU, Nov. 1983.
51. Seitz CL: The Cosmic Cube. *Comm. ACM,* Vol. 28, No. 1, Jan. 1985, pp. 22–33.
52. Smith BJ: Architecture and applications of the HEP multiprocessor computer system. Society of Photo-optical Instrumentation Engineers, Vol. 298, *Real-Time Signal Processing IV,* Aug. 1981, pp. 241–248.
53. Smith AJ: Cache memories. *ACM Computing Surveys,* Vol. 14, No. 3, Sept. 1982, pp. 473–530.
54. Treleven PC, Brownbridge DR, Hopkins RP: Data-driven and demand-driven computer architecture. *Computing Surveys,* Vol. 14, No. 1, March 1982, pp. 93–143.
55. Tucker SG: The IBM 3090 system: An overview. *IBM Systems Journal,* Vol. 25, No. 1, 1986, pp. 4–19.
56. Wilson P: OCCAM architecture eases system design—part I. Computer Design, Nov. 1983, pp. 107–115.
57. Wirth N: Modula: A language for modular multiprogramming. *Softw. Prac. Exper.,* 7, 1977, pp. 3–35.
58. Wulf W, Bell C: C.mmp—a multi-miniprocessor. *AFIPS Proc., FJCC,* Vol. 41, Part 2, 1972, pp. 765–777.
59. Yeh PCCC, Patal JH, Davidson ES: Shared cache for multiple-stream computer system. *IEEE Trans. on Computers,* Vol. C-32, No. 1, Jan. 1983, pp. 38–47.
60. Yew PC, Xu QX: Simulations and analysis for a multiprocessor system with multiprogramming. First Conference on Computers and Applications, Peking, China, June 1984.
61. Zhu C-Q, Yew PC: A synchronization scheme and its applications for large scale multiprocessor systems. *Proc. Conference on Distributed Computing Systems,* San Francisco, CA, May, 1984, pp. 486–491.

5

Parallel Processing

Thomas Schwederski
David G. Meyer
Howard Jay Siegel

5.1 Introduction

Many of today's scientific and industrial problems require enormous processing power. Examples of such computations are weather prediction, fluid dynamics studies, biomedical image processing, robot vision, plasma physics simulations, and VLSI design automation algorithms. To be able to solve these problems in a reasonable time—e.g., calculate a 24-hour weather forecast in less than 24 hours—very powerful computer systems are needed. Many efforts have been made to increase the processing speed of computers. For a long time, most speed increases were achieved by using faster components in the same basic computer structure. Vacuum tubes were replaced by discrete semiconductors, and these discrete components were replaced by integrated circuits. Core memory was replaced by integrated circuit mem-

This work was supported in part by the Air Force Office of Scientific Research under grant F49620-86-K-0006, by the Naval Research Laboratory under grant N00014-85-C-2182, and by the Rome Air Development Center under contract number F30602-83-K-0119.

ory chips. However, today's components seem to be approaching a practical speed limit. Recent developments of gallium–arsenide chips promise gate switching times in the picosecond range. At present, only superconducting elements offer faster speed, but superconducting computers are not expected to appear before mid 1990. A fundamental barrier that limits all computing speed is the velocity of light. Signals cannot propagate through a conductor faster than the speed of light—i.e., roughly 1 ft/ns. Therefore, modern high-speed CPUs tend to be very small (several cubic feet) in order to reduce the length of interconnections and consequently the propagation delay.

Because faster components alone do not satisfy the current demands for high-speed computing, other avenues are being explored. These methods utilize the fact that many computations in a program do not depend on each other and can therefore be executed simultaneously. One such approach is overlap execution or pipelining. Pipelining is used extensively in modern supercomputers like the Cray-1 and Cyber 205. (For a discussion of Cray computer systems, see Chapter 8.) These machines achieve operating speeds of a few hundred million operations per second, but even these processing rates do not always satisfy current computational requirements. Another approach utilized to increase computational speed is the use of parallel processing—i.e., the use of a collection of computers coupled in some way to do faster processing. Many ways to combine computers have been proposed and implemented. They range from multiprocessor systems, where a set of identical or different computers are interconnected, to array computers, where a large number of processors execute the same instruction on different data.

In this chapter, parallel processing systems are introduced. Following a classification of parallel processing systems, software issues are discussed. Case studies describe some of the parallel computer systems that have been proposed or built.

5.2. Classification of Parallel Computer Systems

Many attempts to classify computers have been made; one of the best known is the classification by Flynn (20), which is based on the number of concurrent instruction and data streams in a computer. An instruction stream is the sequence of instructions executed by a computer. The data stream is the sequence of data accessed to be processed by the instructions. Flynn distinguishes four classes:

- SISD   Single Instruction stream–Single Data stream
- SIMD   Single Instruction stream–Multiple Data stream
- MISD   Multiple Instruction stream–Single Data stream
- MIMD   Multiple Instruction stream–Multiple Data stream

In the following subsections these four types will be discussed in detail. (For another classification scheme of multiprocessors, see Chapter 4.)

5.2.1. SISD Machine Architecture

An SISD computer usually consists of a single processor connected to a single memory. It fetches its instructions consecutively, and fetches one data item at a time. Many standard computers fall into this class: microprocessors, minicomputers like Digital Equipment Corporation's VAX superminicomputers, and mainframes like the IBM 360/370. Many modern SISD computers are pipelined to increase computing speed.

5.2.2. SIMD Machine Architecture

An SIMD computer typically consists of a control unit, N processors, N memory modules, and an interconnection network. The control unit broadcasts instructions to the processors, and all processors that are currently active (enabled) execute the same instruction at the same time; this is the single instruction stream. Because each active processor executes the instructions on data stored in its associated memory module, a multiple data stream results. The interconnection network facilitates communication among the processors and memory modules. It is often referred to as an alignment or permutation network. There are many ways to implement such a network; for a detailed discussion of networks, see Chapter 6.

SIMD machines are well suited for exploiting the parallelism of tasks such as matrix multiplication, which involve matrix or vector data, and problem domains such as image processing, where the same operation is performed on many different picture elements (pixels). SIMD machines are sometimes referred to as array processors. Examples of SIMD machines that have been built are the Illiac IV (9), STARAN (3), and MPP (6, 7). IBM's GF11 (8) is an SIMD machine currently under construction. STARAN and MPP are overviewed in Section 5.5 of this chapter.

One way to view the physical structure of an SIMD machine is as a set of N processor/memory pairs called *processing elements* (*PEs*) interconnected by a network and fed instructions by the control unit (Figure 5.1). This configuration is called *processing-element-to-processing-element* (*PE-to-PE*) organization. The network is unidirectional and connects each PE with all or some subset of the other PEs. To move data between two PEs that are not directly connected, the data must be passed through intermediary PEs. For example, assume PE 0 is connected to PE 1, and PE 1 is connected to PE 2. To pass data from PE 0 to PE 2, PE 0 has to send its data to PE 1, and PE 1 passes them on to PE 2. The PE-to-PE configuration is used in the MPP system (6, 7). An alternative SIMD organization is the *processor-to-memory* organization. Here, the network is placed between processors

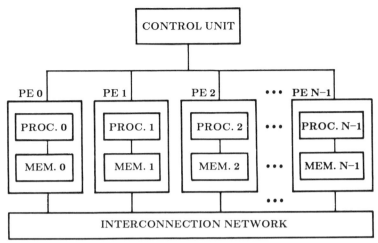

Figure 5.1 Processing-Element-to-Processing-Element SIMD machine configuration with N processing elements (PEs).

and memories as shown in Figure 5.2. The network is bidirectional because it connects both memories to processors and processors to memories. One processor can transfer data to another processor through any memory to which both are connected. To move data between processors, the sending processor writes data into a shared memory and the receiving processor reads the data from that memory. As in the PE-to-PE configuration, multiple transfers involving multiple memories and processors may be necessary for transfers between processors that share no memory.

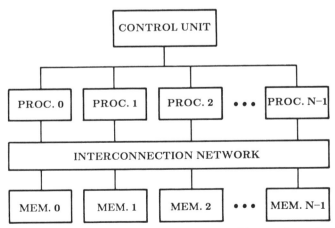

Figure 5.2 Processor-to-Memory SIMD machine configuration with N processors and N memories.

Variations of this scheme have been implemented. The STARAN processor, for example, uses a unidirectional network in a processor-to-memory configuration, as shown in Section 5.5.5.

5.2.3. MISD Machine Architecture

Here, a set of PEs works on the same data item but each PE executes a different instruction. One possible configuration is a macropipeline. Consider an MISD machine with N PEs, numbered 0 through $N - 1$. In such a configuration, the source data stream enters PE 0. PE 0 performs some operation on the data—e.g., it may multiply the data with a constant. The modified data is then passed on to the next processor, which performs a different operation—e.g., a constant may be added. This process of passing data from PE i to PE $i + 1$ continues until the result leaves PE $N - 1$.

5.2.4. MIMD Machine Architecture

MIMD machines are commonly known as multiprocessors. An MIMD machine typically consists of N processors, N memory modules, and an interconnection network. Each of the processors follows its own instructions; these are the multiple instruction streams. Each processor also fetches its own data on which it operates; thus, there are multiple data streams. In an MIMD machine, all processors operate asynchronously, which is more flexible than the lock-step execution of an SIMD machine. On the other hand, additional overhead is necessary if the processors of an MIMD machine need to be synchronized, because the synchronization needs to be done explicitly. In an SIMD system, synchronization is implicit by the lock-step operation. Because of this synchronization-cost/flexibility trade-off, some computational tasks are better suited for the SIMD mode of parallelism, while others are better suited for the MIMD mode of parallelism.

As with an SIMD machine, two basic configurations can be distinguished: the PE-to-PE architecture (see Figure 5.3), and the processor-to-memory architecture (see Figure 5.4). Communication between processors is provided by the interconnection network. Because each processor is executing its own instructions, inputs to the network arrive independently (i.e., asynchronously), in contrast to an SIMD machine, where all inputs to the network arrive at the same time.

Examples of MIMD machines that have been built are Cm* (29, 60, 61), the BBN Butterfly (14), the Cosmic Cube (51), and HEP (25). Proposed MIMD systems include the NYU Ultracomputer (24), Cedar (23), and the IBM RP3 (46). Cm* and Ultracomputer are overviewed in Section 5.5 of this chapter. The Cosmic Cube, HEP, and Cedar are discussed in Chapter 4, HEP and RP3 are discussed in Chapter 8.

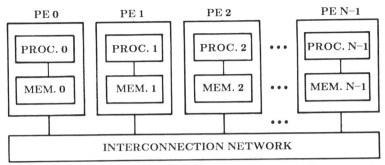

Figure 5.3 Processing-Element-to-Processing-Element MIMD machine configuration with N processing elements (PEs).

5.2.5. Multiple-SIMD Machine (MSIMD) Architecture

An MSIMD machine is a parallel computer that can be dynamically reconfigured to operate as one or more independent virtual SIMD machines of various sizes. Similar to a standard SIMD machine, the processors, memories, and interconnection network can be configured in various ways. Figure 5.5 depicts a general model of an MSIMD machine with a PE-to-PE structure. The control units can be assigned to various PEs by setting the switch appropriately.

The MSIMD concept has various advantages over the standard SIMD machine. For example, faults can be detected by running the same program on more than one virtual machine and comparing the results, and fault tolerance is achieved by not using PEs that are known to be faulty. Multiple users can use the system at the same time; each user is assigned one virtual machine that runs programs independently of the other users. The machine is more efficient because a task that requires only a few PEs need not leave all others idle. Proposed MSIMD systems are MAP (43, 44) and the original design for the Illiac IV (1, 9).

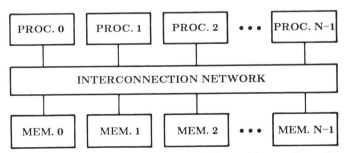

Figure 5.4 Processor-to-Memory MIMD machine configuration with N processors and N memories.

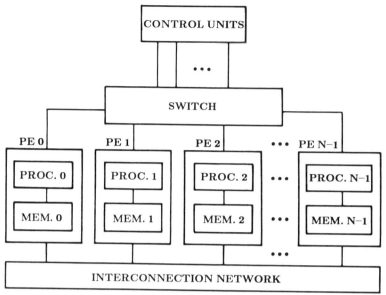

Figure 5.5 General model of a Multiple-SIMD system.

5.2.6. Partitionable-SIMD/MIMD Machine Architecture

A *partitionable-SIMD/MIMD system* is a parallel computer that can be dynamically reconfigured to operate as one or more independent SIMD and/or MIMD machines. Such a system is very similar to an MSIMD machine; it differs in that its PEs can follow not only an instruction stream broadcast by a control unit, but also their own individual instruction stream. Thus, the block diagram of the MSIMD machine also applies to the partitionable-SIMD/MIMD system. Like the MSIMD machines, the processors, memory, and interconnection network can be partitioned to form independent virtual machines. Each virtual machine can work in SIMD or in MIMD mode.

Examples of partionable-SIMD/MIMD systems are PASM (52), TRAC (50), DCA (30), and PM4 (10). PASM and TRAC, both of which are in the prototype stage, are described in Section 5.5.

5.2.7. Chapter Overview

In this chapter, we will concentrate on SIMD and MIMD parallelism. Other approaches to parallel/distributed processing are discussed elsewhere in this book, and in books such as (2, 27, 28, 31, 57, 59). Software problems associated with SIMD and MIMD systems will be discussed in Section 5.3. Section 5.4 provides examples of parallel algorithms. Two MIMD systems (Cm* and Ultracomputer), two SIMD systems (STARAN and MPP), and two partitionable-SIMD/MIMD systems (PASM and TRAC) will be overviewed in Section 5.5.

5.3. Languages for Parallel Processing

5.3.1. Implicit Programming

Parallel computers can be programmed implicitly or explicitly. Implicit programming is done by using an intelligent, parallelizing compiler that accepts programs written in a conventional programming language like FORTRAN or ALGOL. The compiler then analyzes the program and determines which statements can be executed in parallel. For example, consider a program to add vectors **A** and **B**:

FOR $i = 1$ **TO** N **DO** C$[i] := $ A$[i] + $ B$[i]$;

It is obvious that the addition statements are independent of each other, and therefore all additions can be executed in parallel on N processors. This example is typical of the operations performed by a parallelizing compiler. Because the order in which two statements I and J are executed in a sequential program is not preserved if I and J are executed in parallel, three conditions must be met if I and J are to be parallelized. Statement I must not write to locations that statement J reads, and vice versa, and statement I and J must not write to the same location if that location is used by a later statement. Further discussions on parallelism detection can be found in Chapters 4 and 8.

In addition to parallelizing a program, the compiler must allocate the proper hardware to run the program. For example, in an MIMD computer the compiler must determine the optimum number of processors needed for the execution of the program. The compiler also has to allocate data in memory such that the parallel program executes efficiently and delays incurred from data transfers are minimized. This means that in a machine with PE-to-PE organization, all or most of the data a processor needs during program execution should be allocated in its own memory. In the processor-to-memory organization, data should be allocated such that processors get their data from different memory modules because simultaneous accesses to a single shared memory unit by two or more processors can only be served sequentially and will therefore result in a longer access time.

5.3.2. Languages for MIMD Processing

If a parallel machine is programmed explicitly, the programmer must have available a programming language that allows the expression of parallelism in the program. If an MIMD computer is the target machine, a standard assembly or high-level language like Pascal, C, or FORTRAN can be used for programming by adding operating system calls for interprocess communication and synchronization. The programmer has to decide which processor handles what particular subtask, and write the appropriate programs. The programs are then loaded into the processors needed for the task, and the operating system of the machine starts the task and coordinates activities. Many applications, especially in image processing, require a set of processors that all execute the same program. An example is an image processing algorithm in which each processor searches for features in a part of the image. In this case, each processor has its own set of data, but an identical program is executed by each processor. Only one program has to be coded, independent of the number of processors. Depending on the task, this may involve just MIMD operations, just SIMD operations, or both.

If the number of processors varies during task execution, the programming language has to be expanded to include special statements to allocate and deallocate processors. Conway (13) proposed the use of FORK and JOIN instructions. Whenever a FORK is encountered, a new process is created that proceeds independently from the old one. The old and the new processes can be run on different processors. If no processor is available, the new process must be queued until a processor becomes available. If multiprogramming capability is available, two or more processes can be run on the same processor in a time sliced fashion.

Conway proposed three kinds of FORK: FORK A, J, K; FORK A, J; and FORK A. In this implementation, a counter is necessary to keep track of the number of concurrent processes. FORK A creates a new process; the old process continues to execute the instruction following the FORK, and the new process starts at instruction A. The FORK A, J, K instruction sets a counter in memory location J to the value K, then executes FORK A. The programmer is responsible for matching the number of FORKS in the program with the count specified in the FORK A, J, K, because the FORK A alone does not affect the counter. FORK A, J increments counter J by one, then executes a FORK A. This instruction is needed if the decision to fork is made at runtime.

The JOIN statement merges concurrent instruction streams. When a JOIN J is encountered, the counter at location J is decremented. The process that decrements the counter to zero executes the statements following the JOIN; all other processes are terminated, and the processors that ran them are released and become available for other computations.

Figure 5.6 illustrates the use of the three different FORK and the JOIN statements. Process 1 executes a FORK $A, 100, 3$, which sets the counter in memory location 100 to 3 and starts a concurrent process (Process 2). Then Process 1 executes a FORK $B, 100$, which increments the counter in location 100 by one and starts another process, Process 3. Meanwhile, Pro-

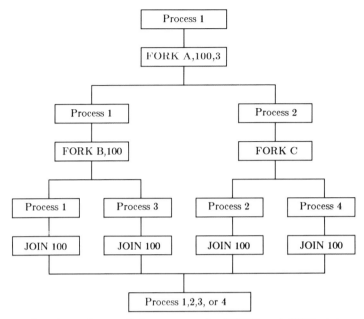

Figure 5.6 Flowchart of a parallel program using FORK and JOIN statements.

cess 2 executes a FORK *C*, generating a fourth process, Process 4. Thus, four concurrent processes are now active. When a process encounters a JOIN 100, it decrements the counter. The process continues if the counter reaches 0, otherwise it ceases. FORK and JOIN are also useful for process synchronization; only after all forked processes have completed their program does the main program continue—this is synchronization.

A more structured way to establish parallel subtasks than the FORK and JOIN instructions was proposed by Dijkstra (16): **parbegin** *S*1; *S*2; . . . *Sn*; defines *S*1 through *Sn* as statements (processes) that can be executed in parallel. The parallel execution is ended when a **parend** is found. Only after all processors executing the parallel statements have reached their **parend** are statements followed the **parend** executed. A program that needs to run two processes in parallel might have the following structure:

parbegin
process1 : **begin**
   statements for process 1
   end;
process2 : **begin**
   statements for process 2
   end;
parend

Another important synchronization mechanism is semaphores. A semaphore S is a shared variable that is accessible only through the operating system calls SIGNAL(S) and WAIT(S). A WAIT(S) reads the value of S and sets S to 1 in a single indivisible operation. If the value of S was found to be 0, the process executing the WAIT can continue. If the value was 1, the process is suspended temporarily. A SIGNAL(S) resets S to 0 and reactivates all processes that have executed a WAIT(S) but were suspended. These processes all execute another WAIT(S); only the first process to do so will read a value of 0 for S and therefore continue; all other processes read a 1 and are suspended again. Semaphores are useful in single CPU, multitasking systems, where they are used for synchronization of processes running in a timesliced mode, and in multiprocessors, where each process runs on a different processor.

Semaphores can be implemented by the test-and-set instruction available in many computers. If a test-and-set is executed on memory location V, a 1 is returned if location V is already set; otherwise a 0 is returned and location V is set to 1. The operation is indivisible. WAIT(X) is accomplished by a test-and-set on X. If X is 1, the process is suspended. If X is 0, the process sets the semaphore to 1 and execution can continue. SIGNAL(X) is performed by simply setting the value of X to 0. In most operating systems, this write operation will cause an interrupt so that the waiting process can resume execution.

Now consider how WAIT(S) and SIGNAL(S) can be used for processor synchronization. Assume processor A runs a program that at some time needs a result that a program running on processor B produces. Thus, A needs to be synchronized with B when it needs B's result. This is accomplished by first allocating a semaphore S with a value of 1. Immediately before A needs the result from B, A executes a WAIT(S), whereas B executes a SIGNAL(S) immediately after it has calculated the result required by A. If B had already computed the result when A executes its WAIT(S), the value of S was reset to 0 by B's SIGNAL(S). Thus, B can immediately use the result and can continue. If, however, B's result was not yet available, A's WAIT(S) would find the value of S to be 1. A would be suspended and reactivated only after B had executed the SIGNAL(S). In this way, synchronization is achieved.

These examples demonstrate two ways of how semaphores can be used. Further information can be found in (26). Another view of synchronization can be found in Chapter 4.

5.3.3. Languages for SIMD Processing

Parallelism of an SIMD computer cannot be expressed explicitly in any conventional programming language, but extensions of existing high-level languages have been proposed—e.g., (11, 12, 35, 37, 42, 45, 48, 49, 58, 63). Such extensions can be machine-dependent or machine-independent.

An example of a machine-dependent language is Glypnir (37), which was specifically developed for the Illiac IV computer and is based on Algol 60. Illiac IV was an SIMD machine with 64 PEs, designed in the 1960s (1, 9). Its fixed interconnection network connects PE i to PEs $i + 1$, $i - 1$, $i + 8$, $i - 8$, all modulo 64, providing a mesh-type interconnection. In Glypnir, variables for PEs and for the control unit can be defined. A PE variable has an element in every PE and is called a super word (*sword*), which always has 64 elements. For example, the statement

PE REAL A, B

declares the variables A and B to be swords.

PE REAL $C(20)$

declares C to be an array of 20 elements in each of the PEs. By using Boolean expressions which include PE variables, PEs can be selectively enabled or disabled. Consider, for example, the statement

if ⟨Boolean expression⟩ **then**
⟨statement1⟩
else
⟨statement2⟩

The Boolean expression will be evaluated in all processors, and the processors finding a true value execute statement1. The others do not participate in the instruction stream broadcast for statement1 but execute only statement2.

Actus (45), a language based on Pascal, is an example of a machine-independent language. It was designed for SIMD machines of arbitrary size. A variable can be declared as parallel, and the extent of parallelism must be specified for each parallel variable. In the range specification of a parallel variable declaration, a colon denotes that a dimension is to be accessed in parallel. For example,

var *array1:* **array** [*1:m, 1..n*] **of** *integer*

declares an array of m by n elements; m elements can be accessed at a time if they are placed in different processors. The underlying operating system takes care of reconfiguring the computer into a machine that can handle the specified parallel variable. **if, case, while,** and **for** statements are expanded for use with parallel variables. Alignment operators are also provided. For example, a **shift** operator moves data within the declared range of parallelism, e.g., [l:m]; a **rotate** shifts data circularly with respect to the extent of parallelism, e.g., [l:m]. Shift and rotate are implemented by using the processor interconnection network.

A programming language to handle both the MIMD and SIMD modes of operation is proposed in (35). It is based on the C programming language. The SIMD features include declarations of parallel variables and functions; an indexing scheme to access and manipulate parallel variables; expressions involving parallel variables; extended control structures using parallel variables as control variables; and functions for PE allocation, data alignment, and I/O. The language supports simple parallel data types like scalars and arrays as well as structured data. For example,

```
parallel [N] int a;
parallel [N] char line[MAXLINE];
struct node {
   char *word; struct node *next;
} parallel [N] nodespace[100], *head;
```

declares, for each of N virtual processors, an integer "a," an array of MAX-LINE characters, an array of 100 nodes, and a node pointer. Indexing along the parallel dimension can be done by using selectors; they enable or disable subsets of the N virtual processors. Functions to send data between processors are provided. They are not part of the language, but are library routines, thus avoiding machine dependence. To facilitate MIMD mode, a few new features and keywords are added, supporting **parbegin, parend,** shared data, synchronization, etc. A preprocessor recognizes these constructs and translates the parallel algorithm into a standard serial C program, which can then be compiled by a standard C compiler and loaded into the program memories of the processors of the MIMD machine.

One of the ways this language implements selectors is based on the use of a *PE address masking* scheme (55). This scheme uses an $n = \log_2 N$-position mask to specify which of the N PEs will be activated. Each position of the mask will either contain a 0, 1, or X ("don't care"), and the only PEs that will be active are those whose addresses match the mask: 0 matches 0, 1 matches 1, and either 0 or 1 matches X. Square brackets denote a mask, superscripts are used as repetition factors. For example, "$[X^{n-1}0]$" activates all even numbered PEs and "$[0^{n-i}X^i]$" activates PEs 0 to $2^i - 1$. A *negative PE address mask* is similar to a regular PE address mask, except that it activates all those PEs that do not match the mask. Negative PE address masks are prefixed with a minus sign to distinguish them from regular PE address masks. For example, for $N = 8$, "$[-0X1]$" activates all PEs except 1 and 3.

5.4. Examples of Parallel Algorithms

As mentioned in the previous section, programming of parallel computer systems can be done explicitly or implicitly. Implicit programming will not be discussed here because only the compiler takes the parallelizing action. Instead, explicit programming examples will be emphasized to illustrate the techniques of restructuring a problem to make it suitable for parallel execution. In this section, SIMD algorithms, associative processing algorithms, and SIMD/MIMD algorithms will be presented.

5.4.1. SIMD Algorithms

As an example of a simple algorithm, consider the *smoothing of an image* (52). The algorithm described here smooths a gray level input image. The aglorithm has I as an input image and S as an output image. Assume both I and S contain 512-by-512 *pixels* (picture elements) for a total of 512^2 pixels each. Each point of I is an 8-bit unsigned integer representing one of 256 gray levels. The gray level of each pixel indicates how "dark" that pixel is, where 0 means white and 255 means black. Each point in the smoothed image, $S(i, j)$, is the average of the gray levels of $I(i, j)$ and its eight nearest neighbors, $I(i - 1, j - 1)$, $I(i - 1, j)$, $I(i - 1, j + 1)$, $I(i, j - 1)$, $I(i, j + 1)$, $I(i + 1, j - 1)$, $I(i + 1, j)$, $I(i + 1, j + 1)$. The top, bottom, left, and right edge pixels of S are set to 0 because their corresponding pixels in I do not have eight adjacent neighbors.

Consider how this could be implemented on an SIMD machine with $N = 1024$ PEs, logically arranged as an array of 32-by-32 PEs as shown in Figure 5.7. Each PE stores a 16-by-16 subimage block of the 512-by-512 image I. Specifically, PE 0 stores the pixels in columns 0 to 15 of rows 0 to 15, PE 1 stores the pixels in columns 16 to 31 of rows 0 to 15, and so on. Each PE smooths its own subimage, with all PEs doing this simultaneously. At the edges of each 16-by-16 subimage, data must be transmitted between

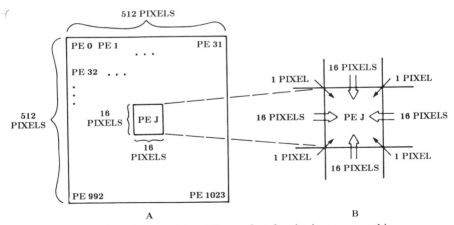

Figure 5.7 Data allocation and inter-PE transfers for the image smoothing algorithm.

PEs in order to calculate the smoothed value. The necessary data transfers are shown for PE J in Figure 5.7. Transfers between different PEs can occur simultaneously—e.g., when PE $J - 1$ sends its upper right corner pixel to PE J, PE J can send its upper right corner pixel to PE $J + 1$, PE $J + 1$ can send its upper right corner pixel to PE $J + 2$, etc.

To perform a smoothing operation on a 512-by-512 image by the parallel smoothing of 1024 subimage blocks of size 16-by-16, $16^2 = 256$ parallel smoothing operations are performed. As described, the neighbors of the subimage edge pixels must be transferred in from adjacent PEs. The total number of parallel data element transfers needed is $(4 \times 16) + 4 = 68$, 16 for each of the top, bottom, left side, and right side edges, and 4 for the corners (see Figure 5.7). The corresponding serial algorithm needs no data transfers between PEs, but $512^2 = 262,144$ smoothing calculations must be performed. If no data transfers were needed, the parallel algorithm would be faster than the serial algorithm by a factor of $262,144/256 = 1024 = N$. If the inter-PE data transfer time is included and it is assumed that each parallel data transfer requires, at most, as much time as one smoothing operation, the time factor improvement is $262,144/324 = 809$. The inter-PE transfer time approximation is conservative. Thus, the overhead of the 68 inter-PE transfers that must be performed in the SIMD machine is negligible compared with the reduction in smoothing operations from 262,144 to 256.

As mentioned, the edge pixels of S are not smoothed. This creates an additional (although negligible) overhead that is to disable the appropriate PEs when the zero values are stored for these edge pixels.

The method of *recursive doubling* is a technique used to speed up parallel computations in a manner that is not straightforward. Consider the problem of summing up all elements of a vector. In a serial computer, a variable would be initialized to the value of the first element of the vector, and all subsequent elements would be added to this variable. If the vector contained N elements, $N - 1$ additions would be required. Assume that on a parallel computer the vector is distributed among processors—i.e., each of N processors holds one element. If the serial method were used on the parallel machine, one processor would accumulate the result, and all other processors would send their element values to this processor. Clearly, this still requires $N - 1$ additions, all performed by the accumulating processor. Thus, no speedup is achieved by using a parallel machine.

The recursive doubling procedure is illustrated in Figure 5.8. Assume that N is a power of 2; in Figure 5.8, $N = 8$. In the first step, all odd-numbered PEs (i.e., 1, 3, 5, 7) send their vector element to an even-numbered PE (i.e., 1 to 0, 3 to 2, etc.). All even-numbered PEs then add the value they received to their own vector element, forming $N/2 (= 4)$ partial results. The odd-numbered PEs do not participate and are disabled. In the next step, this procedure is repeated. PE 2 forwards its partial result to PE 0, while PE 6 sends its result to PE 4. PEs 0 and 4 add the new value to their respective

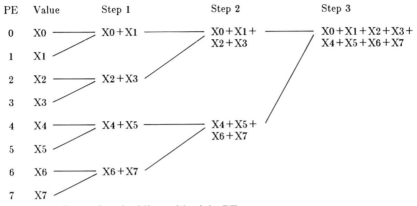

Figure 5.8 Recursive doubling with eight PEs.

partial results, and all other PEs are disabled. In the last step, PE 4 sends its partial result to PE 0. PE 0 adds this value to its own partial result, and the sum is found.

The overall procedure required three transfers and three additions. The example can be expanded to higher values of N. For N a power of 2, $\log_2 N$ additions and data transfer steps are required. This is a significant improvement over the serial algorithm.

Examples of more complex SIMD algorithms for image and speech processing include (28a, 33, 53, 64, 65, 66).

5.4.2. Associative Processing

In this section, associate processing, a special case of SIMD processing, will be introduced. An associative processor achieves its capabilities through the use of a *Content Addressable Memory* (*CAM*). Such a memory is not addressed like a standard random access memory (RAM). Instead, the "address" to the CAM is a value, and all CAM cells that contain this value in a particular field will set a flag indicating that their content matches the input value. A cell may be, for example, 1K bits long. Obviously, only part of the cell should be matched because otherwise no information apart from the already known input value could be provided by the matching cell. This basic CAM operation is illustrated in Figure 5.9.

Assume the match register is initially reset to all zeroes. The CAM memory array contains some information about employees of a company— i.e., the employee name, his or her salary, and the time employed. Each cell could of course contain more information fields than those shown here. If all employees whose salary is higher than $2000 are to be found, a comparand is presented to the memory cells that contains "$2000" in the salary field and "dont't care" elements (represented as X) in all other fields. A

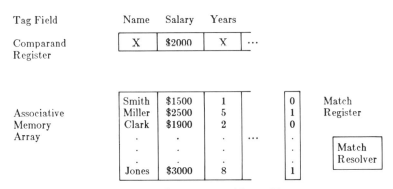

Figure 5.9 Basic operation of a content addressable memory.

controller (not illustrated here) must specify the operation "greater than" to the memory cells; all cells will then compare the salary field of the comparand with their own salary value simultaneously. If a salary higher than $2000 is found, a match bit in the match register will be set to 1; thus, all persons with a salary higher than $2000 will have been found in a single CAM step. If all salaries between $2000 and $3000 are to be found, two steps are necessary. The first step is the one described, and all persons with their salary higher than $2000 are found. To find all persons in the desired range, only those cells that have already found a match should participate in the search for salaries less than $3000. It is therefore desirable that the match register can also be used to select a subset of cells to participate in the operation, making searches like this possible.

The hardware structure is shown in Figure 5.10. All information is encoded in binary. Thus, all fields of the memory array can now be represented as a homogeneous block of memory bits. The rows of this array hold the information records—e.g., the information about the employee as in the earlier example. Thus, each element of a column of the array has the same meaning—e.g., the least significant bit of the employee's salary. The value with which the content of the memory cells is to be compared is written into one or more fields of the comparand register. The mask register holds a 0 if the value of the bit column is to be ignored and a 1 if the bit column is to participate in the operation—i.e., the mask register selects the fields to be used for the search. If a match is found during the operation, the match register bit is set to 1.

Some operations, such as printing of all matching names, necessitate a sequential reading of values. If there is more than one match, the information must be retrieved row by row. A match resolver accomplishes this task by selecting one of the matching rows for retrieval, usually the "first" (i.e., topmost) match. The corresponding match register bit is reset to 0 after the retrieval, then the resolver will select the second element, etc.

Writing to an associative memory is done in a fashion similar to reading.

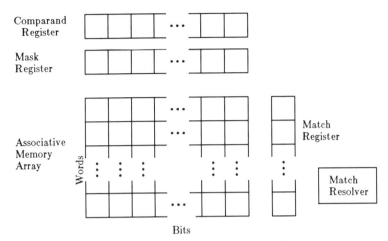

Figure 5.10 Hardware organization of a content addressable memory.

First, some cell is selected for writing by matching it with some comparand, the match resolver selects one specific cell, and the appropriate word is then written into the selected cell. The mask register may be used during the write operation to modify only part of the cell—e.g., just change the salary of an employee. It is also possible to write to all cells that match the comparand simultaneously.

Searches, such as the one described, and arithmetic operations are usually implemented as a series of more primitive hardware operations. A simple example is the addition of 1 to a 16-bit integer in each CAM cell. Let B denote a 16-bit integer field in all CAM cells—i.e., each cell has its own B field value. Let B_j denote bit j of integer B. C denotes a 1-bit carry bit field in each CAM cell. Figure 5.11 illustrates the algorithm to add 1 to each B. The carry bit C is initially set to 1. Then each bit position of the integer is examined in the main loop. If the carry in combination with the integer bit requires a change, this change is performed by a write operation until all bit positions of the integer have been examined. The comparisons of the previous example—e.g., the test for greater then $2000—are also performed by a series of bit equality matches.

This algorithm shows the performance advantage CAMs algorithms have over sequential computers. If there are N integers stored in N CAM cells, each integer with b bits, the time to add 1 to each of the N integers is proportional to b and independent of N. In a sequential computer, the time to execute the algorithm will be proportional to N and independent of b. Thus, in general, if N is larger than b, the CAM will operate faster.

Two basic associative memory structures can be distinguished. A *bit-parallel* CAM performs the search operations in parallel—i.e., an x-bit field match for all words will take a single CAM cycle. This requires that each

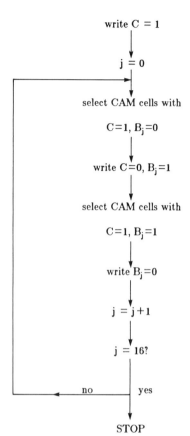

write C = 1

j = 0

select CAM cells with

C=1, B$_j$=0

write C=0, B$_j$=1

select CAM cells with

C=1, B$_j$=1

write B$_j$=0

j = j+1

j = 16?

no   yes

STOP

Figure 5.11 CAM algorithm to add 1 to an integer in all CAM cells.

bit cell of the memory array has the appropriate circuitry necessary for the search operations associated with it. Large bit-parallel memories are very complex and expensive, and are thus not widely used. With today's advanced integrated circuit technology, large integrated bit-parallel CAMs may soon be seen. The bit-parallel organization contrasts with the *bit-serial* CAM as follows. Here, a match is performed one bit at a time: if 20 bits are to be matched, 20 memory cycles are needed. During each of the cycles, one bit slice is compared with the appropriate bit in the comparand register. Bit serial CAMs are slower than their bit-parallel counterparts, but they are much cheaper; in fact, they can be built from standard RAM, as shown in the discussion of the STARAN computer in Section 5.5. For a more detailed description of CAMs and their capabilities, see (21).

5.4.3. SIMD/MIMD Algorithms

Consider an SIMD/MIMD parallel implementation of *contour extraction* (34, 62). A contour in an image is the boundary of some feature of the image.

Two algorithms from a contour extraction task are *edge-guided thresholding* (*EGT*) and *contour tracing*. The EGT algorithm is used to determine a set of optimal thresholds for quantizing the image—i.e., translating each pixel from a gray level value to either black (1) or white (0) (41). The contour tracing algorithm uses the set of thresholds to segment the image and trace the contours. It is assumed that the image to be processed is distributed among the PEs as in the smoothing example.

The EGT algorithm consists of three major steps. First, the Sobel edge operator (17) is used to generate a "Sobel-image" in which gray levels indicate the magnitude of the gradient. The magnitude of the gradient represents the amount of change in the gray level of the original image from one pixel to the next. A figure of merit that indicates how well a given threshold gray level matches edges in the edge image is then computed for every possible threshold. Finally, the maximum value of the figure of merit function is chosen to determine the threshold level. This is done for each PE's subimage independently. Thus, the threshold levels may differ from one subimage to the next. The window-based Sobel operator calculations and inter-PE communications used in the SIMD EGT algorithm are very similar to those discussed earlier for the image smoothing algorithm.

The MIMD contour tracing algorithm has two phases. In Phase I, PEs segment their subimages based on the threshold value each calculated using the EGT algorithm—i.e., each PE converts all pixels of its subimage from gray level values to either black or white. Within each subimage, all contours (collections of connected black pixels) are traced. Some will be closed (complete), others will extend into neighboring subimages (partial). In Phase II, partial contours traced during Phase I are connected.

In Phase I, there is no PE-to-PE communication. Each PE creates a segmented subimage for a particular threshold T by assigning a value of 1 to subimage pixels having a gray level greater than or equal to T, and a value of 0 to the others. Contour tracing starts with each PE scanning the rows of its segmented subimage, beginning with the first pixel of the top row. Scanning stops when a start point of a new contour is found. A start point is a pixel with a value 1 that has a 0-valued neighbor to either or both sides. Contours are traced in either a clockwise or counterclockwise direction and the Freeman direction codes (22) of the "chain" of pixels are recorded. When a pixel from an adjacent subimage is required in order to determine the next direction of the contour, a point of indecision is reached. Such a point is recorded as an end point, and the algorithm returns to the start point to trace the contour in the opposite direction until another point of indecision is reached. Closed contours that are contained within a subimage are traced completely during Phase I.

In Phase II, each PE attempts to connect its partial contours to those located in neighboring PEs. PEs consider each partial contour's end points in turn and try to find a possible extending contour in a neighboring PE. Once such an extended contour is found, the process is repeated, if necessary, by following the contour to the next PE until the contour is closed or cannot be extended. A protocol employing semaphores is necessary to prevent more than one PE from trying to use the same partial contour as an extending contour at the same time. Phase II is complete when all contours have been connected.

The contour extraction demonstrates the advantages of an SIMD/MIMD machine over a pure SIMD machine or pure MIMD machine. The EGT algorithm can be more efficiently executed in SIMD mode, while the tracing algorithm can be more efficiently executed in MIMD mode. Thus, the ability of the PE to operate in either SIMD or MIMD mode allows the most appropriate type of parallelism to be employed by each algorithm in the task.

5.5 Case Studies of Parallel Processing Systems

5.5.1. Introduction

In this section, examples of SIMD and MIMD machines are presented. Brief case studies overviewing six parallel processing systems that have been built or have prototypes under development are given. Different approaches to processor design, processor-to-processor and processor-to-memory communication, and system organization are demonstrated.

5.5.2. The Cm∗ Multiprocessor

The Cm∗ computer was built at Carnegie-Mellon University in the mid-1970s (29, 60, 61). Cm∗ is a shared memory multicomputer consisting of a set of computer modules (*Cm*); each Cm has its own memory and can access the memories of all other Cms through a two-level shared bus system. To provide a distinct address for all memory cells in the system, all memories are part of one large address space of 2^{28} bytes.

The basic Cm∗ block diagram is shown in Figure 5.12. Each Cm in this diagram consists of a commercial LSI-11 microcomputer CPU, a private memory, I/O devices and a *Slocal*. Groups of up to 14 Cms are interconnected through a *Map Bus*. The Slocal determines whether a bus request issued by the CPU is destined for the local memory or for memory in a different Cm (which must be sent to the Map Bus) and routes the request accordingly. It also accepts memory requests from the Map Bus and passes the result of the reference back to the Map Bus. The Map Bus is controlled by the *Kmap* that also routes memory accesses to Cms outside the local group if needed. The group of Cms, the map bus, and the Kmap make up a *cluster*. Clusters are connected by intercluster buses.

A detailed picture of the Kmap is shown in Figure 5.13. The Kmap consists of a *Kbus* that arbitrates and controls the Map Bus, the *Pmap* that

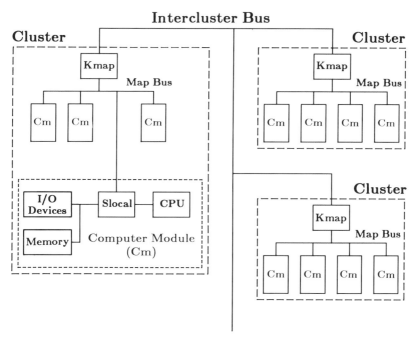

Figure 5.12 Block diagram of a simple 3 cluster Cm* system.

maps the CPU addresses into the 2^{28}-word total address space and vice versa, and the *Linc,* the interface to the intercluster buses.

The Kmap is responsible for handling intracluster and intercluster references. In an intracluster reference, a Cm accesses a memory in the cluster the Cm belongs to, and in an intercluster access, the Cm reference is routed to another cluster. Consider an intracluster read operation. The source Cm issues a memory request, which is received by the Kbus. The Kbus places the request in the run queue, where it is read by the Pmap. The Pmap performs an address translation and places the translated address in the out queue. The Kbus reads the translated address and places it onto the Map Bus, thus forwarding it to the destination Cm. There the Slocal performs the required memory access. The destination Cm then issues a return request to the Kbus, and the Kbus completes the intracluster reference by strobing the data into the source Cm. A write is different in that the data is forwarded with the address, and an acknowledge is passed back instead of the data.

An intercluster reference is more complex. Consider an intercluster read. When the source Cm has issued an intercluster request, the Kbus latches the destination address and places it into the run queue. The Pmap reads the queue, translates the address, and places the new address into one of the Port Send Queues depending on which intercluster bus is used. The Linc reads the Port Send Queue and places the request onto the appropriate

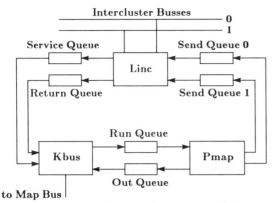

Figure 5.13 Block diagram of the Kmap of Cm∗.

intercluster bus. Because an intercluster memory reference takes up to 20 μs, it is not efficient to start a transaction, then wait for the return to arrive. Instead, the Kmap suspends the current access until a return message is received. The information necessary to reactivate the access is stored in the Pmap.

At the destination Kmap, the intercluster request is received by the Linc and is placed into the Service Queue. This queue is read by the Kbus, which translates the address via the Run Queue, Pmap, and Out Queue. The appropriate memory access is then performed at the destination Cm. The return message (which includes the data) is routed back to the source cluster via the Kbus, Run Queue, Pmap, Port Send Queue, and Linc. At the source cluster, the Linc receives the return message and places it into the Return Queue. The Kbus reads the message from this queue, and places it into the Run Queue. The Pmap then reactivates the access, places the necessary information into the Out Queue, and the Kbus strobes the data into the appropriate memory location, thus completing the intercluster reference. As with intracluster references, a write is different in that the data is forwarded with the address, and an acknowledge is passed back instead of the data.

As seen from this discussion, a memory reference can either be local, intracluster, or intercluster. Because of the rather slow access time to non-local memories, performance of the system degrades unless most of the references are local, especially if many Cms are grouped in a cluster. For example, if all memory references are local, performance increases approximately linearly with the number of processors in a cluster, as could be expected. If no intercluster references are executed, and 40% of the references are inter-Cm references, the performance of a cluster with 16 Cms is only approximately twice as high as a cluster with 4 Cms. This is a rather dramatic decrease in performance, and clearly shows that shared bus systems have only limited application domains. In this limited domain of programs with mostly local references, a system like Cm* has the advantage of easy expandability (Cms can be added to clusters, and new clusters can be added to the system) and low cost (most components like CPU, memory and I/O are commercial products).

5.5.3. The NYU Ultracomputer

The NYU Ultracomputer is a proposed design of a large-scale shared memory MIMD machine (18, 24). It could have as many as 4096 processors connected to 4096 memories through a multistage cube interconnection network; thus, the basic Ultracomputer configuration is of the processor-to-memory type. One of the most important features of the Ultracomputer is the fetch-and-add instruction, denoted F&A (V, e), which provides a simple and efficient way for processor synchronization and is supported by hardware. V is an integer variable and e is an integer expression. The execution of an F&A instruction returns the old value of V and adds to V the value of e. The instruction is indivisible—i.e., while the F&A operation is being performed on V by one processor, no other processor can access V. If two processors A and B try to execute a F&A operation on the same variable at the same time, the effect will be as if one processor preceded the other in time. For example, processor A can receive the old value of V and V will be incremented by the value of e of processor A. Processor B will then receive the new value of V, and V is incremented by the value of e of processor B.

The F&A operation can be used to solve a wide variety of synchronization problems; the following example illustrates its use. Suppose N processors are to be used to each perform a complex operation on an N element array—e.g., calculate the tangent. The first task is to associate one processor with each of the N array elements. This is easily accomplished by initializing a shared variable $V1$ to 0, then having each of the N processors execute an F&A $(V1, 1)$. Each processor will receive a distinct value for $V1$ in the range 0 to $N - 1$; thus, each processor knows the array element it is supposed to handle. Only after all processors have completed their task, can processing that utilizes the result of the computations resume. To ensure this, a second shared variable is set to $N - 1$ before the parallel execution starts. After a processor has completed its task, it executes an F&A $(V2, -1)$. If the returned value is not 0, other processors are still working on their assigned array element. Therefore, the processor simply terminates working on this problem and can be reassigned to other processes. The processor that receives a value of 0 is the last one to complete the task, and this processor continues execution of the program. The example shows similarities between the F&A operation and the FORK and JOIN commands described earlier in this chapter.

The basic fetch-and-add operation can be extended to a fetch-and-ϕ

operation, where ϕ is some function. Here, the old value of V is fetched and replaced by the value of $\phi(V, e)$. An example is the fetch-and-or operation. The value of a variable is fetched, and the value is "or"ed with e. If V and e are binary quantities with $e = 1$, the operation is identical to the previously described test-and-set operation.

If ϕ is the function f_1, such that $f_1(V, e) = V$, a regular load operation is executed. The value of e is not needed and therefore need not be forwarded to the fetch-and-ϕ hardware. A normal store can be accomplished by using the function $f_2(V, e) = e$ and ignoring the value passed back. Thus, a computer providing only fetch-and-ϕ operations can execute all standard memory accesses.

The basic structure of the Ultracomputer is illustrated in Figure 5.14. The N processors are not necessarily identical as in many other designs; at least some of them could be special purpose machines for FFT computations or matrix multiplications, or they could be I/O processors interfacing the system with the outside world. Because of the large number of processors (up to 4096), most of them would very likely be identical one-chip processors with some local memory (cache). The processors interface to the interconnection network through a processor network interface (PNI), and the network is connected to each of the N memories through a memory network interface (MNI).

Much of the processing power of the Ultracomputer originates from the sophisticated interconnection network. The network design is a message-switched multistage omega network that also supports F&A operations and can be expanded to support fetch-and-ϕ. The omega network is a member of the multistage cube family of networks that is described in Chapter 6. The network has $\log_2 N$ interconnected stages, where each stage consists of

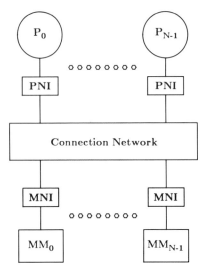

Figure 5.14 Block diagram of the NYU Ultracomputer. (Grajski D, Lawrie D, Kuck D, Sameh S: Cedar. *IEEE Computer Society Spring COMPCON 84*, Feb. 1984, pp. 306–309. © 1984 IEEE.)

$N/2$ 2-input, 2-output switches called *interchange boxes*. By connecting a switch's inputs and output, paths through the network can be established. In this chapter, only the implications of the message switching and the F&A hardware will be discussed.

A message-switched network contrasts with a circuit-switched network in the following manner. *Circuit switching* implies the establishing of a complete path between the source (i.e., the processor) and the destination (i.e., the memory). Once such a path is established, subsequent transfers along the path can be accomplished efficiently at high speed. Problems arise, however, from the possibility of blocking (a path might not be possible because part of the path is used by another, already established path). A *packet-switched* network, often referred to as *message-switched*, does not establish a complete path from source to destination. Instead, data and routing information are collected into a packet, and this packet makes its way from stage to stage, releasing links and interchange boxes immediately after using them. Thus, a packet uses only one interchange box at a time. Because the packets are passed from stage to stage, the travel time of a packet is longer than a transfer along the direct connection in a circuit-switched system. If the processor does not wait for a data item to return after sending a request to the network, but resumes processing—perhaps on a different task—this speed disadvantage need not be serious.

Hardware to implement the F&A operation is provided at two places: adders in the MNI and intelligent switches in the network. When an F&A (Y, e) has passed through the network and reaches the MNI, the value of Y is fetched from memory. This value is passed back through the network to the source of the request, and the value of Y is added to e. The sum is then written back to memory, resulting in the desired F&A operation.

An adder and a local memory is associated with each switch in the network. Whenever two requests for the same memory location—e.g., F&A $(X, e1)$ and F&A $(X, e2)$—arrive at a switch, the switch stores $e1$ in its memory, adds $e1$ and $e2$, and passes a request for F&A $(X, e1 + e2)$ on to the memory. The memory updates the variable X by adding $e1 + e2$ to it, and passes the original value of X back to the network. When this return message reaches the above switch, the switch passes the original value of X back to the location that requested F&A $(X, e1)$, adds the stored value of $e1$ to the value of X, and passes the result back to the second source.

If requests to the same memory location that were combined as described meet at another switch, they can be combined further, thus combining previously combined requests. In this manner, multiple requests to the same memory location can be served in the time of a single request. Interprocessor coordination is therefore not serialized. With appropriate additional hardware, the network can be generalized to facilitate associative fetch-and-ϕ operations.

The Ultracomputer promises to be an extremely powerful computer. It was estimated that a 4096 PE machine could be packaged into a 5 × 5 × 10 ft enclosure using 1990 technology. A 64 processor prototype is currently under development.

5.5.4. The Massively Parallel Processor

The Massively Parallel Processor (MPP) (6, 7) is a very powerful SIMD computer designed by Goodyear Aerospace Corporation and delivered to NASA in 1982. Its processing power originates from 16,384 bit-serial processing elements; the machine can perform up to 6553 million 8-bit integer additions per second.

The basic structure of MPP is shown in Figure 5.15. The Array Unit (ARU) performs array computations under the control of the Array Control Unit, which also executes scalar arithmetic. The overall flow of data and control in the MPP is handled by the Program and Data Management Unit, which is also used to develop programs and perform diagnostic functions. A staging memory and two 128-bit wide I/O interfaces transfer data to and from the ARU through two switches. The staging memory interfaces the ARU with magnetic tape, disk, terminal, line printer, and the external host computer.

The *ARU* consists of an array of 128-by-132 PEs, of which a 128-by-128 square array of PEs is enabled at any given time. The PEs are simple bit-serial processors with 1024 bits of memory each. A subarray of 4-by-2 processors (without the memory) is packaged into a VLSI chip. Four of the columns of the array are included for fault tolerance; four columns were chosen due to the 4-by-2 organization of PEs in the VLSI chips. If no fault exists in the array, an arbitrary set of four columns is disabled. When a fault occurs, the set of the four columns the faulty PE belongs to is disabled, and processing can continue at full speed. Because a fault usually corrupts data, the currently executed program is restarted from the beginning or rerun from a checkpoint at which all data and the machine status were known.

The interprocessor communication in MPP is of the PE-to-PE type, and no shared memory is provided. Because of the very large number of processing elements, the simplicity of each PE, and the expected computational tasks, a rather simple interprocessor communication network was chosen: each processor is connected to its four nearest neighbors. The top and bottom connections can either be left open or be connected within each column. The left and right edges can be left open or be connected within each row, in an open spiral, or in a closed spiral. For the open spiral, PE i is bidirectionally connected to PE $i + 1$, $0 \leq i \leq 16,382$ (i.e., PE 0 and 16,383 are not connected). In the closed spiral mode, PEs 0 and 16,383 are also connected. These modes of the edge connections can be chosen under software control. The choice of edge connections will depend on the algo-

MPP ORGANIZATION

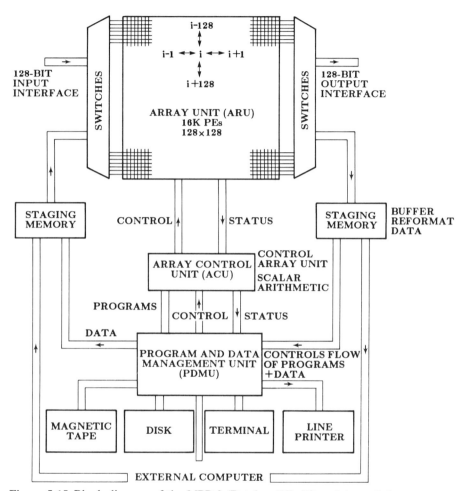

Figure 5.15 Block diagram of the MPP.© (Batcher KE: Bit serial parallel processing systems. *IEEE Trans. on Computers*, Vol. C-31, May 1982, pp. 377–384. © 1982 IEEE.)

rithm being executed. In some cases, multiple data transfers may be required to move data to their intended destination.

The MPP PEs are bit-serial processors; a diagram of a PE is shown in Figure 5.16. The speed of the PEs is one operation per 100 ns. Six one-bit registers—the A, B, G, P, and S registers—are available. They communicate with each other and with the random access memory through a data bus

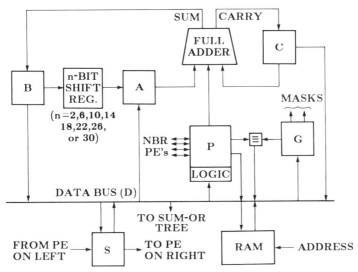

Figure 5.16 Block diagram of an MPP Processing Element.© (Batcher KE: Bit serial parallel processing systems. *IEEE Trans. on Computers*, Vol. C-31, May 1982, pp. 377–384. © 1982 IEEE.)

(*D*). Arithmetic operations are performed by a 1-bit full adder and a shift register of programmable length. The interconnection network interfaces to the *P* register, which has four bidirectional paths to each of its nearest neighbor PEs. To route information, for example, from left to right, each PE shifts the contents of its *P* register into the *P* register of the PE to its right, and thus receives the information from its left neighbor. Additional logic associated with the *P* register (see Figure 5.16) can perform all Boolean operations on the content of the *P* register and the bit currently on the data bus. The result is left in the *P* register. The adder sums the content of the *A* and *P* registers and the carry in the *C* register; it leaves the least significant bit of the result in the *B* register, and the carry in the *C* register. The length of the shift register can be programmed to be 2, 6, 10, 14, 18, 22, 26, and 30 bits. The *A* and *B* registers can be thought of as additional elements of the shift register; the total shift register length is thus a multiple of four. These simple components are sufficient to perform all basic arithmetic operations: addition, subtraction, multiplication, division, and floating point operations.

In many applications (such as in the smoothing example), PEs have to be disabled. To disable PEs, the *G* register is provided. If a *masked* instruction is executed, only those PEs with a 1 in their *G* register participate in the execution.

A comparator ($\equiv$ in Fig. 5.16) speeds up certain algorithms—e.g., normalization of floating point numbers. Global minimum value and maximum value searches and other global operations can be performed by the Sum-

Or-Tree, which is a tree of inclusive-or gates. It has inputs from all PEs, and its output is connected to the Array Control Unit (ACU).

The important role of I/O is handled by the *S*-register of each PE. Together, the 128^2 *S*-registers form a plane that can shift data. Each *S*-register operates independently from the rest of the PE. An *S*-register sends its 1-bit content to its right neighbor and receives the 1-bit content from the *S*-register that is its left neighbor—i.e., 128-bit columns of data are shifted across the *S*-register plane. The 128 bits of data that are simultaneously shifted into the *S*-registers of the leftmost column of PEs originate from the previously mentioned input switches (Figure 5.15). This shifting is done without interrupting normal processing. After 128 shift cycles, a complete 128-by-128 bit plane is loaded into the *S*-registers. Processing is interrupted for a single 100 ns cycle, and this complete data plane of 128-by-128 bits is transferred from the *S*-registers into the PE memories, each *S* register sending 1 bit to its PE. If necessary, all PEs can simultaneously move a memory bit into their associated *S*-register in a second cycle. Then a new plane of 128-by-128 bits can be shifted in and the old plane can be shifted out at the same time. The data that is shifted out of the rightmost PEs is accepted by the output switches, one column (128 bits) per cycle (Figure 5.15). This method of overlapping shift in and shift out provides a very efficient way to get data into and out of the MPP PEs.

Compared with state-of-the-art microprocessors, like the Motorola MC68020 32-bit microprocessor, the MPP PE is a *very* simple CPU indeed, but the large number of PEs result in MPP's tremendous performance. In Table 5.1, MPP's operating speed on integer and floating point data is illustrated (6).

The other components of MPP support the ARU. The *ACU* has the following components: the *main control* executes the main program and performs the necessary scalar arithmetic. It sends all array processing instructions to the *PE control*, which is responsible for broadcasting memory addresses and generating all ARU control signals. The *I/O control* is responsible for the shift operations of the *S*-registers and for interrupting regular processing for transfers between *S*-register and memory.

The *Program and Data Management Unit (PDMU)* is a DEC PDP-11 running the RSX-11M real-time operating system. It controls the overall program and data flow in the system, and is also used for program development.

The *Staging Memory* interfaces the PDMU and the external host to the ARU. Data arriving from the outside world—e.g., from an image sensor—will be organized as a stream of pixel values. The same is true for output—e.g., the output of a smoothed image to an image display device usually needs to be formatted as a stream of pixel values. The PEs, on the other hand, have to be loaded with a bit slice from all 128-by-128 pixel values at once. The staging memory (up to 40 Mbytes capacity) facilitates this

Table 5.1 Processing Speed of MPP

Operations	Execution speed[a]
Addition of Arrays	
8-bit integers (9-bit sum)	6553
12-bit integers (13-bit sum)	4428
32-bit floating point numbers	430
Multiplication of Arrays	
(Element-by-element)	
8-bit integers (16-bit product)	1861
12-bit integers (24-bit product)	910
32-bit floating point numbers	216
Multiplication of array by scalar	
8-bit integers (16-bit product)	2340
12-bit integers (24-bit product)	1260
32-bit floating point numbers	373

[a] Million operations per second (MOPS).
From Batcher KE: Bit serial parallel processing systems. *IEEE Trans. on Computers*, Vol. C-31, May 1982, pp. 377–384.

reformatting process for the input and output data. For error recovery, single-bit error correction and double-bit error detection is provided. The host machine is a DEC VAX-11/780. The VAX is connected to the PDMU and to the staging memory.

5.5.5. The STARAN Associative Processor

One of the first SIMD computers that has been built is the STARAN computer (3, 4, 5, 15, 19). The first STARAN was constructed during the early seventies by Goodyear Aerospace Corporation. STARAN is an SIMD machine, but is further classified as an associative processor. Associative processing was introduced in Section 5.4.2 of this chapter. The heart of the machine consists of up to 32 associative arrays. Each array contains a bit-serial associative memory; 256 bit-serial processors; a mask register; a selector that selects as input the memory, the processors, the mask register, or an input channel; and a flip network that receives its input from the selector and can send its output to the memory, the processors, the mask register, or to an output channel (see Figure 5.17).

The interconnection network used in each STARAN associative array is a 256 input, 256 output, eight-stage network called the *flip network*. Its topology is equivalent to that of the Generalized Cube network described in Chapter 6, with each link being 1-bit wide. Its centralized control scheme is more limited than the approach discussed in that chapter. For further details of the flip network, see (4).

The memory is logically organized as a square array of 256-by-256 bits, and is constructed from commercial LSI memory chips. To facilitate easy

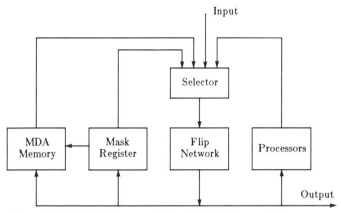

Figure 5.17 Block diagram of the STARAN associative array.

access for associative processing, bit-slice access mode is necessary, but because data arriving from the outside world is usually word-organized (e.g., the complete personal record with name, salary, etc., from the example in Section 5.4.2), word-slice access is also desirable. The STARAN memory not only provides these two access modes but also combinations of the two, and is therefore called the *multidimensional access (MDA) memory*. The data area being fetched from memory is called *access stencil*. Any access stencil always fetches 256 bits. The form and position of the stencil are specified by two 8-bit parameters: the global address G and the stencil mode M. The logical location of a bit in memory is defined by the logical word location W and the logical bit location B. The processor to which a specific bit is routed is denoted by P. If data is not routed to the processors, P designates the bit position in the mask register or the output channel. If the processors access memory at global address G and with access mode M, the hardware for addressing and the network setting generated will cause processor P to read the bit from the following bit and word position:

$$B = (\overline{M}G) \oplus (MP)$$

$$W = (MG) \oplus (\overline{M}P)$$

For example, suppose $M = 0$. Then the equations simplify to

$$B = (\overline{0}G) \oplus (0P) = G \oplus 0 = G$$

$$W = (0G) \oplus (\overline{0}P) = 0 \oplus P = P$$

Thus, all processors receive bit-slice G; $M = 0$ results in bit-slice access. On the other hand, if all bits of M are one, word-slice G is accessed:

$$B = (\overline{1}G) \oplus (1P) = 0 \oplus P = P$$

$$W = (1G) \oplus (\overline{1}P) = G \oplus 0 = G$$

Because *M* and *G* each consist of 8 bits, 256 access modes are possible, as are 256 different positions for each access mode. The theory underlying this is described in (5).

The associative arrays alone do not form the complete computer. Figure 5.18 shows a block diagram of the complete STARAN system. An *associative processor (AP) control module* contains all elements necessary to control the APs—e.g., instruction register, MDA address pointers, counters, etc. The *parallel I/O (PIO Flip) module* for a four AP (Array Module) system consists of a three-stage flip network with eight inputs and eight outputs, and is controlled by the PIO control. The flip network can permute data between its input ports, which are one 256-bit port for each AP module, and additional ports for disks and high-speed I/O. The *Sequential Control* is realized by a PDP-11, and handles peripherals, interfaces to the system console, and performs diagnostic functions. The *external function unit (EXF)* synchronizes the AP, PIO, and Sequential Control. The *Control Memory* holds the instructions for the AP and PIO control. It is also connected to a host computer; thus, STARAN can be considered a high-speed back-end computer.

The use of STARAN has been studied for various applications such as image processing, air traffic control, radar processing, and sonar processing. As an example of the processing speed of STARAN, consider the fast Fourier transform (FFT). A system with four array modules can perform a 1024-point FFT on real data in approximately 3.0 ms. An IBM 360/67 computer, a mainframe widely used when STARAN was designed, needs 446 ms for the same task.

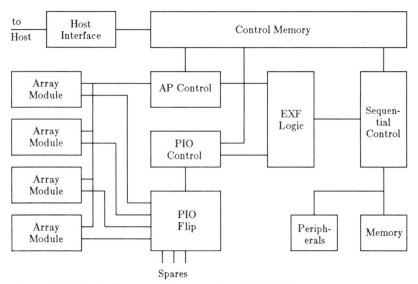

Figure 5.18 Block diagram of the complete STARAN system.

5.5.6. The Texas Reconfigurable Array Computer

TRAC, the Texas Reconfigurable Array Computer (32, 38, 47, 50), is much more flexible than the previously described systems. Not only can it run in SIMD and in MIMD mode, but its processors can be combined to form processors with higher precision (e.g., four 8-bit processors can be combined to form a 32-bit processor). TRAC can therefore be reconfigured in a fashion that is most suitable for the current algorithm. For example, consider the edge tracing algorithm in Section 5.4. Not only can the machine run in SIMD mode and MIMD mode as was required by the algorithm, but the best computational precision can also be selected. The image in the example consisted of 8-bit integers; to do the smoothing and the global edge detection, 16-bit precision is necessary to take care of overflows. After these two operations, the picture consists of 8-bit values again. The calculation of the figure of merit might require the summation of all smoothed values in a subimage; thus, 24-bit or 32-bit integers may be needed if the subimage is big. Additional processors can be allocated to the task to form higher-precision computers. To perform the thresholding, 8-bit numbers have to be compared. No high-precision results occur, so that the operation can be done by using 8-bit processors. Many of the processors necessary to calculate the figure of merit can therefore be released and reassigned to other tasks. The advantages of a system like TRAC become obvious from this discussion. The available processing power is always used in a very efficient manner. However, the flexibility of the machine increases the complexity of the system control.

The basic block diagram of TRAC is shown in Figure 5.19. It does not

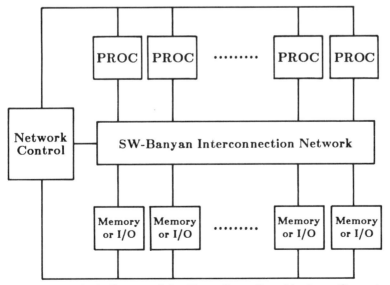

Figure 5.19 Block diagram of the Texas Reconfigurable Array Computer.

differ significantly from the Ultracomputer block diagram. Processors are connected to memory and I/O devices through the interconnection network. The powerful reconfiguration capabilities of TRAC are mainly hidden in the interconnection network.

The network is an *SW-banyan network*, an example of which is shown in Figure 5.20. A banyan network is represented by a graph with three types of nodes: the apex nodes associated with the processors, intermediate nodes representing switches, and base nodes associated with memory or I/O modules. The intermediate nodes all look alike; they all have the same *spread*, where the spread is the number of arcs going toward the apex nodes, and the same *fanout*, where fanout is the number of arcs going towards the base nodes. In Figure 5.20, spread = fanout = 2, and the network is functionally equivalent to the Generalized Cube network in Chapter 6 (39, 56).

The network has two different operating modes—circuit-switched and packet-switched. The two modes are time-multiplexed. This means that during one phase of the system clock, the network is in the circuit-switched

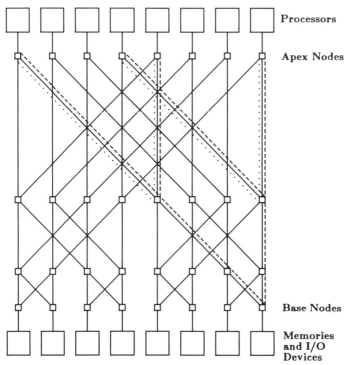

Figure 5.20 Typical banyan interconnection network with spread of 2 and fanout of 2. Solid lines show interconnection links, dashed lines show an instruction tree for a four-processor SIMD machine, dotted lines show carry-propagation paths.

mode, and in the next clock phase it is used in packet-switched mode, resulting in two completely independent networks. The time multiplexing does not decrease the performance of the circuit-switched mode because the packet-switching takes place while the memories execute their read or write cycle.

In SIMD mode, several processors receive the same instruction. In TRAC, this is implemented by an *instruction tree*. The instruction tree forms a path from one memory to the set of all processors that constitute the SIMD machine. If processors are combined to higher-precision machines, a portion of the instruction tree is also used to propagate carry signals through the network. Each processor needs to get data from one or more memories of its own to facilitate the multiple data stream. This is accomplished by forming *data trees* that are independent of the instruction tree. Data trees are analogous to instruction trees except they go from the processor to one or more memories.

In MIMD mode, shared memory is desirable. A *shared memory tree* provides several processors with access to the same memory. Because the memories allow only one access at a given time, arbitration logic is needed that determines the next processor to access the shared memory; this logic uses a simple round-robin priority scheme. The dashed lines in Figure 5.20 could represent a shared memory tree.

The memories contain 4 Kbytes of storage each, and provide important additional features. Several index registers are associated with each memory module, which can be automatically incremented. This has an important implication for program and stack accesses. With the exception of branching conditions, instructions will be fetched consecutively from memory. Thus, the processors do not need to send a memory address but just a request for the next memory word (= instruction); the index registers in the memory will provide the correct word and will be incremented in preparation for the next access. Stack operations that require increment or decrement of the index register after the memory access are simplified as well. Thus, instead of sending a 16-bit memory address through the network (which requires a 16-bit wide network path), only the appropriate index register in memory needs to be specified. This is done by using an 8-bit macroinstruction, and the network path need only have an 8-bit width.

Secondary memory in TRAC is provided by self-managing secondary memory (*SMSM*) modules. The modules are segmented, and the segments can be accessed by name. The search for the segment name is done associatively to speed up accesses. SMSMs connect to base nodes of the network.

A prototype of the system with four processors and nine memories, interconnected by a two-level banyan with a fanout of three and a spread of two, has been constructed.

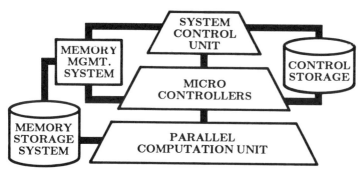

Figure 5.21 Block Diagram of PASM.

5.5.7. The PASM Parallel Processing System

PASM is a multifunction partitionable SIMD/MIMD system being designed at Purdue University (36, 52, 54). A 30-processor prototype has been built (40). A block diagram of the basic components of PASM is shown in Figure 5.21. The *Parallel Computation Unit* (Figure 5.22) contains $N = 2^n$ processors, N memory modules, and an interconnection network. The *processors* are microprocessors that perform the actual SIMD and MIMD operations. The *memory modules* are used by the processors for data storage in SIMD mode and both data and instruction storage in MIMD mode. A mem-

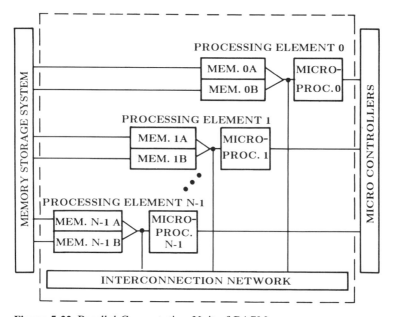

Figure 5.22 Parallel Computation Unit of PASM.

ory module is connected to each processor to form a processor-memory pair called a *Processing Element* (*PE*). The N PEs are numbered from 0 to $N - 1$. A pair of memory units is used for each module to allow data to be moved between one memory unit and secondary storage (the Memory Storage System), while the processor operates on data in the other memory unit. The PASM $N = 16$ prototype uses Motorola MC68010 processors; the final $N = 1024$ system, for which the architecture is designed, will employ sophisticated VLSI processors. The *interconnection network* provides a means for communication among the PEs. Two types of multistage interconnection networks are being considered for PASM: the Generalized Cube and the Augmented Data Manipulator. A fault-tolerant variation of the Cube network, the *Extra Stage Cube* (*ESC*) network, is included in the prototype. An important property of the ESC network is its partitionability—i.e., the ability to divide the network into subnetworks that are completely independent of each other. These networks and their partitionabilities are described in Chapter 6 on Interconnection Networks.

The *Micro Controllers* (*MCs*) are a set of processors that act as the control units for the PEs in SIMD mode and orchestrate the activities of the PEs in MIMD mode. There are $Q = 2^q$ MCs, physically addressed (numbered) from 0 to $Q - 1$. Each MC controls N/Q PEs. PASM is being designed for $Q = 32$ ($Q = 4$ in the prototype). The MCs are multiple control units needed in order to have a partitionable SIMD/MIMD system. Each MC includes a memory module, which consists of a pair of memory units so that memory loading and computations can be overlapped. In SIMD mode, each MC fetches instructions and common data from its memory module, executes the control flow instructions (e.g., branches), and broadcasts the data processing instructions to its PEs. In MIMD mode, each MC gets instructions and common data for coordinating its PEs from its memory.

The partitioning rule in PASM requires all PEs in a partition of size 2^s to agree in their $n - s$ low-order bit positions. The physical addresses of the N/Q processors that are connected to an MC must all have the same low-order q bits so that they are in the same partition. The value of these low-order q bits is the physical address of the MC. A virtual SIMD machine of size RN/Q is obtained by having $R = 2^r$, $0 \le r \le q$, MCs use the same instructions and synchronizing the MCs. The physical addresses of the MCs must have the same low-order $q - r$ bits so that all PEs in the partition have the same low-order $q - r$ physical address bits. A virtual MIMD machine of size RN/Q is obtained similarly. In MIMD mode, the MCs may be used to help coordinate the activities of their PEs. Q is the maximum number of partitions allowable, and N/Q is the size of the smallest partition.

A masking scheme is used in SIMD mode for determining which PEs will be active—i.e., execute instructions broadcast to them by their MC. PASM will use PE address masks as described in Section 5.3.3.

Control Storage contains the programs for the MCs. The loading of programs from Control Storage into the MC memory units is controlled by the System Control Unit.

The *Memory Storage System* provides secondary storage space for the Parallel Computation Unit for data files in SIMD mode, and for data and control instructions in MIMD mode. It consists of N/Q independent *Memory Storage Units*, numbered from 0 to $N/Q - 1$. Each Memory Storage Unit is connected to Q PE memory modules. For $0 \leq i < N/Q$, Memory Storage Unit i is connected to those PE memory modules whose physical addresses have the value i in their $n - q$ high-order bits. Recall that for $0 \leq k < Q$, MC k is connected to those PEs whose physical addresses have the value k in their q low-order bits. This is shown for $N = 32$ and $Q = 4$ in Figure 5.23.

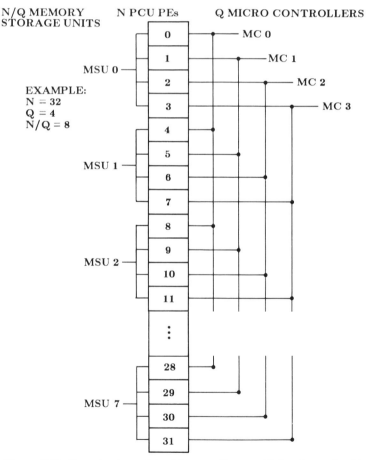

Figure 5.23 Organization of the Memory Storage Unit, shown for $N = 32$ and $Q = 4$. "MSU" is Memory Storage Unit. "PCU" is Parallel Computation Unit.

Consider a virtual machine of RN/Q PEs, $R = 2^r$, $0 \le r \le q$, where the PEs are logically numbered from 0 to $(RN/Q) - 1$, using the $r + n - q$ high-order bits of their physical addresses as their logical addresses. To load such a virtual machine requires only R parallel block moves if the data for the PE memory module whose high-order $n - q$ logical address bits equal i is loaded into Memory Storage Unit i. This is true no matter which group of R MCs (which agree in their low order $q - r$ physical address bits) is chosen. As an example, consider Figure 5.23, and assume that a virtual machine of size 16 is desired. The data for the PE memory modules whose logical addresses are 0 and 1 are loaded into Memory Storage Unit 0, for memory modules 2 and 3 into Unit 1, etc. Assume that the partition of size 16 is chosen to consist of the PEs connected to MCs 1 and 3. The Memory Storage Units first simultaneously load PE memory modules physically addressed 1, 5, 9, 13, 17, 21, 25, and 29 (logically addressed 0, 2, 4, 6, 8, 10, 12, and 14), then simultaneously load PE memory modules physically addressed 3, 7, 11, 15, 19, 23, 27, and 31 (logically addressed 1, 3, 5, 7, 9, 11, 13, and 15). No matter which pair of MCs is chosen (i.e., MCs 1 and 3, or MCs 0 and 2), only two parallel block loads are needed.

The *Memory Management System* controls the transferring of files between the Memory Storage System and the PEs. It is composed of a separate set of microprocessors (four in the prototype) dedicated to performing tasks in a distributed fashion. This distributed processing approach is chosen in order to provide the Memory Management System with a large amount of processing power at low cost. The division of tasks chosen is based on the main functions the Memory Management System must perform.

The *System Control Unit* is responsible for the overall coordination of the other components of PASM. The types of tasks the System Control Unit will perform include program development, job scheduling, and coordination of the loading of the PE memory modules from the Memory Storage System with the loading of the MC memory modules from Control Storage. By carefully choosing which tasks should be assigned to the System Control Unit and which should be assigned to other system components (e.g., the MCs and Memory Management System), the System Control Unit can work effectively and not become a bottleneck. For the $N = 1024$ PASM, the System Control Unit may consist of several processors in order to perform all of its functions efficiently. In the $N = 16$ prototype, the System Control Unit is a microprocessor and the program development functions are performed by a host computer.

5.6. Comparison of the Various Parallel Processing Systems

Although the systems described in this chapter do not have many similarities at first sight, an assessment of the various architectures and some general comments are appropriate. Cm* is the only system of the ones surveyed that employs a shared bus scheme. All other systems use an interconnection network. The complexity of this network ranges from the simple nearest-neighbor approach employed in the MPP to more flexible multistage networks as in STARAN, Ultracomputer, TRAC, and PASM. STARAN uses a centralized control scheme with which multiple network switches are set by the same control signal. In the Ultracomputer, TRAC, and PASM, each switch is controlled individually. The Ultracomputer adds hardware for handling F&A primitives, while TRAC adds hardware for implementing both circuit and packet switching.

Another aspect is the PE-to-PE and the processor-to-memory organization. MPP and PASM are PE-to-PE and TRAC is processor-to-memory. The Ultracomputer is basically a processor-to-memory organization, but because a cache is associated with the processor, the organization becomes hybrid. Machines with a PE-to-PE organization sacrifice the advantage of shared memory. Shared memory is desirable for many parallel processing applications where processors need to access the same data. On the other hand, in a PE-to-PE system local memory accesses are not routed through a network, avoiding potentially sizeable delays for every memory access. Thus, problems that require little communication between PEs can be processed faster.

The problem domain for which the various systems were designed was important for their basic architecture decision. STARAN, TRAC, Cm*, and Ultracomputer are general purpose machines with no preferred problem domain. The design of MPP and PASM was strongly guided by image-processing applications. They will perform image processing especially well, though they are also suited for other parallel computations. For image processing, large amounts of data have to be brought into the machine at high speed. This resulted in the staging memory for MPP and the complex secondary memory system for PASM. Because of its large number of bit-serial PEs and intended applications, a simple interconnection network was chosen for MPP. The Ultracomputer and TRAC can have I/O units that replace some of the memories. TRAC is the only machine of those surveyed that can combine simple processors to achieve higher precision. MPP and STARAN are bit-serial, while TRAC, PASM, and the Ultracomputer use complex processors of 16 or more bits.

A final distinction that will be made here is based on reconfigurability. MPP and STARAN are reconfigurable in a very limited sense: their networks can be reconfigured, and their PEs can be enabled and disabled. They will work in SIMD mode only. Cm* and the Ultracomputer are pure MIMD machines. Because each processor in an MIMD system follows its individual instruction stream, both machines can form one or more virtual MIMD submachines. In Cm*, small virtual machines should not be intercluster because communications along the intercluster buses is slow; the partitions in the

Ultracomputer are arbitrary because of its flexible network. PASM and TRAC are both reconfigurable systems because they can work in both the MIMD and the SIMD mode of operation and can be partitioned into virtual machines.

Trade-offs of the different approaches are application-dependent. Construction and use of the systems will enhance the knowledge of what parallel system features are important for different types of computation.

Problems

1. **a.** Consider the CAM algorithm given in Figure 5.11. Is it possible to exchange the ordering of the two "select CAM cell" operations and their associates "writes"? Why or why not?

   b. Write a CAM algorithm that subtracts 1 from an integer in all CAM cells.

2. Consider a hypothetical Cm* system with the following parameters:

   10 computer modules per cluster
   5 clusters
   2 intercluster buses

   Both the intercluster buses serve all of the 5 clusters. It is found that the average computer module generates 1 million memory references per second; 90% of these are local references, 7% are intracluster, and 3% are intercluster. Local buses (which connect the memory to the Slocal), MAP buses, and intercluster buses can all achieve a maximum throughput rate of 2 million references per second (where a reference consists of both a request and the reply). A reference appearing on an intercluster bus goes to the different clusters with equal likelihood; within a cluster, a reference goes to the different computer modules with equal likelihood.

   a. What is the local bus utilization (actual number of references/maximum references possible)?

   b. What is the MAP bus utilization?

   c. What is the intercluster bus utilization?

3. **a.** In the Ultracomputer, suppose the network supports only F&A operations. Can LOAD and STORE operations be implemented with this network? If so, how?

   b. Recall that network nodes in the Ultracomputer can combine requests. Describe how a network node can combine LOAD and LOAD, LOAD and STORE, and STORE and STORE operations (assume F&ϕ).

4. In MPP, assume a task consists of loading an 8-bit/pixel 128-by-128 pixel image into memory, perform some operation on it, and move the 8-bit/pixel result out of the machine. This task is to be repeated for 200 images. Describe how load, unload, and execution are overlapped. Determine the

maximum number of 100-ns cycles that can be used for execution on any one image so that loading and unloading take place at maximum speed.

5. The access stencil size and location in the STARAN associative processor is determined by formulas given in this chapter. Determine which memory locations are accessed by $M = (00000111)$ and $G = (10000000)$.

6. Consider the PASM system. Assume not N/Q but $(N/Q)/2^d$ distinct Memory Storage Units are available. How many parallel block loads are required to load a virtual machine of size RN/Q? Describe the MSU-to-PE connections. Discuss data allocation.

7. Comment on the various problems associated with using a general purpose, commercially available microprocessor (e.g., Intel 286, Motorola 68010, etc.) as the basis for a PE in an SIMD machine. Consider how instructions are to be broadcast to each PE from the control unit and the difficulties associated with the microprocessor instruction prefetch mechanism. Draw a block diagram of the external hardware required to facilitate instruction broadcast as well as to ensure synchronization among PEs. Describe how processor enabling/disabling could be implemented.

8. As illustrated in this chapter, two distinctly different approaches toward implementation of parallel processing systems are use of simple bit-serial PEs (e.g., STARAN and MPP) and the use of complex microprocessor-based PEs (e.g., PASM). Discuss the trade-offs between these two approaches. Consider such factors as I/O requirements, interconnection complexity, ease of custom VLSI PE design, and amenability to intended applications (e.g., image processing, weather forecasting, etc.).

9. Contrast various problems associated with implicit extraction of parallelism from commonly used high-level languages (C, Pascal, FORTRAN, Ada) with those associated with explicit specification of parallelism using "parallel extensions" of these same languages. Consider such factors as program portability, compiler portability, optimization of compiled code, and ease of programmability.

References

1. Barnes GH, Brown R, Kato M, et al: The Illiac IV computer. *IEEE Trans. on Computers,* Vol. C-17, Aug. 1968, pp. 746–757.
2. Baer J-L: *Computer Systems Architecture,* Computer Science Press, Potomac, MD, 1980.
3. Batcher KE: STARAN parallel processor system hardware. *AFIPS 1974 National Computer Conference,* May 1974, pp. 405–410.
4. Batcher KE: The flip network in STARAN. *1976 International Conference on Parallel Processing,* August 1976, pp. 65–71.
5. Batcher KE: The multidimensional access memory in STARAN. *IEEE Trans. on Computers,* Vol. C-26, Feb. 1977, pp. 174–177.

6. Batcher KE: Design of a massively parallel processor. *IEEE Trans. on Computers*, Vol. C-29, Sept. 1980, pp. 836–844.
7. Batcher KE: Bit serial parallel processing systems. *IEEE Trans. on Computers*, Vol. C-31, May 1982, pp. 377–384.
8. Beetem J, Denneau M, Weingarten D: The GF11 supercomputer. *Twelfth Annual International Symposium on Computer Architecture*, June 1985, pp. 108–115.
9. Bouknight WJ, Denenberg SA, McIntyre DE, et al: The Illiac IV system. *Proc. of the IEEE*, Vol. 60, April 1972, pp. 369–388.
10. Briggs FA, Fu K-S, Hwang K, Patel JH: PM4—a reconfigurable multimicroprocessor system for pattern recognition and image processing. *AFIPS 1979 National Computer Conference*, June 1979, pp. 255–265.
11. Cline C, Siegel HJ: A comparison of parallel language approaches to data representation and data transferral. *Computer Data Engineering Conference (COMPDEC)*, April 1984, pp. 60–66.
12. Cline CL, Siegel HJ: Augmenting Ada for SIMD parallel processing. *IEEE Trans. on Software Engineering*, Vol. SE-11, Sept. 1985, pp. 970–977.
13. Conway ME: A multiprocessor system design. *AFIPS 1963 Fall Joint Computer Conference*, 1963, pp. 139–146.
14. Crowther W, Goodhue J, Thomas R, et al: Performance measurements on a 128-node butterfly parallel processor. *1985 International Conference on Parallel Processing*, Aug. 1985, pp. 531–540.
15. Davis EW: STARAN parallel processor system software. *AFIPS 1974 National Computer Conference*, May 1974, pp. 17–22.
16. Dijkstra EW: Cooperating sequential processes. In Genuys F (ed): *Programming Languages,* Academic Press, New York, 1968, pp. 43–112.
17. Duda RO, Hart PE: *Pattern Classification and Scene Analysis,* John Wiley and Sons, New York, 1973.
18. Edler J, Gottlieb A, Kruskal CP, et al: Issues related to MIMD shared-memory computers: The NYU Ultracomputer approach. *Twelfth Annual International Symposium on Computer Architecture*, June 1985, pp. 126–135.
19. Feldman JD, Fulmer LC: RADCAP—an operational parallel processing facility. *AFIPS 1974 National Computer Conference*, May 1974, pp. 7–15.
20. Flynn MJ: Very high-speed computing systems. *Proc. of the IEEE*, Vol. 54, Dec. 1966, pp. 1901–1909.
21. Foster CA: *Content Addressable Parallel Processors,* Van Nostrand, Reinhold, New York, 1976.
22. Freeman H: Techniques for the digital computer analysis of chain-encoded arbitrary plane curves. *Proc. NEC*, Vol. 17, October 1961, pp. 421–432.
23. Gajski D, Lawrie D, Kuck D, Sameh S: Cedar. *IEEE Computer Society Spring Compcon 84,* Feb. 1984, pp. 306–309.
24. Gottlieb A, Grishman R, Kruskal CP, et al: The NYU Ultracomputer—designing an MIMD shared-memory parallel computer. *IEEE Trans. on Computers*, Vol. C-32, Feb. 1983, pp. 175–189.
25. Hagan MT, Demuth HB, Singgih PH: Parallel signal processing on the HEP. *1985 International Conference on Parallel Processing*, Aug. 1985, pp. 509–606.
26. Habermann AN: *Introduction to Operating System Design,* SRA, Chicago, IL, 1976.

27. Hockney RW, Jeshope CR: *Parallel Computers*, Adam Hilger Ltd., Bristol, England, 1981.

28. Hwang K, Briggs FA: *Computer Architecture and Parallel Processing*, McGraw-Hill, New York, 1984.

28a. Jamieson LH, Mueller PT, Siegel HJ: FFT algorithms for SIMD parallel processing systems. *Journal of Parallel and Distributed Computing*, March 1986, pp. 48–71.

29. Jones AK, Chansler RJ Jr, Durham I, et al: Software management of Cm*—a distributed multiprocessor. *AFIPS 1977 National Computer Conference*, June 1977, pp. 657–663.

30. Kartashev SI, Kartashev SP: A multicomputer system with dynamic architecture. *IEEE Trans. on Computers*, Vol. C-28, Oct. 1979, pp. 704–720.

31. Kartashev SI, Kartashev SP: Designing and Programming Modern Computers and Systems, *Volume I: LSI Modular Computer Systems*. Prentice-Hall, Englewood Cliffs, NJ, 1982.

32. Kapur RN, Premkumar UV, Lipovski GJ: Organization of the TRAC processor-memory subsystem. *AFIPS 1980 National Computer Conference*, June 1980, pp. 623–629.

33. Kuehn JT, Fessler JA, Siegel HJ: Parallel image thinning and vectorization on PASM. *1985 IEEE Computer Society Conference on Computer Vision and Pattern Recognition*, June 1985, pp. 368–374.

34. Kuehn JT, Siegel HJ, Tuomenoksa DL, Adams GB III: The use and design of PASM. In Levialdi S (ed): *Integrated Technology for Parallel Image Processing*, Academic Press, San Diego, 1985, pp. 133–152.

35. Kuehn JT, Siegel HJ: Extensions to the C programming language for SIMD/MIMD parallelism. *1985 International Conference on Parallel Processing*, August 1985, pp. 232–235.

36. Kuehn JT, Schwederski T, Siegel HJ: Design of a 1024-processor PASM system. *First International Conference on Supercomputing Systems*, December 1985, pp. 603–612.

37. Lawrie DH, Layman T, Baer D, Randall JM: Glypnir—a programming language for Illiac IV. *Communications of the ACM*, Vol. 18, March 1975, pp. 157–164.

38. Lipovski GJ: The banyan switch in TRAC, the Texas Reconfigurable Array Computer. *Distributed Processing Technical Committee Newsletter* (*IEEE Computer Society*), Jan. 1984, pp. 13–26.

39. Malek M, Myre WW: A description method of interconnection networks. *IEEE Technical Committee on Distributed Processing Quarterly*, Feb. 1981, pp. 1–6.

40. Meyer DG, Siegel HJ, Schwederski T, et al: The PASM parallel system prototype. *IEEE Computer Society Spring COMPCON 85*, Feb. 1985, pp. 429–434.

41. Mitchell OR, Reeves AP, Fu KS: Shape and texture measurements for automated cartography. *1981 IEEE Computer Society Conference on Pattern Recognition and Image Processing*, Aug. 1981, p. 367.

42. Mueller PT Jr, Siegel LJ, Siegel HJ: A parallel language for image and speech processing. *IEEE Computer Society Fourth International Computer Software and Applications Conference*, Oct. 1980, pp. 476–483.

43. Nutt GJ: Microprocessor implementation of a parallel processor. *Fourth Annual Symposium on Computer Architecture*, March 1977, pp. 147–152.

44. Nutt GJ: A parallel processor operating system comparison. *IEEE Trans. on Software Engineering,* Vol. SE-3, Nov. 1977, pp. 467–475.
45. Perrott RH: A language for array and vector processors. *ACM Trans. on Programming Languages and Systems,* Vol. 1, Oct. 1979, pp. 177–195.
46. Pfister GF, Brantley WC, George DA, et al: The IBM Research Parallel Processor Prototype (RP3): introduction and architecture. *1985 International Conference on Parallel Processing,* Aug. 1985, pp. 764–771.
47. Premkumar UV, Kapur RN, Malek M, et al: Design and implementation of the banyan interconnection network in TRAC. *AFIPS 1980 National Computer Conference,* June 1980, pp. 643–653.
48. Reeves AP, Bruner JD: The programming language Parallel Pascal. *1980 International Conference on Parallel Processing,* Aug. 1980, pp. 5–7.
49. Reddaway SF: DAP—A distributed array processor. *First Annual Symposium on Computer Architecture,* Dec. 1973, pp. 61–65.
50. Sejnowski MC, Upchurch ET, Kapur RN, et al: An overview of the Texas Reconfigurable Array Computer. *AFIPS 1980 National Computer Conference,* June 1980, pp. 631–641.
51. Seitz CL: The Cosmic Cube. *Communications of the ACM,* Jan. 1985, pp. 22–33.
52. Siegel HJ, Siegel LJ, Kemmerer FC, et al: PASM: a partitionable SIMD/MIMD system for image processing and pattern recognition. *IEEE Trans. on Computers,* Vol. C-30, Dec. 1981, pp. 934–947.
53. Siegel LJ, Siegel HJ, Feather AE: Parallel processing approaches to image correlation. *IEEE Trans. on Computers,* Vol. C-31, March 1982, pp. 208–218.
54. Siegel HJ, Schwederski T, Davis NJ IV, Kuehn JT: PASM: a reconfigurable parallel system for image processing. *Workshop on Algorithm-Guided Parallel Architectures for Automatic Target Recognition,* July 1984, pp. 263–291. (Also appears in the ACM SIGARCH newsletter: *Computer Architecture News,* Vol. 12, No. 4, Sept. 1984, pp. 7–19).
55. Siegel HJ: Controlling the active/inactive status of SIMD machine processors. *1977 International Conference on Parallel Processing,* Aug. 1977, p. 183.
56. Siegel HJ: *Interconnection Networks for Large-Scale Parallel Processing: Theory and Case Studies,* Lexington Books, D.C. Heath, Lexington, MA, 1985.
57. Snyder L, Jamieson LH, Gannon DB, Siegel HJ (eds): *Algorithmically Specialized Parallel Computers,* Academic Press, Orlando, FL, 1985.
58. Stevens KG: CFD—A FORTRAN-like language for the Illiac IV. *ACM Conference on Programming Languages and Compilers for Parallel and Vector Machines,* March 1975, pp. 72–76.
59. Stone HS: Parallel computers. In Stone HS (ed): *Introduction to Computer Architecture (second edition),* Science Research Associates, Inc., Chicago, IL, 1980, pp. 363–425.
60. Swan RJ, Bechtolsheim A, Lai KW, Ousterhout JK: The implementation of the Cm* multimicroprocessor. *AFIPS 1977 National Computer Conference,* June 1977, pp. 645–655.
61. Swan RJ, Fuller S, Siewiorek DP: Cm*: a modular multimicroprocessor. *AFIPS 1977 National Computer Conference,* June 1977, pp. 637–644.
62. Tuomenoksa DL, Adams GB III, Siegel HJ, Mitchell OR: A parallel algorithm

for contour extraction: advantages and architectural implications. *1983 IEEE Computer Society Symposium on Computer Vision and Pattern Recognition,* June 1983, pp. 336–344.

63. Uhr L: A language for parallel processing of arrays, embedded in PASCAL. In Duff MJB, Levialdi S (eds): *Languages and Architectures for Image Processing,* Academic Press, London, 1981, pp. 53–88.

64. Warpenburg MR, Siegel LJ: SIMD image resampling. *IEEE Trans. on Computers,* Vol. C-31, Oct. 1982, pp. 934–942.

65. Yoder MA, Jamieson LH: Simulation of a word-recognition system on two parallel architectures. *1985 International Conference on Parallel Processing,* Aug. 1985, pp. 171–179.

66. Yoder MA, Siegel LJ: Dynamic time warping algorithms for SIMD machines and VLSI processor arrays. *1982 International Conference on Acoustics, Speech, and Signal Processing,* May 1982, pp. 1274–1277.

6

Interconnection Networks

Howard Jay Siegel
William Tsun-yuk Hsu

6.1. Introduction

Many tasks require the computational power made possible by parallel processing. The demand for fast computation is usually due to a desire for real-time response and/or the need to process immense data sets. These types of tasks include aerodynamic simulations, air traffic control, chemical reaction simulations, seismic data processing, satellite-collected imagery analysis, missile guidance, ballistic missile defense, weather forecasting, map making, robot vision, and speech understanding. Systems comprising a multitude of tightly coupled, cooperating processors can help provide the computational performance required by these tasks. STARAN (7) and MPP (8) are examples of existing systems with 2^8 and 2^{14} simple processors, re-

Some of the material in this chapter is summarized from *Interconnection Networks for Large-Scale Parallel Processing,* by H. J. Siegel, Lexington Books, D. C. Heath and Company, Lexington, MA, copyright 1985. This project was supported by the Rome Air Development Center, under contract number F30602-83-K-0119, the Institute for Defense Analyses Supercomputing Research Center under contract number MDA 904-85-C-5027, and the Purdue Research Foundation David Ross Grant 1985/86 number 0857.

225

spectively. Ultracomputer (28) is a proposed design for a system consisting of 2^{12} complex processors. This chapter examines methods to provide communications among the processors and memories of such large-scale parallel/distributed systems.

Two models of interprocessor communication networks were introduced in Chapter 5. The *processor-to-memory* model assumes N processors on one side of a bidirectional network and N memory modules on the other side. It is also possible to organize processors and memory modules into processor/memory pairs or *processing elements* (*PEs*). In the PE-to-PE model, PE i is connected to input i and output i of a unidirectional interconnection network. In this chapter, the PE-to-PE model will be used; however, the material presented is also applicable to processor-to-memory systems.

The taxonomy originated by Flynn (26) to describe parallel processors has already been described in Chapter 5. Two of the modes of parallelism described by Flynn are the *SIMD* and *MIMD* modes. SIMD stands for *single instruction stream–multiple data stream*. An SIMD machine may consist of N PEs, an interconnection network that provides communications between PEs, and a single control unit. The control unit broadcasts instructions to all the PEs, and all enabled PEs execute the same instructions simultaneously, hence forming a single instruction stream. Each PE operates on its own data from its memory. Hence, there are multiple data streams. MIMD stands for *multiple instruction stream–multiple data stream*. An MIMD machine may consist of N PEs linked by an interconnection network. Each PE stores and executes its own instructions and operates on its own data. Therefore, there are multiple instruction streams and multiple data streams. In addition, there are *MSIMD* (*multiple-SIMD*) machines and *partitionable SIMD/MIMD* machines. MSIMD machines are systems that can be reconfigured into a number of smaller, independent SIMD machines. Partitionable SIMD/MIMD machines can be partitioned into smaller virtual machines working in SIMD or MIMD mode. These have been covered in Chapter 5.

The task of interconnecting N processors and N memory modules, where N may be in the range 2^6 to 2^{16}, is a nontrivial one. The interconnection scheme must provide fast and flexible communications without unreasonable cost. A single shared bus, as shown in Figure 6.1, is not sufficient because it is often desirable to allow all processors to send data to other processors simultaneously (e.g., from processor i to processor $i - 1$, $1 \le i < N$). The

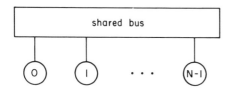

Figure 6.1 A single shared bus used to provide communications for N devices.

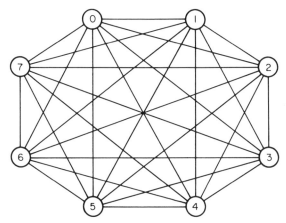

Figure 6.2 A completely connected system for $N = 8$.

ideal situation would be to link directly each processor to every other processor so that the system is completely connected. This is shown for $N = 8$ in Figure 6.2, where one could assume, for example, that each node is a processor with its own memory. Unfortunately, this is highly impractical for large N because it requires $N - 1$ unidirectional lines for each processor. For example, if $N = 2^9$, then $2^9 \times (2^9 - 1) = 261,632$ links would be needed.

An alternative interconnection scheme that allows all processors to communicate simultaneously is the crossbar switch, shown in Figure 6.3. In this example, the processors communicate through the memories. The network can be viewed as a set of intersecting lines, where interconnections between processors and memories are specified by the crosspoint switches at each line intersection (75). The difficulty with crossbar networks is that

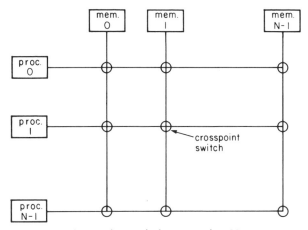

Figure 6.3 A crossbar switch connecting N processors to N memories.

the cost of the network (the number of crosspoint switches) grows with N^2, which, given current technology, makes it infeasible for large systems.

In order to solve the problem of providing fast, efficient communications at a reasonable cost, many different networks between the extremes of the single bus and the completely connected scheme have been proposed in the literature. No single network is generally considered "best." The cost-effectiveness of a particular network design depends on such factors as the computational tasks for which it will be used, the desired speed of inter-processor data transfers, the actual hardware implementation of the network, the number of processors in the system, and any cost constraints on the construction. A variety of networks that have been proposed are overviewed in numerous survey articles and books, e.g., (4, 12, 21, 32, 34, 37, 42, 62, 74, 81).

This chapter is a study of an important collection of network designs that can be used to support large scale parallelism—i.e., these networks can provide the communications needed in a parallel processing system consisting of a large number of processors (e.g., 2^6 to 2^{16}) that are working together to perform a single overall task. Many of these networks can be used in dynamically reconfigurable machines that can perform independent multiple tasks, where each task is processed using parallelism.

The networks examined here are based on the "Shuffle-Exchange," "Cube," "PM2I" (plus-minus 2^i), and "Illiac" (nearest neighbor) interconnection patterns. These networks and their single stage implementations are explored in Section 6.2. Section 6.3 is a study of the multistage Cube/Shuffle-Exchange class of networks. The Generalized Cube network will be discussed as an example of this type of network. A fault-tolerant version of the Generalized Cube network, called the Extra Stage Cube network, is the subject of Section 6.4. Data manipulator type networks, which are multistage implementations of the PM2I connection patterns, will be discussed in Section 6.5.

6.2. Interconnection Functions and Single Stage Networks

6.2.1. Introduction

Assume a parallel system with $N = 2^m$ PEs, numbered (addressed) from 0 to $N - 1$. An *interconnection network* can be described by a set of interconnection functions. Each *interconnection function* is a bijection (permutation) on the set of PE addresses. Interconnection functions represent inter-PE data transfers using mathematical mappings. When an interconnection function f is executed, PE i sends data to PE $f(i)$. If a system is operating in SIMD mode, this means that every PE sends data to exactly one PE, and every PE receives data from exactly one PE (assuming all PEs are active).

Otherwise, the data transfer from PE i to PE $f(i)$ may occur only for a subset of the PEs in the system.

Four types of interconnection networks will be discussed: the Cube, the Illiac, the PM2I, and the Shuffle-Exchange. Interconnection networks can be constructed from a single stage of switches or multiple stages of switches. In a single-stage network, data items may have to be passed through the switches several times before reaching their final destinations. In a multistage network, generally one pass through the multiple (usually m) stages of switches is sufficient to transfer the data items to their final destinations.

An important consideration in the selection of an interconnection network for a system is the partitionability of the network. The *partitionability* of an interconnection network is the ability to divide the network into independent subnetworks of different sizes (60). Each subnetwork of size N' < N must have all of the interconnection capabilities of a complete network of that same type built to be of size N'. Multiple-SIMD systems use partitionable interconnection networks to dynamically reconfigure the system into independent SIMD machines of varying sizes. The multiple-SIMD model will be used as a framework for the partitioning analyses in this chapter. However, the results can be used to partition MIMD and partitionable SIMD/MIMD machines also.

The subject of this section is the single-stage implementation of the Cube, Illiac, PM2I, and Shuffle-Exchange interconnection networks. Each of these networks will be defined, and examples of their operation in both the SIMD and MIMD modes of parallelism will be given. The partitionability of these single stage networks will also be discussed. Further information about these topics is in (59–61, 69).

The following notation will be used: let the binary representation of an arbitrary PE address P be $p_{m-1}p_{m-2} \cdots p_1p_0$, let $\bar{p}_i$ be the complement of p_i, and let the integer n be the square root of N. It is assumed throughout this chapter that $-j$ modulo $N = N - j$ modulo N, for $j > 0$—e.g., -4 modulo $16 = 12$ modulo 16.

6.2.2. The Cube Network

The *Cube* network consists of m interconnection functions defined by:

$$\text{cube}_i(p_{m-1} \cdots p_{i+1}p_ip_{i-1} \cdots p_0) = p_{m-1} \cdots p_{i+1}\bar{p}_ip_{i-1} \cdots p_0$$

for $0 \leq i < m$. For example, $\text{cube}_2(5) = 1$. The Cube interconnection functions for $N = 8$ are shown in Figure 6.4. This network is called the Cube because when the PE addresses are considered as the corners of an m-dimensional cube, using an appropriate labeling, this network connects each PE to its m neighbors, as shown in Figure 6.5 for $N = 8$. In terms of mapping source addresses to destinations, the Cube interconnection function cube_i

A

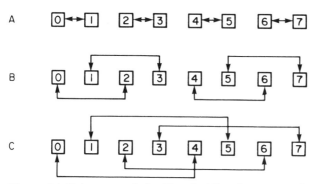

Figure 6.4 Cube network for $N = 8$. (A) $cube_0$ connections. (B) $cube_1$ connections. (C) $cube_2$ connections.

maps the address P to $cube_i(P)$—i.e., the $cube_i$ function sends data from PE P to PE $cube_i(P)$.

The single-stage Cube is used in the Cosmic Cube MIMD machine (57), the proposed CHoPP MIMD machine (72), and the Intel iPSC MIMD machine (35, 76). (The Cosmic Cube and Intel iPSC machines are discussed in Chapter 4.) The Cube network forms the underlying structure of many multistage networks, such as the SW-banyan ($S = F = 2$) (29), STARAN flip (6), Benes (9), indirect binary n-cube (54), Generalized Cube (65, 68), Extra-Stage Cube (1), and the BBN Butterfly (16). Various properties of the single-stage Cube network are discussed in (24, 47–49, 58).

In an SIMD environment, network settings for data transfers can be determined by means of a system control unit. The system control unit simply specifies the data transfer to be performed and the set of PEs that would be involved in the transfer, all as part of the SIMD program. The PE address masking scheme defined in Chapter 5 can be used to enable/disable some subset of the PEs. The system control unit generates an m-position mask with a 0, 1, or X (don't care) in each position, and PEs whose addresses match the mask would perform the specified operation. For example, specifying $cube_0$ $[X^{m-1}1]$ would mean that all odd-numbered PEs send data to the even-numbered PEs whose addresses differ only in the low-order bit

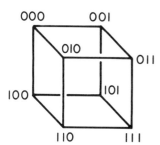

Figure 6.5 Three-dimensional cube structure, with vertices labeled from 0 to 7 in binary.

position. For $N = 8$, PEs 1, 3, 5, and 7 would send data to PEs 0, 2, 4, and 6, respectively.

Consider using the Cube network to perform a "plus one" transfer—i.e., each PE with address ADDR would send data to a PE with address ADDR + 1 modulo N. Intuitively, to add 1 to a binary address, the low-order bit must be complemented, and a "carry-out" may change the values of the higher-order bits. For example, $011 + 1 = 100$, so 3 bits have to be complemented. Moving the data from PE 3 to PE 4 can be viewed mathematically as mapping 3 to 4, by using $cube_2$ to map 3 to 7 (move the data from 3 to 7), then $cube_1$ to map 7 to 5 (move the data from 7 to 5), and then $cube_0$ to map 5 to 4 (move the data from 5 to 4). The following SIMD algorithm uses the Cube functions to make all PEs send data "plus 1." It does this for j going from $m - 1$ down to 0 by mapping P to $cube_j(P)$ if bits $j - 1$ to 0 of P are 1s, meaning that $P + 1$ would have a carry complement the jth bit position. The algorithm is:

for $j = m - 1$ *step* $- 1$ *until* 0 *do* $cube_j [X^{m-j}1^j]$

For example, for $N = 8$, consider PE 1: $cube_2 [X11]$—mask does not match 1, no data movement; $cube_1 [XX1]$—mask matches 1, data goes from PE 1 to PE 3; $cube_0 [XXX]$—mask matches 3, data goes from PE 3 to PE 2.

In an MIMD environment, inter-PE data transfers are less structured. Individual PEs generate their own data and propagate it through the network. There may be several ways to route a message through intermediate PEs. For example, for $N = 8$, to transfer data from PE 3 to PE 5, one possible sequence of $cube_i$ transfers would be $cube_1$ and $cube_2$, moving the data from PE 3 to 1, then to 5. The order of performing the $cube_i$ functions is not important. For example, $cube_2$ then $cube_1$ would move data from PE 3 to 7, then to 5.

The Cube network can be partitioned based on any bit position of the PE addresses. If the use of the $cube_i$ function is disallowed, all PEs with a 0 in the i-th bit of their addresses cannot communicate with PEs with a 1 in the i-th bit of their addresses. Two subnetworks of size $N/2$ are formed, each with $m - 1 = \log_2(N/2)$ Cube functions. Each of these Cube subnetworks can then be further subdivided into smaller partitions.

For example, for $N = 8$, divide the PEs into two groups: GE—those with even physical numbers (0, 2, 4, and 6), and GO—those with odd physical numbers (1, 3, 5, and 7). Within each group, the PEs will be *logically* numbered from 0 to 3. Let logically numbered PEs 0, 1, 2, and 3 in GE be the physical PEs 0, 2, 4, and 6, respectively. Similarly, let logical PEs 0, 1, 2, and 3 of GO be the physical PEs 1, 3, 5, and 7, respectively. If the $cube_0$ function is not used, the two groups are independent and cannot communicate. This is because all PEs in GE have a 0 in the lower-order physical address bit position and all PEs in GO have a 1 in that position. The only way for a PE in GE to communicate with a PE in GO is by using the $cube_0$

connection. Using the logical numbering of the PEs, the physical cube₁ connections act as logical cube₀ connections and the physical cube₂ connections act as logical cube₁ connections. This is shown in Figure 6.6. In a multiple-SIMD environment, if the physically even-numbered PEs are connected to one control unit and the physically odd-numbered PEs are connected to a second control unit, the two partitions can operate independently with complete Cube networks of size four.

As stated, a Cube network can be partitioned in half based on any bit position, then either or both halves can be further subdivided, and so on. In general, the physical addresses of all the PEs in a partition of size σ must agree in the $m - \log_2\sigma$ bit positions not corresponding to the $\log_2\sigma$ Cube functions the partition will use for communications.

6.2.3. The Plus–Minus 2^i (PM2I) Network

The *Plus–Minus* 2^i *(PM2I)* network consists of $2m$ interconnection functions defined by:

$$PM2_{+i}(P) = P + 2^i \text{ modulo } N$$

$$PM2_{-i}(P) = P - 2^i \text{ modulo } N$$

for $0 \le i < m$. For example, $PM2_{+1}(1) = 3$ if $N > 4$. Because $P + 2^{m-1} = P - 2^{m-1}$ modulo N, $PM2_{+(m-1)}$ and $PM2_{-(m-1)}$ are equivalent. Figure 6.7 shows the $PM2_{+i}$ interconnections for $N = 8$; $PM2_{-i}$ is the same as $PM2_{+i}$ except the direction is reversed. This network is called the Plus–Minus 2^i because, in terms of mapping source addresses to destinations, it

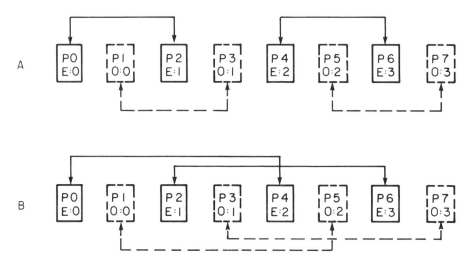

Figure 6.6 Partitioning a size-eight Cube network. (A) Physical cube₁ (logical cube₀). (B) Physical cube₂ (logical cube₁).

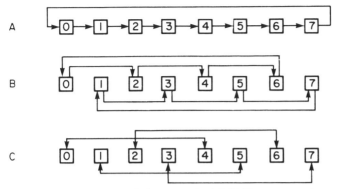

Figure 6.7 PM2I network for $N = 8$. (A) PM2$_{+0}$ connections. (B) PM2$_{+1}$ connections. (C) PM2$_{+2}$ connections.

can add or subtract 2^i from the PE addresses—i.e., it allows PE P to send data to any one of PE $P + 2^i$ or PE $P - 2^i$, arithmetic modulo N, $0 \le i < m$.

A network similar to the PM2I is used in the "Novel Multiprocessor Array" (50) and is included in the network of the Omen computer (31). The interconnection network of the SIMDA machine is similar in concept to that of the PM2I (78). The data manipulator (20), ADM (66), IADM (63), and gamma (52) multistage networks are based on the PM2I connection pattern. Various properties of the single-stage PM2I network are discussed in (24, 56, 58, 67, 70).

Network control in SIMD mode can be achieved by means of a system control unit, as in the Cube network. Suppose the PM2I network is implemented in the hardware, and a cube$_i$ transfer is needed. Mathematically, this means that the i-th bit of each PE address would have to be complemented using PM2I functions—i.e., data needs to be moved from PE P to PE cube$_i(P)$, $0 \le P < N$, using the PM2I connections. One way to do this would be to use the following algorithm:

(S1) PM2$_{+i}[X^m]$:all PEs execute PM2$_{+i}$

(S2) PM2$_{-(i+1)}[X^{m-(i+1)}0X^i]$:active PEs execute PM2$_{-(i+1)}$

In terms of a mathematical mapping, the first statement adds 1 to the i-th bit position of each PE address, thus complementing it. However, if bit i was a 1, the PM2$_{+i}$ operation also affected higher-order bits because a carry (of 2^{i+1}) is produced. Hence, statement 2 "fixes" the PE addresses that had a 1 in the i-th bit position (by subtracting 2^{i+1}). Thus, for $0 \le P < N$, P is mapped to cube$_i(P)$—i.e., PE P sends its data to PE cube$_i(P)$. For example, for $N = 8$ and $i = 0$, consider the data in PE 3: S1 moves the data from PE 3 to 4 because $[XXX]$ matches 3, then S2 moves the data from 4 to 2 (= cube$_0(3)$) because $[XX0]$ matches 4.

Data transfers in MIMD mode can be implemented based on the difference between the source and destination addresses. For example, for N = 16, to route data from PE 2 to PE 15, 13 has to be added to 2. One sequence of PM2I functions that would perform this transfer is $PM2_{+0}$, $PM2_{+2}$, and $PM2_{+3}$, and the message would go through PEs 2, 3, 7, and 15. As in the Cube network, the order of performing the PM2I functions is not important. Also, a different set of PM2I functions may result in the same routing, if the sum of the functions is equal to the difference between the source and destination addresses. For example, it is also possible to use the sequence $PM2_{-2}$ and $PM2_{+0}$ to route data from PE 2 to PE 15.

The PM2I network can be partitioned into two PM2I subnetworks of size $N/2$ by disallowing the $PM2_{\pm0}$ interconnection function. This subdivides the PEs into an even-numbered group and an odd-numbered group, and PEs in one group cannot communicate with PEs in the other group. This is because the only way for PEs in the odd-numbered group to communicate with a PE in the even-numbered group is to use $PM2_{\pm0}$. Each of the two subnetworks formed has $2(m - 1) = 2\log_2(N/2)$ PM2I functions. Each of these subnetworks can be further divided into smaller subnetworks by disallowing $PM2_{\pm1}$, $PM2_{\pm2}$, and so on, in order. An example of partitioning a size eight PM2I network into two subnetworks of size four is shown in Figure 6.8. The two groups and the logical numbering for each are the same as those for the Cube partitioning example. The physical $PM2_{\pm1}$, interconnection functions act as the logical $PM2_{\pm0}$ functions for each partition. Similarly, the physical $PM2_{\pm2}$ function acts as the logical $PM2_{\pm1}$. In a multiple-SIMD

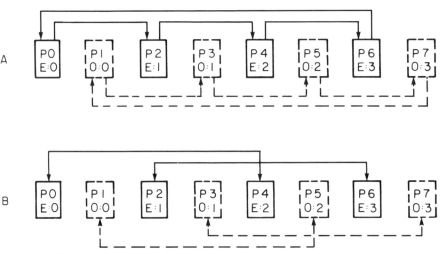

Figure 6.8 Partitioning a size-eight PM2I network. (A) Physical $PM2_{+1}$ (logical $PM2_{+0}$). (B) Physical $PM2_{+2}$ = physical $PM2_{-2}$ (logical $PM2_{+1}$ = logical $PM2_{-1}$).

environment, if the physically even-numbered PEs are connected to one control unit and the physically odd-numbered PEs are connected to a second control unit, the two partitions can operate independently with complete PM2I networks of size four.

In general, the physical addresses of all of the PEs in a partition of size σ must agree in their low order $m - \log_2\sigma$ bit positions. The physical $PM2_{\pm r}$ connections, $m - \log_2\sigma \le r < m$, are used by the partition, as logical connections $PM2_{\pm(r-(m-\log_2\sigma))}$.

6.2.4. The Illiac Network

The *Illiac* network consists of four interconnection functions defined as follows:

$\text{Illiac}_{+1}(P) = P + 1 \text{ modulo } N$

$\text{Illiac}_{-1}(P) = P - 1 \text{ modulo } N$

$\text{Illiac}_{+n}(P) = P + n \text{ modulo } N$

$\text{Illiac}_{-n}(P) = P - n \text{ modulo } N$

where n (the square root of N) is assumed to be an integer. For example, if $N = 16$, $\text{Illiac}_{+n}(1) = 5$. This network allows PE P to send data to any one of PEs $P + 1$, $P - 1$, $P + n$, or $P - n$, arithmetic modulo N. The PEs in an Illiac network may be grouped into an n-by-n array, as shown for $N = 16$ in Figure 6.9, where the "end-around" connections are indicated by the lower case letters. This network is called the Illiac because it was implemented in the Illiac IV SIMD machine, where $N = 64$ (10). It is also referred to as a four nearest neighbor connection pattern. The Illiac network

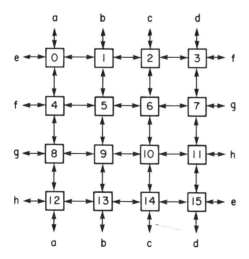

Figure 6.9 Illiac network for $N = 16$. (The actual Illiac IV SIMD machine had $N = 64$.) Vertical lines are $+\sqrt{N}$ and $-\sqrt{N}$. Horizontal lines are $+1$ and -1.

is a subset of the PM2I network—i.e., $\text{Illiac}_{\pm 1} = \text{PM2}_{\pm 0}$, and $\text{Illiac}_{\pm n} = \text{PM2}_{\pm m/2}$.

This type of network is included in the MPP (8) (MPP is discussed in Chapter 5) and DAP (33) SIMD systems. It is similar to the eight nearest neighbor network used in the CLIP4 (19) machine. The "mesh" interconnection network (45–47, 73) is like the Illiac network except there are no "end-around" connections. Various properties and capabilities of the Illiac network are discussed in (10, 27, 51, 58).

Consider the operation of the Illiac network in SIMD mode. Suppose it is desired to perform the PM2I function PM2_{+i}, for $m/2 \leq i < m$, with an Illiac network for all PEs—i.e., an Illiac network is implemented in hardware, and data needs to be moved from PE P to PE $\text{PM2}_{+i}(P)$, $0 \leq P < N$. An algorithm to do this is as follows:

$for\ j = 1\ until\ 2^i/n\ do\ \text{Illiac}_{+n}\ [X^m]$:all PEs execute $\text{Illiac}_{+n}\ 2^i/n$ times

Having all PEs execute $\text{Illiac}_{+n}\ 2^i/n$ times is equivalent to executing PM2_{+i}, $m/2 \leq i < m$. For example, for $N = 16$ and $i = 3$, the data from PE 3 is moved by Illiac_{+4} to 7, then by Illiac_{+4} to 11 ($= \text{PM2}_{+3}(3)$).

To do data transfers in MIMD mode, a sequence of Illiac functions that add up to the difference between the source and destination addresses is used to transfer the data. For example, for $N = 64$, for PE 14 to transmit data to PE 47, one possible sequence would be to execute Illiac_{+n} four times and Illiac_{+1} once. The route taken would be through PEs 14, 22, 30, 38, 46, and 47. As in the PM2I network, the order of performing the transfers is not important, and it is also possible to find different sets of Illiac functions that would perform the same routing—e.g., going from PE 14 to PE 47 could also be accomplished by executing Illiac_{-n} four times and Illiac_{+1} once, and the data would go through PEs 14, 6, 62, 54, 46, and 47.

The Illiac network cannot be partitioned into independent subnetworks, each of which has the properties of a complete Illiac network. In order to have a subnetwork that has the same properties as the Illiac, each PE must have four interconnection functions. Allowing each PE to use all four functions, however, results in the full network.

6.2.5. The Shuffle–Exchange Network

The *Shuffle–Exchange* network consists of a shuffle function and an exchange function. The *shuffle* is defined by:

$$\text{shuffle}(p_{m-1}p_{m-2} \cdots p_1p_0) = p_{m-2}p_{m-3} \cdots p_1p_0p_{m-1}$$

and the *exchange* is defined by:

$$\text{exchange}(p_{m-1}p_{m-2} \cdots p_1p_0) = p_{m-1}p_{m-2} \cdots p_1\bar{p}_0.$$

For example, shuffle(1) = 2 and exchange(5) = 4, for $N \geq 8$. Shuffling a

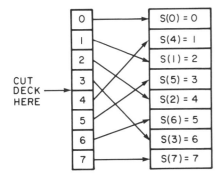

Figure 6.10 Perfectly shuffling a deck of eight cards. "S" stands for "shuffle."

PE's address is equivalent to taking the left cyclic end-around shift of its binary representation. The name "shuffle" has its origin in shuffling cards, by perfectly intermixing two halves of a deck, as shown in Figure 6.10. The exchange function is equivalent to cube$_0$. A Shuffle–Exchange network for $N = 8$ is shown in Figure 6.11.

Mathematical properties of the shuffle are discussed in (30, 36). The multistage omega network is a series of m Shuffle–Exchanges (40). The shuffle is also included in the networks of the Omen (31) and RAP (15) systems. Features of the single-stage Shuffle–Exchange network are discussed in (13, 14, 24, 27, 38, 39, 47, 49, 56, 58, 71, 80).

As an example of the network's operation in SIMD mode, consider using a system that has implemented the Shuffle–Exchange network to perform a cube$_i$ transfer among all PEs—i.e., move data from PE P to PE cube$_i(P)$, $0 \leq P < N$. One way to do this simulation is to "shuffle" the i-th bit of the address into the 0-th bit position, complement it with the exchange function, and shuffle the bits back into the original order. Mathematically, cube$_i(P) = $ shuffle^i(exchange(shuffle$^{m-i}(P)$)), where the superscripts indicate the number of shuffles executed. In algorithm form, this is

(S1) for $j = 1$ until $m - i$ do shuffle $[X^m]$:all PEs execute $m - i$ shuffles

(S2) exchange $[X^m]$:all PEs execute exchange

(S3) for $j = 1$ until i do   shuffle $[X^m]$:all PEs execute i shuffles

For example, for $N = 16$ and $i = 2$, consider the data movement from PE 0110 to cube$_2$(0110) = 0010. The sequence of transfers would be two shuffles

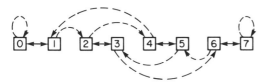

Figure 6.11 Shuffle–Exchange network for $N = 8$. Solid line is exchange; dashed line is shuffle.

(0110 to 1100 to 1001), an exchange (1001 to 1000), and two additional shuffles (1000 to 0001 to 0010).

In MIMD operations, data routing can be based on the algorithm used to simulate the Cube network with the Shuffle–Exchange network. To transform the source address into the destination address, each bit of the address is shuffled into the 0-th bit position and complemented with the exchange function if required. Consider, for $N = 16$, transmitting data from PE 13 (1101) to PE 1 (0001), so bits 3 and 2 have to be complemented. The sequence of transfers would be one shuffle (1101 to 1011), an exchange (1011 to 1010), one shuffle (1010 to 0101), one exchange (0101 to 0100), and two shuffles (0100 to 1000 to 0001). A more efficient algorithm for performing routing in single-stage Shuffle–Exchange networks, which uses extra combinatorial logic or a table to minimize the number of transfers used, is in (82).

A single-stage Shuffle–Exchange network cannot be used to partition the set of PEs into independent groups. The reasoning is similar to that for the Illiac network because the Shuffle–Exchange network also has a constant number of interconnection functions.

6.2.6. Summary

Four sets of interconnection functions—the Cube, Illiac, PM2I and Shuffle–Exchange—and their associated single-stage networks were presented in this section. Multistage networks based on the Cube and Shuffle–Exchange are presented in Sections 6.3 and 6.4. A PM2I-based multistage network is presented in Section 6.5.

6.3. Multistage Cube/Shuffle–Exchange Networks

6.3.1. Introduction

Multistage Cube/Shuffle–Exchange networks are multistage implementations of the Cube and Shuffle–Exchange interconnection networks defined in Section 6.2. The Generalized Cube network will be used in this chapter as a representative of the multistage Cube/Shuffle–Exchange class of networks. This network can operate in the SIMD, multiple-SIMD, MIMD, and partitionable SIMD/MIMD modes of parallelism. The properties of the Generalized Cube network discussed in the chapter—i.e., topology, routing control, and partitionability—are applicable to its operation in any of these modes.

6.3.2. Network Structure

The *Generalized Cube (GC) network* is a multistage Cube-type network topology, which was introduced in (66). As can be seen in (66), this topology is equivalent to that used by the omega (40), indirect binary n-cube (54), STARAN (6), and SW-banyan ($F = S = 2$) (29) networks. Other networks in this family include the delta (53) and baseline (79). This type of network is used or proposed for use in STARAN (7), DISP (25), PASM (68), PUMPS (11), the Ballistic Missile Defense Agency test bed (64), Ultracomputer (28), BBN Butterfly (16), the Burroughs Flow Model Processor for the Numerical Aerodynamic Simulator (5), the IBM Research Parallel Processor Prototype (RP3) (55), and data flow machines (18). (STARAN, PASM, and Ultracomputer are discussed in Chapter 5, and RP3 is discussed in Chapter 8. Ultracomputer is also discussed in Chapter 4.)

Consider a GC network with N inputs and N outputs. Its structure for $N = 8$ PEs is shown in Figure 6.12. It has $m = \log_2 N$ stages, where each stage consists of a set of N lines (*links*) connected to $N/2$ interchange boxes. Each *interchange box* is a two-input, two-output crossbar switch. The links are labeled from 0 to $N - 1$, and the labels of the links entering the upper and lower box inputs have the same labels as the upper and lower outputs, respectively.

The name "Generalized Cube" comes from the fact that this network is a multistage implementation of the Cube interconnection functions defined in the last section that was designed as a standard to represent this family of networks. Stage i of a GC topology has the capabilities of the cube$_i$ interconnection function because it pairs links that differ in the i-th bit position. Each interchange box can be set to one of four legitimate states, as shown in Figure 6.13. Each interchange box will be controlled independently through the use of routing tags.

One-to-one connections in the GC involve just the straight and swap box settings. When an interchange box in stage i is set to swap, it is implementing the cube$_i$ interconnection function. For example, in Figure 6.14 the path from source $S = 2$ to destination $D = 4$ in the Generalized Cube network for $N = 8$ PEs is shown. Consider this path in terms of a mathematical mapping. To map $S = 2 = 010$ to $D = 4 = 100$ using Cube functions, cube$_2$ and cube$_1$ must be applied. By setting the interchange boxes through which

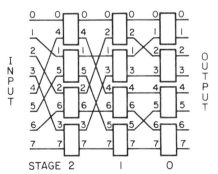

Figure 6.12 Generalized Cube network topology for $N = 8$.

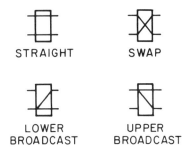

STRAIGHT   SWAP

LOWER   UPPER
BROADCAST   BROADCAST

Figure 6.13 The four legitimate states of an interchange box.

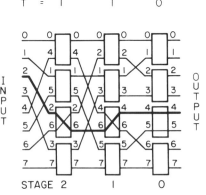

Figure 6.14 The path from input 2 to output 4 in the Generalized Cube network for $N = 8$. T is the routing tag.

the data from source 2 travels to swap in stages 2 and 1, and straight in stage 0, this is accomplished. In general, to go from a source $S = s_{m-1} \ldots s_1 s_0$ to a destination $D = d_{m-1} \ldots d_1 d_0$, the stage i box in the path from S to D must be set to swap (cube$_i$) if $s_i \neq d_i$ and to straight if $s_i = d_i$.

Because stage i corresponds to cube$_i$, the order in which the Cube functions can be applied in a path is determined by the fixed order of the stages, specifically: cube$_{m-1}$, cube$_{m-2}$, . . . , cube$_1$, cube$_0$. Because stage i determines the value of d_i (i.e., if it will be $\bar{s}_i$ or s_i), d_{m-1} is first determined, then d_{m-2}, then d_{m-3}, etc. In general, the stage i output link used in the path from S to D is $d_{m-1} \ldots d_{i+1} d_i s_{i-1} \ldots s_1 s_0$. For the example in Figure 6.14, the links traversed are $s_2 s_1 s_0 = 010$ at the input, $d_2 s_1 s_0 = 110$ after stage 2, $d_2 d_1 s_0 = 100$ after stage 1, and $d_2 d_1 d_0 = 100$ after stage 0. There is only one path from a given source to a given destination because only stage i can change the i-th bit of the address.

Permutation connections, where each input is connected to a single distinct output, are used in SIMD mode. Because each connection in a permutation is one-to-one, only the straight and swap box settings are used. For example, see Figure 6.15. Because each of the $Nm/2$ boxes can be set to straight or swap, the GC can do $2^{Nm/2}$ of the $N!$ different permutations. In general, $2^{Nm/2} \ll N!$; for example, for $N = 8$, $2^{Nm/2} = 4096$, while $N! =$

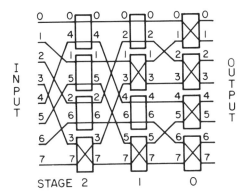

Figure 6.15 The GC for $N = 8$ set to do the permutation input j to output $j + 1$ modulo N, $0 \leq j < N$.

40,320. However, it can do most permutations that are important in SIMD processing (40, 54).

When the lower and/or upper broadcast states of interchange boxes are used in a path, a broadcast (one-to-many) connection is performed. An example is shown in Figure 6.16, where input 5 broadcasts to outputs 2, 3, 6, and 7.

6.3.3. Network Control

A routing tag scheme can be used for controlling the GC network. Using tags allows network control to be distributed among the processors. The routing tags for one-to-one data transfers (not involving broadcasting) consist of m bits. If broadcasts are allowed, $2m$ bits are used. When a message is to be transmitted through the network, a routing tag is added as the first item in the message—i.e., the header. Each interchange box the message enters examines the routing tag to determine how the box should be set,

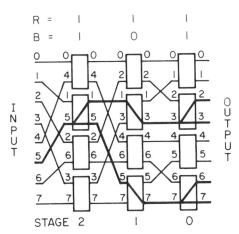

Figure 6.16 The broadcast path from input 5 to outputs 2, 3, 6, and 7 in the Generalized Cube network for $N = 8$. $\{R, B\}$ is the broadcast routing tag.

then sets itself. The data portion of the message follows the routing tag portion through the network.

An m-bit tag for one-to-one (nonbroadcast) connections or permutations can be computed from the input port number and desired output port number. Let $S = s_{m-1} \ldots s_1 s_0$ be the source network address (input port number) and $D = d_{m-1} \ldots d_1 d_0$ be the destination network address (output port number). Then the tag is $T = t_{m-1} \ldots t_1 t_0 = S \oplus D$ (where $\oplus$ means bitwise "exclusive-or") (65); $t_i = 1$ means $s_i \neq d_i$, and $t_i = 0$ means $s_i = d_i$. An interchange box in the network at stage i need only examine t_i. If $t_i = 1$, a swap is performed (i.e., cube$_i$ is performed). If $t_i = 0$, the straight connection is used. If $N = 8$, $S = 2 = 010$, and $D = 4 = 100$, then $T = 110$. The corresponding stage settings are swap, swap, and straight. This is shown in Figure 6.14.

Because each source generates its own tag, it is possible that a conflict will occur in the network—e.g., the tag on the upper input link of a box specifies a swap while the tag on the lower input specifies a straight. In a situation like this, one message must wait until the other has completed its transmission. Both requests cannot be serviced simultaneously. An alternative control scheme, destination tags, is presented in (40).

The routing tags presented here that can be used for broadcasting data are an extension of the exclusive-or routing tag scheme. This broadcast tag scheme allows a source to send a message to 2^j destinations, where there may be at most j bits that disagree among any pair of the addresses. Thus, there are $m - j$ bit positions in which all these addresses agree, and there is a fixed set of j bit positions in which any two destination addresses may disagree. For example, the set of addresses {010, 011, 110, 111} meets this criterion because there are 2^2 addresses and they differ in at most 2-bit positions, the 0-th and the 2nd.

Let the *broadcast routing tag* be specified by $\{R, B\}$, where $R = r_{m-1} \ldots r_1 r_0$ contains the routing information and $B = b_{m-1} \ldots b_1 b_0$ contains the broadcast information (65). To compute the broadcast routing tag, $R = S \oplus D_i$, where D_i is any one of the desired destination addresses, and $B = D_i \oplus D_k$, where D_i and D_k are any two destinations that differ by j bits. For the example given and source $S = 101$, $R = 111$ and $B = 101$. An interchange box at stage i in the network examines r_i and b_i to interpret the broadcast routing tag. If $b_i = 0$, r_i is interpreted exactly as t_i. If $b_i = 1$, r_i is ignored and a broadcast is performed. If a tag where $b_i = 1$ enters the lower input of a stage i box, the box is set to lower broadcast; if it enters the upper input, it is set to upper broadcast. This is shown in Figure 6.16. A similar broadcast routing tag scheme was presented in (77).

6.3.4. Partitioning

In Section 6.2, the partitioning of the Cube single-stage network was described. The partitioning of the GC is related to these results (60, 61, 66, 69).

First, consider partitioning a GC of size N into two independent subnetworks, each of size $N/2$. There are m ways to do this, each based on a different bit position of the input/output port addresses (i.e., a different Cube interconnection function). One way is to force all boxes in stage $m - 1$ to the straight state (i.e., disallow the use of cube$_{m-1}$). This would form two subnetworks, one consisting of those input/output ports with a 0 in the high-order bit position of their addresses and the other consisting of those ports with a 1 in the high-order bit position. These two groups could communicate with each other only by using the swap setting in stage $m - 1$ (i.e., the cube$_{m-1}$ function). By forcing this stage to straight, the subnetworks are independent and have full use of the rest of the network (stages $m - 2$ to 0, corresponding to cube$_{m-2}$ to cube$_0$). This is shown for $N = 8$ in Figure 6.17.

Each subnetwork has the properties of a GC. Therefore, each subnetwork can be further subdivided. Referring to Figure 6.17, Subnetwork B can be further divided using the middle bit position, forming two smaller subgroups of two PEs each, as shown in Figure 6.18. Thus, a size $N/2$ subnetwork can be divided into two size $N/4$ subnetworks by setting all the stage i boxes in the size $N/2$ subnetwork to straight, for any i, $0 \le i < m$,

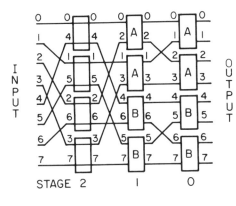

Figure 6.17 Partitioning the GC for N = 8 into two subnetworks of size four (A and B) based on the high-order bit position.

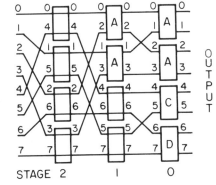

Figure 6.18 Partitioning the GC for N = 8 into one subnetwork of size four (A) and two subnetworks of size two (C and D).

as long as stage i was not used to create the size $N/2$ subnetworks (as stage $m - 1$ was earlier). This process of dividing subnetworks into independent halves can be repeated to create any size subnetwork from 1 to $N/2$. The only constraints are that the size of each subnetwork must be a power of 2, the physical addresses of the input/output ports of a subnetwork of size 2^s must all agree in any fixed set of $m - s$ bit positions, and each input/output port can belong to at most one subnetwork.

It is straightforward to assign logical stage numbers to physical stage numbers, once the network has been partitioned. For a partition of size 2^s, follow any path within the partition from input to output. The first stage containing a box not forced to straight acts as logical stage $s - 1$, the next stage containing a box not forced to straight acts as $s - 2$, etc. For example, consider the A subnetwork in Figure 6.17. By following link number 1 it can be seen that physical stage 1 becomes logical stage 1 and physical stage 0 becomes logical stage 0.

The routing tag control described in the previous section can be used within partitions, in combination with an m-bit partitioning mask. The mask is set to 0 in all the bits that correspond to the stages that are forced to straight in that partition, and all other bits are set to 1. The routing tag is logically ANDed with the mask to force corresponding stages to straight. (If broadcast routing tags are used, the mask is logically ANDed with both R and B.) The properties of the GC make it well-suited for SIMD, MIMD, MSIMD, and partitionable SIMD/MIMD operations.

6.4. The Extra-Stage Cube Network

6.4.1. Introduction

In the last section, it was seen that the Generalized Cube (GC) network is well-suited for large-scale parallel/distributed computer systems. However, it provides only one path from a given network input to a given output. Hence, if there is a single hardware fault, fault-free communication will not be possible between some network input/output pairs. Different approaches to fault tolerant GC-type networks have been studied (2). This section describes the *Extra-Stage Cube* (*ESC*) network, a single fault-tolerant network derived from the GC network, capable of operating in SIMD, MSIMD, MIMD, and partitionable SIMD/MIMD environments (1, 3). The ability of the ESC to overcome single faults is presented.

6.4.2. Network Structure

The ESC network is formed from the GC by adding one extra stage at the input and hardware to allow the bypass, when desired, of the extra stage (stage m) or the output stage (stage 0). Stage m implements the $cube_0$ interconnection function, so there are now two ways of performing the $cube_0$ data transfer. This results in an additional path being available from each source to each destination. An ESC network for $N = 8$ PEs is shown in Figure 6.19.

Because the ESC network is formed by adding an extra stage to the GC, it has all of the interconnecting capabilities of the GC-type networks, as well as the known useful attributes of partitionability and distributed control through the use of routing tags. It will be shown that the ESC network provides fault tolerance for any single failure. A routing tag scheme based on that of the GC provides reliable control even in a faulty environment. The ways in which the ESC network can be partitioned will also be described.

A stage is *enabled* when its interchange boxes can be used to provide $cube_0$ interconnection capability. It is *disabled* when its interchange boxes are being bypassed. Enabling and disabling of stages m and 0 is accomplished by having dual input/output ports, and multiplexers and demultiplexers to select between the input/output lines. Figure 6.20 details interchange boxes from stage m and 0. At stage m, a multiplexer selects between two sets of identical PE output lines, one of which bypasses the stage m box and the other one routes through the box. At stage 0, a demultiplexer gives the option of bypassing the box or routing data through it.

Techniques such as test patterns (17, 22, 23) or dynamic parity checking (65) for fault detection and location have been described for use in the GC topology. It is assumed that the ESC network can be tested to determine

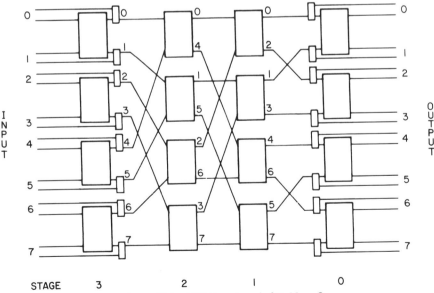

STAGE   3   2   1   0

Figure 6.19 The Extra Stage Cube (ESC) network for $N = 8$.

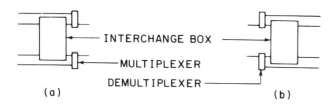

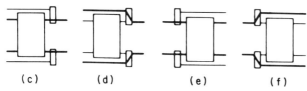

Figure 6.20 (a) Details of stage m interchange box. (b) Details of stage 0 interchange box. (c) Stage m enabled. (d) Stage m disabled. (e) Stage 0 enabled. (f) Stage 0 disabled.

the existence and location of faults; this section is about how to recover once a fault is located. Failures may occur in network interchange boxes, links (lines between interchange boxes), and network input/output lines. Failed components of the network are considered unusable until replaced or repaired.

If an input line connecting a PE to a stage m multiplexer fails, stage m is enabled and forced to straight. Thus, the nonfaulty input line will be used. If the fault is on an input line to a stage m interchange box, that line is currently unused and the system continues to ignore the faulty line. If an output line from a stage 0 box to a PE is faulty, the network is reconfigured as if stage 0 is faulty. If the fault is on an output line from a demultiplexer to a PE, that line is currently unused and the system continues to ignore the faulty line.

Stage m and 0 enabling and disabling may be performed by a system control unit. In normal operation, stage m is disabled (bypassed) and stage 0 is enabled. This fault-free ESC is topologically identical to a GC, as demonstrated by the path from PE 6 to PE 3 shown in Figure 6.21. If after running fault detection and location tests a fault is found, the network is reconfigured. If the fault is in stage 0, stage m is enabled and stage 0 is disabled, and stage m handles the $cube_0$ function instead of stage 0, as shown in Figure 6.22 (a variation of this scheme is discussed in (3)). For faults in a link or box in stages $m - 1$ to 1, both stages m and 0 will be enabled. Stage m of the ESC network allows access to two distinct stage $m - 1$ inputs, S and $cube_0(S)$. Stages $m - 1$ to 0 of the ESC network form a GC topology, so each of the two stage $m - 1$ inputs has a single path to the destination, and these paths are distinct except for the stage m and 0 boxes, which are fault-free in this

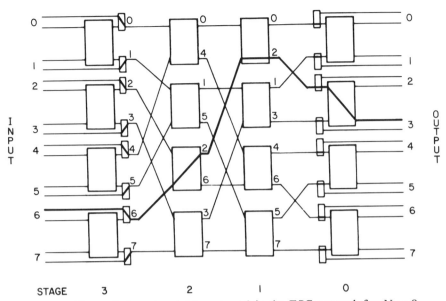

Figure 6.21 The path from input 6 to output 3 in the ESC network for $N = 8$, when stage 3 is disabled and stage 0 is enabled.

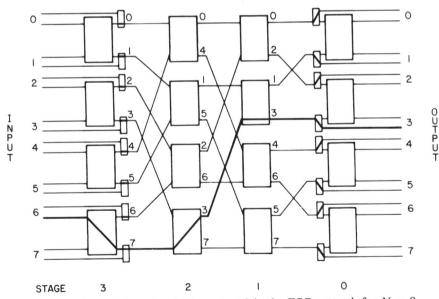

Figure 6.22 The path from input 6 to output 3 in the ESC network for $N = 8$, when stage 3 is enabled and stage 0 is disabled.

case (1). Thus, at least one fault-free path must exist. This is demonstrated for the paths from input 6 to output 3 in Figure 6.23.

The solid line path from 6 to 3 that enters stage 2 in link 6 goes through links with labels that agree with $S = 6$ in the 0-th bit position (it is 0). The dotted line path from 6 to 3 that enters stage 2 on link $cube_0(6) = 7$ goes through links with labels that agree with $cube_0(6) = 7$ in the 0-th bit position (it is 1).

Consider broadcast connections. If the network is fault-free, stage m is bypassed, and the network operates just as the GC does. If stage 0 is faulty, stage m replaces it, as for one-to-one communications. For faults in links or boxes in stages $m - 1$ to 0, the two paths between any source and destination of the ESC network provide single fault tolerance for performing broadcasts as well. For example, consider the broadcast paths from source 2 to destinations 4, 5, 6, and 7 shown in Figure 6.24 for $N = 8$. All the links in the broadcast path marked by the solid line (2, 4, and 6) agree with $S = 2$ in the 0-th bit position (it is 0). All the links in the broadcast path marked by the dotted line (3, 5, and 7) agree with $cube_0(2) = 3$ in the 0-th bit position (it is 1). Both broadcast paths share the same stage $m = 3$ and stage 0 boxes, which are fault-free in this case. Thus, at least one of the broadcast paths must be fault-free.

The ESC network path connecting S to D that bypasses stage m (stage m is disabled) or uses the straight setting in stage m is called the *primary*

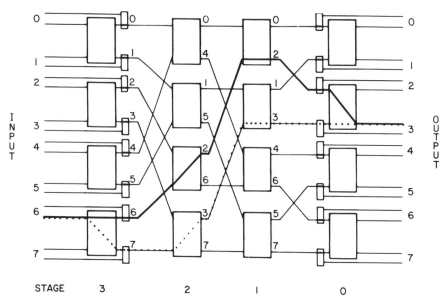

Figure 6.23 The paths from input 6 to output 3 in the ESC network for $N = 8$, when both stages 3 and 0 are enabled.

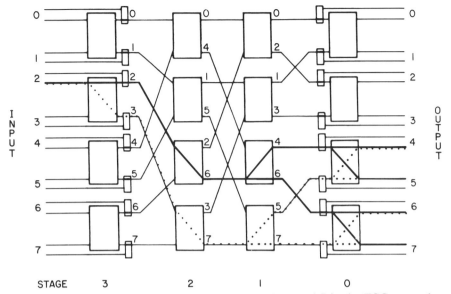

Figure 6.24 The paths from input 2 to outputs 4, 5, 6, and 7 in the ESC network for $N = 8$, when both stages 3 and 0 are enabled.

path. The other path available to connect S to D is the *secondary path*. It must use the swap setting in stage m (stage m is enabled). This is illustrated in Figure 6.23, where the solid line is the primary path and the dotted line is the secondary path.

The concept of primary and secondary paths can be extended for broadcasting. The broadcast path in the ESC analogous to that available in the GC is called the *primary broadcast path*. This is because each path from the source to one of the destinations is a primary path. If every primary path is replaced by its secondary path the result is the *secondary broadcast path*. This is illustrated in Figure 6.24, where the solid lines are the primary broadcast path and the dotted lines are the secondary broadcast path.

6.4.3. Network Control

A routing tag scheme for the ESC network, which takes full advantage of its fault tolerant capabilities, can be derived from the exclusive-or tag scheme for the GC network, described in Section 6.3. The ESC network uses an (m + 1)-bit routing tag $T^* = t_m^* \ldots t_1^* t_0^*$ for one-to-one connections. For broadcast connections, the ESC network uses a ($2m + 2$)-bit broadcast routing tag $\{R^*, B^*\}$, $R^* = r_m^* \ldots r_1^* r_0^*$ and $B^* = b_m^* \ldots b_1^* b_0^*$. In both cases, the ESC tag uses one more bit than the GC tag to control stage m. Actual tag values depend on whether the ESC network has a fault, as well as the source and destination addresses, but are readily computed.

If the network is fault-free, stage m is disabled. Hence, for both routing and broadcast tags, the m-th bit will be ignored. The routing tag is given by $T^* - t_m^* t_{m-1} \ldots t_1 t_0$, where $t_{m-1} \ldots t_1 t_0 = T$, the tag used in the GC. Since the bit t_m^* is ignored, it may be set to any value. Bits $m - 1$ through 0 of T^* are interpreted in the same way as in the GC scheme. For the example in Figure 6.21, $T^* = X101$. The broadcast routing tag comprises $R^* = r_m^* r_{m-1} \ldots r_1 r_0$ and $B^* = b_m^* b_{m-1} \ldots b_1 b_0$, where $r_{m-1} \ldots r_1 r_0 = R$, $b_{m-1} \ldots b_1 b_0 = B$, and $\{R, B\}$ is the broadcast tag used by the GC. r_m^* and b_m^* are arbitrary because they are ignored. Again, $\{R^*, B^*\}$ is interpreted as in the GC. For the example in Figure 6.24, the fault-free path corresponds to the primary path (solid lines), and $R^* = X110$ and $B^* = X011$.

If there is a fault in a network link or box in stages $m - 1$ to 1, stage m is enabled. Bit m of the tags can be used to control stage m and select between the primary and secondary paths. The primary path is used if it is not faulty; if it is, the secondary path is used. For routing tags, $T^* = 0t_{m-1} \ldots t_1 t_0$ yields the primary path, and $T^* = 1t_{m-1} \ldots t_1 \bar{t}_0$ the secondary path. Stage 0 uses $\bar{t}_0$ instead of t_0 to compensate for the swap (cube$_0$) already performed by stage m. For the example in Figure 6.23, $T^* = 0101$ specifies the primary path (solid lines), while $T^* = 1100$ specifies the secondary path (dotted lines). The primary broadcast path is specified by $R^* = 0r_{m-1} \ldots r_1 r_0$ and $B^* = 0b_{m-1} \ldots b_1 b_0$, whereas $R^* = 1r_{m-1} \ldots r_1 \bar{r}_0$ and $B^* = 0b_{m-1} \ldots b_1 b_0$ give the secondary broadcast path. For the example in Figure 6.24, $R^* = 0110$ and $B^* = 0011$ specifies the primary broadcast path (solid lines), while $R^* = 1111$ and $B^* = 0011$ specifies the secondary broadcast path (dotted lines).

The following method is used to determine if a primary path is faulty. If a fault is located in stages $m - 1$ to 1, each PE receives a *fault label* (i, j). If a link labeled j between stages i and $i - 1$ fails, each PE receives the label (i, j). If a box with outputs j and k between stages i and $i - 1$ fails, each PE receives the label (i, j'), where j' has an X ("don't care") in the i-th bit but is identical to j (or k) in all other bit positions. Using the fault labels, it is straightforward to determine whether the primary or secondary path is faulty.

For one-to-one connections, a source S forms $d_{m-1} \ldots d_{i+1} d_i s_{i-1} \ldots s_1 s_0$. Recall from Section 6.3.2 that this is the stage i link label on the primary path from S to D. If this matches j in the fault label, the primary path is faulty; otherwise, it is fault-free. For broadcast connections, S forms $W = w_{m-1} \ldots w_1 w_0$, setting $w_k = s_k$ for $0 \le k < i$, and for $i \le k < m$, if $b_k = 1$, then $w_k = X$ ("don't care"), otherwise $w_k = s_k \oplus r_k$. If W matches j in the fault label, the primary broadcast path is faulty; otherwise, it is fault-free.

If the fault is in stage 0, stage m is enabled and stage 0 disabled. A routing can be accomplished by substituting stage m for stage 0, because both stage m and stage 0 perform cube$_0$. For one-to-one connections, the tag $T^* = t_0 t_{m-1} \ldots t_1 t_0^*$ (setting $t_m^* = t_0$) is used. Now stage m performs the cube$_0$ function if it is needed. t_0^* is ignored because stage 0 is disabled. For the example in Figure 6.22, $T^* = 110X$. For broadcasts, the broadcast routing tag substitutes stage m for stage 0 by assigning $R^* = r_0 r_{m-1} \ldots r_1 r_0^*$ and $B^* = b_0 b_{m-1} \ldots b_1 b_0^*$ (setting $r_m^* = r_0$ and $b_m^* = b_0$). r_0^* and b_0^* are arbitrary because they are ignored. For the example in Figure 6.24, $R^* = 011X$ and $B^* = 101X$, and the path taken is both the solid and dotted lines in stages 3, 2, and 1 (stage 0 is bypassed).

6.4.4. Partitioning

The partitionability of the GC was discussed in Section 6.3. The ESC network can be partitioned in similar ways, with each subnetwork retaining all the properties of an ESC network. However, for each ESC subnetwork to have the redundant paths between each source/destination pair in the partition, partitioning cannot be based on stages m and 0. This is because two stages are needed to implement cube$_0$ to provide the redundant paths. This implies that partitioning cannot be based on bit 0 of the physical port addresses. Nevertheless, the other $m - 1$ bits can still be used for this purpose.

Consider partitioning an ESC network into two subnetworks of size $N/2$. Suppose bit $m - 1$ is used for the partitioning. If all the interchange boxes in stage $m - 1$ are forced to straight, ports with a 0 in bit $m - 1$ of their addresses cannot communicate with ports with a 1 in that bit. Thus, two subgroups of PEs are formed. This is shown in Figure 6.25, for $N =$

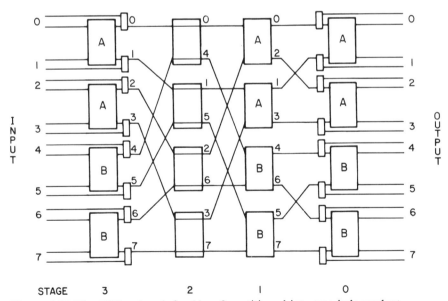

Figure 6.25 The ESC network for $N = 8$ partitioned into two independent subnetworks of size four, based on the high-order bit position. The labels A and B denote the two subnetworks.

8, with stage 2 forced to straight. The two subnetworks are indicated by the labels A and B. Subnetwork A consists of ports 0, 1, 2, and 3, all of which agree in bit 2 (it is 0). Subnetwork B contains ports 4, 5, 6, and 7, all of which agree in bit 2 (it is 1).

The other aspects of partitioning are the same as for the GC—e.g., subdividing subnetworks and the availability of the use of routing tags. The difference is that each ESC subnetwork is fault tolerant. Thus, the ESC can replace any GC-type network when fault tolerance is needed.

6.5. Data Manipulator Networks

6.5.1. Introduction

"Data manipulator" networks are based on the PM2I interconnection functions defined in Section 6.2. Just as the Generalized Cube discussed in Section 6.3 was, in effect, a wired series of Cube interconnection functions, data manipulator networks are a wired series of PM2I interconnection functions. The class of data manipulator networks includes the data manipulator (20), the Augmented Data Manipulator (ADM) (66), the Inverse Augmented Data Manipulator (IADM) (63), and the gamma (52) multistage interconnection networks. This chapter focuses on the ADM network as a representative of this class, examining network topology, routing tag control, and partitionability. These networks can operate in the SIMD, multiple-SIMD, MIMD, and partitionable SIMD/MIMD modes of parallelism.

6.5.2. Network Structure

The *data manipulator* network is shown in Figure 6.26 for $N = 8$. It has m stages. Each *stage* consists of N switching elements (*nodes*) and $3N$ output links, three output links per node. There is also an $(m + 1)$-st column of network output nodes. The stages are ordered from $m - 1$ to 0, where the interconnection functions of stage i are $PM2_{+i}$, $PM2_{-i}$, and the "identity" (straight across). At stage i of the network, $0 \leq i < m$, the first output of node j is connected to node $j - 2^i$ modulo N of stage $i - 1$ (i.e., $PM2_{-i}$), the second output to node j of stage $i - 1$ (i.e., identity), and the third output to node $j + 2^i$ modulo N of stage $i - 1$ (i.e., $PM2_{+i}$). Each node selects one of its input links and connects it either to one of its output links (a one-to-one setting) or to two or three of its output links (a broadcast setting). Because $PM2_{+m-1} = PM2_{-(m-1)}$ ($j - 2^{m-1} = j + 2^{m-1}$ modulo N), an actual network implementation may have only two distinct outputs from each node in stage $m - 1$. The *Augmented Data Manipulator* (*ADM*) network is a data manipulator network with individual switching element control—i.e., each node can be independently set to straight across, -2^i modulo N, or $+2^i$ modulo N (43, 63, 66).

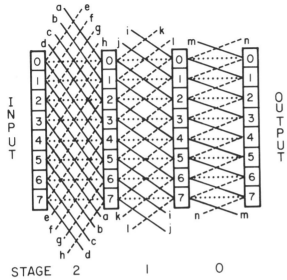

Figure 6.26 The data manipulator network for $N = 8$. Straight connections are shown by the dotted lines, PM2$_{+i}$ by the solid lines, and PM2$_{-i}$ by the dashed lines. The lower-case letters represent "end-around" connections.

To establish a path from an input source (S) of the ADM network to an output destination (D), links whose "sum" modulo N is $D - S$ modulo N are used. For example, in Figure 6.27, a path from $S = 1$ to $D = 6$ is shown. The $+2^2$ connection in stage 2 and $+2^0$ connection in stage 0 sum to $5 = D - S$ (the straight connection in stage 1 contributes nothing to the sum). Relating this to the single-stage PM2I network, PM2$_{+0}$(PM2$_{+2}$(1)) = 6. Other paths between 1 and 6 exist: $+2^2$, $+2^1$, -2^0; and straight, -2^1, -2^0. The only requirement is that the sum of the links in the path equals $D - S$ modulo N. The ADM network can connect any single source to any single destination.

Recall that in the GC there is only one path from a given source to a given destination (Section 6.3). In the ADM network, there are multiple paths between source/destination pairs S and D (unless $S = D$), hence giving it greater flexibility than the GC. This is different from the multiple-path feature of the Extra Stage Cube network, which, with stages m and 0 enabled, has exactly two paths between any source/destination pair.

The ADM network can also perform many permutation connections, where each input is connected to a single different output. The ADM network is different from the GC in that, for many permutations, there exist multiple different network settings that result in the same permutation. Also, the set of permutations performable by the ADM network is a superset of that of

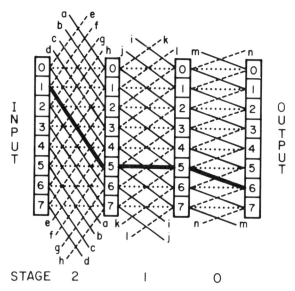

STAGE   2   1   0

Figure 6.27 Example of a one-to-one connection in the ADM network for $N = 8$. The bold line shows one path from input 1 to output 6.

the GC. Details on the number of permutations performable by the ADM network can be found in (41).

When a node in the ADM network selects one of its inputs and connects it to two or three of its outputs, a broadcast (one-to-many) connection is performed. One or more nodes in a path may be set to broadcast. For example, in the ADM network for $N = 8$, input 0 can be connected to outputs 4, 5, 6, and 7 using the node settings shown in Figure 6.28. In some cases, there are multiple paths for broadcasts as there are for one-to-one connections.

6.5.3. Network Control

To specify arbitrary paths in an ADM network, full routing tags can be used. These tags would be message headers, as for the GC. A *full routing tag, F* $= f_{2m-1} \ldots f_0$, uses the m low-order bits to represent the magnitudes of the route and the m high-order bits to represent the signs corresponding to the magnitudes. At stage i, a given switching element examines bits i and $m + i$ of the full tag. If $f_i = 0$, the straight link is used regardless of the value of f_{m+i}. If $f_i = 1$, the corresponding sign bit is examined. If $f_{m+i} = 0$, the $+2^i$ link is used. If $f_{m+i} = 1$, the -2^i link is used. For example, in the ADM network, for $N = 16$, if the source is 1 and the destination is 6, the routing tag $F = 00111011$ might be used. The path traversed is $+2^3$, straight, -2^1, -2^0. Obviously, because of the existence of multiple paths

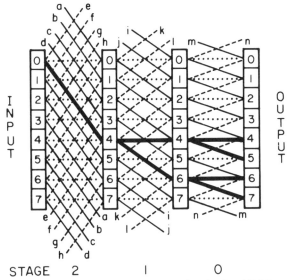

STAGE   2   1   0

Figure 6.28 Example of broadcasting in the ADM network for $N = 8$. Input 0 is connected to outputs 4, 5, 6, and 7.

in the ADM network, for most source/destination pairs different tags can be used to route from a given source to a given destination. One way to calculate a full tag F from source S to destination D is to set bits 0 to $m - 1$ of F to $S \oplus D$ and bits m to $2m - 1$ to $\overline{SD}$ (63). For the previous example, with $S = 1$ and $D = 6$, this produces $F = 00010111$, which is the path $+2^2$, $+2^1$, -2^0.

It is possible to use a more compact routing tag to control network settings, if some flexibility is sacrificed. A *natural routing tag* uses only one bit for the sign. All the links traversed are forced to be of the same sign. Thus, the new tag requires only $m + 1$ bits, and $T = t_m \ldots t_0$, where t_m is the sign bit. Let S denote the source address and D the destination address. An $m + 1$ bit routing tag is formed by computing the *signed magnitude* difference between the destination and the source: $T = t_m \ldots t_0 = D - S$. The *sign bit* is t_m, where $t_m = 0$ indicates positive or zero (i.e., $D \geq S$), and $t_m = 1$ indicates negative (i.e., $D < S$). Bits $t_{m-1} \ldots t_0$ equal the absolute value of $D - S$, the *magnitude* of the difference. For example, if $N = 16$, $S = 13$, and $D = 6$, $T = -7 = 10111$.

To route a message through the ADM network, stage i need examine only bits t_m and t_i in the routing tag. The natural routing tag is interpreted in the same way as the full routing tag, except t_m is used as the sign bit at every stage. In the previous example, with $T = 10111$, when a message enters the ADM network at stage 3, the sequence of connections traversed from port 13 to 6 is straight, -2^2, -2^1, -2^0.

A route consisting of only straight or $+2^i$ connections is called *positive dominant* and a route consisting of only straight or -2^i connections is called *negative dominant*. Two tags, T_1 and T_2, are *equivalent* (denoted $T_1 \simeq T_2$) if and only if they route a message from the same source address to the same destination address—i.e., given $T_1(S) \rightarrow D_1$ and $T_2(S) \rightarrow D_2$, $T_1 \simeq T_2$ if and only if $D_1 = D_2$. A characteristic of the routing tag scheme is that for any arbitrary natural tag, an equivalent routing tag can be computed that uses links of the opposite sign. For example, for $N = 16$, consider the positive dominant tag $T_1 = 00010 = +2$. T_1 is equivalent to the negative dominant tag $T_2 = 11110 = -14$, because -14 modulo $16 = +2$. In general, if T' is the 2's complement of T, $T \neq 0$, then $T' \simeq T$. This allows conversion from a positive dominant tag to a negative dominant tag, and vice versa. These ideas are extended in (43) to develop techniques for routing around faulty or busy switches.

One way to add a broadcast capability to either the full or natural routing tags is to include an $m + 1$ bit broadcast mask. The *broadcast routing tag* is denoted by {R, B}, where R is the *routing control* and B is the *broadcast mask*. R corresponds to F if full routing tags are used or to T if natural routing tags are used. For this discussion, it will be assumed that $R = T$.

This broadcast routing tag scheme allows a switching node to send the same message out on two links (it does not include facilities for sending the same message on all three of its links). Two kinds of broadcasts can be performed. A 2^i-*type* broadcast uses one straight link and one of the remaining nonstraight links. A 2^{i+1}-*type* broadcast uses the $+2^i$ link and the -2^i link.

A broadcast tag is interpreted by a node in stage i as follows. If the i-th bit of B, b_i ($0 \leq i < m$), is 0, no broadcast is performed and R is treated exactly as T would be (interpreted as a normal route). If b_i is a 1, the i-th bit of R is ignored and a broadcast is performed. The high-order bit of B, b_m, specifies a 2^i-type broadcast if equal to 0 and a 2^{i+1}-type broadcast if equal to 1. If a 2^i-type broadcast is specified, the sign bit of R, r_m, specifies which nonstraight link to use. Various properties of 2^i-type broadcasting are examined in the rest of this section. More information about 2^{i+1}-type broadcasts is in (43).

Using 2^i-type broadcast routing tags, 2^j destinations, each separated by a distance of 2^k, can receive a message from any source S. To do this, set bits k through $k + j - 1$ of B to 1 (all others to 0), and set R to $q - S$, where q is one of the desired destinations. As an example, consider the broadcast connections in Figure 6.28, where $N = 8$, $S = 0$, $q = 4$, $k = 0$, and $j = 2$. Then $B = 0011$ and $R = 0100$. The four destination addresses are 4 (100), 5 (101), 6 (110), and 7 (111). The broadcast path used by this tag is shown for the ADM network by the solid lines in Figure 6.28.

If $r_m = 0$, the routing control is positive dominant, and {R, B} is a *positive dominant broadcast route*. Similarly, if $r_m = 1$, {R, B} is a *negative dominant broadcast route*. Thus, equivalent broadcast routes can be computed in a fashion analogous to that for one-to-one connections (43).

In the discussion, it was assumed that the 1s in B were adjacent. This assumption was to simplify the description and is not a restriction on the broadcast capabilities of this scheme.

6.5.4. Partitioning

In Section 6.2, the partitioning of the PM2I single stage network was described. The partitioning of the ADM is related to these results (60, 61, 66, 69).

Consider partitioning an ADM network of size N into two independent subnetworks, each of size $N/2$. The only way to do this is to treat the even-numbered input/output ports as one subnetwork (A) and the odd-numbered ports as the other (B). This is shown in Figure 6.29 for $N = 8$. By setting all of the stage 0 connections to straight, no PE attached to subnetwork A can communicate with a PE attached to subnetwork B, and vice-versa. This is because the only way a PE with a 0 in the 0-th bit of its address can route data to a PE with a 1 in the 0-th bit of its address is by using a $+2^0$ or -2^0 connection at stage 0. Thus, by setting stage 0 to all straight connections, a size N ADM network can be partitioned into two size $N/2$ ADM networks. Each subnetwork has the properties of a complete ADM network of size $N/2$.

Because each subnetwork of size $N/2$ is a complete ADM network of size $N/2$, with all the properties of an ADM network, this process of dividing subnetworks into two independent halves can be repeated to create a subnetwork of any size from 1 to $N/2$. The only constraints are that the size of each subnetwork must be a power of 2, and the physical addresses of the input/output ports of a subnetwork of size 2^s must agree in their low-order $m - s$ bit positions.

In general, if input/output port j is in a subnetwork (partition) of size 2^s, switch j in stages 0, 1, . . . , $(m - s) - 1$ must be set to straight. This prevents input port j from accessing an output port that differs from it in any of the low order $m - s$ bit positions of its address. Each input/output port in the subnetwork can be logically numbered by the s high-order bits of its physical address (number). Physical stage i acts as logical stage $i - (m - s)$ for the partition, just as physical $\text{PM2}_{\pm i}$, would act as logical $\text{PM2}_{\pm(i-(m-s))}$ for the single-stage PM2I network.

The partitioning of the ADM network can be enforced using the routing tag schemes described in Section 6.5.3. If full routing tags are used, construct a $2m$-bit partitioning mask whose high-order m-bits are all 1s and whose low-order bits contain a 0 in those bit positions that correspond to stages that should be set to straight and 1s elsewhere. If this partitioning mask is logically ANDed with a tag before it is used, the partitioning will be guaranteed. The

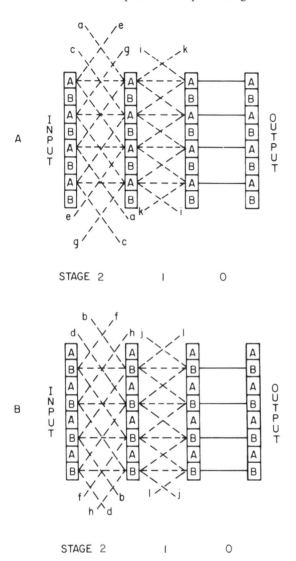

Figure 6.29 Partitioning a size-eight ADM network into two independent size four networks. (A) The A subnetwork, input/output ports 0, 2, 4, and 6. (B) The B subnetwork, input/output ports 1, 3, 5, and 7.

$(m + 1)$-bit partitioning mask for natural routing tags is similar, where the high-order bit is set to 1 and the low-order m-bits are set in the same way.

Thus, the ADM is partitionable and controllable by routing tags, as is the GC. The ADM is a more flexible network, but also more costly to implement (44).

6.6. Summary

This chapter introduced an important set of interconnection networks. In Section 6.2, four basic interconnection networks, the Cube, Illiac, PM2I, and Shuffle–Exchange, were defined, and single-stage implementations of these networks were studied. Section 6.3 explored the Generalized Cube network, a representative of the multistage Cube/Shuffle–Exchange class of networks. The Extra-Stage Cube network, a variant of the Generalized Cube network, which has fault-tolerant capabilities, was presented in Section 6.4. Finally, the properties of data manipulator networks, which are multistage implementations of the PM2I functions, were covered in Section 6.5.

This chapter will aid in the understanding of the related networks referenced here, as well as the existing and proposed systems that use these types of networks. For a more detailed treatment of this material, see (61).

Problems

1. Write an algorithm using the single-stage cube network to do a "$+2$" shift—i.e., PE P sends data to PE $P + 2$ modulo N, $0 \le P < N$.
2. Write an algorithm using the Illiac network to perform a PM2_{-i} transfer, for $0 \le i < m/2$ ($m = \log_2 N$), for all PEs.
3. In the algorithm using the PM2I network to do cube$_i$, $0 \le i \le m - 2$, if statement $S1$ is changed to

   ($S1$) PM$2_{-i}[X^m]$

   what would statement $S2$ have to be to make the algorithm correct?
4. Show how to partition the single-stage cube network for $N = 16$, forming subnetworks of sizes 8, 4, 2, and 2.
5. Consider a GC variant for $N = 8$ where the stages are ordered 1, 2, and 0 from input to output. Devise a routing tag scheme (including broadcasts) for this new network. Compute routing tags for (i) $S = 1$, $D = 5$ and (ii) $S = 0$, $D = \{4, 5, 6, 7\}$. How many permutations can this variant network perform?
6. Show how to partition the GC network for $N = 16$ into three subnetworks containing the I/O ports $\{0, 2, 4, 6, 8, 10, 12, 14\}$, $\{1, 5, 9, 13\}$, and $\{3, 7, 11, 15\}$, respectively.
7. Consider the ESC network for $N = 8$. Compute the routing tag T^* for $S = 5$ and $D = 2$ when
   (i) there is no fault in the network;
   (ii) stage 0 is faulty;
   (iii) a stage 2 box is faulty but it is not on the primary path from S to D;

    (iv) a stage 2 box is faulty and it is on the primary path from S to D;

    (v) stage 3 is faulty.

8. Consider the ESC network for $N = 16$. Compute the broadcast routing tag $\{R^*, B^*\}$ for $S = 5$ and $D = \{0, 1, 2, 3\}$ when

    (i) there is no fault in the network;

    (ii) stage 0 is faulty;

    (iii) a stage 2 box is faulty but it is not on the primary path from S to D;

    (iv) a stage 2 box is faulty and it is on the primary path from S to D;

    (v) stage 3 is faulty.

9. Consider an ADM network for $N = 16$.

    (i) Compute the positive dominant tag for $S = 13$, $D = 2$.

    (ii) Compute the equivalent negative dominant tag.

    (iii) Compute an equivalent full routing tag using both positive and negative links.

10. Consider an ADM network for $N = 8$. Compute a broadcast routing tag for $S = 0$, $D = \{1, 3, 5, 7\}$.

References

1. Adams GB III, Siegel HJ: The extra-stage cube: a fault-tolerant interconnection network for supersystems. *IEEE Trans. on Computers,* Vol. C-31, May 1982, pp. 443–454.
2. Adams GB III, Siegel HJ: A survey of fault-tolerant multistage networks and comparison to the extra stage cube. *Seventeenth Annual Hawaii International Conference on System Sciences,* Dec. 1984, pp. 268–277.
3. Adams GB III, Siegel HJ: Modifications to improve the fault tolerance of the extra-stage cube interconnection network. *1984 International Conference on Parallel Processing,* Aug. 1984, pp. 169–173.
4. Baer J-L: *Computer Systems Architecture,* Computer Science Press, Potomac, MD, 1980.
5. Barnes GH, Lundstrom SF: Design and validation of a connection network for many-processor multiprocessor systems. *Computer,* Vol. 14, Dec. 1981, pp. 31–41.
6. Batcher KE: The flip network in STARAN, *1976 International Conference on Parallel Processing,* Aug. 1976, pp. 65–71.
7. Batcher KE: STARAN series E. *1977 International Conference on Parallel Processing,* Aug. 1977, pp. 140–143.
8. Batcher KE: Bit serial parallel processing systems. *IEEE Trans. on Computers,* Vol. C-31, May 1982, pp. 377–384.
9. Benes VE: *Mathematical Theory of Connecting Networks and Telephone Traffic,* Academic Press, New York, 1965.
10. Bouknight WJ, Denenberg SA, McIntyre DE, et al: The Illiac IV system. *Proc. IEEE,* Vol. 60, April 1972, pp. 369–388.

11. Briggs, FA, Fu K-S, Hwang K, Wah BW: PUMPS architecture for pattern analysis and image database management. *IEEE Trans. on Computers,* Vol. C-31, Oct. 1982, pp. 969–982.

12. Broomell G, Heath JR: Classification categories and historical development of circuit switching topologies. *ACM Computing Surveys,* Vol. 15, No. 2, June 1983, pp. 95–133.

13. Chen P-Y, Lawrie DH, Yew P-C, Padua DA: Interconnection networks using shuffles. *Computer,* Vol. 14, Dec. 1981, pp. 55–64.

14. Chen P-Y, Yew P-C, Lawrie DH: Performance of packet switching in buffered single-stage shuffle-exchange networks. *Third International Conference on Distributed Computing Systems,* Oct. 1982, pp. 622–627.

15. Couranz GR, Gerhardt MS, Young CJ: Programmable RADAR signal processing using the RAP. *1974 Sagamore Computer Conference on Parallel Processing,* Aug. 1974, pp. 37–52.

16. Crowther W, Goodhue J, Starr E, et al: Performance measurements on a 128-node Butterfly parallel processor. *1985 International Conference on Parallel Processing,* Aug. 1985, pp. 531–540.

17. Davis NJ IV, Hsu WT-Y, Siegel HJ: Fault location techniques for distributed control interconnection networks. *IEEE Trans. on Computers,* Oct. 1985, pp. 902–910.

18. Dennis JB, Boughton GA, Leung CKC: Building blocks for data flow prototypes. *Seventh Annual Symposium on Computer Architecture,* May 1980, pp. 1–8.

19. Duff MJB: Real applications on CLIP4. In Levialdi S (ed): *Integrated Technology for Parallel Image Processing,* Academic Press, Orlando, Florida, 1985, pp. 153–165.

20. Feng TY: Data manipulating functions in parallel processors and their implementations. *IEEE Trans. on Computers,* Vol. C-23, March 1974, pp. 309–318.

21. Feng TY: A survey of interconnection networks. *Computer,* Vol. 14, Dec. 1981, pp. 12–27.

22. Feng TY, Wu C-L: Fault-diagnosis for a class of multistage interconnection networks. *IEEE Trans. on Computers,* Vol. C-30, Oct. 1981, pp. 743–758.

23. Feng TY, Zhang Q: Fault diagnosis of multistage interconnection networks with four valid states. *Fifth International Conference on Distributed Computing Systems,* May 1985, pp. 218–226.

24. Fishburn JP, Finkel RA: Quotient networks. *IEEE Trans. on Computers,* Vol. C-31, April 1982, pp. 288–295.

25. Filip AE: A distributed signal processing architecture. *Third International Conference on Distributed Computing Systems,* Oct. 1982, pp. 49–55.

26. Flynn MJ: Very high-speed computing systems. *Proc. IEEE,* Vol. 54, Dec. 1966, pp. 1901–1909.

27. Gentleman WM: Some complexity results for matrix computations on parallel processors. *Journal of the ACM,* Vol. 25, Jan. 1978, pp. 112–115.

28. Gottlieb A, Grishman R, Kruskal CP, et al: The NYU Ultracomputer—designing an MIMD shared-memory parallel computer. *IEEE Trans. on Computers,* Vol. C-32, Feb. 1983, pp. 175–189.

29. Goke GR, Lipovski GJ: Banyan networks for partitioning multiprocessor systems. *First Annual Symposium on Computer Architecture,* Dec. 1973, pp. 21–28.

30. Golomb SW: Permutations by cutting and shuffling. *SIAM Review,* Vol. 3, Oct. 1961, pp. 293–297.
31. Higbie LC: The Omen computer: associative array processor. *IEEE Computer Society COMPCON 72,* Sept. 1972, pp. 287–290.
32. Hockney RW, Jeshope CR: *Parallel Computers,* Adam Hilger Ltd., Bristol, England, 1981.
33. Hunt DJ: The ICL DAP and its application to image processing. In Duff MJB, Levialdi S (eds): *Languages and Architectures for Image Processing,* Academic Press, London, England, 1981, pp. 275–282.
34. Hwang K, Briggs F: *Computer Architecture and Parallel Processing,* McGraw-Hill, New York, 1984.
35. Intel Corporation: *A New Direction in Scientific Computing,* Order #28009-001, Intel Corporation, 1985.
36. Johnson PB: Congruences and card shuffling. *American Mathematical Monthly,* Vol. 63, Dec. 1956, pp. 718–719.
37. Kuck DJ: *The Structure of Computers and Computations, Vol. 1,* John Wiley & Sons, New York, 1978.
38. Lang T: Interconnections between processors and memory modules using the shuffle–exchange network. *IEEE Trans. on Computers,* Vol. C-25, May 1976, pp. 496–503.
39. Lang T, Stone HS: A shuffle–exchange network with simplified control. *IEEE Trans. on Computers,* Vol. C-25, Jan. 1976, pp. 55–66.
40. Lawrie DH: Access and alignment of data in an array processor. *IEEE Trans. on Computers,* Vol. C-24, Dec. 1975, pp. 1145–1155.
41. Leland MDP: On the power of the Augmented Data Manipulator network. *1985 International Conference on Parallel Processing,* Aug. 1985, pp. 74–78.
42. Masson GM, Gingher GC, Nakamura S: A sampler of circuit switching networks. *Computer,* Vol. 12, June 1979, pp. 32–48.
43. McMillen RJ, Siegel HJ: Routing schemes for the augmented data manipulator network in an MIMD system. *IEEE Trans. on Computers,* Vol. C-31, Dec. 1982, pp. 1202–1214.
44. McMillen RJ, Siegel HJ: Evaluation of cube and data manipulator networks. *Journal Parallel and Distributed Computing,* Vol. 2, Feb. 1985, pp. 79–107.
45. Nassimi D, Sahni S: Bitonic sort on a mesh-connected parallel computer. *IEEE Trans. on Computers,* Vol. C-28, Jan. 1979, pp. 2–7.
46. Nassimi D, Sahni S: An optimal routing algorithm for mesh-connected parallel computers. *Journal of the ACM,* Vol. 27, Jan. 1980, pp. 6–29.
47. Nassimi D, Sahni S: Data broadcasting in SIMD computers. *IEEE Trans. on Computers,* Vol. C-30, Feb. 1981, pp. 101–107.
48. Nassimi D, Sahni S: Optimal BPC permutations on a cube-connected SIMD computer. *IEEE Trans. on Computers,* Vol. C-31, April 1982, pp. 338–341.
49. Nassimi D, Sahni S: Parallel permutation and sorting algorithms and a new generalized connection network. *Journal of the ACM,* Vol. 29, July 1982, pp. 642–667.
50. Okada Y, Tajima H, Mori R: A reconfigurable parallel processor with microprogram control. *IEEE Micro,* Vol. 2, Nov. 1982, pp. 48–60.
51. Orcutt SE: Implementation of permutation functions in Illiac IV-type computers. *IEEE Trans. on Computers,* Vol. C-25, Sept. 1976, pp. 929–936.

52. Parker DS, Raghavendra CS: The gamma network: a multiprocessor interconnection network with redundant paths. *Ninth Annual Symposium on Computer Architecture,* April 1982, pp. 73–80.

53. Patel JH: Performance of processor-memory interconnections for multiprocessors, *IEEE Trans. on Computers,* Vol. C-30, Oct. 1981, pp. 771–780.

54. Pease MC III: The indirect binary n-cube microprocessor array. *IEEE Trans. on Computers,* Vol. C-26, May 1977, pp. 458–473.

55. Pfister GF, Brantley WC, George DA, et al: The IBM Research Parallel Processor Prototype (RP3): Introduction and architecture. *1985 International Conference on Parallel Processing,* Aug. 1985, pp. 764–771.

56. Pradhan DK, Kodandapani KL: A uniform representation of single- and multistage interconnection networks used in SIMD machines. *IEEE Trans. on Computers,* Vol. C-29, Sept. 1980, pp. 777–791.

57. Seitz CL: The Cosmic Cube. *Comm. ACM,* Jan. 1985, pp. 22–33.

58. Siegel HJ: Analysis techniques for SIMD machine interconnection networks and the effects of processor address masks. *IEEE Trans. on Computers,* Vol. C-26, Feb. 1977, pp. 153–161.

59. Siegel HJ: A model of SIMD machines and a comparison of various interconnection networks. *IEEE Trans. on Computers,* Vol. C-28, Dec. 1979, pp. 907–917.

60. Siegel HJ: The theory underlying the partitioning of permutation networks. *IEEE Trans. on Computers,* Vol. C-29, Sept. 1980, pp. 791–801.

61. Siegel HJ: *Interconnection Networks for Large-Scale Parallel Processing: Theory and Case Studies,* Lexington Books, D. C. Heath and Company, Lexington, MA, 1985.

62. Siegel HJ, McMillen RJ, Mueller PT Jr: A survey of interconnection methods for reconfigurable parallel processing systems. *AFIPS 1979 National Computer Conference,* June 1979, pp. 529–542.

63. Siegel HJ, McMillen RJ: Using the Augmented Data Manipulator network in PASM. *Computer,* Vol. 14, Feb. 1981, pp. 25–33.

64. Siegel HJ, McMillen RJ: The cube network as a distributed processing test bed switch. *Second International Conference on Distributed Computing Systems,* April 1981, pp. 377–387.

65. Siegel HJ, McMillen RJ: The multistage cube: a versatile interconnection network. *Computer,* Vol. 14, Dec. 1981, pp. 65–76.

66. Siegel HJ, Smith SD: Study of multistage SIMD interconnection networks. *Fifth Annual Symposium on Computer Architecture,* April 1978, pp. 223–229.

67. Siegel HJ, Smith SD: An interconnection network for multimicroprocessor emulator systems. *First International Conference on Distributed Computing Systems,* Oct. 1979, pp. 772–782.

68. Siegel HJ, Siegel LJ, Kemmerer FC, et al: PASM: a partitionable SIMD/MIMD system for image processing and pattern recognition. *IEEE Trans. on Computers,* Vol. C-30, Dec. 1981, pp. 934–947.

69. Smith SD, Siegel HJ: Recirculating, pipelined, and multistage SIMD interconnection networks. *1978 International Conference on Parallel Processing,* Aug. 1978, pp. 206–214.

70. Smith SD, Siegel HJ: An emulator network for SIMD machine interconnection

networks. *Sixth Annual Symposium on Computer Architecture*, April 1979, pp. 232–241.

71. Stone HS: Parallel processing with the perfect shuffle. *IEEE Trans. on Computers*, Vol. C-20, Feb. 1971, pp. 153–161.

72. Sullivan H, Bashkow TR, Klappholz K: A large-scale homogeneous, fully distributed parallel machine. *Fourth Annual Symposium on Computer Architecture*, March 1977, pp. 105–124.

73. Thompson CD, Kung HT: Sorting on a mesh-connected parallel computer. *Comm. of the ACM*, Vol. 20, April 1977, pp. 263–271.

74. Thurber KJ, Masson GM: *Distributed-Processor Communication Architecture*, Lexington Books, D. C. Heath and Company, Lexington, MA, 1979.

75. Thurber KJ: Parallel processor architectures—part 1: general purpose systems. *Computer Design*, Vol. 18, Jan. 1979, pp. 89–97.

76. Weiss R: Multiple-processor systems and emerging architectures take the lead at NCC. *Electronic Design*, June 27, 1985.

77. Wen KY: *Interprocessor Connections—Capabilities, Exploitation, and Effectiveness*, PhD Thesis, University of Illinois at Urbana-Champaign, Department of Computer Science Report No. 76-830, 1976.

78. Wester AH: Special features in SIMDA. *1972 Sagamore Computer Conference on Parallel Processing*, Aug. 1972, pp. 29–40.

79. Wu C-L, Feng TY: On a class of multistage interconnection networks. *IEEE Trans. on Computers*, Vol. C-29, Aug. 1980, pp. 694–702.

80. Wu C-L, Feng TY: The universality of the shuffle–exchange network. *IEEE Trans. on Computers*, Vol. C-30, May 1981, pp. 324–332.

81. Wu C-L, Feng TY: *Tutorial: Interconnection Networks for Parallel and Distributed Processing*, IEEE Computer Society Press, Silver Spring, MD, 1984.

82. Yew P-C: *On the Design of Interconnection Networks for Parallel and Multiprocessor Systems*. PhD Thesis, University of Illinois at Urbana-Champaign, Department of Computer Science Report No. 81-1059, March 1981.

7

Resource Allocation for Local Computer Systems

Jie-Yong Juang
Benjamin W. Wah

7.1. Introduction

Because of the rapid advances in microelectronics and Very-Large-Scale-Integrated (VLSI) circuit design technologies, the cost of computer hardware has dropped drastically and the processing and communication speeds have approached some physical limitations. These technological advances, coupled with the explosion in size and complexity of new applications, have led to the development of *resource sharing computer systems*. Such systems usually consist of a large number of general- and special-purpose processors interconnected together by a communication network called the *resource-sharing interconnection network* (64).

A resource in a computer network is a processor that performs computation functions or manipulates data objects. It may generate requests to

Research supported partially by CIDMAC, a research unit of Purdue University, sponsored by Purdue, Cincinnati Milicron Corporation, Control Data Corporation, Cummins Engine Company, Ransburg Corporation, and TRW, and by National Science Foundation Grant DMC-85 19649.

265

utilize other resources. A system featuring resource sharing should support *dynamic task migration,* a scheme that allows tasks to be relocated dynamically. Depending on the system status, a task originally allocated to a processor may be migrated to another processor and executed remotely. Reasons for the migration of a task include: (1) the local processor is unable to execute the task because it does not support the designated computing functions; (2) the required data are not available locally and have to be retrieved from a remote site; (3) the workload of the local processor is heavier than that of the remote processor—i.e., the remote processor has better turnaround time; or (4) the local processor is unavailable because of hardware or software failures.

For convenience, the following terms are defined. The processor receiving a migrated task is called a *resource* to this task, and the processor from which the task is migrated is called a *request generator.* A processor may play the roles both of a request generator and a resource. For example, a general-purpose processor may request for migrating a fast-Fourier-transformation (FFT) task to a special-purpose processor. At the same time, it may accept a language-translation task from another processor that has a heavier workload.

7.1.1. A Generic Model of Resource-Sharing Computer System

The resource-allocation problem involves the scheduling of resources in resource-sharing computer systems. To study the resource allocation problem, a generic model that helps to grasp the instantaneous configuration of such systems is devised and shown in Figure 7.1. The model consists of a pool of resources and a set of request generators. These resources and processors are connected by an interconnection network. This model is the logical construction of resource-sharing computer systems. A computational device that makes requests is represented by a processor in the processor pool, and a computational device that can receive and service tasks is represented by a resource in the resource pool. A device may be either a processor or a resource in this model because of its dual roles as a resource and a request generator. Those devices not involved in resource allocation are not represented in the model.

According to the network selected and the characteristics of processors, the proposed model may represent different classes of resource-sharing systems. It includes multiprocessors, local computer networks, or long-haul computer networks. The model addresses the issues of global resource allocation and excludes the details of local scheduling. If a set of tightly coupled processors is connected by a fast network, the cluster of processors is represented by a single-request generator or resource in the model. The resource scheduling algorithms developed in this chapter may be applied recursively to the scheduling within the cluster.

Systems that can be characterized by the generic model have the fol-

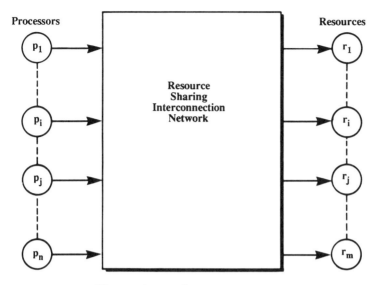

Processors

Resources

Resource
Sharing
Interconnection
Network

p_i - i'th request generating processor;
r_j - j'th resource for executing a designated task.

Figure 7.1 A generic model of resource sharing computer systems (Arrow K, Pesotchinsky L, Sobel M: On partitioning a sample with binary-type quetions in lieu of collecting observations. *Journal of the American Statistical Association,* Vol. 76, No. 324, June 1981, pp. 402–409.

lowing properties:

1. The global status information of the system is not available to the individual processors.
2. The interconnection network is the only intercommunication facility among processors.
3. A request may be dispatched to any one in the set of available resources that is capable of carrying out the designated task.
4. A resource is accessible by any request-generating processors.

A resource-sharing system with these characteristics has the following advantages:

1. Tasks may be executed in parallel, and workload of processors may be distributed evenly.
2. Efficient architectures for performing special tasks may be included in the system.
3. Modifications to include new functions or increased performance can be done easily because of the system's modularity.
4. Malfunctional devices may be removed from the system without stopping the entire system.

Consequently, the performance of such a system may be improved by increasing the number of resources or replacing an existing resource by a more efficient one. The system is also highly reliable and maintainable.

A shared resource may manipulate data objects or provide computational service on request. Issues on sharing data have been studied intensively in recent years. Many schemes have been proposed to deal with the synchronization and data-coherence problems. Examples include monitors and synchronization schemes in operating systems (13, 23), cache coherence schemes in multiprocessors (14), and the methods of maintaining data integrity in distributed database managements systems (51). However, as discussed in Section 7.2, schemes for sharing computational devices are less developed. Most existing schemes are based on centralized control or simple distributed extensions of centralized control. The characteristics of the network are usually not incorporated in the design of resource-sharing schemes.

This generic model encompasses many existing or proposed systems. The dynamic task migration is the basic feature of many proposed distributed programming languages such as Hoare's Cooperating Sequential Processes (24, 53), CLU developed at MIT (39, 40), and Brinch Hansen's distributed processes (21). New operating system designs also provide mechanisms to support dynamic task migrations. Examples include pipes in MEDUSA (47) and UNIX (50). Many architectures also exhibit the characteristics of this generic model. Examples include local computer networks with load balancing such as the ECN (26) and LOCUS (69), VLSI-systolic array multiprocessors (5, 35), and dataflow supercomputers (11). Because resources of these architectures represent different levels of abstraction, it is instructive to describe them and to indicate their mappings to the generic model.

Example 1: Local Computer Network with Load Balancing. Load balancing is a scheme that engages communication facilities in supporting remote job execution in a user-transparent manner, so the turnaround time is reduced through the enhancement of resource sharing. Depending on the workload of processors, the network operating system may distribute jobs to a remote processor or may schedule them for local execution. A local computer network with load balancing is illustrated in Figure 7.2 (26, 63). Corresponding to the model, those processors of heavy workloads are request-generators, and those processors of light workloads are resources. The resources in this system are job-level processors.

Example 2: VLSI-Systolic Array Multiprocessors. A VLSI systolic array is a parallel pipeline architecture for evaluating a recursive function, such as FIR filtering, matrix multiplication, and FFT. Such VLSI chips are usually organized as attached processors to host computers as shown in Figure 7.3 (35). In this organization, requests are generated from processors and routed to systolic arrays through the system bus. The resources in such systems are process-level special-purpose processors.

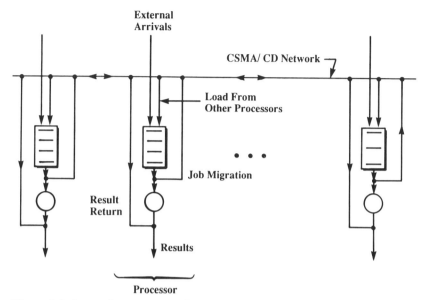

Figure 7.2 A queuing representation of local computer network with load balancing.

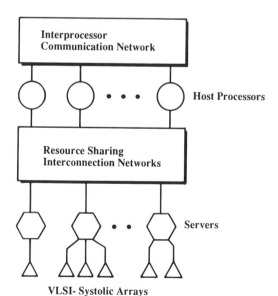

VLSI- Systolic Arrays

Figure 7.3 An organization of VLSI systolic-array multiprocessors.

Example 3: Dataflow Supercomputers. In contrast to the conventional von Neumann machine, there are no sequence-control mechanisms in a dataflow machine. The execution of an instruction is driven by the availability of its input data. An instruction is active when all its input arguments are ready. An active instruction is executed at a processing unit. The outputs of this instruction will activate other instructions for the subsequent executions. A typical dataflow multiprocessor is shown in Figure 7.4 (11). For a detailed discussion, see Chapter 9.

In this architecture, instructions are allocated in the activity store and waiting for their inputs. Once an instruction becomes active, it is routed through an arbitration network to a processing element and executed there. The output is then routed back to the activity store through a distribution network. The activity store is divided into cell blocks, and active instructions in a cell block are requests. The processing units are arithmetic and logical devices, hence they are instruction-level resources.

7.1.2. Resource Scheduling

Resource scheduling entails the allocation of resources (including communication facilities), so task migrations can be carried out efficiently. In general, the migration of a task in a distributed resource-sharing system is divided into three phases: resource-bidding, task-migration, and result-return. In the first phase, the local processor has to make a request for utilizing a

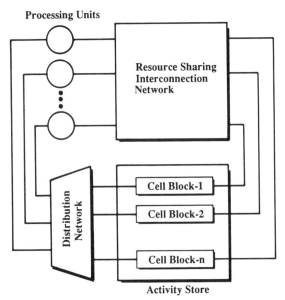

Figure 7.4 A dataflow multiprocessor.

resource. In the second phase, the body of the task, including the task control, program code, and data, are transferred to the resource allocated and executed remotely. In the last phase, the results generated from the execution of the task are routed back to the original processor. Basically, only data transmission is involved during the migration and result-return phases. Resource scheduling is carried out in the resource-bidding phase. In this phase, system status information has to be collected, and the decision of resource allocation has to be made.

Issues of Resource Scheduling

The central issue of resource scheduling is to determine a resource mapping that maps requests to resources. Resources will be allocated to associated requests determined by the mapping. Because a task can be allocated to one of a set of free resources, and multiple requests may contend for the same resource, multiple requests may be allocated the same resource while other resources are idle. This problem is called *resource conflict*. If the resource has local buffers, the tasks may still be migrated and queued at the resource regardless of conflicts. This causes no error in operation but may deteriorate resource utilization because of the imbalance of workload. If the resource has no buffering capability, every request except one has to be rescheduled again.

In addition to resource conflict, a bad resource allocation may degrade the performance of the network. Depending on the characteristics of the system, a physical communication link may be assigned to every processor-resource allocation and operate in a circuit-switching mode, or links may be shared in a packet-switching mode. A resource-allocation scheme that minimizes resource conflicts is not necessarily optimal because there may be many paths being blocked in the circuit-switching mode, and packets may be congested in the packet-switching mode.

In summary, three major issues will affect resource utilization in resource-sharing computer systems. These include network blocking (or packet congestions), request conflicts, and imbalanced workload. Unless the scheduling algorithm is carefully designed and implemented, there may be many adverse effects on the benefits of resource sharing.

Efficiency of Resource Scheduling

To illustrate the effects of these issues, a resource-sharing system may be transformed into a queuing network as shown in Figure 7.5. In this queuing model, a processor is represented by an arrival process with arrival rate λ_i, while a resource is represented by a server R_j with service rate μ_j. An additional server S is introduced to model the resource-allocation mechanism and the communication network. A branch from the output of server S feeds back to the input of this server and represents the unsuccessful resource allocations due to network blockages or resource conflicts. Although the

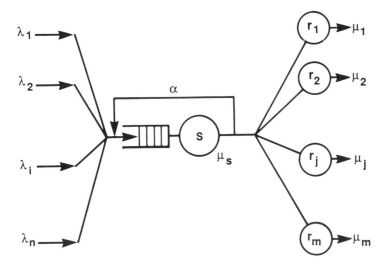

S — A server represents the resource allocation mechanism;
α — the probability of network blocking and resource conflicts;
λ_i — request generation rate of processor p_i ;
μ_j — Service rate of resource r_j;
μ_s — Scheduling rate of S.

Figure 7.5 A queuing model for resource sharing computer systems.

scheduling mechanism is represented by a single server, it does not imply centralized control. Instead, it may be realized in many alternative ways as will be described in Section 7.2. Task-transmission delays in the network are considered part of scheduling overhead.

In a word, the service rate of S depends on two factors: the speed of the scheduler and the delay of task transmissions. According to the results of queuing theory (32), the service rate of server S is crucial to the overall system performance. Thus, improving the efficiency of resource allocation is translated to increasing the service rate of S and reducing its feedback probability. These may be achieved (1) by a good design of a high-speed resource allocation mechanism, (2) by utilizing a good scheduling algorithm that generates a good resource mapping, and (3) by using a high-speed communication network.

Scheduling Disciplines
Depending on the scheduling disciplines, requests and resources may be characterized by multiple attributes. A request may be represented by the types of task it requests, expected execution time, and priority level. On the other hand, resources may be modeled by its speed, load, and reliability.

A scheduling algorithm has to evaluate the allocation costs based on these attributes.

Consider a scheduling example that consists of two types of requests: matrix computations and scalar computations. Suppose that requests for matrix computations have higher priority than requests for scalar computations, that all vector processors are busy, and that only pipelined processors are available. Then requests for matrix computations would be allocated if the requests are scheduled according to their priorities. On the other hand, matrix computations may be executed more efficiently on a vector processor than that of a pipelined processor. Hence, requests for matrix computations may not be allocated if the requests are scheduled according to the preferences of resources.

In this chapter, we consider only the class of scheduling disciplines in which multiple attributes are combined into a single parameter. The parameter that characterizes a request is called the *priority* of the request, and the parameter that characterizes a resource is called the *preference* of the resource. Our objective is to investigate the design of efficient resource-scheduling mechanisms for resource-sharing computer systems, and explore the integration of the scheduling algorithms and computer networks. Several goals are to be pursued:

1. A feasible scheduling strategy for improving resource utilization in resource-sharing computer systems will be studied.
2. The distribution of scheduling intelligence will be investigated.
3. Fast implementation for the scheduling mechanisms will be developed.

A unified design methodology is employed to incorporate these three design goals. However, we consider only those scheduling schemes that allocate one resource to a request at a time. When multiple resources are requested by a single request, they have to be allocated sequentially.

7.2. A Taxonomy of Resource-Allocation Schemes

In the design of resource allocation schemes, achieving high-speed scheduling and obtaining an optimal mapping are usually two mutually conflicting goals. Compromises between the optimality of the scheduling decision and the overhead of collecting system status information are reached in many ways. Resource allocation schemes can be characterized by the trade-off between these two goals. In this section, a taxonomy of these resource-allocation schemes is presented. The advantages and disadvantages of each class of resource-allocation schemes in the taxonomy are explored. This leads to the conclusion that a distributed state-dependent allocation scheme is preferable. To tackle the complex design problems of distributed state-dependent resource allocation schemes, a systematic design methodology is proposed in this section.

7.2.1. A Taxonomy of Resource-Allocation Schemes

A taxonomy that categorizes most resource-allocation schemes is given in Figure 7.6. Resource-allocation schemes may be classified into two classes depending on whether global status information is used or not, and whether they are *state-dependent* or *state-independent*.

In the class of state-independent scheduling schemes, resource allocation is carried out by the individual request-generator. Each request-generator determines the resource to bid for based on the local information available. This information may include the statistics of the system's operating history, piggy-backed information carried by the return message of previous requests, and the specifications of individual resources. If the processor chooses a resource randomly, the scheduling scheme is a *random scheduling* scheme. On the other hand, if the statistics on previous requests and resource specifications are inputs to the scheduling decision, the scheduling scheme is a *probabilistic scheduling* scheme. Because requesting processors do not communicate, resource conflicts are unavoidable. Conflicting requests have to contend for the resource they bid for. Queuing-network analysis has been applied intensively to analyze the efficiency of this class of scheduling schemes (45, 59, 70).

On the other hand, in the class of state-dependent scheduling schemes, the global status information is crucial. Among them, a *localized state-de-*

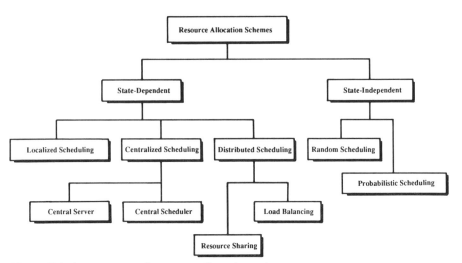

Figure 7.6 A taxonomy of resource allocation schemes.

pendent scheduling scheme requires every processor to maintain a copy of the global state information and to determine the resource allocation independently. In contrast, in *centralized state-dependent scheduling* schemes, the status information is collected by a central control node that determines the resource mapping to be distributed to all requesting processors. A scheduling scheme with this kind of organization is called a *central scheduler*. Essentially, only the tasks of resource bidding are carried out in the central control node. Task migrations and result returns are carried out independently. However, the central control node may be also responsible for buffering tasks and dispatching them to resources. In this sense, the scheduler becomes a *central server*. A central server is usually found in systems in which resources do not have local memories. Some master–slave multiprocessors belong to this class (15).

A *distributed scheduling* scheme differs from localized and centralized scheduling schemes in the way that global status information is collected and utilized. In a distributed scheduling scheme, only partial status information is maintained by each processor, and the scheduling decision is made cooperatively through exchanging information. The amount of information flow is usually lower than that of the previous two approaches.

Most existing resource scheduling schemes belong to the class of state-independent schemes (10, 27, 37, 38): The resource sharing protocol of AR-PANET is a typical example in which task migrations are determined by end users (57). This class of resource scheduling schemes is simple and incurs relatively little overhead. Nevertheless, the problem of low resource utilization remains unsolved. Centralized state-dependent scheduling schemes can be found in many multiprocessor systems with master–slave structure (2, 15, 22). However, adopting this approach to distributed systems tends to eliminate their advantages. Localized state-dependent scheduling schemes are the direct distributed extensions of centralized control. The load balancing schemes of ECN and LOCUS belong to this class. Although this approach can be implemented in an existing network, it incurs a large amount of redundant information flow and is hard to maintain a consistent state information because of the network delay. Consequently, a resource mapping generated by an optimal scheduling algorithm is not necessarily the optimal one because inaccurate information may be used.

Distributed state-dependent scheduling schemes are generally preferable for the following reasons: (1) the information flow in maintaining the global information is reduced because status information is utilized efficiently; (2) they can achieve optimal resource allocation; and (3) their speed may be increased because of the concurrent execution of scheduling tasks. Only a few simple distributed state-dependent schemes have been proposed (29, 30, 41, 62–64). It is still an open area of study. We focus on the design of distributed state-dependent resource scheduling schemes in this chapter.

7.2.2. Implementation Considerations and a Design Methodology

In general, a resource-scheduling algorithm generates a resource mapping according to the system status information. A good resource mapping is one that minimizes a cost function under the network constraints. The cost function is usually determined by the scheduling disciplines. It is usually easier to optimize the cost function regardless of the constraints imposed by the network. As a result, many processors may not be allocated a scheduled resource because of conflicts in the network. To reduce this probability, a high-bandwidth network is usually used (16). A crossbar network has been used in systems such as the C.mmp (15, 18). It does not have the network blocking problem. However, the cost of a crossbar network is $O(n^2)$, where n is the number of devices connected, and is not practical when the system is large. A multistage interconnection network is a cost-effective choice (64), but blocking probability may be as high as 60% if resources are not allocated properly (17, 48). These observations indicate that a good resource-scheduling algorithm should incorporate network constraints in the optimization of a given scheduling discipline. The following design methodology is proposed:

1. Formulate the resource-scheduling problem into a constrainted optimization problem.
2. Design a distributed algorithm to solve the problem.
3. Identify primitive operations of each process in the distributed algorithm.
4. Integrate the primitive operations into the network.

The cost of collecting status information may also be included in the objective function, so trade-offs can be made between the amount of status information used and the efficiency of the scheduling algorithm. A well-designed distributed algorithm should reduce unnecessary message passing. The crucial speedup of the scheduling scheme lies in implementing the primitive operation into the network. This approach essentially shifts the responsibility of scheduling requests by the request generators to the network.

We will show the application of the methodology to the design of resource scheduling schemes for a single contention-bus network. Resource allocation is studied with respect to requests that need one resource only; multiple resources needed by a request are allocated sequentially. The network is assumed to be a *reliable multiaccess bus* with the *broadcast capability*. *Carrier-sense-multiaccess networks* with *collision detection* (CSMA/CD networks) belong to this class, and are exemplified by the Ethernet (56) (Figure 7.7a).

CSMA/CD networks evolved from CSMA networks, which have listen-before-talk protocols to avoid overlapping transmissions. The collision-detection capability of CSMA/CD networks allows processors to additionally listen-while-talk, so collisions resulting from simultaneous transmissions can

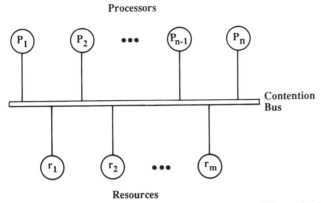

Figure 7.7a A resource-sharing system connected by a single multiaccess bus.

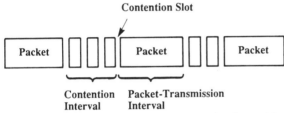

Figure 7.7b The operations of a contention bus with altering phases.

be detected and stopped immediately. The time for a processor to assert that there are no overlapping transmissions is the end-to-end propagation delay on the bus and is called a *contention slot*. To avoid repeated collisions, a contention-resolution protocol is used to control transmissions and to eventually isolate one station for transmitting the message. The operation of the bus is thus divided into two alternating phases, the contention-resolution phase consisting of a sequence of contention slots, and the data-transmission phase consisting of the message transmission (Figure 7.17b). Many contention-resolution protocols have been proposed and implemented (4, 7, 8, 19, 25, 28, 33, 34, 36, 42, 44, 60, 63). They are distinguished by the different transmission control.

7.3. Optimal Resource-Allocation Algorithms

The optimal resource-allocation problem can be considered as an optimization problem that optimizes the system performance or cost subject to constraints of the network. Let P be the set of request generators and R be the set of resources. Each request generator $p \in P$ is characterized by a priority x_p, which measures the urgency that the request generated has to be serviced. Similarly, each resource $r \in R$ is characterized by a preference y_r, which measures its capability to service a generated request. Because there is only one communication channel in a single-bus system, only one resource can be allocated at a time, and the scheduling problem is reduced to finding a pair of request generator and resource that optimize the system performance or cost. The optimization can be represented as

$$\min_{(p,r)\in P\times R} H(x_p, y_r) \tag{7.1}$$

where H is a cost function defined with respect to a given scheduling discipline.

In general, the cost function H depends on the characteristics of tasks and resources, as well as the interconnection network. It may be very complex and difficult to optimize. We will only study a special class of the cost functions that are monotonic with respect to x_p and y_r. That is,

$$\frac{\partial}{\partial x_p} H(x_p, y_r) \text{ is either positive or negative for all } x_p \text{ and } y_r \tag{7.2a}$$

$$\frac{\partial}{\partial y_r} H(x_p, y_r) \text{ is either positive or negative for all } x_p \text{ and } y_r \tag{7.2b}$$

These conditions imply that, for a given resource, the cost is minimized by servicing a task of the highest priority (if Eq. (7.2a) is negative), or one with the lowest priority (if Eq. (7.2a) is positive). Similarly, for a given request, the cost is minimized by choosing a resource of the highest preference (if Eq. (7.2b) is negative), or one with the lowest preference (if Eq. (2b) is positive). For instance, if

$$\frac{\partial}{\partial x_p} H(x_p, y_r) \leq 0 \text{ and } \frac{\partial}{\partial y_r} H(x_p, y_r) \geq 0$$

it follows directly from Eqs. (7.1) and (7.2) that

$$\min_{(p,r)\in P\times R} H(x_p, y_r) = H(\max_{p\in P}(x_p), \min_{r\in R}(y_r)) \tag{7.3}$$

Optimal resource scheduling can thus be considered as choosing a request generator p with the maximum x_p and a resource r with the minimum y_r independently.

Many existing resource-scheduling problems can be solved by independently selecting the task to be serviced and the resource to service the task. Some notable examples are given here.

1. *Random-Access Protocols in CSMA Networks*. In CSMA networks, all processors share a single communication channel to communicate with each other. Processors with message to transmit are request generators, and the communication channel is the only shared resource. Contention-reso-

lution protocols in CSMA networks are designed to resolve contentions in using the channel. Because each request generator has equal right to access the channel, its priority can be considered as a random number in $(0, 1]$, and the cost function $H(x_p, y_r) = x_p$. The request generator with the minimum number generated is given the access right to the channel.

2. *First-Come-First-Served Discipline in CSMA Networks.* The channel is the only resource to be scheduled. The priority level x_p is an increasing function of the task arrival time. The cost function $H(x_p, y_r) = x_p$.

3. *Shortest-Job-First Discipline in CSMA Networks.* The channel is the only resource to be scheduled. The priority level x_p is an increasing function of size of the job. The cost function $H(x_p, y_r) = x_p$, and the scheduler selects the smallest job.

4. *Priority Scheduling.* Messages in the network are divided into priority classes (levels), and the channel is allocated to service messages in decreasing order of priority levels. Several CSMA protocols for handling priority messages have been suggested recently (20, 46, 55, 58). They may be classified as linear protocols and logarithmic protocols. Each station is assigned the highest priority of the local messages. In a linear protocol, a slot is reserved for each priority level during the resolution of priorities. An active station contends during the slot reserved for the local priority level. When the station(s) with the highest priority level is determined, the process is switched to identifying a unique station within this priority level. This scheme is good when high-priority messages are predominantly sent. A logarithmic protocol determines the highest priority level in $O(\log_2 P)$ steps by a binary-divide scheme, where P is the maximum number of priority levels (46). This assumes that the highest priority level is equally likely to be any one of the P priority levels. Neither of these schemes is able to adapt to the various traffic patterns.

Resource scheduling in this case can be carried out in two phases. The first phase determines the highest priority level present in the network. A cost function $H(x_p, y_r) = -x_p$ is assumed. There may be multiple stations in this priority level, and scheduling for these stations is done in the second phase using one of the preceding criteria.

5. *Resource Sharing of a Pool of Identical Resources.* The priority of a request generator is an integer between 1 and P. The preference of a resource can be a random number in $[0, 1]$ indicating its status (0 indicates that it is busy; any number between 0 and 1 indicates that it is free). Resource scheduling is carried out in two phases. The first phase identifies a request generator with the highest priority. The second phase identifies a free resource to service the task. Examples of cost function $H(x_p, y_r)$ that can be used are $(-x_p - y_r)$ or $(-x_p y_r)$.

6. *Load Balancing.* This uses the communication facility to support remote job execution in a user-transparent fashion to improve resource utilization and to minimize response time. A decision to load balance a job is

made if the job is likely to be finished sooner when executed remotely than when executed locally. Resource scheduling is performed in two phases. In the first phase, processors are treated as request generators and are assigned priority equal to the average response time of executing a job locally. The processor with the highest response time is chosen as the request generator to send the job. In the second phase, processors are treated as resources and are assigned preferences equal to the sum of the average transmission time of sending a job across the network and the average response time of executing a job locally. The processor with the lowest preference is chosen. The cost function $H(x_p, y_r) = -x_p + y_r$ is the reduction in response time of executing a job remotely at processor r.

In these examples, only linear functions on x_p and y_r are defined. In general, they can be any function satisfying Eqs. (7.2a) and (7.2b).

A general organization of a resource scheduler is shown in Figure 7.8. There may be multiple classes of problems in resource sharing and they will be assigned different priorities in scheduling. For example, the network may be designed primarily for message transfers, and load balancing may be its secondary function. The resource scheduler will schedule all message transmissions before initiating load balancing for the system. For this example,

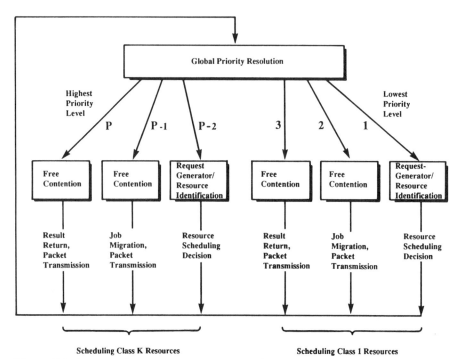

Figure 7.8 A protocol to support resource sharing of multiple classes of resources connected by a multiaccess bus.

$P = 6$ and $K = 2$ in Figure 7.8. Class 1 tasks refer to load-balancing operations, and Class 2 tasks refer to message transmissions. Generally, within a class of resource-scheduling problem, the return of results from a previously migrated job, if any, is given a higher priority than the migration of a new request because any delay in returning results contributes to an increase in response time, while an earlier transmission of a request to a remote resource may not reduce the response time unless the remote resource is idle. The migration of a request is given a higher priority than the identification of a new request-generator/resource pair because a request must be completely sent before it can be processed, and any delay in completing a job transfer may tie up valuable buffer space unnecessarily and reduce the resource utilization.

7.4. A Distributed Minimum-Search Algorithm

The operations of the resource scheduler in Figure 7.8 can be reduced to the primitive operation of identifying the extremum from a set of physically dispersed random numbers called *contention parameters*. The generation of these parameters may be dependent on each other, and may also be site-dependent. For tractability reasons, the parameters are assumed to be independently generated and possibly site-dependent in this section. Specifically, the identification of the task with the highest priority in Figure 7.8 can be considered as the search of the maximum priority level from a set of priority levels, one from each processor. Similarly, the transmission of a message (result or job) can be regarded as the selection of a ready station from a set of ready stations, each of which generates a contention parameter from a uniform distribution between 0 and 1. Likewise, the identification of a request generator or resource is again the selection of the station with the maximum or minimum parameter.

Conventionally, the implementation of an extremum-search algorithm relies on the message-passing mechanism to collect all information to a central site. This requires $O(n)$ messages, where n is the number of stations. In this section, an efficient distributed protocol for identifying the minimum is presented. The algorithm for searching the maximum is similar. The proposed algorithm has a load-independent behavior, which is important for resource-sharing applications because the number of processors to participate in identifying the extremum is usually large. Conventional contention-resolution algorithms, such as Ethernet's Binary Exponential Backoff algorithm, is load-dependent, but performs satisfactorily because the channel load is normally low for point-to-point message transmissions. Moreover, these algorithms cannot be directly applied to identify the extremum.

It is assumed that each processor in the network is capable of maintaining a global reference interval or *window*, and counting whether there

```
procedure window_protocol_station_i:
/* procedure to find window boundaries for isolating one of the contending stations */
[ /* window - function to calculate window size w,
    random - function to generate local contention parameter,
    estimate - function to estimate channel load,
    transmit_signal - function to send signal to bus with
        other stations synchronously,
    detect - function to detect whether there is collision on the bus (three-state),
    r_i - local contention parameter,
    n̂ - estimated channel load,
    lb_minimum - lower bound of interval containing minimum (minimum is L),
    ub_minimum - upper bound of interval containing minimum (maximum is U),
    contending - boolean to continue the contention process,
    state - state of collision detect, can be collision, idle, or success
        (for three-state collision detection). */
  lb_minimum := L;
  ub_minimum :=U;
  r_i ;- random (L,U);
  n̂ := estimate ();
  w := window (lb_minimum, ub_minimum, n̂);
  contending := true;
  while (contending) do [
      if (r_i > lb_minimum and r_i ≤ w) then [
              /* parameter is inside window, contend for bus */
              transmit_signal();
              /* test for unique station in the window */
              state := detect ();
              if state = collision then
                      /* update upper bound of interval containing minimum */
                      ub_minimum := w;
                  else /* successful isolation of minimum */
                      return (lb_minimum, ub_minimum);
                  w := window (lb_minimum, ub_minimum, n̂) ]
          else [
                  state := detect();
              if state = idle then
                      /* all parameters are outside window */
                      /* update lower bound of interval containing minimum */
                      lb_minimum := w ;
                      w: = window (lb_minimum, ub_minimum, n̂)
]
                  else
                      /* some other parameters are inside window, stop contending */
                      contending := false ]
      return (failure)
]
```

Figure 7.9 Procedure illustrating the basic steps executed in each station for contending the channel with a three-state collision-detection mechanism.

is none, one, or more than one contention parameter falling in the window. A global window can be maintained in all stations if they start in the same initial state, receive identical information from the bus, and execute the same control algorithm in updating the window with information received from the bus. Suppose that the set of contention parameters is $\{x_1, \ldots, x_n\}$ in the interval between L and U, and that y_i is the i-th smallest of the x_js. To search for the minimum, an initial window is chosen with the lower bound at L and the upper bound between L and U. There can be zero, one, or more than one contention parameter in this window. If there is exactly one contention parameter in the window, it can be verified as the minimum, y_1. Otherwise, the window has to be updated: it is moved if it is empty, or shrunk to a smaller size if it contains more than one number. This process is repeated until the minimum is uniquely isolated in the window. An implementation of the distributed window-search scheme at Station i, $1 \leq i \leq n$, on a multiaccess bus with a three-state collision-detection mechanism is shown in Figure 7.9.

Figure 7.10 illustrates the steps involved in the window-search scheme. Initially, five stations are ready, and they sense that the bus is free. Each

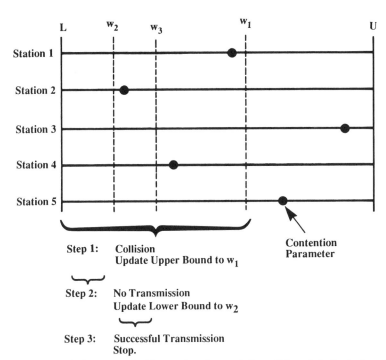

Figure 7.10 An example illustrating the updates of the global window to isolate the station with the minimum contention parameter. (Braces indicate windows used in different steps.)

of them generates a random contention parameter in $(L, U]$, sets the window as $(L, w_1]$, and transmits in the next contention slot if its contention parameter falls in the window. Station 3 is eliminated in the first iteration. As Stations 1, 2, 4, and 5 transmit, collision is detected. The stations reduce the upper bound of the interval to w_1 and set the windows to $(L, w_2]$ (identical for all stations as they use identical window-control algorithms and inputs). In the second iteration, no transmission is detected because all contention parameters are outside the window. The lower bound of the interval is set at w_2, and all stations set the windows as $(w_2, w_3]$. In the third iteration, successful transmission is detected, and the process terminates.

The concept of window protocols has been proposed with respect to contention resolution on multiaccess networks, but has not been developed for resource sharing and extremum search in general. Moreover, efficient and practical window-control algorithms have not been found. The optimization of the window size in the Urn Protocol (34) was studied by Hluchyj (25), who formulated it into a Markov decision process with an exponentially large number of states. Mosley and Humblet proposed to use the generation times of messages as a basis for the transmission order on the bus (44). This protocol is a generalization of Gallagher's procedure (19), which is itself based on an idea from Hayes (22) and Capetanakis (6). Towsley and Venkatesh (60) and Kurose and Schwartz (36) further extended Mosley and Humblet's algorithm by developing new heuristics. Mosley and Humblet also proposed that stations can generate random numbers as the contention parameters (44). The throughput was analyzed according to an infinite-population assumption.

The basic operations required for the proposed window-search scheme can be implemented easily either in hardware or in software on an existing multiaccess network such as the Ethernet. The global window can be maintained by updating an initially identical window with a common algorithm and using identical information broadcast on the bus. Assuming that information broadcast is received correctly by all stations, the global window will be synchronized at all sites.

To count the number of contention parameters falling in the window, the collision-detection capability of the network interface can be used effectively to detect whether the previous contention slot was empty, successful, or had collision. Stations with parameters inside the window contend for the bus in a contention slot. If there is more than one station with a parameter in the window, a collision will be detected. If there is exactly one station with a parameter in the window, a successful transmission will be detected. If there is no station with a parameter in the window, an empty slot will be detected. Each iteration of the protocol in Figure 7.9 will be completed in one contention slot. Hardware implementation will be discussed in Section 7.4.7 after the window-control algorithms are presented.

In systems where modification to existing hardware is impossible, the window protocol can be implemented in software. Software implementation is only necessary for applications that select a station based on the meaning of the contention parameter (such as identifying the station with the maximum response time). For applications that need to randomly select a station, such as identifying a free resource, the existing interface suffices. Suppose that an existing Ethernet for point-to-point and broadcast transmissions is available. Stations with parameters inside the window contend for the bus. The station that is granted the bus will broadcast its parameter. However, in this case, it is not clear whether exactly one station or more than one station have parameters inside the window. (This is equivalent to a network with a two-state collision-detection capability.) Hence, a verification phase must follow to assert that the broadcast parameter is the minimum. This verification phase can be implemented as a timeout period, so other stations with smaller parameters can continue to contend and broadcast a smaller parameter inside this timeout period. In each iteration of the window protocol, the channel has to be contended twice, and two broadcasts of contention parameters have to be made. By suitably adjusting the timeout period according to the channel load, the station with the minimum parameter can be isolated with a high degree of certainty and without significant degradation in performance. The window will be adjusted according to the minimum of the two broadcast contention parameters.

7.5. Window-Control Algorithms

To minimize the number of iterations in the protocol, to identify the minimum, the window used in each step must be chosen appropriately. Given the lower and upper bounds of the interval containing the minimum contention parameter, the lower bound of the window is set at the lower bound of this interval, and the upper bound of the window is to be chosen. The contention parameters are assumed to be independently generated from a uniform distribution in $(0, 1]$. When the distribution functions are identical but nonuniform, the contention parameters can be transformed by the distribution function into uniformly distributed parameters. Four algorithms to determine the upper bound of the window are described in this section. These algorithms assume that the channel load and the distribution functions from which the contention parameters are generated are exactly known. Methods to estimate the channel load will be presented in Section 7.5.5. The performance is worse when the channel load is estimated. Lastly, issues on finding the distribution functions and implementation are discussed.

7.5.1. Binary-Divide Window Control

A straightforward way to choose the upper bound of the window in each iteration is to set it midway in the interval containing the minimum. Binary search is applied in each iteration to eliminate half of the remaining interval. This method provides a lower bound on the performance.

The overhead is analyzed in terms of the number of iterations of the protocol to determine the minimum. In any given step, if the window size is greater than the distance between the two smallest parameters, y_1 and y_2, the minimum may be isolated depending on the relative positions of y_1, y_2, and the window (Figures 7.11a and 7.11b). On the other hand, if the window is reduced to a size smaller than the distance between y_1 and y_2, and the bounds of the window are updated according to the procedure in Figure 7.9, the minimum will always be isolated in such a window. This is illustrated in Figure 7.11c. Hence, the maximum number of iterations to resolve the minimum never exceeds the number of steps to reduce the window to a size smaller than the distance between y_1 and y_2. Assuming that k steps are required, the following condition holds:

$$2^{-k} < y_2 - y_1 < 2^{-(k-1)} \tag{7.4}$$

Taking the logarithm of the inequality in Eq. (7.4) and rearranging it,

$$\left[-\frac{\log_e(y_2 - y_1)}{\log_e 2} \right] < k < \left[1 - \frac{\log_e(y_2 - y_1)}{\log_e 2} \right] \tag{7.5}$$

This inequality gives the upper bounds of the binary-divide window-control rule for given y_1 and y_2.

From the theory of ordered statistics (9), if the $y_i s$ are uniformly distributed in (0,1], then the joint probability density function of y_1 and y_2 is

$$f_{Y_1 Y_2}(y_1, y_2) = \begin{cases} \dfrac{n!}{(n-2)!} (1 - y_2)^{n-2} & \text{for } 1 \geq y_2 > y_1 \geq 0 \\[2mm] 0 & \text{otherwise} \end{cases} \tag{7.6}$$

From Eqs. (7.5) and (7.6), $E(k)$, the average number of iterations to resolve contentions in the binary-divide window-control rule, can be obtained by integrating the weighted upper bound over the domains of y_1 and y_2.

$$E(K) < \int_0^1 \int_0^{y_2} \left[1 - \frac{\log_e(y_2 - y_1)}{\log_e 2} \right] \frac{n!}{(n-2)!} (1 - y_2)^{n-2} \, dy_1 dy_2$$

$$= 1 - \frac{n!}{(n-2)! \log_e 2} \int_0^1 \left[\int_0^{y_2} \log_e(y_2 - y_1) \, dy_1 \right] (1 - y_2)^{n-2} \, dy_2 \tag{7.7}$$

Because $\int_0^{y_2} \log_e(y_2 - y_1) \, dy_1 = y_2 \log_e y_2 - y_2$, Eq. (7.7) can be simplified as

$$E(K) < 1 - \frac{n!}{(n-2)! \log_e 2} \int_0^1 (1 - y_2)^{n-2} (y_2 \log_e y_2 - y_2) \, dy_2 \tag{7.8}$$

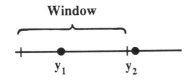

(a)   Contention is resolved by
a window with size greater
than (y_2-y_1).

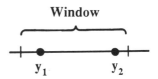

(b)   Contention is not resolved
by a window with size
greater than (y_2-y_1).

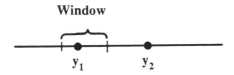

(c)   Contention is always resolved
if size of window is smaller
than (y_2-y_1) and lower bound
of window is smaller than y_1.

Figure 7.11 Possible sizes and positions of a window during a contention step.

The integration in Eq. (7.8) can be evaluated to become

$$\int_0^1 (1 - y_2)^{n-2}y_2 \log_e y_2 \, dy_2 = H_n - H_{n-1} \tag{7.9}$$

where H_n is the harmonic mean of the series $\{1, 2, \ldots, n\}$, i.e.,

$$H_n = \frac{1}{n} \sum_{i=1}^n \frac{1}{i} \tag{7.10}$$

The harmonic mean is approximately equal to $[\log_e n + \gamma + O(1/n)]/n$ (49),
where γ is a constant. Hence, from Eqs. (7.7) through (7.10), we obtain

$$E(k) < 1 - \frac{n(n-1)}{\log_e 2}\left[\left(\frac{\log_e n}{n} - \frac{\log_e(n-1)}{n-1}\right)\right.$$
$$\left. + \left(\frac{1}{n} - \frac{1}{n-1}\right)\right] \tag{7.11}$$

Because $\log_e n \approx \log_e(n-1)$ for large n, Eq. (7.11) may be reduced to

$$E(k) < 1 + \frac{n(n-1)}{\log_e 2}\frac{(1 + \log_e n)}{n(n-1)} < 3 + \log_2 n \tag{7.12}$$

Hence,

$$E(K) = O(\log_2 n) \tag{7.13}$$

In addition to the preceding analysis, simulations have been conducted to evaluate the performance of the binary-divide window-control rule. The simulation program was written in FORTRAN 77 and was executed on a DEC VAX 11/780 computer. In each simulation run, N random numbers were first generated in $(0, 1]$, and successive windows were generated until the station with the minimum parameter was obtained. A 95% confidence interval of ± 0.1 was used in the simulations. The results are plotted in Figure 7.12. Note that the average number of iterations is smaller than $O(\log_2 n)$, which confirms that $O(\log_2 n)$ is the upper bound of the average performance.

7.5.2. Dynamic-Programming Window Control

The size of the window in each iteration of the window protocol can be controlled by a dynamic-programming algorithm that minimizes the expected total number of iterations before the minimum is isolated. The following notations are first defined:

$N(a, b)$ the minimum expected number of iterations to resolve con-

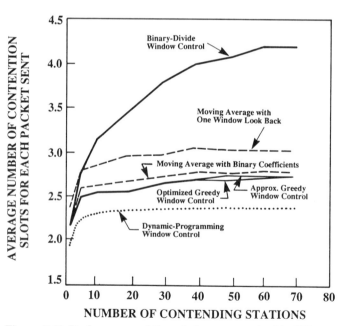

Figure 7.12 Performance of the window protocol with different window-control and load-estimation methods. (Solid lines assume that the channel load is exactly known; for dashed lines, the channel load is evaluated from previous experience.)

tention given that there are n contention parameters in $(a, U]$ and collision occurs in the current window $(a, b]$

$g(w, n, a, b)$ probability of *success* in the next iteration if a window of $(a, w]$, $a < w < b$, is used

$\ell(w, n, a, b)$ probability of *collision* in the next iteration if a window of $(a, w]$, $a < w < b$, is used

$r(w, n, a, b)$ probability of *no transmission* in the next iteration if a window of $(a, w]$, $a < w < b$, is used

It follows directly from the preceding definitions that

$$\ell(w, n, a, b) + g(w, n, a, b) + r(w, n, a, b) = 1 \tag{7.14}$$

As the Principle of Optimality is satisfied, the problem of minimizing the expected total number of iterations is reduced to that of finding w that minimizes the expected number of future iterations should collision or no transmission be detected in the current iteration. The problem can be formulated recursively as

$$N(a, b) = \min_{a < w < b} \{1 + 0 \cdot g(w, n, a, b)$$

$$+ N(a, w) \cdot \ell(w, n, a, b) + N(w, b) \cdot \gamma(w, n, a, b)\} \tag{7.15}$$

The probabilities $g(w, n, a, b)$, $\ell(w, n, a, b)$, and $r(w, n, a, b)$ can be derived from the distributions of the contention parameters and the state of contention. When transmission is unsuccessful, it is always possible to identify a window $(a, b]$ such that at least two of the $x_i s$ lie in $(a, b]$ and no x_i is smaller than a. This condition is designated as event A.

$A = \{$at least two $x_i s$ are in $(a, b]$, given that all $x_i s$ are in $(a, U]\}$

Suppose that the window is reduced to $(a, w]$, $a < w < b$, in the next iteration, three mutually exclusive events corresponding to three possible outcomes can be identified:

$B = \{$exactly one of the $x_i s$ is in $(a, w]$, given that all $x_i s$ are in $(a, U]\}$

$C = \{$no x_i is in $(a, w]$, given that all $x_i s$ are in $(a, U]\}$

$D = \{$more than one x_i is in $(a, w]$, given that all $x_i s$ are in $(a, U]\}$

From these events, the probabilities can be expressed as

$$g(w, n, a, B) = Pr\{B \mid A\} = \frac{Pr\{A \cap B\}}{Pr\{A\}} \tag{7.16}$$

$$r(w, n, a, b) = Pr\{C \mid A\} = \frac{Pr\{A \cap C\}}{Pr\{A\}} \tag{7.17}$$

The set $A \cap B$ represents the events that exactly one of the x_is is in $(a, w]$, that at least one x_i is in $(w, b]$, and that all others are in $(w, U]$. The set $A \cap C$ represents the event that at least two x_is are in $(w, b]$, given that all x_is are in $(w, U]$.

Let $F_i(x)$ (resp. $f_i(x)$) be the distribution (resp. density) function that governs the generation of x_i, $1 \leq i \leq n$, where n is the number of contending stations. Then event A occurs with probability:

$$Pr(A) =$$

$$\frac{\prod_{i=1}^{n} [1 - F_i(a)] - \sum_{i=1}^{n} \left\{ [F_i(b) - F_i(a)] \prod_{\substack{j=1 \\ j \neq i}}^{n} [1 - F_j(b)] \right\} - \prod_{i=1}^{n} [1 - F_i(b)]}{\prod_{i=1}^{n} (1 - F_i(a))}$$

(7.18)

The first and last terms of Eq. (7.18) indicate the probabilities that all x_is are greater than a and b, respectively. The second term is the probability that exactly one of the x_is is in the window $(a, b]$. Similarly,

$$g(w, n, a, b) =$$

$$\frac{\sum_{i=1}^{n} [F_i(w) - F_i(a)] \times \left\{ \prod_{\substack{j=1 \\ j \neq i}}^{n} [1 - F_j(w)] - \prod_{\substack{j=1 \\ j \neq i}}^{n} [1 - F_j(b)] \right\}}{Pr(A) \prod_{i=1}^{n} (1 - F_i(a))}$$

(7.19)

$$r(w, n, a, b) =$$

$$\frac{\prod_{i=1}^{n} [1 - F_i(w)] - \sum_{i=1}^{n} \left[[F_i(b) - F_i(w)] \prod_{\substack{j=1 \\ j \neq i}}^{n} [1 - F_j(b)] \right] - \prod_{i=1}^{n} [1 - F_i(b)]}{Pr(A) \prod_{i=1}^{n} (1 - F_i(a))}$$

(7.20)

It follows that an optimal window can be derived in each iteration once the channel load and the distributions of contention parameters are known. However, the dynamic-programming formulation is continuous and requires infinite levels of recursion. Boundary conditions must be set to terminate the evaluations after a reasonable number of levels. In practice, the x_is may represent indistinguishable physical measures when their difference is less than δ. It is assumed that when the window size is small than δ, the probability that two stations have generated parameters in this interval is so small that contention can always be resolved in one step. The following boundary condition is included:

$$N(a, b) = 1 \qquad \text{for all } (b - a) < \delta$$

The value of δ was set to $1/(10 \times n)$ in our evaluations for continuous distributions, and to 1 for discrete distributions. The results of the evaluation are plotted in Figure 7.12, which shows that the average number of iterations is bounded by 2.4, independent of the number of contending stations. This performance is much better than that of the Binary Exponential Backoff Protocol of Ethernet (52) as shown in the simulation results in Figure 7.13. It must be pointed out the simulation results for the proposed window protocol assume that the number of contending stations is known, while those of the Binary Exponential Backoff protocol start out with one contending station. However, the advantage of the window protocol is that the channel load can be estimated easily from previous windows (Section 7.5.5), provided that the arrival rate does not change abruptly and that the degradation in performance with estimated loads is negligible. In case the channel load cannot be estimated and the binary-divide window-control protocol has to be used, the performance is still much better than that of Ethernet.

Arrow et al. had studied a similar problem with the difference that the number of contending stations in a collided window is assumed to be known exactly (1, 54). The problem was formulated into a *finite* recursion, and an

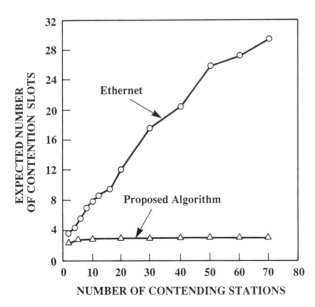

Figure 7.13 Comparison of Ethernet's Binary Exponential Backoff Protocol with the proposed window protocol.

asymptotic bound of 2.4 iterations was obtained by numerical evaluations. We have obtained comparable results when only ternary information on collision is available and the infinite dynamic programming tree is truncated. This shows that the information on the exact number of contending stations is insignificant.

Although optimal, the dynamic programming algorithm has a high computational complexity, which makes the algorithm impractical for real-time applications. As an example, the execution time to evaluate Eq. (7.15) on a DEC VAX 11/780 computer is 1.3 s for $n = 20$, and increases to 828 s for $n = 100$. Efficient hardware implementations will be discussed in Section 7.5.7.

7.5.3. Optimal Greedy Window Control

The optimization of window control using dynamic programming requires a high computational overhead because it examines the entire sequence of possible future windows to determine the window to be used in the next iteration. To reduce this overhead, only one future window may be examined. An optimal greedy window-control scheme is one that finds a window to maximize the probability of success, $g(w, n, a, b)$, in the next iteration. When the contention parameters have identical continuous distributions, $F(x)$, $g(w, n, a, b)$ can be expressed in a simple form as

$$g(w, n, a, b) = K[F(w) - F(a)]\{[1 - F(w)]^{n-1} - [1 - F(b)]^{n-1}\} \tag{7.21}$$

where $K = n/\{Pr(A)[1 - F(A)]^n\}$. It can be shown that Eq. (7.21) is unimodal between a and b, so a maximum exists in the window $(a, b]$. To find the optimal value of w, we set $(\partial/\partial w)g(w, n, a, b) = 0$ and solve for w. This derivation leads to the following equation if $f(w) \neq 0$:

$$[1 - F(w)]^{n-1} - [1 - F(b)]^{n-1}$$
$$= (n - 1)[F(w) - F(a)][1 - F(w)]^{n-2} \tag{7.22}$$

If $z = 1 - F(w)$, Eq. (7.22) becomes

$$z^{n-1} - \frac{(n - 1)[1 - F(a)]z^{n-2}}{n} - \frac{[1 - F(b)]^{n-1}}{n} = 0 \tag{7.23}$$

It can be shown that a real root of Eq. (7.23) exists and satisfies the inequality $(1 - F(b)) < z_o < (1 - F(a))$. There is no closed-form solution to Eq. (7.23), and z_o has to be solved numerically. Once z_o is obtained, w_o, the upper boundary of the window, can be computed directly from z_o as

$$w_o = F^{-1}(1 - z_o) \tag{7.24}$$

The performance of the greedy scheme is measured by the average number of iterations expended before the minimum is identified. It has been proved that the average number of iterations to resolve contention is bounded by 2.7 when the contention parameters are generated from a single distribution function [see Figure 7.12 (62)]. The computational overhead to solve Eq. (7.23) numerically is independent of n and is less than 1 s of CPU time on the DEC VAX 11/780 in most cases.

It is worth noting that a binary-divide window-control scheme is derived from the optimal greedy window-control scheme by setting n to 2. When n is 2, Eq. (7.23) is evaluated to become $F(w_o) = [F(a) + F(b)]/2$. If $F(y)$ is uniformly distributed in (0, 1], then $w_o = (a + b)/2$. The binary-divide control rule can also be used as a heuristic for window control with general distribution functions. It can be interpreted as one that always predicts that there are two contending stations. As a result, it performs well when the channel is lightly loaded, and degrades to have an $O(\log_2 n)$ performance when the channel load is heavy.

7.5.4. Approximate Greedy Window Control

The approximately greedy window-control scheme is similar to the optimal greedy window-control scheme except that an approximate equation on success probability is used. Eq. (7.21) may be rewritten as

$$g(w, n, a, b) = K[F(w) - F(a)][F(b) - F(w)][1 - F(w)]^{n-2} \sum_{i=0}^{n-2} v^i$$

$$(7.25)$$

where $v = [1 - F(b)]/[1 - F(w)]$. A function $\hat{g}(w, n, a, b)$ that has a maximum very close to that of $g(w, n, a, b)$, can be obtained by replacing the term $[\sum_{i=0}^{n-2} v^i]$ with $(n - 1)$. That is,

$$\hat{g}(w, n, a, b) = K'[F(w) - F(a)][F(b) - F(w)][1 - F(w)]^{n-2} \qquad (7.26)$$

where $K' = (n - 1)K$. By solving $(\partial/\partial w) \log_e \hat{g}(w, n, a, b)] = 0$, we obtain

$$\frac{f(w)}{F(w) - F(a)} + \frac{f(w)}{F(w) - F(b)} + \frac{(n - 2)f(w)}{F(w) - 1} = 0 \qquad (7.27)$$

or, equivalently,

$$[F(w)^2 + C[F(w)] + D = 0 \qquad (7.28)$$

where

$$C = \frac{(n - 1)[F(a) + F(b)] + 2}{n}$$

$$D = \frac{F(a) + F(b) + (n - 2)F(a)F(b)}{n}$$

A solution to Eq. (7.28) in the window $(F(a), F(b)]$ is given by

$$F(w_a) = \frac{-C - \sqrt{C^2 - 4D}}{2} \tag{7.29}$$

The approximate window w_a as calculated from Eq. (7.29) gives a performance that is nearly as good as that of the optimal greedy scheme (see Figure 7.12). The computational overhead to calculate Eq. (7.29) is independent of n and can be done in less than 100 μs on the DEC VAX 11/780.

7.5.5. Load Estimations

Before the window-control protocol is carried out, the number of contending processors must be estimated from the distributions of the contention parameters and the statistics of previous channel activities. This information is essential in estimating an initial window and in controlling the dynamic changes in window sizes in the current contention period. A method based on maximum-likelihood estimation is described here.

After the t-th message is transmitted, the window $(L, w(t)]$ that successfully isolates the station with the minimum is known to all processors. A maximum-likelihood estimate of $n(t)$, the number of stations that have participated in the contention, can be computed from a likelihood function on the probability of success that the minimum lies in $(L, w(t)]$. Assuming that the contention parameters are independently and uniformly distributed in $(0, 1]$, the likelihood function is derived as

$$LK(\hat{n}(t), w(t), 0) = Pr(0 < Y_1 < w(t) < Y_2)$$

$$= \hat{n}(t)w(t)(1 - w(t))^{\hat{n}(t)-1} \tag{7.30}$$

$LK(n(t), w(t), 0)$ is maximized at

$$\hat{n}(t) = \left[\frac{-1}{\log_e(1 - w(t))} \right] \quad 0 < w(t) < 1 \tag{7.31}$$

The number of contending stations to transmit the $(t + 1)$-th message can be obtained by adding to $\hat{n}(t)$ the difference between the possible arrivals after the t-th message has been transmitted. The average number of iterations to resolve contentions using this load-estimation method is 3.1 as shown in Figure 7.12.

Because the extremum is readily available when contention is resolved, this information can be "piggybacked" in the packet transmitted. Hence, an alternative estimate is based on the density function of this statistics. The conditional density of y_1 is

$$f_{Y_1}(y_1 \mid 0 < Y_1 < w < Y_2) = \frac{\int_w^1 f_{Y_1Y_2}(y_1, y_2)\, dy_2}{\int_0^w \int_w^1 f_{Y_1Y_2}(y_1, y_2)\, dy_2 dy_1} \tag{7.32}$$

Because the contention parameters are independently and uniformly distributed in (0, 1],

$$f_{Y_1 Y_2}(y_1, y_2) = (n - 1)(1 - y_2)^{n-2} \tag{7.33}$$

Substituting Eq. (7.33) into Eq. (7.32) yields

$$f_{Y_1}(y_1 \mid 0 < Y_1 < w < Y_2) = \frac{1}{w} \tag{7.34}$$

This result shows that the distribution of y_1 is determined once the window $(0, w]$ is known. Therefore, no new information is gained by using this first-order statistic in estimating n.

The accuracy on load estimation can be improved by using information on previous windows that successfully isolate a single station. A technique in time-series analysis called Auto-Regressive-Moving-Average (ARMA) model can be applied to obtain an estimated window based on all previous windows, $w(1)$, $w(2)$, . . . , $w(t)$. A simple example is computing a moving average, $w_{mv}(t)$, using the following formula:

$$w_{mv}(t) = \frac{w_{mv}(t - 1) + w(t)}{2} \tag{7.35}$$

The value of $w_{mv}(t)$ is then used in Eq. (7.30) to estimate the channel load. The performance of using ARMA load estimation is very close to that when the channel load is exactly known (see Figure 7.12).

7.5.6. Estimating the Distribution Functions of Contention Parameters

In applications such as load balancing and finding the highest-priority class, the distribution functions from which the contention parameters are generated are unknown and have to be estimated dynamically. Generally, the distribution functions are assumed, and parameters of the distribution functions are estimated from statistics collected. Because information on the distribution functions is essential and must be consistent for all sites to optimize the window search, independent monitoring of local information and information broadcast on the bus may be insufficient and may lead to unstable operations.

For loading balancing, a single site is responsible for collecting the distribution functions on local response times and distributing them to other sites (3). For scheduling transmissions with the highest-priority level, information on the priority levels of messages transmitted can be observed on the bus. As an example, let λ_i be the arrival rate of messages to the i-th priority level and t_i be the arrival time of the most recent packet in the i-th level that has been transmitted. Assuming a Poisson process for the packet arrivals, the probability that at least one station has a message in the i-th priority level is

$$p_i = 1 \int_{T-t_1}^{\infty} \lambda_i e^{-\lambda_i t} \, dt = e^{-\lambda_i(T-t_i)} \tag{7.36}$$

where T is the current time. The distribution that a station generates a message in the i-th priority level is

$$F_i(k) = \begin{cases} 0 & k < i \\ e^{-\lambda_i(T-t_i)} & i \leqslant k \leqslant P \\ 1 & k > P \end{cases} \tag{7.37}$$

where P is the total number of priority levels in the system. The arrival time of a packet may be acquired by piggybacking this information on the packet transmitted. The packet arrival rate may be estimated by observing the packet arrival times.

The proposed window-control algorithms are quite robust with respect to changes in the distribution functions. Experiments on variations of the parameter of a Poisson distribution did not lead to any significant degradation in performance. However, there is always a delay between the time that the distribution function is changed and the time that this change is propagated to all sites. The optimization in the window protocol may be unstable if changes cannot be disseminated in time. The method for estimating the distribution functions is highly problem-dependent and is currently a problem under investigation.

7.5.7. Implementation of the Window Protocol on Ethernet Interfaces

We have presented four window-control protocols in this section. Window control using dynamic programming requires a high computational overhead, while the other window-control algorithms require less computations but give poorer performance. The implementation on Ethernet-type interfaces has a stringent real-time requirement because each contention slot has a duration of less than 60 μs on a 10-Mbps network (12). The direct computation of the binary-divide and approximately greedy window-control schemes can satisfy this timing requirement. In this section, we describe a lookup-table method for implementing the dynamic-programming window control.

The sequence of windows evaluated by dynamic programming can be precomputed and stored in a lookup table. Given a channel load n, the sequence of optimal windows derived from Eq. (7.15) constitutes a binary decision tree (Figure 7.14a). The root of a subtree represents a window. The optimal window for the next iteration will reside in the left subtree if collision is detected in the current iteration. It will be in the right subtree if no trans-

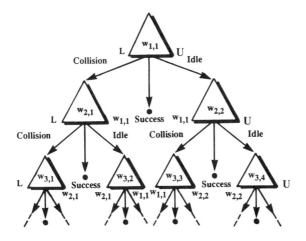

(a) Binary Decision Tree

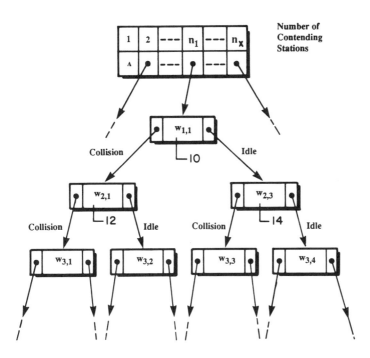

(b) Corresponding Data Structure

Figure 7.14 Lookup-table implementation of dynamic-programming window control. (a) Binary decision tree. (b) Corresponding data structure.

mission is detected. A set of binary trees, each of which corresponds to a channel load, can be constructed and stored as a lookup table in each station. The data structure for implementing the binary decision tree is shown in Figure 7.14b. The optimal window in each iteration can be retrieved efficiently in real time. The windows are evaluated based on a uniform distribution of the contention parameters. In applications where the contention parameters have identical but nonuniform distributions, they must be transformed by the distribution function into the uniform distribution before the lookup table is used.

One problem with the lookup-table method lies in the large memory space required. Since the average number of iterations is small, some subtrees can be pruned to reduce the memory space without significant degradation to performance. Window boundaries in the pruned subtrees have to be obtained by interpolation techniques. Likewise, for those channel loads for which no decision trees are stored, interpolation has to be used to obtain the window boundaries.

The lookup-table method has been designed on existing Ethernet interfaces (65, 68). A microcontroller, Intel MCS 8396, is placed between the Ethernet-protocol chip, Intel 82586, and the collision-detection chip, Intel 82501. A decision tree of four levels as evaluated by dynamic programming is used, and the microcontroller switches to binary-divide window control when more than four contention slots are needed. Sixteen-bit random numbers are used for the contention parameters and the entries of the decision tree. The channel load is assumed to vary from 1 to 100 stations. Hence, the total space required for storing the lookup table is 3 kbytes, which can fit in the 8-kbyte read-only memory of the MCS 8396. The performance of the truncated decision-tree method is less than 3.0 contention slots when n = 100 (Figure 7.12) as the number of slots to resolve contention is normally less than four.

The balanced binary tree in the preceding implementation simplifies the data structure. However, the performance can be improved if a skewed binary tree is used. The reasoning behind the skewed tree is that when a collision occurs, the left subtree is traversed and the size of the interval containing the minimum is small. In this case, a binary-divide control works well. On the other hand, when no transmission is detected, the right subtree is traversed and the size of the interval containing the minimum is not reduced significantly. In this case, the binary-divide control does not work well. Experimental results indicate that less than 2.5 slots are required to resolve a contention when a skewed binary tree with a height equal to n and a height of 1 for the left subtree of every nonterminal node (n is exactly known) is used. This means that $2n$ words are required for every dynamic programming tree. The total memory space required for n ranging from 1 to 60 stations is 7.3 kbytes.

7.6. Conclusions

In this chapter, we have shown that a class of resource-allocation problems for a local computer system connected by a multiaccess bus can be reduced to the problem of determining the extremum from a set of physically distributed random numbers. A distributed algorithm to identify the extremum in a constant average time independent of the number of contending stations is proposed. The correspondence between the properties of our design and the proposed methodology is summarized in Table 7.1. The load-independent behavior of the proposed algorithm is important because the number of contending stations to identify the extremum is usually large. Most existing contention-resolution algorithms, such as the Binary Exponential Backoff algorithm of Ethernet, are load-dependent and cannot be used to identify the extremum. The proposed algorithm can be implemented in hardware on a contention bus with the collision-detection capability. The overhead in each iteration is the time for a contention slot. On the other hand, it can also be implemented in software on existing multiaccess networks. In this case, two messages have to be transmitted in each iteration. It must be pointed out that the proposed window control is optimal in the sense of minimizing the number of iterations before the extremum is found, but is not optimal in minimizing the expected delay or maximizing the average throughput of the network.

The proposed algorithm requires the reliable transmission of collision and broadcast information to all processors. This may be difficult if the channel is noisy. Incorrect information received may cause indefinite contentions and the inability to identify the extremum. The problem can be resolved by broadcasting the extremum after it is found. Further, the proposed algorithm has a predictable average behavior. Significant deviation from this behavior can be used to indicate an unreliable channel.

Besides the resource-sharing applications discussed in this section, the

Table 7.1 Application of the Methodology to Design the Proposed Resource-Allocation Scheme in a Single Contention-Bus Network

Methodology	Design
Optimal allocation	$\begin{cases} \text{Request of highest priority} \\ \text{Resource of highest preference} \end{cases}$
Distributed algorithm	Distributed minimum-search
Primitive operation	Window search
Implementation	Collision detection
Results	$\begin{cases} \text{No explicit message transfer} \\ \text{2.4 contention slots (optimal)} \end{cases}$

proposed algorithm can be extended to resolve contentions for multiple multiaccess or bit-parallel buses (31, 43, 61, 65), maintain consistency and process queries in distributed databases (66), and unify many existing adaptive CSMA protocols (28).

Problems

1. What are the advantages and disadvantages of maintaining a queue at each resource? Discuss the issue with respect to the processing speed of the resource and message delays in the resource-sharing interconnection network.
2. In a resource-sharing system with a central scheduler, status information of a request is obtained by transferring messages through a message-transfer subsystem. Assuming N requests are pending for service, how many message transfers are necessary for the scheduler to determine the request of the highest priority? If the distributed minimum-search algorithm is applied, how many message transfers are necessary?
3. If the resource-sharing interconnection network comprises multiple contention buses, multiple requests can be transmitted simultaneously. As a result, t requests of the highest priority have to be identified when there are t buses available. Modify the distributed minimum-search algorithm such that multiple buses can be utilized to search these requests in parallel.
4. After the successful completion of the distributed minimum-search algorithm, three events can be identified: (1) no x_i is in the interval $[L, a]$; (2) the minimum of $x_i s$ is in the interval $(a, w]$; and (3) the second minimum is in $(w, b]$. Formulate a maximum likelihood estimate of $\hat{n}$ based on these three events.
5. Suppose that the number of processors involved in the distributed minimum-search procedure is governed by a Poisson process. Use this a priori information together with the three events described in Problem (4) to formulate a Bayes estimate of $\hat{n}$.
6. In dynamic-programming window control, a boundary condition is included that results in a truncated dynamic programming tree. Show that the number of nodes in a truncated tree is proportional to the number of contending stations.

References

1. Arrow K, Pesotchinsky L, Sobel M: On partitioning a sample with binary-type questions in lieu of collecting observations. *Journal of the American Statistical Association*, Vol. 76, No. 374, June 1981, pp. 402–409.

2. Baer JL: *Computer Systems Architecture*. Computer Science Press, Rockville, MD, 1980.

3. Baumgartner KM, Wah BW: The effects of load balancing on response time for local computer systems with a multiaccess network. *Proc. International Conference on Communications, IEEE*, June 1985, pp. 10.1.1–10.1.5.

4. Berger T, Mehrauari N, Towsley D, Wolf JK: Random multiple access and group testing. *Trans. on Communications, Vol. COM-34, No. 7, IEEE*, July 1984, pp. 769–779.

5. Briggs FA, Fu KS, Hwang K, Wah BW: PUMPS architecture for pattern analysis and image database management. *Trans. on Computers, IEEE*, Vol. C-31, No. 10, Oct. 1982, pp. 969–983.

6. Capetanakis J: The Multiple-Access Broadcast Channel: Protocol and Capacity Considerations, Ph.D. Thesis, Massachusetts Institute of Technology, 1977.

7. Capetanakis J: Tree algorithm for packet broadcast channels. *Trans. on Information Theory, IEEE*, Vol. IT-25, No. 5, Sept. 1979, pp. 505–515.

8. Capetanakis J: Generalized TDMA: The multi-accessing tree protocol. *Trans. on Communications, IEEE*, Vol. COM-27, No. 10, Oct. 1979, pp. 1479–1484.

9. David HA: *Order Statistics*. John Wiley & Sons, New York, 1970.

10. Day JD: Resource sharing protocols. *Computer, IEEE*, Vol. 10, No. 9, Sept. 1977, pp. 47–56.

11. Dennis JB: Data flow supercomputers. *Computer, IEEE*, Vol. 13, No. 11, Nov. 1980, pp. 48–56.

12. Digital Equipment Corp., Intel Corp., and Xerox Corp., Ethernet: Local Area Network Data-Link Layer and Physical Layer Specifications, Version 1.0, Sept. 30, 1980.

13. Dijkstra EW: Cooperating Sequential Processes. In Genuys F (ed): *Programming Languages*, Academic Press, New York, 1968.

14. Dubois M, Briggs FA: Effects of cache coherency in multiprocessors. *Trans. on Computers, IEEE*, Vol. C-31, No. 11, Nov. 1982.

15. Enslow PH: Multiprocessor organization. *Computing Surveys, ACM*, Vol. 9, March 1977, pp. 103–129.

16. Feng TY: A survey of interconnection networks. *Computer, IEEE*, Dec. 1981, pp. 12–27.

17. Frankovich JM: A bandwidth analysis of baseline networks. *Proc. International Conference on Distributed Computing Systems, IEEE*, Oct. 1982, pp. 572–578.

18. Fuller SH, Harbison SP: The C.mmp Multiprocessor, Technical Report, Carnegie-Mellon University, Pittsburgh, PA, 1978.

19. Gallagher RG: Conflict resolution in random access broadcast networks. *Proc. AFOSR Workshop Communication Theory and Applications*, Sept. 17–20, 1978, pp. 74–76.

20. Gold YI, Franta WR: An efficient collision-free protocol for prioritized access-control of cable radio channels. *Computer Networks*, North-Holland, Amsterdam, Vol. 7, pp. 83–98.

21. Hansen PB: Distributed processes: A concurrent programming concept. *Communications of ACM*, Vol. 21, Nov. 1978, pp. 934–941.

22. Hayes JH: An adaptive technique for local distribution. *Trans. Communications, IEEE*, Vol. COM-26, No. 8, Aug. 1978.

23. Hoare CAR: Monitor: An operating system structure concept. *Communications of ACM,* Vol. 17, No. 10, Oct. 1974, pp. 549–557.
24. Hoare CAR: Communicating sequential processes. *Communication of ACM,* Vol. 21, No. 8, Aug. 1978, pp. 666–667.
25. Hluchyj MG: Multiple Access Communication: The Finite User Population Problem, Massachusetts Institute of Technology, Cambridge, MA, Nov. 1981.
26. Hwang K, et al: A Unix-based local computer network with load balancing. *Computer, IEEE,* Vol. 15, No. 4, April 1982, pp. 55–66.
27. Jayaraman B, Keller RH: Resource expressions for applicative language. *Proc. 1982 International Conference on Parallel Processing, IEEE,* Aug. 1982, pp. 162–167.
28. Juang JY, Wah BW: Unified window protocol for local multiaccess networks. *Proc. Third Annual Joint Conference of the IEEE Computer and Communication Societies, IEEE,* April 1984, pp. 97–104.
29. Juang JY, Wah BW: A multi-access bus-arbitration scheme for VLSI-densed distributed systems. *Proc. National Computer Conference,* AFIPS Press, Vol. 53, July 1984, pp. 13–22.
30. Juang JY, Wah BW: Optimal scheduling algorithms for resource sharing interconnection networks. *Proc. Eighth International Computer Software and Applications Conference, IEEE,* Nov. 1984, pp. 217–225.
31. Juang JY: Resource Allocation in Computer Networks, Ph.D. Thesis, Purdue University, West Lafayette, IN, Aug. 1985.
32. Kleinrock L: *Queueing Theory, 1,* Addison-Wesley, Reading, MA, 1972.
33. Kleinrock L, Tobagi FA: Packet switching in radio channels: Part 1—carrier sense multiple access modes and their throughput-delay characteristics. *Trans. on Communications, IEEE,* Vol. COM-23, No. 12, Dec. 1975, pp. 1400–1416.
34. Kleinrock L, Yemini Y: An optimal adaptive scheme for multiple access broadcast communication. *Proc. International Conference on Communications, IEEE,* 1978, pp. 7.2.1–7.2.5.
35. Kung HT: Why systolic architectures. *Computer, IEEE,* Vol. 15, No. 10, Jan. 1982, pp. 37–46.
36. Kurose JF, Schwartz M: A family of window protocols for time-constrained applications in CSMA networks. *Proc. Second Joint Conference of Computer and Communication Societies, IEEE,* 1983, pp. 405–413.
37. Leinbaugh DW: High-level specifications of resource sharing. *Proc. International Conference on Parallel Processing, IEEE,* Aug. 1981, pp. 162–163.
38. Leinbaugh DW: Selector: High-level resource schedulers. *Trans. on Software Engineering, IEEE,* Vol. SE-10, No. 11, Nov. 1984, pp. 810–824.
39. Liskov BH, et al: CLU Reference Manual (Lecture notes in Computer Science), 114, Springer-Verlag, 1981.
40. Liskov BH: On linguistic support for distributed programs. *Trans. on Software Engineering, IEEE,* Vol. SE-8, No. 3, May 1982, pp. 203–210.
41. Manner R: Hardware task/processor scheduling in a polyprocessor environment. *Trans. on Computers, IEEE,* Vol. C-33, No. 7, July 1984, pp. 626–636.
42. Metcalfe RM, Boggs DR: Ethernet: Distributed packet switching for local computer networks. *Comm. of the ACM,* Vol. 19, No. 7, July 1976, pp. 395–404.
43. Mok AK, Ward SW: Distributed broadcast channel access. *Computer Networks,* Vol. 3, 1979, pp. 327–335.

44. Mosley J, Hamblet P: A class of efficient contention resolution algorithms for multiple access channels. *Trans. on Communications, IEEE,* Vol. C-35, Feb. 1985, pp. 145–157.
45. Li MN, Hwang K: Optimal load balancing strategies for a multiple processor system. *Proc. Tenth International Conference on Parallel Processing, IEEE,* Aug. 1981, pp. 352–357.
46. Ni LM, Li X: Prioritizing packet transmission in local multiaccess networks. *Proc. Eighth Data Communications Symposium, IEEE,* 1983.
47. Ousterhout JK, Scelza DA, Sindhu PS: MEDUSA: An experiment in distributed operating system structure. *Communications of ACM,* Vol. 23, No. 2, Feb. 1980, pp. 92–105.
48. Patel JH: Performance of processor-memory interconnections for multiprocessors. *Trans. on Computers, IEEE,* Oct. 1981, pp. 771–780.
49. Reingold EM, Nievergelt JN, Deo N: *Combinatorial Algorithms*, Prentice-Hall, Englewood Cliffs, NJ, 1979.
50. Riche DM, Thompson K: The Unix time-sharing system. *Communications, ACM,* Vol. 17, No. 7, July 1974, pp. 1278–1308.
51. Selinger PG: State-of-the-art issues in distributed databases. *Trans. on Software Engineering, IEEE,* Vol. SE-9, No. 3, May 1983, pp. 218–219.
52. Shock JF, et al: Evolution of the Ethernet local computer network. *Computer, IEEE,* Vol. 15, No. 8, Aug. 1982, pp. 10–27.
53. Silberschatz A: Extending CSP to allow dynamic resource management. *Trans. on Software Engineering, IEEE,* Vol. SE-9, No. 4, July 1983, pp. 527–530.
54. Sobel M, Groll PA: Group testing to eliminate efficiently all defectives in a binomial sample. *Bell Systems Technical Journal,* Sept. 1959, pp. 1179–1252.
55. Shacham N: A protocol for preferred access in packet-switching radio networks. *Trans. on Communications, IEEE,* Vol. COM-31, No. 2, Feb. 1983, pp. 253–264.
56. Tanenbaum AS: *Computer Networks.* Prentice-Hall, Englewood Cliffs, NJ, 1981.
57. Thomas RH: A resource sharing executive for the ARPANET. *Proc. National Computer Conference,* AFIPS Press, 1973, pp. 155–163.
58. Tobagi FA; Carrier sense multiple access with message-based priority functions. *Trans. on Communications, IEEE,* Vol. COM-30, No. 1, Jan. 1982.
59. Towsley D: Queueing network models with state-dependent routing. *Journal of ACM,* Vol. 27, No. 2, April 1980, pp. 323–337.
60. Towsley D, Venkatesh G: Window random-access protocols for local computer networks. *Trans. on Computers, IEEE,* Vol. C-31, No. 8, Aug. 1982, pp. 715–722.
61. Towsley D, Wolf JK: On adaptive polling algorithms. *Trans. on Communications, IEEE,* Vol. COM-32, Dec. 1984, pp. 1294–1298.
62. Wah BW, Hicks A: Distributed scheduling of resources on Interconnection networks. *Proc. National Computer Conference,* AFIPS Press, 1982, pp. 697–709.
63. Wah BW, Juang JY: Load balancing on local multiaccess networks. *Proc. Eighth Conference on Local Computer Networks, IEEE,* Oct. 1983, pp. 56–66.
64. Wah BW: A comparative study of distributed resource sharing on multiprocessors. *Trans. on Computers, IEEE,* Vol. C-33, No. 8, Aug. 1984, pp. 700–711.

65. Wah BW, Juang FY: An efficient contention-resolution protocol for local multiaccess networks. Pending patent application, Sept. 1984.
66. Wah BW, Licn YN: Design of distributed databases on local computer systems with multiaccess network. *Trans. on Software Engineering, IEEE,* Vol. SE-11, No. 7, July 1985, pp. 606–619.
67. Wah BW, Juang JY: Resource sharing for local computer systems with a single multiaccess network. *Trans. on Computers, IEEE,* Vol. C-34, Dec. 1985.
68. Wah BW, Li WQ: Interface design for efficient multiaccess networks, in press.
69. Walker B, et al: The LOCUS distributed operating system. *Proc. Ninth ACM Symposium on Operating System Principles, ACM,* 1983, pp. 49–70.
70. Wang YT, Morris JT: Load sharing in distributed systems. *Trans. on Computers, IEEE,* Vol. C-34, March 1985, pp. 204–217.

PART III

From Concepts to Systems

8

Supercomputers and Artificial Intelligence Machines

Kai Hwang
Joydeep Ghosh

8.1. Introduction

This chapter presents recent advances in supercomputers and artificial intelligence (AI) machines. Architectural features of representative systems are presented along with their application domains. A comparison of numerical and symbolic processing requirements yields different architectural characteristics for their support. These features are highlighted in several case studies, which include commercial systems such as the Cray series, HEP and Connection Machine, as well as research projects such as the Dado, Remps, and Japan's PIM. Finally, research issues and future trends in supercomputing and AI architectures are discussed.

High-performance and intelligent computers are becoming indispensable for tackling complex problems in the areas of structural analysis, weather forecasting, fusion energy research, petroleum exploration, aerodynamic simulations, electronic circuit design, remote sensing, medical di-

This project was supported in part by NSF grant DMC-84-21022 and in part by AFOSR grant 86-0008.

agnosis, artificial intelligence, advanced automation, military defense and weapons design, expert systems, genetic engineering, and socioeconomics (19). The demand for these systems arises from a wide range of scientific, technological, and business applications that require the processing of huge volumes of data/knowledge and the inclusion of artificial intelligence (AI) features along with enormous numerical and symbolic computing power.

The value of intelligent supercomputing has been recognized in three important directions (7). First, these computers aid in *knowledge acquisition* via the treatment of complexity within a reasonable time. Knowledge examples include logical inference, expert systems, partial differential equations, and extraordinary phenomena such as fusion, geophysics, oceanography, atmospheric science, and material science. Second, they provide *computational tractability* in instrumentation, predictive simulations, energy resource exploration, general circulation modeling, weapons effects, atmospheric testing, etc. Third, they *promote productivity* in systems optimization, computer-aided design (CAD) and manufacturing (CAM), VLSI circuit design, etc. A large range of supporting services are being engendered via supercomputing and machine intelligence (37, 81).

The mainstream use of computers is experiencing a trend of four ascending levels of sophistication. We started with the use of computers for *data processing*, in which number crunching is the major task performed. The next level is for *information processing*, in which related data items are processed in a structured manner. Most of today's computers are still being used for data and/or information processing, and the term "supercomputers" is applied today to a machine that can perform hundreds of millions of floating point operations per second (100 Mflops) with a word length of approximately 64 bits and a main memory capacity of millions of words (37, 38, 58, 66).

Computer scientists have long predicted that the use of computers for *knowledge processing* would be the major thrust in the 1990s. In knowledge processing, semantic meaning is added to items of information. Knowledge-based information processing requires intensive use of nonnumerical symbol manipulations. Ultimately, we want to use computers for *intelligence processing*, in which new knowledge can be acquired through computers learning from large-scale, accumulated knowledge databases. Such computers should also be able to communicate with humans intelligently through speech, written languages, pictures, and images, and to reason through logical inference or distributed problem solving.

We are witnessing the emergence of a new generation of computers to satisfy the demand for knowledge and intelligence processing. These are the AI-oriented machines (78, 81). The objective here is to create intelligent machines with smart interfaces: machines that can listen to us, help program themselves, make logical inferences, translate among different languages (84), see and understand images, learn from their own experience, and search through large-scale databases to find useful and pertinent information (4). Can we build a "Hal" by 2001 A.D. (9)? Can we ever synthesize a machine that can imitate the human brain?

8.2. Numerical Versus Symbolic Processing

Supercomputers for numerical processing and computers for AI-oriented applications are characterized and differentiated in this section. The conventional von Neumann computers are designed for deterministic numerical computations. AI-oriented computers must be able to process symbolic information nondeterministically. Consequently, the two architectures are quite different. However, to achieve high performance, both types of computer systems demand parallel processing and/or distributed computing.

8.2.1. Numerical Supercomputing

The efficiency of a numerical supercomputer greatly depends on its ability to operate on large vectors, arrays, and matrices, where the data is highly structured and regular. It is also influenced by the ability to execute scalar, vector, and I/O operations concurrently and swiftly. Besides having adequate hardware to support high memory and I/O bandwidths and to perform fast arithmetic operations, numerical supercomputers should be able to perform parallel processing at all possible levels.

Parallelism can be exploited at four programmatic levels: job or program level, task or procedure level, interinstruction level, and intrainstruction level. Based on the form of parallel processing emphasized, supercomputers are structured in three architectural classes: pipelined computers, array processors, and multiprocessor systems. A pipelined computer performs overlapping computations to exploit temporal parallelism at the inter- and intrainstruction levels. An array processor uses multiple arithmetic/logic units to achieve spatial parallelism. A multiprocessor system executes multiple instruction streams over multiple data streams using interactive processors with shared resources.

These three approaches to supercomputer design are not mutually exclusive. Pipelined multiprocessors represent the state-of-the-art in supercomputer design and exploit parallel processing at all four levels. Many of the supercomputer manufacturers are taking this route in upgrading their high-end models. Pipelined and array supercomputers are designed mainly for vector processing of large arrays of data. At present, most of the commercially available supercomputers are pipelined machines.

The usefulness of a supercomputer is not entirely determined by its hardware capabilities. In fact, the efficiency is to a large extent dependent on the availability of supersoftware which, while easy to use, is capable of exploiting the maximum parallelism from user programs. First, a sophisticated automatic vectorizer is needed to convert DO loops into vector code. Vectorization should be done even for complicated loops continuing IF statements, intrinsic functions, and list vectors (37). Dynamic register allocation and code optimization via program flow analysis are desired. An intelligent compiler must also be developed to detect the concurrency among scalar instructions that can be realized with pipelined or array multiprocessors, and to exploit multitasking among multiple instruction streams on multiprocessors. At present, high-level languages used on supercomputers are mostly sequential. Hence, a good *vectorizing and/or multitasking compiler* is needed to regain the parallelism lost when an algorithm is expressed in a sequential language. Most existing vector machines are FORTRAN-based, and the effectiveness of FORTRAN compilers has greatly influenced the performance of contemporary supercomputers.

Table 8.1 compares the speed of modern supercomputers in millions of floating-point operations per second (Mflops). The expected minimum and peak performances are shown. Of course, the actual speed depends on the application and algorithmic implementation. In general, the performance tends to be lower for mixed application problems. The Cray 1, introduced in 1976, marked the beginning of the present generation of supercomputers. The CDC Cyber-20 is tuned to the processing of long vectors. The three Japanese supercomputers have peak speeds ranging from 800 to 1300 Mflops. Denelcor's HEP-1 is a multiprocessor system with as many as 16 processors. The Cray X-MP/2 is a dual-processor system, upgraded from the Cray 1.

Table 8.1 Speed Performance of Present and Future Supercomputers

		Speed range (Mflops)	
Year of introduction	Manufacturer and model	Expected minimum	Peak speed
1976	Cray 1	30	160
1981	CDC Cyber 205	15	400
1983	Cray X-MP	60	700
1984	Fujitsu VP-200	30	800
1984	Hitachi S810	30	900
1985	Cray 2	120	2000
1985	NEC SX2	?	1300
1987	ETA/GF10	200	10,000
1988	Cray 3	?	16,000
1991	ETA/GF30	3000	30,000

Data from Fernbach S: Supercomputers: Past, present, and prospects. J. of Future Generation Computer Systems, North-Holland, Vol. 1, No. 1, 1984, pp.23–30; Wah BW, Li GJ (eds): Computers for Artificial Intelligence Applications. IEEE Computer Society Press, March 1986; and Lubeck O, Moore J, Mendez R: A benchmark comparison of three supercomputers: Fujitsu VP-200, Hitachi S810/20, and Cray X-MP/2. IEEE Computer Magazine, Dec. 1985, pp. 10–29. © IEEE.

The X-MP/4 and Cray-2 have four processors each. In early 1986, about 150 supercomputer installations were extant worldwide. We will examine the Cray supercomputers (Cray X-MP, Cray 2, and Cray 3), Denelcor's HEP system, the IBM/RP3 Project, and the USC/Remps in Section 8.4.

Some future supercomputer systems are shown at the bottom of Table 8.1. The ETA-GF10 being developed by ETA Systems will be an eight-processor system targeted for a performance of 10 Gflops (10^{10} flops). The Cray-3 will use 16 processors to attain even higher speeds. The Japanese national supercomputer project is targeted to be a 10 Gflops machine. The U.S. Strategic Computing project demands a supercomputer that can perform 1 Tflops (10^{12} flops). These supercomputers may appear within the next decade (19, 35, 36). Applications of these future systems will be assessed in later sections.

8.2.2. Computers for Symbolic Processing

Symbolic processing for AI applications differs from numerical processing in several fundamental ways. Consequently, these applications have different architectural requirements. In fact, von Neumann computers and their speed-up techniques, like vector processing and pipelining, may not be suitable for most AI applications. In this section, we examine the characteristics of typical processes in AI and assess special architectural requirements for their efficient execution.

The acquisition, representation, and intelligent use of information and knowledge is fundamental to AI processing (4). A system can acquire information from external sources: visual, vocal, or written. These inputs are often incomplete, imprecise, or even contradictory. Proper recognition and understanding of images and speech is required. At a higher level of capability, intelligent machines should learn on their own by applying their cognitive capabilities on accumulated knowledge and experiences.

Knowledge representation involves the encoding of information regarding objects, relations, goals, actions, and processes into data structures and procedures. The encoding should facilitate the addition, alteration, and manipulation of knowledge. Prominent among current approaches to knowledge representation are semantic nets, frames, scripts, production systems, predicate logic, and relational databases.

Knowledge is used for problem solving, logic inferencing, and information retrieval. Methods to achieve these include state space traversal, problem reduction, forward and backward reasoning, resolution, planning, heuristic search, and pruning. Most of these are I/O bound—i.e., the amount of memory accesses and I/O activities required outweighs computational needs. Furthermore, the operations are often global and are carried out over large knowledge bases.

A von Neumann architecture with centralized control provides a processor/memory bottleneck for intensive and irregular memory-access patterns. A distributed database with localized computations is needed to reduce the interprocess communication traffic. This leads to architectures with "intelligent memories." Here, memory units are endowed with processing capabilities so that they can manipulate and modify their contents without much help from outside. For VLSI implementation, the communication network should have a regular topology, such as a Boolean n-Cube or a two- or three-dimensional array. The logical interconnection pattern, however, needs to be flexible enough to adapt to the changing needs of the message traffic, which is highly irregular in terms of volume and destination. Packet switching networks are indicated. An alternative is to use buses or rings to connect all the processor/memory elements. The architecture itself should be able to adapt to changes in the granularity and data formats of various applications.

Parallel and nondeterministic AI processing emphasizes dynamic allocation and load-balancing techniques. Efficient garbage collection becomes vital when storage is allocated dynamically. Furthermore, frequent interprocessor communication or broadcasting may be needed. For example, in the branch and bound technique for combinatorial search problems, whenever a processor finds a better solution than the current "best solution," it needs to transmit this as the new "best solution" to all other processors so that they know when to "bound." Similarly, end-of-computation signals (success/failure) need to be broadcast globally. This can be facilitated by having a global bus or shared data register (82). An alternative is to have the global message passed from one processor to its neighbors in a distributed manner. This is clearly slower, though it can be somewhat alleviated by pipelining techniques.

Associative memory can be used for parallel search and retrieval of patterns. Associative arrays processors can execute a pattern-matching operation simultaneously at different points in the knowledge base, or can pursue several hypothesis in parallel (54). Hardware stacks are useful for storing information about previous states that needs to be recovered quickly for backtracking and other operations.

AI processing often requires logical set operations such as union, intersection, and negation of sets. For example, the elements in a database that fit a set of observed features can be determined by associating with each feature a set of elements that satisfy that feature, then taking their intersection. The ability to operate on status flags associated with data and/ or processes is very useful for these purposes. Tagged mechanisms can also be used to denote contexts. Data and operations (rules) that are invalid in a given context can be marked with flags/tags. Masks can then be used to temporarily ignore them. Masking techniques can also be used to temporarily relax some constraints when we have to make decisions based on insufficient or uncertain data.

AI machines also need some rudimentary arithmetic capabilities. These are used to evaluate cost functions (make best decision), manipulate certainty factors, etc. In vision, the problem is often to recognize a whole object (pattern) even if it has undergone a complex transformation. Thus, we might need to apply transformation like translation, rotation, and scaling. Vision problems usually incorporate both symbolic and numerical processing, with the numerical component gaining predominance during low-level image processing (53, 63).

All the architectural requirements mentioned have been inferred from knowledge representation and manipulation schemes. This is a *knowledge approach* to AI architecture design. The other approach is to design an architecture to efficiently support some high-level AI language. This *language approach* has given birth to Lisp (30, 51, 55, 77) and Prolog machines. They incorporate special mechanisms to efficiently implement primitive operations of the language(s) they support. Prolog machines have hardware units for matching and unification of goals with heads of clauses. A dataflow implementation of primitive operations in Lisp (cons, car, cdr, atom, and eq) has been reported (2).

No AI machine can support all of these features. Based on current technology and techniques, it is impractical to create a general-purpose AI machine. Currently, extensive research is being carried out in designing efficient AI architectures (31, 58). Future AI architectures are expected to incorporate existing concepts like dataflow processing, stack machines, tagging, direct execution of high-level languages, database machines, multiprocessing, and distributed processing with totally new concepts in computer architecture. Intelligent computers that have been proposed for solving AI problems will be further elaborated on in Section 8.5.

8.3. Supercomputing and AI Applications

In this section, we review advanced applications of supercomputers and AI machines. We first examine the impact on science and engineering. Then we check the application of these systems for predictive modeling and energy resource exploration. Military and medical uses are then assessed. Finally, we examine the applications of AI-oriented computers (38, 81).

8.3.1. Science and Engineering

Basic research in almost every scientific area demands the use of supercomputers—for example, computational physicists and chemists study quantum mechanics, fluid dynamics, molecular dynamics, and crystal growth using supercomputers. Breakthroughs in many of these advanced scientific applications depend on the availability of reliable computing systems that are capable of suggesting new theories, interpreting experiments, modeling real processes, and providing accurate calculations within a reasonable time.

In structural engineering, supercomputers are used to solve large systems of algebraic equations arising from finite-element analysis. Computational aerodynamics offers an economic alternative for designing advanced aircrafts without building an expensive wind tunnel. Supercomputers are in demand for the advancement of AI and design automation, which involves signal/image processing, pattern and speech recognition, computer vision and graphics, logical inference for developing knowledge databases and expert systems, CAD/CAM for industrial automation, intelligent robotics, remote sensing for earth-resource management, etc. Semiconductor manufacturers use supercomputers to aid in the analysis and synthesis of VLSI circuits. Vectorized SPICE code has been developed to aid large-scale circuit analysis.

8.3.2. Prediction and Exploration

Predictive modeling demands extensive simulation experiments on high-performance computers. Often we need to perform large-scale numerical computations on tremendous volumes of data arrays in order to achieve the desired accuracy and turnaround time for weather forecasting, climate prediction, oceanographic studies, astrophysical explanations, modeling of world economics, government censuses, and biological system simulations. Present-day computers have not been able to satisfy the demand for computational speeds required for these predictive simulations.

Supercomputers are being used for discovering oil and gas and managing their recovery, for developing workable plasma-related fusion energy sources, and for ensuring nuclear reactor safety. The use of computer technology for energy exploration has resulted in lower production costs and better safety measures. Both seismic signal processing and oil-field reservoir modeling demand the use of supercomputers to provide accuracy and to save processing time. Magnetic fusion research programs are being aided by vector supercomputers at the Lawrence Livermore National Laboratory. The potential for fusion energy has increased as a result of the Tokamak experiments being supported by computational simulation programs. The U. S. National Magnetic Fusion Energy Computer Center is currently using a CDC 7600 and two Cray 1 machines for controlled plasma experiments. Nuclear reactor design and safety control can also be aided by real-time computer simulations.

8.3.3. Military and Medicine

Weapons research agencies have used most of the available supercomputers in the design of multiwarhead missiles, in the study of atomic weapon effects, and in intelligence gathering, antiballistic programs, cartographic surveys, robotics warfare, etc. The U. S. strategic defense initiative (SDI) project needs intelligent supercomputers for "star wars." Basic operations required for battle management include keeping track of the positions, courses, and identities of all boosters, warheads, and assorted decoys, etc., keeping track of the status and position of all defensive weapons and sensors, allocating weapons to threats, and maintaining database consistency (1). Each of these operations demands computing powers and intelligence that are orders of magnitude greater than what is attainable at present. The prospects of maintaining consistency in a huge, globally distributed (literally!) database and running 6–10 million lines of code (20) in a foolproof manner under stringent real-time constraints and in an extremely hostile environment seem extremely remote, even with the development of intelligent supercomputers and supersoftware.

Supercomputers are in great demand in modern medical diagnosis, such as in developing fast computer-assisted tomographic scanners for generating three-dimensional and stop-action pictures of a human heart. Genetic engineers demand fast computers and expert systems for studying molecular biology, for artificial synthesis of protein, and for gel matching in estimating the mutation rate of the human species.

8.3.4. Machine Intelligence

Computer vision and image understanding, together with understanding and processing of natural languages and speech, are aimed at enabling the computer to interface with the external world (and vice versa) in a more effective and natural manner. We need intelligent computers for automated reasoning, automatic programming, planning, problem solving, and theorem proving. In the process of developing and using such systems, we hope to improve our understanding of cognition, learning, and reasoning in humans as well.

Machines for knowledge-base management and expert systems for consulting and computer-aided instruction help us in managing, pooling, and using our huge warehouse of knowledge more easily and effectively. Robotics enables us to delegate mundane, repetitive, and/or precision jobs such as component assembly, as well as dangerous jobs such as handling of radioactive material in nuclear reactors, to robots, thereby freeing our energies for more creative activities. AI applications lead to a systematic approach to knowledge engineering. We demand future computers to serve as unbiased experts that can be consulted for making critical decisions in very complicated tasks (18).

8.4. Multiprocessing Supercomputers

Multiprocessor systems, which have more than one processor sharing memory space and peripherals under the supervision of a single integrated operating system, have been developed to improve throughput, reliability, flexibility, and availability. Multiprocessor system organization is determined primarily by the interconnection patterns between processors, memory modules, and peripheral devices. Most commercial machines have used time-shared common buses, crossbar switch networks, multiported memories, or the hypercube topology for interconnecting processors and memories. The processors need to communicate so that they can cooperatively solve a given large problem. This is achieved through a shared memory or by a message-passing mechanism. Accordingly, multiprocessors are characterized as tightly coupled or loosely coupled systems.

Multiprocessors should be designed to perform multitasking—i.e., the concurrent execution of procedures or tasks within the same program or job. Pipelined multiprocessor supercomputers are able to do parallel processing at all four programmatic levels. Their effective use requires the development of parallel algorithms, parallel language features, and compilers for the detection of parallelism in user programs. To enable the processors to cooperate effectively and to regulate the use of shared resources, multiprocessor operating systems include protection schemes, system deadlock resolution methods, interprocess communication mechanisms, and various multiple processor scheduling strategies. (A more detailed discussion of partitioning, scheduling, and synchronization in multiprocessors is given in Chapter 4.)

One of the limiting factors to the expansion of a tightly coupled system is the performance degradation due to memory contentions that occur when two or more processors attempt to access the same memory unit concurrently. This problem can be alleviated by interleaving the shared memory and by having a home memory for each processor. However, this requires careful partitioning of instructions and data and their allocation to appropriate memory modules. Another limiting factor is the bandwidth restrictions in the processor–memory interconnection network. Effective bandwidth can be increased by the incorporation of private caches for the processors. However, this leads to multicache coherency problems. An easy way to tackle this is for the compiler to prespecify data as cacheable/uncacheable. An implementation of this mechanism in the IBM/RP3 will be described later in this section.

We describe next the Cray series of supercomputers—namely, the Cray 1, Cray X-MP, Cray 2, and Cray 3. This series is currently the most popular one among supercomputer users (36). The HEP, though not so successful commercially, incorporates many interesting features such as packet-switched data forwarding and extremely fast context-switching. The following sections elaborate on the salient features of these systems. We then describe two MIMD systems that are in the research stage: The RP3 system being developed by IBM highlights some of the design issues particular to MIMD systems and proposes some innovative solutions for them. The

Remps multiprocessor at the University of Southern California is distinguished by its extreme flexibility and reconfigurability for a wide variety of scientific computations.

8.4.1. Cray Supercomputers

Table 8.2 lists some of the interesting system parameters of four Cray supercomputers. All four systems have a register-to-register multipipelined architecture that can be used for effectively processing scalars, short vectors, and long vectors in a concurrent manner. The Cray 1 is now being replaced by Cray X-MP/1. ECL technology has been used in the first three systems. The Cray 3 will be based on the new GaAs technology and have a 10-fold increase in the basic clock rate. The Cray 1 and Cray X-MP run on the Cray Operating System (COS), while the Cray 2 uses the UNIX System V operating system. The main memory has been increased from 1M to 256M words in the 10 years from the Cray 1 to Cray 2. The cooling technology has advanced from liquid refrigerants to liquid immersion in the same period.

Cray X-MP has one, two, or four identical CPUs that share memory and an I/O subsystem. The system can execute multiple jobs at various levels. The X-MP series design combines high-speed scalar and vector processing with multiple processors, large and fast memories and high-performance I/O. Beside vectorization through the use of multipipelines in each CPU, the system can support either multiprocessing or multitasking. The X-MP/1 systems provide the user with 1.5 to 2.5 times the power of a Cray 1. Each CPU has a 9.5-ns cycle time. The X-MP/48 has four CPUs and 8M

Table 8.2 Key Parameters of Cray Supercomputers

Feature	Cray 1 (1976)	X-MP (1983)	Cray 2 (1985)	Cray 3 (1988 ?)
Technology and basic clock rate (ns)	SSI/ECL 12.5 ns	MSI/ECL 9.5 ns	MSI/ECL 3-D circuit packages 4.1 ns	GaAs 1 ns
No. of processors used	1	1, 2, 4 plus an I/O subsystem	4 background processors, 1 foreground processor	16
Speed range (Mflops)	30–160	60–700	120–2000	up to 16,000
Max. main memory (Mwords)	1M	16M with 128M of SSD	256M plus 16k local memory per processor	2000M
Operating system	COS	COS	UNIX System V	UNIX
Cooling	Liquid refrigerant	Liquid refrigerant	Liquid immersion	(unknown)

words of ECL bipolar memory, and is 10 times faster than the Cray 1. The Cray X-MP/416 configuration offers 16M words of main memory.

The X-MP/48 multiprocessor structure is depicted in Figure 8.1. The mainframe consists of the CPUs, bipolar or MOS central memory, and various I/O channels. The I/O subsystem contains various I/O controllers for external disks, front-ends, and magnetic tape units. The Solid-State Storage Device (SSD) is an extended central memory with a capacity ranging from 64 to 1024 Mbytes. The central memory is shared by four CPU's with a memory bank cycle time of 38 ns. The memory provides four parallel access ports per processor and thus achieves more than 16 times the bandwidth of the Cray 1. Two of the ports are for vector fetch, one is for vector write, and one is for independent I/O operations. This means that each processor of an X-MP system has four times the memory bandwidth of a Cray 1. The memory is 32-way interleaved to support high-speed CPU and I/O operations in parallel.

Each X-MP processor offers very fast scalar processing as well as high-speed processing of long and short vectors. Multiprocessor models enable the user to exploit multitasking too. The scalar performance of each processor is attributable to its fast clock cycle, short memory-access time, and large instruction buffers. Vector performance is supported by the fast clock,

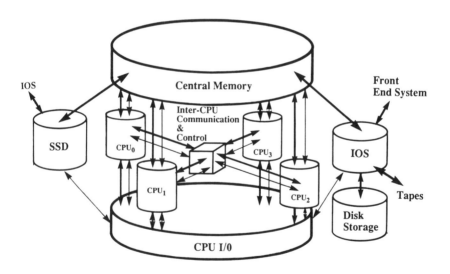

Figure 8.1 Cray X-MP-4 overall system organization. (Courtesy of Cray Research, Inc., 1984.)

parallel memory ports, and flexible hardware chaining. These features allow simultaneous execution of memory fetches, arithmetic operations, and memory stores in a series of linked vector operations. The internal structure of each CPU in the X-MP is an enhancement of the Cray-1 design, and contains 13 functional units in addition to register files and instruction buffers. The functional units are divided into four groups: address, scalar, vector, and floating point. The X-MP guarantees chaining of linked vector operations. Hardware support of *gather/scatter* operations (chainable from other vector memory *fetches* and *stores*) and compressed index generation are also provided to facilitate the execution of various conditioned vector operations.

The SSD is incorporated in the Cray X-MP in the place of disks for providing large amounts of data memory. This device can be used to store large datasets that are generated and manipulated repetitively by user programs. The SSD can also be used to store system programs, and provides a significant improvement for applications that are I/O bound. The IOS is integrated into the system to offer control and buffering capabilities for other auxiliary storage and front-end systems. A disk cache of up to 8M words of MOS memory can be configured in the IOS to reduce data access time.

The four CPUs in the X-MP/4 intercommunicate and synchronize via five clusters of shared registers. The operating system allocates the clusters to the CPUs. An allocated cluster may be accessed in either user or supervisor mode. The COS has been designed to support concurrent execution of independent tasks of different jobs as well as related tasks of a single job on multiple precessors. Loosely coupled tasks can communicate through shared memory, while shared registers are provided for communications among tightly coupled tasks. The Cray FORTRAN compiler (CFT) allows vectorizing optimizations. Front-end connections for the X-MP can use IBM/MVS, CDC/NOS, DEC, Honeywell, Sperry, or NSC network adapters.

In order to provide flexible and efficient multitasking capabilities, special hardware and software features have been built into the Cray supercomputers. These features allow one or more processors to access shared memory or high-speed shared registers for rapid communication and data transmission between CPUs. Hardware provides built-in detection of deadlocks within a cluster of processes. Experience shows that multitasked applications running on X-MP/48 computers can realize speedups of 3.5 to 3.8 times over the uniprocessor X-MP (10).

The Cray 2, introduced in 1985, has an effective throughput 6–12 times that of the Cray 1 (11). The main memory has 256M words and the processor cycle time is only 4.1 ns. As depicted in Figure 8.2, the Cray 2 consists of four foreground processors, which can operate independently on separate jobs or concurrently on a single problem. Each processor has an architecture similar to that of the Cray 1 or Cray X-MP. However, the instruction buffers are enlarged, and a local memory of 16K words is built into each processor for storing temporary scalar and vector operands during computations. The

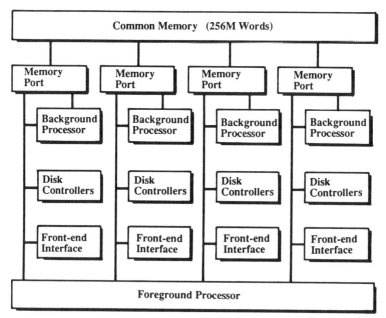

Figure 8.2 The system architecture of Cray 2. (Courtesy of Cray Research, Inc., 1985.)

foreground processor supervizes overall systems activity among all five processors, the common memory, and peripheral controllers. System communications occur through four synchronous data channels.

Technological innovations in the Cray 2 include the use of liquid immersion cooling and three-dimensional circuit modules. The entire system consists of 320 pluggable modules, each of which contains about 750 IC packages mounted on eight layers of PC-boards. Circuit interconnections are made in all three dimensions within each module. Only 16-gate MSI/ECL packages are used. The major software improvement of the Cray 2 over earlier Cray machines lies in the use of the UNIX System V. This OS greatly enhances I/O processing and manipulates very large data files efficiently. Other important enhancements include the support of asynchronous I/O, multiprocessing, and user multitasking in FORTRAN and C languages.

Very little is known about the Cray 3 at the time of writing, except that we see a major switch from silicon technology to gallium arsenide (GaAs) circuits. The Cray 3 is expected to use 16 processors with 2 Gwords of main memory, and attempts to attain a peak performance of 16 Gflops.

8.4.2. The HEP Multiprocessor

The Heterogeneous Element Processor (HEP) has been produced by Denelcor Inc. in the United States. The HEP-1 system consists of 1 to 16 processors connected to 128 data memory modules through a packet-switched network. Each processor has 1 million words of program memory, and each memory module can store 128 million words of 64 bits each. A functional block diagram of the HEP architecture is shown in Figure 8.3a. The HEP is an intrinsic MIMD computer that can support tightly coupled multiprocessing at the process level. The processors and the packet-switching network are highly pipelined. The system allows modular growth to keep pace with growing computational demands.

The system provides unlimited addressing and eliminates data dependency delays by fast context switching among concurrent processes and by direct internal data forwarding. Synchronization is done by using tagged memory words and registers. The system uses ANSI FORTRAN 77 with extensions. The performance of the system can be linearly increased up to 160 Mips. Fifty instruction streams (processes) are allowed per processor, with a maximum of 800 user instruction streams for the entire HEP system.

The HEP executes multiple instruction streams over multiple data streams in a highly pipelined fashion. This technique is called *MIMD pipelining* among instructions from different streams. An example is shown in Figure 8.3b, where an *add* operation is in progress for one process, a *multiply* for another, a *divide* for a third, and a *branch* for a fourth. Because instructions being executed concurrently are independent of each other, execution of one instruction does not influence the execution of other instructions. Thus, fill-in parallelism, as obtained by fast-context switching, is used to increase processor utilization. Arbitrarily structured parallelism is applicable to codes that do not vectorize well. The concept of MIMD pipelining makes HEP very attractive for solving PDE problems characterized by large sparse matrices.

More information about the HEP supercomputer and its applications can be found in *Parallel MIMD Computations*, edited by Kowalik (47). This book contains interesting articles dealing with the HEP's architectural development, programming of HEP to solve PDEs, linear algebraic and boundary-value problems, and some performance characterizations of the HEP. Unfortunately, the HEP system is no longer in production because of financial difficulties.

8.4.3. The IBM/RP3 Project

The Research Parallel Processor Project (RP3) is being undertaken by the IBM Watson Research Center (60) in cooperation with the Ultracomputer Project of the Courant Institute of New York University (25). This experimental project aims at investigating the hardware and software aspects of highly parallel computations.

The RP3 is an MIMD system consisting of 512 Processor-Memory Elements (PMEs) and a fast interconnection network (Figure 8.4). Each PME

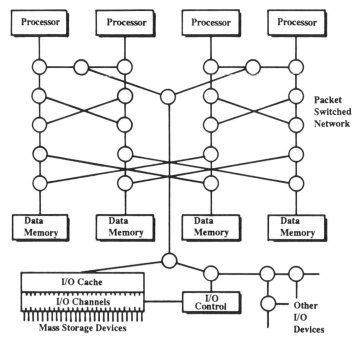

(a) The Architecture of HEP with Four Processors

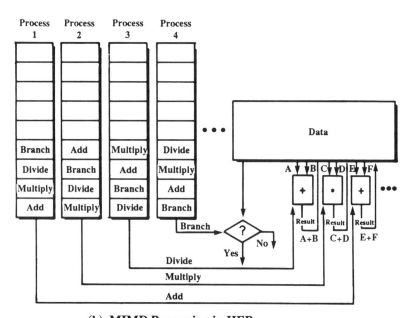

(b) MIMD Processing in HEP

Figure 8.3 HEP architecture and MIMD processing. (a) The architecture of HEP with four processors. (b) MIMD processing in HEP. (Courtesy of Denelcor, Inc., 1982.)

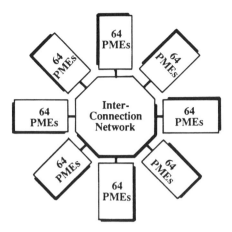

(a) The Global Architecture

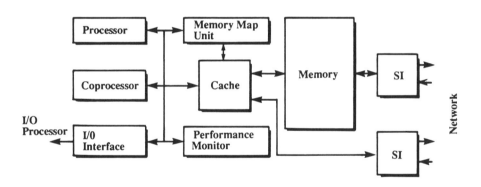

(b) Design of Each Processor-Memory Element (PME)

Figure 8.4 System architecture of the RP3 multiprocessor. (a) The global architecture. (b) Design of each processor-memory element (PME).

contains an IBM 801-like microprocessor, 32K-byte cache, vector floating point unit, and 4M bytes of memory. Switch interfaces (SI) are needed between each PME and the interconnection network for logic-level conversions and data-formating. Special I/O processors are used for I/O and performance monitoring, system initialization, and configuration. Each I/O processor supports eight PMEs through a bus attachment that is independent of the main network. The full configuration will provide up to 1300 Mips or 800 Mflops. The system will run on a modified version of the BSD 4.2 UNIX operating system.

The experimental nature of the RP3 project is reflected in its highly flexible organization. The RP3 can be configured as a shared memory system, as a message-passing system with localized memories, or as mixtures of these two paradigms chosen at run time. Furthermore, the system can be partitioned into completely independent submachines by controlling the degree of memory interleaving. Extensive hardware support for monitoring allows measurement of many performance-related parameters.

The instruction sets of the processors in each PME are augmented for a parallel environment and include seven fetch-and-OP instructions such as fetch-and-add and fetch-and-min, which are used for process coordination and synchronization. Also provided are cache control instructions that can efficiently invalidate logical blocks of data in the cache.

The floating point unit is a coprocessor used to perform arithmetic functions. Vector operations are of the form memory-to-memory. Registers internal to the coprocessor can be used for register-to-register or mixed (register-to-memory/memory-to-register) operations on scalars. This coprocessor works independent of and asynchronously with the processor. Each coprocessor can deliver up to 1.5 Mflops for single precision and 0.9 Mflops for double precision operands. A vector length of 20 is sufficient to cross 90% of the peak performance.

Figure 8.5a shows how the global address space is distributed across the PMEs. Part of each PME's memory is allocated to form the global memory. True local memory is accessed via the cache without going through the interconnection network. The dynamic partitioning of memory is determined at run time. Moving the local/global boundary to the far right makes RP3 a pure shared-memory machine like the NYU Ultracomputer. Moving it to the far left makes it a pure local-memory multiprocessor using message-passing for interprocessor communication. Intermediate boundary positions provide a "mixed-mode" computation. The architecture allows shared-memory oriented applications to allocate private data locally to improve efficiency, while message-oriented applications use the global memory to balance the work load. In the address translation process (Figure 8.5b), the interleaving degree can range between 0 and 9. The interleave transformation causes n consecutive addresses within a page to be interleaved across 2^n memory modules, where n is the interleaving degree.

A critical issue for using multiple caches in a multiprocessor environment is that of cache coherency. The RP3 solves the cache coherence problem in software, with hardware assistance. The cacheable/noncacheable attribute of a datum is determined during compile time. However, this attribute can be changed between program segments if, for example, the usage of a datum changes from shared read-write to read-only or vice versa. To support this scheme, the system requires cache control instructions and an efficient technique for cache invalidation of logical blocks of data. The compiler determines the cacheability and volatility attributes of data and stores them in

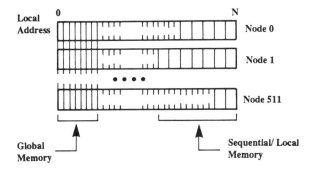

(a) Local vs. Global Memory Allocation

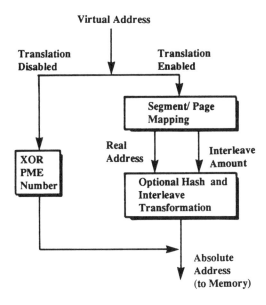

(b) The Address Translation Process

Figure 8.5 Memory space and addressing in RP3. (a) Local vs. global memory allocation. (b) The address translation process. (From Brantley WC, McAuliffe KP, Weiss J: RP3 processor-memory element. *Proc. 1985 International Conference on Parallel Processing*, Aug. 1985, pp. 782–789; Pfister GJ, et al: The IBM research parallel processor prototype (RP3): Introduction and architecture. *Proc. 1985 International Conference on Parallel Processing*, Aug. 1985, pp. 764–771.)

a memory map. The volatility attribute is used to indicate temporarily cacheable pages and/or segments, which can be removed by an "invalidate volatile data" command.

The PMEs are interconnected by two multistage networks. One is a high-speed network designed with bipolar technology to provide quick responses to memory requests. This low-latency network is a rectangular SW banyan (24). The other network is slower, but can combine memory access operations (25). Usually, memory access requests for synchronization operations such as fetch-and-OP are sent by the PMEs to the combining network; all other requests are sent to the low-latency network. The combining network has the geometry of an Omega network (49). If two or more read/write requests to the same memory location arrive at a switch in the network, only one is forwarded and the others are satisfied indirectly. For example, two read requests can be combined at a switch by locally storing the return address of one of them and forwarding the other to the appropriate memory module. When the result of the read operation passes by this switch on its way back to the requesting PE, a copy of it is also sent to the other PE whose address had been stored locally.

Each switch also includes an ALU to implement fetch-and-OP oper-

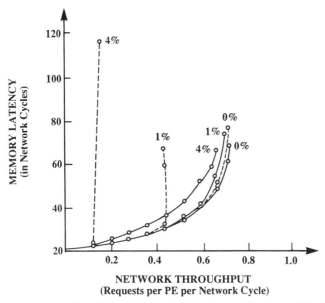

Figure 8.6 The effect of hot-spots on memory latency. Single hot-spot used with intensity of 0, 1, and 4% of total network traffic. Dashed lines are obtained when combining of memory accesses is not implemented. (From Pfister GJ, Norton VA: "Hot spot" contention and combining in multistage interconnection networks. *Proc. 1985 International Conference on Parallel Processing*, Aug. 1985, pp. 790–797.)

ations. This increases the switch cost, but is very effective for coping with the problem of hot spots. A hot spot is said to occur at a memory module if the module receives more than the average number of memory references from the processors. Hot spots are expected to occur in multiprocessor systems with shared memory, typically at shared memory locations that contain synchronization mechanisms, shared data, common queues, etc., and are therefore accessed by more than one processor concurrently.

Figure 8.6 reflects the degrading effect of hot spots on average memory latency and how this problem can be alleviated by combining memory accesses. For both the solid and dashed lines, the rightmost curves are obtained when the memory-access pattern is assumed to be uniform over all shared memory modules. The other curves are obtained by superimposing a single hot spot, representing 1% and 4% of the total memory references, on a background of uniform traffic. Since most data that cause hot spots are not cacheable and have to reside in the global memory, the data traffic to hot spots is expected to be high enough (5–20% of total network traffic) to warrant the design of a separate combining network in the RP3.

The performance of RP3 is a function of instruction and data cache miss ratios. For typical scientific application codes, instruction miss ratios are expected to be in the 1–2% range and data miss ratios to be about 20%. With these assumptions, RP3 should have a performance of approximately 1 Mflops with 512 PMEs. Much of the details of the RP3 multiprocessor can be found in articles (5, 59–61) reported by IBM researchers.

8.4.4. The Remps Vector Multiprocessor

A reconfigurable vector multiprocessor, called Remps, has been proposed at the University of Southern California (42). This multiprocessor is generalized from the aforementioned supercomputers. We briefly describe the Remps architecture and show how it can be used to simulate other supercomputers. The Remps is an MIMD vector multiprocessor with shared resources, as illustrated in Figure 8.7. An $n \times m$ configuration of Remps has n processors, each of which has m pipelined functional units. At the global level, the machine is a macro-dataflow computer, while at the local level, each processor is a multipipeline control-flow system. The flexibility attained by the use of several interconnection networks makes Remps suitable for scientific computations that demand both vectorization and multitasking.

The shared memory consists of multiple modules, each of which can be used to store a number of tasks for execution. A high-bandwidth network is used to interface the global memory with the processors. Tasks may be assigned to multiple processors for concurrent processing. Each processor has a local memory, some local I/O devices, a large register file, and multifunctional pipelined units (PEs) that can operate in parallel. The PEs are identical in structure, but they do not have to operate in a lockstep manner.

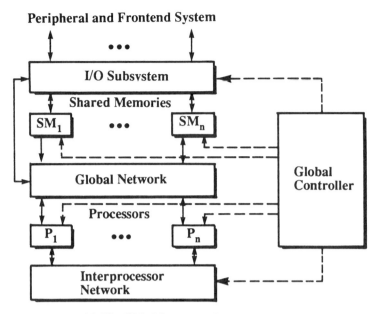

(a) The Global Structure of Remps

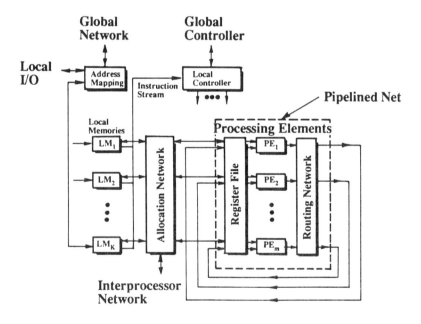

(b) The Detailed Structure of Each Processor

Figure 8.7 The system architecture of Remps. (a) The global structure of Remps. (b) The detailed structure of each processor. (From Hwang K, Xu ZW: Remps: A reconfigurable multiprocessor for scientific supercomputing. *Proc. International Conference on Parallel Processing*, Aug. 1985, pp. 102–111.)

Different functions can be performed at different PEs at the same time, similar to those multiple functional pipelines used in IBM 360/91, CDC 7600, or Cray supercomputers.

The I/O subsystem is connected to the shared memories for the input/output of large programs, data sets, or result sets. For small jobs, these operations can be directly handled by the local I/O facilities attached to each processor. The interprocessor network provides direct communication paths between processors. This network contains shared data registers and special semaphore registers. Thus, multitasking is supported with both shared memory and direct interrupt mechanisms. The global controller is responsible for macrolevel task scheduling, memory management, multiprogramming, synchronization, and other housekeeping functions.

The Remps is being designed to realize macro-dataflow computations at the process or task level. A compiler is needed to partition a large job into a number of communicating tasks or processes to be processed by multiple processors. The large-grain task-dependence graph is formed at compile time and used by the global controller. Multi-PE networking can be implemented within each processor using the routing network to provide dynamic systolization among the PEs (43). The collection of the register file, the PEs, and the routing network forms a *dynamic pipeline net*, which is different from the static connections in a static systolic array (48). One major disadvantage of static systolic arrays is the lack of application flexibility with its fixed topology. Both switch lattices (73) and the pipelined nets in Remps can assume multiple configurations under program control. A comparison of the pipeline nets with systolic arrays and switch lattice is made in Table 8.3 (41).

The Remps is primarily designed for scientific predictive simulations and for solving PDE problems. The idea is to support arbitrary parallelism (multitasking) at the macro-dataflow level using multiple processors with shared memories and to support regular parallelism (vector/array computations) within each processor using multipipeline networking. It should be noted that when all the PEs in each processor are synchronized to perform the same function, the pipeline net operates in an SIMD mode. In this sense,

Table 8.3 Comparisons Among Systolic Arrays, Switch Lattices, and Pipeline Nets

Features	Systolic arrays [Kung & Leiserson (48)]	Switch lattices [Snyder (73)]	Pipeline nets [Hwang & Xu (42, 43)]
Connection	Local	Local	Local or global
Topology	Fixed	Reconfigurable	Reconfigurable
Pipelining	One-level or two-level	One-level	Two-level
Application	Special purpose	Limited	General purpose

Remps is a reconfigurable MIMD/SIMD/multiple SIMD computer, similar to that claimed in the Cedar project at the University of Illinois (23).

Figure 8.7 demonstrates how the Remps can be reconfigured to simulate the operational configurations of the HEP and the Cray X-MP. The Remps extends the pipeline chaining operations in X-MP to pipeline networking and offers MIMD pipelining at the macro-dataflow level rather than at the process level as implemented in the HEP.

8.5. Multiprocessors for Artificial Intelligence

Parallel processing plays a major role in AI applications, as shown in Section 8.2.2. Multiprocessors have been suggested for a number of AI applications. Parallel machines have been proposed for supporting AI Languages such as Lisp and Prolog (28, 56). Other multiprocessors have been considered for implementing database machines and production systems (22). Most of the AI-oriented systems are designed for symbolic processing, information retrieval, logic inference, theorem proving, knowledge engineering computer vision and speech and language understanding. We give next an overview of major AI-oriented computers, and discuss some representative systems— namely, the Connection Machine, the DADO and NON-VON multiprocessors, and Japan's Parallel Inference Machine.

8.5.1. An Overview of AI Machines

AI-oriented computers are mainly used for symbolic processing. Parallel and distributed processing of AI information is often practiced. Many AI algorithms are nondeterministic in nature. Dynamic resource allocation and load balancing become crucial for AI information processing. Management of large knowledge bases is often required. Most AI architectures are software oriented. Many new approaches to computer architecture have been proposed or experimented with for AI systems. Candidate architectures include dataflow, reduction, direct-execution of high-level languages, data/knowledge-base machines, and logic machines (79).

Key issues in developing AI-oriented computers include AI programming languages and their applications, parallel algorithms for unification and logic programming, multiprocessing of combinatorial search problems, functional programming systems, logic machine architectures, parallel production systems, semantic networks, distributed problem solving, logic inference mechanisms, and intelligent man-machine interfaces. Interested readers may refer to the tutorial by Wah and Li for relevant literature (81).

In Table 8.4, we have compiled a list of 11 representative AI-oriented computers that have been built or are under development in various countries. The designers, architecture model, languages, and main applications

Table 8.4 Computers for AI Processing

System	Architecture; execution model	Applications
ALICE, England (12, 62)	Multiprocessor with 16 × 16 crossbar for P-M connections and two rings for direct interprocessor communications; data-driven dataflow execution of HOPE.	Processing of high-level applicative languages (HOPE).
AMPS, Univ. of Utah (46)	Binary tree-structured multiprocessor with internal nodes for communication and load balancing and leaf nodes for processors/memory; demand-driven execution of Flow-Graph Lisp.	Parallel Lisp processing and other AI applications.
Connection Machine, Thinking Machines, Inc. (32, 33)	Massively parallel fine-grained SIMD system using a hypercube network, and executing Connection Machine Lisp (CmLisp).	Processing of knowledge represented by semantic networks.
DADO, Columbia Univ. (74, 75)	A binary tree-structure multiprocessor for SIMD/MIMD/multiple SIMD operations using Intel 8751 microprocessors and PL/M language.	Implementing production systems and expert systems, Prolog language.
NON-VON, Columbia Univ. (34, 71, 72)	Aggregate of fine-grained binary trees with mesh-connected leaves serve as active memories for microcomputers at the roots. Runs in a Lisp-like environment.	General purpose AI machine (knowledge-base management, image processing, production systems).
FAIM-1, Fairchild Corp. (13, 14)	Hexagonal mesh of identical RISC processors that have hardware stacks, tags, unification units, and intelligent storage, and communicate by message passing; supports stream, OR and AND parallelism using a high-level language called OIL.	Theorem-proving, knowledge-based systems and parallel execution of logic programs.
Guzman Machine, National Univ. of Mexico (28)	Grill memory contains functions and variables that are sent via a FIFO queue and distributor to eight Lisp processors connected by a bus, and running Lisp interpreters.	Parallel Lisp processing.
PIM-D, ICOT, Japan (55, 56)	Multiple processors with tagged architecture access shared structured data from structure memories, and use streams for asynchronous producer-consumer communication: nondeterministic goal-driven execution of Prolog programs based on the unfolding interpreter.	Parallel execution of logic programs such as Prolog and C-Prolog.
SNAP, USC, Los Angeles (54)	2-D mesh augmented by global buses connect processors having content addressable memories, hardware flags, and microprogrammed control; combines associative and cellular	Pattern matching, production systems, discrete relaxation for vision.

(Continued)

Table 8.4 Computers for AI Processing (*continued*)

System	Architecture; execution model	Applications
	array processing using a set of primitive instructions.	
THRISTLE, CMU Pittsburgh (17)	Massively parallel, fine-grained distributed processing with both marker and value passing mechanisms; local representation and manipulation of knowledge.	Processing of semantic nets, iterative relaxation algorithms for low-level vision.
ZMOB, Univ. of Maryland (64, 65, 83)	256 Z-80 based processors communicating through a fast slotted ring.	Image processing and artificial intelligence research.

of these AI machines are identified in the table. Key references to each prototype system are also given. This list is by no means exhaustive. Of the AI machines to be reviewed, the Connection Machine is presently designed as an SIMD machine and not a multiprocessor in the traditional sense. The DADO machine is designed to implement production systems. The Japanese PIM-R machine is a language-based design of a machine for efficient execution of logic programs.

One of the reasons for developing AI-oriented computers is to facilitate the construction of expert systems. An expert system is meant to solve very difficult or tedious problems at the expert level using a comprehensive knowledge base. An expert system must possess a learning mechanism to correct, expand, and update the knowledge base and have the ability to interpret and explain its decisions. Eventually, we would like to create ideal consultants that can make intelligent and unbiased decisions.

More than 50 knowlege-based expert systems are now available for various special-purpose applications. For example, MYCIN is used for diagnosis of blood diseases, XCON is for cost-effective configuration of VAX computers, DIPMETER helps in oil exploration, and SPERIL estimates earthquake damages. Expert systems are often implemented using rule-based production systems. Pattern matching is by far the most frequently performed operation for such systems. Concurrent operations on parallel production systems and their mapping onto multiprocessor configurations are important and interesting topics of research (53, 79).

Knowledge retrieval in AI involves more than just looking up a fact in a table. If the knowledge is stored as a semantic network, finding the relevant information may involve searching the entire network. If the desired fact is not stored explicitly, it may have to be deduced from other stored information. Programs for knowledge retrieval often spend most of their time repeating a few basic operations. These include:

1. Sorting a set according to some parameter. For instance, a program may need to order goals in terms of importance.

2. Finding a perfect match or best match between a pattern and the given knowledge structure. For example, the problem of finding an analogy to a situation can be reformulated in terms of searching a graph for a subgraph with a specified structure.
3. Deducing facts from semantic inheritance networks like KLONE and NETL (16).

For fast manipulation of knowledge represented by semantic networks, we would like to simultaneously initiate these operations from many nodes of the network. Ideally, each concept (node) should be allocated to a distinct processor, and the interconnections between these processors should be flexible enough to represent the relationships between the corresponding concepts. This requires a large number of processor elements with programmable logical connections so that the topology can be configured to suit the problem. So if the silicon area is fixed, the processors must be simpler and have little local memory. However, the memory is now distributed throughout the machine and is more intelligent because it can modify itself in many places simultaneously through the local processors. The fundamental inefficiency of the von Neumann memory, where only a few locations can change state at any given time, is thus avoided. These considerations are reflected in the architecture of the Connection Machine, examined next.

8.5.2. The Connection Machine

The Connection Machine (CM) was conceived at MIT's AI Laboratory (32) for concurrent manipulation of knowledge stored in semantic networks. This computer operates with a large number of simple processor/memory cells. A prototype SIMD machine, called CM-1, has 64K of such cells linked by a 12-dimensional hypercube network, and is currently being constructed by the Thinking Machines Corporation of Cambridge, Massachusetts. The processing cells are logically connected in data-dependent patterns that are used to both represent and process the data. An external host computer stores these data structures into the CM, orchestrates their activities, and reads the results. Thus, the host computer accesses the CM as it would a conventional memory. However, this access has three basic differences. First, all processing cells can perform local computations simultaneously. Second, information is also stored in the general intercommunications network that can connect all the cells in an arbitrary (programmable) pattern. Finally, the CM can transfer data to and from peripheral devices directly by using a high-bandwidth I/O channel. These features are designed to avoid the von Neumann processor/memory bottleneck.

A connection is established between two processor/memory cells by storing a pointer in the memory. These connections can be set up by the host, loaded through the I/O channel, or determined dynamically by the CM

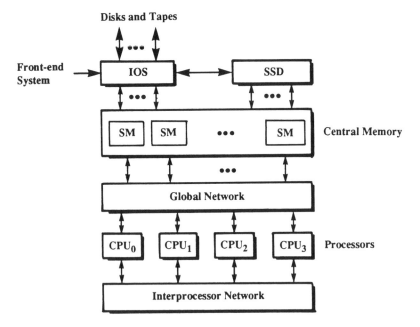

(a) Simulating Cray X-MP/ 4.

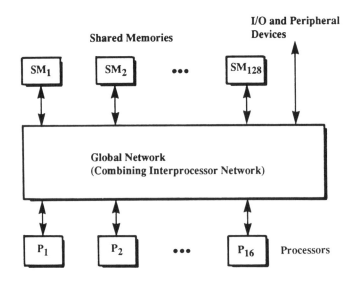

(b) Simulating HEP Using Remps.

Figure 8.8 Reconfiguration of Remps for simulating X-MP/4 and HEP. (a) Simulating Cray X-MP/4. (b) Simulating HEP using Remps.

itself. Figure 8.9a shows the block diagram of the CM-1, a prototype Connection Machine. This prototype has 64K processor/memory cells, with 4K bits of memory per cell. In this SIMD system, the host sends high-level instructions to the special-purpose microcontroller, which converts them into sequences of simpler instructions that can be executed directly by the processors. For example, the host might specify a 32-bit addition sequence by a single command to the microcontroller, which would translate it into 32 individual bit operations to be executed directly by the cells. Thus, the microcontroller acts effectively as a bandwidth amplifier for the instruction stream coming from the host.

The basic building blocks are custom CMOS chips, each containing 16 processor cells and one router unit. The chip control unit decodes nanoinstructions received through the instruction pins and produces signals to control the processor array and the router, using an externally supplied clock for synchronization. The router is responsible for routing messages between chips. The chips are physically connected as a 12-dimensional hypercube. The hypercube topology is distinguished by its symmetry, small diameter, and multiplicity of paths between any two nodes, and is amenable to a layout with high packing density and short average wire length. Within a chip, the processors are connected in a 4×4 grid. Each processor cell can communicate directly with its North, East, West, and South neighbors, without involving the router. This two-dimentional grid pattern can be extended across multiple chips.

Figure 8.9b shows the interior design of a single processor cell. All data paths are 1-bit wide. Each processor has only 16 bits of state information, stored in 16 1-bit flags. The processor cell has an extreme RISC architecture with only one simple but powerful instruction. This instruction takes in three 1-bit operands: two from the external memory and one flag, and produces two output bits, one to be written in the external memory, the other to update a flag. The outputs are found by a memory/flag table lookup. One of 256 possible functions is chosen from each table. All processors receive the same instruction from the control unit, but each processor can be independently masked off if so desired.

Message transfer is controlled by 4096 routers of the CM. Each router handles messages for 16 processing cells that share the same chip. The routers are connected by bidirectional wires to form the hypercube. Suppose a processor $P_{i,j}$ on chip i wants to communicate with processor $P_{k,l}$ on chip k. It first injects the message to the router R_i on its own chip, using a simple hand-shaking mechanism. This router forwards the message to router R_k on chip k. Finally, R_k delivers the message to the appropriate memory location. The routine algorithm used by the router can be broken into repeating cycles called petit cycles. Each petit cycle can be further divided into 12-dimension cycles. During a petit cycle, messages are moved across each of the 12 dimensions in sequence. If there are no conflicts, a message will reach its

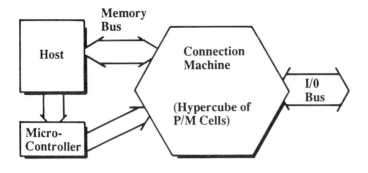

(a) Conceptual System Architecture

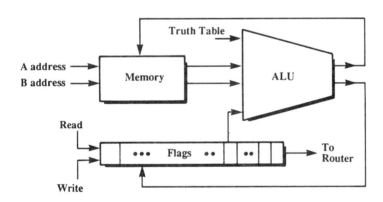

(b) Each Processing Cell.

Figure 8.9 The connection machine. (a) Conceptual system architecture. (b) Each processing cell. (From Hillis, WD: The connection machine: A computer architecture based on cellular automata. *Physica*, North-Holland, 1984, pp. 213–238; Hillis WD: *The Connection Machine*. Massachusetts Institute of Technology Press, Cambridge, MA, 1985.)

destination in one petit cycle because any vertex of the cube can be reached from any other by traversing no more than 12 edges.

Highly concurrent computations are carried out on the CM by matching the interconnection of the PEs to the natural data structure of the problem environment. For image processing and computer vision, one processor is assigned per pixel to form a 2-D array processor. For VLSI simulation, one processor is used to simulate each transistor. The processors are connected in the pattern of the circuit shown in Figure 8.10. To process a semantic

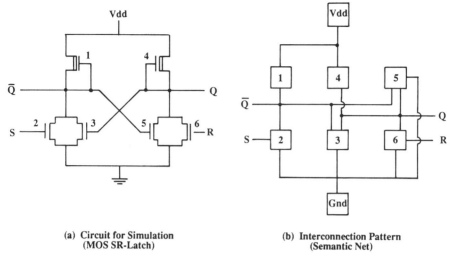

(a) Circuit for Simulation
(MOS SR-Latch)

(b) Interconnection Pattern
(Semantic Net)

Figure 8.10 Interconnection of processors for VLSI simulation. (a) Circuit for simulation (MOS SR-latch). (b) Interconnection pattern (Semantic net).

network, one processor is assigned to each semantic node, and the connections among the processing cells represent the relationships among them. The interconnections are controlled by software. There must be enough processing cells for the machine to match the size of typical problems. The CM, once fully completed, may use 2^{20} processing cells to handle real AI problems (15).

8.5.3. DADO and NON-VON Multiprocessors

The DADO machine, being developed at Columbia University (75), is a binary tree-structured multiprocessor system as shown in Figure 8.11. It is primarily designed to execute production systems. Each node represents a PE based on an 8-bit microcomputer (Intel 8751), and includes about 16K bytes of RAM and a specialized I/O switch. The DADO1 prototype with 15 PEs has been operational since 1983. The DADO2 incorporates 1023 PEs to be of the hardware complexity of a VAX 11/750, and is targeted to perform 600 Mips.

Each PE is capable of executing in SIMD or MIMD mode. In the SIMD mode, the PE executes instructions broadcast by an ancestor PE. If a PE is disabled, it bypasses the instructions being broadcast to its enabled descendants, which will receive and execute such instructions. In MIMD mode, the PE executes instructions stored in its own memory. A special control processor adjacent to the root of the tree controls the operation of the complete ensemble.

The DADO machine has been specifically designed for the execution

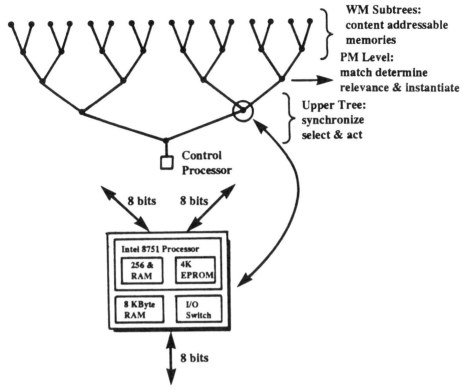

Figure 8.11 The DADO multiprocessor. (From Stolfo SJ, Miranker DP: DADO: A parallel processor for expert systems. *Proc. International Joint Conference on Parallel Processing*, Aug. 1984, pp. 74–82; Stolfo SJ, Miranker D, Shaw DE: Architecture and applications of DADO: A large-scale parallel computer for artificial intelligence. *Proc. International Joint Conference on Artificial Intelligence*, 1983.)

knowledge-based expert systems implemented as production systems. The binary tree topology is logically partitioned into three levels. Each rule is assigned to one PE at the PM level. This level determines the relevance of rules and instantiates the application of appropriate rules. The upper trees are used to synchronize the multiple-SIMD or MIMD operations. The PEs at the WM subtrees operate in SIMD mode using associative memories for fast-searching and pattern-matching operations. Alternate execution schemes and performance characteristics are given in (26, 74).

The NON-VON supercomputer, also being developed at Columbia University, is intended to be a general-purpose AI machine. Application areas include rule-based inferencing, low- and intermediate-level computer vision, and knowledge-base management. The NON-VON project has been influenced by DADO but differs from it in certain crucial aspects. Figure 8.12 shows the organization of the general NON-VON machine.

A Small Processing Element (SPE) is essentially a small memory element of about 256 bytes, enhanced by some processing logic, registers, flags, and a specialized I/O switch. A tree of SPEs forms an intelligent active memory for the Large Processing Element (LPE) attached at its root. Each LPE is based on an off-the-shelf 32-bit microprocessor and has a significant amount of local RAM. It uses its active memory in the SIMD mode for associative search and other parallel operations. The LPEs can be synchronized by the host through the LPE network so that the whole system works as an SIMD machine. Alternatively, the LPEs can operate independently in an MIMD or multiple-SIMD fashion.

The metaphor of an "intelligent record" is useful in describing the operation of the NON-VON. Each record should be able to manipulate its contents and report results according to instructions from a central controller. The size of an SPE has been chosen to match that of an average record. Larger or smaller records can be mapped onto the SPEs by the controlling LPE using spanning or packing methods in a user-transparent manner.

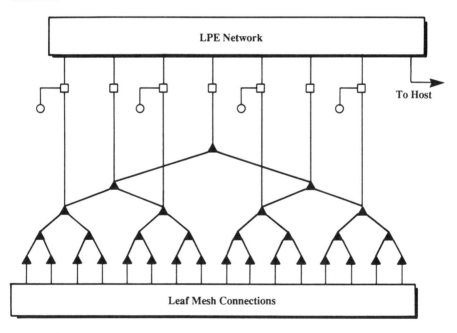

Figure 8.12 Organization of the NON-VON machine. (From Hillyer BK, Shaw DE: Execution of OPS5 production systems on a massively parallel machine. *Journal of Parallel and Distributed Computing*, Vol. 3, No. 2, June 1986, pp. 236–268.)

There are several types of communications between the PEs. First, the tree connections are typically used for broadcasting and propagation/collection of results. Second, the I/O switches of the SPEs can be dynamically configured to support linear neighbor connections—i.e., connections between any pair of nodes that would be adjacent in an in-order enumeration of the active memory tree. This is used for mapping and manipulation of linear arrays of records. Third, the 2-D mesh connections at the leaves are particularly useful for several image processing algorithms where the image is stored at the leaves, one for every pixel, and the inner nodes are used for higher-level representations. Thus, hierarchical data structures such as the multiresolution pyramid and binary image tree can be easily implemented.

Each SPE has an 8-bit comparison unit that can set one of two 1-bit flags depending on the outcome of a COMPARE instruction. By storing the result in the ENABLE flag, one can selectively disable SPEs depending on the results of the comparison test. Larger patterns can be matched byte by byte by ANDing the results of a series of comparison tests. The RESOLVE instruction chooses the first SPE (determined by in-order enumeration) from the candidate set of enabled PEs. The REPORT instruction can be used to transfer the contents of the accumulator of this SPE to the central controller. Finally, by saving the (remaining) candidate set before every REPORT, sequential processing of all candidates is possible. Thus, the entire active memory is content-addressable, and a pattern can be searched for in time proportional to its length, irrespective of the size of the search space. Also, a candidate set can be examined in time proportional to its size.

The I/O subsystem consists of a bank of disk drives whose heads contain a small amount of processing hardware so that they can filter out irrelevant data "on the fly" and do simple operations like hash-coding (70) on the data passing beneath them. An intelligent parallel interface is thus obtained.

The first prototype, NON-VON1, was fabricated and tested in a Lisp-like environment in 1985. It consisted of a tree of seven SPEs whose root was connected to a VAX 11/750 that acted as the central controller. The current version, NON-VON4, will have 32 LPEs based on Motorola 68020s, and 16K SPEs each with 256 bytes of RAM and an 8-bit ALU. The tree paths are 8 bits wide, and the leaves are connected by a bit-wide mesh. With this configuration, an order of magnitude speedup is expected over current database machines when executing knowledge-base primitives such as relational join and aggregation (72).

More spectacular are the projections for the execution of production systems, which show two orders of magnitude speedup over uniprocessors of comparable hardware complexity (34). To achieve this, a parallel adaptation of the RETE algorithm (21) is implemented. Production system rules consist of a set of clauses (the left-hand side) which, if satisfied by the working memory (representing the current "state of the world"), allow a set of actions (the right-hand side) to be executed in order to modify the working memory. Figure 8.13a shows a production rule written in OPS5. This rule might be used to select a team for a mountaineering expedition. Attribute names are prefixed with an up-arrow. The execution cycle for a production system consists of a match phase, where the left-hand sides of all the rules are compared with the active memory. The conflict set consists of all rules that have successful matches and are thus eligible to be fired. The select and act phases will choose one rule out of the conflict phase and execute it.

The RETE algorithm is based on the observation that the firing of a rule affects very few members of both the working memory and the conflict set. Production rules are compiled into dataflow graphs. The state of the system, which includes lists of all working elements that satisfy each rule clause (stored in α-memory nodes) and elements that satisfy sets clauses belonging to the same rule (stored in β-memory nodes), are stored in the internal nodes of these graphs. Changes in the working memory form the input tokens, and the output tokens represent the changes in the conflict set. The dataflow graph for the rule in Figure 13a is shown in Figure 13b.

The "parallel" RETE algorithm is implemented on the NON-VON as follows: The host is the master controller, which first partitions the set of rules among the LPEs. Each LPE compiles the dataflow graphs for its own set of rules. The clauses, α and β nodes, relevant bindings of variables, conflict set, etc. for these rules are stored in the active memory tree. The match phase is effected by the LPEs, which broadcast instructions to their memory trees in an SIMD mode for large-scale associative search in parallel. The LPEs report the changes in the conflict set to the host, which then selects a rule and fires it by sending the changes to be made in the working memory as "add/delete ⟨element⟩" tokens to all the LPEs, which begin the next match phase by using these tokens to associatively match all clauses, update all the α-memory nodes, and determine the changes in the β-memory nodes. Based on statistical characteristics of production systems obtained in (27), this implementation on the NON-VON4 would fire about 900 rules per second. By comparison, a Lisp-based OPS5 interpreter executing the sequential Rete match algorithm on a VAX 11/780 typically fires between 1 and 5 rules per second, while a Bliss-based interpreter executes between 5 and 12 rules per second (34).

8.5.4. Japan's Parallel Inference Machine

The Fifth Generation Computer System is being developed by Tokyo's Institute for New Generation Computer Technology (ICOT) (56). The system is geared toward information and knowledge processing, which requires an efficient knowledge-base management system as well as mechanisms for problem solving and for making inferences based on a knowledge base. At

342

```
(p    select
        (adult ↑name <x> ↑age >18)        ; If the person is over 18,
        (health↑name <x> ↑fit  yes)       ; and he is physically fit,
        -(status ↑name <x> ↑chosen yes)   ; and he has not already been selected
        – – – →                                   then
        (MAKE member ↑name <x>)           ; add his name to list of members
        (MODIFY 3 ↑chosen yes))           ; and update his status.
```

(a) A Production Rule in OPS5

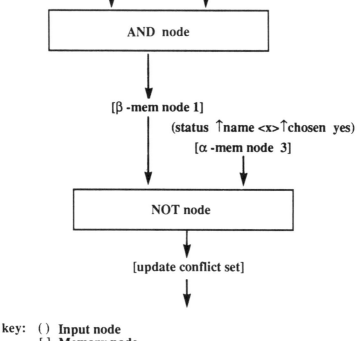

(adult ↑name <x>↑age 18)

[α -mem node 1]

(health ↑name <x>↑fit yes)

[α -mem node 2]

AND node

[β -mem node 1]

(status ↑name <x>↑chosen yes)

[α -mem node 3]

NOT node

[update conflict set]

key: ( ) Input node
      [ ] Memory node
      ▭ Two-input node

(b) Dataflow Graph Corresponding to Rule in (a).

Figure 8.13 Representation of rules as dataflow graphs in the NON-VON. (a) A
production rule in OPS5. (b) Dataflow graph corresponding to rule in (a).

the heart of the fifth generation computer is a machine capable of making logical inferences in parallel. We shall examine the PIM-R, a parallel inference machine based on the reduction mechanism (57).

The reduction mechanism executes Prolog programs in OR parallel and Concurrent Prolog programs in AND parallel. Consider the following goal sequence and clauses:

$G:$ $\leftarrow p_1, p_2, p_3$
$C_1:p_1 \leftarrow q_1, q_2$
$C_2:p_1 \leftarrow q_3, q_4, q_5$

A Prolog or C-Prolog program generates resolvents from a goal and a clause. The clause is used as a rule to modify the goal. This process of self-modification enables the use of the reduction process as a model of execution.

Figure 8.14 shows the logical design of the PIM-R. The goals are kept in a process pool. The goals are executed sequentially from left to right. First, p_1 is sent to the unification unit, which contains a clause pool. This

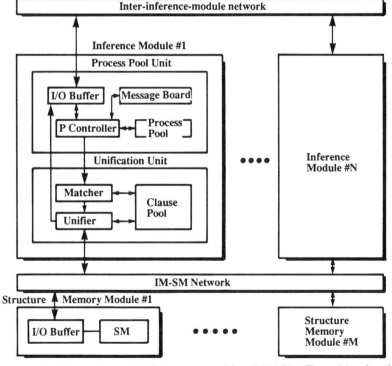

Figure 8.14 Japan's parallel inference machine (PIM-R). (From Murakami K, et al: Research on parallel machine architecture for fifth-generation computer systems. *IEEE Computer*, June 1985, pp. 76–92. © 1985 IEEE.)

clause pool stores the same set of clauses in each inference module. The PIM-R uses the structure-copy method to increase the independence of individual processes and to decrease the network traffic caused by structure sharing. The matcher now compares p_1 with the heads of all clauses in the clause pool. Clauses C_1 and C_2 are then fetched and unified with p_1 to generate two resolvents: q_1, q_2, and q_3, q_4. The results of the unification are then sent back to the process pool unit, where a child process will be created for each resolvent. In OR parallelism, if more than one unification with a rule clause succeeds, the results can be distributed and processed among other inference modules in parallel.

A process consists of the goal sequence as well as status and control information, which counts the number of child processes generated by it. A child process returns the solution it obtains to its parent process. In the preceding example, the parent process is the one that has p_1, p_2, p_3 as its goal sequence. If all children of a process fail, it enters the garbage state and signals failure to its own parent. The process controller is responsible for garbage collection as well as for suspension of processes, message-board operation, and commit operation for C-Prolog. It also regulates the amount of AND/OR forking, handles failed AND/OR operations, and selects the reducible process to be sent to the unification unit next.

The message board is essentially a memory to store channel variables in C-Prolog programs and coordinate producer and consumer processes. The structure memory module stores long, structured data containing no undefined variables, such as lists and vectors, and passes these structured data to the unification unit in the inference module on request. A read request is made only if all unifications between arguments that do not reference the structured memory modules have succeeded.

The success of the parallel logic inference machine depends heavily on how efficiently the concurrent execution of unification operations can be carried out. Ideally, all unification units should be busy fetching goal frames, performing unification with definition clauses and generating child goal frames. All of these must exploit a high degree of concurrency in order to achieve a speed of over 1 million *logical inferences per second* (Lips) as required to support the fifth-generation computer systems.

8.6. Future Perspectives

Assessed next are future perspectives of supercomputers and AI machines and their impact on modern civilization. Computer scientists have been constantly searching for new approaches to designing high-performance machines. Artificial intelligence, software engineering, innovative architectures and VLSI technology are making a great impact on the development of future computers (79). Powerful Lisp machines such as the TI Explorer (77), Lambda (51), the Symbolics 3600 series (55), and ALPHA (30), are already commercially available. Dataflow techniques, systolic arrays, and VLSI technology are mutually supportive approaches for fine-grained parallel machines. The mechanisms needed for parallel computing models and the associated high-level languages are still in the research domain. Large-scale VLSI processor arrays have been experimented with for both numerical computations and symbolic manipulations (80). Techniques for directly mapping parallel algorithms into silicon chips using silicon compilers are in great demand. This necessitates the use of VLSI/CAD tools for developing future generations of computers.

The rapid advent of VLSI technology has created a new architectural horizon. The new high-resolution lithographic technique has made possible the fabrication of 200,000 transistors in a single CMOS chip (such as in the Motorola 32-bit MC68020 microprocessor). It has been projected that by the late 1980s it will be possible to fabricate VLSI chips that contain more than 10^7 individual transistors. One such chip may be capable of more functions than one of today's large minicomputers. VLSI-based multiprocessors are expected to have regular interconnections (40). VLSI arithmetic devices have been proposed by vector and matrix computations (38). Packet-switching networks are also suggested for VLSI-based multiprocessors (8).

University projects in the U.S. for developing multiprocessor systems include the Ultracomputer at New York University (25, 67), Cedar at the University of Illinois (23), and Remps at the University of Southern California. Several multiprocessor projects, such as the Pumps for image processing (6), emphasize reconfiguration between multiple SIMD and MIMD operations. A prototype of PASM, a partitionable SIMD/MIMD system for image processing and pattern recognition (52, 68), is currently under construction at Purdue University. At the California Institute of Technology, a research group has developed a hypercube multiprocessor system (69), which has been commercialized by Intel (44).

In addition to university research efforts, three huge R&D programs in microelectronics and supercomputing have been launched in the United States in recent years. The Microelectronics and Computer Technology Corp. has been established by a dozen U.S. corporations as a nonprofit, joint venture to develop long-range research on the new generation of computers. The Semiconductor Research Corp. is another joint venture by over a dozen U.S. chip manufacturers and computer companies for exploring automatic synthesis and fabrication of VLSI circuits. The Defense Advanced Research Project Agency (DARPA) has announced a Strategic Computing project to push for advanced supercomputing and artificial intelligence technologies. This strategic computing project, once completed, will provide a broad and advanced base of machine intelligence technology to reinforce the nation's security. Potential military applications include autonomous systems such as the autonomous land vehicle, pilot's associate, and battle management.

In Japan, a national project is under way to develop a 10-Gflops computer system (45). Major applications of Japan's supercomputer project include meteorology, nuclear energy, and aerodynamics. This project demands both new computer architectures and new device technologies. This should be distinguished from the well-publicized fifth-generation computer systems project, which is a separate scheme aimed at developing logic inference supercomputers for implementing knowledge-based systems.

The computational requirements for many supercomputing problems, and the search space in knowledge-based systems, often grow exponentially with the input size. Tightly coupled multiprocessors can only realize a constant speedup that is not enough to tackle such NP-Complete problems. However, good approximations can be made by probabilistic approaches, heuristics, simulated annealing, distributed computing, etc. The proper representation of knowledge is crucial. Humans have the remarkable ability to select relevant patterns from a host of external stimuli and internally stored information. This is fundamentally dependent on the way knowledge is represented and processed in our brains. Computing mechanisms modelled on neural networks have been proposed recently (84, 85).

Computers operate on models, and thus base their results on a reduced and simplified version of reality. They are therefore inherently limited by the comprehensiveness of these models. This poses problems if reality cannot be quantified satisfactorily. How many bits are required to characterize a personality? The fuzzy logic approach offers initial steps to bring the computing model closer to human reasoning, and Dr. Zadeh expects future computers to play important roles in three key areas: *numerical analysis, large databases,* and *knowledge engineering* (44). However, it seems difficult to achieve a qualitative jump in machine intelligence through present methods of representing and manipulating knowledge. This does not detract from the pivotal role of computers in improving our standards of living. We should only be aware that, like us, computers also have limitations on their suitability for certain activities.

8.7. Conclusions

Supercomputers and AI machines are crucial and indispensable to many scientific and business applications. We can soon expect fundamental changes in the microelectronics technology and in computer architecture. However, these changes will be based on previous achievements and on continued research and development efforts among universities, industry, and government research agencies. We have come a long way from the stone age to a supercomputer era. We still have a long way to go before we have supercomputers that not only can perform laborious numerical computations quickly and accurately but can also acquire knowledge systematically with little human intervention. Building superintelligent computers will push human civilization to new levels. Multinational efforts will save development overhead. It is imperative that computers and data communication technologies be integrated in today's knowledge-based society.

Problems

1. Some experts feel that using special-purpose machines attached to a conventional host processor is more suitable for AI applications than having a general-purpose AI machine like NON-VON. Thus, a robot might have special modules for vision, speech, reasoning, etc., with a central coordinator. Compare the two approaches and identify suitable applications areas for each.

2. Suppose a task is divided among i processors with probability f_i, so that the load on each processor is $1/i$ units. If it was executed on a uniprocessor, it would have caused a load of 1 unit. Thus, no overheads are incurred in the distribution of tasks among different processors, synchronization, accumulation of results, etc. Give the speedups obtained in using an n processor system under the above assumptions, for the following three cases:

   a. $f_i = 1/n$ $\qquad\qquad\qquad 1 \leq i \leq n$

   b. $f_i = i / \left(\sum_{j=1}^{n} j \right)$ $\qquad 1 \leq i \leq n$

   c. $f_i = (n - i + 1) / \left(\sum_{j=1}^{n} j \right)$ $\qquad 1 \leq i \leq n$

   The first case treats all possible task divisions equally. The second favors the assignment of the computing task to a larger number of processors, whereas the third favors the assignment to a smaller number of processors. Plot the speedup vs. number of processors n for the three cases. Find the limiting values as n becomes unbounded, if they exist.

3. Consider a multiprocessor system with n processors. Let δ be the fraction of code that can be multitasked in a given program and β be the lumped overhead required to install the multitasking. Suppose multitasked code sections are evenly distributed among the n processors. Show that the speedup of using this system over a uniprocessor with execution time = 1, is equal to $S = 1/[\delta/n + (1 - \delta) + \beta]$.

4. The four parallel memory access ports per processor in the Cray X-MP allow simultaneous memory fetches, arithmetic, and memory-store op-

erations. This contrasts with Cray 1, which has unidirectional vector fetch/store and fixed chaining. Consequently, certain vector computation sequences that require several chains in Cray 1, can be executed in a single pipelined chain in the X-MP. Consider the sequence of vector computations given below:

$$A = (B + C) \times s$$
$$D = s \times B \times C$$
$$E = C \times (C - B)$$

This requires the following 11 vector operations, provided all vectors are already in memory and the scalar s is in a working register.

1. Load **B**
2. Load **C**
3. Add **B** + **C**
4. Multiply s
5. Store **A**
6. Multiply $s \times$ **B**
7. Multiply **C**
8. Store **D**
9. Subtract **C** − **B**
10. Multiply **C**
11. Store **E**

Show that it takes 7 *chimes* (*Ch*ained vector t*imes*) to implement the above 11 vector instructions on the Cray 1, and 5 *chimes* on the X-MP.

5. What are the extra capabilities obtained by MIMD pipelining as introduced in HEP, over conventional SISD pipelining?

6. Consider a three-stage shuffle exchange network using 2×2 switches, which connects 8 processors to 8 memories. Each switch has an infinite "waiting queue" at its input ports, and can combine an incoming packet with a packet in the queue if they have the same destination address.

   a. For this network, explore the effect of a single hot spot with intensities of 0, 1, and 5% on the average memory latency when the background traffic is uniform with 0.5 memory requests per processor per network cycle.

   b. Repeat (a) with wait buffers of size 2 at each input port and the policy that a switch refuses to accept an incoming packet if its buffers are full.

7. Consider a NON-VON tree with a controlling LPE at the root. Each SPE contains a number in a fixed location in its memory. Give a sequence of commands such as COMPARE, REPORT, ENABLE/DISABLE, GET FROM LCHILD, etc., to obtain the maximum of these numbers in $O(\log n)$ steps, where n is the number of SPEs.

8. The performance of the routing algorithm in the connection machine de-

pends on the number and pattern of messages. Consider a "reduced" connection machine where 16 PEs are connected into a four-dimensional hypercube. Estimate the number of petit cycles required to achieve the following permutations with one unit of data per processor:

1. Exchange
2. Perfect shuffle
3. Bit reversal

9. Complete the table below to show the differences between numerical and symbolic processing.

Algorithm features	Numerical	Symbolic
Data representation		
Commonly used operations		
Control flow		
Memory requirements		
Data dependencies		
Data communication patterns		
Suitable architectures		

References

1. Adam JA, Fischetti MA: STAR-WARS—SDI: The grand experiment. *IEEE Spectrum,* Sept. 1985, pp. 34–64.
2. Amamiya M, et al: A list processing-oriented data-flow machine architecture. *AFIPS Proc. NCC,* 1982, pp. 143–151.
3. Arbib M, Hansen AR: *Vision, Brain and Cooperative Computation.* MIT Press, Cambridge, MA, 1985.
4. Barr A, Feigenbaum EA (eds): *The Handbook of Artificial Intelligence.* Vols. 1, 2, and 3, William Kaufmann, Los Altos, CA, 1982.
5. Brantley WC, McAuliffe KP, Weiss J: RP3 processor-memory element. *Proc. 1985 International Conference on Parallel Processing,* Aug. 1985, pp. 782–789.
6. Briggs FA, Fu KS, Hwang K, Wah BW: PUMPS architecture for pattern analysis and image database management. *IEEE Trans. on Computers,* Vol. C-31, No. 10, Oct. 1982, pp. 969–982.
7. Buzbee BL: Supercomputing values and trends. Unpublished slide presentation, Los Alamos National Lab., 1983.
8. Chin CY, Hwang K: Packet switching networks for multiprocessors and dataflow computers. *IEEE Trans. on Computers, Special Issue on Parallel Processing,* Nov. 1984, pp. 991–1003.
9. Clark AC: *2001: A Space Odyssey.* Signet Books, New York, 1968.
10. Cray Research Inc.: *The Cray X-MP Series of Computer Systems.* Technical Brochure, Aug. 1985.
11. Cray Research Inc.: *The Cray-2 Computer System.* Technical Brochure, 1985.

12. Darlington J, Reeve M: ALICE and the parallel execution of logic programs. Preliminary draft, Department of Computing, Imperial College of Science and Technology, London, June 1983.
13. Davis A, Robison SV: The FAIM-1 symbolic multiprocessing system. *Proc. COMPCON Spring, IEEE*, 1985, pp. 370–375.
14. Deering MF: *Architecture for AI. Byte*, McGraw-Hill, April 1985, pp. 193–206.
15. Dongarra JJ and Hinds A: Comparison of the Cray X-MP-4, Fujitsu VP-200 and Hitachi S-810/20. in *Supercomputers and AI Machines* (Hwang and DeGroot, eds), McGraw-Hill, 1988 (in press).
16. Fahlman SE: NETL: *A System for Representing and Using Real-World Knowledge*. Massachusetts Institute of Technology Press, Cambridge, MA, 1979.
17. Fahlman SE, Hinton GE: Massively parallel architectures for AI. NETL, Thistle, and Boltzmann machines. *Proc. National Conference on Artificial Intelligence*, August 1983, pp. 109–113.
18. Feigenbaum EA: Knowledge engineering: The applied side of artificial intelligence. Department of Computer Science, Stanford University (Memo, No. HPP-80-21). 1980.
19. Fernbach S: Supercomputers: Past, present and prospects. *Journal of Future Generation Computer Systems,* North-Holland, Vol. 1, No. 1, 1984, pp. 23–30.
20. Fletcher J, et al: Battle management, communications, and data processing. Report of the study on eliminating the threat posed by nuclear ballistic missiles. Vol. 5, U.S. Department of Defense, Feb. 1984.
21. Forgy CL: Rete: A fast algorithm for the many pattern/many object pattern match problem. *Artificial Intelligence*, Sept. 1982, pp. 17–37.
22. Forgy CL, et al: Initial assessment of architectures for production systems. *Proc. National Conference on Artificial Intelligence*. AAAI, Aug. 1984, pp. 116–120.
23. Gajski DD, Milutinović VM, Siegel HJ, Furht BP (ed): *Tutorial on Computer Architecture*, IEEE Computer Society Press, 1986.
24. Goke LR, Lipovsky GJ: Banyan networks for partitioning multiprocessing systems. *Proc. First Annual Symposium on Computer Architecture*, 1973, pp. 21–28.
25. Gottlieb A, Grishman R, Kruskal CP, et al: The NYU ultracomputer—designing and MIMD shared-memory parallel computer. *IEEE Trans. on Computers*, Feb. 1983, pp. 175–189.
26. Gupta A: Implementing OPS5 production systems on DADO. *Proc. International Conference on Parallel Processing*, Aug. 1984, pp. 83–91.
27. Gupta A, Forgy CL: Measurements on production systems. Technical Report, Carnegie-Mellon Computer Science Department, 1983 (undated).
28. Guzman A: A parallel heterarchical machine for high-level language processing. In Duff Levialdi (eds): *Languages on Architectures for Image Processing*, Academic Press, New York, 1981.
29. Handler W, Schreiber H, Sigmund V: Computation structures reflected in general purpose and special purpose multiprocessor systems. *Proc. International Conference on Parallel Processing*, Aug. 1979, pp. 95–102.
30. Hayashi H, et al: ALPHA: A high-performance Lisp machine equipped with a new stack structure and garbage collection system. *Proc. Tenth Annual Symposium on Computer Architecture, IEEE/ACM*, June 1983, pp. 342–348.

31. Hewitt C, Lieberman H: Design issues in parallel architectures for artificial intelligence. *Proc. COMPCON Spring, IEEE*, Feb. 1984, pp. 418–423.
32. Hillis WD, Steele GL: Data parallel algorithms. *Comm. of the ACM*, Dec. 1986, pp. 1170–1183.
33. Hillis WD: *The Connection Machine*. Massachusetts Institute of Technology Press, Cambridge, MA, 1985.
34. Hillyer BK, Shaw DE: Execution of OPS5 production systems on a massively parallel machine. *Journal of Parallel and Distributed Computing*, Vol. 3, No. 2, June 1986, pp. 236–268.
35. Hwang K: Advanced parallel processing with supercomputer architectures. *Proceedings of the IEEE*, October 1987.
36. Hwang K, Briggs FA: *Computer Architecture and Parallel Processing*, McGraw-Hill, New York, 1984.
37. Hwang K, Cheng YH: Partitioned matrix algorithms for VLSI arithmetic systems. *IEEE Trans. on Computers*, Dec. 1982, pp. 1215–1224.
38. Hwang K, DeGroot D (eds): *Supercomputers and AI Machines*. McGraw-Hill, New York, 1988 (in press).
39. Hwang K, Ghosh J, Chowkwanyun R: Computer architectures for artificial intelligence processing. *IEEE Computer, Special Issue on Special Purpose Computers for Artificial Intelligence*, in press.
40. Hwang K, Ghosh J: Hypernet: a communication-efficient architecture for constructing massively parallel computers. *IEEE Trans. Computers*, special issue on Supercomputing, Dec. 1987.
41. Hwang K, Tseng PS, Kim D: An orthogonal multiprocessor for efficient parallel processing. *IEEE Trans. Computers*, to appear 1988.
42. Hwang K, Xu Z, Louri A: Remps: an electro-optical supercomputer for parallel solution of PDE problems. *Proc. of the Second International Conf. on Supercomputing*, Santa Clara, Ca. May 5–8, 1987.
43. Hwang K, Xu Z: Pipeline nets for compound vector supercomputing, *IEEE Trans. Computers*, January 1988.
44. Intel Corp: iPSC: A new direction in scientific computing. Technical Brochure, 1985.
45. Karplus WJ (ed.): *Multiprocessors and Array Processors*, The Society of Computer Simulation, San Diego, Ca. Jan. 1987.
46. Keller RM, et al: A loosely coupled applicative multiple-processing system. *Proc. National Computer Conference, AFIPS*, 1979, pp. 613–622.
47. Kowalik JS (ed): *Parallel MIMD computation: HEP Supercomputer and its Applications*, Massachusetts Institute of Technology Press, Cambridge, MA, 1985.
48. Kuck DJ, Davidson ES, Lawrie DH, Sameh AH: Parallel supercomputing today and the Cedar approach. *Science*, Feb. 1986, pp. 967–974.
49. Kung HT, Leiserson CE: Systolic arrays (for VLSI). *SIAM Sparse Matrix Proceedings* (Duff et al, eds), 1978, pp. 245–282.
50. Lubeck O, Moore J, Mendez R: A benchmark comparison of three supercomputers: Fujitsu VP-200, Hitachi S810/20 and Cray X-MP/2. *IEEE Computer Magazine*, Dec. 1985, pp. 10–29.
51. Manuel T: Lisp and Prolog machines are proliferating. *Electronics*, McGraw-Hill, Nov. 1983, pp. 132–137.

52. Meyer DG, et al: The PASM parallel system prototype. *Proc. COMPCON Spring, IEEE*, Feb. 1985, pp. 429–434.

53. Moldovan DI, Tung YW: SNAP: A VLSI architecture for artificial intelligence processing. *J. of Parallel and Distributed Computing*, May 1985, pp. 109–131.

54. Moon DA: Architecture of the symbolics 3600. *Proc. Twelfth Annual International Symposium on Computer Architecture, IEEE/ACM*, June 1985, pp. 76–83.

55. Moto-oka T, Stone HS: Fifth-generation computer systems: A Japanese project. *IEEE Computer*, March 1983, pp. 6–13.

56. Murakami K, et al: Research on parallel machine architecture for fifth-generation computer systems. *IEEE Computer*, June 1985, pp. 76–92.

57. Ni L, Hwang K: Vector reduction technique for arithmetic systems, *IEEE Trans. Computers*, May 1985, pp. 404–411.

58. Norrie C: Supercomputers for superproblems: An architectural introduction. *IEEE Computer*, March 1984, pp. 62–74.

59. Norton A, Pfister GF: A methodology for predicting multiprocessor performance. *Proc. 1985 International Conference on Parallel Processing*, Aug. 1985, pp. 772–781.

60. Pfister GF, et al: The IBM research parallel processor prototype (RP3): Introduction and architecture. *Proc. 1985 International Conference on Parallel Processing*, Aug. 1985, pp. 764–771.

61. Pfister GF, Norton VA: "Hot spot" contention and combining in multistage interconnection networks. *Proc. 1985 International Conference on Parallel Processing*, Aug. 1985, pp. 790–797.

62. Pountain D: Parallel processing: A look at the ALICE hardware and HOPE language. *Byte*, May 1985, pp. 385–395.

63. Preston K Jr., Uhr L (eds): *Multicomputers and Image Processing Algorithms and Programs*. Academic Press, New York, 1982.

64. Rieger C: Zmob: A mob of 256 cooperative Z80-based microcomputers. *Proc. of the DARPA Image Understanding Workshop*, Los Angeles, CA, 1979.

65. Rieger C, et al: Zmob: A new computing engine for AI. *Proc. Seventh International Joint Conference on Artificial Intelligence, IJCAI*, Aug. 1981, pp. 955–960.

66. Rodrigue G, Giroux ED, Pratt M: Perspective on large-scale scientific computations. *IEEE Computer*, Oct. 1980, pp. 65–80.

67. Schwartz JT: Ultra-computers. *ACM Trans. Programming Languages and Systems*, Vol. 2, No. 4, 1980, pp. 484–521.

68. Seigel HJ, et al: PASM: A partitionable SIMD/MIMD system for image processing and pattern recognition. *IEEE Trans. on Computers*, Vol. C-30, No. 12, Dec. 1981, pp. 934–946.

69. Seitz CL: *The Cosmic Cube. Comm. of ACM*, Jan. 1985, pp. 22–33.

70. Shaw DE: Knowledge-based retrieval on a relational database machine, Ph.D. Thesis, Dept. of Computer Science, Stanford University, 1980.

71. Shaw DE: Organization and operation of a massively parallel machine. Rabbat G (ed): *Computers and Technology*, Elsevier/North-Holland, New York, 1986, in press.

72. Shaw DE: On the range of applicability of an artificial intelligence machine, *Artificial Intelligence*, 1986 (in press).

73. Snyder L: Introduction on the configurable highly parallel computer. *IEEE Computer,* January 1982, pp. 47–64.
74. Stolfo SJ, Miranker DP: DADO: A parallel processor for expert systems. *Proc. International Joint Conference on Parallel Processing,* Aug. 1984, pp. 74–82.
75. Stolfo SJ, Miranker D, Shaw DE: Architecture and applications of DADO: A large-scale parallel computer for artificial intelligence. *Proc. International Joint Conference on Artificial Intelligence,* 1983.
76. Tenorio MFM: Parallel processing techniques for production systems. Ph.D. Thesis, Dept. of Electrical Engineering, University of Southern California, Los Angeles, 1986.
77. Texas Instruments Inc.: *Texas Instruments EXPLORER.* Technical Summary, 1984.
78. Treleaven PC: The new generation of computer architecture. *Proc. Tenth Annual International Symposium on Computer Architecture. IEEE/ACM,* June 1983, pp. 402–409.
79. Treleaven PC, Lima LG: Future computers: Logic, data flow, . . . , control flow. *IEEE Computer,* March 1984, pp. 47–56.
80. Uhr L: *Multicomputer Architectures for Artificial Intelligence,* Wiley Interscience, New York, 1987.
81. Wah BW, Li GJ (eds): *Computers for Artificial Intelligence Applications.* IEEE Computer Society Press, March 1986.
82. Wah BW, Li GJ, Yu CF: Multiprocessing of combinatorial search problems. *IEEE Computer,* June 1985, pp. 93–108.
83. Weisen M, et al: Status and performance of the Zmob parallel processing system. *Proc. COMPCON Spring, IEEE,* Feb. 1985, pp. 71–73.
84. Xu Z, Hwang K: Molecules: a language construct for layered development of parallel programs. *IEEE Trans. Software Engineering,* to appear 1988.
85. Zadeh LA: Coping with the imprecision of the real world. *Comm. of ACM,* Vol. 27, April 1984, pp. 304–311.

9

Dataflow Computation: A Case Study

Jack B. Dennis

9.1. Introduction

In this chapter we consider an important area for the application of new computing technology, the area of large-scale scientific computing. There is increasing recognition that the lower cost of computation in prospect augurs for much wider application of high-performance computers to engineering and scientific problems, and that the possibilities offered by VLSI technology and parallelism are great. This chapter presents one promising unconventional approach to high-performance machines: the use of dataflow computer architecture and the functional programming language Val. Parallel processing using multiple conventional processing units is surveyed by Schwederski, Meyer, and Siegel in Chapter 5, and a more conceptual treatment of the programming methodologies used in multiprocessor computers is given by Gajski and Peir in Chapter 4. Contemporary high-performance machines—the products of Cray Research in particular—are described by Hwang and Ghosh in Chapter 8.

The dataflow model of computation has been under study in the Computation Structures Group of the MIT Laboratory for Computer Science since "program graphs" were introduced as a useful program representation by Jorge Rodriguez in 1966 (33). The research led to the computing model known as *dataflow program graphs* (11, 18), then to a series of proposals for computers using the dataflow model as their underlying mechanism for program representation and execution.

In the dataflow model, data values involved in a computation are carried by *tokens* placed on the arcs of a graph. The nodes of the graph are *actors* that respond to the presence of tokens on their input arcs by "firing"—applying an operator to the values carried by the input tokens. The results are carried by tokens placed on each output arc of the actor. In the *static* dataflow model that is the focus of this chapter, an arc may carry no more than one token. Other dataflow models allow more general behavior— for example, the *tagged token* model espoused by Arvind (6) and used by the Manchester University group as the basis for their experimental machine (21).

In a dataflow model, there is no notion of sequential control flow as in conventional computers. Many actors of a dataflow graph may be ready to fire at the same time. To the extent permitted by the computational algorithm, this opens the possibility of large-scale parallelism in machines designed to execute programs represented by dataflow graphs—machines with hundreds or thousands of dataflow processing elements.

The choice of programming language for use with highly parallel machines for scientific computation is a controversial topic. FORTRAN is currently the language of choice, but even with the substantial effort devoted to "vectorizing" compilers, these compilers have failed to achieve more than a fraction of peak performance, even on machines using a small number of conventional processors. Functional programming languages such as Val are more appropriate for expressing problems for highly parallel machines. These languages have the property that the flow of data values from definition to use is directly expressed by the program text and structure, and no difficult analysis by a compiler is required to identify this information flow. A discussion of functional programming languages and a comparison of the various architectures proposed for executing programs expressed in these languages will be found in Chapter 10 by Vegdahl.

To evaluate a radically different computer concept such as dataflow architecture, a different approach must be used than for a new implementation of a conventional architecture. The performance of the machine must be judged by how well the potential of the hardware can be applied to application tasks. Of course, the efficiency of the hardware design in allowing full utilization of processing elements and memory is important, but the principal issue is the ability of a compiler to transform high-level language programs into dataflow machine code that makes the best possible use of machine resources.

The sections that follow are intended to illustrate the effectiveness of the static dataflow architecture and the functional programming language Val for an application of considerable interest, the simulation of three-dimensional flow fields for studying the aerodynamics of aircraft parts. We begin with some predictions about the nature of high-performance computers for the 1990s based on the technologies—VLSI and parallelism—that will be employed. Then follows a brief introduction to dataflow graphs and the principles of static dataflow architecture. Some examples illustrate the use and importance of pipelining in structuring dataflow programs, and the general principles proposed for implementing a "program-transforming" compiler.

This sets the stage for analysis of a full-scale application. We introduce the aerodynamic simulation problem, which is based on a system of partial differential equations. We describe the computational scheme and its overall structure as a program in Val. There follows an analysis of the program as we envision it would be carried out by a program-transforming compiler, and a performance estimate is given for the problem running on a 256-processing element dataflow machine. We include a detailed treatment of the program module that solves block tridiagonal linear systems and accounts for most of the arithmetic operations performed.

Throughout the chapter, program examples are given in the Val language, substantially as described in (2). Val and its features are also discussed in (1, 26), and its unique features for error handling are presented in (37). We have taken the liberty of omitting type declarations when the meaning is clear. This amounts to assuming a very reasonable degree of type-inference capability on the part of the compiler.

The concluding section discusses prospects for static dataflow architecture in other application areas, and the prospects for generalizing dataflow concepts for broader application in data management, office automation, and knowledge-based systems.

9.2. Some Predictions

The supercomputers of the 1990s will be very different from those of the past, for the advance of integrated circuit technology has paved the way for a genuine revolution in the way problems are formulated, programs developed, and computations carried out.

First Prediction: Supercomputers in the 1990s will support massive parallelism—thousand-fold parallelism—exploited by the hardware. In this way they will gain high performance, not through use of fast circuits, but by means of high-density devices with many thousands of gates. Four-, eight-, or sixteen-fold parallelism is not enough. There is so much to be gained from massive parallelism that the problems of building and programming such highly parallel machines will be addressed and solved. Dataflow concepts provide a viable conceptual approach for these computers.

Second Prediction: The supercomputers of the 1990s will use high-density custom chips containing many thousands of gates apiece. Manufacturers have shifted their attention from bipolar technology to devices that have greater density of gates on a chip and therefore better performance for the space occupied and power consumed.

The highly parallel architectures will perform best using program structures radically different from those tailored for conventional concepts of program execution. Very different approaches to program development and to translating programs into efficient machine code structures will be used.

Third Prediction: In the 1990s, programs for supercomputers will be written in functional programming languages. The massive parallelism present in most large-scale scientific computations is very evident when the program is expressed in a functional language. While it is true that one can discover parallelism in FORTRAN programs through data flow analysis, and that many FORTRAN programs can be successfully vectorized, it is questionable whether these techniques can succeed for ordinary programs when the degree of parallelism needed is many thousand-fold.

9.3 Dataflow Models for Computation

In thinking about computer systems and how they will be programmed, it is important to have a *model of computation* as a guide. For conventional computers, one does not usually think of there being an abstract model—the abstraction is so familiar and implicit. Yet, the model of the store (or address space) and program counter is at the heart of all conventional computers and the languages used to prepare programs to run on them.

For highly parallel machines, new models of computation are required, and little guidance may be had from past experience with programming for conventional machines. Conventional ideas about machine program structure and the compilation of efficient code must be replaced with ideas appropriate to the new architectures. Dataflow models of computation provide this guidance for a class of machines capable of supporting massively parallel computation (4).

To illustrate the static dataflow model, let us consider the well-known quadratic formula for the roots of a second-order algebraic equation with real coefficients:

$$az^2 + bz + c = 0$$

The complex roots of the quadratic are given by

$$z = \frac{-b \pm \sqrt{b^2 - 4ac}}{2a}$$

A Val program to compute the two complex root values is shown in Figure 9.1. The complex values are represented with a user-defined record type having fields for the real and imaginary components.

```
function Quadratic (
      a, b, c:  real)
      returns (complex, complex)
      type complex = record [re, im: real];
      let    D := b * b -  4.0 * a * c;
             Y := 1 / (2.0 * a );
      in     if D ≥ 0.0
             then
                    let x := SqRt (D)
                    in     record [re: (−b + X) * Y; im: 0.0],
                           record [re: (−b − X) * Y; im: 0.0]
                    endlet
             else
                    let X := SqRt (−D)
                    in     record [re: −b * Y; im: X * Y]
                           record [re: −b * Y; im: −X * Y]
                    endlet
             endif
      endlet
endfun
```

Figure 9.1 The quadratic formula written in Val.

A dataflow graph for this computation is given in Figure 9.2. The graph consists of *actors* connected by *links* that indicate the flow of data from one actor to another. The actors that represent constants and arithmetic operators are self-explanatory. The diamond-shaped actor is a *decider* that performs a test on its data input and sends the resulting Boolean truth value to its successors. The circles inscribed with T or F are *gates* that pass a data value if and only if the Boolean control input matches the label. Finally, at the bottom of the graph are four *merge* actors that pass one value from the specified data input for each Boolean token received. Except for the merge actor, all actors behave according to the same simple *firing rule*: an actor is *enabled* if and only if a token is present on each input link and there is no token on the output link. The merge actor is special: it is enabled only when a Boolean token is present and a data token is present at the input corresponding to the truth value carried by the Boolean token (the output link must be empty).

One may easily verify that the dataflow graph in Figure 9.2 has the correct behavior, generating one set of output data for each set of input data supplied. Furthermore, the final configuration of tokens in the graph and the values they carry are independent of the order in which enabled actors are fired. This property is called *determinacy*,[1] and reflects the fact that a

---

[1] The property of determinacy has been studied by Van Horn (34), Karp and Miller (24), Kahn (23), and Patil (29), among others. Van Horn published an early proof of the determinacy of a parallel computation model. The development of Patil is the most directly applicable to dataflow graphs.

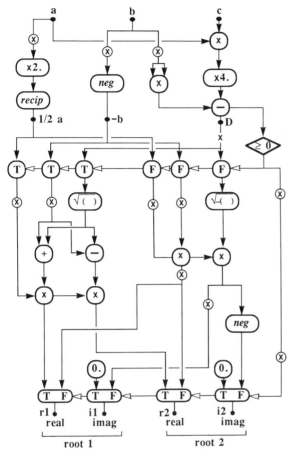

Figure 9.2 The quadratic formula as a dataflow graph. The Xs mark points where buffering may be introduced to allow maximally pipelined operation.

functional programming language expresses parallelism without admitting the timing hazards and races that make the debugging of conventional multiprocess programs very taxing.

An idea that is of great importance in dataflow computation is *pipelining*—the processing of data by successive stages of a computing mechanism so that each stage is usefully busy in every cycle of operation. This scheme is used in the high-performance arithmetic units of conventional supercomputers where the stages are subcomponents of an arithmetic operation such as floating point addition or multiplication (25). When a computation is pipelined on a static dataflow computer, the stages of the pipeline are successive groups of actors in a dataflow graph—each stage comprises a set of perhaps many arithmetic operations. Note that whereas the interconnection of stages is "hardwired" in the typical conventional arithmetic unit, these connections in a dataflow program are the links between dataflow actors and are part of the stored program.

The rule that the arcs of a dataflow graph can hold, at most, one token makes pipelined operation the natural mode of operation of static dataflow graphs. Yet, to achieve the highest computation rate, every path through a dataflow graph must contain exactly the same number of actors. A dataflow graph arranged to support this sort of pipelined behavior is said to be *maximally pipelined* (20).

An acyclic dataflow graph can always be made into a maximally pipelined graph by the addition of identity actors (see 27, 19). For example, Figure 9.2 includes an indication of where identity actors may be inserted so that the graph supports full throughput. In a *balanced graph*, the actors divide into stages such that every path is incident on one actor in each stage. Then all actors in even stages may fire alternately with all actors in odd stages, and each actor fires as often as is possible.

We will not go into further detail here about dataflow program graphs, but go directly to a discussion of their representation as dataflow machine code. Further discussion of dataflow graphs may be found in the literature (10, 11).

9.4. Static Dataflow Architecture

Many approaches to the organization of computing machines for executing dataflow programs have been published. A major dichotomy exists between proposals of machines for large-scale scientific computation on the one hand, and for general purpose applications on the other. We consider here only architectures able to compete with other high-performance machines for scientific computation. Most of these machines might be classified as distributed memory multiprocessors. They have the general organization shown in Figure 9.3, and consist of a number of processing elements (PEs) and an interconnection network that supports the transmission of information packets from any PE to any other PE. Many routing network structures are suitable for use in a dataflow computer. Because high throughput is important and minor transmission delays are masked by parallelism, packet switched networks are superior to circuit switched networks for dataflow machines. A discussion of some network topologies is given by Siegel and Hsu in Chapter 6.

Most dataflow architectures proposed for scientific computation fall into two categories: *static* architecture and *tagged token* architecture. The two categories differ in the way instructions are recognized as available for execution. In the static architecture—the subject of this chapter—each dataflow instruction is signalled by the completion of specific predecessor in-

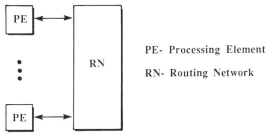

Figure 9.3 General organization of static dataflow computer for scientific computation.

structions, and is activated when the right number of signals have been counted. The signals indicate that the data on which the instruction will operate are available at specific memory locations. At any time there can be, at most, one instance of execution of an instruction.

In the tagged token architecture (5, 6, 36), result packets (tokens) created within or arriving at a processing element are held in a *matching store* until a matching token arrives. A matching pair of tokens contains the two operand values required by a specific instruction in the PE's memory. The advantage of the tagged token architecture is the ability of a PE to support several simultaneous activations of one instruction, a feat not possible in the static architecture but that provides flexibility in the implementation of function activations. A disadvantage is the relatively costly associative mechanism needed to implement the matching store.

Several experimental and commercial prototypes of dataflow machines have been built (8, 21, 28, 35, 38). Whether tagged token or not, most of these machines are static in the sense that once the dataflow instructions for a problem are loaded into the machine, no reallocation of the instructions takes place. An immediate consequence is that all allocation of dataflow instructions to PEs and within PEs must be done prior to program execution—that is, by the compiler. The compiler must translate an application program into an optimized dataflow graph, partition it into sections, and code each section into dataflow instructions for each processing element.

In this chapter we consider a proposed static dataflow multiprocessor composed of 256 processing elements, where each PE is capable of performing 10 Mflops, for a total peak performance of 2560 Mflops.

Each processing element requires storage for dataflow instructions, memory for the data values on which the instructions operate, functional units capable of performing the basic scalar operations, and a mechanism for controlling activation of instructions. In early proposals for dataflow processors (8, 12, 15), each instruction included space for its operands and special bits to control the "firing" of the instruction. However, the availability of commercial, pipelined floating point chips for 64-bit addition and multiplication has led to new proposals for processing element structure, proposals that make a greater separation between the instruction sequencing mechanism on the one hand and the data paths, functional units, and memory used for instruction execution on the other. This separation allows the close coupling of the floating point functional units to the data memory necessary to achieve an efficient processing element design for scientific computation.

Figure 9.4 shows a recent proposal for a dataflow processing element. It has two sections: (1) the Instruction Execution System (IES), consisting of memories and functional units, together with a control system (IECS); and (2) the Signal System (SS). The components of the IES are familiar, but the SS is a departure from conventional computer architecture. It implements the dataflow control mechanism. Communication between the two sections is by "fire" signals that command the IECS to execute a specific instruction, and "done" signals that inform the SS that execution of an instruction has completed.

In correspondence with the processing element structure, the instruction format (Figure 9.5) has two parts: one part contains the information used by the IES to direct instruction execution; the other part contains information used by the SS to control the enabling of other instructions. The former part is similar to a conventional three-address instruction format. It specifies an operation that takes operand values from and stores a result

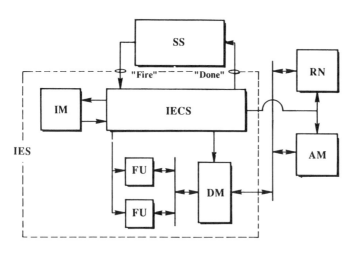

SS - Signal System   IES- Instruction Execution
IM - Instruction Memory   System
FU - Functional Unit   IECS- Instruction Execution
DM- Data Memory   Control System
RN- Routing Network   AM- Array Memory

Figure 9.4 Structure of a processing element for a static dataflow architecture.

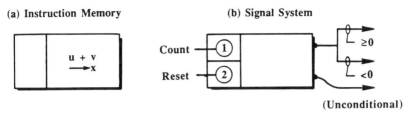

(a) Instruction Memory

(b) Signal System

(Unconditional)

Figure 9.5 Elements of dataflow instructions. (a) Execution information (opcode and three addresses) kept in instruction memory. (b) Sequencing information held in the signal system.

value in the data memory. The control part consists of a *signal list*, a *count* field, and a *reset* field. The signal list is a specification of which instructions are to be sent signals upon completion of instruction execution.

The SS operates as follows: For each "done" command received from the IECS, the signal system processes the signal list of the instruction just completed. Whenever a signal is sent to instruction i its count field is decremented by 1. If the count becomes 0, instruction i is marked as "enabled" and the count field is set to the value of the reset field. Using a "fair" selection rule, the SS sends fire commands to the IES for instructions marked "enabled."

Using the notations illustrated in Figure 9.5, a dataflow machine program takes the form of a directed graph in which nodes denote instructions and arcs represent the sequencing information contained in the signal lists. A simple example is shown in Figure 9.6. This dataflow code performs the computation

$$z: = (x * y + 3.5) * (x * y - 5.2)$$

This code is pipelined—that is, each instruction signals its successor instructions to indicate that its result has been stored, and signals its predecessor instructions to indicate readiness to handle new data. The code shown

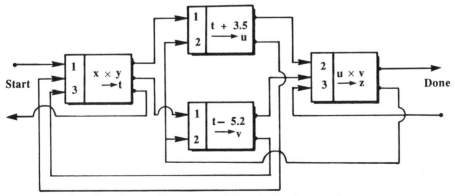

Figure 9.6 Dataflow instructions arranged for pipelined execution.

is *maximally pipelined* because each path through the code is incident on exactly one instruction in each stage.

A crucial property is the *instruction execution period*, the time interval from the instant a fire command is delivered to the IES to the time fire commands for the successor and predecessor instructions are issued by the SS, assuming other instructions impose no constraint on the frequency with which an instruction may be repeatedly executed. The instruction execution period will depend on the details of the IES and will probably vary for different classes of instructions. The period will also depend on character-istics of the SS and on how large the pool of enabled instructions is. A conservative estimate for this time is about 10 μs, allowing 5 μs for the IES and another 5 for the SS.

The instruction execution period places an upper bound on the com-putation rate of pipelined code. The rate cannot exceed the limit imposed by any simple cycle in the machine code graph. In Figure 9.6, every cycle is incident on two instructions, so each instruction may fire, at most, once every 20 μs, giving a computation rate of 50 kHz. This should not be regarded as slow. At this rate, a processing element holding 400 instructions in pipe-lined code would be running at 20 MIPS. If half of these instructions were floating point operations, 10 Mflops performance would be achieved.

Figure 9.7 shows a coding of the quadratic function. Most of this code can be understood by comparing it with the dataflow graph in Figure 9.2. The major difference is that the gate and merge actors do not appear as distinct instruction cells. Because the arms of the conditional expression are each built of two pipelined stages, two separate tests of D are needed. These are implemented by cells *c2-1* and *c3-1*. For example, cell *c2-1* instructs the SS to fire cell *c2-4* or *c2-5*, depending on whether D ≥ 0.0 or D < 0.0. Cell *c3-1* performs the same function for the second pipeline stage of the con-ditional arms. The merge is implemented simply by having the cells of each conditional arm (cells *c3-4* through *c3-7* for the **true** arm and cells *c3-10* through *c-13* for the **false** arm) write into the same locations of data memory. It is not that simple, however, because skew in timing might lead one arm to write its result too early or too late, yielding nondeterminate behavior. To prevent this, cell *c3-1* selects just one group of cells as the next in line to write into the result locations.

Figure 9.7 is another example of pipelined dataflow machine code. The acknowledge signals that indicate completion of work units by each of the three stages are identified in the diagram. Signal *ack-2*, for example, tells stage 3 to begin processing the work unit just completed by stage 2, and also tells stage 1 that it is permitted to begin processing its next work unit. This code is not maximally pipelined because the paths through each stage contain one, two, or three instruction cells instead of only one. A maximally pipe-lined version of the code could be constructed, but the number of signal arcs required would make the code difficult to comprehend.

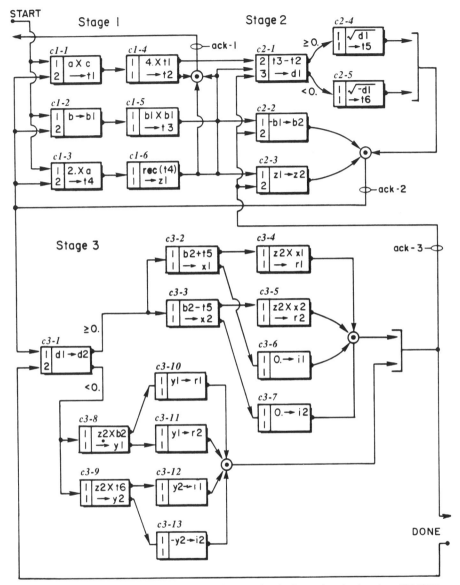

Figure 9.7 Dataflow machine code for the quadratic formula. A signal at START means that locations a, b, and c have been properly set. An acknowledge signal at START means the producer may set a, b, and c again. Similarly at DONE. A bracket indicates signals are to be treated to implement the logical **or** operation; a circled dot indicates treatment to implement the **and** operation.

Instruction cells $c2\text{-}2$, $c2\text{-}3$, and $c3\text{-}1$, whose primary function is to copy values generated by other instructions, are included in the machine code to balance the pipeline. The need for these "overhead" cells can be avoided by using the *result queueing* scheme explained in Figure 9.8. In Figure 9.8a, cell $c2$ serves as a buffer for cell $c1$ so that $c1$ may fire again before $z2$ is used by cell $c3$. The same advantage may be obtained by providing cell $c1$ with a result queue as in Figure 9.8b. Cells $c1$ and $c3$ use index counters Ⓐ and Ⓑ to address elements of the queue. The notation ⟨+A⟩ means that the index counter Ⓐ is incremented by one before it is used to fetch or store each element in the queue. Note that with only the signalling indicated in Figure 9.8b, counter Ⓑ can never advance beyond counter Ⓐ, so no element of the queue will be read before it is written. Although Ⓐ may advance arbitrarily far ahead of Ⓑ in principle, it usually happens that the code includes other constraints that limit the distance to a small integer. In this case, the result queue may be implemented as a ring buffer in the data memory of a processing element.

Use of the result queue mechanism would eliminate three cells from the machine code of Figure 9.7. The code would then consist of 21 cells, of which 14 are used by each work unit as it passes down the pipeline, and the average number of arithmetic operations performed per work unit is 10.

(a)

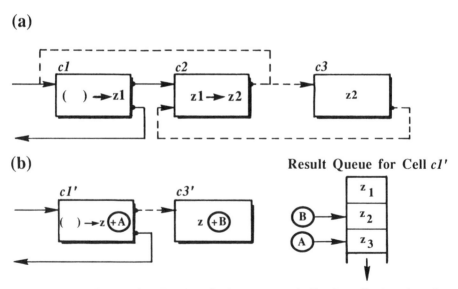

(b)   **Result Queue for Cell $c1'$**

Figure 9.8 Result queueing. In (a), cell $c2$ serves as a buffer for cell $c1$ so that $c1$ may fire again before $z2$ is used by cell $c3$. The same advantage may be obtained by providing cell $c1$ with a result queue as shown in (b). The two index counters Ⓐ and Ⓑ control the insertion and removal of items in the queue.

9.5. Computation with Arrays

Large-scale scientific computation generally makes use of large arrays of data. Hence, the efficient processing of large volumes of data in this form must be supported in a practical dataflow computer. In dataflow computation, it is not satisfactory to view arrays as in FORTRAN—as a set of values occupying successive locations in a memory. Two alternative views useful in dataflow computation are illustrated in Figure 9.9. In one, an array is regarded as a set of scalar values carried simultaneously by several dataflow arcs—the array is spread out in space. In the second view, the array is regarded as the set of successive values carried by tokens traversing a single dataflow arc—the array is spread out in time.

The choice between spreading in space or time is an important choice available to a compiler for matching parallelism in the program to the parallelism supportable by the dataflow computer. In the aerodynamic simulation code, as in many other large-scale codes, the amount of parallelism available in the algorithm is so great that spreading most arrays out in time is necessary to achieve balanced use of machine resources.

The following example illustrates this point. It shows how dataflow machine code in the form of a pipelined code body is a very effective implementation of a process that consumes one or more large multidimensional arrays and generates a multidimensional array as its result.

The example is Smooth, a module from the aerodynamic simulation code. This module accounts for about 3% of all arithmetic operations performed in a run. Imagine a cubical grid divided by 100 intervals along each of three coordinate directions. Five physical quantities are associated with each of the $100 \times 100 \times 100$ grid points. The purpose of Smooth is to produce new data for the grid by applying a smoothing formula at sets of adjacent

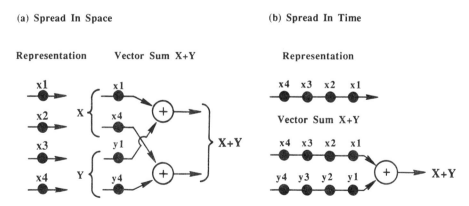

Figure 9.9 Two views of arrays. (a) Spread in space. (b) Spread in time.

points. To compute the new data for point (l, k, j), the old values at distances ± 2, ± 1, and 0 parallel to one of the coordinates are used in a weighted sum. Simpler formulas are used at the boundaries. The smoothing process is carried out as a separate computation for each direction, each computation using the result of the previous computation as shown in Figure 9.10.

The Val program in Figure 9.11 defines the smoothing process for the coordinate associated with index j, and for just one of the five physical quantities. This program makes good use of the Val **forall** construct, which defines a new array value in terms of existing value definitions. For example, the element-by-element sum of two vectors may be written as

forall i **in** $[1, n]$ **construct** $A[i] + B[i]$ **endall**

Let us consider how the Smooth module might be implemented as machine code for a static dataflow supercomputer. An immediate observation is that the amount of data involved is very large, much too large to be held in the data memories of the processing elements. Moreover, the program modules that perform the smoothing operation in the two other directions need access to the data in a different order, at least if the formulas are to be effectively pipelined. For this reason, it is not workable to operate the three modules as a cascade of producer/consumer pairs. Instead, each module must generate and store its results completely before the next module may begin. The array memory, a large and therefore slower memory than the data memory, is provided in each processing element to hold large data objects such as the arrays of intermediate data needed in this example.

A dataflow machine program for the Smooth module is shown in Figure 9.12. A few new instructions and coding tricks need explanation. In successive firings, the instruction Generate(a,b) produces elements of the se-

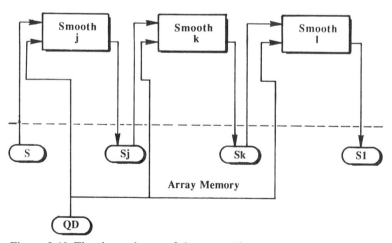

Figure 9.10 The three phases of the smoothing process.

```
function Smooth(
       Q: Grid;        % state values
       S: Grid;        % residuals
       D: Grid;        % Jacobian
       smu: real;      % smoothing parameter
       n: integer)     % grid size
       returns (Grid)      %Smoothed data


    type Grid = array[array[array[real]]];


    let
          sm1: real := .5 * smu;
    in
          for all j in [1,n], k in [1, n], l in [1,n]
          construct
                if j = 1 | k = 1 | l = 1 | j = n | k = n | l = n
                then % boundary point — no change
                      S[j, k, l]
                elseif j = 2 | j = n − 1
                then % point is next to boundary in j−direction
                      % — use second order formula
                      S[j, k, l] + sm1 * (
                            + Q[j + 1, k, l] * D[j + 1, k, l]
                            − 2.0 * Q[j, k, l] * D[j, k, l]
                            + Q[j − 1, k, l] * D[j − 1, k, l]
                            ) / D[j, k, l]
                else % interior point — use fourth order formula
                      S[j, k, l] − smu * (
                            + Q[j + 2, k, l] * D[j + 2, k, l]
                            − 4.0 * Q[j + 1, k, l] * D[j + 1, k, l]
                            + 6.0 * Q[j, k, l] * D[j, k, l]
                            − 4.0 * Q[j − 1, k, l] * D[j − 1, k, l]
                            + Q[j − 2,  k, l] * D[j − 2, k, l]
                            ) / D[j, k, l]
                endif
          endall;
    endlet
endfun
```

Figure 9.11 The Smooth function written in Val for one physical quantity and for one direction of processing.

quence $(a, \ldots, b, *)$, where $a, \ldots, b$ is the sequence of integers starting with a and ending with b, and the symbol $*$ indicates completion of each cycle. Subsequent firing, repeat the entire cycle endlessly. The signal list of a generate instruction may condition transmission of a signal on the integer value it produces, or on the presence or absence of the symbol $*$. For example, a signal arc labelled (5..100) sends a signal if the integer generated is in the indicated range. The set notation {1,2} is used to specify that a target instruction is to be signalled if the integer belongs to the set.

370

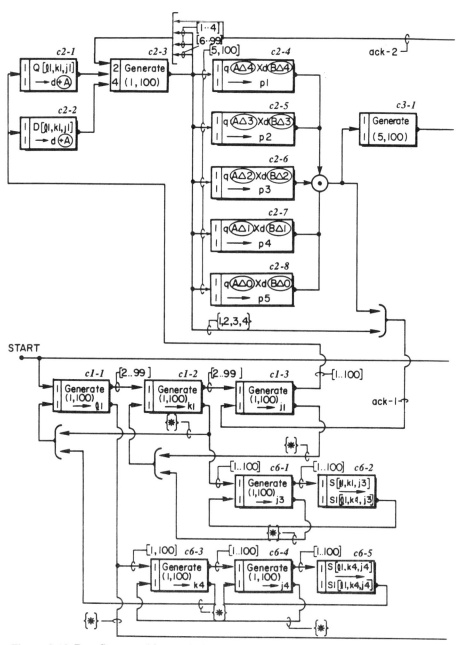

Figure 9.12 Dataflow machine code for the Smooth module.

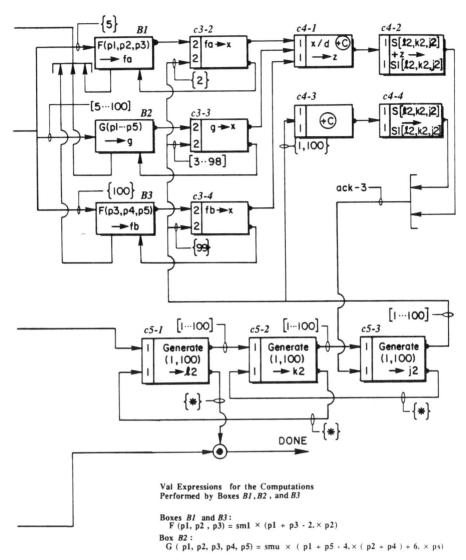

Figure 9.12 (*continued*).

Some instruction cells call for accessing operand values from array memory, or storing result values in array memory. These options are indicated by the usual array indexing notation. This overlooks the problem of implementing array accesses when array elements are distributed over several PEs, a problem that is outside the scope of this chapter.

An overview of the operation of this code is as follows: Three of the generate instructions on the left set indices *l1*, *k1*, and *j1* to successive points of the grid, with *j1* being the fast index. Array memory fetch cells *c2-1* and *c2-2* move elements of Q and D into result queues in data memory. Note that the generate instruction *c2-3* waits for five values to enter each of the result queues before signalling the product cells *c2-4*, . . . , *c2-8*. In the product cells, the notation (A△4) means that the element four items earlier than the one at (A) in the result queue is to be read. This accomplishes the desired offset addressing so that all five product terms may be computed at once.

The three boxes *B1*, *B1*, and *B3* contain the instruction cells for evaluating the two body expressions F and G—two copies of F and one copy of G. Box *B1* handles only element 2 of each row; box *B2* handles elements 3 through 98, and *B3* handles element 99. Figure 9.13 shows how the signalling arrangement ensures that each of these boxes receives the correct product values.

Instruction cells *c3-2*, . . . , *c3-4* and the generate instruction *c5-3* implement the determinate merging of results of the conditional arms. Cells *c4-1* and *c4-2* perform the final computation steps and store the results in the array memory. Cells *c4-3* and *c4-4* store values of the first and last elements of each row.

To remain in step, each of the three index counters (A), (B), and (C) must be stepped the same number of times in the processing of each row, so extra steps must be inserted where data items held in a result queue are not referenced. Thus, cell *c4-3* is included to step counter (C) for elements 1 and 100 of the *d* array produced by cell *c2-2*.

The three generate instructions on the right are needed to ensure that the DONE signal is not sent before all result values have been stashed safely away in the array memories. The remaining instruction cells on the left, *c6-1* through *c6-5*, store old data values in the boundary elements of the new array as called for by the Val program.

A remaining question is the amount of data memory required for the two result queues. For values of *q* produced by cell *c2-1*, five locations are necessary and sufficient because once the first five values have been produced, the signalling allows further values to be produced only as queue elements are released by firings of the product cells. Determining the size of the result queue for cell *c2-2* is more subtle. We must determine how

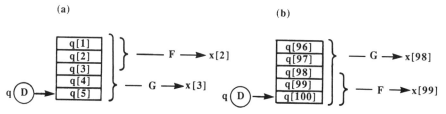

Figure 9.13 Conditions of the result queue for cell *c2-1*. (a) Just after the first five values have been read and cells *c2-4* through *c2-8* receive their first signal. (b) Just when cells *c2-4* through *c2-8* receive their last signal.

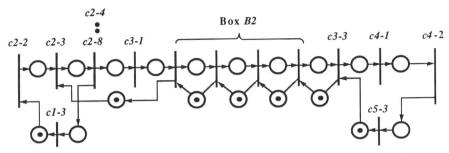

Figure 9.14 Petri net for determining the size of the result queue for cell $c2-2$.

many values of d may be produced in advance of their use by cell $c4-1$. The Petri net (30, 32) in Figure 9.14 helps find the answer. Each transition models the firing of the indicated instruction cell in Figure 9.12, and the placement of tokens corresponds to the initial count and reset values in the machine code. (The number of transitions used to represent $B2$ reflects the depth of the expression for G, which is four.) Examination of the Petri net shows that transition $c2-2$ can fire, at most, seven times before the first firing of $c4-1$, and therefore a queue of seven elements is sufficient.

To complete our discussion of the Smooth module, let us consider its performance parameters and how we can arrange that its implementation can use the full performance of a dataflow machine with 256 processing elements. For the smoothing of all five physical quantities of the problem, the counts of arithmetic operations and array memory read and write operations are as follows (the Jacobian D need be read only once):

adds	multiplies	divides	reads	writes
$25\,n^3$	$40\,n^3$	$5\,n^3$	$11\,n^3$	$5\,n^3$

Because three data memory cycles are required for each arithmetic operation, the ratio of data memory accesses to array memory accesses is $(3 \times 70)/16 = 13.1$. This is in keeping with the processing element architecture.

The rate at which actors in the machine code can fire is controlled by the simple cycle that has the greatest total time for the sequence of actions in the cycle to occur. There are three simple cycles of four instruction cells in the graph as shown in Figure 9.15.

These cycles involve generate instructions, result queue manipulation, and array memory accesses, as well as arithmetic operations. Probably the most limiting cycle is Cycle 3 as it contains a division and also has a read and write of array memory in one cell. The time for a cell firing has two parts, that due to the SS and that due to the IES. The former component probably depends on how many enabled instructions are available to a PE, and the latter component will depend on the complexity of the instruction executed. Let us take as a reasonable estimate a cycle time of 30 μs for Cycle 3, and suppose it is this cycle that limits the rate of computation.

Cycle 1

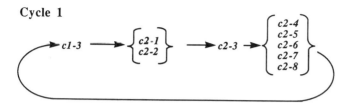

Cycle 2

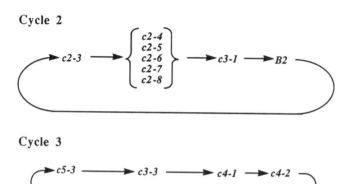

Cycle 3

Figure 9.15 The cycles that may limit the firing rate of dataflow instructions in the Smooth module implementation.

The total number of floating point arithmetic operations performed for each work unit entering the pipeline is 70. Assuming a repetition cycle of 30 μs duration, these instructions can support $70/(30 \times 10^{-6}) = 2.33$ mops, not enough to keep one processing element busy, let alone 256. The solution to this mismatch is to use many copies of the code. Using four copies in each PE will support $4 \times 2.33 = 9.32$ Mflops of performance for each PE, which is close to the peak performance of the machine.

9.6. The Val Compiler

The Val language has a straightforward and clear interpretation and lacks the complexity of many popular languages. Thus, the main issue in building an effective Val compiler for high-performance scientific computation is getting the most performance from the target machine or system. When the target system is a dataflow multiprocessor, the compiler must produce machine code structures that keep all processing elements usefully busy while faithfully implementing the computation expressed by the source program. Building a successful dataflow compiler requires unconventional approaches to the processes of program analysis and generation of machine code structures. The code structures generated must be a function not only of the corresponding source program text, but also of the amount of memory and number of processors of the target machine, and of the global program context in which the code appears.

In conventional optimizing compilers, attention is focused on one section of code at a time, and a speed improvement in one section almost always yields an improvement in the overall performance of the code. In contrast, the construction of efficient machine code for a dataflow computer (or any highly parallel computer, for that matter) is primarily concerned with the overall or global structure of the program. How the major blocks of code are divided among the computing elements and how their intercommunication is supported are two of the important issues.

Figure 9.16 shows the suggested organization of a "program transforming" compiler for Val. The Front End is conventional and performs the usual functions of syntax analysis, type-checking, and other static semantic checks. The result is a program module (a Val function) represented in an intermediate form. The Graph phase encodes the Val module as a dataflow graph, retaining all structural information of use to later phases of the compiler.

In the Link step, all modules—user-written and library—that together define a computation to be run on the target machine, are linked together in preparation for global optimization.

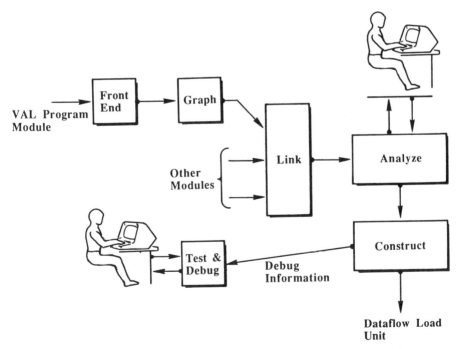

Figure 9.16 Organization of a smart compiler/programming environment for a dataflow computer.

The heart of the proposed compiler consists of the Analyze and Construct modules. The purpose of the Analyze module is to formulate a strategy for structuring dataflow machine code and allocating it among the processing elements so as to achieve the best possible overall performance. The purpose of the Construct module is to structure the dataflow machine code according to the strategy.

In many programs for large-scale computation, sufficient information may be extracted from the program text to determine many quantitative measures of the resources required by program parts. This information includes the dimensions of arrays defined by the program, the range of index values in **forall** expressions, the number of cycles performed by **for .. iter** loops, and the conditions that control evaluation of **if .. then .. else** expressions. The Analyze phase extracts this information from the linked set of program modules and also determines scalar operation counts for each program part to the best of its ability.

The analysis will be more or less successful depending on the kind of program being processed. If information derived from the program text is not sufficient to determine good measures of the program's resource requirements, the user, through conversational interaction with the Analyze module, may supply additional information such as the range of cycles taken by an iteration, the typical size of an array, or the frequency of selection of the alternative arms of a conditional expression.

On the basis of this information, the Analyze module formulates a strategy for constructing machine code and calculates bounds on the anticipated performance of the compiled code. The objective for choice of strategy is that the machine code structure specified for each component of the source program should, when executed together with other parts of the target code, achieve balanced utilization of the machine's resources. In Section 9.8 we show how this approach works for the aerodynamics simulation problem, and how the use of pipelined dataflow machine code is able to achieve the goals of the compiler. A simpler problem, choosing a strategy for the Smooth module, is treated in detail in Section 9.7.

Two basic problems must be dealt with by the Analyze module in formulating strategy. These are the division of the program over space— that is, how the machine code should be *partitioned* over the processing elements—and the division of the computation over time—that is, how the computation should be divided into *phases*, each of which will make full use of the processing elements for a certain time interval. The examples that follow illustrate the principles used to address these problems in the design of the Val compiler.

An important feature of any compiler is provision of information that permits users to test and correct programs by inspecting intermediate results produced during a computation. The convenience of being able to carry out this inspection in terms of source-language names and constructs has become mandatory for efficient program development. To support this feature, the proposed compiler will provide information relating names occurring in the Val source program to the memory locations to which the associated values and code have been allocated in the machine.

9.7. Analysis of Program Structure

The Analyze module of the compiler must gather information about the linked program graph to answer such questions as: Can the program be run as a whole (as a single phase) or must it be divided into parts (several phases) that are allocated use of the processing elements in turn? What trade-off between time and space will provide the best match of parallelism in the machine to that of the application? Which pairs of program modules can communicate without requiring the use of array memory? How much data, array, and program memory will be required to run the compiled code?

Here we use the Smooth program module to illustrate how the analyzer of the Val compiler would specify the construction of appropriate dataflow machine code. The function of the analyzer can be divided into three parts: first, analysis, collecting information from the program text that measures the resource requirements of the various program modules; second, strategy formulation, using the collected information to formulate a plan for constructing the target code; and third, performance calculation, deriving from the analysis and the strategy the level of performance to be expected from the compiled code.

The first step is to construct a *description tree* that contains all information about the module that will be used in determining the strategy. For programs written in Val we may associate the needed information with a structural description of the Val program. Such a structural description is a tree in which the nodes correspond to the various phrase types of the language:

for .. iter	the loop construct
forall .. construct	the principal array constructor
for .. eval	the array generic reduction operator
if .. then .. else	the conditional expression

Each of these node types corresponds to a block of Val code that defines one or more values, each of which may be an array of any order from a single scalar to a multidimensional grid. Two major expression types of the Val language do not appear in the list. One is the **let .. in** expression. This is omitted because **let** expressions merely indicate connections between operations, and disappear when a program is transformed into a dataflow graph. The other missing expression form is function application. In the present discussion, we assume that the dataflow graphs of function bodies are copied

Table 9.1 Node Types Used in Program Description Trees

Node Type	Remarks
Graph	Describes an acyclic interconnection of component program elements.
ForAll	Represents Val **forall** expression and gives the order and index ranges of its result arrays.
Iteration	Represents a Val **for ... iter** expression and gives the number of evaluations of its body.
Conditional	Describes a Val conditional expression by references to its arm and test expressions.
SubRange	Describes a conditional expression where the tests divide an index range into manifest subranges.
ArrayExp	Describes an expression containing only scalar operators and references to array elements, and having a result of type **real**.
SimpleExp	Describes an expression containing only scalar operators and a result of type **real**.
Boolean	Describes an expression having a result of type **Boolean**.

in place wherever the function is called so **apply** actors do not exist in the linked dataflow graph.[2]

The result of program analysis is a program description tree with nodes in correspondence with the program tree. The node types used in a description are listed in Table 9.1 along with some remarks about the information they hold. An **Iteration** node includes information about the number of cycles the loop will execute. A **Conditional** node gives the relative frequencies with which each arm of the conditional is chosen for evaluation. The nodes that describe expressions give the number and types of the scalar operations performed for each evaluation. In the case of expressions that contain array references, the description node includes information about the range of index values for each input array used by the expression.

It may not be possible to obtain all of this information by algorithmic analysis of the source program text. For instance, the termination condition for an iteration may be dependent on problem data. This is why user interaction is suggested. The user can supply reasonable estimates on ranges for the number of loop cycles, or the dimensions of arrays, where this information is not evident from the program text.

It is convenient to express the analysis data as ranges of values written such as [4..8], and to use problem parameters of the program text such as the parameter n specifying the size of the data arrays in the Smooth module. Such parameters are usually integer variables, and the analyzer can easily identify those that derive from program inputs and are therefore appropriate parameters for expressing the results of analysis. Of course, it may not be

---

[2] The **case** expression of Val is not considered here. It would be treated by analogy with the conditional expression. Recursion and shared program modules will be treated in future publications.

possible to completely determine the program construction strategy until any such parameters have been assigned numerical values.

Figure 9.17 shows a description tree for the Smooth program as given in Figure 9.11. The top-level node describes the **forall** expression. It gives the index ranges for the three-dimensional result array derived from the **forall** header, and has a link to the description tree node for its body. The body is a conditional expression, and its description tree node simply refers to the subtrees that describe the two tests and three arms that make up the conditional. The two tests are simple Boolean expressions. The description node for each of the arm expressions gives operation counts and a characterization of all references to input arrays. In this example, the index offset is 0 for all references except those to array Q for index *j*. By "offset" we mean the difference between the index value used to access an input array and the index value of the element of the output array being computed. The

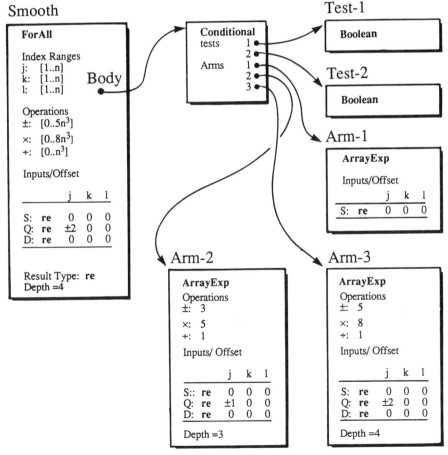

Figure 9.17 Description tree for the Smooth module.

Smooth   Body

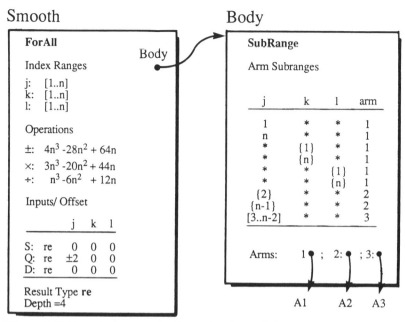

Figure 9.18 Description tree for Smooth using a SubRange node.

description indicates that Arm-2 accesses Q with j-indexes between $j - 1$ and $j + 1$, and that Arm-3 uses j-indexes between $j - 2$ and $j + 2$. The information about offset indexing of the input arrays is summarized in the top-level node. This node also shows the best that can be said about the operation counts without knowledge of how the tests in the conditional expression turn out. The extremes correspond to the case that Arm-1 is always selected and that Arm-3 is always selected.

To construct the machine code in Figure 9.12, a deeper analysis is necessary. Note that the conditional arms are selected by known subranges of the integers. This allows a more informative representation of the conditional by a special type of node called a *subrange* node. Using this device, the description tree for Smooth becomes that shown in Figure 9.18.

Each line in the "arm subrange" list specifies a combination of index ranges (* means no restriction, [..] gives a sequence, and { } indicates a set) for which the indicated arm is chosen. Because several lines may specify the same arm, the definable index sets for an arm include any finite union of rectangular subarrays of a multidimensional array. The nodes describing the arms are just as before. This information is sufficient to compute the exact number of operations performed in an execution of Smooth.

Arm	Adds	Multiplies	Divides	Evaluation Count
Arm-1	0	0	0	$n^3 - (n - 2)^3$
Arm-2	3	5	1	$2(n - 2)^2$
Arm-3	5	8	1	$(n - 2)(n - 2)(n - 4)$

In this example, no interaction with the user is needed to obtain a complete analysis because all needed information is available from the program text. As we shall see, the same is true for all modules of the aerodynamic simulation code, and is likely to be true for many complete programs for scientific computation.

The next steps constitute strategy formulation. It is evident that each of the three arms of the conditional are readily pipelined with a small requirement for buffer storage because the offsets of the input array indices are small and fixed. If the parameter n is given as 100, as in the benchmark computation, it is evident that the $100 \times 100 \times 100 \times 5$ result array must be stored in array memory. Since the second sweep of smoothing accesses the data in a different sequence, the two sweeps cannot communicate as a pipelined producer/consumer pair, and each must run as a separate phase of the computation. From this analysis, the code replication and partitioning described in Section 9.5 follows.

9.8. Aerodynamic Simulation

A problem of considerable importance is the study of air flow around the elements of aircraft structures: wings, fuselage, engines, tail assemblies. The increasing power and economy of large-scale computation has made it increasingly attractive to study these problems using computers rather than to use conventional wind tunnel experiments. As the capacity of supercomputers further improves, more ambitious calculations become feasible. Of particular interest to aeronautical engineers is the study of turbulence, which requires three-dimensional flow models to adequately represent the physical process.

The physical quantities of interest are density ρ, the velocity components u_1, u_2, and u_3, internal energy e, temperature T, and pressure p. The continuum mechanics of a fluid are described by a set of five partial differential equations that derive from the conservation laws for mass, momentum in three directions, and energy. The equation for mass conservation is the familiar continuity equation:

$$\frac{\partial \rho}{\partial t} + \sum_{k=1}^{3} \frac{\partial}{\partial x_k}(\rho u_k) = 0 \tag{9.1a}$$

Conservation of momentum is expressed by a group of three equations, one for each coordinate direction x_1, x_2, and x_3:

$$\rho \frac{\partial u_j}{\partial t} + \rho \sum_{k=1}^{3} u_k \frac{\partial u_j}{\partial x_k} + \frac{\partial p}{\partial x_j} = 0, \qquad (j = 1, 2, 3) \tag{9.1b}$$

These equations model the ability of a compressible medium to absorb impulse from nearby fluid mass. For simplicity, we have omitted the terms that express the viscous or dissipative transfer of energy in the fluid. The fifth equation expresses conservation of energy:

$$\rho \frac{\partial e}{\partial t} + \rho \sum_{k=1}^{3} u_k \frac{\partial e}{\partial x_k} + \rho \sum_{k=1}^{3} \frac{\partial u_k}{\partial x_k} - \sum_{k=1}^{3} \frac{\partial}{\partial x_k} \left(K \frac{\partial T}{\partial x_k} \right) = 0 \qquad (9.1c)$$

in which K is the coefficient of thermal conductivity.

These five equations constitute the *governing equations* for a compressible fluid (9). They involve seven unkown variables, so two additional relationships are needed to constrain the problem to a definite behavior. The missing relationships are the equations of state that express the temperature and pressure in terms of the remaining five variables:

$$T = \frac{1}{c_v} \left[\rho e - \frac{1}{2} (u_1^2 + u_2^2 + u_3^2) \right]$$

$$P = (\gamma - 1) \left[e - \frac{1}{2} (\rho u_1^2 + \rho u_2^2 + \rho u_3^2) \right] \qquad (9.2)$$

where c_v is the specific heat at constant volume and γ is the ratio of specific heats.

When viscous terms are included in the momentum and energy equations, the set is known as the *Navier-Stokes equations*. Although the viscous property of air is essential in modeling turbulence, incorporation of viscous effects into the equations does not significantly change the nature of the mathematical problem or the applicability of the computational procedures of interest. Therefore, our study considers the governing equations without the viscous terms.

The set of governing equations can be written in a very compact form by representing the five physical quantities by a vector $\mathbf{q}$ and writing the terms using three vector-valued functions of $\mathbf{q}$ denoted E, F, and G. The pressure and temperature variables are eliminated by incorporating the state equations into these functions. It is usual to use the product of density and velocity instead of unscaled velocity because this choice leads to simpler equations.

$$\frac{\partial \mathbf{q}}{\partial t} = \frac{\partial E(\mathbf{q})}{\partial x_1} + \frac{\partial F(\mathbf{q})}{\partial x_2} + \frac{\partial G(\mathbf{q})}{\partial x_3}, \qquad \mathbf{q} = \begin{bmatrix} \rho \\ \rho u_1 \\ \rho u_2 \\ \rho u_3 \\ e \end{bmatrix} \qquad (9.3)$$

A typical problem to be solved concerns a rigid body (such as an airfoil) situated in a stream of air. The initial state is specified by giving the characteristics of the undisturbed air stream (with the body absent) and the conditions imposed at the boundary between the body and the air stream. The objective may be to determine the steady-state behavior of the flow, or, if turbulence is being studied, the variation of the flow with time.

Several steps are required to turn the analytical equations into a practical computational scheme. First, a discrete approximation to the contin-

uous mathematics must be chosen. A computational scheme for advancing
the solution by steps in time is needed along with a method of imposing the
boundary conditions. The scheme must be computationally efficient and yet
converge to answers with the required precision.

Typically, the computation is performed on a rectangular grid. Partial
derivatives in the analytical form of the equations are replaced by difference
operators in the computational form. The equations are "integrated" by
solving the resulting system of difference equations to obtain the state matrix
$\mathbf{q}^{n+1}$ for time t_{n+1} from the state matrix $\mathbf{q}^n$ for time t_n, where t_n means $n\Delta t$.
Each of the five components of $\mathbf{q}$ is now a three-dimensional array of values.

The method used in the implementation considered here is an implicit
scheme—that is, an integration formula is written in terms of $\mathbf{q}^n$ and $\mathbf{q}^{n+1}$
and a rule devised for computing $\mathbf{q}^{n+1}$ when $\mathbf{q}^n$ is known. For illustration,
consider the trapezoidal integration rule,

$$\mathbf{q}^{n+1} - \mathbf{q}^n = \frac{\Delta t}{2} \left[\left(\frac{\partial \mathbf{q}}{\partial t} \right)^n + \left(\frac{\partial \mathbf{q}}{\partial t} \right)^{n+1} \right] \tag{9.4a}$$

Let us apply this rule to Eq. 9.3. For simplicity we use the two-dimensional
case where the third velocity component is dropped from $\mathbf{q}$ and the term in
G is deleted.

$$\mathbf{q}^{n+1} - \mathbf{q}^n = \frac{\Delta t}{2} \left[\left(\frac{\partial E}{\partial x_1} \right)^n + \left(\frac{\partial E}{\partial x_1} \right)^{n+1} \right]$$

$$+ \frac{\Delta t}{2} \left[\left(\frac{\partial F}{\partial x_2} \right)^n + \left(\frac{\partial F}{\partial x_2} \right)^{n+1} \right] \tag{9.5}$$

Before considering a solution technique, let us deal with the nonlinearity of
the functions E and F. Because only small excursions of the physical quantities from their mean values are expected, an approximation based on a
Taylor expansion of these functions is reasonable.

$$E^{n+1} \approx E^n + \mathbf{A}^n(\mathbf{q}^{n+1} - \mathbf{q}^n), \qquad \mathbf{A} = \frac{\partial E}{\partial \mathbf{q}}$$

$$F^{n+1} \approx F^n + \mathbf{B}^n(\mathbf{q}^{n+1} - \mathbf{q}^n), \qquad \mathbf{B} = \frac{\partial F}{\partial \mathbf{q}} \tag{9.6}$$

The coefficients $\mathbf{A}$ and $\mathbf{B}$ are four-by-four matrices. Using this approximation
in Eq. 9.5, we obtain

$$\mathbf{q}^{n+1} - \mathbf{q}^n = \Delta t \left[\left(\frac{\partial E}{\partial x_1} \right)^n + \left(\frac{\partial F}{\partial x_2} \right)^n \right]$$

$$+ \frac{\Delta t}{2} \left[\frac{\partial}{\partial x_1} \mathbf{A}^n(\mathbf{q}^{n+1} - \mathbf{q}^n) \right]$$

$$+ \frac{\Delta t}{2} \left[\frac{\partial}{\partial x_2} \mathbf{B}^n(\mathbf{q}^{n+1} - \mathbf{q}^n) \right] \tag{9.7}$$

or, with terms in q^n and q^{n+1} separated and collected,

$$\left[I + \frac{\Delta t}{2} \left(\frac{\partial}{\partial x_1} A^n + \frac{\partial}{\partial x_2} B^n \right) \right] q^{n+1} - \left[I + \frac{\Delta t}{2} \left(\frac{\partial}{\partial x_1} A^n + \frac{\partial}{\partial x_2} B^n \right) \right] q^n$$

$$= \Delta t \left[\left(\frac{\partial E}{\partial x_1} \right)^n + \left(\frac{\partial F}{\partial x_2} \right)^n \right] \quad (9.8)$$

The next step would be to replace the spatial derivatives with difference operators. Imagining that this has been done, the resulting system of linear algebraic equations in unknowns q^{n+1} would have one equation and one unknown for each point in the grid. For a three-dimensional grid of size 100, the system would have 1 million equations and unknowns! Fortunately, methods are available that avoid having to solve directly such large linear systems. One of these is the *method of alternating directions* (17), which we derive now for a two-dimensional grid having n rows and n columns.

Eq. 9.8 has the form

$$(I + C + D)q^{n+1} = H \quad (9.9a)$$

where

$$C = \frac{\Delta t}{2} \frac{\partial}{\partial x_1} A^n \qquad D = \frac{\Delta t}{2} \frac{\partial}{\partial x_2} B^n$$

$$H = \Delta t \left[\left(\frac{\partial E}{\partial x_1} \right)^n + \left(\frac{\partial F}{\partial x_2} \right)^n \right] + [I + C + D]q^n \Bigg\} \quad (9.9b)$$

As we will see below, this system (9.9a) can be solved by the following rule: First solve the system

$$(I + C)q^a = H - Dq^n \quad (9.10a)$$

for q^a. Then solve

$$(I + D)q^{n+1} = q^a + Dq^n \quad (9.10b)$$

for q^{n+1}.

Because the operator C will be approximated by differences in the x-direction only, system 9.10a separates into n systems of n equations, each associated with one row of the grid. Likewise, system 9.10b separates into n systems of n equations associated with the columns of the grid. Each individual system has five unknowns for each row or column and therefore is of a size that is readily handled computationally. Moreover, if the difference operators chosen are central differences (using only immediately adjacent grid points), the equation systems have the form called *block tridiagonal*, for which particularly efficient algorithms are known. These are discussed in Section 9.10.

That the alternating direction scheme (9.10) works can be verified as follows. Write Eq. 9.10b as

$$\mathbf{q}^a = (\mathbf{I} + \mathbf{D})\mathbf{q}^{n+1} - \mathbf{D}\mathbf{q}^n \tag{9.11}$$

Using the right-hand side for $\mathbf{q}^a$ in Eq. 9.10a and rearranging terms, we obtain

$$(\mathbf{I} + \mathbf{C} + \mathbf{D})\mathbf{q}^{n+1} + \mathbf{C}\mathbf{D}(\mathbf{q}^{n+1} - \mathbf{q}^n) = \mathbf{H} \tag{9.12}$$

This is exactly the equation to be solved (9.9a) with the added term $\mathbf{C}\mathbf{D}(\mathbf{q}^{n+1} - \mathbf{q}^n)$ which, being of higher order in Δt, may be neglected.[3]

Handling the boundary conditions poses problems, especially when the subject of study is an irregular-shaped object such as an aircraft fuselage. A successful general approach is to employ a coordinate transformation such that one face of the computational grid is mapped onto the surface of the body. This scheme, although it adds some complexity to the solution method, has the advantage that the grid lines converge toward the surface of the body, automatically providing greater density of computational elements where they are most needed.

The mapping of the computational grid onto the physical space is described by a function

$$G: \mathbf{N} \times \mathbf{N} \times \mathbf{N} \rightarrow \mathbf{R} \times \mathbf{R} \times \mathbf{R}$$

which associates a point in physical three-space with each triple of coordinate indices in the computational space. Whenever spatial differences are used, the computational scheme must make use of difference approximations to the partial derivatives of G. These could be calculated once and stored, but in the application code under discussion the expense of calculating them as needed is preferred to an increased memory requirement. Nevertheless, the Jacobian D of the function G,

$$D: \mathbf{N} \times \mathbf{N} \times \mathbf{N} \rightarrow \mathbf{R}$$

which measures the volume of physical space corresponding to a cell of the computational grid, is needed throughout the computation, and is computed and stored before computation of time steps begins.[4]

9.9. Structure of AeroSim

The program AeroSim applies the alternating direction method to the governing equations for a compressible fluid. It uses a mapping function from the cubical computational grid to the physical space such that the boundary surface of the body under study corresponds to the $l = 1$ face of the com-

---

[3] For further details and an analysis of stability and consistency, see (17).

[4] A detailed computational method based on this development is described in (31). For further explanation of the principles, see (9, 7).

```
function AeroSim (
        n: integer;            % Grid size
        p: integer)            % Time steps to be performed

    returns ( GridMap, Data )

    type Grid = array[array[array[real]]];
    type Data = array[Grid];
    type GridMap = record[x, y, z: Grid]

    % Initialization

    let
        % Generate grid
        G0 : GridMap := DefineGrid ();

        % Compute Jacobian of the grid
        D: Grid := Jacob (G0);

        % Set grid data for initial conditions
        Q0: Data := InitialData ();

        % The main interation
        Gf, Q1 :=
            for r, Gi, Qi := 1, G0, Q0
            do
                    if r > p then Gi, Qi
                    else
                        let
                            Gn, Qn := Step (Qi, Gi, D)
                        in
                            iter
                                r, Gi Qi := r+1, Gn, Qn
                            enditer
                        endlet
                    endif
            endfor;

        % Unscale by Jacobian
        Qf: Data := Unscale (Q1, D)

    in Gf, Qf
    endlet
endfun
```

Figure 9.19 Top level of the aerodynamic simulation code.

putational grid. The overall structure of the program is displayed in Figures
9.19 through 9.24.[5] The diagrams show the flow of information among the
major submodules and indicate the types and amounts of data passed between modules as large arrays.

---

[5] The code expressed in Val was derived from a FORTRAN benchmark code named
ARC3D obtained from the National Aeronautics and Space Administration Ames Research
Center, Moffett Field, CA.

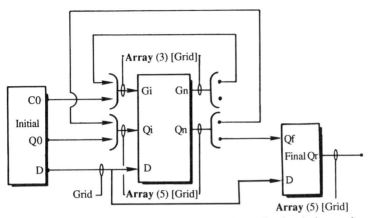

Figure 9.20 Dataflow diagram for the aerodynamic simulation code.

```
function Step (
              Qi: Data;             % Grid data
              Gi: GridMap;          %Grid map
              D: Grid )             % Jacobian
        returns (
              GridMap,              % final gridmap
              Data )               %Final Q

    let
              % Modify gridmap to reflect rotation of body
              Gn := Spin (Gi)

              % Boundary Values of Q
              Q1 := BoundaryConditions (Gn, Qi);

              % Compute Right Hand Side
              S0 := RightHandSide (Gn, Q1);

              % Smooth
              S1 := Smooth (S0, Q1);

              % Implicit integration
              S2 := XPass (Gn, S1, Q1, D);
              S3 := YPass (Gn, S2, Q1, D);
              Qn := ZPass (Gn, S3, Q1, D);

        in Qn

        endlet
endfun
```

Figure 9.21 The body of the main iteration.

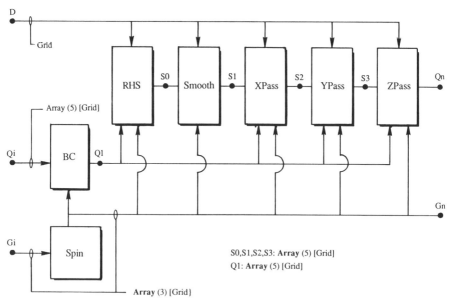

Figure 9.22 Dataflow diagram for the main iteration body.

The main program module (Figures 9.19 and 9.20) generates the initial grid and data arrays and computes the Jacobian of the grid. This is followed by the main iteration in which the Step module is called p times to carry out the alternating direction method. Finally, the data, which have been scaled by the Jacobian to simplify the computation, are unscaled for interpretation.

The Step module (Figures 9.21 and 9.22) computes a modified grid array that reflects rotation of the body, and a new data array of physical data that is the result of advancing the solution one time step. Within the body of Step, module BC fills in the faces of the current data array with values satisfying the desired boundary conditions. Module RHS calculates the right-hand-side arrays of the linear systems to be solved. The Smooth module, analyzed earlier, is used to permit use of a larger time increment which ensuring stability of the computational algorithm. Modules XPass, YPass, and ZPass solve the three sets of linear systems corresponding to the three spatial dimensions of the grid; they are responsible for the bulk of the computation.

The XPass module is expanded in Figures 9.23 and 9.24. Modules XM, AMat, and ABCSet compute the coefficient matrices for a set of block tri-diagonal equation systems, which are solved by Solve. One block tridiagonal system is set up and solved for each combination of indices k and l. Nearly all of the arithmetic operations performed are in the implementation of Solve, which is the subject of Section 9.10.

```
function XPass (
            G: GridMap;    % Grid map
            S: Data;       %
            Q: Data;       %
            D: Grid )      % Jacobian
    returns (Data)             % new Q

      let
          X :=
                  forall k in [2, n−1], l in [2, n−1]

                  H: Grid :=
                          forall j in [1, n]
                                  Xmet := XM (G, D, j, k, l)
                          construct
                                  AMat (Q[j, k, l], Xmet)
                          endall;

                  A, B, C :=
                          forall j in [2, n−1]
                          construct
                                  ABCSet (H[j−1], H[j+1], D[j,k,l], D[j−1,k,l], D[j+1,k,l])
                          endall;

                  F :=
                          forall j in [2, n−1]
                          construct S[j,k,l]
                          endall;

                  construct Solve (B,C,A,F,n)
                  endall;

      in
              forall j in [2, n−1], k in [2, n−1], l in [2, n−1],
              construct S[j,k,l] + X[j,k,l]
              endall;

      endlet
endfun
```

Figure 9.23 The XPass module written in Val.

Figure 9.25 shows the results of program analysis as the top levels of a program description tree for AeroSim. The analysis data are expressed in terms of program input parameters n and p, which define the size of the computational grid and the number of steps to be performed. A complete analysis of the various program modules yields the summary in Table 9.2, which gives operation counts, depth of pipelined code, and the sizes of the arrays generated by each module.

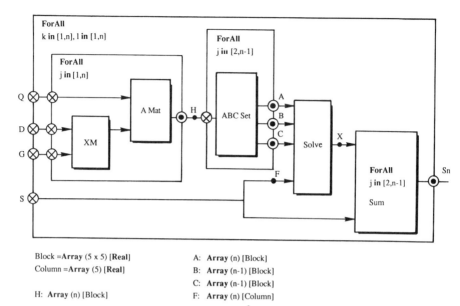

Block =Array (5 x 5) [Real]   A: Array (n) [Block]
Column =Array (5) [Real]   B: Array (n-1) [Block]
                                     C: Array (n-1) [Block]
H: Array (n) [Block]   F: Array (n) [Column]

Figure 9.24 Dataflow diagram for the XPass module.

The next step is to determine how the computation will be split into phases. Because it is evident that practically all of the computation is done by the main iteration, the resource requirements of the Step module must be considered primary. Each component of the Step module in Figure 9.22 generates a large array of new data, so large (for $n = 100$) that it cannot be

Table 9.2 Summary of the Results of Program Analysis

Program AeroSim

Phase	Adds	Multiplies	Divides	Depth	Data generated
Spin	$2n^3$	$4n^3$	0	2	n^3
BC	$447n^2$	$496n^2$	$38n^2$	$105 + 18 \log n$	$6n^2$
RHS	$59n^3$	$105n^3$	0	23	$20n^3$
Smooth	$75n^3$	$120n^3$	$15n^3$	3×8	$15n^3$
XPass	$888n^3$	$1064n^3$	$11n^3$	$18 + 70 \log n$	$5n^3$
YPass	$888n^3$	$1064n^3$	$11n^3$	$18 + 70 \log n$	$5n^3$
ZPass	$888n^3$	$1064n^3$	$11n^3$	$18 + 70 \log n$	$5n^3$
Total	$3247n^3$	$3917n^3$	$86n^3$		$57n^3$

XPass, YPass, ZPass

Component	Adds	Multiplies	Divides	Depth
XM	$7n^3$	$13n^3$	0	9
AMat	$21n^3$	$56n^3$	n^3	7
ABCSet	$15n^3$	$15n^3$	0	2
Solve	$845n^3$	$980n^3$	$10n^3$	$70 \log n$
Total	$888n^3$	$1064n^3$	$11n^3$	$18 + 70 \log n$

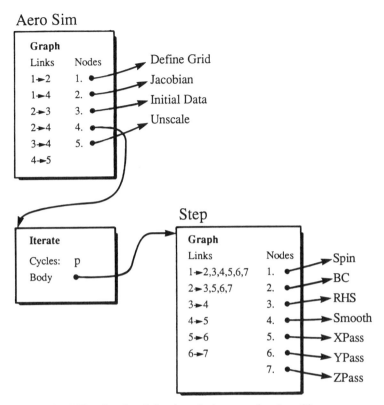

Figure 9.25 Top levels of the description tree for AeroSim.

held in the data memory of the processing elements. If the elements of these arrays could be generated in the same sequence that they would be consumed by successor modules, the use of array memory might be avoided. Because this is not the case for the arrays generated by the components of Step, each module must write its result array into the array memory of the machine. This reasoning applies to arrays Gn, $Q1$, $Q3$ and $S0, \ldots, S3$. It follows that each module in Figure 9.22 must belong to a separate phase of computation and must, by itself, utilize as much of the machine's processing resources as possible.

We have seen how this can be done for the Smooth module. The RHS module is amenable to similar treatment and involves about the same number of dataflow instructions and pipeline depth. Modules Spin and BC account for such a small fraction of the computation that their effect on overall performance is not material. Nevertheless, utilizing the parallelism available in the boundary condition module (BC) is essential, otherwise this module would be an embarrasing bottleneck in the code.

Within the XPass module (Figure 9.24), intermodule communication is in a more fortunate pattern. Module XM can produce values as needed by AMat, and AMat in turn generates the H array in the order required by ABCSet. As explained in Section 9.10, the Solve module may be implemented as one huge piece of pipelined dataflow code that accepts one linear systems specification (7840 numerical values) as each work unit. To match the input requirements of Solve, the other three modules must be expanded in space in the j-index, and the entire XPass module should be pipelined in the k and l indices. Thus, the entire XPass module can operate as a single pipeline, using array memory only for accessing the input arrays and for writing the final results. The YPass and ZPass code blocks operate in the same way.

One performance issue yet to be addressed is the start-up and shut-down times of the pipelined program modules. As shown in Figure 9.26, the rate of instruction execution for a pipeline ramps up as the first work units to enter the pipe activate successive pipeline stages. The duration of this start-up period is the depth of the pipe divided by the instruction repetition rate for the pipeline. The time interval from the beginning of start-up to the beginning of shut-down (the time for all work units to enter the pipe) is the number of work units fed to the pipe divided by the instruction repetition rate. If the pipeline can keep its share of the machine's processing elements busy when full, the efficiency of the pipeline is approximately

$$w/(w + d)$$

where d is the depth of the pipeline and w is the number of work units fed to it. Note that this calculation applies separately to each copy of a pipelined code module when multiple copies are required to use the full performance of the machine.

Table 9.3 gives the efficiency of each component of Step. For example, the largest pipelines, XPass, YPass, and ZPass, each have a depth of $18 + 70 \log n = 488$, and the number of work units is 100^2. Because a single copy is more than sufficient to keep the machine busy, the machine should achieve 95% of full performance in executing these phases of the computation.

In the case of the Smooth module, we noted earlier that it is necessary to load each processing element with four copies of the pipelined code to keep the machine fully busy once the pipes are full. In this case, the number

Activity

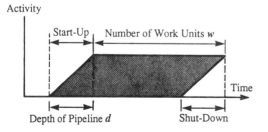

Time

Figure 9.26 Start-up and shut-down of a pipeline and its effect on performance.

Table 9.3 Pipeline Efficiencies of the Cmpets of the Step Module

Phase	Operations	Depth	Work Units	Copies	Efficiency (%)
Spin	$6n^3$	2	n^3	1×256	100
BC	$981n^2$	$105 + 18 \log n$	n^3	(see text)	13.8
RHS	$164n^3$	23	n^3	4×256	97.7
Smooth	$210n^3$	3×8	n^3	4×256	99.2
XPass	$1963n^3$	$18 + 70 \log n$	n^2	1	95.2

of work units per pipe is $100^3/(4 \times 256)$, or 977, but because the pipeline depth for each section of Smooth is only 8, pipeline efficiency is better than 99%. The worst situation is the boundary condition computation. For most of its subcomponents the number of work units is 100^2, but this must be distributed over all the processing elements, yielding only 37 work units per copy of the code. Because pipeline depth is $105 + 18 \log n = 231$, its efficiency is only 14%.

In spite of the weakness in Module BC, overall performance of the entire AeroSim program structure can be very high. If the dataflow processing elements can achieve 10 Mflops of performance apiece, and if the routing network and array memories can support the required traffic, the computation for one time step would run at 95% utilization of the processing elements. It would run in 2.7 s at an average rate of 2437 Mflops.

9.10. Block Tridiagonal Systems and Solvers

The special class of linear algebraic equation systems called *block tridiagonal systems* arises when simple difference methods are applied to linear partial differential equations. These systems have the form

$$
\begin{vmatrix}
B_1 & C_1 & & \\
A_2 & B_2 & C_2 & \\
& \cdot & \cdot & \cdot \\
& & \cdot & \cdot & \cdot \\
& & & A_n & B_n
\end{vmatrix}
\begin{vmatrix}
X_1 \\
X_2 \\
\cdot \\
\cdot \\
X_n
\end{vmatrix}
=
\begin{vmatrix}
F_1 \\
F_2 \\
\cdot \\
\cdot \\
F_n
\end{vmatrix}
$$

in which the only nonzero elements lie on the main diagonal (the Bs), the upper diagonal (the Cs), and the lower diagonal (the As). For application in the AeroSim program, each of the elements is a five-by-five block of values, the number five arising from the five physical quantities associated with each grid point.

In the following, we explain and compare two methods for computing solutions for such systems, *linear reduction* and *cyclic reduction*. For our explanation, it is convenient to consider, first, *tridiagonal* systems in which each block is a simple value, then extend the algorithms to the block tridiagonal case.

Linear reduction is straightforward: The first equation of the system may be used to eliminate X_1 from the second equation, so the second becomes

$$B_2^n X_2 + C_2^n X_3 = F_2$$

where

$$B_2^n = B_2 - A_2(1./B_1)C_1$$

$$F_2^n = F_2 - A_2(1./B_1)F_1$$

$$C_2^n = C_2$$

The new second equation may now be used to remove X_2 from the third, and so on. In general, a series of $n - 1$ steps yields a system with only main and upper diagonal elements defined by

$$
\begin{aligned}
B_i^n &= B_i - A_i(1./B_{i-1}^n)C_{i-1}, & i &= 2, \ldots, n \\
&= B_i, & i &= 1 \\
C_i^n &= C_i, & i &= 1, \ldots, n-1 \\
F_i^n &= F_i - A_i(1./B_{i-1}^n)F_{i-1}^n & i &= 2, \ldots, n \\
&= F_i, & i &= 1
\end{aligned}
$$

This system is easily solved by finding X_n from the n-th equation and substituting successively in equations $n - 1$, $n - 2$, etc.

Application of the method to a block tridiagonal system is done simply by using matrix multiplication and addition in place of the corresponding scalar operations, and substituting matrix inversion for taking the reciprocal. One must be careful about the order of operations because the matrix operations do not always commute. To evaluate a term of the form $B^{-1}A$, it is efficient to use the technique of "upper/lower" decomposition to find the solution of the linear equation system $BY = A$. This amounts to using the equivalence shown in Figure 9.27, where the *decompose* and *substitute* operators (written out for a five-by-five system) have the operation counts and pipeline depth given in the figure. Figure 9.28a shows a dataflow diagram of the complete linear reduction calculation. The whole diagram may be operated as a dataflow pipeline if many similar systems must be solved, as in the AeroSim program. Note, however, that the amount of FIFO buffering required to balance the pipeline is very large, on the order of $1870 \times n^2$ words of memory for systems with n five-by-five blocks, or 18.5 million words if n is 100.

The cyclic reduction method has the advantage that it requires a pipeline of depth proportional to $\log n$ instead of n, cutting the buffering needs by the factor $(\log n)/n$, that is, 5.6% of the memory required for linear re-

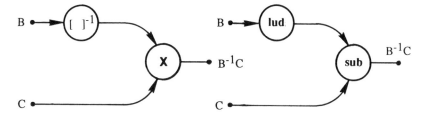

Operator	Adds	Multiplies	Divides	Depth
Decompose (**lud**)	30	40	5	16
Substitute (**sub**)	100	125	0	21

Figure 9.27 Operators for upper/lower decomposition and their performance characteristics for matrices of order five.

duction. On the other hand, it uses more arithmetic operations. To derive the method, consider three successive equations from a tridiagonal system.

$$A_{i-1}X_{i-2} + B_{i-1}X_{i-1} + C_{i-1}X_i \qquad\qquad = F_{i-1}$$
$$A_iX_{i-1} \quad + B_iX_i \quad + C_iX_{i+1} \qquad\qquad = F_i$$
$$A_{i+1}X_i + B_{i+1}X_{i+1} + C_{i+1}X_{i+2} = F_{i+1}$$

We can form a new equation in X_{i-2}, X_i, and X_{i+2} by multiplying the first equation by $A_i(1./B_{i-1})$, the third by $C_i(1./B_{i+1})$, and subtracting the sum from the second equation.

$$- A_i(1./B_{i-1})A_{i-1}X_{i-2} - A_i(1./B_{i-1})C_{i-1}X_i$$
$$+ B_iX_i$$
$$- C_i(1./B_{i+1})A_{i+1}X_i - C_i(1./B_{i+1})C_{i+1}X_{i+2}$$
$$= F_i - A_i(1./B_{i-1})F_{i-1} - C_i(1./B_{i+1})F_{i+1}$$

If we do the same for $i = 2, 4, \ldots, n - 1$ and n is odd, the result is a system of $(n - 1)/2$ equations in $X_2, \ldots, X_{n-1}$. Substitution of the solution of this simpler system in equations of the original system yields the values of the remaining unknowns. If n is one less than a power of 2, then $nn = (n - 1)/2$ is also odd and one less than a power of 2, so the process may be continued recursively until a system of one equation results, which is solved trivially. A slight modification will adapt the algorithm for arbitrary n.

 Let us number the equations of a reduced system $1, \ldots, nn$. Then equations $i - 1$, i, and $i + 1$ of the previous system yield equation k of the

(a) Linear Reduction

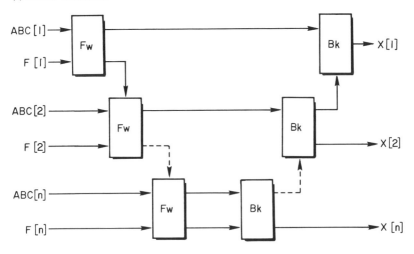

(b) Cyclic Reduction

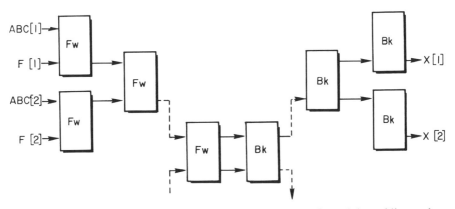

Figure 9.28(a,b) Flow diagrams of two pipelined schemes for solving tridiagonal systems.

reduced system where $i = 2k$. The formulas for the coefficients and right hand side of the new system are

$$A_k^n = - A_i(1./B_{i-1})A_{i-1}$$

$$B_k^n = B_i - A_i(1./B_{i-1})C_{i-1} - C_i(1./B_{i+1})A_{i+1}$$

$$C_k^n = - C_i(1./B_{i+1})C_{i+1}$$

$$F_k^n = F_i - A_i(1./B_{i-1})F_{i-1} - C_i(1./B_{i+1})F_{i+1}$$

A program in Val for this algorithm is shown in Figure 9.29.

```
function Solve (
            n: integer;              % size of problem: one less than
                                     % a power of two
            A: array[real];          % lower diagonal)
            B: array[real];          % main diagonal) main elements
            C: array[real];          % upper diagonal)
            F: array[real];          % right hand side )
     returns
            ( array[real] )          % solution
     if mod (n, 2 ) = 0 then undef
     elseif n = 1 then [1: (1./B[1] ) * F[1]]
     else
            let nn := (n−1)/2;
                An := forall k in [2, nn]
                      i := 2*k
                      construct − A[i] * 1 ./B[i−1] * A[i−1]
                      endall;
                Bn := forall k in [1, nn]
                      i := 2*k
                      construct
                      B[i] − A[i] * 1./B[i−1] * C[i−1] − C[i] * 1./B[i+1] * A[i+1]
                Cn := forall k in [1, nn−1]
                      i := 2*k
                      construct − C[i] * 1./B[i+1] * C[i+1]
                      endall;
                Fn := forall k in [1,nn]
                      i := 2*k
                      construct
                      F[i] − A[i] * 1./B[i−1] * F[i−1] − C[i] * 1./B[i+1] * F[i+1]
                      endall;
                Xn := Solve (nn, An, Bn, Cn, Fn);
            in forall i in [1,n]
                      k := ( (i−1) / 2 ) + 1 ;
                      even := if mod (i, 2) = 0 then true else false endif;
                construct
                      if even then Xn[k]
                      elseif k = n then
                            1./B[i] * ( F[i] − A[i] * Xn[k] )
                      else
                            1./B[i] * ( F[i] − A[i] * Xn[k] − C[i] * Xn[k+1] )
                      endif
                endall
            endlet
     endif
endfun
```

Figure 9.29 The cyclic reduction algorithm written in Val for scalar elements.

Table 9.4 Comparative Performance Parameters for Two Block Tridiagonal Solvers.

Method	Adds	Multiplies	Divides	Depth
Linear	$375 (n - 1)$	$430 (n - 1)$	$10 (n - 1)$	$68 n$
Cyclic	$845 (n - 1)$	$980 (n - 1)$	$10 (n - 1)$	$70 \log n$

As before, this method extends to block equation systems by replacing scalar operations with matrix operations. For example, the term $(1./B_{i-1})A_{i-1}$ becomes $B_{i-1}^{-1}A_{i-1}$, which may be evaluated by solving the linear system

$$B_{i-1} Y = A_{i-1}$$

for Y. Similarly, $B_{i-1}^{-1}F_{i-1}$ may be evaluated by solving

$$B_{i-1} G = F_{i-1}$$

for G. A dataflow diagram of the computation is shown in Figure 9.28b.

Table 9.4 compares the two methods. Note that for $n = 100$, the delay through the computational pipeline is not the most important parameter for the AeroSim program because for either method the delay is only a tiny fraction of the time for all 10,000 work units to enter the pipe. Rather, the choice of method depends on the relative availability of arithmetic and memory resources in the computer system. Either method might be preferred.

9.11. Concluding Remarks

Our aim in this chapter has been to illustrate application of static dataflow computation to large-scale scientific problems. We have outlined the general principles that could be used to structure machine-level programs for running a three-dimensional aerodynamic simulation problem on a dataflow supercomputer. Our analysis gives reasonable expectation that a machine having 256 processing elements could carry out the computations at better than two Gflops. Such a computer could be built using a few thousand custom LSI parts and inexpensive high-density memory components. It would be smaller than conventional supercomputers and consume less than 10 W of power for each Mflop of performance.

Other large-scale scientific computing problems have also been used as benchmarks for dataflow computation. Work on a global weather simulation model was reported in (14), and the Livermore Laboratory Simple code, a hydrodynamics problem, has been the subject of several studies. Less extensive analyses of the particle-in-cell computation for plasma simulation and an object recognition problem have been carried out. In addition, several teams brought their applications to a dataflow workshop held in the fall of 1984. Parts of each problem were programmed in Val, and each was found to be feasible for effective use of a dataflow machine of appropriate size (3).

Some issues have not been addressed in these studies: The codes studied represent the computationally intensive core of each problem, and do not include support for entering and checking data or for presenting and analyzing computed results. Although provisions for problem backup and fault tolerance have not been considered, the main concepts of fault-tolerant computer architecture are just as applicable to dataflow computers as they are to conventional machines, and may even be utilized at less cost. The fundamentals and typical applications of fault-tolerant design are covered by Siewiorek and Maxion in Chapter 12. The primary work needed to bring high-performance dataflow computers into practical use for scientific computation is the development of a compiler that can generate machine code structures of the sort illustrated here. This requires further development of appropriate theory and algorithms for transforming, optimizing, and genrating machine code from programs expressed in Val.

It remains to be seen how broadly applicable are the techniques we have described. Clearly, they will work best in application to computations that have a regular structure such as a main loop that performs nearly the same amount of computation on similarly structured data on each cycle. Yet there are important problems that do not have this form. Language processing, symbol manipulation, and various problems in artificial intelligence are examples. Some "artificial intelligence" applications such as image analysis and speech recognition may profit from use of the numerical techniques of scientific computation. An example is current work in speech recognition that makes use of "hidden Markov models" (22) that involve large amounts of numerical computation, both to construct and verify the models and to carry out the recognition task. Preliminary study of this application indicates that it is amenable to high-performance dataflow implementation.

How broadly applicable is dataflow computation? Discussions of supercomputer research programs have concerned two major areas of development: supercomputers for scientific computation that will be able to perform the same sorts of computations as existing supercomputers but with substantially increased performance, and supercomputers for "knowledge-based" pattern recognition and problem-solving—areas that are not application areas for contemporary supercomputers. The first area is the extension to massively parallel systems of computations for which algorithms and solution techniques are well known. Enough work has been completed in this area that highly parallel forms of many important algorithms are known, programming languages exist in which these algorithms can be elegantly expressed, and machine architectures have been proposed that can perform them effectively. In contrast, the area of knowledge-based applications calls for development of a new conceptual basis for computation before successful massively parallel system architectures will evolve.

Dataflow concepts are applicable to both areas. For knowledge-based systems, research is at a relatively primitive stage. There is at present no sound and accepted conceptual model for the massively parallel execution of general "artificial intelligence" computations, and there have been no studies or research results that show how supercomputer levels of performance can be achieved for these problems. Yet, dataflow concepts show promise of providing a sound semantic foundation for computer systems applicable to a broad range of applications (13), including knowledge-based systems. In contrast to the static dataflow architecture studied in this chapter, a general purpose dataflow computer system must be able to dynamically manage very large collections of information in an online storage hierarchy. Such a machine will serve many users at once and will have to be very flexible in its management of resources. Decisions about memory and processor allocation will be made by the system during program execution rather than in advance by the compiler. These are the characteristics needed to realize "fifth generation" computers. The Vim project at MIT (16) is pursuing fundamental research toward the realization of practical systems having these characteristics and using dataflow principles.

9.12. Acknowledgments

The work leading to the concepts of high-performance dataflow computation reported here was done mostly by the Computation Structures Group of the MIT Laboratory for Computer Science, in which more than 25 graduate students have carried out their doctoral research. We appreciate the assistance of Ken Stevens and Tom Pulliam of the NASA Ames Research Center in supplying and helping us understand the FORTRAN program on which the work reported here was based. We thank Bill Ackerman, Ken Todd, and Gao Guang-Rong for their work on recasting the code in Val and assisting in its analysis.

Our work on dataflow concepts began with the graph model of Jorge Rodriguez published in 1967 (33). Since then, we have enjoyed support from the Advanced Research Projects Agency, the National Science Foundation, the Lawrence Livermore Laboratory, the Basic Sciences Program of the Department of Energy, and the NASA Ames Research Center. Through this period, the interest and support of the directors of the Laboratory for Computer Science, especially Robert Fano and Michael Dertouzos, has been helpful and encouraging.

Problems

1. In scientific computation, conditional expressions often present difficulties for conventional vectorizing compilers. Consider the following Val

conditional expression:

if $x + y > 3$ **then** $x*y$ **else** $x - y$ **endif**

a. Construct the static dataflow graph for the conditional expression.
b. Construct dataflow machine code for the graph in part a, using the notation for dataflow instructions suggested in the text. Give careful attention to how the switch and merge gates are implemented.
2. Balance both the dataflow graph and the machine code you constructed in Problem 1. Identify the cycle with the longest length in both cases. What are the pipelined throughput rates for the two cases? (Assume that 10 μs are required for the complete execution of one instruction or the firing of an actor.)
3. The following **forall** expression performs a two-dimensional relaxation computation:

```
X: = forall i in [0, m + 1]
        construct
            if i = 0 then A[i]
            elseif i = m + 1 then A[i]
            else
                forall j in [0, n + 1]
                construct
                    if j = 0 then A[i, j]
                    elseif j = n + 1 then A[i, j]
                    else
                        (A[i, j − 1] + A[i, j + 1]
                         + A[i − 1, j] + A[i + 1, j])/4
                    endif
                endall
            endif
        endall
```

Assume this computation is to be implemented by using one dataflow pipeline for the body, and by spreading the arrays in time in both dimensions.
a. Give a balanced dataflow graph for the conditional expression that is the body of the inner **forall** expression. (Use the dataflow *select* actor v = A[i] to select array elements.)
b. Construct dataflow machine code for the complete nested **forall** expression. Use generate instructions and result queueing as in the text example. (Assume that array A is held in array memory at the beginning of execution and arrange that X is in array memory at completion.)
4. The following Val **for-iter** expression computes a first-order linear

recurrence:

```
X: = for
        T = array_empty;
        i = 0;
        x = B[1];
    do
        if i > n then T
        else
            iter
                T = T[i:x];
                i = i + 1;
                x = A[i]*T[i - 1] + B[i];
            enditer
        endif
    endfor
```

The internal array T is initialized to an empty array denoted by the constant expression **array-empty**. The evaluation of the expression is conducted iteratively, controlled by the simple test expression $i > n$. If $i \leq n$, the iteration is continued and T and i are redefined as specified in the **iter** arm of the body. When the test expression returns false, (i.e., $i > n$), the evaluation of the **for-iter** expression is completed by returning the array T as the result array X.

a. Construct a dataflow graph for the above **for-iter** expression using gate and merge actors to implement the iteration and select and append (B = A[i:x]) actors for array access and construction.

b. What aspect of your dataflow graph would limit computation rate on a static dataflow computer?

c. The linear recurrence can be transformed so the dependence of x_i on x_{i-1} is replaced by dependence on x_{i-2} or, in general, x_{i-k}. Using this fact, can you transform the program such that the corresponding dataflow graph can be maximally pipelined? Discuss the trade-offs of your approach. Can it be generalized?

5. In this chapter, we have described a new way of implementing computations that involve construction of arrays (vectors) of data. We have shown how massive parallelism can be effectively exploited in a fine-grain dataflow computer by using pipelined machine code. Compare this approach with conventional vector processing as performed using machines such as Cray or CDC supercomputers. Some areas to be consider are: the complexity of implementing code blocks (such as Smooth and Solve in the aerodynamic simulation code) on multiple pipelined hardware function units; the issues of vector register allocation and pipeline startup time; and possibilities for concurrent processing of multiple code blocks.

References

1. Ackerman WB: Data flow languages. *Computer 15*, 2 Feb. 1982. Previously appeared in *Proc. of the 1979 Nat. Comp. Conf.*, August 1979.

2. Ackerman WB, Dennis JB: VAL—A Value-oriented algorithmic language: Preliminary reference manual. Report MIT/LCS/TR-218, Laboratory for Computer Science, 545 Technology Sq., Cambridge, MA, June 1978.

3. Adams GB, Brown RL, Denning PJ: Report on an evaluation study of dataflow computation. Research Institute for Advanced Computer Science, Moffet Field, CA, April, 1985.

4. Agerwala, T. and Arvind, eds. Special issue on data flow systems. *Computer 15*. 2 Feb. 1982.

5. Arvind, Gostelow KP: A computer capable of exchanging processors for time. *Information processing 77: Proc. of IFIP Congress 77*, Toronto, Canada, August, 1977, pp. 849–853.

6. Arvind, Kathail V: A Multiple processor dataflow machine that supports generalized procedures. *Proc. of the Eighth Annual Arch. Conference*, May, 1981.

7. Beam R, Warming RF: An Implicit finite-difference algorithm for hyperbolic systems in conservation-law-form. *J. Comp. Physics*, Sept. 1976.

8. Cornish M et al: The TI data flow architectures: The power of concurrency for avionics. *Proc. of the Third Digital Avionics Systems Conference*, November, 1979, pp. 19–25.

9. Currie IG: *Fundamental Mechanics of Fluids*. McGraw-Hill, New York, 1974.

10. Davis AL, Keller RM: Dataflow program graphs. *Computer 15*, 2 Feb. 1982, pp. 26–41.

11. Dennis JB: First version of a data flow procedure language. In Robinet B (ed): *Programming Symposium*, Lecture Notes in Computer Science 19: Springer-Verlag, Berlin, Heidelberg, New York, 1974.

12. Dennis JB: Data flow supercomputers. *Computer 13*, 11 Nov. 1980.

13. Dennis JB: An operational semantics for a language with early completion data structures. In *Formal Descriptions of Programming Concepts*, Springer-Verlag, Berlin, Heidelberg, New York, 1981.

14. Dennis JB, Gao GR, Todd KR: Modeling the weather with a data flow supercomputer. IEEE Trans. on Computers C-33, 7 (July 1984), pp. 592–603.

15. Dennis JB, Misunas DP: A preliminary architecture for a basic data flow computer. *Proc. of the Second Annual Symposium on Computer Architecture*, IEEE, New York, 1975.

16. Dennis JB, Stoy JE, Guharoy B: VIM: An experimental multi-user system supporting functional programming. Proc. of the Workshop on High-level Computer Architecture, Los Angeles, May 1984.

17. Douglas J Jr, Gunn JE: A General Formulation of Alternating Direction Methods. *Numer. Math. 4*, 1964, p. 428.

18. Fosseen JB: Representation of algorithms by maximally parallel schemata. Master's thesis, Dept. of Electrical Engineering and Computer Science, MIT, Cambridge, Mass., June 1972.

19. Gao GR: An implementation scheme for array operations in static data flow computers. MIT/LCS/TR-280, Laboratory for Computer Science, Cambridge, MA, 1982.

20. Gao GR: A Pipelined Code Mapping Scheme for Data Flow Computers. MIT/LCS/TR-371, Laboratory for Computer Science, Cambridge, MA, August 1985.
21. Gurd JR, Kirkham CC, Watson I: The Manchester dataflow prototype computer. *Communications of the ACM 28*, 1 January 1985, pp. 34–52.
22. Jelinek F: Continuous speech recognition by statistical methods. *Proc. IEEE*, April 1976.
23. Kahn G: The semantics of a simple language for parallel programming. Information Processing 74: *Proc. of the IFIP Congress 74*, North Holland, Amsterdam, 1974, pp. 471–475.
24. Karp RM, Miller RE: Properties of a model for parallel computations: Determinancy, termination and queueing. *SIAM Journal of Applied Math. 14*, Nov. 1966.
25. Kogge PM: *The Architecture of Pipelined Computers*. McGraw-Hill, New York, 1981.
26. McGraw J: The Val language: Description and analysis. *Trans. on Programming Languages and Systems* 4, 1, Jan. 1982.
27. Montz L: Safety and optimization transformations for data flow programs. MIT/LCS/TR-240, Laboratory for Computer Science, Cambridge, MA, July 1980.
28. NEC Electronics, Inc. *Advanced Product Information User's Manual: μPD7281 Image Pipelined Processor*. Mountain View, CA, 1985.
29. Patil SS: Closure properties of interconnections of determinate systems. Record of the Project MAC Conference on Concurrent Systems and Parallel Computation, ACM, New York, NY, 1970.
30. Peterson JL: *Petri Net Theory and the Modeling of Systems*. Prentice-Hall, Englewood Cliffs, NJ, 1981.
31. Pulliam TH, Steger JL: On implicit finite-difference simulations of three dimensional flow. American Institute of Aeronautics and Astronautics, New York, Jan. 1978.
32. Ramchandani C: On The Computation Rate of Asynchronous Computation Systems. Proc. of the Seventh Annual Princeton Conference on Information Sciences and Systems, 1973.
33. Rodriguez JE: *A Graph Model For Parallel Computation*. Ph.D. thesis, Massachusetts Institute of Technology, Sept. 1967.
34. Van Horn E: Computer Design for Asynchronously Reproducible Multiprocessing. MAC/TR-34, Project MAC, Massachusetts Institute of Technology, Cambridge, MA, Nov. 1966.
35. Vedder R, Campbell M, Tucker G: The Hughes data flow multiprocessor. Proc. of the Fifth International Conference on Distributed Computing Systems, Denver, CO, 1985, pp. 2–9.
36. Watson I, Gurd J: A Practical Data Flow Computer. *Computer 15*, 2 Feb. 1982, pp. 51–57.
37. Wetherell CS: Error data values in the data-flow language VAL. *Trans. on Programming Languages and Systems 4*, 2 April 1982, pp. 226–238.
38. Yuba T, Shimada T, Hiraki K, Kashiwagi H: Sigma-1: A dataflow computer for scientific computation. Electrotechnical Laboratory, 1-1-4 Umesono, Sakuramura, Niiharigun, Ibaraki 305, Japan, 1984.

10

Architectures That Support Functional Programming Languages

Steven R. Vegdahl

In recent years, a number of scientists have advocated the use of functional programming (FP) as a means of increasing programmer productivity, enhancing the clarity of programs, and reducing the difficulty of program verification. A major drawback of using functional languages has been that they are perceived to run slowly on von Neumann computer architectures.

The first section of this chapter discusses functional programming languages and their advantages and disadvantages from the viewpoint of both the programmer and systems implementor. The second section discusses many of the architectural issues that arise in attempting to design hardware that executes functional languages efficiently. The third section discusses selected architectures in more detail in order to give the reader a picture of some of some of the actual design decisions that have been made. The final section is a summary. Sections 10.1, 10.2, and 10.4 are based on a paper previously published by the author (88).

10.1. Functional Programming Languages

The terms *functional language, applicative language, dataflow language,* and *reduction language* have been used somewhat interchangeably in the literature to refer to languages that are based on function application and therefore free of side effects. The term *functional language* is used here for the purpose of clarity. This section characterizes functional languages by defining and comparing them with (traditional) imperative ones and by discussing issues that arise when programming, implementing, and executing them.

10.1.1. Characterization of Imperative and Functional Languages

Advocates of functional programming contend that imperative programming languages (e.g., FORTRAN, Pascal) are simply "high-level versions" of the von Neumann computer. Their principal operations involve changing the state of the computation in much the same way a machine-language program does (6):

- Program variables imitate machine words. Programmers think of them as locations in which a value can be saved.
- Control statements imitate jumps. For example, *if-then-else* has the semantics: "Test the condition. If true, go and execute the 'then' statements; otherwise go and execute the 'else' statements."
- The assignment statement imitates fetch and store instructions of the underlying machine.

Central to an imperative model of computing is the concept of a *present state,* which encompasses the program counter, the values of all variables, the stack, etc. According to advocates of functional programming, thinking of program execution in terms of a *present state* has a number of undesirable consequences (6, 7):

- Two widely separated pieces of code may reference a common global variable and therefore have an "unanticipated" interaction. A programmer must also be concerned with issues such as aliasing, which can increase program complexity.
- A programmer concentrates on data manipulation, not on the essential algorithm.
- It is difficult to characterize parallel execution when several independent asynchronous processes can have side effects on one another.
- Program proof and transformation are more difficult because the imperative model does not lend itself to easy mathematical characterization. For example, a name in a given context can have different meanings at different times, because of invocation of an operation that produces a side effect.

On the other hand, it may also be argued that many common computer applications (e.g., updating a database) are inherently imperative in nature, and that imperative programming languages are well-suited to such tasks.

Functional programs contain no notion of a *present state, program counter,* or *storage.* Rather, the "program" is a *function* in the true mathematical sense: it is applied to the input of the program, and the resulting value is the program's output. For example, if the "program" *Plus* computes the sum of two numbers, then 3 + 4 can be computed by applying *Plus* to the input ⟨3, 4⟩:

Plus: ⟨3, 4⟩ → 7

Because a function's argument(s) and output value(s) may be list structures, a function can define quite complex operations on its input.

Essential to functional programming is the notion of *referential transparency* (10, 50): the value of an expression depends only on its textual context, *not* on computational history. The value of *Plus:* ⟨3, 4⟩ is determined only by the static definitions of *Plus, 3,* and *4.* Another way of viewing this is that the *output* is another form of the *function and input*; 7 and *Plus:* ⟨3, 4⟩ are simply different forms of the same object. The purpose of the computation is to *reduce* an *expression* to an equivalent *constant expression.*

The basic operation, then, in functional programming is function application. Data dependencies exist only as a result of function application, the value of a function being completely determined by its arguments. Notions such as *time-dependence, side effect,* and *writable memory* do not exist.

Examples of functional languages are pure Lisp, Backus' FP (6), Hope (10), Val (62), Id (4), KRC (86), and ML (32). Some, like FP, have no assignment statement. Others, such as Val and Id, are known as *single-assignment languages,* in which an "assignment statement" is simply a notational convenience for binding an expression to an identifier.

According to Backus, programs are constructed in an imperative language by writing simple statements—such as the assignment statement—and "gluing them together" with control structures—such as *if-then-else*; programs in a functional language are composed by writing functions and "gluing them together" with *functional forms.* The major components of his system are (6):

1. A set of *objects.*
2. A set of *functions* that map objects into objects. These functions are analogous to built-in functions and operators in imperative programming languages.
3. A set of *functional forms* that combine existing functions or objects to form new functions. An example of a functional form is the *reduction* operator of APL.[1]

---

[1] Some functional languages (85) allow higher-order functions—that is, functions that can be applied to functions—obviating the need for *functional forms.*

As an example of the functional style of programming, consider a functional program for computing the inner product of two vectors using a notation similar to that of Backus (6):

IP = *(Reduce Plus)* ∘ *(Map Times)*

Map is a functional form that applies an n-ary function to n vectors of equal length, resulting in a single vector of that length. *Reduce* is identical to the operator of the same name in APL. Thus,

IP:⟨⟨2, 3, −2⟩, ⟨3, 1, 5⟩⟩

   = *(Reduce Plus)* ∘ *(Map Times)*:⟨⟨2, 3, −2⟩, ⟨3, 1, 5⟩⟩

   = *(Reduce Plus)*:⟨6, 3, −10⟩

   = −1

Similarly, matrix multiplication may be defined as

MM = *(ApplyToAll(ApplyToAll IP))* ∘ *Pair* ∘ [*First, Transpose* ∘ *Second*]

ApplyToAll applies a unary function to each element of a vector, resulting in a vector of identical length. *Pair* is a function that creates a matrix of pairs of elements of its two arguments; *First* and *Second* are functions that select the first and second elements of a vector, respectively. Thus the multiplication of a 2 × 3 matrix and a 3 × 2 matrix,

MM:⟨⟨⟨0, 3, 2⟩, ⟨1, −4, 4⟩⟩, ⟨⟨1, 0⟩, ⟨3, −2⟩, ⟨5, 1⟩⟩⟩

   = *(ApplyToAll(ApplyToAll IP))* ∘ *Pair* ∘ [*First, Transpose* ∘ *Second*]:

      ⟨⟨⟨0, 3, 2⟩, ⟨1, −4, 4⟩⟩, ⟨⟨1, 0⟩, ⟨3, −2⟩, ⟨5, 1⟩⟩⟩

   = *(ApplyToAll(ApplyToAll IP))* ∘ *Pair*:

      ⟨⟨⟨0, 3, 2⟩, ⟨1, −4, 4⟩⟩, ⟨⟨1, 3, 5⟩, ⟨0, −2, 1⟩⟩⟩

   = *(ApplyToAll(ApplyToAll IP))*:

      ⟨⟨⟨⟨0, 3, 2⟩, ⟨1, 3, 5⟩⟩, ⟨⟨0, 3, 2⟩, ⟨0, −2, 1⟩⟩⟩,

      ⟨⟨⟨1, −4, 4⟩, ⟨1, 3, 5⟩⟩, ⟨⟨1, −4, 4⟩, ⟨0, −2, 1⟩⟩⟩⟩

   = ⟨⟨19, −4⟩, ⟨9, 12⟩⟩

results in a 2 × 2 matrix.

The functional programming style can thus be characterized as the building of complex functions from simpler ones by using *functional forms*; the notion of the *state* of a computation is absent.

10.1.2. The Programmer's Perspective

The use of functional languages has been advocated by a number of scientists (6, 29). Claims have been made that the use of functional programs increases programmer productivity, program lucidity, and ease of verification. Morris et al. (64), however, question whether functional programming is well-suited to someone who must make a living programming, or if it is primarily for "metaprogrammers," who study programming?

If functional programming is to become commonplace in the "real world," a number of issues must be resolved; the most significant, perhaps, is whether real applications are suited to functional programming. Can a text editor, operating system, or video game be easily constructed in a functional language? If not, can the domain of its practicality be characterized?

Many people argue in favor of functional programming languages by comparing them with conventional languages, such as FORTRAN or Pascal (6). There has recently, however, been much interest in object-oriented languages such as Smalltalk (31) and CLU (55). Productivity claims similar to those about functional languages have also been made about object-oriented languages (41), and indeed many of their features are similar. Thus, the question must be raised whether most of the high productivity attributed to functional programming is due to referential transparency, or to other properties, such as abstraction, extensibility, higher-order functions, and heap-allocated memory. Finally, there is the question of whether functional languages can be mapped onto computer hardware and executed with reasonable efficiency, a topic that is discussed later in this section.

Advantages of the Functional Programming Style

Proponents of functional programming claim that correct functional programs are easier to produce than equivalent imperative ones. Advantages cited include:

- Programs can be written at a higher level; a programmer can get the "big picture" rather than specifying a computation "a word at a time," as is typical in imperative languages (6, 7). Time can be spent concentrating on the algorithm rather than on the details of its implementation.
- Its compact, lucid notation allows more "algorithm" to be expressed per line of code. Evidence suggests that the *number of lines of correct code per day* is roughly constant for a given programmer, independent of the language used (93). Assuming this to be true, a functional language would increase productivity because an algorithm can generally be expressed more concisely in a functional language than in an imperative one (85).
- Functional languages are free of side effects. A programmer can construct a program without being concerned about *aliasing* or "unexpected" modifications to variables by other routines. A consequence of this is that the

procedure parameter passing mechanisms *call-by-value* and *call-by-name* have the same semantics, providing the computation terminates (7).

- Functional programs are easier to verify because proofs can be based on the rather well-understood concept of a function rather on the more cumbersome notion of a von Neumann computer (6).
- Functional programs often contain a great deal of implicit and easily detected parallelism (29). Explicitly specifying parallelism on a von Neumann system can be quite difficult (44).

Programming experience seems to indicate that languages with FP features do in fact increase programmer productivity. APL has long been known as a language in which programs can be quickly constructed (56). Poplar (64), a functional string-processing language, has been used by a number of people to create a report-generation system, family-budget maintainer, and a purchase-order management system. The consensus among programmers was that the use of Poplar significantly decreased programming time. Users and designers of other functional languages have made similar claims about productivity (10, 85).

Although functional languages can be quite powerful, there is nothing "magic" about them. An "imperative" program can be written in a functional language by defining a structure that encodes the values of all variables and passing this structure as a parameter to every function, where every function returns a modified version. Such modifications would correspond to changes in the values of variables in the imperative program.

Another way of saying this is that both functional and imperative languages are Turing-equivalent; any computation expressed in a functional language can be expressed in an imperative one, and vice versa. Furthermore, sloppy, unstructured programs can be written in either style; program maintenance issues—and other "programming in the large" issues—arise in either style.

Problems with the Functional Programming Style
One of the potential drawbacks of programming in a functional language is the difficulty—or at least the different approach—one encounters when programming an inherently sequential algorithm, such as one that consists largely of I/O operations. Consider an imperative program in which a file is opened and a pointer to it is passed among procedures, each reading a record from the file, then returning to the main program. A functional program, because it is free of side effects, would be somewhat awkward to write in this (imperative) style. If function *A* is to read a record from the input file, and function *B* is to read the next record, functions must be written so that *B* calls *A* (either directly or indirectly), and *A* must return both the *main result* and the *modified versions of all files it uses*. Performing I/O in this manner has much the flavor of simulating a von Neumann machine by "passing the whole machine state around from function to function."

The method of handling I/O that seems to have gained the widest acceptance among functional programming advocates is that of using *streams,* which were originally proposed by Landin (54) and later incorporated into a dataflow language by Weng (96). A stream is a representation of a list structure in that is implemented by passing the elements sequentially; the use of streams can allow functional programs to be specified in a natural way, at least for simple input–output behavior. Examples have also been given in which streams can be used to model more complex sequential events in a functional language (5). The question of whether the stream model is as general and as natural as its proponents claim will likely remain unanswered until a significant number of "real applications" are written in functional languages.

Debugging Functional Programs
The debugging of functional programs is another issue that requires further exploration. The experience of several scientists indicates that debugging may actually be easier when using a functional language (10, 64). Although one cannot examine the state of the computation—there is no state—it certainly seems feasible to trace one or more paths down the "execution tree," examining the inputs and outputs of each function (see Figure 10.1). This type of debugging seems well-suited to functional programs, because such a tree is a static object for a given input; an imperative program, on the other hand, has a state that changes with time. Debugging a functional program in a traditional way (setting break points, etc.) could be a confusing

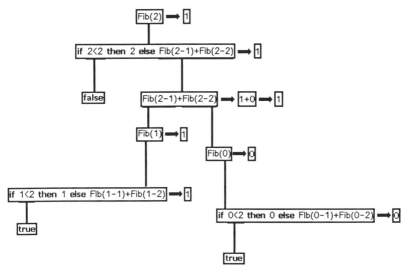

Figure 10.1 Execution tree of a simple functional program.

undertaking if *lazy evaluation* (38) (see Section 10.2.2) is employed because the order of evaluation may be nonintuitive (64).

The *equality assertion* feature of Poplar (64) seems well-suited to functional programs, and has been shown to be useful in allowing the compiler to aid in debugging. This feature allows the programmer to specify a *test input* for the function along with *values at intermediate points* of the computation and *the output value* for the chosen test input. The assertions act as comments, giving a reader an intuitive feel for what the program is doing. In addition, they are executed by the compiler to ensure that they are consistent with the actual code.

Summary
There is evidence that functional programs can be used to express a number of algorithms concisely and lucidly, requiring less effort than programming in an imperative language. Additional experience is required before it can be determined how much of the "functional programming advantage" is due to the lack of side effects and how much is due to other features that are common to many functional languages.

10.1.3. Efficiency Considerations

We now turn our attention from programming issues to those of efficiency. Many FP proponents contend that whether or not functional programming increases programmer productivity, it produces programs that are highly suitable for parallel processing. On the other hand, functional programs have gained a reputation for running slowly.

Potential for Concurrent Execution
Functional programs often contain a great deal of implicit parallelism, making them attractive candidates for execution on parallel processors. Arguments of a function (29) and distinct elements in a dynamically created structure (29) can all be evaluated concurrently and independently. In addition, a reduction (as in APL) with an associative operator can be evaluated as a tree rather than as a list, decreasing its running time from linear to logarithmic if sufficient processors are available (62, 89) (see Figure 10.2). Finally, if the programmer (or system) is willing to spend computing time on

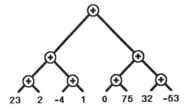

Figure 10.2 Parallel execution of a plus-reduction.

results that may not be needed, all three clauses of a conditional expression can even be evaluated concurrently (70).

Proponents also argue that functional programs are also attractive for parallel processing because data dependencies are localized; the value of a function depends only on values of its arguments, giving rise to the possibility that communication overhead can be minimized by arranging for the evaluation of a function to occur "near" the evaluation of its arguments. Proposals for implementing this typically involve attempting to make the function-hierarchy graph correspond roughly to the physical graph of processors.

Efficiency Problems

The power of parallel processing may be overshadowed by the allegedly inherent inefficiencies of functional programs. Reasons cited for the lack of speed in functional languages have included (42, 65, 67, 90):

- The use of linked lists instead of arrays. A random access to an "array" element takes linear time rather than constant time.
- The high frequency of function calls and the resulting overhead for parameter passing, etc.
- Garbage-collection overhead.
- Lack of destructive updating. To return a modified version of a structure, it is necessary (logically) to return a new copy of the structure with the modification.
- Listful style. Some functional languages encourage the passing of intermediate list structures between composed functions. The use of such structures causes additional storage allocation and dereferencing operations to be performed, and increases garbage-collection overhead.

Although several of these reasons reflect the fact that functional languages are not as "close" to von Neumann computers as are imperative languages, others reflect only that many *implementations* have been inefficient. Fateman (27) points out that one of the reasons functional languages have their reputation for inefficiency is that they have typically been run interpretively rather than compiled.

Although the use of linked lists is ideal for some operations, it is quite poor for array-like random accesses. It has been suggested that a tree representation of a sequential structure might be a good compromise between a linked list and an array (33, 48); this would also allow destructive updating to be performed in logarithmic time. In some cases, the use of contiguous arrays is also appropriate.

Another problem is that most FP computations are performed on structures, not scalar values, diminishing the effectiveness of arranging for functions to compute their values "near" the evaluation of their arguments. When a structure is represented by a pointer, accessing its elements may still require a large number of remote references.

A more serious issue affecting efficiency is that the functional programming style encourages programmers to operate on large structures
rather than "a word at a time." If *A* and *B* are arrays, an imperative programmer might write

$A[i] + B[i]$

while an APL programmer would likely write

$(A + B)[i]$

which, although more concise, causes a completely new array, $A + B$, to
be created when evaluated in a straightforward manner. Similarly, to compute the third largest element in a list *L*, an APL programmer might write

(*Reverse Sort L*)[3]

rather than running through a loop and keeping track of the three largest
values. The general problem is that the evaluation of functions that operate
on large structures can be inefficient. (The use of *lazy evaluation* (38) can
lead to substantial improvement in some cases, at the cost of higher space
and speed overhead—see Section 10.2.2.)

Another potential inefficiency is the performing of the same computation repeatedly. Consider the recursive program to compute the *n*-th Fibonacci number:

Fib = *(Leq* 1) → *Ident*; *Plus* ∘ [*Fib* ∘ (*Sub* 1), *Fib* ∘ (*Sub* 2)]

Although mathematically concise, this function takes exponential time when
executed in the straightforward manner. The recursive program to determine
whether a number is prime,

IsPrime = (*Reduce Or*) ∘ (*ApplyToAll Divides*) ∘ *Distl* ∘

[(*Filter IsPrime*) ∘ *Upto* ∘ [2, *Floor* ∘ *Sqrt*], *Ident*]

also invokes *IsPrime* multiple times for several values.

The fundamental problem seems to be that it can be quite difficult to
detect at compile-time when a function will be invoked with the same arguments, so that the result can be saved the first time it is computed, and
looked up during subsequent calls (49). An imperative program can explicitly
save values that are known to be needed later. Keller and Sleep (50) have
proposed a mechanism by which a programmer can specify when a result
is to be cached. A totally automatic caching scheme introduces a number
of implementation problems (see Section 10.2.5).

Compile-Time Techniques for Improving Efficiency
Compiler optimization techniques can be used to solve some of the inefficiency problems of functional programs. Although not the subject of this

chapter, compiler techniques are a promising area of research, and are sometimes ignored by FP machine designers. Solving an efficiency problem by program transformation should at least be considered before a complex piece of hardware is designed.

Two approaches are being explored in the area of functional program transformation. *Discovery methods* employ a small number of transformations: a heuristic search is performed, applying the transformations in an attempt to improve the efficiency of the program. *Schema methods* employ a larger collection of transformations, but without searching.

Discovery methods (9, 49, 60, 77, 90) are generally variants of an unfolding–folding technique, which coalesces operations and attempts to minimize the number of intermediate list structures. A function is first *unfolded* by expanding some of its functions, replacing each with its definition. The goal is to extract "an atomic step" of a recursive function, and to transform the remainder of the function into an instance of the function itself. Tail-recursion may often be eliminated to transform the function into iterative form (81).

Schema methods (52, 72, 89) do not perform heuristic searching; instead, a collection of predefined transformation templates are applied to transform the program. These methods are generally faster than discovery methods—no searching is done—but less general, as all transformations must be predefined. Schemas have been developed for APL compilers that "understand" certain array manipulation/permutation operations such as transpose and sort, and can optimize such operations as

Reverse Reverse x → *x*

and

(Sort x)[3] → '*third smallest element in x*'

Compiler techniques for improving functional programs have generally concentrated on removing overhead such as intermediate list creation. While these techniques clearly improve performance on a von Neumann architecture, there is the possibility that such transformations may reduce the potential for parallelism. If it is necessary to perform a complex operation on each element of a list, performing the operations iteratively so that the list does not have to be physically created may not be the most efficient method on a multiprocessor architecture. The cost of storage management must be weighed against the potential speedup of concurrent evaluation. Such analysis by a compiler will not always be practical.

On the other hand, when an effective, well-understood compiler technique is discovered to solve a particular efficiency problem, it should be used rather than building additional hardware to solve the problem. Hardware solutions should generally be applied only when compiler solutions are inadequate.

Summary
There is a great deal of inherent parallelism in many functional programs. Because of their freedom from side effects, they are attractive candidates for execution on parallel architectures. Efficiency problems, however, still exist. Some may be classified as "overhead" (e.g., intermediate list construction), while others are more fundamental (e.g., programming style). Whether parallelism and/or compiler techniques can compensate for or solve these problems remains an open research issue.

10.2. Design Issues for FP Machines

This section compares and contrasts design decisions that have been made by architects of various FP machines along these dimensions:

- The physical interconnection of the processors, which vary from uniprocessor systems to cube-interconnection networks.
- The method used to "drive" the computation.
- The representation of program and data. Most machines use a list or graph structure for both program and data.
- How parallelism is invoked and controlled. There are many issues here, including when to invoke parallelism, the mapping of processes to processors, and deadlock avoidance.
- Optimization techniques. Some proposed machines use evaluation strategies that attempt to avoid unnecessary and/or redundant computations.

In this section, the issues will be discussed in general terms; selected architectures will be examined with respect to these issues in Section 10.3.

Not all machines mentioned here were designed to execute purely *functional* languages. A number of them, particularly Lisp and APL machines, were designed for the execution of a nonfunctional language that contains a large functional subset; we refer to such languages as *quasifunctional*. Such machines are included to reflect points in the design space that would otherwise be overlooked. Although multiprocessors are the primary emphasis, a number of uniprocessors are included to present a richer view of the design space.

10.2.1. Physical Interconnection of Processors

The selection of a processor interconnection scheme in a multiprocessing environment is an important design decision. The subject has been one of great interest for designers of von Neumann multiprocessors (37), and the trade-offs involved apply to FP multiprocessors as well. (Chapter 6 gives an extensive treatment of this topic.)

Generally, a richer interconnection offers higher performance and flexibility at a greater hardware expense.[2] A complete interconnection is generally infeasible, however, because FP machine designers envision systems of hundreds or thousands of processors (11, 17). At the other end of the spectrum are uniprocessor systems. While some have interesting features with respect to functional program implementation, they are not of particular interest in discussing interconnection strategies.

Shared Buses
The concurrent-Lisp processor (82) and Rumbaugh's dataflow machine (75) each use a shared bus interconnection (see Figure 10.3). The concurrent-Lisp processor has several memory banks, each attached to a single bus, with each processor directly connected to each memory bus, and processor communication done via the shared memory. Rumbaugh's system has two global memory banks—one for instructions and one for structure values—and local memories in each processor, used for caching. Bandwidth requirements make a shared bus approach feasible for only a small number of processors.

Ring
The *ZMOB* multiprocessing system (74) and the TI-dataflow machine (43) each use a ring network in which data flows in one direction (see Figure 10.4). Like shared bus architectures, bandwidth can become a bottleneck when the number of processors is large. The communication bandwidth of the 256 processor *ZMOB* network, for example, is only about 1 bit/μs per processor.

Tree
A number of designers have proposed tree-structured architectures (19, 46, 57, 68) (see Figure 10.5). For a *reduction machine,* in which the problem can be decomposed into independent, parallel subproblems, there is a natural mapping between the hardware (tree) and the software (tree of processes). Unfortunately, it is often necessary to copy data (e.g., parameter values) to

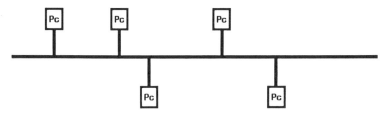

Figure 10.3 Shared bus interconnection.

---

[2] Richer interconnections may also have other advantages, such as higher reliability, but such a topic is beyond the scope of this chapter.

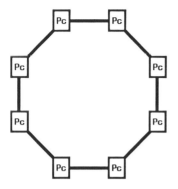

Figure 10.4 Ring network.

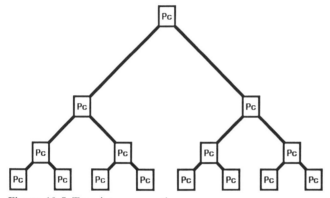

Figure 10.5 Tree interconnection.

each of a number of independent computations, making the bottleneck near the root of the tree a potentially serious problem. Sorting, for example, requires linear time on a tree, but can be performed in $O(\log^2 n)$ on a richer network (87). Another problem is that the physical tree of processors has a finite depth, so that the resources at a leaf node may be insufficient for solving a large subproblem if the problem decomposes into a structure that is deeper than the physical tree.

A tree architecture may also be used in an SIMD (Single Instruction, Multiple Data) manner, in which the tree is used as an associative memory and as a data shifter (58, 68); lists may be stored across the leaves of the tree rather than in linked form. When insertion or deletion is required, some of the elements in the list are shifted to their neighbors; a single data shift among leaves of a tree may be performed in logarithmic time (73).

Hierarchical

A two-level hierarchical system (see Figure 10.6) has been proposed for the *ALICE* multiprocessor (15, 17) in which the processors are divided into

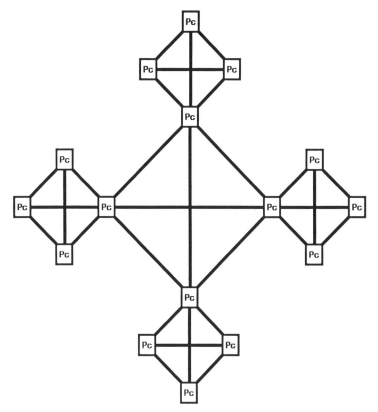

Figure 10.6 Hierarchical interconnection.

tightly coupled *clusters* (of size two in the prototype version), which are
then interconnected as a routing network. Parallelism unfolds dynamically,
requiring the mapping of processes onto processors at runtime. The experience with the Cm[*] multiprocessor (44), also a clustered system but programmed imperatively, has shown that locality—important for good performance—is not easy to achieve. The performance of such a structure
should be no worse than that of a tree, however, because a tree can be
viewed as a special case of a hierarchical interconnection.

Routing Networks
Several architectures employ a routing network (see Figure 10.7) for communication between a set of processing elements and a set of memories (24).
The network used for Dennis' dataflow project consists of $\log_2 N$ layers of
N routers for an N-element system, each receiving packets at two input
ports and transmitting them to one of two output ports. Two-way communication between processing elements and memories is achieved using a pair

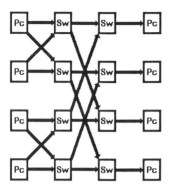

Figure 10.7 Routing network.

of tree routing networks. Although there is a rather large delay for a single-memory access, such architectures are often designed primarily for total throughput. For large systems, however, network contention can easily degrade system throughput by 75% (71), though this can be improved by introducing buffering into the network (26). (Section 6.3 of Chapter 6 discusses this extensively.)

Hypertorus

Hewitt (39) suggests a hypertorus (see Figure 10.8) interconnection—each processor being a member of *n* orthogonal ring networks, where *n* is the dimension of the hypertorus—in which all processors contain local memory and are homogeneous. Attractive features of such a scheme are that the *maximum distance* between any two processors is proportional to the *n-th* root of the number of processors, and that the interconnection structure is quite rich.

N-cube

N-cube interconnections (see Figure 10.9) have also been suggested for FP architectures (3, 11). The connectivity of an N-cube is similar to that of a

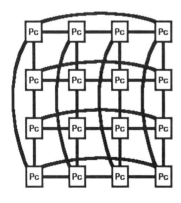

Figure 10.8 Two-dimensional hypertorus interconnection.

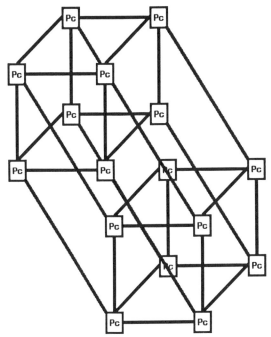

Figure 10.9 Four-cube (four-dimensional N-cube) interconnection.

routing network, but each node contains a processor with memory rather than just a switch. The maximum distance between any two processors is logarithmic in the number of processors. Akers and Krishnamurthy (2) have proposed "group graphs," a family of interconnection networks that allegedly have higher performance than even N-cubes.

Summary
Although functional programs may exhibit a fair amount of locality, it is important for a processor to have reasonably efficient access to any other processor in the system if structures are to be shared. The shared bus, tree, and ring have bottlenecks that make them less desirable candidates as *general* FP engines. One-way routing networks cannot take advantage of any locality, while the *cluster* approach has "arbitrary" locality boundaries. The N-cube and hypertorus give "gracefully degrading locality" and a rich interconnection structure, but still require the overhead of dynamic routing.

10.2.2. Method of Driving the Computation

Functions in an FP machine may be evaluated either top-down—where a function is evaluated when requested by another function that requires it as an argument—or bottom-up—where a function is evaluated as soon as its arguments are available. (Also discussed in Section 4.2 of Chapter 4.) The bottom-up approach is known as *data-driven* computation, with each function (node) in a dataflow graph being scheduled for evaluation as soon as its arguments arrive. Sequential and demand-driven evaluation are top-down—the arguments of function are not evaluated until a request is made that the function itself be evaluated.

Demand-Driven Evaluation

The *demand-driven* evaluation strategy makes use of the fact that *call-by-value* and *call-by-name* always return the same value in functional program (with *call-by-name* actually possessing better termination properties). A function's arguments are passed by name, and each is evaluated—again in a demand-driven fashion—the first time its value is needed; subsequent references to the argument use the already-evaluated form. This results in *unreduced* or *partially reduced* structures being passed among functions as arguments, each function application performing only the reductions necessary for its own evaluation. Demand-driven evaluation was used by Abrams (1) in his APL machine, and has been used in many implementations since. It is also known as *lazy evaluation* (38) or *call-by-need* (66, 91).

Demand-driven evaluation generally introduces a fair amount of overhead. When a structure element is accessed, it must be determined whether it has already been reduced; if not, additional computation may be required. In a multiprocessor environment, several concurrent processes may simultaneously need the same structure to be reduced, requiring the synchronization and/or blocking (17). The designers of Poplar note that in the cases where all elements of a structure were eventually required, lazy evaluation slowed programs in their (uniprocessor) implementation by a factor of about two (64). In a multiprocessor system, communication and synchronization overhead may cause this factor to be even higher.

The advantages of the demand-driven evaluation include the potential for eliminating a vast amount of computation by evaluating only what is necessary for computing the result, and the handling of infinite list structures in a natural way (28). The infinite list of positive integer perfect squares, for example, may be expressed as

SquareList: 1

where *SquareList* is defined as

$SquareList = Square \; \square \; (SquareList \circ (Plus \; 1))$

where "$\square$" is a right-associative list construction operator (analogous to "cons" in Lisp). If the third element of the list is needed, lazy evaluation can invoke *SquareList* and *Square* until the third element is reduced:

SquareList: 1 → (*Square*: 1) □ (*SquareList*: 2)

→ (*Square*: 1) □ (*Square*: 2) □ (*SquareList*: 3)

→ (*Square*: 1) □ (*Square*: 2) □ (*Square*: 3) □ (*SquareList*: 4)

→ (*Square*: 1) □ (*Square*: 2) □ 9 □ (*SquareList*: 4)

Whether lazy evaluation *may* be used—or *must* be used—depends on the semantics of the particular functional language being implemented.

Data-Driven Evaluation
A data-driven system incurs relatively little time overhead, with each operator node remaining inactive until *fired*—that is, when all its inputs have arrived. Parallelism is thus inhibited only by direct data dependencies; it is not inhibited because the result of a computation is not needed, as in demand-driven evaluation. Potential problems that appear in data driven systems are:

- Too much parallelism might be generated. Memory could become swamped with partial results that are not yet used, causing deadlock. Decisions about suspending processes are more difficult because control passes from the bottom up.
- It is not possible to evaluate *structures* in a *lazy* manner because a dataflow node only deals with fully evaluated structures; conceptually infinite structures therefore cannot be represented as data entities. Weng (96) applied the *stream* construct (54) to dataflow computers, allowing conceptually infinite structures to be produced by sending them through data flow nodes one element at a time. This requires the user/compiler to deal with two disjoint representations of the same concept: *structures*, which can be manipulated efficiently, and *streams*, which must be manipulated serially but can represent infinite objects.
- In a purely data-driven system, all three subexpressions of a conditional statement would be evaluated in parallel, causing unnecessary computation to be performed. In practice, *switch* and *merge* nodes are inserted into the data paths of a conditional execution to delay the execution of the *then* or *else* expressions until after the condition is evaluated (24). This amounts to lazy evaluation at the top level of a conditional expression, demonstrating that lazy evaluation can occur among function arguments—but not for structure elements—in a purely data-driven system. For this reason, a number of data-driven systems (3, 8) have introduced an element of demand-drive for structure elements.

In this example, a data-driven system would evaluate *SquareList* :1 completely before its result is passed to the node that uses the third element, requiring an infinite amount of computation. (See Chapter 9 for a detailed description of a data-driven architecture, along with examples of execution and analysis.)

Sequential Evaluation

The power and efficiency of sequential evaluation (in terms of both overhead and total computation) is closer to data-driven evaluation than to demand-driven. Treleaven et al. (83) argue that sequential evaluation is computationally equivalent to data-driven evaluation because both completely evaluate arguments before calling a function. Sequential evaluation differs from data-driven evaluation in that it is top-down, so parallelism is more easily inhibited. There may be, however, more overhead because control must pass down the "computation graph" before results are passed up; in a data-driven scheme, the data elements (at the bottom of the computation graph) flow up the graph. Additionally, parallelism is not as natural to express in the sequential model.

Summary

Demand-driven evaluation requires more overhead than data-driven evaluation, but allows better control of parallelism, more selective evaluation, and a natural way of handling infinite structures. Data-driven evaluation is more efficient locally, but its "good performance" is limited to a narrower spectrum of computations—namely, those that are data intensive and do not "blow up" when maximal parallelism is invoked. Sequential evaluation is similar to data-driven evaluation, but parallelism cannot be expressed as naturally.

10.2.3. Representation of Program Structures

Several methods have been proposed for representing programs and data in an FP system. The most popular seems to be the use of graph or list structures, although a number of architectures use other representations for either or both.[3]

Program Representation and Execution Method

The representation of the program depends largely on the method used for program evaluation:

- *Sequential execution.* In a (traditional) sequential program, code and data are separated, and instructions are executed sequentially; code can be considered an active agent that transforms the passive data. This method of execution is often used when the source language is quasifunctional.

---

[3] The use of list structures as program and data representation was introduced by McCarthy in the Lisp language. He considers having both program and data structures represented in the same way to be one of Lisp's great strengths (61).

- *Dataflow.* In this case, the data elements can be considered the active agent, moving through the "code graph" as it is transformed into the final result. The code representation is a dataflow graph, possibly augmented by auxiliary dataflow graphs that represent user-defined functions.
- *Reduction.* A reduction machine takes the view that the *source-and-input* and *output* are merely two different forms of the same object, the output being the *reduced* form of the original program and input. An *object* in a reduction system is a structure, the base elements of which are atoms and functions; a *reduced object* is one in which all base elements are atoms. The reduction process, then, consists of applying transformations to an object until it is in reduced form. Many reduction machines use graphs to represent structures and user-defined functions, although strings are sometimes used. Primitive functions—and sometimes even user-defined functions—are generally represented in machine code.

Traditional Machine Code
Several processors use traditional machine code for machine language (1, 34). Many are uniprocessors that are microcoded for improved performance of quasifunctional programs. However, several designs for pure-reduction architectures have been proposed that use machine language (47, 53). Generally, the purpose of such compilation is to decrease overhead at the expense of reducing the potential for fine-grained parallelism.

Graph-structured Program Representation
Most of the current and proposed functional machines use some form of graph or list structure to represent the program, normally either list-structured machine code (reduction graph), a combinator graph, or a dataflow graph.

    Graph-structured machine code, often used in interpretive Lisp systems, is a variation of sequential code in which a graph structure is used to represent the program's structure. The machine executes instructions by traversing the list structure rather than by using a program counter. Reduction machines also use graphs of this form, but the mode of execution differs. In the former case, the environment is kept in a separate structure such as a display or association list, while in the latter case, the data becomes intermingled with the program as function definitions are inserted during the graph transformation.

    A combinator graph is a version of the source program in which all variable and function references have been removed by applying combinator transformations (16). Turner (84) developed an interpreter that reduces combinator graphs; this prompted several hardware combinator-reduction designs, including SKIM (14), Norma (76), and the G-Machine (53) (see Section 10.3.1). Analysis by Jones (45) suggests that combinator reduction generally outperforms lamda-reduction.

A *dataflow graph* is similar to list-structured machine code with its pointers reversed to reflect bottom-up execution. The classical dataflow program consists of a static graph that transforms data elements as they pass through, recursive programs not being representable (43). To allow recursive functions, the MIT Tagged Token Dataflow Architecture (3) and Manchester dataflow machine (8) replace a *function node* with a copy of its definition whenever it is invoked, each copy having a *label* to identify it. (Chapter 9 gives examples of dataflow (graph) programs.)

Token-String Program Representation
Berkling and Magó (7, 58) have proposed reduction machines that represent an expression by a string. The job of the processor(s) is to recognize patterns that can be reduced, then to reduce them. Berkling's uniprocessor system evaluates Polish prefix expressions using a stack, while Magó's tree-structured machines groups data segments by associating each token in the string with a nesting level.

Data Representation Issues
The manner in which data is represented and accessed in a machine has a great bearing on the efficiency of a program. For accessing a structure, it is desirable to have the *random access* efficiency that an array representation would provide. On the other hand, data manipulations like concatenation and transposition—generally faster on list-structured data—should also be efficient.

Depending on the representation used, the question of whether to use monolithic data structures or pointers must also be resolved. A policy of always copying whole structures does not appear to be a good idea if large amounts of data are involved.

Methods of Representing Data
Traditionally, functional and quasifunctional systems have represented structures as linked linear lists of substructures. Although this has the advantage that many structure-manipulation operations can be done quickly, *random access* to a structure element takes linear time. Another alternative, typically used in imperative languages, is to represent structures as arrays, allowing fast random access, but having the disadvantages that operations such as insertion take linear time and that memory can become fragmented when data blocks differ in size.

Some systems (34) use both lists and arrays under programmer control, giving the programmer some of the "best of both worlds" at the expense of requiring him to be concerned with another "programming detail." This method still does not solve the problem if a single structure must have both types of operations performed on it.

It has been suggested that a tree be used to represent linear structures

(33, 48), allowing most access and manipulation operations to be performed in logarithmic time. This approach has the disadvantage that the complexity of many simple access and data manipulation operations is increased, especially if the tree is required to remain balanced. Additional advantages of using a tree are that nondestructive updating of a structure can be performed in logarithmic time, and that reductions applying an associative operator can be performed in logarithmic time on a parallel architecture; a list structure requires linear time simply to access the elements in a list.

Some architectures represent all structures as token strings. This has the disadvantage that random access can be efficient only for the lowest-level structures, other data manipulation operations being expensive. An advantage, in a multiprocessor system with distributed memory, is that storage management can be simplified, as each processor can maintain its own address space.

Copying Structures

Trade-offs exist between *copying pointers* and *copying data* strategies in multiprocessor systems (69). Copying large data structures among processors can be expensive in terms of time, bus contention, and memory utilization if only a few elements of a structure are needed. On the other hand, copying data incurs less overhead if all the data are eventually going to be used, and allows storage management to be performed at the individual processor level.

The decision whether to copy data or pointers is an instance of a general problem in FP systems: the program is written at a high enough level that the programmer is freed from making—and the system is required to make—the decision. In an imperative program, the copying of data or pointers is generally specified explicitly.

Dennis (22) suggested a hybrid scheme in which a pointer is cached in any processor to which it is copied, effectively building a copy of the structure in the remote processor as it is accessed. (Such caching is perfectly safe on a functional machine because a structure is never modified once it is created.) In the case where the remote processor has the only reference to a structure, it gradually migrates toward the remote processor; accessed portions of the structure in the local processor are reclaimed by the storage manager. To reduce communication overhead, pointers (or atoms) might be sent in groups rather than singly.

Storage Management

When the pointers are used to implement structures, it is necessary to reclaim storage that has become unreferenceable. Referencing counting is often used when graphs are known to contain no cycles. Otherwise, a strategy such as marking or copying is generally employed. Friedman and Wise (30) have shown that when the graph cycles are created only by the language system—not by the programs written in the language—reference counting technique can be modified so that cyclic structures are caught. Deb (21) has discovered an algorithm that combines reference counts and local graph-searching, that also locates cyclic structures.

Although cycles are not necessary in data graphs—a purely functional langauge has no destructive operators—the optimization of certain graph representations can introduce cyclic list structures (17, 84). In such cases, any additional garbage-collection overhead and complexity must be weighed against the increased efficiency of structure access.

The drawbacks of a reference-count strategy are that space is taken for a count field in each structure and that counts must be updated when pointers are copied or deleted. The advantage is that space can often be recovered more quickly and that reference counting is more easily performed asynchronously.

Halstead and Ward (35, 92) suggested a storage-management strategy that uses *reference trees,* data structures linking together all references to a particular object in the system. Their approach allows garbage collection to occur on a local processor basis only, while finding global cyclic list structures through a strategy of migrating connected nodes to a common processor.

A popular method of decreasing storage-reclamation overhead on uni-processors is to build a second "storage-management" processor (53, 76, 97). In the G-Machine (53), for example, the main processor is responsible only for notifying the storage processor when a pointer is copied or over-written, or when a function call occurs. All other storage management—including the maintenance of a hardware queue of free nodes that is used by a primitive "allocate node" instruction—is handled by the hardware.

Magó's machine (58) necessarily approaches storage management in a different manner because there are no pointers; the problem in this case is what to do when the leaves of the subtree are about to overflow, full. The method employed to alleviate the problem is to shift computations across the leaves of the tree; this is rather expensive if the amount of data and the distance to shift is large. If the entire tree becomes full, some computations are suspended, stored in secondary memory, and restarted at a later time.

10.2.4. Parallelism Issues

Design decisions about process communication, load balancing, control of parallelism, and other software issues very substantially among multiprocessor FP systems. Although many systems are limited by the underlying architecture—a tree machine would not make good use of a global process list because efficient execution on a tree machine depends greatly on locality of reference (46), for example—there are generally many variations to consider.

Many multiprocessor FP machines have a fine grain of parallelism, with every node in the program graph represented by a process containing a small amount of state. (Granularity of parallelism is also discussed in Section 4.4 of Chapter 4.) A process node in the Dennis dataflow machine (23, 24) contains four words: an opcode, two data words, and the name of the successor instruction. Each node in the *ALICE* reduction machine (15, 17) contains six fields: its name, the function name, argument list pointers, process state information, a reference count, and signal list for blocked processes. On such machines, a process tends to be active for a short period of time, performing a simple transformation.

Other methods of defining granularity include:

- Each node acting as a uniprocessor, reducing its own portion of the graph. When parallelism is desired (e.g., due to a function needing two operands evaluated), a new node may be created to perform the collateral evaluation (29).
- Each data item (as well as each operator) acting as a process (39, 58).
- Requiring the user to program parallelism explicitly (82).
- Reducing the overhead of fine-grained parallelism by grouping several reduction nodes together and executing it as a single von Neumann process (47, 53).

Although fine-grain parallelism is conceptually simple, it can lead to a great deal of process management and communication overhead. In particular, as the grain of parallelism becomes finer, less "intelligence" can be applied in making scheduling decisions. Fine-grain parallelism also generally leads to better load balancing (11). Again, this must be weighed against the increased overhead cost.

Mapping of Processes Onto the Hardware
The mapping of processes onto a machine's processors involves attempting to attain several (sometimes conflicting) goals. On the one hand, it is desirable to keep a process close to its data and to keep communicating processes close together. On the other hand, work should be shifted from overloaded processors to underloaded processors. This problem is compounded when the grain of parallelism is fine, and it is therefore not cost-effective to spend much computing time deciding where to execute a process.

Simple strategies at opposite ends of the spectrum are the uniprocessor approach in which all processes and data are kept in the same processor—clearly unacceptable in a multiprocessor system—and keeping a global list of processes from which an idle processor can choose a process to execute. The latter strategy spreads the workload evenly over all processors, but takes no advantage of locality.

Dataflow machines at MIT (24) and Manchester (94) use routing networks in which the data (packets) and processors are separated. Locality is not an issue in process mapping on these systems because an instruction travels the same distance, once around the routing network, regardless of which processor it "uses."

Friedman and Wise (29) propose a strategy, called *colonel and sergeants,* that also uses a global process list. One process, the *colonel,* begins reducing the graph in *normal* order—that is, performing depth-first traversal, visiting the leftmost son first. When the colonel reaches a point where parallelism could be invoked, a *sergeant* (if available) begins the secondary computation. The pending processes that are "close" to the colonel have the highest priority, so locality tends to be maintained in the sense that most processors in the system are working "close to one another."

A compromise between the *global list* and *uniprocessor* approaches involves the use of local lists of processes, either shared by a group of processors or unique to each processor. The *ZAPP* system (11) uses the latter approach, but allows a processor to "steal" a pending process from a neighboring processor when its own process list becomes empty. This strategy encourages processes to migrate to neighboring processors, and allows trees of processes to spread out all over the system while ensuring that no process is more than one processor away from its immediate offspring. The *Rediflow* system (47, 51) uses a similar strategy, employing a "pressure model" to balance processor load among neighbors.

The tree architectures generally map the process tree directly onto the processor tree, resulting in a great deal of process locality. In AMPS (46), each leaf processor has its own list of pending processes, while in Magó's machine (58), each atomic symbol resides in a unique leaf processor; symbols are mapped onto the sequence of leaf processors in the order in which they occur in the expression.

Invoking and Controlling Parallelism

Because functional programs tend to contain a great deal of implicit parallelism, the problem can arise that the system becomes swamped with processes. Another problem with excess concurrency is that it is possible that all memory might become tied up holding intermediate results for computations that are in progress, thereby creating a deadlock situation.

The conservative approach, of course, is never to invoke parallelism; this can be done on reduction machines by performing a *normal-order reduction* order—traversing the reduction tree in a depth-first manner, visiting the leftmost son first. A common strategy is to invoke parallelism only on *strict* operators and to refrain from invoking it for *non-strict* operators.[4]

---

[4] A *strict* operator is one that requires all its arguments to be completely evaluated before it is applied; a *non-strict* operator contains at least one argument that need not be evaluated before it is applied. *If-then-else* is generally non-strict: if the first argument is true (false), the third (second) argument is never evaluated. *Cons* may or may not be strict, depending upon the semantics of the programming language.

Maximal concurrency, of course, is obtained by evaluating expressions *eagerly*—invoking parallelism even for arguments of non-strict operators. While such a strategy is optimal given an infinite number of processors, it is likely to cause a great deal of wasted computation, slowing down a system of finite capacity.

Systems that perform *eager evaluation* therefore generally constrain it in some way. The *AMPS* and *ALICE* systems (15, 46) allow the programmer to state explicitly whether a non-strict operator is to be evaluated eagerly. *ALICE* additionally constrains eagerness by allowing it only when the compiler can determine that the eager computation will terminate (66).

The system of Friedman and Wise (29) invokes parallelism whenever there is an idle processor available. This may require that a stray process be purged, in the case where it can be determined that the process is performing an unnecessary or divergent computation.

In the *ZAPP* (11) and *Rediflow* (47) systems, the amount of parallelism is determined by the processor load. Breadth-first expansion—which encourages parallelism—is employed when load is light, depth-first when it is heavy. This is implemented in *ZAPP* on a local basis by maintaining a list of processes—each ordered according to its depth in the computation tree—and giving shallow processes priority over deep ones only when the load is light. The amount of *eager* evaluation is constrained by allowing *unsafe* computations—computations that may never terminate—a limit on the amount of processing that they are allowed to perform (79). A process may be terminated when it exhausts its "budget," presumably leaving behind a partially reduced graph that becomes subject to garbage collection; alternatively, the budget may be extended if system load is light enough, allowing the unsafe computation to continue, again with a (revised) bound on its computation time.

On data-driven machines, the evaluation of arguments is performed before the operator node is encountered, making it difficult to use properties of the operator in dynamically constraining eager evaluation. One possible solution would be to introduce top-down *demand tokens* (20), allowing parallelism to be controlled more finely at the expense of introducing more overhead. Another is a *throttling mechanism* suggested by Bohm, Gurd, and Sargeant (8) (see Section 10.3.3).

Deadlock Avoidance

The problem of deadlock in FP multiprocessing systems seems to be more easily solved in demand-driven than in data-driven systems because parallelism is more easily constrained. *ZAPP*'s strategy (11) of basing their expansion (depth-first vs. breadth-first) on system load is part of their method of deadlock prevention. If the assumption is made that there is always enough memory in any processor to evaluate an expression in *normal order,* this strategy does in fact prevent deadlock by forcing each processor to act as a uniprocessor, evaluating an expression in normal order, when system load becomes extremely high. Such an assumption is valid in cases where the computation tree remains small.

Another possible approach in concurrent FP systems is to wait until deadlock occurs, then to free some memory by selecting certain process trees for purging. Because FP computations have no side effects, purging a partially completed computation means only that it may have to be recomputed later. In the extreme case, the computation tree would be pruned to the extent that a single process is active and is performing normal-order reduction.

10.2.5. Additional Optimizations

In Section 10.2.2, it was seen that *lazy evaluation* can potentially increase the efficiency of a functional program by reducing the amount of unnecessary computation. This section discusses two other dynamic optimizations that have been suggested. Compile-time versions of each are also possible.

Avoiding Unnecessary Data Manipulations

Operations such as transposition, rotation, and slicing can involve a great deal of data manipulation, yet occur frequently in functional programs. In designing his APL machine, Abrams proposed the use of a technique called *beating* (1), in which certain data-manipulation operations are implemented by performing transformations on *array descriptors* rather than on arrays themselves. An array transposition might be implemented by exchanging indices in the array descriptor, for example.

It is not clear whether the generalization of this technique to linear list structures would be effective because the effectiveness of *beating* is diminished in the absence of *random access* to structure elements. In systems where arrays—or other structures with efficient random access—are present, optimizations similar to beating may be worthwhile.

Avoiding Redundant Computations

A potential source of inefficiency in functional programs is that their straightforward execution often causes the same computation to be performed repeatedly (50). For example, although most evaluators would evaluate *Transpose*:x only once in

[$Fcn1$, $Fcn2$] ∘ $Transpose$: x

it would probably be necessary for a compiler to discover the common expression in

[$Fcn1$ ∘ $Transpose$, $Fcn2$ ∘ $Transpose$]: x

Even more difficult is the recognition that [Fib: 2] and [Fib: 1] (dynamically)

occur more than once in

Fib: 4 → *Plus* ∘ [*Fib*: 3, *Fib*: 2]

Fib: 3 → *Plus* ∘ [*Fib*: 2, *Fib*: 1]

Fib: 2 → *Plus* ∘ [*Fib*: 1, *Fib*: 0]

In this particular case, dynamic recognition of common expressions could reduce an exponential algorithm to a linear one.

Most FP systems share the result of the common computation in the first case, and could be augmented to do so in the second. Doing so in the third case probably requires some type of result-catching, although combinator reductions sometimes recognize these in simple cases (not in *Fib*, however). As a result, the default strategy for result-sharing tends be sharing in the first two cases but recomputing in the third.

The policy of saving the result if the common expression is easy to detect, and recomputing it otherwise is not always the most effective. The *Fib* example demonstrates that it is sometimes desirable to detect "difficult" common expressions. Convesely, it may sometimes be desirable to ignore easily detected common expressions. Consider the evaluation of an expression in which a list is traversed in different orders by two functions:

[*Trasverses-forward, Traverses-backward*] ∘ *From-1-to-1000000*

The cost of recomputing the common function *From-1-to-1000000* may be relatively small, while keeping its value in memory would use a large number (1000000) of cells. If *lazy* evaluation and an *appropriate* method of representing structures were used, the necessary number of cells might be reduced to a handful.

The profitability of sharing a computation thus seems to be somewhat independent of the ease of common-expression recognition. The only way of sharing results in a general manner appears to through caching (63), which introduces a number of new issues to consider (50):

- What results should be cached? If the result of every intermediate computation is cached, it seems that memory could be quickly swamped. If not everything is cached, on what basis does one decide what to cache?
- How should the cache directory be structured? How are the cached values mapped onto the processor(s)? How much extra interprocessor traffic will be generated by cache lookup requests? Can cache lookup be made efficient enough that it does not slow up "fast" operations?
- What replacement algorithm should be used to determine what entries to purge when the cache becomes full? How much overhead does this algorithm introduce? Ideally, one would like to account for factors such as the complexity of the computation, the amount of storage it takes to cache results, the number of "recent" references, and whether there are out-

standing computations waiting for the result. It is probably not desirable, however, to spend a great deal of time performing cache management.

- Should *easily detected* common expressions be subject to the same purging strategy as cached ones, so that a function like *From-1-to-1000000* does effectively generate its elements twice if memory becomes scarce?
- Should cache lookup be done in parallel with computation? If this strategy is adopted, the process(es) performing the computation should be aborted if the cache lookup is successful.

The caching issue seems to be another instance of a potential problem because an FP language is at a higher level then an imperative language. In a typical imperative language, the programmer has explicit control over the decisions about whether a value should be saved or recomputed, basing these decisions on the complexity of the computation, the likelihood of needing to reuse the value, etc. In a functional program, such issues are generally transparent to the user, the system being responsible for deciding whether to save a value. The most practical approach thus far proposed is that the programmer be responsible for specifying which results should be cached (50).

Harbison's analysis (36) of a von Neumann architecture that caches expression values suggest that a moderately sized cache (512 entries) can significantly improve performance. Caching in a functional multiprocessor architecture is likely to be complicated, however, by the cache being distributed over the entire system and by comparisons being performed on structure values rather than scalar values and variable names.

10.3. Examples of FP Architectures

In this section, we examine in greater detail four architectures that represent widely different points in the design space of functional architectures. The first architecture is a uniprocessor combinator-reduction machine. The second is tree-structured, and performs token-string reduction. The third is a data-driven architecture in which processors communicate via a routing network. The last is a multiprocessor-reduction architecture.

All four of these architectures are experimental. In fact, only the Manchester machine has hardware implementation at this writing; the others are implemented with simulators. Nevertheless, each illustrates interesting ideas and concrete design decisions that have been made.

10.3.1. The G-Machine

The G-machine, which is being designed at the Oregon Graduate Center, is a uniprocessor combinator-reduction architecture (53). It is based on the abstract machine architecture use by Johnsson and Augustsson in the design of a compiler for a lazy, functional language; this, in turn was inspired by the combinator-reduction architecture proposed by Turner (84) and subsequent extensions by Hughes (40).

Combinator Reduction

Before describing the machine itself, we shall compare combinator-reduction architectures with the more traditional lambda-reduction architectures. In any programming language that allows variables (to represent arguments of a function, for example), it is necessary to evaluate the function in the context of an environment. The representation of the environment, and the passing of parameters during the computation, is often a significant cost of execution of a functional language (12).

Turner (84) applied a result from logic to show that any applicative program can be translated into a variable-free notation by introducing a modest number of additional constants called *combinators*. The translation process, while fairly straightforward to implement on a computer, produces an "object code" that is virtually unreadable by humans. An interpreter for such combinator code, however, can be implemented rather easily. What is required is that for each primitive (including combinators), a routine be written (or hardware be built) that performs a moderately simple graph transformation that corresponds to the semantics of the primitive.

As an example, let us define the S, K, I, B, and C combinators that were used by Turner[5]:

$$((S\ f)g)x = (f\ x)(g\ x)$$

$$(K\ x)y = x$$

$$I\ x = x$$

$$((B\ f)g)x = f(g\ x)$$

$$((C\ f)g)x = (f\ x)g$$

The combinator code for the function $foo\ x = (x + 1)(x - 1)$ is

$$foo = (S((B\ times)((C\ plus)1)))((C\ minus)1)$$

The evaluation of $foo\ 7$ would then proceed as follows:

$$((S((B\ times)((C\ plus)1)))((C\ minus)1))7$$

$$= (((B\ times)((C\ plus)1))7)(((C\ minus)1)7)$$

$$= (times(((C\ plus)1)7))(((C\ minus)1)7)$$

$$= (times((plus\ 7)1))(((C\ minus)1)7)$$

---

[5] Here, all functions are "curried"—that is, $f(x, y)$ is written $(f\ x)y$; $f(x, y, z)$ is written $((f\ x)y)z$, etc.

$= (times\ 8)((((C\ minus)1)7)$

$= (times\ 8)(((minus\ 7)1)$

$= (times\ 8)6$

$= 48$

Advantages of compiling into combinator code include:

- An elegant, efficient method of parameter passing.
- The ability to support lazy evaluation with little overhead.
- The overhead incurred when adding levels of functional abstraction is eliminated.

Object code can be produced for any program using just the S, K, and I combinators; however, the addition of more combinators greatly reduces the number of reductions that need be performed during execution. Hughes (40) proposed *super-combinators,* in which user-defined functions can be directly compiled as "primitive" combinators. This leads to a combinator-reduction machine in which execution occurs in much the same manner as in a conventional machine—by executing sequential machine instructions—except that some of the machine instructions are stack and graph-manipulation instructions.

The Design of the G-Machine

The G-machine is designed to be a programmable, graph-reduction engine. Its components include:

- A tagged, dynamically allocable list-structured memory that contains the graph being transformed.
- A stack memory (P-stack) that contains pointers to nodes in the *normal* path of the program graph.
- A concurrent memory-management processor that minimizes the overhead of storage reclamation.

During execution, the program graph is traversed, the path from the root being stored in the P-stack, which is the sole source of addresses for the G-machine's access to graph memory. Because simulations have shown that stack instructions account for 20–25% of G-code generated, the top 24 cells of the stack are cached in high-speed memory and are available to the processor in a single internal clock cycle. The P-stack is also used for storing the program counter during a function call. A second, working stack is associated with the ALU, which is of conventional design.

As mentioned, the architecture does not employ a fixed number of combinators as in Turner's model. Rather, user functions are compiled into machine code that effect similar transformations on the graph as Turner's machine would have. The advantage is that the graph need not be "interpreted," and optimizations can be performed on the code. Additionally, the designers expect to allow "unwrapped" versions of functions, which would pass their arguments in the stack registers instead of using the G-memory.

The G-memory is a collection of nodes, each containing 2 32-bit data cells, 16 reference count bits, and 8 auxiliary bits. The latter contain storage-management information, and flags that indicate whether a node is evaluated, which is necessary when lazy evaluation is employed.

Because dynamic memory allocation is of critical importance in a graph-reduction architecture, the machine has a primitive instruction that allocates a memory node. A hardware queue is used to hold a small number of free cells so that the allocation instruction can execute quickly. Storage reclamation is performed by a memory controller, which operates in parallel. The only storage-reclamation activities that are performed by main processor are notifying the memory controller when a pointer is copied or destroyed, or when a function call or return occurs.

The storage-reclamation scheme is a variation of reference counting that allows cyclic structures to be reclaimed (21). The memory controller performs two tasks. First, it modifies a node's reference count whenever a pointer is copied or destroyed. Second, it performs a storage reclamation when the G-processor executes a function return. During storage reclamation, it examines each node that had been allocated since the function call began; each node whose reference count is zero is immediately reclaimed. A local graph-traversed algorithm is applied to any nonzero nodes, which finds local cycles.

10.3.2. Magó's Tree Machine

The tree architecture of Magó and his colleagues at the Univesity of North Carolina (57, 58) was one of the first multiprocessors designed for executing functional programs (6). Illustrated here is the use of the architecture to support the execution of Backus' FP language (6). Others have proposed ways in which the architecture could be used for other languages (80).

Both the program and data are represented by token strings, which reside in the leaves. Computation consists of reductions, each being performed by one or more interior nodes that transform the leaves. Initially, the program (expression) resides in the leaf cells (L-cells) of the tree, with (at most) one symbol per node (see Figure 10.10). The expression is reduced in a bottom-up (i.e., data-driven) fashion, with the L-cells containing the data, and the interior nodes (T-cells) combining data and moving it among the L-cells and performing storage management.

The expression-string is stored in the L-cells in prefix-Polish form. In addition, each symbol in an L-cell has a number that denotes its nesting level in the expression; delimiters (e.g., parentheses) can therefore be represented without requiring a separate L-cell. There are four types of

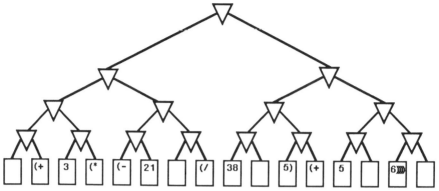

Figure 10.10 Magó's tree machine.

expressions:

- *Atomic symbols* such as integers or Booleans.
- *Primitive expressions,* whose operator (leftmost symbol) is the name of a function that is a system primitive.
- *Defined expressions,* whose operator is the name of a user-defined function.
- A *composition* of elements into a list of elements.

There are effectively two types of *primitive expressions.* One type combines data, but its result expression does not exceed the size of the original expression. An example of this type of expression would be an addition. The other type of expression is one that manipulates data, without combining it; in this case, however, the expression may grow in size. When such an application is reduced, storage management may be required to make room for the application.

Defined expressions are similar to the data-manipulation expressions; when such an application is reduced, the operator is replaced by its definition, (usually) causing the expression to grow in size.

Execution occurs in phases. The purpose of the first phase is to locate reducible applications—that is, sequences of L-cells that are unreduced expressions, but whose subexpressions have been reduced. Figure 10.11 shows an expression with two reducible applications, whose root T-cells are marked **A** and **B** respectively. Scanning to the right of the application symbol whose nesting level is *i*, one does not reach an application symbol with a nesting level greater than *i* unless there is an intervening symbol whose nesting level is less or equal to that *i*. This is done by passing information about operators and nesting-levels up the tree (see Problems, p. 448).

After the reducible applications are located, the L-cells for each are loaded with a small *microprogram,* which is loaded from an I/O T-cell (typi-

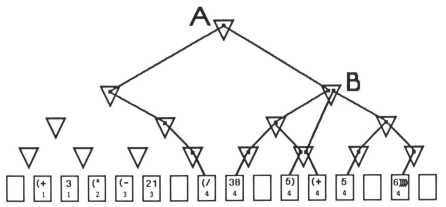

Figure 10.11 Reducible applications in Magó's tree machine.

cally, the root). The microprograms specify to each group L-cells (i.e., reducible application) the behavior necessary to implement the given operation.

The next phase is the *data movement* phase. Each reducible application is then associated with a *root* T-cell—that is, the deepest T-cell whose subnodes completely contain it. Magó has shown that each T-cell will be the root of, at most, four reducible applications (57). The execution phase consists of each L-cell of a reducible application sending its data to its root.

Once it has its data, the root of a reducible application can compute the amount of additional storage it might need; this leads to the *storage-management* phase. During this phase, tokens in the L-cells are shifted to make room for new data. The designers of this system have discovered a clever way to use the T-cells to shift an arbitrary amount of data in time that is proportional to the distance the data moves, but is independent of the amount of data shifted. When data is "shifted" off the end of the L-cell array, it is temporarily stored in secondary memory.

Once space has been made for new data, it is broadcast down the T-cells; each L-cell listens for the broadcast of its root T-cell and updates itself when appropriate. At this point, the tree is ready for another cycle, in which new reducible applications are located and executed.

This architecture has a couple of drawbacks for the general execution of functional programs, unless suitable modifications are made. One is the bottleneck encountered when data moves up the tree. If a reducible application contains a large amount of reduced data (as would occur in the transposition of a large matrix), the amount of parallelism would be reduced as a large amount of data is funneled through single T-cell. It would be possible, however, to extend the architecture so that the T-cells near the root of the tree had a richer interconnection structure (59).

Another potential drawback is that all data is stored as token strings; there exist no pointers. Although this greatly simplifies storage management, data sharing is relatively inefficient.

10.3.3. Manchester Dataflow Machine

The Manchester dataflow machine (94, 95) is an extension of the ideas of Dennis (24, 25), whose machine contains programs that are static dataflow graphs which perform computation as tokens flow through them. For clarity, we begin by briefly describing an early version of the architecture of Dennis. (See Chapter 9 for a more detailed description.) We then discuss extensions incorporated into the Manchester machine.

In the dataflow machine of Dennis, there is (logically) a single memory element that holds representations for each instruction cell—that is, for each

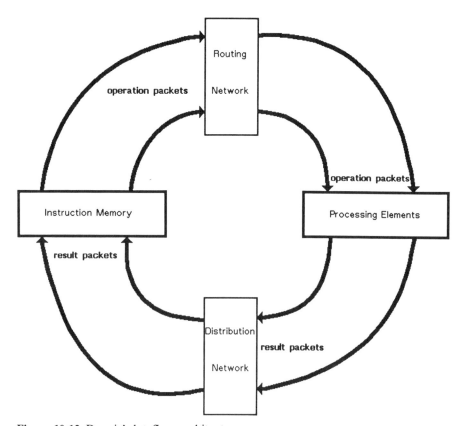

Figure 10.12 Dennis' dataflow architecture.

node in the dataflow graph. A instruction cell consists of an *operator* that specifies the computation to be performed, and one or more destination addresses that specify where the result is to be sent.

The second major component in the Dennis machine is the processing elements, which receive *instruction packets* from the instruction memory and send *result packets* back to the instructions. Processing elements and instruction cells communicate by sending data through two routing networks. One network transmits instruction packets from the instruction cells to the processing elements; the other transmits result packets back to the instruction cells. A simplified view of the architecture can be seen in Figure 10.12.

Each instruction cell contains one or more slots in which a result can be stored. When all such slots have received a result packet, the instruction cell becomes *fireable,* and is sent to a processing element; data slots in the instruction cell are then marked as "empty," and are available to receive new result packets.

As an example of the execution of a dataflow program, consider the program to compute the expression, $(i + j)*k$. The dataflow graph for such a program can be seen in Figure 10.13. Initially, the values i and j are sent to the first and second slots of the $+$ node, respectively, and the value for k is sent to the second slot of the $*$ node. The sending of i and j makes the $+$ node fireable, so an instruction packet containing the values for i and j is sent to a processing element that is capable of performing an addition. The processing element computes $i + j$, and sends the resulting value in a result packet to the first slot of the instruction packet representing the $*$ node, causing it to become fireable. An instruction packet containing the $*$ node is then sent to an instruction processor, which computes the final result. In Figure 10.13, i and k have already received their values; the computation is waiting for a value for j.

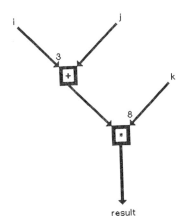

result   **Figure 10.13** A dataflow graph.

The architecture of Dennis also allows loops and conditional tests. Loops are implemented by simply making the dataflow graph cyclic; tests are implemented by a *switch node,* in which the a given result is sent to one of two possible destinations, depending on the value of a second (Boolean) input.

One of the problems with the design of Dennis is that a program must be represented by a static dataflow graph. In particular, all function calls must be expanded inline; this disallows recursive functions, except in the case where the maximum recursion depth is known at compile time. To this end, a group led by Watson and Gurd at the University of Manchester embarked on a project that would solve this problem. (Independently, a group led by Arvind at MIT is designing a similar machine (3).)

Their strategy for introducing parallelism was to represent the program by a static dataflow graph, but to allow multiple copies of a single instruction to exist simultaneously. This is implemented by marking instruction instances with a label that distinguishes the particular function invocation with which it is associated. This is implemented by inserting a *matching store* into the routing network between the processing elements and the instruction cells (see Figure 10.14). The matching store contains the "variable" portion of the instruction instance, while the *node store* contains the "constant" portion. Result packets, then, get sent to the matching store, where they are required to match on both the *instruction* and the *label.*

To maintain system integrity, unique tags must be created. This is handled by introducing a token queue into the network, which maintains a list of tokens that are no longer in use.

When a result packet arrives at the matching store, its destination instruction instance may or may not physically exist in the matching store, depending on whether it was the first packet to arrive for its destination. In order to find the instruction quickly, a parallel-hash lookup is performed on the matching store hardware; if a match is found, the packet's data is stored in the matching instruction instance. If a match is not found, a space is allocated for it.

Another aspect of the Manchester architecture that is not present in many earlier dataflow machines' designs is that it supports structured data. The implementation of structures is supported by a *structure store* that can receive messages from processing elements via a *switch unit.* The structure store performs both structure-manipulation operation and storage management.

As mentioned earlier, parallelism seems more difficult to constrain in a data-driven system. The designers of this architecture are considering a *throttling mechanism,* in which an *intelligent token queue* is used to give priority to tokens in an order that would either encourage or discourage parallelism.

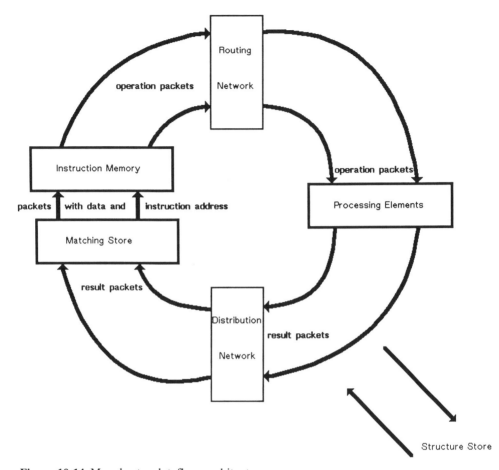

Figure 10.14 Manchester dataflow architecture.

10.3.4. ZAPP

ZAPP (11) is a proposed demand-driven reduction architecture that is configured as a binary N-cube (see Figure 10.9). Both data and program are represented by a graph/list structure. Parallelism is fine-grained; there is effectively a process for every node in the reduction graph.

The normal mode of operation on the *ZAPP* system consists of each processor working on independent computation, adding processes to its local process list as it reduces a subgraph. Thus, a small computation will likely execute completely on one processor. When a processor is underloaded, it steals processes from neighboring processors; this tends to inhibit movement of processes across the system when system load is heavy, but encourages it when system load is light. A process is not allowed to migrate more than a single processor from its parent, maintaining some degree of locality. From a software perspective, the designers consider the architecture to be a "virtual tree of processors"; in other words, the N-cube interconnection is viewed to be tree of infinite depth that is "folded upon itself." Simulations have been run for systems of up to 64 processors, although the designers envision processes of hundreds or thousands of processors.

Execution consists of processors evaluating nodes from their own process lists, suspending them when it is necessary to wait for data from other processes. Simultaneously, a processor communicates with its neighbors. Neighboring processors communicate by exchanging fixed-size packets on each *communication cycle*; a dummy packet is sent if a processor has no useful information to communicate. Typically, a communication cycle consists of a large number of machine cycles.

One of the noteworthy features of *ZAPP* is its method of controlling parallelism. Ideally, parallelism should be encouraged when system load is light and discouraged when it is heavy. This is implemented by giving the highest priority to shallow processes (according to depth in the computation tree) when load is light, and to deep processes when load is heavy. These correspond to performing computation breadth-first (which tends to spawn of many new processes) and depth-first (which is similar to uniprocessor evaluation), respectively.

Another interesting idea proposed for the architecture is that it allows subexpressions of non-strict operators to be evaluated. Such expressions would therefore not necessarily be attempted during a *normal-order* reduction because full evaluation of such expressions could cause the computation to diverge. When such a potentially divergent computation is spawned, it is allocated a "renewable budget"—an amount of computing it may apply toward the evaluation of the expression. When it exhausts its budget, it is required to request additional processor time from the system, which honors or rejects the request depending on factors such as system load.

Simulations of this architecture on several problems indicate that there is reason to be optimistic (13). For large trees, processor utilization was over 99%. Performance for problems that have a large amount of data sharing across the network remains to be seen.

10.4. Conclusions

Can machines be built that will efficiently execute functional programs? Although many architectures have been built or proposed, it has yet to be demonstrated that functional programs can be competitive with von Neumann systems. No architecture executing a purely functional language has had widespread use for solving real problems.

A major issue in answering the preceding question is the high level at which functional programs are written, which may be a blessing during programming but a curse during execution. The "system" is required to make many decisions that an imperative programmer—or his programming language—would specify explicitly on a case-by-case basis, including:

- Should data be copied or should pointers be used?
- Should results be stored and reused, or should they be recomputed?
- How should data be represented?
- When should parallelism be invoked?
- At what granularity should parallelism be invoked?
- How should processes be mapped onto processors?

For a language that is directly executed on hardware, these decisions are likely to be system-wide, and will clearly be "wrong" sometimes. Although it is possible for a compiler to make intelligent decisions in some instances, many questions are yet to be answered in this area as well (90). Optimizations involving parallelism appear to be particularly difficult for a compiler to perform as they often involve making use of dynamic information; difficult problems still remain in this area even for imperative languages (78). On the other hand, other issues, such as synchronizing multiple list traversals, do seem well-suited to compile-time analysis.

Allowing a compiler to make decisions about the manner in which data is represented also has ramifications with respect to separate compilation: What happens when two separately compiled programs expect data to be in different forms?

10.4.1. Desirable Elements of an FP Machine

What features would an "ideal" FP machine have? Based on the discussion in this chapter, the following would be desirable:

- A multiprocessor system with a rich interconnection structure.

  A multiprocessor allows the system to take advantage of the inherent concurrency in functional programs. A rich interconnection of processors seems to be essential if there is any hope of spreading work throughout the system while maintaining moderately efficient access to remote data.

- Representation of list structures balanced trees, if this does not add too much complexity to the system.

  Although a tree is a more complex object than an array or list, the efficiency with which random access, structure manipulation, and destructive updating can be performed makes it an attractive candidate for data representation. This is particularly true if the compiler does not decide the type of data structure to be used.

- Hardware support for demand-driven execution.

Although demand-driven execution can often speed up a computation substantially, it has generated a great deal of overhead on currently built systems; hardware support to decrease this overhead is desirable.

- Hardware support for low-overhead process creation.

It is highly desirable that parallel execution be the norm, not the exception, when a functional program is being evaluated. If the mechanism for invoking parallelism is not efficient, program performance will be unacceptably slow.

- Hardware support for storage management.

The extensive use of structures in functional programs makes hardware support for storage management very attractive. If hardware/firmware support for storage management is not available, system overhead is likely to be markedly higher.

Of the architectures currently proposed, none meets all of these criteria; most lack a rich interconnection structure or support for demand-driven execution. Of those remaining, *ZAPP* and *Rediflow* are the only architectures whose processor interconnection and process-to-processor mapping methodology are well specified.

10.4.2. Open Questions

The question of how efficiently functional programs can run on hardware is still largely unanswered. The following are some key issues that have been raised—but not fully answered—in the literature.

Compiler Techniques
A major issue, which has not been addressed here, is that of compiler optimization. How much can program transformation and data structure selection improve program performance? Can compiler techniques be as effective when the program is to run on a multiprocessor?

Interconnection Structure
What processor interconnections are most effective? N-cube and hypertorus machines have rich interconnection structures, yet have the potential to take advantage of locality. Given that pieces of a structure are likely to be distributed across the system, how much does locality buy? If not much, a routing network—or a routing network of clusters—may be more appropriate.

Controlling Parallelism
How should parallelism be controlled? Data-driven architectures seem to be at a disadvantage here, but even those with demand drive have not dem-

onstrated that the problem is solved. The method employed in *ZAPP* (11) and *Rediflow* (47) looks promising, but is largely untested.

Granularity of Parallelism
Many proposed FP machines have a very fine grain of parallelism. Can hardware be built to support this efficiently, or will process creation and synchronization costs be unacceptably high? Perhaps a somewhat coarser granularity is more appropriate.

Tree Representation of Lists
Can lists be effectively represented by balanced trees? Are the logarithmic times for operations such as random access and insertion efficient enough that it is not necessary to consider using arrays and lists? How much overhead is involved in keeping trees balanced?

Caching
How big a problem is the recomputation of results? Are the current methods for handling it adequate? If not, can an effective caching scheme be developed?

10.4.3. Summary

There is promising evidence that programmer productivity can be increased for some classes of programs by the use of functional programming. Additionally, functional languages seem especially suited to parallel architectures because they lack side effects, giving rise to the possibility that functional programs may run more quickly than their imperative counterparts unless the imperative programmer is willing to specify parallelism explicitly.

The efficient execution of functional programs on uniprocessor and multiprocessor systems is currently under active investigation. As of this writing, too few FP multiprocessors and compilers have been completely implemented, hence it is not possible to answer the question until more experimentation is done.

10.4.4. Further Reading

Backus (6) gives a good introduction to FP languages, and makes a strong case for considering their use. The collection of papers edited by Darlington, Henderson, and Turner (18) considers many functional programming issues in greater depth. Turner (84) gives an excellent introduction to the use of combinators in implementing functional languages. Particularly informative articles on individual architectures have been written by Magó (57, 58), Dennis (24), Cripps, Field, and Reeve (15), Arvind et al. (3), Watson and

Gurd (95), Keller and Lin (47), Burton, Sleep, and Huntbach (11, 13), and Kieburtz (53). A discussion of lazy evaluation is given by Friedman and Wise (28).

Problems

1. Perform combinator reductions for the program $((S \; times)((B(plus \; 1))I))4$, which computes $foo \; 4$, where $foo \; x = x*(1 + x)$.
2. The entries for the matching store in the Manchester dataflow machine (logically) vary in size because operators differ in the number of input operands they have. Physically the entries are (presumably) of the same size; this limits the number of arguments a user function can have. Propose a method (hardware, software, or a combination) of avoiding this restriction.
3. In the Manchester dataflow machine, why is it unnecessary for result packets whose destinations are unary functions to be entered into the matching store? Could currying, which makes all functions unary, be used to obviate the need for the matching store?
4. Show that a T-cell in Magó's machine can be the root of, at most, four reducible applications.
5. Formulate a parallel algorithm (one that runs on all T-cells, another that runs on all L-cells) for Magó's machine that finds all reducible applications.
6. Consider a caching scheme where hashing is used to ensure that primitive objects are unique—i.e., there is, at most, one instance of any given primitive in the system. The hash value of a "cons" cell can then be computed as a function of the hash value of its arguments; thus, structures can be made to be unique as well. This would allow even "hard-to-detect" caching problems like Fibonacci to be detected automatically. What potential problems might be encountered? Consider an implementation of this in light of a finite amount of memory, garbage collection, cyclic structures, and lazy evaluation.

References

1. Abrams PS: *An APL Machine,* PhD Thesis, Stanford University, Feb. 1970.
2. Akers SB, Krishnamurthy B: Group graphs as interconnection networks. *Proc. 14th International Conference on Fault-Tolerant Computing,* 1984, pp. 422–427.
3. Arvind, Culler DE, Iannucci RA, et al: The tagged token dataflow architecture. Technical Report, MIT, 1985.
4. Arvind, Gostelow KP, Plouffe W: An asynchronous programming language and computing machine. Technical Report 114a, University of California at Irvine, Dec. 1978.

5. Arvind and Brock JD: Streams and managers. Computation Structure Group Memo 217, MIT, June 1982.

6. Backus J: Can programming be liberated from the von Neumann style? A functional style and its algebra of programs. *Communications of the ACM*, 21(8), pp. 613–641, Aug. 1978.

7. Berkling KJ: Reduction languages for reduction machines. *Proc. International Symposium on Computer Architecture*, Houston, Jan. 1975, pp. 133–140, IEEE.

8. Bohm APW, Gurd JR, Sargeant J: Hardware and software enhancement of the Manchester dataflow machine. *Proc. IEEE COMPCON*, Feb. 1985, pp. 420–423.

9. Burstall RM, Darlington J: A transformation system for developing recursive programs. *Journal of the ACM*, Vol. 24, No. 1, Jan. 1977.

10. Burstall RM, MacQueen DB, Sannella DT: HOPE: An experimental applicative language. *Lisp Conference Record*, Stanford University, 1980, pp. 136–143.

11. Burton FW, Sleep MR: Executing functional programs on a virtual tree of processors. *Proc. Conference on Functional Programming Languages and Computer Architecture*, ACM 1981, pp. 187–194.

12. Burton FW: Controlling speculative computation in a parallel functional programming language. *Proc. Fifth International Conference on Distributed Computing Systems*, May 1985.

13. Burton FW, Huntbach MM: Virtual tree machines. *IEEE Trans. on Computers*, Vol. C-33, No. 3, March 1984, pp. 278–280.

14. Clarke TJW, Gladstone PJS, MacLean CD, Norman AC: SKIM—The S, K, I reduction machine. *Lisp Conference Record*, Stanford University, 1980, pp. 128–135.

15. Cripps MD, Field AJ, Reeve MJ: The design and implementation of ALICE: A parallel graph reduction machine. *Byte*, Vol. 10, No. 8, Aug. 1985.

16. Curry HB, Feys R: Combinator Logic, North Holland, Amsterdam, 1958.

17. Darlington J, Reeve M: ALICE—a multi-processor reduction machine for the parallel evaluation of applicative languages. *Proc. Conference on Functional Programming Languages and Computer Architecture*, ACM 1981.

18. Darlington J, Henderson P, Turner DA: Functional Programming and its Applications. An Advanced Course, Cambridge University Press, 1982.

19. Davis AL: The architecture and system method of DDMI: A recursively structured data-driven machine. *Proc. International Symposium on Computer Architecture*, April 1978, pp. 210–215.

20. Davis AL, Keller RM: Data flow program graphs. *IEEE Computer*, Vol. 15, No. 2, Feb. 1982, pp. 26–41.

21. Deb A: An efficient garbage collector for graph machines. CS/E Technical Report 84-003, Oregon Graduate Center, 1984.

22. Dennis JB: First version of a data-flow procedure language. In Lecture Notes in Computer Science, Springer Verlag, New York, 1974.

23. Dennis JB: The varieties of data flow computers. *Proc. International Conference on Distributed Computing Systems*, IEEE, 1979, pp. 430–439.

24. Dennis JB: Data flow supercomputers. *IEEE Computer*, Vol. 13, No. 11, Nov. 1980, pp. 48–56.

25. Dennis JB, Gao GR, Todd KW: Modeling the weather with a data flow supercomputer. *IEEE Trans. on Computers*, Vol. C-33, No. 7, July 1984, pp. 592–603.

26. Dias DM, Jump JR: Analysis and simulation of buffered delta networks. *IEEE Trans. on Computers,* Vol. C-30, No. 4, April 1981, pp. 273–282.

27. Fateman RJ: Reply to an editorial. *SigSAM Bulletin,* vol. 25, March 1973, pp. 9–11.

28. Friedman DP, Wise DS: Cons should not evaluate its arguments. In Michaelson and Miller (eds): *Automata, Languages, and Programming,* Edinburgh University Press, pp. 257–284.

29. Friedman DP, Wise DS: Aspects of applicative programming for parallel processing. *IEEE Trans. on Computers,* Vol. C-27, No. 4, April 1978, pp. 289–296.

30. Friedman DP, Wise DS: Reference counting can manage the circular environments of mutual recursion. Information Processing Letters, Vol. 8, No. 1, Jan. 1979, pp. 41–45.

31. Goldberg A, Robson D: Smalltalk-80: The Language and its Implementation. Addison-Wesley, Reading, MA 1983.

32. Gordon M, Milner R, Morris L, et al: A metalanguage for interactive proof in LCF. *Proc. ACM Symposium on the Principles of Programming Languages,* 1978, pp. 119–130.

33. Gostelow KP, Thomas RE: A view of dataflow. *Proc. National Computer Conference,* Vol. 48, AFIPS 1979, pp. 629–636.

34. Greenblatt R, et al: Lisp machine progress report. A.I. Memo 444, Massachusetts Institute of Technology, Aug. 1977.

35. Halstead RH Jr: Object management on distributed systems. *Proc. Texas Conference on Computing Systems,* University of Houston, 1978, pp. 7.7–7.14.

36. Harbison SP: A computer architecture for the dynamic optimization of high-level language programs. Ph.D. Thesis, Carnegie-Mellon University, Sept. 1980.

37. Haynes LS, Lau RL, Siewiorek DP, Mizell DW: A survey of highly parallel computing. *IEEE Computer,* Vol. 15, No. 1, Jan. 1982, pp. 9–24.

38. Henderson P, Morris JH: A lazy evaluator. *Proc. ACM Symposium on the Principles of Programming Languages,* ACM 1976, pp. 95–103.

39. Hewitt C: The apiary network architecture for knowledgeable systems. *Lisp Conference Record,* Stanford University, 1980, pp. 107–117.

40. Hughes RJM: Super-combinators: A new implementation method for applicative languages. *Conference Record of the 1982 ACM Symposium on Lisp and Functional Programming,* Carnegie-Mellon University, Aug. 1982, pp. 1–10.

41. Ingalls DHH: Design principles behind Smalltalk. *Byte,* Vol. 6, No. 8, Aug. 1981, pp. 286–298.

42. Jenks RD, Griesmer JH: Editor's comment. *SigSAM Bulletin,* No. 24, Oct. 1972, pp. 2–3.

43. Johnson D, et al: Automatic partitioning of programs in multiprocessor systems. *Proc. IEEE COMPCON,* 1980, pp. 175–178.

44. Jones AK, Chansler RJ Jr, Durham I, et al: Programming issues raised by a multiprocessor. *Proc. IEEE,* Vol. 66, No. 2, Feb. 1978, pp. 229–237.

45. Jones SLP: An investigation of the relative efficiencies of combinators and lambda-expressions. *Conference Record of the 1982 ACM Symposium on Lisp and Functional Programming,* Carnegie-Mellon University, Aug. 1982, pp. 150–158.

46. Keller RM, Lindstrom G, Patil S: A loosely coupled applicative multi-processing system. *Proc. National Computer Conference,* Vol. 48, AFIPS, 1979, pp. 613–622.

47. Keller RM, Lin FCH: Simulated performance of a reduction-based multiprocessor. *IEEE Computer,* Vol. 17, No. 7, July 1984, pp. 70–82.

48. Keller RM: Divide and CONCer: Data structuring in applicative multiprocessor systems. *Lisp Conference Record,* Stanford University, 1980, pp. 196–202.

49. Keller RM, Lindstrom G: Applications of feedback in functional programming. *Proc. Conference on Functional Programming Languages and Computer Architecture,* ACM, 1981, pp. 123–130.

50. Keller RM, Sleep MR: Applicative caching. *Proc. Conference on Functional Programming Languages and Computer Architecture,* ACM, 1981, pp. 131–140.

51. Keller RM, Lin FCH, Tanaka J: Rediflow multiprocessing. *Proc. IEEE COMPCON,* Feb. 1984, pp. 410–417.

52. Kieburtz RB, Shultis J: Transformations of FP program schemes. *Proc. Conference on Functional Programming Languages and Computer Architecture,* ACM, 1981, pp. 41–48.

53. Kieburtz RB: The G-machine: A fast graph-reduction processor. CS/E Technical Report 85-002, Oregon Graduate Center, 1985.

54. Landin PJ: A correspondence between Algol 60 and Church's lambda notation: Part I. Communications of the ACM, Vol. 8, No. 2, Feb. 1965, pp. 89–100.

55. Liskov B, et al: CLU reference manual. In Goos and Hartmanis (eds): Lecture Notes in Computer Science, Springer-Verlag, New York, 1981.

56. McLean ER: The use of APL for production applications: The concept of throwaway code. *Proc. APL Conference,* ACM-STAPL 1976, pp. 303–307.

57. Magó GA: A network of microprocessors to execute reduction languages, Part I. *International Journal of Computer and Information Sciences,* Vol. 8, No. 5, Oct. 1979, pp. 349–385.

58. Magó GA: A cellular computer architecture for functional programming. *Proc. IEEE COMPCON,* Feb. 1980, pp. 179–187.

59. Magó GA: Private Communication, 1985.

60. Manna Z, Waldinger T: Synthesis: Dreams ⇒ Programs. *IEEE Trans. on Software Engineering,* Vol. SE-5, No. 4, July 1979, pp. 157–164.

61. McCarthy J: Lisp—notes on its past and future. *Lisp Conference Record,* Stanford University, 1980, pp. v–viii.

62. McGraw JR: Data flow computing: Software development. *Proc. International Conference on Distributed Computing Systems,* IEEE, 1979, pp. 242–251.

63. Michie D: "Memo" functions and machine learning. *Nature,* Vol. 218, April 1968, pp. 19–22.

64. Morris JH, Schmidt E, Wadler PL: Experience with an applicative string processing language. *Proc. ACM Symposium on the Principles of Programming Languages,* ACM, July 1980, pp. 32–46.

65. Morris JH: Real programming in functional languages. In Darlington, Henderson, and Turner (ed): *Functional Programming and its Applications. An Advanced Course,* Cambridge University Press, 1982.

66. Mycroft A: The theory and practice of transforming call-by-need into call-by-value, *Proc. Fourth International Colloquium on Programming,* 1980.

67. Mycroft A: Abstract interpretation and optimising transformations for applicative programs. Ph.D. Thesis, University of Edinburgh. 1981.

68. O'Donnell JT: A systolic associative Lisp computer architecture with incremental parallel storage management. Ph.D. Thesis, University of Iowa, 1981.

69. Ousterhout JK: Partitioning and cooperation in a distributed multiprocessor operating system: Medusa. Ph.D. Thesis, Carnegie-Mellon University, April 1980.
70. Page RL, Conant MG, Grit DH: If-then-else as a concurrency inhibitor in eager beaver evaluation of recursive program, *Proc. Conference* on *Functional Programming Languages* and *Computer Architecture*, ACM 1981, pp. 179–186.
71. Patel JH: Processor-memory interconnections for multiprocessors. *Proc. Symposium on Computer Architecture*, IEEE, 1979, pp. 168–177.
72. Perlis AJ: Steps toward an APL compiler—updated. Technical Report 24, Yale University, March 1975.
73. Presnell HA, Pargas RP: Communication along shortest paths in a tree machine. *Proc. Conference on Functional Programming Languages and Computer Architecture*, ACM, 1981, pp. 107–114.
74. Rieger C, Trigg R, Bane B: ZMOB: A new computing engine for AI. *Proc. IJCAI*, University of British Columbia, 1981, pp. 955–960.
75. Rumbaugh JE: A data flow multiprocessor. *IEEE Trans. on Computers,* Vol. C-26, No. 2, Feb. 1977, pp. 138–146.
76. Scheevel M: Private communication 1985.
77. Scherlis WL: Expression procedures and program derivation. Ph.D. Thesis, Stanford University, Aug. 1980.
78. Schwans K: Tailoring software for multiple processor systems. Ph.D. Thesis, Carnegie-Mellon University, 1982.
79. Sleep MR: Applicative languages, dataflow and pure combinatory code. *Proc. IEEE COMPCON,* Feb. 1980, pp. 112–115.
80. Smith B: Logic programming on an FFP machine. *International Symposium on Logic Programming,* Feb. 1984, pp. 177–186.
81. Steele GL Jr: Debunking the expensive procedure call myth, or, procedure call implementations considered harmful, or, LAMBDA: The ultimate goto. *Proc. ACM Annual Conference,* Oct. 1977, pp. 153–162.
82. Sugimoto S, Koichi T, Kiyoshi A, Ohno Y: Concurrent Lisp on a multi-microprocessor system. *Proc. IJCAI,* University of British Columbia, 1981, pp. 949–954.
83. Treleaven PC, Brownbridge DR, Hopkins RP: Data-driven and demand-driven computer architecture. *ACM Computing Surveys,* Vol. 14, No. 1, March 1982, pp. 93–143.
84. Turner DA: A new implementation technique for applicative languages. *Software—Practice and Experience,* Vol. 9, Jan. 1979, pp. 31–49.
85. Turner DA: The semantic elegance of applicative languages. *Proc. Conference on Functional Programming Languages and Computer Architecture,* ACM 1981, pp. 85–92.
86. Turner DA: Recursion equations as a programming language. In Darlington, Henderson, and Turner (eds): *Functional Programming and its Applications. An Advanced Course.* Cambridge University Press, 1982.
87. Ullman JD: Some thoughts about supercomputer organization. *Proc. IEEE COMPCON,* Feb. 1984, pp. 424–432.
88. Vegdahl SR: A survey of proposed architectures for the execution of functional languages. *IEEE Trans. on Computers.* Vol. C-33, No. 12, Dec. 1984, pp. 1050–1072. Copyright © 1984 IEEE.
89. Wadler PL: Applicative style programming, program transformation, and list

operators. *Proc. Conference on Functional Programming Languages and Computer Architecture,* ACM, 1981, pp. 25–32.
90. Wadler PL: Listless is better than laziness: An algorithm that transforms applicative programs to eliminate intermediate lists. Ph.D. Thesis, Carnegie-Mellon University, 1985.
91. Wadsworth C: Semantics and pragmatics of lambda-calculus. Ph.D. Thesis, Oxford University, 1971.
92. Ward S: The MuNet: A multiprocessor message-passing system architecture. *Proc. Texas Conference on Computing Systems,* University of Houston, 1978.
93. Wasserman AI, Gutz S: The future of programming. *Communication of the ACM,* Vol. 25, No. 3, March 1982, pp. 196–206.
94. Watson I, Gurd J: A prototype data flow computer with token labeling. *Proc. National Computer Conference,* Vol. 48, AFIPS, 1979, pp. 623–628.
95. Watson I, Gurd J: A practical data flow computer. *IEEE Computer,* Vol. 15, No. 2, Feb. 1982, pp. 51–57.
96. Weng KS: Stream-oriented computation in recursive data flow schemes. Technical Report MTMM-68, Massachusetts Institute of Technology, Oct. 1975.
97. Wise DS: Design for a multiprocessing heap with on-board reference counting. CSD Technical Report No. 163, Indiana University, 1985.

11

Systematic Design Approaches for Algorithmically Specified Systolic Arrays

José A. B. Fortes
King-Sun Fu*
Benjamin W. Wah

11.1. INTRODUCTION

The evolution in Very-Large-Scale-Integration (VLSI) technology has had a great impact on computer architecture (114). Many existing algorithms in pattern recognition and image and signal processing can be implemented on a VLSI chip using multiple, regularly connected processing elements (PEs) to exploit the great potential of pipelining and multiprocessing in applications in command, control, and communications systems (4). This type of array processor has been referred to as a *systolic array,* and the concept was introduced in the pioneering paper of H. T. Kung and C. E. Leiserson (67, 69). A good survey on the state of the art is provided by Ullman (116). A list of the sample problems for which systolic solutions exist is shown in Table 11.1 (46).

* Deceased.

Research supported by National Science Foundation Grants ECS 80-16580, DMC 85-19649, and DMC 84-19745, and was also supported by the Innovative Science and Technology Office of the Strategic Defense Initiative Organization and was administered through the Office of Naval Research under contract no. 00014-85-k-0588.

Table 11.1 A Sample of the Applications for Which Systolic Arrays Are Available

Signal and image processing and pattern recognition
    FIR, IIR filtering and 1-D convolution[21–24,33,57,69,82]
    2-D convolution and correlation[18,64,65,73,77,92]
    discrete Fourier transform[9,21,22,57,58,69,71,123]
    interpolation[18]
    1-D and 2-D median filtering[72]
    geometric warping[6,18,124]
    feature extraction[11]
    order statistics[72,82]
    counters[82]
    minimum distance classifier[12]
    covariance matrix computation[36]
    template and pattern matching[22,36,82]
    seismic signal classification
    cluster analysis[120]
    syntactic pattern recognition[54,89]
    radar signal processing[30,90,91]
    curve detection[103]
    dynamic scene analysis[31]
    image resampling[44]
    scene matching[30]

Matrix arithmetic
    Toeplitz matrix–vector multiplication[69]
    matrix–matrix multiplication[3,34,69,82,119]
    matrix triangularization[35,52,69]
    QR and LU decompositions[1,35,49,52,82,112,115]
    sparse-matrix operations[53]
    solution of triangular linear systems[1,49,82]
    polynomial multiplication/division[33]

Nonnumeric applications
    data structures—stacks and queues,[14] searching,[10,76,92,94] sorting and priority queues
    graph algorithms—transitive closure,[51] minimum spanning trees,[8] connected components[105]
    language recognition[7,50,82,107,109,111]
    dynamic programming[42,43,51]
    arithmetic arrays[2,3,45]
    relational database operations[10,32,51,66,113]
    algebra[51,93]

An example of a systolic array for multiplying matrices A and B to form C is shown in Figure 11.1. The dataflows of the three rhomboidal data blocks are in three directions: A moves toward the north, B moves toward −120° north, and C moves toward −60° north. During a clock cycle, each PE receives three data items from three different pipes and executes a multiply-add operation. These data items advance into neighboring PEs along their own pipes synchronously in the next clock cycle.

456

(a)

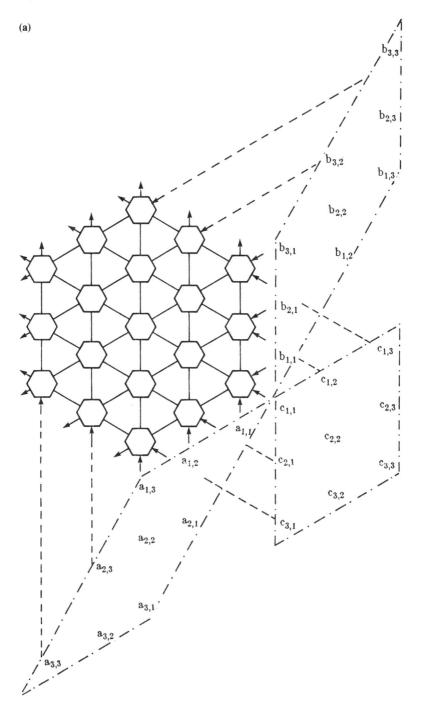

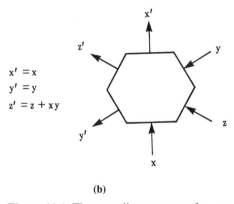

$$x' = x$$
$$y' = y$$
$$z' = z + xy$$

(b)

Figure 11.1 The systolic processor for two-dimensional matrix multiplication. (a) Systolic processor. (b) Structure of PE.

One of the many advantages of the systolic approach is that each input-data item can be used a number of times once it is accessed, and thus a high computational throughput can be achieved with only a modest bandwidth. Other advantages include modular expandability, simple and regular data and control flows, and simplicity and uniformity of PEs.

Systolic arrays have been classified into semisystolic arrays with global data communications and pure systolic arrays without global data communications (67). In a *semisystolic array,* a data item accessed from memory is broadcast to and used by a number of possibly nonidentical PEs concurrently. Although this approach is potentially faster than systolic arrays without data broadcast, providing (or collecting) a data item to (or from) all the PEs in each cycle requires the use of a global bus that may eventually slow down the processing speed as the number of PEs increases. On the other hand, a *pure systolic array* eliminates the use of broadcast buses and implements the algorithm in pipelines extending in different directions. Several data items flowing along different pipes with the same or different rates may meet and interact. The PEs operate synchronously with one or more clocks, and all the necessary operands to be processed by a PE in each computational step must arrive at this PE simultaneously. This mode of pipelining is referred to as *systolic processing.*

One of the important design problems in systolic processing is the development of a systematic methodology for transforming an algorithm represented in some high-level constructs into a systolic architecture specified by the timing of data movements and the interconnection of processing elements such that the design requirements are satisfied. In this chapter, we survey 19 methodologies proposed in the literature. The applicability, capabilities, and results derived for each methodology are identified.

11.2. Systematic Methodologies for Designing Systolic Arrays

The common characteristic of most previously proposed methodologies is the use of a transformational approach—i.e., systolic architectures are derived by transforming the original algorithm descriptions that are unsuitable for direct VLSI implementation. Distinct transformational systems for systolic-architecture design (hereafter referred to as transformational systems) can be characterized by how algorithms are described, what formal models are used, how systolic architectures are specified, and what types of transformations are used on and between these resprentations. In other words, we can visualize each transformational system as a three-dimensional space, where dimensions (or axes) are associated with the algorithm representation, algorithm model, and architecture specification. To the axis of algorithm representation, we associate different forms or levels to present an algorithm to the transformational system. The axis of algorithm model shows different levels of abstraction used to represent relevant features of the algorithm. The axis of architecture specification is associated with the hardware model or level of design in which the systolic array is described.

This three-dimensional space can be graphically depicted as a Y chart (Figure 11.2), where directed arcs can be drawn to illustrate transformations that map a given representation into another representation in the same axis and level (a self loop), in the same axis and different level, or between distinct dimensions.[1] Arcs drawn in full lines represent systematic transformations, whereas those drawn in broken lines represent ad hoc transformations. The Y charts allow us to classify and describe the large number of approaches taken to design systolic arrays. Before we do this, we will use the Y chart in Figure 11.3 to explain Kuhn's approach (63).

Kuhn's methodology starts with a naive high-level language cyclic-loop program—i.e., an algorithm written without regard to how it is implemented in VLSI. In an ad hoc manner, additional subscripts for variable referencing are introduced such that the possibility of broadcasts of variables does not exist. The algorithm model assumed in Kuhn's method is a set of computation nodes (which correspond to the loop-body assignment statements) indexed by the vector value of the indices of the iteration when they are computed (Figure 11.3). The structural information is modeled by the dimensionality of the iteration space and the dependency vectors (which are the vector difference of the indices of dependent computation nodes). The geometry of the algorithm is represented by the iteration space and how different variables are associated to points in that space. This model is derived from the program in a systematic manner by using analysis techniques

---

[1] We borrowed from Gajski's paper (47) the idea of using Y charts to improve the clarity of our presentation; however, our Y charts are minimally related to those used in that reference.

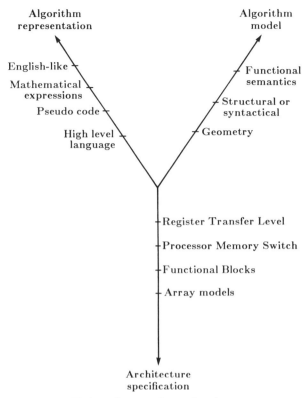

Algorithm
representation

Algorithm
model

English-like

Mathematical
expressions

Pseudo code

High level
language

Functional
semantics

Structural or
syntactical

Geometry

Register Transfer Level

Processor Memory Switch

Functional Blocks

Array models

Architecture
specification

Figure 11.2 Y-chart for transformational systems.

similar to those used in optimizing compilers. A re-indexing transformation
is then sought in an ad hoc fashion until a favorable set of dependencies is
obtained. Once this transformation is known, one can systematically generate not only the new dependency vectors but also the range of the new
indices of the loops and the subscript functions used to reference variables.
By projecting the new iteration set into all but one of its dimensions, and
by identifying the iterations in which input variables are used, the size,
dimension, and input/output ports of the architecture can be systematically
generated.

Each point in the projected space corresponds to a PE in the array
whose function is totally described by the statements in the loop body. The
interconnections and the direction, speed, and timing of data movements
are systematically derived from the new set of dependencies that resulted
from applying the re-indexing transformation. This completes our example
of the use of Y-charts to explain a methodology. We defer the analysis of
the capabilities of Kuhn's method until after we introduce a classification
of the different approaches in terms of the Y-charts.

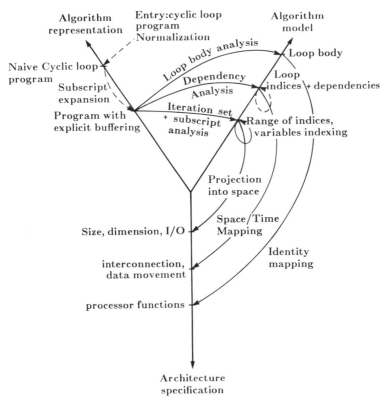

Figure 11.3 Kuhn's method.

The various methodologies can be grouped into the following classes:[2]

1. Those that allow transformations to be performed at the algorithm-re-presentation level and that advocate a direct mapping from this level to the architecture specification. These include:
   Cohen, Johnsson, Weiser, and Davis' method
   Lam and Mostow's method
2. Methods that prescribe transformations at the algorithm-model level and that require procedures for deriving the model from the algorithm repre-sentation (analysis) and for mapping the model into hardware (synthesis). These include:
   Gannon's method
   H. T. Kung and Lin's method
   Kuhn's method
   Moldovan and Fortes' method

---

[2] The order in which the methodologies are described is chosen at random.

Miranker and Winkler's method
Cappello and Steiglitz's method
S. Y. Kung's method
Quinton's method
Ramakrishnan, Fussell, and Sillberschatz's method
Li and Wah's method
Cheng and Fu's method
Jover and Kailath's method
Schwartz and Barnwell's method
Ibarra, Kim, and Palis' method

3. Methods that transform a previously designed architecture into a new architecture. We will consider only one work in this class:

Leiserson, Rose, and Saxe's method

4. Methods that abstract the function implemented by a given systolic architecture and that use symbolic manipulations and transformations to prove the correctness of the design. Two studies in this class are considered:

Chen and Mead's method
Kuo, Levy, and Musicus' method

In the following sections, we will describe these methods in an arbitrary order, show their applicability, discuss their capabilities, and summarize the major results. The discussion in some of these studies may be vague, and we have tried to infer their results from our understanding of the published work.

11.2.1. Cohen, Johnsson, Weiser and Davis' Method (33, 57–59, 119)

Description

Starting from a mathematical expression involving subscripted variables, which conceptually represent data sequenced in time or space, this method begins by deriving a new expression where a well-defined operator Z is used to model displacements in time (e.g., the storage of data) or shifts in space (e.g., the allocation of a data stream to PEs). Symbolic manipulation is used to transform the derived mathematical expression into equivalent ones by using the properties of the Z operator and the functional operators in the expression. From a particular expression, the execution order of the operations can be derived from known precedence rules. The number, placement, and interconnection of operator PEs can also be derived. Timing and storage requirements are inferred from the placement of delay PEs (which correspond to the Z operators) (Figure 11.4).

Applicability

This method seems to be best applicable to algorithms that can be described by relatively simple and concise mathematical expressions.

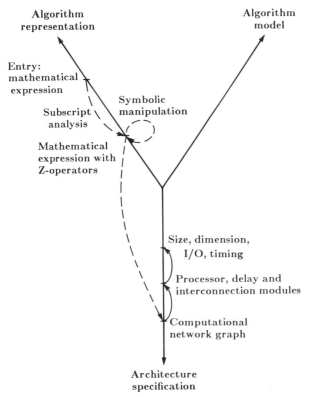

Figure 11.4 Cohen, Johnsson, Weiser, and Davis' method.

Capabilities
Computational rate, performance, delay, modularity, and size can be easily derived from the equations; interconnection and communication character- istics can also be derived when the architecture is regular. This method may yield implementations with both parallel and sequential features, requiring hardware of a size smaller than the problem size. The method treats control signals in the same way as data signals. The optimal design is searched in an ad hoc manner.

Results
Formal derivations have been reported for architectures intended for the following problems: finite-impulse-response (FIR) filters, discrete Fourier transform (DFT), matrix-vector product, string matching, solution of tri- angular linear equations, product of band matrices, synthetic aperture radar (SAR), and multiplication and division of polynomials. A set of data-set operators defined in terms of the Z operator was also proposed for treating

sets of data as wavefront entities in expressions and their graphical representation.

11.2.2. Lam and Mostow's Method (SYS) (78, 101)

Description

SYS accepts as input an algorithm suitable for systolic implementation— i.e., an algorithm obtained by software transformations from a high-level specification that results in segments of code executed repeatedly with a regular pattern of data accesses. The algorithm is mapped into a systolic design described by a structure and a driver. The structure describes the hardware PEs (which are functionally equivalent to code segments), interconnections, and input–output ports. The driver defines data streams in terms of the original variables in the algorithm. The mapping of iterative algorithms uses three basic allocation schemes named sequential, parallel, and compositional. SYS has a special language for representing a given design. Initially, SYS generates a simple-minded implementation of the given algorithm. Systematic and user determined transformations are then used to optimize and to obtain new designs (Figure 11.5).

Applicability

SYS can process algorithms with simple FOR loops and BEGIN-END blocks, simple unnested function calls, and scalar and array variables. As reported in the references, SYS cannot deal with conditional execution, computed iteration bounds and array indices, and other high-level software constructs.

Capabilities

SYS can derive the structure and driver of a systolic design. Specification of the structure includes the number and dimensionality of ports of PEs, hierarchical definition of PEs, arrays and compounds of PEs, and interconnections among them, including broadcasts and directional links. The driver describes data streams and timing schemes that include delay, skew of streams, and ready time (time allowed between two consecutive inputs to the structure).

Results

Reported designs obtained by SYS include two systolic arrays for polynomial evaluation and a circuit for computing the greatest common divisor of two polynomials. Other nonsystolic designs using a transformational system related to SYS include a chip for color shading and hidden-surface elimination and a multichip switching network for marker passing semantic networks. All designs were previously known.

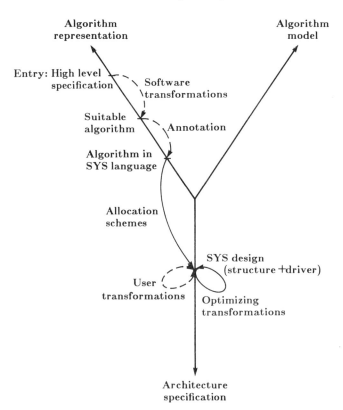

Figure 11.5 Lam and Mostow's method.

11.2.3. Gannon's Method (48)

Description

From a given algorithm, a functional specification is derived by using vector operators that explicitly represent parallelism. These vector operators are defined in terms of basic functions that correspond to small units of sequential computation and that map directly into the functional specification of the PEs of the systolic architecture. The vector operators include a product operator, which represents the concurrent operation of basic functions, permutation and data-movement operators; a chain operator, which represents the iterative composition of basic functions; and the systolic-iteration operator, which describes basic functions that are "reused." The global functional specification of the algorithm is viewed as a dataflow graph which, depending on the properties of the functions and operators used, can be mapped into a systolic architecture. Different architectures result from expressing the same algorithm with different operators (Figure 11.6).

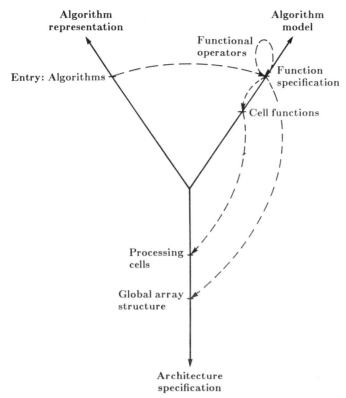

Figure 11.6 Gannon's method.

Applicability

This method seems to be suitable to those algorithms that can be reexpressed by vector operators. For these algorithms, the methodology seems hard to apply without human assistance.

Capabilities

The functional description of PEs and the interconnection topology can be easily derived. Additional information such as data movement and timing is present in implicit form.

Results

A previously known design of a recurrence solver was rederived. The formalism used proved the theoretical result that systolic versions of computation graphs perform asymptotically as fast as fully concurrent execution of the original dataflow graph.

11.2.4. H. T. Kung and Lin's Method (70)

Description

This method starts by deriving a straightforward and obviously correct algebraic representation from the mathematical representation of the algorithm. The canonical algebraic representation consists of two matrical expressions of the form (a) $v \leftarrow Av + bx$, and (b) $y = c^T v$, where x represents the input, y represents the output, and v represents variables generated by implicit functions. The $(n \times n)$ matrix A and the column vectors b and c represent the delay cycles between the availability and the use of variables, and each entry is either 0 or Z^{-k}, where k corresponds to the number of delays. For example, the i-th component of v in Expression (a) is

$$v_i \leftarrow Z^{-a_{i,1}} v_1 + \cdots + Z^{-a_{i,n}} v_n + Z^{-b_i} x,$$

which means that

$$v_i(t) = f_i[v_1(t - a_{i,1}), \ldots, v_n(t - a_{i,n}), x(t - b_i)]$$

for some implicit function f_i associated with node v_i. To this canonical representation, algebraic transformations are then applied. There are two major types of transformations, retiming and "k-slowing," which can also be described algebraically. These transformations determine the distribution of delays and the input/output periods of the systolic architecture. There exists a direct correspondence between the algebraic representations and a hardware-related representation denoted as the Z-graph. The Z-graph has an edge for each variable and a node for each computation. Each edge is labeled by Z^{-k} if k delay cycles (i.e., registers) exist between the availability of the variable and its use as an operand or output (Figure 11.7).

Applicability

The method is suitable for algorithms for which a canonical algebraic representation can be found.

Capabilities

Functional description of PEs, interconnections, and timing for input/output and data communication can be derived systematically; designs and transformations can be expressed algebraically; theoretical results on retiming and k-slowed designs can be proved easily by algebraic manipulation.

Results

Designs for FIR and IIR filters and matrix–matrix multiplication were derived. New results include the derivation of two-level pipelined systolic arrays and systolic architectures for LU decomposition.

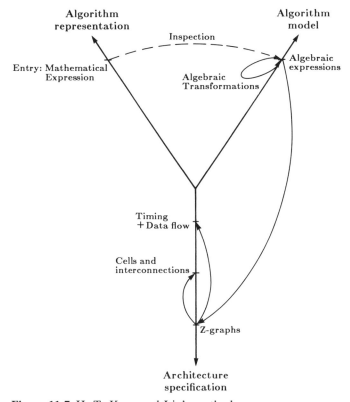

Figure 11.7 H. T. Kung and Lin's method.

11.2.5. Kuhn's Method (62, 63)

Description
As described early in this chapter.

Applicability
This method is best suited for algorithms described as cyclic-loop programs with constant execution time and dependencies in loop bodies.

Capabilities
Size, dimension, topology, input–output ports, execution time, data movement, timing, and functional descriptions of PEs of an architecture can be systematically derived. However, nothing can be said about the optimality of the design, and the choice of transformations is done in an ad hoc manner.

Results

Designs for the following problems were derived using this method: matrix–matrix multiplication, matrix–vector multiplication, recurrence evaluation, solution of triangular linear systems, constant-time priority queue, on-line sort, transitive closure, and LU decomposition.

11.2.6. Moldovan and Fortes' Method (37–41, 96–99, 100, 104)

Description

From a program or a set of recurrence equations, an algebraic model of the algorithm is derived by using systematic techniques similar to those used in software compilers. This model consists of a structured set of indexed computations that operate on a set of inputs to obtain a set of outputs. Typically, programs include loops, and indexing of computations is related to the loop indices. However, unlike Kuhn's approach, which associates the body of loops with the corresponding loop indices, each computation has an index. The algebraic representation of the algorithm is then transformed by local and global transformations. Local transformations are used to rewrite computations that are mapped into the functional and structural specifications of the PEs of the systolic architecture. Global transformations composed of time and space transformations are used to restructure the algorithm. They are chosen in such a way that the new algorithm has a set of dependencies that favors VLSI implementation. Time transformations determine the execution time of the algorithm and the timing for data communication. Space transformations determine the interconnections and the direction of data movement. The projection of the index set of the algorithm into space determines the size, dimension, I/O ports, and geometry of the architecture (Figure 11.8).

Applicability

This method is best suited to algorithms described by either programs with loops or recurrence equations.

Capabilities

Because this method is an extension of Kuhn's approach, it has the same capabilities as that method. Additionally, it allows or eliminates broadcasting, designs fixed-size architectures for arbitrarily large algorithms, implements fault-tolerance schemes, and optimizes execution time.

Results

Systematically obtained designs have been reported for matrix–matrix multiplication, LU Gaussian elimination, dynamic programming, partitioned matrix–vector multiplication, convolution, partitioned QR-eigenvalue de-

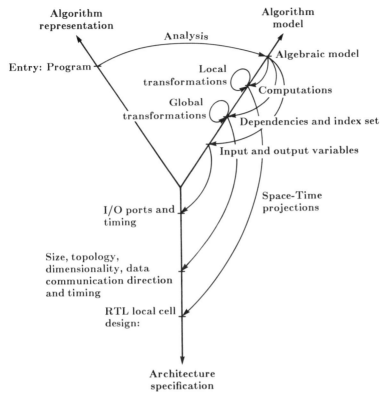

Figure 11.8 Moldovan and Fortes' method.

composition, and partial differential equations. Theoretical results include the necessary and sufficient conditions for the existence of global transformations and broadcasts, sufficient conditions for the partitionability of algorithms, and a method for finding optimal linear schedules for systolic algorithms.

11.2.7. Miranker and Winkler's Method (95)

Description

This method is an extension of Kuhn's method and is similar to Moldovan's method. An algorithm is represented as either a mathematical expression or a cyclic-loop program. One extension is to allow the rewriting of mathematical expressions by using the properties of the operators in an ad hoc fashion. The other extension is to use the graph embeddings based on the knowledge of the longest path of the computation graph when this graph is too irregular and simple matrix transformations are not useful (Figure 11.9).

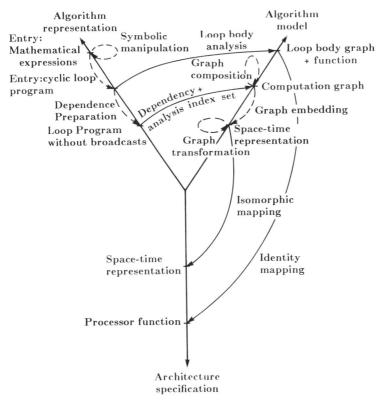

Figure 11.9 Miranker and Winkler's method.

Applicability
Theoretically, it can be applied to any algorithm, although systematic design seems possible only for those algorithms described by programs with loops.

Capabilities
Size, dimension, topology, data movement, timing, functional description of PEs, and execution time can be systematically derived.

Results
Designs of architectures for the computation of discrete Fourier transform and the solution of a triangular linear system of equations were systematically derived.

11.2.8. Cappello and Steiglitz's Method (15–17)

Description
Starting from a set of recurrence equations describing the algorithm, a canonical representation is obtained by adjoining an index representing time

to the definition of the recurrence. Each index is associated with a dimension of a geometric space, where each point corresponds to a tuple of indices on which the recurrence is defined. To each such point, a primitive computation is associated, and its implementation is left unspecified. Primitive computations are mapped directly into functional specifications of PEs in the systolic architecture. From the geometric representation and an ordering rule, the topology and size of the architecture and the timing and direction of dataflows are derived systematically. By selecting different geometric transformations, distinct geometric representations and their corresponding architectures can be derived (Figure 11.10).

Applicability
This method is best suited to algorithms described by recurrence equations.

Capabilities
Geometric representations help the designer's understanding of a systolic architecture, and geometric transformations are easily and succinctly rep-

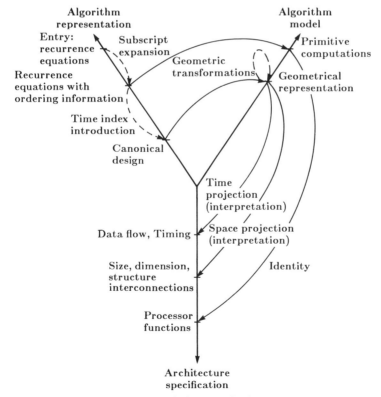

Figure 11.10 Cappello and Steiglitz's method.

resented as matrix transformations. The presence of broadcasts, data pipelining, topology, area, and timing of the architecture are easily perceived from the geometric representation.

Results
Designs of architectures for matrix–vector multiplication, convolution, matrix–matrix product, and matrix transposition were formally related and rederived. For some, it was shown that they are asymptomatically optimal, and for others, alternative designs were provided.

11.2.9. S.Y. Kung's Method (74, 75)

Description
Given a Signal Flow Graph (SFG) representing an algorithm, this method starts by choosing basic operational modules that correspond to the functional description of PEs of the architecture. Localization rules are then applied to derive a regular and temporally localized SFG. The localization procedure consists of selecting cut-sets of the SFG and reallocating scaled delays to edges "leaving" and "entering" the cut-set in such a way that at least one unit of time is allowed for communicating a signal between two nodes. Delays are combined with operational modules to obtain a full description of the operation of a basic systolic module. The resulting SFG maps straightforwardly into the systolic array by mapping basic modules into PEs and edges into interconnections. Timing and data movements can be derived from the basic modules due to the localized spatial and temporal characteristics of the SFG (Figure 11.11).

Applicability
This method is applicable to all algorithms described by computable SFGs with some regularity.

Capabilities
Size, dimension, functional, and structural description of PEs, timing, direction of dataflow, and interconnections of the architecture can be derived from the SFG of the algorithm. Design verification can be done by applying Z-transform techniques to the SFG.

Results
Systolic arrays have been derived from SFGs for autoregressive filter, matrix multiplication, banded-matrix–full-matrix product, banded-matrix multiplication, and LU-matrix decomposition. Theoretical results include the proof that all computable SFGs are temporally localizable and the equivalence between SFGs and dataflow graphs.

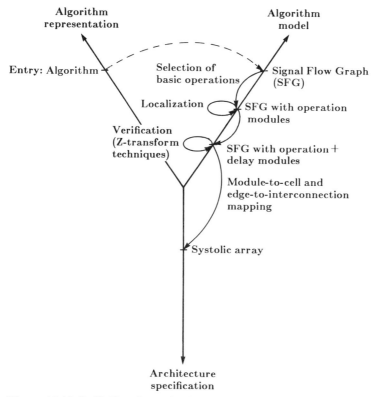

Figure 11.11 S. Y. Kung's method.

11.2.10. Quinton's Method (106, 107)

Description

Given a system of n uniform recurrence equations defined over some convex subset D in Z^M and with some characteristic dependency vectors, (which, together define a dependency graph), this method starts by finding a timing function that maps points of D into time. This requires the identification of a convex space of feasible timing functions from which one can be chosen heuristically. Such space can be found systematically from the knowledge of the dependency vectors and D (D can be thought of as the index set of the recurrence). Next, an allocation function is chosen, which projects D into space along a preselected direction such that two points in D with the same image under the timing function do not map into the same point in space. Once the timing and allocation functions (which are quasi-affine functions) are known, the systolic array can be systematically generated from D. Each point of D is mapped into a PE that computes the recurrence function, and receives and sends data from and to PEs that are the image of points dependent and depending on the point under consideration, with delays given by the timing function (Figure 11.12).

Applicability
The method is specifically intended for algorithms described by uniform recurrence equations.

Capabilities
The functional description of PEs, the size, dimension, and topology of the array, and the execution time, direction, and timing of data communication can all be derived systematically.

Results
Derived architectures include arrays for convolution (including a block convolver and a ring convolver) and matrix product. Extensions of the method allow the derivation of arrays for LU decomposition and dynamic programming.

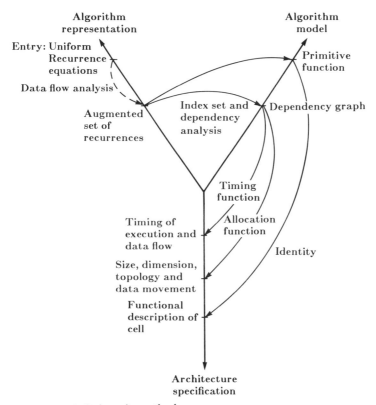

Figure 11.12 Quinton's method.

11.2.11. Ramakrishnan, Fussell, and Sillberschatz's Method (108, 118)

Description
This method starts with a dataflow description of the algorithm (an acyclic program graph), which is partitioned into sets of vertices that are mapped into the same PE (this partitioning is called diagonalization). A syntactically correct mapping is then used to map computation vertices onto PEs and time steps, and the labels and edges to map communication delays and interconnections (Figure 11.13).

Applicability
The method applies only to homogeneous graphs with connectged subgraphs that satisfy certain properties. Moreover, the method can only be used to generate linear arrays.

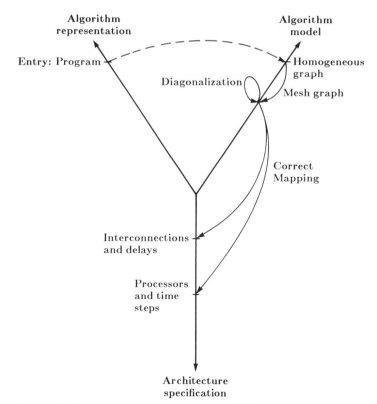

Figure 11.13 Ramakrishnan, Fussell, and Sillberschatz's method.

Capabilities
The method yields the number of PEs, their functional description, and the number of I/O ports. Additionally, it gives the direction of data communication, time used, and timing.

Results
Linear-array designs were synthesized for band matrix–vector multiplication, convolution, dynamic programming, and transitive closure.

11.2.12. Li and Wah's Method (85–88)

Description
Starting from an algorithm described as a set of linear recurrence equations, this method derives three classes of parameters: velocities of dataflows, spatial distributions of data, and periods of computations. The relationships among these parameters are represented as constraint vector equations that must be satisfied in a correct design. The performance of a design can also be expressed in terms of the defined parameters. Performance can be defined as execution time or the product of the square of execution time and the number of PEs. Optimal designs are then searched in the space of solutions that satisfy the constraint equations. This search is done by ordered enumeration over a limited search space in time polynomial to the problem size. The functional description of the PEs is derived from the definition of the recurrence equations. The interconnections among PEs are found from the defined parameters (Figure 11.14).

Applicability
The method is best suited to algorithms that can be described by sets of linear recurrences.

Capabilities
Functional description of PEs, timing and spatial distribution of dataflows, execution time, number of PEs, and interconnections can be systematically derived. Optimal designs can be found.

Results
Systematically derived architectures include systolic arrays for finite-impulse-response (FIR) filtering, matrix multiplication, discrete Fourier transform, polynomial multiplication, deconvolution, triangular matrix inversion, and tuple comparison.

11.2.13. Cheng and Fu's Method (26–30)

Description
Starting from a recursive formula with several indices or a program-loop with a simple expression, this method starts by designing the basic PE to

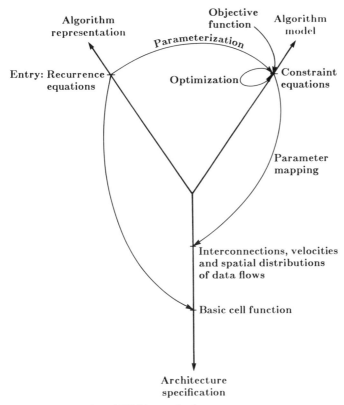

Figure 11.14 Li and Wah's method.

compute the simple expression. This basic PE is then expanded in time and space in such a way that indices of the loop (or recursion) become associated with time and space. This expansion is done according to rules that maintain the consistency of time and space. Time-space expansion can be applied in any degree varying from full-time expansion (i.e., purely sequential single-processor architecture) to full-space expansion (i.e., fully parallel single-time execution). Time and space expansions implicitly determine dataflow timing and direction as well as PE interconnections (Figure 11.15). The method can be implemented at the gate level, register level, processing-unit level, and system level. Because there is no restriction on the dimensionality of the processing array, the method can be applied to design high-dimensional VLSI architectures. A computational model and partition rules can be derived that partition any problem suitable for the method and implement the problem on a fixed-size VLSI architecture.

Applicability
The method is suitable for algorithms described by recurrence expressions or programs with loops.

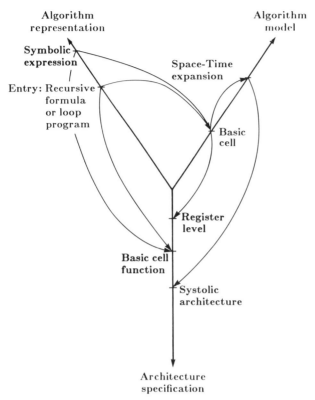

Figure 11.15 Cheng and Fu's method.

Capabilities
Functional description of PEs, timing and directions of dataflows, interconnections, execution time, and number of PEs can be systematically generated.

Results
This method has been applied to construct computational structures for computing vector inner product, matrix multiplication, convolution, comparison operations in relational databases, fast Fourier transform, hierarchical scene matching, transitive closure, string matching, pattern matching, recognition of hand-written signals, and recognition of context-free languages.

11.2.14. Jover and Kailath's Method (60)

Description
This method is based on the use of Lines Of Computation (LOCs) to determine whether a given topology is suitable for VLSI implementation. LOCs

are directional straight lines with several equally spaced nodes, and can be interpreted either as the history of how a given value was computed or as a stream of values in different stages of a computation. Because of the properties of LOCs, one can easily check if the LOCs chosen for a given algorithm define a systolic array or a systolic-type array (not necessarily planar and fully regular) (Figure 11.16).

Applicability
Suitable for algorithms from which one can easily identify LOCs.

Capabilities
The topology of the systolic array can be easily derived from LOCs. Additionally, throughput, efficiency, data interval, initial conditions, interval and external delays, and pipeline ability can also be found from LOCs and the knowledge of execution times of basic operations.

Results
Three designs for matrix multiplication were derived.

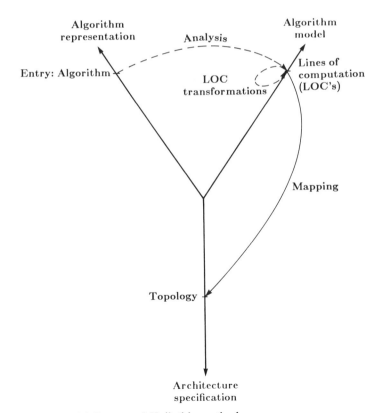

Figure 11.16 Jover and Kailath's method.

11.2.15. Schwartz and Barnwell's Method (5, 110)

Description

This method starts with an algorithm described as a fully specified flow graph—i.e., a directed graph in which nodes represent operations and edges represent signal paths. Node operations are fundamental operations performed by the PEs of the architecture. For a given flow graph, it is possible to derive a bound in the sampling period and a bound in the static-pipeline sampling period (i.e., the minimum sampling period achievable if the graph is implemented as a static pipeline). Different systolic solutions are generated by distributing delay nodes throughout the flow graph such that correctness is preserved and data transfers can be simultaneous. The transformations of flow graphs consist of data interleaving and the cut-set of delay transformation that are shown to preserve equivalence. The transformed flow graph is mapped into a systolic array by mapping nodes into PEs and delays and edges into interconnections (Figure 11.17).

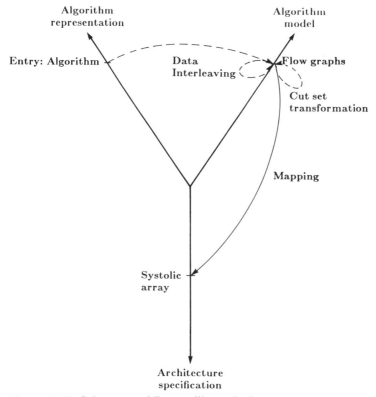

Figure 11.17 Schwartz and Barnwell's method.

Applicability
This method can be used with algorithms representable as shift-invariant flow graphs.

Capabilities
The following information about the systolic architecture can be systematically derived: number and functional description of PEs, interconnections, data movement, and time. The optimality of the resulting designs can be analyzed.

Results
Previously known and new architectures have been derived for FIR and IIR filters and two multiplier Markel–Gray lattice filters.

11.2.16. Ibarra, Palis, and Kim's Method (55, 56)

Description
Sequential-Machine (SM) models are used to simulate linear and orthogonal Systolic Arrays (SAs). Given an algorithm, this methodology starts by generating an SM characterization that consists of a serial program for a simple sequential machine with a single PE and an infinite array of registers (called the "worktape(s)"). SM characterizations that are obtained heuristically are easier to program and analyze than their SA counterparts. The conversions from SM to SA characterizations and vice versa are done systematically (Figure 11.18).

Applicability
This method seems to be best applicable to algorithms that can be easily programmed in an SM model. These are likely to be relatively simple and regular algorithms.

Capabilities
Because one starts with a given type of systolic array, certain features of the architecture (e.g., number, placement, direction of interconnections, and inputs) are known beforehand. In this sense, the methodology synthesizes or maps a given algorithm into a type of systolic array. From the SM program, the functional description of the PEs and the direction and timing of data movement can be derived automatically. The search and selection of the best type of systolic array and the best SM algorithm is done in an ad hoc manner.

Results
Systolic architectures and algorithms have been reported for priority queues, real-time bitwise multiplication, and language recognition. For linear systolic

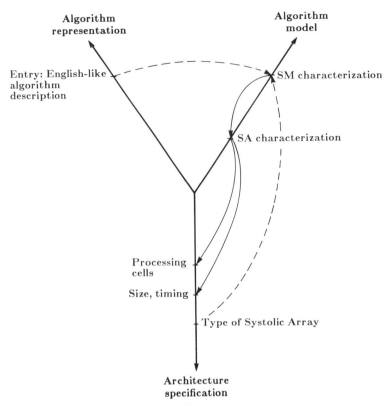

Figure 11.18 Ibarra, Kim, and Palis' method.

arrays, several general results on speedup, computational power, the effects of adding global control, and the use of one- and two-way communications were reported.

11.2.17. Leiserson, Rose, and Saxe's Method (81–84)

Description

This method starts with the design of a synchronous circuit (not necessarily systolic) whose correctness is either obvious or easily verifiable. This design is modeled as a finite, rooted, vertex-weighted, edge-weighted, directed multigraph, where nodes represent functional PEs and edges represent interconnections. Weights represent delays of nodes and register delays of interconnections. Transformations are then applied to the original design to obtain a systolic design without global broadcasts (Figure 11.19). The transformations applied include retiming, k-slowdown, broadcast and census elimination, coalescing, interlacing, code motion, resetting, register elimination, and parallel/serial compromises.

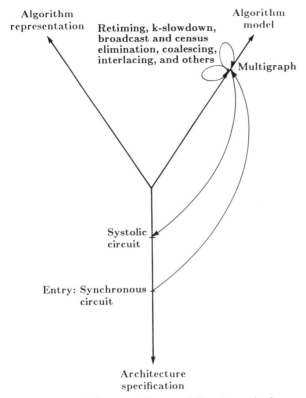

Figure 11.19 Leiserson, Rose, and Saxe's method.

Applicability
It applies to any synchronous system.

Capabilities
The function of PEs, layout, and number of pins are preserved by the transformations. Optimal retiming transformations can be selected either by reducing this problem to an efficiently solvable mixed-integer linear-programming problem such that the transformed circuit has the smallest clock period, or by solving a linear-programming dual of a minimum-cost flow problem such that the total number of registers is minimum. Extensions of the optimization procedures used can also take into account fanout, interconnection-bus width, multiple hosts, host timing constraints, and geometric constraints like the number of registers per interconnection.

Results
Systolic designs were derived from synchronous versions of a digital correlator and palindrome recognizer. Other derived circuits include priority

queues, search trees, priority multiqueue, counters, matrix–vector multiplication, matrix–matrix multiplication, and LU decomposition.

11.2.18. Chen and Mead's Method (19, 25)

Description
The goal is to verify that a given systolic design computes the function for which it was intended instead of the generation of a systolic architecture to compute a given function. However, one can see this method as the verification component of a design methodology in which systolic architectures are designed heuristically. Given a systolic architecture, the method generates a CRYSTAL program that describes the algorithm executed by the architecture as a set of space-time equations (19). This representation consists of several equations describing processes executed by local PEs, equations describing connections between PEs, functions representing data streams, and functions describing the relation between the structure of input and output data and the systolic-array structure. From fixed-point theory, the minimum solution of the system of recursive equations is the function computed by the systolic architecture (Figure 11.20).

Applicability
The generality and power of the formalism used makes the methodology widely applicable; however, for the same reason, it is not clear how practical and feasible it is to automate the steps and reasoning involved in this method.

Capabilities
Any systolic array with homogeneous or heterogeneous PEs and interconnections, and synchronous and self-timed systems can be verified.

Results
The method has been demonstrated in verifying the correctness of published designs for synchronous and self-timed systolic architectures for matrix–matrix multiplication.

11.2.19. Kuo, Levy, and Musicus' Method (20)

Description
This method starts from the knowledge of the action and position of each PE in the systolic array, the data "waves" present, their movements, and the way their components are indexed. A "wave" is simply a collection of related data that moves as a block during execution such that the relative positions are preserved (e.g., a matrix). By inspection, Space-Time-Data (STD) equations can be derived for each data wave. These equations relate

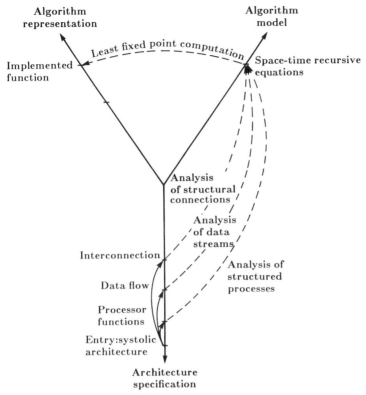

Figure 11.20 Chen and Mead's method.

the PE coordinates, time, and indices of data for each wave. Two functions can be derived from the STD equations: the position function and the memory function. The position function gives the coordinates of the PE at which some indexed data arrive at a given instant of time. The memory function is the inverse of the position function and gives the index of the data that arrives at a given PE at a given time. The direction and speed of data movement are described by velocity vectors that correspond to the difference between the coordinates of a PE receiving the data and those of the PE sending the same data. Verification is done by simulating the systolic network to either (a) track the activity of each PE over time by using the memory functions to identify the data being used at any given time, or (b) track each wave of data through the array by using the position functions to identify the PE being visited by a piece of data and the memory functions to identify other data present in that PE. If this simulation does exactly the same operations on the same data as the original algorithm, systolic algorithm is correct (Figure 11.21).

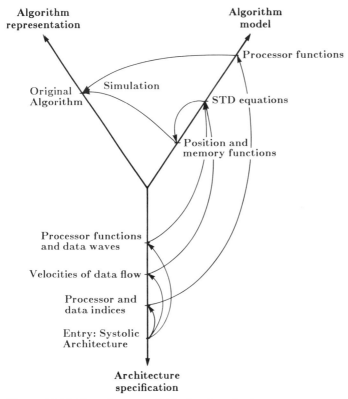

Figure 11.21 Kuo, Levy, and Musicus' method.

Applicability

This methodology is best suited for verifying spatially invariant systolic arrays for which data flows are independent of the values computed by the PEs. In practice, this means that the systolic algorithms must have regular dataflows through an array with regular geometry.

Capabilities

Computational wavefronts can be rigorously described by position and memory functions that are linear functions of time, data indices, and PE coordinates.

Results

The verification of matrix–matrix multiplication on a hexagonal array has been reported.

11.3. Final Remarks

In this chapter, we have surveyed 19 systematic methods for synthesizing algorithmically specified VLSI computational arrays. From a global point of view, it is clearly indicated that the two greatest limitations in the state of the art of existing transformational systems are the nonexistence of powerful systematic semantic transformations and the inability to systematically achieve optimality in the resulting designs. This will be the directions of future research in designing better methodologies.

Problems

1. Starting with an algorithmic description of matrix–matrix multiplication, derive the systolic array design of Figure 11.1 using the following methods: (a) Moldovan and Fortes' method, (b) Li and Wah's method, and (c) S. Y. Kung's method. (Hint—review references (75, 88, and 96.)

2. In "A mathematical model for the verification of systolic networks" by R. G. Mehlem and W. C. Rheinboldt (SIAM J. Comp., Vol. 13, No. 3, August 1984), a methodology is proposed for the verification of the correctness of systolic designs. Derive the Y-chart for this method and compare it with the verification methods mentioned in this chapter.

3. In reference (67), six systolic designs are described for the convolution problem. For each of the methodologies mentioned in this chapter, rederive those designs. (Review the relevant references for each methodology because most of them consider convolution as an example.)

4. (Project.) For each of the applications mentioned in Table 11.1, use the methods described in this chapter to verify, design, or redesign the systolic architectures described in the corresponding references. Compare the power, versatility, and effectiveness of the methods with respect to each application. List the main limitations and advantages of each method.

References

1. Agrawal DP, Pathak GC: Design of VLSI based multicomputer architecture for dynamic scene analysis. In Fu KS (ed): *VLSI for Pattern Recognition and Image Processing,* Springer-Verlag, New York, 1984.

2. Apostolico A, Negro A: Systolic algorithms for string manipulations. *Trans. on Computers,* Vol. C-33, No. 4, April 1984, pp. 361–364.

3. Banatre JP, Frison P, Quinton P: A network for the detection of words in continuous speech. *Acta Informatica,* Vol. 18, 1983, pp. 431–448.

4. Barbe DF: VHSIC systems and technology. *Computer,* Vol. 14, No. 2, Feb. 1981, pp. 13–22.
5. Barnwell TP III, Schwartz DA: Optimal implementations of flow graphs on synchronous multiprocessors. *Proc. 1983 Asilomar Conference on Circuits and Systems,* Pacific Grove, CA, Nov. 1983.
6. Baudet GM, Preparata FP, Vuillemin JE: Area-time optimal VLSI circuits for convolution. *Trans. on Computers,* Vol. C-32, No. 7, July 1983, pp. 684–688.
7. Bentley JL: A parallel algorithm for constructing minimum spanning trees. *Journal of Algorithms,* Jan. 1980, pp. 51–59.
8. Bentley JL, Kung HT: A tree machine for searching problems. *Proc. International Conference on Parallel Processing,* Aug. 1979, pp. 257–266.
9. Blackmer J, Kuekes P, Frank G: A 200 MOPS systolic processor. *Proc. SPIE: Real-Time Signal Processing IV,* Vol. 298, SPIE, 1981.
10. Bojanczyk A, Brent RP, Kung HT: Numerically stable solution of dense systems of linear equations using mesh-connected processors. *Journal on Scientific and Statistical Computing,* Vol. 5, No. 1, March 1984, pp. 95–104.
11. Bongiovanni G: A VLSI network for variable size FFTs. *Trans. on Computers,* Vol. C-32, No. 8, Aug. 1983, pp. 756–760.
12. Bongiovanni G: Two VLSI structures for the discrete Fourier transform. *Trans. on Computers,* Vol. C-32, No. 8, Aug. 1983, pp. 750–754.
13. Brent RP, Kung HT: Systolic VLSI arrays for linear-time GCD computation. In Anceau F, Aas EJ (eds): *VLSI '83,* North-Holland, Aug. 1983.
14. Brent RP, Luk FT, Loan CV: Computation of the singular value decomposition using mesh-connected processors, Technical Report 82-528, Cornell University, Ithaca, NY, March 1983.
15. Capello PR: VLSI Architecture for Digital Signal Processing. Ph.D. Thesis, Princeton University, Princeton, NJ, 1982.
16. Cappello PR, Steiglitz K: Unifying VLSI array designs with geometric transformations. *Proc. International Conference on Parallel Processing,* 1983, pp. 448–457.
17. Cappello PR, Steiglitz K: Unifying VLSI array design with linear transformations of space-time. In Preparata F (ed): *Advances in Computing Research,* JAI Press, Inc., 1984, pp. 23–65.
18. Cappello PR, Steiglitz K: Digital signal processing applications of systolic algorithms. In Kung HT, Sproull RR, Steele G Jr. (eds): *VLSI Systems and Applications,* Computer Science Press, Rockville, MD, 1981.
19. Chen M: Space-Time Algorithms: Semantics and Methodology. Technical Report 5090:TR:83, California Institute of Technology, May 1983.
20. Chen MC: A Methodology for Hierarchical simulation of VLSI Systems. Research Report, YALEU/DCS/RR-325, Yale University, New Haven, CT, Aug. 1984.
21. Chen MC: A Synthesis Method for Systolic Design. Research Report YALEU/DCS/RR-334, Yale University, New Haven, CT, Jan. 1985.
22. Chen MC: Synthesizing Systolic Designs. Research Report YALEU/DCS/RR-374, Yale University, New Haven, CT, March 1985.
23. Chen MC: The Generation of a Class of Multipliers: A Synthesis Approach to the Design of Highly Parallel Algorithms in VLSI. Research Report YALEU/DCS/RR-406, Yale University, New Haven, CT, July 1985.

24. Chen MC: A Parallel Language and its Compilation to Multiprocessor Machines or VLSI. Research Report YALEU/DCS/RR-412, Yale University, New Haven, CT, Aug. 1985.
25. Chen MC, Mead CA: Concurrent algorithms as space-time recursion equations. *Proc. USC Workshop on VLSI and Modern Signal Processing,* University of Southern California, Los Angeles, CA, Nov. 1982, pp. 31–52.
26. Cheng HD: Space-time domain expansion approach to VLSI and its application to pattern recognition and image processing. Ph.D. Thesis, Purdue University, West Lafayette, IN, 1985.
27. Cheng HD, and Fu KS: Algorithm partition for a fixed-size VLSI architecture using space-time domain expansion. *Proc. Seventh Symposium on Computer Arithmetic,* IEEE, June 1985.
28. Cheng HD, Fu KS: VLSI architectures for pattern matching using space-time domain expansion approach. *Proc. International Conference on Computer Design: VLSI in Computers,* IEEE 1985.
29. Cheng HD, Lin WC, Fu KS: *Proc. Seventh International Conference on Pattern Recognition,* IEEE, July 1984.
30. Cheng HD, Lin WC, Fu KS: Space-time domain expansion approach to VLSI and its application to hierarchical scene matching. *Trans. on Pattern Analysis and Machine Intelligence,* IEEE, May 1985, pp. 306–319.
31. Chiang YP, Fu KS: Parallel parsing algorithms and VLSI implementations for syntactic pattern recognition. *Trans. on Pattern Analysis and Machine Intelligence,* IEEE, Vol. PAMI-6, No. 5, May 1984, pp. 578–580.
32. Clarke MJ, Dyer CR: Systolic array for a dynamic programming application. *Proc. 12th Workshop on Applied Imagery Pattern Recognition,* IEEE, 1983.
33. Cohen D: Mathematical approach to iterative computation networks. *Proc. Fourth Symposium on Computer Arithmetic,* IEEE, 1978, pp. 226–238.
34. Cohen D, Tyree V: VLSI system for synthetic aperture radar (SAR) processing. In *Digital Processing of Aerial Images,* Vol. 186, SPIE, May 1979, pp. 166–177.
35. Dyer CR, Clarke MJ: Optimal curve detection in VLSI. *Proc. Conference on Computer Vision and Pattern Recognition,* IEEE, 1983, pp. 161–162.
36. Fisher AL: Systolic algorithms for running order statistics. In Kung HT, et al. (eds): *Signal and Image Processing VLSI Systems and Computations,* Computer Science Press, Rockville, MD, Oct. 1981, pp. 265–271.
37. Fortes JAB: Algorithm transformations for parallel processing and VLSI architecture design. Ph.D. Thesis, University of Southern California, Los Angeles, Dec. 1983.
38. Fortes JAB, Parisi-Presicce F: Optimal linear schedules for the parallel execution of algorithms. *Proc. International Conference on Parallel Processing,* IEEE, Aug. 1984.
39. Fortes JAB, Raghavendra CS: Dynamically reconfigurable fault-tolerant array processors. *Proc. 14th International Conference on Fault-Tolerant Computing,* IEEE, 1984.
40. Fortes JAB, Moldovan DI: Parallelism detection and transformation techniques useful for VLSI algorithms. *Journal of Parallel and Distributed Computing,* Vol. 2, Academic Press, 1985.
41. Fortes JAB, Moldovan DI: Data broadcasting in linearly scheduled array pro-

cessors. *Proc. 11th Annual Symposium on Computer Architecture,* ACM/ IEEE, 1984, pp. 224–231.

42. Foster MJ, Kung HT: The design of special-purpose VLSI chips. *Computer,* Vol. 13, No. 1, Jan. 1980, pp. 26–40.

43. Foster MJ, Kung HT: Recognize regular languages with programmable building blocks. In *VLSI 81,* Academic Press, Aug. 1981, pp. 75–84.

44. Fouse SD, Nudd GR, Cumming AD: A VLSI architecture for pattern recognition using residue arithmetic. *Proc. Sixth International Conference on Pattern Recognition,* IEEE, 1982.

45. Frison P, Quinton P: A VLSI parallel machine for speech recognition. *Proc. ICASSP,* 1984, pp. 25B.3.1–25B.3.4.

46. Fu KS: VLSI for Pattern Recognition and Image Processing, Springer-Verlag, New York, 1984.

47. Gajski DD, Kuhn RH: Guest editor's introduction: New VLSI tools. *Computer,* Vol. 16, No. 12, Dec. 1983, pp. 11–14.

48. Gannon D: Pipelining array computations for MIMD parallelism: A functional specification. *Proc. International Conference on Parallel Processing,* 1982, pp. 284–286.

49. Gentleman WM, Kung HT: Matrix triangularization by systolic arrays. *Proc. SPIE: Real-Time Signal Processing IV,* Vol. 298, 1981.

50. Guibas LJ, Kung HT, Thompson CD: Direct VLSI implementation of combinatorial algorithms. *Proc. Conference Very Large Scale Integration,* California Institute of Technology, Jan. 1979, pp. 509–525.

51. Guibas LJ, Liang FM: Systolic stacks, queues, and counters. *Proc. Conference on Advanced Research in VLSI,* Massachusetts Institute of Technology, Jan. 1982.

52. Horowitz E: VLSI architecture for matrix computations. *Proc. International Conference on Parallel Processing,* Aug. 1979, pp. 124–127.

53. Hwang K, Cheng YH: VLSI computing structure for solving large-scale linear system of equations. *Proc. International Conference on Parallel Processing,* Aug. 1980, pp. 217–227.

54. Hwang K, Su SP: VLSI architectures for feature extraction and pattern classification. *International Journal on Computer Vision, Graphics, and Image Processing,* Vol. 24, Academic Press, Nov. 1983, pp. 215–228.

55. Ibarra O, Kim S, Palis M: Designing systolic algorithms using sequential machines. *Proc. 25th Annual Symposium on Foundations of Computer Science,* ACM, Oct. 1984, pp. 46–55.

56. Ibarra O, Kim S, Palis M: Some results concerning linear iterative (systolic) arrays. *Journal of Parallel and Distributed Computing,* Vol. 2, 1985, pp. 182–218.

57. Johnsson L, Cohen D: Mathematical approach to modeling the flow of data and control in computational Networks. In Kung HT, et al (eds): *VLSI Systems and Computations,* Computer Science Press, Rockville, MD, 1981, pp. 213–225.

58. Johnsson L, Cohen D: Computational arrays for the discrete Fourier transform. *Proc COMPCON,* 1981, pp. 236–244.

59. Johnsson L, Weiser U, Cohen D, Davis A: Towards a formal treatment of VLSI arrays. *Proc. Second Caltech Conference on VLSI,* California Institute of Technology, Jan. 1981.

60. Jover JM, Kailath T: Design framework for systolic-type arrays. *Proc. ICASSP,* 1984, pp. 8.5.1–8.5.4.

61. Jutand F, Demassieux N, Viard D, Chollet G: VLSI architectures for dynamic time warping using systolic arrays. *Proc. ICASSP*, pp. 34A.5.1–34A.5.4, IEEE, 1984.

62. Kuhn RH: Transforming algorithms for single-stage and VLSI architectures. *Proc. Workshop on Interconnection Networks for Parallel and Distributed Processing,* April 1980, pp. 11–19.

63. Kuhn RH: Optimization and interconnection complexity for parallel processors, single stage networks and decision trees, Ph.D. Thesis, Technical Report 80-1009, University of Illinois, Urbana-Champaign, IL, 1980.

64. Kung HT: Special-purpose devices for signal and image processing: An opportunity in VLSI. *Proc. SPIE: Real-Time Signal Processing III,* Vol. 241, July 1980, pp. 76–84.

65. Kung HT: Highly concurrent systems introduction to VLSI system. In Mead CA, Conway LA (eds): *Introduction to VLSI Systems,* Addison-Wesley, 1980.

66. Kung HT: Use of VLSI in algebraic computation: Some suggestions. *Proc. Symposium on Symbolic and Algebraic Computation.* ACM SIGSAM, Aug. 1981, pp. 218–222.

67. Kung HT: Why systolic architecture. *Computer,* Vol. 15, No. 1, Jan. 1982, pp. 37–46.

68. Kung HT, Lehman PL: Systolic (VLSI) arrays for relational database operations. *Proc. International Conference Management of Data,* ACM SIGMOD, May 1980, pp. 105–116.

69. Kung HT, Leiserson CE: Systolic arrays (for VLSI). In Sparse Matrix Proc. 1978, pp. 256–282.

70. Kung HT, Lin WT: An algebra for VLSI algorithm design. *Proc. Conference on Elliptic Problem Solvers,* Monterey, CA, 1983.

71. Kung HT, Picard RL: Hardware pipelines for multi-dimensional convolution and resampling. *Proc. Computer Society Workshop on Computer Architecture for Pattern Analysis and Image Database Management,* Nov. 1981, pp. 273–278.

72. Kung HT, Ruance LM, Yen DWL: A two-level pipelined systolic array for convolutions. In Kung HT, et al (eds): *VLSI Systems and Computations,* Computer Science Press, Rockville, MD, Oct. 1981, pp. 255–264.

73. Kung HT, Song SW: A systolic 2-D convolution chip, Technical Report CMU-CS-81-110, Carnegie-Mellon University, Pittsburgh, PA, March 1981.

74. Kung SY: From transversal filter to VLSI wavefront array. *Proc. Internationala Conference on VLSI,* IFIP, 1983.

75. Kung SY: On supercomputing with systolic/wavefront array processors. *Proc. IEEE,* Vol. 72, No. 7, 1984.

76. Kung SY, Hu YH: A highly concurrent algorithm and pipelined architecture for solving toeplitz systems. *Trans. on Acoustics, Speech, and Signal Processing,* Vol. ASSP-31, No. 1, Feb. 1983, pp. 66–76.

77. Kuo CJ, Levy BC, Musicus BR: The specification and verification of systolic wave algorithms. In *VLSI Signal Processing,* IEEE Press, 1984.

78. Lam M, Mostow J: A transformational model of VLSI systolic design. *IFIP Sixth International Symposium on Computer Hardware Descriptive Languages and their Applications,* Carnegie-Mellon University, Pittsburgh, PA, May 1983.

79. Lehman PL: A systolic (VLSI) array for processing simple relational queries. In Kung HT, Sproull RF, Steele GI (eds): *VLSI Systems and Computations,* Computer Science Press, Rockville, MD, 1981.
80. Leiserson CE: Systolic priority queues. *Proc. Conference on Very Large Scale Integration,* California Institute of Technology, Jan. 1979, pp. 199–214.
81. Leiserson CE: Systolic and semisystolic design (extended abstract). *Proc. International Conference on Computer Design/VLSI in Computers,* IEEE 1983.
82. Leiserson CE: Area-efficient VLSI Computations. Massachusetts Institute of Technology Press, Cambridge, MA, 1983.
83. Leiserson CE, Rose FM, Saxe JB: Optimizing synchronous circuitry by retiming. In Bryant R (ed): *Proc. Third Caltech Conference on Very Large Scale Integration,* Computer Science Press, Rockville, MD, 1983.
84. Leiserson CE, Saxe JB: Optimizing synchronous systems. *Twenty-second Annual Symposium on Foundations of Computer Science,* ACM, Oct. 1981, pp. 23–36.
85. Li GJ: Array pipelining algorithms and pipelined array processors. M.Sc. Thesis, Institute of Computer Technology, Chinese Academy of Science, Beijing, China, 1981.
86. Li GJ, Wah BW: Optimal design of systolic arrays for image processing. *Proc. Workshop on Computer Architecture for Pattern Analysis and Image Database Management,* IEEE, Oct. 1983, pp. 134–141.
87. Li GJ, Wah BW: The design of optimal systolic algorithms. *Proc. Computer Software and Applications Conference,* IEEE, 1983, pp. 310–319.
88. Li GJ, Wah BW: The design of optimal systolic arrays. *Trans. on Computers,* Vol. C-34, No. 10, Jan. 1985, pp. 66–77.
89. Liu HH, Hu KS: VLSI algorithm for minimum distance classification. *Proc. International Conference on Computer Design,* IEEE, 1983.
90. Liu HH, Fu KS: A VLSI systolic processor for fast seismic signal classification. *Proc. International Symposium on VLSI Technology, Systems and Applications,* Taipei, Taiwan, March 30–April 1, 1983.
91. Liu PS, Young TY: VLSI array architecture for picture processing. In Fu KS, Kunii TL (eds): *Picture Engineering,* Springer Verlag, New York, Vol. 6, 1982.
92. McCanny JV, McWhirter JG: Implementation of signal processing functions using 1-bit systolic arrays. *Electronic Letters,* Vol. 18, No. 6, March 1982, pp. 241–243.
93. McCanny JV, McWhirter JG: Completely iterative, pipelined multiplier array suitable for VLSI. *Proc. IEEE,* Vol. 129, No. 2, April 1982, pp. 40–46.
94. McWhirter JG: Systolic array for recursive least-square minimization. *Electronics Letters,* Vol. 19, No. 18, Sept. 1983, pp. 729–730.
95. Miranker WL, Winkler A: Space-time representations of computational structures. *Computing,* Vol. 32, 1984, pp. 93–114.
96. Moldovan DI: On the analysis and synthesis of VLSI algorithms. *Trans. on Computers,* Vol. C-31, No. 11, Nov. 1982, pp. 1121–1126.
97. Moldovan DI: On the design of algorithms for VLSI systolic arrays. *Proc. IEEE,* Vol. 71, No. 1, Jan. 1983, pp. 113–120.
98. Moldovan DI, Fortes JAB: Partitioning of algorithms for fixed size VLSI architectures. Technical Report PPP-83-5, Department of Electrical Engineering Systems, University of Southern California, Los Angeles, CA, 1983.

99. Moldovan DI, Varma A: Design of algorithmically specialized VLSI devices. *Proc. International Conference on Computer Design: VLSI in Computers,* 1983, pp. 88–91.
100. Moldovan DI, Wu CI, Fortes JAB: Mapping an arbitrarily large QR algorithm into a fixed size VLSI array. *Proc. International Conference on Parallel Processing,* Aug. 1984.
101. Mostow J, Lam M: Transformational VLSI design: A progress report. Unpublished manuscript.
102. Narayan SS, Nash JG, Nudd GR: VLSI processor array for adaptive radar applications. *Proc. of SPIE 27th International Technical Symposium,* 1983.
103. Ni LM, Jain AK: Design of a pattern cluster using two-level pipelined systolic array. In Fu KS (ed): *VLSI for Pattern Recognition and Image Processing,* Springer-Verlag, New York, 1984.
104. Nishida S: Application of mapping algorithm to VLSI architectures, Technical Report, Department of Engineering Systems, University of Southern California, Los Angeles, 1984.
105. Ottmann T, Rosenberg AL, Stockmeyer LJ: A dictionary machine (for VLSI). Technical Report RC9060, IBM T. J. Watson Research Center, Yorktown Heights, NY, 1981.
106. Quinton P: The systematic design of systolic arrays. Technical Report 193, IRISA, April 1983.
107. Quinton P: Automatic synthesis of systolic arrays from uniform recurrent equations. *Proc. 11th Annual Symposium on Computer Architecture,* ACM/IEEE, 1984, pp. 208–214.
108. Ramakrishnan IV, Fussell DS, Sillberschatz A: On mapping homogeneous graphs on a linear array-processor model. *Proc. International Conference on Parallel Processing.* IEEE, 1983, pp. 440–447.
109. Savage C: A systolic data structure chip for connectivity problems. In Kung HT, Sproull RF, Steele GL Jr. (eds): *VLSI Systems and Computations,* Computer Science Press, Rockville, MD, 1981.
110. Schwartz DA, Barnwell TP III: A graph theoretic technique for the generation of systolic implementations for shift-invariant flow graphs. *Proc. ICASSP, IEEE,* 1984, pp. 8.3.1–8.3.4.
111. Song SW: On a high-performance VLSI solution to database problems. Ph.D. Dissertation Carnegie-Mellon University, Pittsburgh, PA, July 1981.
112. Stroll Z, Kang SC: VLSI-based image resampling for electronic publishing. In Fu KS (ed): *VLSI for Pattern Recognition and Image Processing,* Springer-Verlag, New York, 1984.
113. Travassos RT: Real-time implementation of systolic Kalman filters. Technical Report, Systolic Systems Inc., 1983.
114. Treleaven PC: VLSI processor architectures. *Computer,* Vol. 15, No. 6, June 1982, pp. 33–45.
115. Tur M, Goodman JW, Moslehi B, et al: Fiber-optic signal processor with applications to matrix-vector multiplication and lattice filtering. *Optics Letters,* Vol. 7, No. 9, Sept. 1982, pp. 463–465.
116. Ullman JD: Computational Aspects of VLSI, Computer Science Press, Rockville, MD, 1984.
117. Varman PJ, Fussell DS, Ramakrishnan IV, Sillberschatz A: Robust systolic

algorithms for relational database operations. *Proc. Symposium on Real Time Systems,* Dec. 1983.
118. Varman PJ, Ramakrishnan IV: Dynamic programming and transitive closure on linear pipelines. *Proc. International Conference on Parallel Processing,* 1984, pp. 359–364.
119. Weiser V, Davis A: A wavefront notion tool for VLSI array design. In Kung HT, et al (eds): *VLSI Systems and Computations,* Computer Science Press, Rockville, MD, 1981.
120. Weste V, Burr DJ, Ackland BD: Dynamic time warp pattern matching using an integrated multiprocessing array. *Trans. On Computers,* Vol. C-32, No. 8, Aug. 1983, pp. 731–744.
121. Wing O: A content-addressable systolic array for sparse matrix computation. Technical Report, Columbia University, New York, 1983.
122. Yeh CS, Reed IS, Truong TK: Systolic multipliers for finite fields. *Trans. on Computers,* Vol. C-33, No. 4, April 1984, pp. 357–360.
123. Yen DWL, Kulkarni AV: Systolic processing and an implementation for signal and image processing. *Trans. on Computers,* Vol. C-31, No. 10, Oct. 1982, pp. 1000–1008.
124. Zhang CN, Yun DYY: An area-time optimal systolic network for discrete Fourier transform. *Proc. 11th Annual International Symposium on Computer Architecture,* ACM/IEEE, June 1984.

12

Principles and Structures for Fault-Tolerant Computer Architectures

Daniel P. Siewiorek
Roy A. Maxion

12.1. Fault-Tolerance: Example and Overview

Fault-tolerant computing is a discipline that has evolved from early interest in system reliability. It is sometimes regarded as the survival attribute of digital systems (2). System reliability has been a major concern since the beginning of the electronic computer age. The earliest computers were constructed of components such as relays and vacuum tubes that would fail to operate correctly as often as once every 100,000 or 1 million cycles. This error rate was far too large to ensure correct completion of even modest calculations requiring tens of millions of operating cycles. Reliability features in these early computers focused almost exclusively on detection of errors. Recovery from failure was only achievable by restarting the software program.

Dependence on computing systems has grown to the extent that it is becoming difficult to return to less-sophisticated mechanisms. For example, automation pervades industries like banking and communications to the extent that system functions cannot be handled by humans. Humans cannot cope with the high data and throughput requirements of today's automated society. It is no longer possible to perform manually such tasks as assigning airline seats from a manual checklist or even typing, addressing, and mailing credit card bills each month. System failures can result in the loss of millions of dollars (19), loss of sensitive communication links (19), or loss of life (20). Thus, systems whose functions are highly automated must also be equipped with automated error-detection and failure-recovery mechanisms.

Today, interest in reliability permeates the computer industry, from large mainframe manufacturers to semiconductor fabricators who produce not only reliability-specific chips (such as error-correcting coders and decoders), but also entire systems. Because customer reliability expectations grow with each passing computer generation, computer designers must be students of reliability as well as students of design.

This chapter provides an introduction to principles and structures for fault-tolerant computer architectures. Topics covered include:

- **Attributes of reliable computing and their definitions.** Fundamental definitions are given. The role of reliability in the design process is delineated.
- **Fundamental reliability theory.** Before systems can be built to handle faults, designers need to understand the sources of faults and their manifestations in systems. The cause–effect sequence of faults is defined. Both hardware and software faults are considered. The stages of fault handling are described. These stages are used in developing a taxonomy of reliability-enhancement techniques.
- **Design for reliability.** Examples will be given on translating reliability requirements into hardware system specifications. Fault-handling techniques are surveyed and evaluation criteria for performing design trade-offs are defined. Structures for fault-tolerant systems are presented.
- **Commercial architectures.** Selected examples from IBM, Univac, Bell Systems, Tandem, Stratus, etc., are presented.

12.2. Concepts and Measures in Fault-Tolerant Systems

The discipline of fault-tolerant computing has evolved over the course of almost two decades. In the formative years of fault-tolerant computing, practitioners were primarily concerned with the design of reliable systems. Their goal was to reduce failure rates by whatever means were available, and without particularly distinguishing one class of methods from another. Many of the early methods of reliable design (which are still used) included conservative design practices like component burn-in, careful circuit routing, and use of high-quality components. Faults were avoided by using these methods, thereby reducing the occurrence of faults and simultaneously increasing reliability, but those inevitable faults that eventually occurred were not tolerated by the system—i.e., they still caused catastrophic system failure. In response to this, methods were developed to enable systems to detect their own faults. This provided sufficient warning so that systems could take remedial action based on the nature of the failure (e.g., try the failed operation again), but still there was no tolerance of the failure in the sense that the system could essentially ignore altogether the presence of the fault. Later, methods based on redundancy were developed, and these methods showed that faults could be tolerated with little or no adverse effect on system performance. From these approaches arose the two principal methods of increasing system reliability: fault-avoidance and fault-tolerance. *Fault-avoidance* is the prevention of fault occurrence by careful construction of systems, thereby improving system reliability. *Fault-tolerance* involves the application of special techniques, like redundancy, to provide a level of service complying with the system goals, despite faults having occurred or being present. These ideas will be discussed in Section 12.4.

12.2.1. Terminology

As the discipline of fault-tolerant computing has evolved, so has its terminology. As more is learned about computer systems and their behaviors under exceptional conditions, definitions evolve to become more precise. The term *fault-tolerance* suggests a host of concepts: *dependability* and impairments to it such as *faults, errors,* and *failures*; the *means* for achieving dependability such as *fault-tolerance, fault-avoidance, error removal,* and *error forecasting*; and *measures* of dependability such as *reliability, availability, maintainability, diagnosability,* and *safety*. These terms are not always used consistently. Establishing a common terminology is important, especially in a field so intrinsically given to complexity as computer design. Consequently, an effort to standardize the terminology is in progress under the auspices of IFIP Working Group 10.4 on reliable computing and fault-tolerance. This section draws on their terminology as given in (15).

Service and Dependability

At the highest level of abstraction, the system can be viewed from the user's or client's vantage point, which is that the system provides a service on which clients depend to accomplish their own objectives. Service and dependability are, at an intuitive level, exactly what one would expect. The computer system provides a *service* to users. This service could be word processing, numerical or symbolic computation, billing, transaction processing as in airline reservation making, or monitoring and/or control of critical processes like chemical plants, air traffic control systems, or spacecraft.

User or clients in any of these situations come to place an expectation, a reliance, or a trust in the level of service offered by the system. That is, they expect the system—indeed, depend on the system—to perform calculations on demand, print the invoices on time, operate at a particular minimum throughput, and be available for any use throughout specified periods during the day or week. The extent to which the system delivers service according to user expectations can be qualitatively measured in terms of the system's *dependability*. A good example illustrating this is an automated bank teller machine. Both bank officials and bank customers have certain needs and expectations that they demand of automated tellers, and people have come to depend on these machines to the extent that when the machines deny desired services, banks are likely to lose customers.

Using dependability as a system performance yardstick permits a separation of the general perception of reliability as a qualitative system attribute from the more quantitative sense of reliability as a system measure. Dependability lies at the root of Laprie's taxonomy, suggesting three main classes of attributes, decribed below, and shown graphically in Figure 12.1.

- **Impairments to dependability.** These are undesired (not necessarily unexpected) circumstances causing or resulting from undependability. System dependability can be impaired by faults, errors, and failures.
- **Means to dependability.** These are the methods, tools, and solutions that provide a system with the ability to deliver a service on which reliance can be placed. Two of the most cogent examples of such methods are fault-avoidance and fault-tolerance.
- **Measures of dependability.** Measurements of system dependability are needed as a means of appraising the quality of service delivered by a system. The usual metrics for such assessments are reliability and availability.

Computer system *dependability* refers to the quality of service provided by the system such that reliance can *justifiably* be placed on the service. Service is dependent on the application because some applications demand higher levels of service than others. The expected level of service to be delivered by a system is usually specified in terms of the extent to which service can be delayed or denied. When no service degradation can be tolerated, as in a deep space mission, a highly reliable system is de-

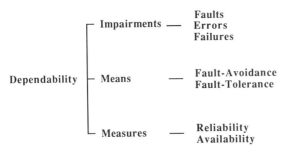

Figure 12.1 Partial taxonomy of fault-tolerance.

manded. A highly reliable system never does "the wrong thing." When short service degradations can be tolerated, as in many transaction processing systems, a highly available system is demanded. A highly available system does "the right thing" within a specified response time. Critical applications like air traffic control, chemical plant process automation, and hospital patient monitoring may suffer catastrophic consequences from even temporary interruptions or degradations in service, hence their demand for high reliability. Alternatively, an airline reservation system can tolerate service degradations, like slowdowns, though it may be unable to tolerate complete outages.[1]

System dependability can be impaired by faults, errors, and failures, each of which has a distinct meaning. A wide range of techniques for overcoming the adverse effects of fault, errors, and failures is broken roughly into two classes: fault-avoidance methods and fault-tolerance methods. The success of applying these means of achieving system dependability is usually measured in terms of reliability and availability. Each of these concepts is discussed in the following sections.

Faults, Errors, and Failures

Fault classes were originally introduced by Avizienis (2), who classified faults as being either physical faults or human-made faults. Laprie has classified faults into two broad categories as follows:

- **Physical faults.** Physical faults are adverse physical phenomena, either internal or external. Examples of internal physical faults are threshold changes, short circuits, open circuits, stuck-at-one, stuck-at-zero, etc. Examples of external faults are effects due to temperature or humidity change, to lightning strikes or electromagnetic disturbances, and other environmental perturbations.
- **Human-made faults.** Examples of human-made faults are design faults and interaction faults. Design faults are introduced during system design. Interaction faults are inadvertant or deliberate violations of operating or maintenance procedures.

Thus, a *fault* is a physical perturbation of some part of the system. One example of a physical fault is the mechanism (e.g., short circuit) by which a memory bit becomes stuck at one value, say zero. When a memory bit is stuck, it cannot be changed from the stuck value by the normal means of writing to memory. The fact that the bit is stuck is an *error*. This is the *manifestation* of the fault. Errors can be latent or active, depending on whether or not the system comes into active contact with them. Using the

---

[1] A major airline can lose as much as $36,000 for each *minute* of downtime. It is easy to see why. A customer wishing to reserve space on a flight will call another airline if his or her reservation request is denied because "the computer is down."

example of the stuck memory bit, the stuck-at error is considered latent if either the bit is never accessed in the course of normal computation, or the bit *is* accessed and the stuck-at value of zero happens to be what would have been stored at that location anyway. A latent error turns into an effective error when the error affects some operation in the system. Again using the stuck-at memory bit as an example, when a program uses the value in the stuck-at memory bit, and that value is wrong, that *effective error* causes a failure. Hence, a *failure* can be considered to be an active encounter with a latent defect. The failure occurs when the error affects the service delivered by the system, such as when the wrong memory value causes the execution of an invalid instruction, halting the machine. Notice that errors can cycle between latent and effective states. An effective error may (and often does) propagate from one component to another, creating a cascade of errors along the way. Laprie gives several illustrative examples:

• A programmer's mistake is a fault. The consequence is a (latent) error in the written software (erroneous instruction or piece of data); upon activation (activation of the module where the error resides and an appropriate input pattern activating the erroneous instruction, instruction sequence or piece of data), the error becomes effective. When this effective error produces erroneous data (in value or in the timing of their delivery) that affect the delivered service, a failure occurs.

• A short-circuit occurring in an integrated circuit is a fault. The consequence (connection stuck at a Boolean value, modification of the circuit function, etc.) is an error that will remain latent as long as it is not activated, the continuation of the process being identical to the previous example.

• An electromagnetic perturbation of sufficient energy is a fault when, for instance, acting on a memory's inputs, it will create an error if active when the memory is in the write position. The error will remain latent until the erroneous memory location(s) is (are) read, etc.

• An inappropriate man–machine interaction performed (inadvertently or deliberately) by an operator during the operation of the system is a fault. The resulting altered data is an error, etc.

• A maintenance or operating manual writer's mistake is a fault. The consequence is an error in the corresponding manual (erroneous directives) that will remain latent as long as the directives are not acted upon in order to face a given situation, etc.

From these examples, it is evident that the duration of error latency may vary considerably, depending on the fault, the system utilization, and so forth. These examples also illustrate why an error is defined as being liable to lead to a failure. Whether or not an error will effectively lead to a failure depends on several factors: the activation conditions of the error, the system configuration, and the amount of available redundancy.

Fault-Avoidance and Fault-Tolerance

Fault-avoidance and fault-tolerance are two means by which reliability and dependability can be improved. Intuitively, these two terms mean exactly what one would expect, as explained next.

Fault-avoidance. Fault-avoidance is a preemptive measure taken to avoid the occurrences of faults in the first place. Fault-avoidance employs conservative design practices such as the use of high-quality components, careful signal routing, shielding and equipment grounding, and static reduction via filters and grounds. Some machines (e.g., VAX-8600) are equipped with wrist and ankle ground straps that technicians must don before touching the inside of the cabinet. Limiting the fanout of gates can decrease power dissipation and, hence, thermal effects. It also decreases the possibility of transient faults by limiting the effective noise margin. Also of concern is the avoidance of human errors through careful construction of drawings, documentation, and maintenance procedures. Fault-avoidance can be enhanced by manipulating factors that affect the failure rate such as the environment of the system, the quality of its components, and its complexity.

Environmental conditions consist of several factors, the most important of which is probably heat. While the operating environment is usually beyond the designer's control, there are design issues that can address temperature concerns. Gate junction temperature, for example, is a function of ambient air temperature, heat transfer from the chip to its package to the air, and power consumption on the chip itself. These factors can be modified through the use of fans, air conditioners, or coolants; heat sinking of boards and chips; and limited fan-out designs.

Sometimes, circuit boards develop "hot spots" due to several factors. One condition is that hot chips are on the leeward side of components that block airflow. Another is that several hot chips are placed together on a board instead of being dispersed. Sometimes, turbulence due to nonuniform surfaces causes hot spots, the solution for which is to make the board as uniform as possible, perhaps by using dummy packages to fill empty areas (26).

Changing the quality of system components is a common fault-avoidance technique. High reliability can be achieved by careful screening of components during system manufacture (be sure the chip works before installing it on a board), and by burn-in, in which failures due to infant mortality will be corrected before the system is delivered to a customer.

When components are integrated at higher levels (e.g., LSI), a number of advantages are obtained. There are fewer chips at high integration levels, hence fewer solder joints and fewer boards. Moreover, component failure rates do not increase linearly with the number of gates or bits on a chip, so failure rates decrease as gate counts go up.

When fault-avoidance techniques are employed in reliable system design, the effects of many environmental and design factors can be mitigated. It is noted in (26, page 77) that roughly a 5 to 1 improvement in mean time to failure can be attained solely through the use of fault-avoidance techniques.

Fault-tolerance.   Fault-tolerance is carried out by automatic or operator-assisted error processing whose constituent phases are: processing effective errors and processing latent errors. The goal of processing effective errors is to return an effective error to a latent state before the occurrence of a failure. The goal of processing latent errors is to ensure that a latent error does not become effective by virtue of making the error passive, possibly through reconfiguring the system so that the portion of the system containing the error is no longer part of the active system. An example of this is the use of parity in memory systems.

Processing effective errors takes two forms: error recovery and error compensation. In general, error recovery is the substitution of an error-free state for an erroneous state. That is, when it is discovered that a system is in an erroneous state, recovery is effected by returning the system to a known good state. One typical way of accomplishing this is backward error recovery. Rollback and journaling (discussed in Section 12.7) are backward recovery methods of returning systems to error-free conditions by virtue of resetting the system to a known good state, and continuing processing from there.

Error compensation can take place when the error state contains enough redundancy to overcome the effects of the error, thereby enabling the delivery of error-free service despite the presence of the error. This is distinct from error recovery in that error recovery methods actually reset parts of the system, whereas error compensation techniques are essentially able to ignore the presence of errors. Typically this is accomplished through masking (see Section 12.4).

Reliability and Availability
Reliability is a measure of the capacity of a piece of equipment to operate without failure when put into service. Reliability is the probability that a device will perform adequately or as expected, for the period of time intended under the operating conditions encountered. Reliability is always a probability associated with a no-failure performance of a device (from chips to entire large systems) after an accumulated time (from very short switching times to very long mission times) in specific environments over a given period of operation with some desired level of confidence.

Reliability can be classified into predicted reliability, inherent reliability, and demonstrated reliability. *Predicted reliability* represents the performance expected of a system after its design has been reviewed and corrected. Predicted reliability can be calculated using design parameters before final assembly or system test. *Inherent reliability* is an intrinsic function of design, and can change only if the design is changed or if the system degrades during operation. *Demonstrated reliability* is derived from field tests, and is constrained by both time and economics. Demonstrated reliability cannot be established for a system until the system matures to a stable state.

Reliability is not used to predict discrete events. Only probabilities can be predicted. Reliability will not predict that a system will operate for a certain time interval before failing. Rather, reliability predicts that a system will, on average, experience some number of failures in a given period, or that a certain average time will elapse between failures. A well-designed highly reliable system might fail within minutes of being turned on, or it might run without failure for an abnormally long time, but reliability does not predict which of these will happen. Reliability is a general statement of the set of expectations placed on a system.

In summary, reliability is the meaure that imparts a sense of confidence in the nonfailure of any part of a system. It suggests a high level of assurance that the system will continuously deliver its expected service throughout the life of its particular mission. Reliability is of great importance to users of law-office word processors as well as controllers of spacecraft as computers face harsher environments, novice users, and increasing maintenance costs. Everyone pays for unreliability, from manufacturers and their service organizations to end-users.

Availability is often used as a figure of merit in systems in which service (in the sense discussed, not in the sense of service as maintenance) can be delayed or denied for brief periods without serious consequences. This means essentialy that some amount of downtime can be tolerated under prescribed conditions. High-availability systems strive to keep downtime to a minimum, as well as to distribute downtime in prescribed ways.

The goal of minimizing downtime is important because the cost of downtime can be quite severe. Aside from the obvious consequences of loss of life due to failure (downtime) of systems controlling or monitoring hospital patient monitors, nuclear or chemical plants, or spacecraft, other losses can occur as a result of downtime even in mundane applications.

The anatomy of a typical outage is interesting. Consider a conventional, well-managed transaction processing system such as a banking system or airline reservation system. Such systems typically fail about once a week, incurring roughly a 90-minute outage. Figure 12.2 portrays a time line for the outage.[2] Assume, as is usually the case, that an operations error or software error caused the outage. It takes a few minutes for someone to realize that there is a problem and that a restart is the only obvious solution. It takes the operator about 5 minutes to snapshot the system state for later analysis. Then the restart can begin. For a large system, the operating system

---

[2] This scenario is from (6).

Minutes
<pre>
 0   Problem occurs
 3   Operator decides problem requires dump/restart
 8   Operator completes dump
12   OS restart complete; begin DB/DC restart
17   DB restart complete (assume no tape handling)
30   Network restart continuing
40   Network restart continuing
50   Network restart continuing
60   Network restart continuing
70   DC restart complete; begin user restart
80   User restart continuing
90   User restart complete
</pre>

Figure 12.2 A simple failure mushrooms into a 90-minute outage.

takes a few minutes to get started. Then the database and data communications systems begin their restart. The database restart completes within a few minutes, but it may take an hour to restart a 5000 terminal network. Once the network is up, the users take a while to refocus on the tasks they had been performing. After restart, much work has been saved for the system to perform, so the transient load presented at restart is the peak load. This affects system sizing.

Ninety minutes of downtime per week translates into 99.2% availability. This might *sound* very good, but hospital patients, people living near nuclear or chemical plants, and users of automated tellers and reservation systems do not share this view. A system that fails once a week is unacceptable for these applications.

It is interesting to see how a change in availability of just .1% can affect a commercial operation. Consider a reservation system for a major airline. Downtime for such an application can cost $36,000 each minute. For 90 minutes of downtime, the cost is $3.24 million per week. Considering that a .1% change in availability means a 10-minute weekly reduction in downtime, the money saved is $360,000. That startling figure demonstrates not so subtly how important availability is. The cost of downtime cannot always be measured directly in terms of dollars. Other aspects are lost work, lost opportunity, lost accounts, loss of credibility, and increased maintenance costs.

Only two basic measures have been considered—reliability and availability—whereas a third one—maintainability—is usually considered, and may be defined as a measure of the continuous service interruption or, equivalently, of the time to restoration. This measure is no less important than those previously defined; it was not introduced earlier because it may, at least conceptually, be deduced from the other two.

Coverage

If a machine boasted 100% *coverage*, it would mean that absolutely every aspect—every circuit, every gate, every data path—was covered by some mechanism for tolerating faults. It is not likely that any such system exists, but coverage is still a useful concept for gauging the extent of fault-tolerance attributed to a system.

Coverage is a concept serving diverse purposes with two major meanings, quantitative and qualitative. The quantitative meaning is used most often in reliability modeling of redundant systems. In its quantitative sense, coverage is the probability that the system successfully recovers from a specified failure. Quite often, coverage is the probability that a particular class of fault is successfully detected before complete system corruption occurs. Other typical uses include the probability of successful takeover by backup systems, and noncorruption of checkpoint variables.

The qualitative meaning of coverage specifies the types of errors against which a particular redundancy scheme guards. For example, the coverage of a Hamming single-error-correcting double-error-detecting code is correction for all single-bit errors in a code word and detection of all double-bit errors and some multiple-bit errors. This measure of coverage has been developed for a variety of both error-detection and correction techniques (11).

12.2.2. Measurements in Fault-Tolerant Systems

Any scheme for measuring computer system dependability, reliability or availability requires a method of evaluating the goodness of the measurement for the sake of comparing one system against another. This section briefly introduces some criteria for evaluation of fault-tolerant systems by qualifying the system attributes discussed.

It is of interest to first note how one's perception of reliability and availability changes according to the application domain of the system. To a banker, an automated teller is reliable if it never (or seldom) prevents a customer from depositing or withdrawing money (as well as being error-free in recording the transaction). To a researcher, a system is reliable if it has the space and computing power available for processing experimental data. Reliability to a word processing operator means that the system never loses files. Finally, an air traffic control system is reliable if it is never responsible for fatal consequences resulting from bad decisions or unavailability.

Interestingly, similar application dependencies also apply to availability. An automated teller is considered sufficiently available if it is never inaccessible long enough to make customers leave (about 3 minutes, according to bank surveys). An airline ticket agent considers a system to be suitably available if it processes reservation requests within a reasonable amount of time, but word processing operators regard slowdowns as a lack of availability, because when the system cannot keep up with input keystrokes, the system is essentially unavailable.

When system specifications are written, they often include reliability and availability requirements. A typical requirement might be that the system should have a maximum unavailability of 30 minutes per day. Notice that the 30 minutes can be split in various ways. For example, the specification might call for a maximum of one outage per day, but if the outage actually occurred, a duration of 30 minutes would be tolerable. Alternatively, the 30 minutes could be broken into 10 intervals of no longer than 3 minutes each. This first situation would be unacceptable for automated tellers; the second situation would not. However, a word processing operator would much prefer a single outage of moderate duration each day as opposed to 10 short outages.

There are a number of criteria for evaluating the dependability of computing structures. Often, several measures are required to describe a system adequately. Table 12.1 shows several system evaluation criteria, though only a subset of these will be discussed here. For additional information, see (26).

Failure rates of electronic components vary with time. Time-dependent failure rates are called *hazard functions,* hazard rates, or mortality rates, and are usually measured in failures per million hours. For electronic components on the normal-life portion of the bathtub curve (Figure 12.3), the failure rate is assumed to be constant. The exponential hazard function then is

$$z(t) = \lambda$$

Table 12.1 Evaluation Criteria

Deterministic
    Survive at least k component failures

Probabilistic functions
    Hazard function (failure rate): $z(t)$
    Reliability: $R(t)$
    Mission time: $MT(r)$
    Repair rate: μ
    Availability: $A(t)$

Single parameters
    Mean Time to Failure (MTTF)
    Mean Time to Repair (MTTR)
    Mean Time Between Failures (MTBF)
    Coverage

Comparative measures
    Reliability difference: $R_2(t) - R_1(t)$
    Reliability gain: $R_2(t)/R_1(t)$
    Mission time improvement: $MT_2(r)/MT_1(r)$

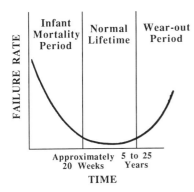

Figure 12.3 Failure rate versus age.

where the parameter λ is referred to as the *failure rate* because it describes the rate at which failures occur in time.

Reliability can be quantified as the probability that the device or system will not fail before a given time period elapses. R(t), a function of time, is the conditional probability that the system has survived a specific interval, given that the system was operational at the beginning of the interval.

Reliability is a measure used to describe systems in which repair is not possible (e.g., space missions) or in which the system is serving a critical function and cannot be lost even for the short time it may take for a repair (e.g., aircraft flight computers) or in which the repair is prohibitively expensive. In general, building highly reliable computers is difficult because of the stringent requirements imposed by the reliability definition.

Because reliability and availability equations are often too complex to comprehend, even for simple systems, several single-parameter metrics have been proposed to summarize the continuous-time equations.

MTTF

The mean time to failure, specifically the mean time to first failure. Like the MTTF for components, the MTTF of a system is the expected time to the first system failure in a population of identical systems given successful startup at time zero. It assumes a perfect system at time zero. For the special case of nonredundant systems with a constant failure rate, $R(t) = e^{-\lambda t}$ and MTTF $= 1/\lambda$. Although, in theory, MTTF applies only to large populations, it is also a useful measure for only a single design with a population of one. The MTTF for a constant hazard rate can be calculated as (length of interval)/ (average number of failures per interval).

MTBF

Strictly speaking, mean time to failure should be used when measuring the expected time of first failure of a population of systems. Mean time between failures is used with repairable systems. MTBF includes the mean time between two successive component failures, though the components need not be identical, plus the time to repair and restore the system to an operational state. A simple approximation for MTBF is MTBF = MTTF + MTTR, where MTTR is the reciprocal of a constant repair rate (μ) for an exponential distribution.

Availability

For systems that can be repaired, a measure called availability is often used. Availability, A(t), is the probability that the system is operational at any given time. Availability differs from reliability in that any number of system failures can have occurred prior to time t, but the system is available if all those failures have been repaired. With reliability, the system is considered reliable only if *no* system failures have occurred prior to that time. As a result, the availability function has a steady-state term (a nonzero constant). For a constant failure rate λ (i.e., nonredundant system following a Poisson distribution) and a constant repair rate μ, the steady state availability can be expressed as $A_{ss} = \mu/(\lambda + \mu)$, where λ is the constant failure rate and μ is the constant repair rate.

Steady state availability can also be found in terms of MTTF and MTTR. MTTR is used to measure system repairability, and is the expected time for repair of a failed system. For exponential distributions where MTTF = $1/\lambda$ and MTTR = $1/\mu$, the steady state availability can be calculated as A_{ss} = MTTF/(MTTF + MTTR).

12.3. How Systems Fail

When designing fault-tolerant systems, it is first useful to know the origins of faults so that system design can circumvent errors when faults occur. Faults can be due to physical changes, design inadequacies, environmental influences, or human error. In addition to the faults, errors, and failures described in Section 12.2, Avizienis (2) has made the following characterizations:

- **Permanent.** Describes a fault, error, or failure that is continuous and stable. In hardware, permanent failure reflects an irreversible physical change. The word *hard* is used interchangeably with *permanent*.
- **Intermittent.** Describes a fault or error that is only occasionally present due to unstable hardware or varying hardware or software states (e.g., as a function of load or activity).
- **Transient.** Describes a fault or error resulting from temporary environmental conditions (e.g., alpha-particle perturbation of memory bits). The word *soft* is used interchangeably with *transient*.

Figure 12.4 shows the possible sources of failure. Intermittent errors can be caused by unstable or marginally stable hardware, or incorrect de-

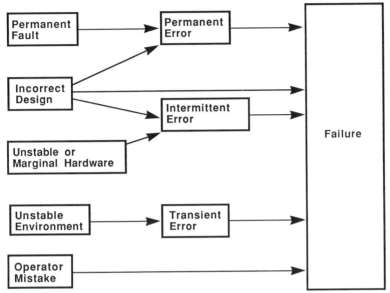

Figure 12.4 Sources of failure.

signs. Environmental conditions can lead to transient errors. Operator mistakes can produce failures. Errors resulting from physical conditions or repeated environmental conditions are usually easily detected and repaired. Errors due to temporary environmental or timing conditions are not repairable because the hardware is undamaged. It is this attribute of transient errors that magnifies their importance.

Permanent or *intermittent* errors may be repaired by the replacement of a physical component. Transients, on the other hand, may be due to environmental factors (e.g., static electricity, noisy power supplies, cosmic rays, etc.) or to design errors (e.g., timing errors). They may not be repaired by physically replacing a component with an identical component. A US Air Force study (25) showed that 80% of electronic failures in computers were intermittent. These kinds of failures are particularly nettlesome to field service organizations because roughly 40% of their time is spent in attempting to trace faults that will never be found. This can be extremely costly for a maintenance operation.

There are numerous ways for errors to occur. Some are due to physical manufacturing defects. Others are due to normal operational stresses or to heavy loads on the system. Transients are often due to a combination of local phenomena such as ground loops, static, and thermal effects, and universal phenomena such as alpha particles, cosmic rays, and power surges.

In addition to physical defects, faults can manifest themselves as logical errors. Logic values in gates and pins can become *stuck-at* either 0 or 1. *Bridging* occurs when signal lines are physically shorted together. *Shorts* and *opens* correspond to unwanted additional connections and undesired missing connections, respectively.

At the system level, faults are usually manifested as operation retries or as system crashes. Timing problems (e.g., race conditions) are often suspected, but extremely difficult to track down. See (26) for additional details.

12.4. Stages and Techniques for Fault-Tolerance[3]

The function of fault-tolerance is to preserve delivery of expected system services even in the presence of errors caused by faults either internal or external to the system itself. At an abstract level, this goal is accomplished by providing the system with extra resources that nearly always take the form of redundancy in one of three domains: time, space, and information. Redundancy in time suggests repetition of computational operations that can be checked against one another or can be continually repeated until an error-free execution is achieved. Redundancy in space suggests extra hardware so that parallel computations can be voted upon, errors can be masked out, or duplicate hardware can be switched automatically to replace failed hardware. Redundancy in information suggests software replications in which different algorithms are employed to compute the same result, which is voted upon immediately after the computation terminates.

There are at least 10 stages a system must progress through to eliminate the effect of a fault or error. Note that not all stages need be present in a fault-tolerant system. A major design decision facing the designer is how many of these stages are implemented in hardware and how many in software.

- **Fault/error confinement.** When faults/errors occur, it is desirable to limit the scope of their effects. Fault/error confinement is achieved by limiting the spread of fault/error effects to one area of the system, thereby preventing contamination of other areas. Fault/error confinement can be achieved through liberal use of fault and error detection circuits, through consistency checks before performing a function ("mutual suspicion"), and through multiple requests/confirmations before performing a function. These techniques may be applied in both hardware and software.
- **Fault/error detection.** Most faults eventually result in logical errors. Many techniques are available to detect faults/errors, such as parity, consistency checking, and protocol violation. Unfortunately, these techniques are not perfect, and an arbitrary period of time may pass before detection occurs. This time is called "error latency." Fault-detection techniques are of two major classes: off-line detection and on-line detection. With off-line de-

---

[3] This section draws from Ref. 26, Chapter 3.

tection, the device is not able to perform useful work while under test. Diagnostic programs, for example, run in a stand-alone fashion even if executed on idle devices or multiplexed with the operations software. Thus, off-line detection assures integrity before and possibly at intervals during operation, not during the entire time of operation. On-line detection, on the other hand, provides a real-time detection capability, because it is performed concurrently with useful work. On-line techniques include parity detection and duplication.

- **Fault/error masking.** Fault/error-masking techniques hide the effects of faults. In a sense, the redundant information outweighs the incorrect information. In its pure form, masking provides no detection. However, many fault-masking techniques can be extended to provide on-line detection as well. Otherwise, off-line detection techniques are needed to discover faults. Majority voting is an example of fault masking.
- **Re-try.** In many cases, a second attempt at an operation may be successful. This is particularly true of a transient error that causes no physical damage.
- **Diagnosis.** If the fault/error-detection technique does not provide information about the fault location and/or properties, a diagnostic step may be required.
- **Reconfiguration.** If a fault/error is detected and a permanent fault located, the system may be able to reconfigure its components to replace the failed component or to isolate it from the rest of the system. The component may be replaced by backup spares. Alternatively, it may simply be switched off and the system capability degraded. This process is called "graceful degradation."
- **Recovery.** After detection and (if necessary) reconfiguration, the effects of errors must be eliminated. Normally, the system operation is backed up to some point in its processing that preceded the fault/error detection, and operation recommences from this point. This form of recovery, often called "rollback," usually entails strategies using backup files, checkpointing, and journaling. In recovery, error latency becomes an important issue because the rollback must go far enough to avoid the effects of undetected errors that occurred before the detected one.
- **Restart.** Recovery may not be possible if too much information is damaged by an error, or if the system is not designed for recovery. A "hot" restart— that is, a resumption of all operations from the point of fault/error detection—is possible only if no damage has occurred. A "warm" restart implies that only some of the processes can be resumed without loss. A "cold" restart corresponds to a complete reload of the system, with no processes surviving.
- **Repair.** When a component is diagnosed as "failed," it is replaced. As with detection, repair (replacing defective components) can be either on-line or off-line. In off-line repair, either the failed component is not necessary for system operation and can be removed without bringing down

the system, or the entire system must be brought down to perform the diagnosis and repair. In on-line repair, the component may be replaced immediately by a backup spare in a procedure equivalent to reconfiguration, or operation may continue without the component as is the case with masking redundancy or graceful degradation. In either case of on-line repair, the failed component may be physically replaced or repaired without interrupting system operation.

* **Reintegration.** After the physical replacement of a component, the repaired module must be reintegrated into the system. For on-line repair, reintegration must be accomplished without interrupting system operation.

Because this section focuses on major architectural differences in fault-tolerant systems, time-redundant methods will be discussed only briefly, and information-redundant methods not at all. For a discussion of software fault-tolerance, see (3) and (1) for more information about time-redundancy using various recovery schemes, see (26) for fault-tolerance in design, see (3) and (14), and for user interface fault-tolerance, see (17).

The major techniques addressed here are masking redundancy and dynamic redundancy. Error detection plays a role, too, in that once an error is detected, recovery by re-try can be invoked from a previous checkpoint in the system at whose time the system's state was known to be good. These recovery methods are generally referred to as "rollbacks" because the system, upon detecting an error, rolls itself back in time to a point before the error, then begins computation again from that point. Such techniques can be successful when the fault is transient, but they will fail for permanent faults. See Table 12.2 for a summary of reliability techniques. This section will only discuss four stages in fault/error handling: detection, masking, reconfiguration, and recovery.

12.4.1. Fault/Error Detection Techniques

Fault/error detection techniques are employed primarily to invoke some kind of corrective action when faults and errors are detected. This action can range from retrying the operation, to switching in replacement parts, to ignoring the erroneous results (the bad data are simply not used). Attempts at correction through rollback or reconfiguration are also possible.

Duplication. Duplication is probably the simplest detection technique. Two identical copies of hardware run the same computations, then results are checked. At such time as the results do not match, an error has occurred. Duplication is a popular detection technique because of its simplicity and its applicability to all areas and levels of computer design. Its only drawback is a susceptibility to common mode errors that may not produce identical data to be presented to the comparator, though there are mechanisms for avoiding this contingency, too. Duplication, however, is expensive because

Table 12.2 Reliability and Fault-Tolerance Techniques

Region	*Technique*
Fault avoidance	Environment modification
	Quality changes
	Component integration level
Fault detection	Duplication
	Error detection codes
	Parity
	Check sums
	Arithmetic codes
	Cyclic codes
	Self-checking and fail-safe logic
	Watchdog timers and time-outs
	Consistency and capability checks
Masking redundancy	Voting
	Error correcting codes
	Hamming DED/SEC
	Other codes
	Masking logic
	Interwoven logic
	Coded-state machines
Dynamic redundancy	Reconfigurable duplication
	Reconfigurable NMR
	Backup sparing
	Graceful degradation
	Reconfiguration
	Recovery

it requires replication of the simplex system plus a comparison element. This, too, can be avoided by using the same hardware to perform redundant operations (time redundancy), though this doubles execution time and is more susceptible to hardware faults. Transients would be less problematic.

Error-Detection Codes. Error-detection codes utilize information redundancy. For example, parity codes involve the addition of an extra bit to represent the number of ones or zeroes in a group of bits. If the group of bits has an even number of ones, it is defined as having even parity; otherwise, it is of odd parity. The choice of even or odd depends on the dominant fault mode. Even parity does not detect all zeroes. A number of variations on parity are discussed in (26).

Checksums. The checksum for a block of words is formed by adding together all of the words in the block module n, where n is arbitrary. The block of words and its checksum together constitute a code. This code is recomputed each time the block of words is retransmitted, and compared to the last computation. If the two do not match, there is an error. More complete information on checksumming and its variations can be found in (11).

Watchdog Timers. A watchdog timer is maintained as a process separate from the one it checks. The timer is set when the timed process begins. If the timer is not reset within the time limit imposed by the timer, the corresponding process is assumed to have failed in some way. The idea underlying this mechanism is that any failure or corruption of the timed process will cause it to miss resetting its watchdog. Watchdog timers can be implemented in hardware or software.

Consistency and Capability Checking. Consistency checks require minimal hardware redundancy. The check is done by testing to ensure that interim or final results are reasonable either on an absolute basis or as a simple function of the inputs. One example is a range check, which confirms that a compared value is within a reasonable range, such as paychecks not exceeding some maximum value. The most common uses of consistency checking are address checking, opcode checking, and arithmetic operation checking. Capability checking is usually embedded in the operating system. Access to resources is limited to clients with proper authorization. Resources might include memory segments and I/O devices; clients might themselves be processes.

12.4.2. Masking Redundancy

Masking redundancy, sometimes known as static redundancy, uses extra components in such a way as to obscure, or mask, the effect of a faulty component.

Fault masking provides fault-tolerance either by isolating faults or by correcting them before they propagate to module outputs. Masking is an apt term because under this scheme the errors do not go away; rather, their effects are hidden from clients. Because masking does not involve spares, when the masking redundancy in a circuit is exhausted by faults or errors in the module, any further exceptions will cause errors at the output.

In pure fault masking, the effects of faults are essentially neutralized with no specific notification of their occurrence. This concepts is also employed in situations like steam heating systems with pressure relief valves. If the system overheats, the pressure is automatically released through the valve with no warning necessary. Examples of fault masking are voting and error correcting codes.

The most general hardware masking technique is triple modular redundancy (TMR). This is illustrated in Figure 12.5, where three identical modules provide a voting element with their separate results. This is an instance of extended duplication: three modules instead of two. The modules may be at any level from adders or gates to microprocessors or entire systems. The voting element accepts outputs from the three modules and delivers the majority vote as its output. This technique originated with vonNeumann (31).

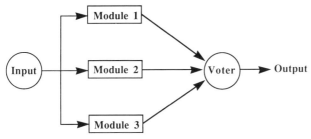

Figure 12.5 Triple modular redundancy.

The concept of TMR can be expanded to include as many redundant modules as needed, providing an N-modular redundancy (NMR) system. To avoid uncertainty due to tie votes, N is usually chosen to be odd. The TMR configuration shown in Figure 12.5 has a single point of failure—the voter. This means that the system will fail if the voter fails, whether or not the other modules fail. The reliability of the voter in the basic TMR architecture can be improved by using three copies of the voter, too, in addition to the replicated modules. As shown in Figure 12.6, this architecture is called triplicated TMR. System outputs are correct only if two out of three replicated voters function properly.

If a module fails in a TMR system, both of the remaining modules must continue to function properly. Once a module has failed, the reliability of the TMR system is lower than that of an individual module, in which case the reliability becomes R_n^2, where R_n is the reliability of a single module. In this condition, reliability can be improved by disabling one of the remaining good modules together with the faulty module, and operating the system in simplex mode.

There are several advantages to using triple modular redundancy. First, all faults are masked immediately. This is true for either permanent faults (which are merely masked all the time) or for transient faults (which are masked instantaneously as they occur). Second, no special fault detection

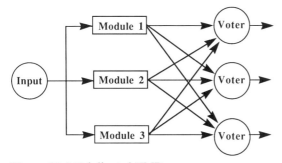

Figure 12.6 Triplicated TMR.

is necessary outside the voter. Finally, making the conversion to a TMR system from a nonredundant system is relatively simple.

Error-correcting codes (ECC) can be used to provide fault detection, fault location, and fault masking. ECC is the most commonly used means of masking redundancy. One form of ECC, called Hamming single-error-correcting (SEC) code, is used extensively in primary memory designs to increase the reliability of information stored in memory. SEC coded memories are inexpensive in terms of both cost and performance overhead. The redundancy of SEC codes ranges from 10 to 40% depending on the design. Encoding and decoding delays are relatively small.

Because high-density RAM chips are particularly prone to soft errors, and because RAM chips constitute an increasingly large proportion of digital system, they can contribute 60 to 70% of system failure rates. Special SEC detection/correction chips are now available for easy implementation of SEC codes in memories. Hamming SEC codes are commonly used in computer systems, and most implementations of Hamming codes use an extra check bit to provide for detection of double-bit errors, in addition to single-bit correction.

One drawback to the use of SEC codes is that when they are used purely for masking purposes, the system hardware may be deteriorating unbeknown to system maintainers because there need not be any notification if an error is correctable. Most implementations of Hamming coded memory systems include the ability to report the occurrence of correctable errors. This aids in the diagnosis of memory problems. Reference (17a) is a good general reference on coding theory as it applies to digital systems. A general discussion of error codes (properties, applications, limitations), including an extensive bibliography on codes and applications can be found in (22).

Fault-masking techniques improve system reliability by allowing the system to operate correctly in the presence of errors. Small amounts of extra redundancy can add fault-detection benefits like error flagging and rapid diagnosis. Fault masking, however, is limited by its static nature. Systems using fault masking can hide their errors but they cannot heal themselves. When errors accumulate to the point where the masking ability becomes saturated, the system will fail.

12.4.3. Reconfiguration

System reliability can be increased when redundancy is used dynamically as well as statically. Dynamic redundancy techniques involve the *reconfiguration* of system components in response to failures. The reconfiguration—removing or replacing damaged units—prevents errors from contributing their effects to the system operation.

Reconfiguration is triggered either by internal detection of errors in the damaged subunit, or by detection of errors in its output. The reconfiguration itself can occur either automatically by the system itself (on-line repair) or manually by technical personnel (off-line repair). Error-detection techniques form the basis for dynamic redundancy, and a system's chance of successful reconfiguration is largely dependent on its error-detection ability.

Three main issues for error detection in reconfigurable systems are: the confinement of error effects before unrecoverable damage occurs; error detection; and correct diagnosis of the error location so that the appropriate unit is marked for removal or replacement.

Reconfigurable Duplication
A static duplicated system provides for detection of disagreements, but it does not provide fault-tolerance. Fault-tolerance can be provided to a duplicate system, however, via two enhancements. Needed first is the ability to discern which of the duplicated modules is faulty when a disagreement is detected. The second requirement is the ability to disconnect the faulty module and simultaneously disable the comparison unit. Figure 12.7 depicts reconfigurable duplication. The active unit (selected arbitrarily) is connected to the output. The standby unit functions in parallel with the active unit, but is not connected to the system output.

When an error is detected, there are several means of determining which copy is defective and switching it out. One method is to run a diagnostic program. If the diagnostic fails, control is passed to the standby unit. Another method is to include self-checking in each module so that the joint occurrence of a mismatch and an internally detected error immediately determines the faulty copy. In the event that a mismatch occurs without detection of internal errors, both processors are taken off-line and forced to

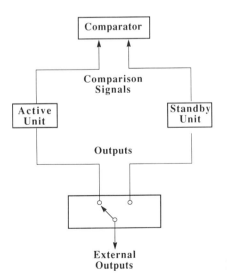

External
Outputs

Figure 12.7 Reconfigurable duplication.

run diagnostics; the first to finish successfully is designated the active processor. Watchdog timers can also be used in determining the faulty processor. If the active processor fails to reset a timer, the timer automatically invokes a change of control to the standby processor. Finally, an outside arbiter can be used to control the configuration.

Hybrid Redundancy
Hybrid redundancy combines static and dynamic redundancy by virtue of being a combination of NMR with voting, and backup sparing. Hybrid redundancy marries a TMR (NMR) system with a set of spare modules. When one of the TMR modules fails, it is replaced by a spare, so that the basic TMR configuration can continue. Figure 12.8 shows the basic concept.

A core of N identical modules is in use at any one time, and bad modules are replaced by an equivalent number of spares. Initially the system contains a total of $N + S$ modules (N initials and S space). The system can tolerate the failure of $P = t + s$ modules as long as there are never more than $t = N/2$ failed modules in the core before configuration can take place.

Adaptive Voting
Most voting schemes place equal weight on voter input, but in adaptive voting, the voter inputs are weighted by an accumulated history of disagreements of error detection. Hybrid redundancy can be regarded as a form of adaptive voting with the weights determined by the switch. The NMR/simplex architecture discussed in the section on TMR is an example of this.

Backup Sparing
Backup sparing is a method of spares switching. A typical backup sparing architecture uses N modules, as shown in Figure 12.9, each of whose outputs is connected to an error-detection mechanism and an output selection switch.

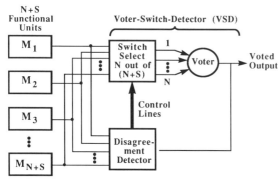

Figure 12.8 Hybrid redundancy.

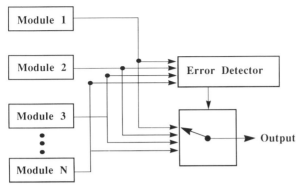

Figure 12.9 Backup sparing.

Though all modules run in parallel, only one is directly connected to output at any given moment. If the detector senses an error on the current module, it switches to another module. Detection can be achieved through such mechanisms as watchdog timers, periodic diagnostic tests, and self-checking circuits.

It is interesting to note that reliability does not increase as a linear function of the number of redundant modules. Losq (16) showed that for a given mission time there is a best number of spares for each of the many dynamic redundancy architectures.

The redundant units used for error detection, correction, or replacement of bad units in the various dynamic redundancy architectures perform no useful work until the moment they are switched into active service. Graceful degradation techniques use the redundant hardware as part of the system's resources as a matter of course. There are two distinct perspectives on graceful degradation, and they originate in the motivation for having included fault-tolerance in a system. If a cost/performance goal needs to be met, along with some ability to continue operating (perhaps without regard to performance, as in timesharing systems), then system resources are designed so that continuous (though perhaps degraded) operation is possible in the event of failure. This is a situation where degraded operation is preferable to no operation at all.

The second perspective is that any performance below a certain level is not acceptable, such as in real-time control systems for aircraft. In this context, extra resources are added to a system to ensure that a minimum performance level can be met with high probability. While the extra hardware is not being used in overcoming error effects, it can be used to boost performance over the minimum requirements. In either case—cost/performance or minimum service level—the goal is to permit system performance to degrade gracefully instead of having it go out with a bang.

12.4.4. Recovery

Special recovery techniques are often employed when errors occur, so that enough of the system state can be restored to permit execution to continue without performing a complete restart and without significant loss of state information or data. There are two basic approaches: forward and backward recovery. Forward error recovery is usually highly application-dependent. For a brief discussion of forward error recovery, see (23).

Backward recovery techniques require some redundant process and state information to be recorded as the computations progress. This information is used to "roll back" an interrupted process to a point for which correct information is available. Three such techniques are retry, checkpoint, and journaling.

Retry techniques are the fastest form of error recovery, and conceptually the simplest. Immediately after an error is detected, retry effects the necessary repairs. If the error is transient, the system will pause long enough for the transient to die away, then retry. For hard failures, reconfiguration is attempted, as in mapping disk bad spots to bad page tables. Retry techniques require immediate error detection to be successful, and they usually require substantial dedicated hardware.

Another recovery technique, checkpointing, can withstand some amount of error detection latency, because its methodology provides for the errant process to be backed up to an earlier point in its processing when the integrity of the process and its data were not suspect. In checkpointing, some subset of the system is saved at specific "checkpoints" during the process execution. The checkpointed information consists of whatever system state is necessary to complete the process after the checkpoint. Rollback, part of the actual recovery process, consists of resetting the system to the state stored at the latest checkpoint. The only loss incurred is due to the extra time taken to perform the operation, and whatever data was received during the interval that cannot be recreated. One issue about checkpointing is the question of making the correct choice of checkpoint locations. If the checkpoints are taken too frequently, unnecessary system overhead may be incurred. If the checkpoints are too infrequent, much computation time can be lost in excessively long rollbacks. Another issue is how to choose the minimum state information that must be saved at each checkpoint.

A third recovery mechanism, journaling, is the simplest but least efficient of the three methods discussed. In journaling, a copy of the initial database is saved when the process begins. As the process executes (e.g., an editing session), a record is kept of all transactions that affect the data. If the process fails, its effect can be recreated by running a copy of the backup data through the transactions a second time (after the fault has been removed). Recovery by journaling takes almost as long as the original transaction does, except that it takes slightly less time because human delays are not involved.

12.5. System Types

Fault-tolerance techniques can be applied for a number of purposes to a broad range of systems. Fault-tolerance can be a part of a general purpose commercial system, a specifically high-availability system, a long-life system, or a critical environment system. This section, drawn from (24), describes briefly each of these types of systems. In Section 12.7, examples are given for each type of system.

12.5.1. High Availability

High-availability systems share resources when the occasional loss of a single user is acceptable but a systemwide outage or common data base destruction is unacceptable. These systems are most frequently oriented toward general-purpose computing, executing a variety of user programs whose demands cannot be anticipated. Because they are targeted for the cost-sensitive commercial marketplace, these systems use minimal modifications to existing designs. Hamming-coded memory, bus parity, timeout counters, diagnostics, and software reasonability checks are the primary redundance techniques. Thus, coverage is low. In multiple-processor systems, however, the fault can be isolated once it is identified, and the system can continue operation, perhaps in degraded mode. Examples of high-availability systems include Tandem and Pluribus.

12.5.2. Long Life

Long-life systems, such as unmanned spacecraft, cannot be manually maintained over the system operating life (frequently 5 or more years). Often, as in spacecraft monitoring of planets, the peak computational requirement comes at the end of the system life. These systems are highly redundant, equipped with enough spares to survive the mission with the required computational power. Redundancy management may be performed automatically (on the spacecraft) or remotely (from ground stations). STAR is an example of long-life spacecraft systems.

12.5.3. Postponed Maintenance

Closely related to long-life systems are systems designed to survive faults until periodic maintenances can be performed. For small systems like spacecraft, maintenance could be postponed for the entire system life. For other systems in which on-site repair is difficult, redundancy is more cost-effective than unscheduled maintenance. There are many mobile systems that depart from a central facility for a period of time and return. Stocking spares and maintenance expertise are most cost-effective if maintenance can be postponed until the mobile unit returns to the central facility. Such systems include mass transit, ships, airplanes, and tanks.

12.5.4. High-Performance Computing

High-performance computing systems (such as signal processing) are very susceptible to transient errors (due to close timing margins) and permanent faults (due to complexity). As performance demands increase, fault-tolerance may be the only way of building systems with sufficient Mean Time To Error (MTTE) to allow useful computation. Occasional errors that disrupt processing for several seconds are tolerable as long as automatic recovery follows.

12.5.5. Critical Computations

The most stringent requirement for fault tolerance is realtime control systems in which faulty computations can jeopardize human life or have high economic impact. Not only must computations be correct, but also recovery time from faults must be minimized. Specially designed hardware operates with concurrent error detection so that incorrect data never leave the faulty module. SIFT and FTMP are examples of avionic computers designed to control dynamically unstable aircraft. Their design goal is a failure probability of less than 10^{-9} for a 10-hour mission.

Before presenting example fault-tolerant systems, we will first develop a computer structure taxonomy to provide an overall framework.

12.6. Structures in Fault-Tolerant Systems

In order to develop a framework for mapping fault-tolerant architectures, let us first examine a taxonomy of nonredundant computer structures. Figure 12.10 depicts the canonical uniprocessor using the PMS notation in (27). In

Figure 12.10 Serial uniprocessor structure.

Figure 12.11 Interleaved memory structure.

PMS, major architectural components are represented by single capital letters, with P standing for Processor, M for memory, S for switch, L for link, D for data operator, K for controller, T for transducer, and C for computer. Components can have modifying attributes such as P.central for central processor, abbreviated as Pc. Other commonly used attributes are p for primary (e.g., Mp) and s for secondary (e.g., Ms).

Figure 12.10 expands the processor into a data part, containing arithmetic units, and a control part containing instruction decoders and interpreters. While input/output (I/O) has been left out of Figure 12.10 to simplify our discussion, one should not underestimate the significance of I/O. Higher performance computer structures can be derived by replicating various combinations of M, D, and K.

By replicating memory modules as in Figure 12.11, overlap can be achieved in memory accessing. The addresses between the memory modules can be interleaved by assigning consecutive words to different memory modules. For the example in Figure 12.11, even-address memory words would reside in the left-hand M, while odd-address memory words would reside in the right-hand M. The memory could thus provide two words at the same time.

By replicating the data operators as shown in Figure 12.12, a pipeline organization results. There are several distinct phases to the execution of an instruction: instruction fetch, instruction decode, effective-address calculation, operand fetching, execution, and storage of results. Normally, these operations are carried on sequentially in time on the same set of hardware (in temporal sequencing). However, if specialized hardware operators are provided for each phase, as shown in Figure 12.12, instructions can move between phases (in spacial sequencing) and several instructions can be in various phases of completion at one time. Each operator starts the next instruction as soon as it has completed its current instruction. The pipeline

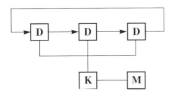

Figure 12.12 Uniprocessor vector structure.

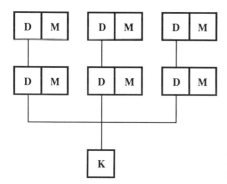

Figure 12.13 Uniprocessor array structure.

is limited by, and lockstepped to, the slowest operator. An instruction is completed in every cycle of the slowest data operator.

By providing each data operator with its own memory, an array processor results as depicted in Figure 12.13. Called processing elements (PEs), the data-memory units are able to communicate via direct connections to a subset of the other data-memory units. The single controller fetches, decodes, and broadcasts control signals to all the PEs in what is sometimes referred to as a Single Instruction Multiple Data (SIMD) organization. See Chapter 5 parallel processing for details of SISD, SIMD, MISD, and MIMD organizations. All operations proceed in lockstep. PEs can be selectively disabled from taking part in the computation.

Replication of all three components (with the control and data yielding a processor) leads to the multicomputer organization in Figure 12.14. Each element is a complete computer with its own operating system. Computers communicate through a local area network or a high-speed backplane. Any intercomputer communication must go through multiple copies of the operating system (i.e., both sender and receiver), greatly increasing the overhead of cooperation. Multicomputers have most often been used in fault-tolerant systems where the physical separation of computers is believed to minimize the possibility of multiple, simultaneous hardware failures.

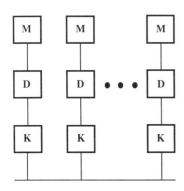

Figure 12.14 Multiple processor: multicomputer structure.

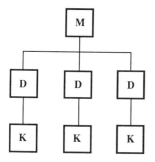

Figure 12.15 Multiple processor: multiprocessor structure.

Finally, replicating controller-data operators that share a large main memory yields the multiprocessor configuration of Figure 12.15. All processors have equal access to a shared memory, meaning that resources can be effectively shared (i.e., there needs to be only one copy of the operating system rather than one for each processor as in the multicomputer), and programs can cooperate with a minimum of overhead (i.e., processors can check flags in memory without involving the operating system).

The taxonomy of computer structures is summarized in Figure 12.16

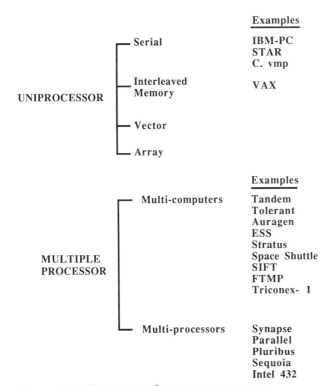

Figure 12.16 Taxonomy of computer structures.

with examples discussed in this chapter. The taxonomy divides computer structures into a uniprocessor branch and a multiple processor branch.

Orthogonal to the dimensions of computer structure are the dimensions of system fault-tolerant strategies. A taxonomy of the strategies discussed in Section 12.4 is shown in Figure 12.17. Figure 12.17 is a simplification of a more comprehensive taxonomy contained in (26). There are two approaches to increased reliability: fault avoidance and fault-tolerance. Fault avoidance results from conservative design practices such as the use of high-reliability components, component burn-in, and careful signal path routing. The goal of fault avoidance is to reduce the possibility of a failure. Even with the most careful fault avoidance, however, failures will eventually occur and result in system failure (hence the name fault-intolerance).

In fault-tolerant designs, redundancy is used to provide the information needed to negate the effects of failures. The redundancy is manifested in one of two ways: extra time or extra components. One form of time redundancy involves extra executions of the same calculation, perhaps by different methods. Comparison or other operations on the multiple results (identical when no errors are present) provide the basis for subsequent action. Two major forms of redundancy are dynamic and masking.

The left-most branch of Figure 12.17 covers those systems whose configuration can be dynamically changed in response to a fault, or in which masking redundancy, supplemented by on-line fault detection, allows on-line repair. Dynamic redundancy techniques involve the reconfiguration of system components in response to failures. The reconfiguration prevents failures from contributing their effects to system operation. In many instances, reconfiguration amounts to disconnecting the damaged units from the system. Reconfiguration is triggered either by internal detection of faults in the damaged subunit or detection of errors in its output. Thus, fault-detection techniques form the basis of dynamic redundancy.

Masking redundancy, also called static redundancy, tolerates failures but gives no warning of them. In its pure form, fault masking does not provide fault detection. The effects of faults are automatically neutralized without notification of their occurrence. The logical interconnection of the circuit elements remains fixed and no intervention occurs from elements outside the module. Thus, when the masking redundancy is exhausted by faults in

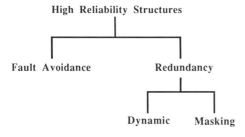

Figure 12.17 Strategies used in high-reliability systems.

the module, any further faults will cause errors at the output. When supplemented with on-line fault detection, fault masking can dynamically reconfigure to produce on-line repair. These systems are a "hybrid" of dynamic and masking redundancy.

A system's chance of successful reconfiguration is greatly dependent on its fault-detection ability. Three issues are involved in the employment of fault detection in configurable systems. First is the confinement of fault effects before unrecoverable damage occurs, second is fault detection, and third is correct diagnosis of the failure location, so that the faulty unit—and only the faulty unit—is marked for remedial action (removal and/or replacement). Thus, the two fault-detection criteria of coverage and diagnosability are important factors in the choice of a detection technique. Detection coverage, in particular, is commonly used in deriving the reliability formula of a dynamically redundant system. In modeling dynamically redundant systems, coverage is often generalized to mean the probability of successful reconfiguration; successful fault detection then becomes only one of the factors in determining coverage along with the probabilities of successful error confinement and resource switching. A more detailed discussion of fault tolerant strategies, including a dictionary of reliability techniques, can be found in (26).

12.7. Examples of Fault-Tolerant Systems[4]

The ultimate system goals affect design philosophy and design trade-offs. The cost of fault-tolerance must be weighed against the cost of error or failure. Error costs include down time as well as incorrect computation. Some system goals that affect the design philosophy include: Is the system to be highly reliable or highly available? Do all outputs have to be correct, or only data committed to long-term storage? How familiar must the user be with the architecture and software redundancy? Is the system dedicated so that attributes of the application can be used to simplify fault-tolerant techniques? Is the system constrained to use existing components? Even if the design is new, what is the cost and/or performance penalty to the user who does not require fault-tolerance? Is the design stand-alone, or are there other processors that can be called upon to assist in times of failure? For each of the example systems in this section we will identify in general as many of the goals that influenced the design and illustrate in particular how attributes of the intended application are used to increase reliability.

This section will describe a number of fault-tolerant systems mapped against the architectural taxonomy given in Figure 12.16 and the high-reliability strategies taxonomy given in Figure 12.17. To simplify the discussion we will not describe power supplies or physical packaging. All fault-tolerant

---

[4] This section is based upon the introduction to Part 2 of Ref. 26.

systems have redundant power supplies and packaging to facilitate repair. As a further simplification, only two stages in the response to the occurrence of a failure that were given in Section 12.4 will be considered: the stages of detection and recovery. In general, almost all stages of responses to failure can be implemented in either hardware or software. For example, consider fault detection. A simple example of hardware fault detection would consist of redundant copies of the processor whose outputs are being compared every clock cycle. Sometimes called "functional redundancy checking" or "self-checking modules," duplication and comparison has been used in the Stratus FT 200, Intel 432, and Bell Systems ESS systems. An example of software fault detection is a watchdog timer. The software periodically sets a countdown timer to an initial value. The initial value is selected to be close to the time required during normal execution to reach another portion of code that can reset the timer. If the countdown timer reaches zero before the software has a chance to reset it, an error in operation is detected. The watchdog timer generates an interrupt, which initiates fault diagnosis and recovery procedures.

As with fault detection, recovery can be either hardware- or software-based. As an example of hardware recovery, consider two copies of a processor, each one employing functional redundancy checking, as shown in Figure 12.18. Thus there are two pairs of two processors acting as a single logical processor. If one pair of processors detects a disagreement, the computation can be picked up by the other pair of processors and continued without interruption. Because all four processors are executing the same program, their internal states are identical and no other recovery action is required. Now consider software recovery techniques for a transaction processing application. In transaction processing, modifications are made to a shared data base, and the integrity of the data base is of paramount importance.

Consider two computers which are cooperating to maintain the integrity of the data base, as shown in Figure 12.19. One computer is the master and the second is the backup. Periodically the master sends checkpoint information that represents its internal state. If a failure should occur, the backup processor will commence execution at the internal state represented by the last checkpoint information received. In addition, there will be two identical copies of the data base on physically disjoint secondary storage. When modifications are made to one copy, the results are "mirrored" to the second copy. This form of redundancy has been used in Tandem Computer's NONSTOP system, Synapse's N + 1, and Tolerant Transaction

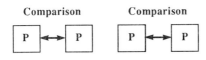

Comparison   Comparison

Figure 12.18 Hardware recovery based upon dual functional redundancy checking blocks.

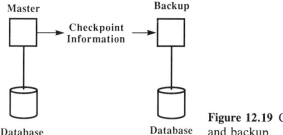

Master   Backup

Checkpoint
Information

Database   Database

Figure 12.19 Checkpointing with master and backup.

Systems' Eternity computer.[5] Checkpointing and mirroring requires an overhead of 20–30% (i.e., 1.2 or 1.3 processors are required to deliver the logical power of a single processor) compared with the dual functional redundancy checking blocks in Figure 12.18, employed by Stratus and Intel, which has an overhead of 300%.

A more economical approach to software error recovery in transaction processing systems is called journaling. Again, there are two copies of the data base. When one processor makes any modifications to the data base, the commands that trigger these modifications are stored in a special journal file. If the processor should crash, a second processor can take the non-updated second copy of the data base and execute the commands in the journal file to update the second data base to the state just prior to the first processor's crash. Journaling has been used in Auragen Systems Corporation System 4000.[6] The overhead for journaling is only about 5%.

Table 12.3 categorizes several fault-tolerant systems using dynamic redundancy. The four uniprocessor subbranches of the taxonomy in Figure 12.16 have been lumped together as a single entity called uniprocessor. Most fault-tolerant systems use multiple processors; hence, both multiple processor branches in the taxonomy in Figure 12.16 are reproduced in Table 12.3. Table 12.3 represents the dynamic redundancy branch of the fault-tolerant strategies taxonomy shown in Figure 12.17. The detection and recovery stages in fault handling are listed along with whether the detection and/or recovery techniques are performed in software or hardware. In practice, the earlier stages of fault handling that were described in Section 12.4 are performed in hardware, while the later stages are performed in software. Because the earlier stages are more real-time oriented than the later stages, the early stages are typically implemented in hardware, with the later stages implemented in software. Thus, Table 12.3 does not include software fault detection and hardware recovery. If a system had devoted the resources to

---

[5] NONSTOP, N + 1, and Eternity are trademarks of Tandem, Synapse, and Tolerant Transaction Systems, respectively.

[6] System 4000 is a trademark of Auragen Systems Corporation.

Table 12.3 Categories of Dynamic Redundancy

Uniprocessor			
Detection	SW	HW	HW
Recovery	SW	SW	HW
Example	IBM-PC	VAX	STAR
	[standard commercial systems]		
Multicomputer			
Detection	SW	HW	HW
Recovery	SW	SW	HW
Examples	Tandem Tolerant Auragen	ESS	Stratus
Multiprocessor			
Detection	SW	HW	HW
Recovery	SW	SW	HW
Examples	Synapse Parallel	Sequoia Pluribus	Intel 432

the hardware fault recovery, it would make little sense to leave fault detection to software. Software typically has lower fault coverage than hardware. Furthermore, the cost for fault detection is typically lower than that for fault recovery, so most of the cost would have already been allocated to hardware fault recovery.

12.7.1. General-purpose Uniprocessors

Typical commercial systems consist of a uniprocessor with minimal dynamic redundancy for fault-tolerance. Personal computers, such as the IBM PC, have only limited software fault detection. Because there is no spacial redundancy, these commercial systems use temporal redundancy to recover from transient or intermittent faults. The recovery mechanism may be as simple as rebooting and rerunning the application program. Many minicomputers and mainframe systems have built in hardware error-detection and reporting mechanisms. For example, a Digital Equipment Corporation VAX specifies three types of exceptions: aborts, faults, and traps. Aborts are the most severe form of exception. When an instruction is aborted, the machine registers and memory may be left in an indeterminate state. Because system status is destroyed, the instruction cannot be correctly restarted, completed, simulated, or undone. Faults, on the other hand, leave the machine registers and memory in a consistent state. Once the fault is eliminated, the instruction may be restarted and the correct results obtained. Faults restore only enough state to allow restarting. The state of the process may not be the same as before the fault occurred. Finally, a trap occurs at the end of the instruction causing the exception. The machine registers and memory are consistent, and the address of the next instruction to execute is stored on the machine stack. The process can be restarted with the same status as before the trap occurred. Exceptions include: machine check, kernel stack not valid, power fail, attempted execution of reserved or privileged instruction, attempted execution of reserved addressing mode, memory management access-control violation, arithmetic overflow/underflow/divide-by-zero, and uncorrectable memory errors.

The primary error-detection mechanism is parity. Typically, parity is included on control store, translation buffer, cache, and memory backplane buses. Software-based recovery is limited to attempts to restart software processes after a fault or trap has occurred. Further examples of error detection and recovery in the VAX can be found in Chapter 8 of (26), the IBM System/360 System/370 in (8), and the Univac 1100/60 (7).

12.7.2. STAR—Self Testing and Repairing Computer

Figure 12.20 depicts the Self Testing and Repairing (STAR) experimental computer developed by the Jet Propulsion Laboratory (JPL). The STAR was intended to be a prototype for real-time satellite control computers targeted for a 10-year mission to the outer planets of the solar system. STAR primarily used hardware-subsystem fault-tolerant techniques such as functional unit redundancy, voting, power switching of spares (units are removed by turning off power, and are connected by turning power on), error coding, and self-checks.

STAR consisted of a COP (control processor) containing the program counter and index registers, the LOP (logic processor) performing logical operations, the MAP (main arithmetic processor) containing arithmetic operators, ROM (read only memory), RWM (read write memory), IOP (input/output processor), IRP (interrupt processor), and TARP (test and repair processor), which monitored the operation of the computer and implemented recovery. The functional units communicated by means of the M-I (memory in) and M-O (memory out) buses. Control signals are sent from the TARP

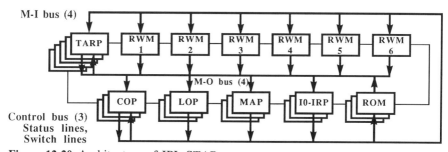

Figure 12.20 Architecture of JPL STAR computer.

to synchronize the functional units and to initiate recovery. The principal method of fault detection in the STAR is validation that every unit is active at the proper time. The TARP receives unit status information from each of the functional units. These messages include "output active," "disagree with bus," and "internal fault." By predicting the sequence of active units and observing the status messages from the functional units, the TARP can detect abnormal operation. The TARP initiates recovery by power switching of spares. User applications checkpoint the internal state periodically so that the computations can be rolled back to the last valid checkpoint upon detection of a fault in reconfiguration. Because the TARP was so fundamental to the recovery of the system, it employed a combination of masking and dynamic redundancy termed "hybrid redundancy." Three copies of TARP would be simultaneously active with their outputs being voted upon. If any TARP disagreed with the voted output, it would be replaced (dynamically) by a spare. A more detailed description of STAR can be found in (4).

Typically, uniprocessors have not been made fault-tolerant. Because in excess of 90% of the hardware associated with a uniprocessor must be operational before even a single instruction can be executed, there are very few techniques, short of replicating the entire processor, for tolerating failures. Thus, multiple processor structures are preferred for fault-tolerance because the extra processors can be used to increase throughput during the time of no failure. When a failure does occur, intelligence in the form of the other processors is available for assisting with fault recovery.

12.7.3. Tandem

Tandem Computers Incorporated was founded in 1976 for the purpose of building high-availability computer systems for commercial transaction processing.

Database applications are well-suited to software recovery. The database is duplicated on two physically different magnetic media. The software needs only insure that the database is always consistent. Each transaction is either always completed or aborted without modifying the database. Only one copy of the database is modified at a time, leaving the other consistent. The Tandem 16 was the first commercially available, modularly expandable system designed specifically for high availability. As shown in Figure 12.21, Tandem consists of up to 16 computers interconnected by two message-oriented Dynabuses. A loosely coupled architecture was selected instead of a tightly coupled, shared memory architecture because it was felt that the former allowed for more complete fault containment. While there was some built-in hardware fault detection (e.g., parity on data bus and error correcting code memory), Tandem primarily relied upon software fault detection and recovery. Data integrity is maintained through the mechanism of I/O "process pairs." One I/O process is designated as primary and the

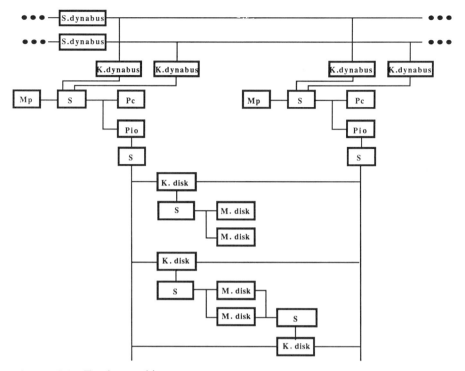

Figure 12.21 Tandem architecture.

other is designated as a backup. All file-modification messages are delivered to the primary I/O process. The primary sends a message with checkpoint information to the backup so that it can take over if the primary's processor or access paths to the I/O device fails. Files can also be duplicated on physically distinct devices controlled by an I/O processor pair on physically distinct processors. All file-modification messages are delivered to both I/O proceses. Thus, in the event of physical failure or isolation of the primary, the backup file is up to date and available.

User applications can also use the process pair mechanism. Consider a nonstop application program **A** in Figure 12.22. **A** starts a backup process **Ab** in another processor. There are also duplicate file images, one designated primary and the other backup. All file activity by **A** is performed on both the primary and backup file copies. Program **A** periodically (at user specified points) sends checkpoint information to **Ab**. **Ab** is the same program as **A**, but **Ab** knows that it is a backup program. **Ab** reads checkpoint messages to update its data area, file status, and program counter. **Ab** loads and executes if the system reports that **A**'s processor is down (error message is sent from **A**'s operating system image or **A**'s processor fails to respond to a periodic "I'm alive" message). When **Ab** starts to execute from the last

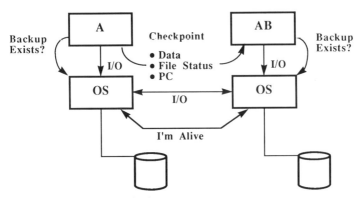

Figure 12.22 Tandem shadow processor.

checkpoint, it may attempt to repeat an I/O operation successfully completed by **A**. The system file handler will recognize this and send **Ab** a successful-completion I/O message. **A** periodically asks the operating system if the backup process exists. Because one no longer does, it can request the creation and initialization of a copy of both the process and file structure. The process pair mechanism requires approximately 1.2 to 1.3 physical processors to deliver one logical processor worth of performance. While the overhead is low, the user has the responsibility of selecting checkpoints and specifying checkpoint data for correct recovery under all possible fault conditions. More information can be found on the operating system and the programming of NONSTOP applications in (6).

12.7.4. Tolerant

Tolerant Systems, Inc. Eternity series updates the Tandem approach to on-line transaction processing by incorporating single chip VLSI microprocessors. Two 32-bit microprocessors execute the user and operating systems code, while two other microprocessors handle I/O. The four processors plus a shared memory form a single System Building Block (SBB). Up to 15 SBBs can be configured in a loosely coupled network with a transparent network operating system. The network operating system allows application software to access services through a single global name space. Thus, the application software need not know the physical location of the service. The operating system automatically balances load among servers as well as attempting to associate clients with their physically nearest server.

Fault-tolerance is achieved through process images and system logs. The user can select which processes should have virtual images. If selected, a process has three images: active user process, primary image, and secondary image. The two backup images—primary and secondary—are required for fail-safe operation, while the backup images are being updated.

The disk storage for all three images is kept in a file system that has been replicated on three or more physical disk drives, each with its own controller.

Upon a process failure, the primary backup process becomes the active process and affected files are rolled back to the state prior to the beginning of the last transaction. The system is then rolled forward to the point of failure. If the program is driven by terminal input, the input for rolling forward is taken from the terminal log.

12.7.5. ESS

The Electronic Switching Systems (ESS) developed by Bell Laboratories over the last two decades are the most numerous fault-tolerant digital systems. The ESSs handle routing of telephone calls through central offices. They have an aggressive availability goal: 2 hours downtime in 40 years (3 minutes per year). Telephone switching can take advantage of some natural redundancies in the network and in the data—that is, telephone users will redial if they get a wrong number or are disconnected. However, there is a user aggravation level that must be avoided: users will redial as long as errors do not happen too frequently. User aggravation thresholds are different for failure to establish a call (moderately high) and disconnection of an established call (very low). Thus, an ESS follows a staged failure recovery process as presented in Table 12.4.

A typical ESS processor consists of a program store (PS), a call store (CS, also called the transient memory), and a central computer (CC). These units are duplicated and their outputs matched during real-time execution, as depicted in Figure 12.23.

Large-scale ESS systems allow various combinations of the three components to form a single operational system. Smaller systems would swap the entire computer complex, as depicted in Figure 12.23. Error detection

Table 12.4 Staged Recovery in ESS

Phase	Recovery action	Effect
1	Initialize specific transient memory	Temporary storage affected No calls lost
2	Reconfigure peripheral hardware Initialize all transient memory	Lose calls being established Calls in progress not lost
3	Verify memory operation, establish a workable processor configuration, verify program, configure peripheral hardware, initialize all transient memory.	Lose calls being established Calls in progress not affected
4	Establish a workable processor configuration, configure peripheral hardware, initialize all memory.	All calls lost

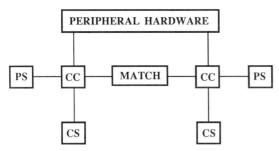

Figure 12.23 ESS processor structure.

was achieved primarily by comparing the values of various internal nodes during instruction execution. The set of internal nodes varied as a function of the instruction under execution. Because the application software is very repetitive, heavy use was made of watchdog timers to detect common failure modes that affected both processors identically. Once an error was detected by mismatch, the system would enter a "maze" program that the processor must successfully navigate against tight time constraints in order to be declared operational. A separate hardware mechanism would step the system through different hardware configuration states until one configuration was found that could successfully navigate the maze program. It is interesting to note that these telephone switching systems have not only met, but indeed have surpassed, their availability goals.

A more complete description of ESS processors can be found in (30). Alternative duplication and match architectures inspired by the Bell ESS processors include the UDET 7116 telephone switching system central computer (18), the COMTRAK railroad traffic computer (10), and the AXE telephone switching computer (21).

12.7.6. Stratus FT 200

The Stratus architecture consists of up to 32 logical processors communicating over a local area network called the Stratus Link. Stratus systems are aimed at the same on-line transaction processing market pioneered by Tandem. As with Tandem, Stratus employs a backup computer for recovery. Fault detection, however, uses hardware duplication and match.

Figure 12.24 illustrates one logical processor module. The Stratus architecture takes advantage of the low cost and high density of VLSI microprocessors.[7] One pair of processors executes application software, while the

---

[7] By way of contrast, Tandem processors use bit-sliced LSI and MSI technology to implement a custom-designed instruction set. This difference in approach is primarily due to the four or five-year gap between the founding of the two companies and the technology available at the time of founding.

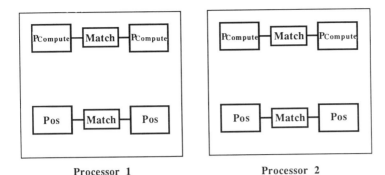

Processor 1   Processor 2

Figure 12.24 Dual duplication employed in Stratus systems.

other pair executes the operating system. The separation between operating system and application functions is primarily due to the inability of early microprocessors to recover from page faults. Each processor has its outputs checked through matching with its redundant counterpart. Four processors, labelled Processor 1 in Figure 12.24, form a "functional redundancy checking" or "self-checking" module. Any disagreement between matched processor pairs causes a signal to be sent to all other processors, as well as an LED (light emitting diode) to be lit on the edge of the processor card. In this case, Processor 2 could pick up the computation because it had been performing the identical internal computations as Processor 1. When a new processor is selected as the backup, it is reeducated so that its internal state is brought into agreement with that of its primary processor.

While each logical processor consists of four separate microprocessors, the extra cost for processor-level replication is small. However, Stratus systems can have up to 32 Mbytes of physical memory. Memory may be too large and too costly to depend on duplication and matching. Memory is a regular structure to which error-correcting codes can be readily applied. Thus the memory subsystems rely on error-correcting codes to detect and correct failures. Memory may be duplicated for critical applications.

12.7.7. Synapse N + 1

The Synapse N + 1 system is also targeted for on-line transaction processing. However, the Synapse N + 1 differs from Tandem and Stratus in that it utilizes the advantages of the multiprocessor structure to increase throughput and decrease overhead.

Because memory is shared between the processors, processors can create new work by placing a task on a job queue. Processors are self-scheduling in that upon completion of the current task, the processor accesses the job queue for the next piece of work. The operating system and application tasks are kept small. Checkpoint information is automatically generated at the output of each software task. Thus checkpointing is done frequently and the amount of checkpoint data is kept small. The checkpoint data consists of a time stamp, a pointer to the next program module, and some status information on the application and user display. If a processor fails during the execution of a program module, recovery software merely reenters the task on the job queue to be executed by the first available free processor.

Fault detection is primarily in software through protection enforced by the operating system. Software is layered in levels, including the kernel operating system, a relational database management system, extended operating system, the transaction processing manager, and user programs. Each of the higher layers has direct "call" access to the services of the lower levels. Privileges of any level are dynamically determined by the sequence of calls that a process used to arrive at that level. For example, if a user program called the transaction processing manager, which in turn called the kernel operating system, the kernel operating system could only manipulate its own data or the data in the transaction processing manager or the user application. The Synapse N + 1 system also has fast boot and system initialization software, which allow the system to rapidly recover from common mode failures.

12.7.8. Parallel

The Parallel Computer, Inc. Parallel 300 XR is a commercial office system using VLSI microprocessors in a duplicated architecture. The system architecture, depicted in Figure 12.25, assembles industrial standards (such as Motorola 68000 microprocessor, Unix operating system, and IEEE Standard 796 Multibus) into a fault-tolerant structure. In a structure reminiscent of the duplex ESS, all tasks are executed simultaneously on both processors. If a fault is detected, the faulty processor is transparently removed by the operating system fault-management core while the application continues to run on the second processor.

All files are mirrored on duplicated disk drives. If a disk error occurs

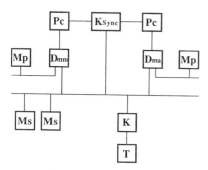

Figure 12.25 Architecture of Parallel 300 system.

because of a defective medium, the bad track is mapped out and the data is automatically updated from the good drive. If a hard failure occurs, the affected disk subsystem is logically configured out.

Duplicated power supplies with integrated batteries isolate the system from power-source transients. This configuration greatly reduces the occurrence of disk head crashes and transient disk writes, often caused by external power fluctuations. The batteries are sufficient to keep the entire system, including disk drives, operational for up to 90 minutes. This is in contrast to most battery back-up systems, which only provide several minutes of power to primary memory. The power supplies have sufficient capacity to completely power the system even if one supply should fail.

12.7.9. Pluribus

Pluribus was conceived as a modular highly available multiprocessor for message switching in the ARPANET. The Pluribus is configured by interconnecting processor buses, memory buses, and I/O buses as depicted in Figure 12.26. Interconnections are made by bus couplers denoted by Ks in the figure. Processors have a small amount of local memory for storage of frequently executed code. All other shared code and data resides on the memory buses. Memory uses parity for error detection. Parity is also computed and checked across all bus coupler paths. "Feedback" parity is used for writes to I/O buses. The I/O bus sends the parity it computed from the received word back to the processor bus for comparison. The process is reversed for reads. The Pluribus software also assists in fault detection through the use of periodic software diagnostics, redundancy in data structures, and watchdog timers.

Most of the Pluribus fault recovery is achieved in software. Several levels of protocol are employed in the ARPANET, each with its own error detection and recovery. If a failure in a Pluribus occurs, all the in-progress messages are buffered at other ARPANET nodes until positively acknowledged. These messages are eventually rerouted past the failed Pluribus. Thus the ARPANET application requires only that the Pluribus recover gracefully from a failure. This goal can be achieved by quick system reinitialization with omission of questionable components. The Pluribus operating system recovers in stages:

- Checksum local memory code, initialize local interrupt vectors and enable interrupts, and discover a real-time clock for system timing.
- Discover all usable common memory pages and establish a page for communication between processors.
- Checksum the common memory code to be used in the next three stages.
- Discover all common buses in real-time clocks.
- Discover all processor bus couplers and processors.

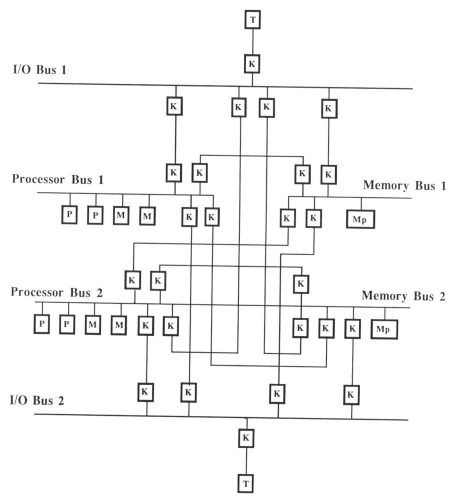

Figure 12.26 An example of Pluribus configuration.

- Checksum code to be used in the rest of initialization.
- Checksum all of local code.
- Checksum common memory code and develop page allocation map.
- Discover common I/O interfaces.

The network structure allows for remote diagnosis from the Network Control Center. Even in the case of total destruction of memory contents, the Pluribus can request that the code be transmitted from the Network Control Center or other Pluribuses in the network. Any transitory messages lost will be restored via the retransmission mechanism in the network protocol. Because data integrity in messages is assured through network level protocols, the Pluribus can rotate hardware (e.g., either new or repaired) into use. Any problematic hardware will appear only as a transient to the system because the offender will be quickly configured out. More information on Pluribus can be found in (13).

12.7.10. Sequoia

The Sequoia System architecture is a modularly expandable multiprocessor, as illustrated in Figure 12.27. Faults are detected by error-correcting codes, duplication, and protocol monitoring:

- Byte parity protects data stored in processor caches, input/output processor buffers, and bus address/data transfers. Main memory employs error-correcting code.
- Every processor, memory, and input/output processor is duplicated with several internal points of comparison every clock cycle. If a mismatch is detected, the element electrically isolates itself from the rest of the system.
- Each element involved in a bus transaction monitors the protocol for logical consistency. A set of watchdog timers monitor protocols for temporal consistency. Monitoring circuitry is periodically tested under operating system control.

Fault recovery is performed by the operating system. After reconfiguration, suspended processes are restarted. Maintaining a consistent image of each process in main memory is crucial to correct recovery. The processor caches use a deferred write policy where data modifications are only stored in the cache. Periodically, the cache is flushed to update main memory. Process images are mirrored in memory. Thus, a processor flushes its cache twice, once to the primary and once to the backup.[8] So even if a processor fails during a cache flush, there is always one consistent process image. The

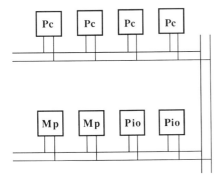

Figure 12.27 Sequoia architecture.

---

[8] Note the similarity of process mirroring in memory to database mirroring on disks.

mirroring of modified data in memory also permits toleration of memory failures.

Code and unmodified data are backed up on disk and not mirrored in memory. Thus, if a memory module fails, its contents can be reconstructed by information stored on disk and in mirrored memory. Disks can also be mirrored to tolerate disk failures.

12.7.11. Intel 432

The Intel 432 was designed as a set of building blocks from which high-availability and high-reliability systems could be built. By adding a small amount of extra hardware to a VLSI chip set, a wide range of system types are possible.

The basic components in the Intel 432 are shown in Figure 12.28 along with the fault-confinement regions. In order to limit the spread of errors, carefully defined fault-confinement regions were designed, primarily at chip boundaries. Hardware checks data as it leaves a confinement region. If an error is detected, it is assumed that the fault is contained in this fault-confinement region.

Figure 12.29 depicts a typical Intel 432 system using duplication and matching as the primary fault-detection mechanism. One processor is designated master by enabling a pin on the processor chip. Only the master processor drives the bus, but both processors receive data from the bus. Thus, the checker receives data from the bus, performs the appropriate internal computation, and compares its output to that which the master has put on the bus. Functional redundancy checking is also used on the memory array controllers. The memory arrays are not duplicated, rather they depend on error-correcting codes to tolerate failures.

There is also a dedicated hardware error-logging mechanism that facilitates automatic recovery from failures in hardware. For example, assume that there is a break in bus 1 between the processors and memory in Figure 12.29. Further assume that the memory controllers detected the fault via a violation in the bus protocol. A separate error-reporting network is used to transmit this information to all modules in the system. During the first phase of the error reporting, all modules on bus 1 are notified of the problem.

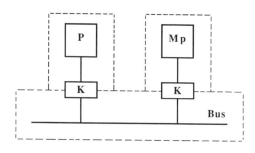

Figure 12.28 Basic building blocks of the Intel 432 with fault confinement regions indicated.

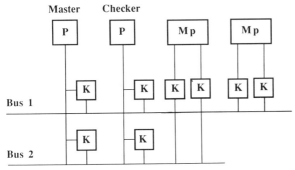

Master   Checker

Bus 1

Bus 2

Figure 12.29 Functional redundancy checking in the Intel 432.

During phase 2, the master and checker processors are notified of the problem. Finally, during phase 3 all other bus interfaces attached to the master and checker processors are notified. Thus, in three cycles of the error-reporting system all modules would know the unique source of the problem. Recovery is a completely local activity—in this case, all the bus interfaces attached to bus 1 would turn themselves off.

Automatic recovery from processor and/or memory failure uses the primary/backup matching scheme employed by Stratus. Error detection, reporting, and recovery mechanisms are periodically exercised through software that forces error conditions and waits to observe the results. More information on the Intel 432 can be found in Chapter 18 of (26) and (12).

12.7.12. Masking Redundancy in Uniprocessors

Table 12.5 depicts uniprocessor and multicomputer examples of masking redundancy. Because by definition, masking redundancy corrects faults before they reach module outputs, detection and recovery are part of the same process. Pure fault masking thus give no warning of a deteriorating hardware state until enough faults have accumulated to cause a failure. Because of this problem, most fault-masking techniques are extended to provide fault detection as well. The additional redundancy needed for this purpose is

Table 12.5 Categories of Masking Redundancy

Uniprocessor		
Detection and Recovery	SW	HW
Examples	Any uniprocessor	C.vmp
Multicomputer		
Detection and Recovery	SW	HW
Examples	Space Shuttle	FTMP
	SIFT	Triconex-1

usually only a minor increase. For example, consider triplication and voting. The voter is usually a circuit whose output is "on" when two or more of its inputs are "on." When the voter output is "on," we do not know whether all three inputs are "on" or two out of three are "on." Separate disagreement detectors would be required to determine if each input coincided with the output value. Thus, fault detection in masking-redundancy systems is either not present or is a simple adjunct to the basic recovery mechanism. For these reasons, Table 12.5 considers detection and recovery as part of the same basic mechanism, with only the options of being implemented in software or hardware.

On uniprocessors, fault masking can take the form of either temporal or spatial replication. In principle, any uniprocessor can be programmed to perform a computation three times, followed by a vote to calculate the majority results. Yang et al. (34) discuss the implementation of software voting on a uniprocessor and calibrate its effectiveness by experimentally inserting faults. Interestingly enough, there were some single failures that caused the triplicated system to fail. These faults dealt with the message communication subsystem in that nonmessage-based instructions under faulty conditions could be changed to a message instruction, causing a spurious message to be sent and modifying arbitrary memory locations (34).

12.7.13. C. vmp

Figure 12.30 depicts the architecture of C.vmp, which uses off-the-shelf components and a custom-designed voter to achieve fault-tolerance. Voting occurs every time the processors access the bus to either send or retrieve information. C.vmp in fact consists of three separate machines capable of operating in independent mode and executing three separate programs. Under the control of an external event or under the control of one of the processors, C.vmp can synchronize its redundant hardware and start executing the critical section of code. With the voter active, the three buses are voted upon and the result of the vote is sent out. Any disagreements among the processors will therefore not propagate to the memories and vice versa. Because voting is a simple act of comparison, the voter is memoryless. Voting is done in parallel on a bit-by-bit basis. A computer can have a failure

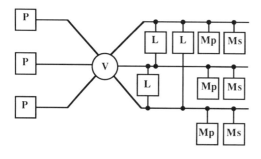

Figure 12.30 Architecture of C.vmp.

on a certain bit in one bus, and, provided that the other two buses have the correct information for that bit, operation will continue. There are cases, therefore, where failures in all three buses can occur simultaneously and the computer would still be functioning correctly.

Bus-level voting works only if information passes through the voter. Any internal state of the processor must periodically circulate through the voter to clean up errors. Traces of actual programs indicate that the internal processor state is frequently written to memory during normal program and operating system behavior. C.vmp runs an unmodified version of a commercial operating system. Thus, the fault-tolerant properties of the architecture are achieved in a manner transparent to the software (i.e., no modifications need to be made in the operating system or application software). In addition to the obvious overhead of having three copies of all the components, actual measurements on the system indicate a further degradation of 15% in performance due to the added delays induced by the voter sitting between the processor and memories. More information on C.vmp can be found in (28).

12.7.14. Space Shuttle

Multicomputer systems have also used fault-masking redundancy. A straightforward extension to software voting on a uniprocessor is to provide a separate computer for each redundant computation. Messages between computers can convey the results of a computation to be voted upon before use by the next software task. Software voting has been used on the Space Shuttle primary flight computer (5, 29). In the Space Shuttle, four computers perform identical computations and broadcast their results to each other. Each computer is responsible for picking up the results from the other three computers and computing a majority vote prior to executing the next software task. In this scheme, the Space Shuttle can actually lose two computers and still operate correctly. After two computer failures, the two remaining computers operate in a duplicate and match mode. When the third failure occurs, it is detected but it is uncertain as to which computer is in failure, thus the phrase "fail soft." Thus, the Space Shuttle had to be "fail safe, fail safe, fail soft." The shuttle computer actually has a fifth backup, which runs different software that has been programmed by a different contractor. The fifth computer represents a "sanity check" on the other four and guards against a common mode failure (i.e., program bug) in the software of the four main voting computers.

12.7.15. SIFT—Software Implemented Fault-Tolerance

SIFT was designed by SRI International (32, 33) for real-time control of aircraft. The hardware consists of independent computers communicating over dedicated links. SIFT software is divided into tasks. The input to a task is produced by the output of a collection of tasks.

Computer 1   Computer 2   Computer 3

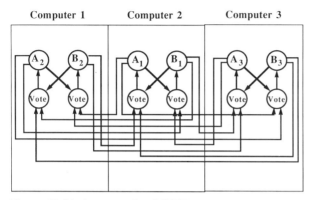

Figure 12.31 An example of SIFT.

Figure 12.31 depicts the cooperation between two software tasks (e.g., A and B) on the SIFT architecture. Task A feeds its output to Task B, which does some computations prior to creating new input for Task A. As depicted in Figure 12.31, the tasks residing on different computers broadcast their results to voters to calculate the correct majority value input for the next task. Voting is only performed on the input to each task rather than partial results. If all copies of the output are not identical, an error has been detected. Such errors are recorded for use by the operating system to determine faulty units and system reconfiguration.

12.7.16. FTMP

Just as hardware voting techniques can be used instead of software voting on uniprocessors, hardware techniques can be used in multicomputer configurations. Figure 12.32 depicts the structure of FTMP (Fault-Tolerant Multiprocessor). Basic elements are processor memory pairs with common memory modules. A set of redundant serial buses interconnects the ele-

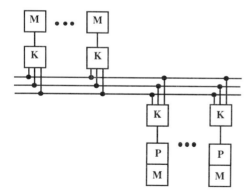

Figure 12.32 Simplified diagram of FTMP.

ments. Basic elements combine into triads as determined by status information in the bus control units.

Applications software is divided into tasks. A task is initialized when a processor memory triad reads input data from a common memory triad. The bus controllers are set up so that the processors read from the appropriate three common memories over the appropriate three buses. Each common memory drives a different active bus. The bus controllers vote on the information prior to loading it into the local processor's memory. The processors then independently execute the program. Upon completion, the output data is written into the common memory module triad, with each processor driving a different active bus and each memory module voting on the contents of the three active buses. When an element of the triad fails, its status is detected by the voting mechanism and can be configured out by reprogramming the bus interfaces. The reprogramming is done by reconfiguration management software. Thus, any element can serve as a spare for any triad. More can be found on FTMP in (9).

12.7.17. Tricon-1

Triconex Corporation integrated many of the concepts in SIFT, FTMP, C.vmp. and ESS into a real-time process controller with an availability goal of .99999 (i.e., less than 1 hour downtime in 12.5 years of operation). There are three independent channels consisting of an input processor (Pi), a central processor (Pc), and an output processor (Po). The central processors are connected to each other by a dual serial bus over which control, status, and data are exchanged.

Each central processor runs its own operating system copy as well as an identical copy of the process control algorithm. The central processor clocks are skewed so that transient faults do not form a single point (in time) failure. If a transient fault affects all three processors, the processors will be executing a different portion of the control algorithm and the error will be caught during voting.

Both inputs and outputs are voted on. When it is time to vote, one central processor's clock is selected for the exchange of data. Each processor forms a software majority vote of the received data. Each processor compares its calculation with the outcome of the majority vote. If there is a disagreement, the processor marks itself in error and places itself into an inactive state. The other two processors continue the process control algorithm in duplex mode. While in the inactive state, the processor executes a sanity test in which it must complete complex functions. The functions are arranged in a maze in which there is only one correct path. A hardware watchdog timer is set at the beginning of the maze. If the maze is completed before the timer reaches zero, the processor is declared sane.

To assure correct sequencing through the maze, a baton-passing scheme is used. A relay checkpoint is set up between functional blocks of the maze program. These checkpoints consist of conditional statements to check whether the baton variable has a valid value. If the value is correct, the old baton variable is cleared and a new baton variable is initialized with the value to be checked at the next relay checkpoint. If the program flow erroneously jumps ahead, the baton variable will not have the correct value at the relay checkpoint. If the program flow erroneously backtracks, the baton variable was cleared on the first passage through the relay checkpoint and the error will be discovered. Once the sanity test is passed the processor can return to normal processing. As long as the sanity test is not passed, the processor remains in the inactive state.

To increase error detection in the active state, the application program is automatically augmented, in a manner transparent to the user, with settings for a watchdog timer and relay checkpoints. Error detection is further enhanced by appending a portion of the sanity test program and a portion of the diagnostics to the application program. If there is a disagreement in duplex mode, both active processors execute the sanity test and diagnostics. If no errors are discovered, both processors return to active status. If only one processor passes the sanity test, it returns to active status to accomplish an orderly shutdown of the physical process (30). Processors are restored to active operation by "reeducation" whereby data is passed between the processors in a special mode. Thus, processors can be replaced without loss of process control.

Control information generated by the output processors is also voted on. So that the transducer that sets the physical control point does not become a single point of failure, a quad arrangement of switches is used that can still function correctly even if one switch is failed.

12.8. Conclusions

With increased customer interest in fault-tolerance and constantly decreasing hardware costs, there is a significant trend to implement more fault-tolerance in hardware. Hardware error tolerance has many advantages:

• Simplifies recovery for software and user applications
• Saves time
• Provides transparency to the user
• Increases probability of successful recovery, given early detection
• Decreases MTTR
• Increases MTTF, MTTE (Mean Time To Error), and MTTC (Mean Time To Crash)
• Simplifies software recovery and reduces dependence on implementation

- Error-detection logic can help isolate design errors so that future implementations are even more reliable

By starting from first principles, we can design a fault-tolerant architecture that achieves better reliability and availability, at better cost effectiveness than an ad hoc, add-on approach. Several examples in this chapter demonstrate that it is possible to build systems in which the activities of fault detection, diagnosis, and recovery are completely automated and transparent to the user.

Problems

1. Discuss the advantages and disadvantages for fault-tolerance of loosely coupled vs. tightly coupled architectures.
2. Show how you would extend hardware fault-tolerance concepts for multiprocessors to provide fault-tolerance in parallel machines such as the Cosmic Cube (Intel Hypercube) or the HEP (Denelcor Heterogeneous Element Processor). Do the same for a massively parallel architecture such as the Connection Machine; for data flow machines.
3. Describe how you would design/implement a rollback recovery procedure for a multiprocessor under at least two different data-level synchronization schemes (as described in Chapter 4 on multiprocessing) such as Cray's chaining, test&set used in the IBM 360/70, or others of your choice. What special difficulties are encountered under each scheme?
4. Consider a Tandem NonStop system with four processors. An engineering change order (ECO) is issued to revise a particular piece of hardware (or a certain section of software). Revising the hardware or the software requires taking the processor down. This is not a problem because the system can operate despite one processor's being down. After the ECO is installed, the processor is brought up, and a second processor is taken down for ECO installation. At this point, three processors are active, two running the old version of hardware (or software) and one running the new. How will the NonStop system handle this? What suggestions do you have to mitigate this kind of problem?
5. Explain why some schemes for fault-tolerance are particularly effective for some applications and not for others (e.g., transaction processing or telephone switching). What kinds of trade-offs are required between application requirements and technology limitations? Comment on the applicability of the Tandem architecture for telephone switching systems; on the applicability of ESS for transaction processing.
6. Select a computer system for which the processor and operating system documentation is available to you. Analyze the fault-tolerance and re-

covery techniques and capabilities of the hardware/software system. What (low-cost) improvementts might be made?

7. Choose one of the system architectures presented in this (or another) chapter and show how its design for fault-tolerance could be improved. Comment on the cost, performance, and fault-detection ability of your improved design. Compare and contrast the original design against your design on the bases of reliability, availability, and maintainability. Alternatively, perform the same analysis comparing any two extant systems, either from this book or from other information available to you.

References

1. Anderson T, Lee PA: Fault Tolerance: Principles and Practice. Prentice-Hall, Englewood Cliffs, NJ, 1981.
2. Avizienis A: Fault-tolerance: The survival attribute of digital systems. *Proc. of the IEEE 66,* Oct. 1978, pp. 1109–1125.
3. Avizienis A, Kelly JPJ: Fault-tolerance by design diversity: Concepts and Experiments. *IEEE Computer,* Vol. 17, No. 8, Aug. 1984, pp. 67–80.
4. Avizienis A, Gilley GC, Mathur FP, et al: The STAR (self-testing and repairing) computer: An investigation on the theory and practice of fault-tolerant computer design. *IEEE Trans. on Computers,* Vol. C-20, Oct. 1971, pp. 1312–1321.
5. Velocity, Altitude Regimes to Push Computer Limits. *Aviation Week and Space Technology,* April 1981, pp. 49–51.
6. Bartlett JF: A 'non-stop' operating system. In *Hawaii International Conference on System Sciences,* 1978, Honolulu, Hawaii, pp. 103–119.
7. Boone LA, Liebergot HL, Sedmak RM: Availability, reliability, and maintainability aspects of the Sperry Univac 1100/60. In *Digest of Tenth International Fault-Tolerant Computing Symposium,* IEEE Computer Society, Kyoto, Japan, 1980, pp. 3–8.
8. Droulette DL: Recovery through programming System/360 System/370. In *SJCC AFIPS Conference Proceedings,* AFIPS Press, 1971, pp. 467–476.
9. Hopkins AL, Jr., Smith TB III, Lala JH: FTMP—A highly reliable fault-tolerant multiprocessor for aircraft. In *Proc. of the IEEE Computers,* Oct. 1978, pp. 1221–1239.
10. Ihara H, Fukuoka K, Kubo Y, Yokota S: Fault-tolerant computer system with three symmetric computers, *Proc. of the IEEE,* Oct. 1978, pp. 1160–1177.
11. Jack LA, Berg RO, Kinney LL, Prom GJ: Coverage analysis of self-test techniques for semiconductor memories. Technical Report MR 12399, Honeywell Corporation, Minneapolis, MN, 1975.
12. Johnson D: Error reporting in the Intel iAPX 432. In *Proc. of the 14th International Fault-Tolerant Computing Symposium,* IEEE Computer Society, 1984, pp. 24–28.
13. Katsuke D, Elsam ES, Mann WF, et al: Pluribus—an operational fault-tolerant multiprocessor. In *Proc. of the IEEE,* Oct. 1978, pp. 1146–1159.
14. Knight JC, Leveson NF, St. Jean, LD: A large-scale experiment in N-version

programming. In *15th International Symposium on Fault-Tolerant Computing,* IEEE, Ann Arbor, MI, June 1985, pp. 135–139.

15. Laprie JC: Dependable computing and fault-tolerance: Concepts and terminology. In *15th Annual International Symposium on Fault-Tolerant Computing,* IEEE, Ann Arbor, MI, June 1985, pp. 2–11.

16. Losq J: A highly efficient redundancy scheme: Self-purging redundancy. Technical Report 62, Stanford University, 1975.

17. Maxion RA: Toward fault-tolerant user interfaces. Proc. of the Fifth IFAC International Conference on Safety of Computer Central Systems, Sarcat, France, Oct. 1986, pp. 117–122.

17a. MacWilliams FJ, Sloane NJA: The Theory of Error-Correcting Codes. North-Holland, New York, 1978.

18. Morganti M, Coppadoro G, Ceru S: UDET 7116—Common control for PCM telephone exchange: Diagnostic software design and availability evaluation. In *Eighth International Fault-Tolerant Computing Symposium,* IEEE Computer Society, Toulouse, France, 1978, pp. 16–23.

19. Neumann PG: Risks to the public in computer systems. *ACM SigSoft/Software Engineering Notes,* Vol. 10, No. 3, July 1985, p. 8.

20. Neumann PG: Risks to the Public in Computer Systems. *ACM SigSoft/Software Engineering Notes,* Vol. 10, No. 5, Oct. 1985, p. 8.

21. Ossfeldt BE, Jonsson I: Recovery and diagnostics in the central control of the AXE switching system. *IEEE Trans. on Computers,* Vol. C-29, June 1980, pp. 482–491.

22. Pradhan DK, Reddy SM: Error-correcting codes and self-check circuits. *Computer,* Vol. 13, No. 3, March 1980, pp. 27–37.

23. Randell BP, Lee PA, Treleaven PC: Reliability issues in computer system design. *Computing Surveys,* Vol. 10, No. 2, June 1978, pp. 123–165.

24. Rennels DA: Distributed fault-tolerant computer systems. *Computer,* Vol. 13, No. 3, March 1980, pp. 55–65.

25. Roth JP, Bouricius WG, Carter WC, Schneider PR: Phase II of an architectural study for a self-repairing computer. Technical Report, SAMSO-TR-67-106, U.S. Air Force Space and Missile Division, El Segundo, CA, 1967.

26. Siewiorek DP, Swarz RS: *The Theory and Practice of Reliable System Design.* Digital Press, Bedford, MA, 1982.

27. Siewiorek DP, Bell CG, Newell A: *Computer Structures: Principles and Examples.* McGraw-Hill, New York, 1982.

28. Siewiorek DP, Kini V, Mashburn H, et al: A case study of C.mmp, Cm*, and C.vmp: Part I—experience with fault-tolerance in multiprocessor systems. *Proc. of the IEEE,* Vol. 66, No. 10, Oct. 1978, pp. 1178–1199.

29. Sklaroff JR: Redundancy management technique for space shuttle computers. *IBM Journal of Research and Development,* Vol. 20, No. 1, Jan. 1976, pp. 20–28.

30. Toy WN: Fault-tolerant design of local ESS processors. *Proc. of the IEEE,* Vol. 66, No. 10, Oct. 1978, pp. 1126–1145.

31. von Neumann J: Probabilistic logistics and the synthesis of reliable organisms from unreliable components. *Automata Studies,* Princeton University Press, Princeton, NJ, 1956, pp. 43–98.

32. Wensley JH: SIFT software implemented fault-tolerance. In *FJCC AFIPS Conference Proceeding,* AFIPS Press, 1972, pp. 243–253.
33. Wensley JH, Lamport L, Goldberg J, et al: SIFT: Design and analysis of a fault-tolerant computer for aircraft control. In *Proc. of the IEEE Computers,* Oct. 1978, pp. 1240–1255.
34. Yang X, York G, Birmingham W, Siewiorek D: Fault recovery of triplicated software in the Intel iAPX 432. in *IEEE Fifth International Conference on Distributed Computing Systems,* Denver, CO, 1985.

Index

Note: f = figure; t = table

A

Access stencil, definition, 209
Actus, machine-independent language for SIMD machine, 189
Adder design, gallium arsenide, 103–104
Aerodynamic simulation, dataflow computation for, 381–385
AeroSim, 385–393
  program analysis of, 390t
Algol, for parallel processing, 185
ALICE, architecture, applications, 331t
ALICE multiprocessor, two-level heirarchical system, 418–419
ALICE system, determining parallelism in, 431
ALPHA, 345
ALU, 77
AMPS
  architecture, applications, 331t
  determining parallelism in, 431
APL Machine. *See* IBM APL Machine
Applicative language, 405
Applicative model of computation, 138
Approximate greedy window control, 293–294
AR-PANET, resource scheduling in, 275
Architecture, computer
  goals of, 49–52
  hardware requirements, 51
  language features, 50–51
  trends, 52–56
Architectures
  advanced microprocessors, 3–47
  ALICE, 331t
  AMPS, 331t
  combinator-reduction, 435
  Connection Machine, 331t, 336f
  Cray 2, 320f
  DADO, 331t, 338f

dataflow (Dennis), 440f
DEL model for execution, 41f
direct execution, 5, 42–45
FAIM-1, 331t
fault-tolerant computers, 495–552
functional programming, 434–444
functional programming supported by, 415–453
G-machine, 434–437
Guzman Machine, 331t
HEP-1, 322f
high-level language processors, 3–47
HLL computers, classification of, 4–6
IBM/RP3, 321–323
implementation issues, 74–80 (*see also* specific terms)
indirect execution, 5
lambda-reduction, 435
language-corresponding, 6, 34–42
language-directed, 6, 24–34
Mago's tree machine, 437–440
  Manchester dataflow machine, 440–442, 443f
MIMD machine, 182
MISD machine, 182
MIT Scheme-79/81, 36f
multiple-SIMID machine, 183
multiprocessor, 135–177
NON-VON supercomputer, 331t, 339f
packaging constraints on, 79–80
parallel interference machine, 343f
partitionable-SIMD/MIMD machine, 184
PIM-D, ICOT, 331t
Pluribus, 540f
reduced instruction set computer (RISC), 48–83
Remps, 328f
Sequoia, 541f
SIMD machine, 180–182
SISD machine, 180
SNAP, 331t

553